World Health Organization

GLOBAL STATUS REPORT ON ROAD SAFETY 2018

Global status report on road safety 2018

ISBN 978-92-4-156568-4

Suggested citation. Global status report on road safety 2018. Geneva: World Health Organization; 2018. Licence: CC BY-NC-SA 3.0 IGO.

Cataloguing-in-Publication (CIP) data. CIP data are available at http://apps.who.int/iris.

Design and layout by Paprika

Printed in France

Made possible through funding from Bloomberg Philanthropies.

Contents

Acknowledgements

The *Global status report on road safety 2018* benefited from the contributions of a number of WHO staff and collaborators. Nhan Tran coordinated the writing of the report with contributions by Jeanne Breene, Meleckidzedeck Khayesi, Rob McInerney, Anesh Sukhai, Tamitza Toroyan and David Ward. Kacem Iaych was responsible for data management and statistical analysis; Joëlle Auert was responsible for the legislation data management and analysis. Strategic direction on the report was provided by Etienne Krug.

Regional data coordinators were responsible for trainings, data collection and validation: Anneli Heimann and Martial-Manfred Missimikim (African Region), Alessandra Senisse (Region of the Americas), Rania Saad (Eastern Mediterranean Region and South-East Asian Region), Yongjie Yon (European Region), Maria Angela Pestaño and Whitney Skowronski (Western Pacific Region). Further support at regional level was provided by: Hala Sakr, Dinesh Sethi, Eugenia Rodrigues, Jonathon Passmore, Patanjali Nayar and Jatinder Pal Singh Chhatwal. WHO Representatives and staff at country level facilitated this work and their contribution is gratefully acknowledged. Other WHO staff who contributed include: Elena Altieri, Angelita Ruth Dee, Doris Ma Fat, Colin Mathers, Evelyn Murphy, Florence Rusciano, Zoe Brillantes and Teri Reynolds.

Country level data could not have been obtained without the invaluable input of: the National Data Coordinators (see Table A1 in the Statistical Annex); all respondents who participated in data collection and the country level consensus meetings; government officials who supported the project and provided official clearance of the information for inclusion in this report.

WHO also wishes to thank the following contributors whose expertise made this document possible: Adrienne Pizatella, Jennifer Ellis, Kelly Larson, and Kelly Henning from Bloomberg Philanthropies; Leslie Zellers for her support in reviewing and analysing legislative documents for the region of the Americas; Saul Billingsley, Lotte Brondum, Soames Job, Adnan Hyder, Rob McInerney, and David Ward, for serving on the advisory committee for this report; Abdul Bachani, Judy Fleiter, and Margie Peden, for review comments; Alejandro Furas and Jessica Truong for support on collecting and interpreting data on vehicle standards; Isaac Botchey for assisting with checking of country profiles; Claudia Adriazola-Steil, Matts-Ake Belin and Judy Williams for providing material for boxes; Eric Thuo for assisting with literature review on child restraints; Hal Inada for the checking of references; Kaitlyn Friedman for assisting with data processing; Tony Price who edited the report; the team of translators from Alboum for support with translations of legislation; and graphic designers from Paprika who produced the design and layout of the report.

This report is in memoriam of Dominique Rurangirwa, the National Data Coordinator in Rwanda who lost his life in a road traffic crash earlier this year. His death was most unexpected and he will be sadly missed by all his colleagues, both locally and internationally. This tragedy serves as a reminder of the importance of this work and that more must still be done to strengthen road transport systems to prevent the needless loss of life.

Finally, the WHO wishes to thank Bloomberg Philanthropies for its generous financial support for the development and publication of this report.

FOREWORD

Is there anyone we can call for you?

There is a phone call or a knock on the door that we all dread, in which we are told that a loved one has been killed or seriously injured in a road traffic crash.

We shiver as emergency vehicles speed past us on the road to attend a crash. Our hearts miss a beat as we hear about a "road accident" on the news.

But road traffic crashes are not "accidents". They are completely preventable.

This report shows that the problem is getting worse. Deaths from road traffic crashes have increased to 1.35 million a year. That's nearly 3 700 people dying on the world's roads every day.

Tens of millions more are injured or disabled every year, people who suffer life-altering injuries with long-lasting effects. These losses take a huge toll on families and communities. The cost of emergency response, health care and human grief is immense.

There are many reasons for this trend: rapid urbanization, poor safety standards, lack of enforcement, people driving distracted or fatigued, others under the influence of drugs or alcohol, speeding and a failure to wear seat-belts or helmets.

One of the most heart-breaking statistics in this report is that road traffic injury is the leading cause of death for people aged between 5 and 29 years. No child should die or be seriously injured while they walk, cycle or play.

We must return our streets to our children. They have a right to feel safe on them.

In the Sustainable Development Goals, world leaders have committed to halve the number of deaths from road crashes by 2020. This report shows that three years on, far too little progress has been made towards this goal. There is an urgent need to scale up evidence-based interventions and investment.

Development is an opportunity for low- and middle-income countries to avoid the costly mistakes made in the past by high-income countries. We need to create cities and transport systems that reduce reliance on cars. We must apply the lessons we have learned about safe road design. With the right leadership and investment, countries can build in the safeguards and best practices to save lives.

WHO is committed to working with countries to reduce the needless death and disability caused by road traffic crashes.

WHO's General Programme of Work 2019–2023 – our five-year strategic plan – includes road safety goals that are underpinned by 12 voluntary performance targets agreed upon by world leaders last year. These are designed to provide guidance to WHO Member States on key interventions.

It is one thing, of course, to set goals and targets. It's another to achieve them.

Experience shows that sustainable road safety must be planned and requires long-term investment and appropriate management capacity for effective delivery. International organizations, donors and the public and private sectors need to work together to make things happen.

This report highlights the increasing number of countries and cities that are making progress with effective and affordable interventions. My hope is that this report will save lives, prevent injuries and mean fewer emergency responders knock on doors with messages they should never have to deliver.

Dr Tedros Adhanom Ghebreyesus
Director-General, World Health Organization

FOREWORD

Road safety is an issue that does not receive anywhere near the attention it deserves – and it really is one of our great opportunities to save lives around the world.

The numbers are staggering. Road traffic crashes now represent the eighth leading cause of death globally. They claim more than 1.35 million lives each year and cause up to 50 million injuries. And, the fact is, every one of those deaths and injuries is preventable.

We know which interventions work. Strong policies and enforcement, smart road design, and powerful public awareness campaigns can save millions of lives over the coming decades. To spread those interventions to more countries, it is critically important for partners to target our resources effectively and hold each other accountable for our results.

The data show that low- and middle-income countries bear the greatest burden of road traffic fatalities and injuries. So, over the past decade, Bloomberg Philanthropies has worked closely with the World Health Organization, government agencies, and road safety organizations and invested US$ 259 million to help implement evidence-based solutions. Together we have promoted the use of helmets and seat-belts, combatted speeding and drunk driving, redesigned city streets to make them safer, and advocated for safer vehicles.

Overall, we have made important policy progress since WHO issued its last road safety report in 2015. Twenty-two countries have amended their road safety laws, bringing them in line with best practices. These laws cover more than one billion people, or 14% of the world's population.

At the same time, we have also focused our intervention efforts on cities. The opportunity for cities is enormous, because they are home to more than half the world's population. And, once cities demonstrate something works, national governments tend to be more willing to scale up a proven solution. To cite just a few leading cities: Accra is using data to improve pedestrian safety, and Ho Chi Minh City is taking cost-effective steps to make more than 150 high-risk intersections safer. Cities in countries such as Brazil and India have reduced traffic crashes, and through media campaigns and stronger enforcement, more cities have cut drunk driving.

These are encouraging trends, and public support for road safety policies is only growing. However, there is still much more work to be done, and Bloomberg Philanthropies will continue to raise awareness of road safety and the need for more action by governments.

Reducing road traffic deaths and injuries is one of the United Nations Sustainable Development Goals – and, given everything we know about the problem and its solutions, that goal is achievable if governments prioritize road safety. WHO is helping to drive the progress we are making, and all of us at Bloomberg Philanthropies thank Dr Tedros, WHO Director-General, his colleagues, and our allies around the world for their continued partnership.

We invite you to learn more about the status of road safety in this important report.

Michael R. Bloomberg
Founder, Bloomberg L.P. & Bloomberg Philanthropies
WHO Global Ambassador for Noncommunicable Diseases and Injuries

EXECUTIVE SUMMARY

The number of road traffic deaths continues to climb, reaching 1.35 million in 2016. However, the rates of death relative to the size of the world's population has stabilized in recent years. The data presented in this report show that progress has been achieved in important areas such as legislation, vehicle standards and improving access to post-crash care. This progress has not, however, occurred at a pace fast enough to compensate for the rising population and rapid motorization of transport taking place in many parts of the world. At this rate, the Sustainable Development Goals (SDG) target 3.6 to halve road traffic deaths by 2020 will not be met.

Road traffic injury is now the leading cause of death for children and young adults aged 5–29 years, signalling a need for a shift in the current child health agenda, which has largely neglected road safety. It is the eighth leading cause of death for all age groups surpassing HIV/AIDS, tuberculosis and diarrhoeal diseases. The burden of road traffic injuries and deaths is disproportionately borne by vulnerable road users and those living in low- and middle-income countries, where the growing number of deaths is fuelled by transport that is increasingly motorized. Between 2013 and 2016, no reductions in the number of road traffic deaths were observed in any low-income country, while some reductions were observed in 48 middle- and high-income countries. Overall, the number of deaths increased in 104 countries during this period.

Strengthening legislation to mitigate key risk factors is recognized by the majority of governments as an important strategy to improve road safety, as evidenced by the 149 countries that have designated lead agencies with responsibilities that include enacting and assessing traffic laws. While too many countries still lack legislation that appropriately addresses risks such as speeding, drink-driving, the use of helmets, seat-belts and child restraints, since 2014 progress has been made in a number of these areas. Overall 22 additional countries have amended their laws on one or more risk factors to bring them in line with best practice. This translates to an additional one billion people who are now covered by effective road traffic laws.

Of the 175 countries participating in this report, 123 have road traffic laws that meet best practice for one or more key risk factors. During this review period, ten additional countries (45 in total) have aligned with best practice on drink-driving legislation, five additional countries (49 in total) on motorcycle helmet use, four additional countries (33 in total) have aligned with best practice on the use of child restraint systems, and three additional countries (105 in total) on the use of seat-belts. Less progress has been made on adopting best practice on speed limits, despite the importance of speed as a major cause of death and serious injury.

The enforcement of laws and adoption of safety standards — such as the availability of seat-belts and fitments for car occupants in both front and rear seats, remain challenging in many parts of the world. Despite the benefits of vehicle safety measures, only 40 countries have implemented seven or eight of the priority UN vehicle safety standards. There are, however, signs of progress. For example, India, the world's fourth largest car manufacturer, is producing its first four-star (out of a possible five-stars) vehicle and phasing out production of a popular model, which consistently failed safety crash tests.

Some progress is also evident in the planning, design and operation of roads and roadsides, and in the take-up of a range of tools, notably the International Road Assessment Program (iRAP), which is a star rating tool for road networks. One hundred and fourteen countries are currently carrying out systematic assessments or star ratings of existing roads. These assessments and the implementation of appropriate road standards are particularly important as the majority of travel by road users such as pedestrians, cyclists and motorcyclists, occur on roads that are inherently unsafe for them.

There are also some signs of progress in improving access to post-crash care to reduce the consequences and severity of injury once a crash occurs. One hundred and nine countries now have access to a telephone number to contact emergency care and 97 countries have a formal process to train and certify prehospital care providers. More work is needed, however, to ensure access to quality emergency care. Approximately half of all countries have speciality training pathways in emergency medicine and trauma surgery while 78 reported having national or subnational trauma registries in place.

Although the progress towards reducing the number of road traffic deaths has not met global expectations, there are nonetheless signs of improvement. Accelerating the rate of this progress and bringing to scale the benefits of effective legislation, safer vehicles, safer roads, and increasing access to quality emergency care is the main challenge moving forward. There is an urgent need for governments to scale up their road safety efforts in order to live up to their commitments made in the Sustainable Development Agenda 2030. The upcoming Third Global Ministerial Conference on Road Safety in Sweden in February 2020 will be a key opportunity to take a strategic view and set a road safety agenda for the next decade, including setting a new global target on fatalities.

INTRODUCTION

Deaths and injuries resulting from road traffic crashes remain a serious problem globally and current trends suggest that this will continue to be the case in the foreseeable future (1,2). Accelerating progress can, however, be achieved through an integrated approach that includes putting in place and enforcing effective measures such as safety standards for roads and vehicles, legislation to mitigate high-risk behaviours such as speeding, as well as ensuring timely access to professional emergency care (3). Key to this approach is the availability of reliable and comprehensive data on the burden, and risks of road traffic crashes, injuries and deaths to target and monitor progress (4,5).

Without knowledge of the magnitude of the problem and the risks of death and injury, the ability to implement context-specific and appropriate interventions is severely limited. Moreover, as highlighted in previous and current editions of this report, the under-reporting of road traffic deaths is pervasive in many parts of the world and results in a lower priority being given to road safety as compared to other public health challenges (6). Even though the number of people dying annually as a result of road traffic injury surpasses those dying from HIV/AIDS, tuberculosis and diarrhoeal diseases, the political commitment and financial investments in road safety is only a small fraction of that made to combat these diseases (7).

This report is intended to stimulate country actions to improve road safety in countries through the identification of key gaps and opportunities. As we approach the end of the Decade of Action for Road Safety 2011–2020 and the deadline for SDG target 3.6, it is intended to serve as an advocacy tool to generate further political action, as well as a resource to guide implementation by relevant government actors including ministries of health, transport, finance, education, and interior, as well as local authorities in provinces and cities (5,8,9). The specific objectives of this report are to:

→ document the annual number of deaths resulting from road traffic injury in order to establish an assessment of progress towards the UN goals for road safety and the Decade of Action;

→ review institutional management practices as well as target setting;

→ present an analysis of national legislation on key road safety risk factors using best practice criteria;

→ summarize the current state of vehicle standards and regulations as well as road infrastructure, and

→ examine current progress and challenges in improving post-crash care.

What's new?

The criteria used to determine best practices for legislation have been updated along with the classifications of countries as those with laws that conform to best practice, those with laws that do not conform to best practice, those without laws, and those in which the laws are not applicable. In some instances, new criteria have been introduced based on the latest evidence, to capture the nuanced aspects of road safety legislation in different countries more effectively.

Using the updated criteria, legislation from 2014 (used for the 2015 report) was retrospectively analysed and compared with the analysis of 2017 (used for this report) legislation. Changes (both upgrades and downgrades) have been documented and are presented in the findings of this report. In addition to grouping those countries with laws that conform to best practice, this report also shows which countries have made improvements, which have stayed the same, and which (in a few instances) have made changes that have moved their laws out of alignment with current best practice.

Methods

This series of global status reports on road safety has been developed through an iterative and consultative process with participating Member States. In the first phase, requests for data were sent out through a survey administered in 2017 by the WHO Headquarters to Regional and National Data Coordinators (R/NDC) appointed in each region or country. The self-administered survey contained questions relating to the status of the five pillars of the Decade of Action. With coordination by the NDCs, experts from different sectors within each country discussed and came to an agreement on the responses to the survey questions using information available.

Based on the reported number of road traffic deaths and the source of data, adjustments were made to account for the potential under-reporting due to differences in definitions as well as limitations in the Civil Registration and Vital Statistics (CRVS) in many countries. This process resulted in an estimated number of fatalities, which is presented along with the reported figure. Following this, a final consultation was carried out to allow Member States to respond to any changes that resulted from the verification and validation process. This consultation also provided Member States an opportunity to comment on the WHO estimates for road traffic fatalities, which is often much higher than the official statistics.

Data sources

Three primary sources of data were used in the development of this report: 1) data collected from the self-administered surveys for which responses were received from 175 Member States; 2) data collected through publicly accessible databases, including the UN Economic Commission for Europe database on road traffic conventions, government websites, as well as specialised entities such as the Global New Car Assessment Programme and road inspection data collected by the International Road Assessment Programme to measure the level of safety for different road users; and 3) Global Health Estimates generated by the WHO Department for Information, Evidence and Research. For this report, 2018 data were used for the review of vehicle standards; 2017 data were used for the review of legislation, road standards and post-crash care; fatality estimates were based on data from 2016.

SECTION 1

CURRENT STATE OF GLOBAL ROAD SAFETY

CHAPTER 1

THE GLOBAL BURDEN OF ROAD TRAFFIC DEATHS

Key messages

- The number of road traffic deaths on the world's roads remains unacceptably high.
- Road traffic injuries are the leading killer of children and young adults.
- More than half of global road traffic deaths are amongst pedestrians, cyclists and motorcyclists who are still too often neglected in road traffic system design in many countries.
- There is progress being made, however, it is far from uniform across countries.
- SDG 3.6 target to halve road deaths and injuries by 2020 will not be met without drastic action.

1.35
million deaths each year

8th
leading cause of death for people of all ages

#1
cause of death for children and young adults 5–29 years of age

3
times higher death rates in low-income countries than in high-income countries

The number of road traffic deaths continues to climb, reaching a high of 1.35 million in 2016. However, the rate of death relative to the size of the world's population has stabilized and declined relative to the number of motor vehicles in recent years (10). As shown in Figure 1, despite the increase in absolute numbers, the rate of road traffic deaths has remained fairly constant at around 18 deaths per 100,000 population over the last 15 years. While this does suggest that the problem is not worsening, the world is far from achieving SDG target 3.6, which calls for a reduction in the number of deaths by a half by 2020 (8). Insufficient progress is being made.

Road traffic injuries are the 8th leading cause of death for people of all ages.

Figure 1: Number and rate of road traffic death per 100,000 population: 2000–2016

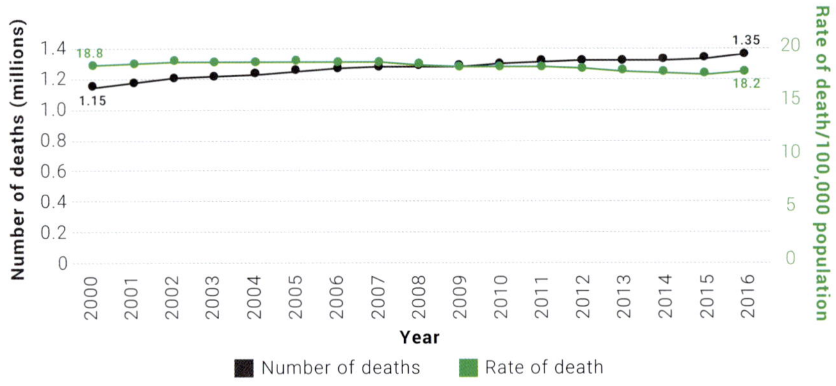

During the same period the number of vehicles worldwide has steadily increased, while death rates declined from 135 deaths for every 100,000 vehicles in 2000 to approximately 64 deaths for every 100,000 vehicles in 2016 (Figure 2). This represents a reduction of more than 50% in the last 15 years suggesting some progress in mitigating the adverse effects of increasing motorized transport. Although progress has been made, these data show that it has not occurred at a pace fast enough to compensate for rapid population growth and increasing motorization worldwide.

Figure 2: Number of motor vehicles and rate of road traffic death per 100,000 vehicles: 2000–2016

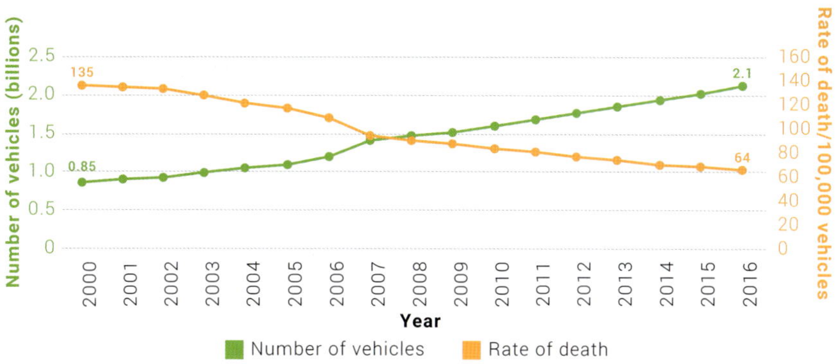

The number of deaths on the world's roads remains unacceptably high with **1.35 million people** dying each year.

A leading killer of children

Road traffic injury is the 8th leading cause of death for all age groups, up from the 9th leading cause of death (10). It is also now the leading cause of death for children and young adults aged 5–29 years, signalling a need for a shift in the current child health agenda, which has largely neglected the road safety (11). As progress is made in the prevention and control of infectious diseases, the relative contribution of deaths from noncommunicable diseases and injuries increases (10,11). More people now die as a result of road traffic injuries than from HIV/AIDS, tuberculosis and diarrhoeal diseases (10).

In addition to the injuries and disabilities resulting from road traffic crashes, the safety of roads (or lack thereof) also impacts other public health issues as it contributes to inactivity. People are less likely to walk, cycle, or use public transportation when conditions are unsafe and this has a bearing on other leading causes of death shown in Table 1 (12). These include ischaemic heart disease, stroke, chronic obstructive pulmonary disease, and diabetes, while increasing motorization has also been linked with respiratory illnesses. Simultaneously preventing road traffic deaths and encouraging active travel in safe environments will contribute to reducing the overall burden of preventable deaths.

Road traffic injuries are now the leading cause of death for children and young adults aged 5–29 years.

Table 1: Leading causes of death, all ages, 2016

Rank	Cause	% of total deaths
	All Causes	
1	Ischaemic heart disease	16.6
2	Stroke	10.2
3	Chronic obstructive pulmonary disease	5.4
4	Lower respiratory infections	5.2
5	Alzheimer's disease and other dementias	3.5
6	Trachea, bronchus, lung cancers	3.0
7	Diabetes mellitus	2.8
8	Road traffic injuries	2.5
9	Diarrhoeal diseases	2.4
10	Tuberculosis	2.3

2016 WHO Global Health Estimates

Progress is not uniform across regions and income levels

Progress in reducing road traffic deaths over the last few years varies significantly between the different regions and countries of the world. There continues to be a strong association between the risk of a road traffic death and the income level of countries. With an average rate of 27.5 deaths per 100,000 population, the risk is more than 3 times higher in low-income countries than in high-income countries where the average rate is 8.3 deaths 100,000 population. As shown in Figure 3, the burden of road traffic deaths is disproportionately high among low- and middle-income countries in relation to the size of their populations and the number of motor vehicles in circulation. Although only 1% of the world's motor vehicles are in low-income countries, 13% of deaths occur in these countries.

Figure 3: Proportion of population, road traffic deaths, and registered motor vehicles by country income category*, 2016

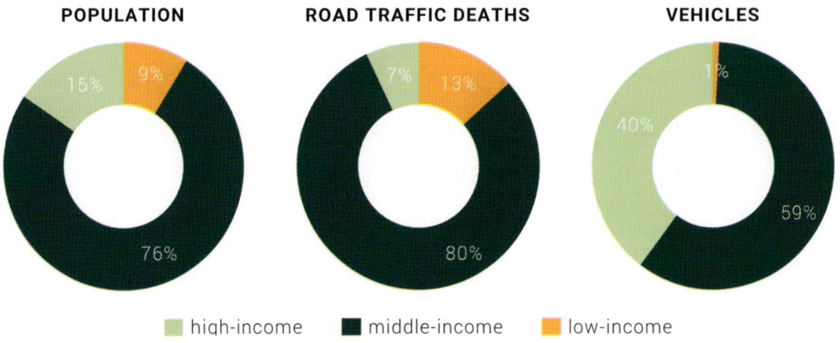

*income levels are based on 2017 World Bank classifications.

There has been no reduction in the number of road traffic deaths in any low-income country since 2013.

There has also been more progress in reducing the number of road traffic deaths among middle- and high-income countries than low-income countries. As shown in Figure 4, between 2013 and 2016, no reductions in the number of road traffic deaths were observed in any low-income country, while some reductions were observed in 48 middle- and high-income countries. Overall, the number of deaths increased in 104 countries during this period.

Figure 4: Number of countries where a change in the number of road traffic deaths has been observed since 2013*

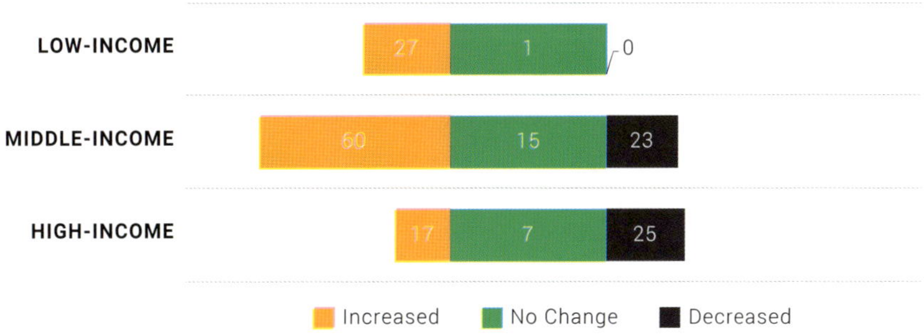

*These data represent countries that have seen more than a 2% change in their number of deaths since 2013, and excludes countries with populations under 200 000. The income levels are based on 2017 World Bank classifications.

The rates of road traffic death are highest in Africa (26.6/100,000 people) and South-East Asia (20.7/100,000 people).

Inequalities across regions

Countries in Africa and South-East Asia have regional rates of road traffic deaths higher than the global rate with 26.6 and 20.7 deaths per 100,000 population respectively. This is followed by countries in the Eastern Mediterranean and Western Pacific, which have regional rates comparable with the global rate with 18 and 16.9 deaths per 100,000 population respectively. Countries in the Americas and Europe have the lowest regional rates of 15.6 and 9.3 deaths per 100,000 people respectively. In terms of progress made, in three of the six regions (Americas, Europe, Western Pacific), the rates of death have decreased since 2013.

Figure 5: Rates of road traffic death per 100,000 population by WHO regions: 2013, 2016

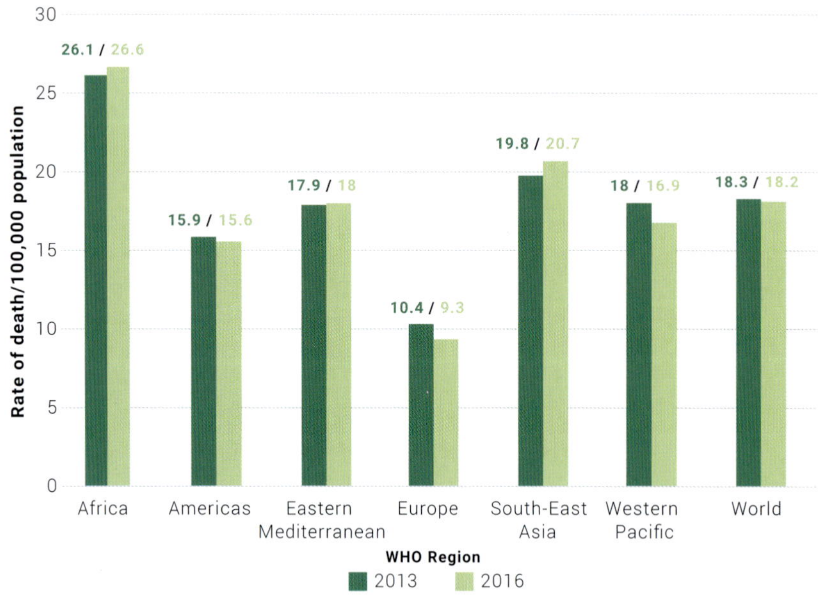

With the exception of the Eastern Mediterranean region, the rate of road traffic deaths per 100,000 population generally decreases as income increases (13). In the Americas, for example, the rate of road traffic deaths among high-income countries is 11.8 per 100,000

population, while it is 18.3 among low-income countries. In Africa there is an observable difference between middle-income countries, which have a rate of death of 23.6 per 100,000 population and low-income countries, where the rate is 29.3 per 100,000 population. At the other end of the continuum, in Europe, the rate of road traffic deaths in middle-income countries (14.4 deaths per 100,000 population) is nearly three times higher than in high-income countries, where there are 5.1 road traffic deaths per 100,000 population.

Vulnerable road users disproportionately impacted

More than half of all road traffic deaths are among vulnerable road users: pedestrians, cyclists and motorcyclists.

The variation in rates of deaths observed across regions and countries also corresponds with differences in the types of road users most affected. Globally, pedestrians and cyclists represent 26% of all deaths, with those using motorized two- and three-wheelers comprising another 28%. Car occupants make up 29% of all deaths and the remaining 17% are unidentified road users[1]. Africa has the highest proportion of pedestrian and cyclist mortalities with 44% of deaths. In South-East Asia and the Western Pacific, the majority of deaths are among riders of motorized two- and three-wheelers who represent 43% and 36% of all deaths respectively.

Although pedestrians, cyclists and riders of motorized two- and three-wheelers-are more vulnerable as a result of being less protected than car occupants, the heavy burden of deaths borne by these road users is also a reflection of infrastructure and vehicle design that prioritizes cars and other motorized transport (14). Despite the prominence of vulnerable road users in many parts of the world, many of whom cannot afford or do not have access to the safest vehicles, they are still largely ignored in the planning, design and operation of roads. In many countries, roads still lack separate lanes for cyclists or adequate crossings for pedestrians and allow motor vehicle speeds that are too high (15). Similarly, while vehicle standards have been developed for car occupants, many are not widely implemented in vehicles sold in low- and middle-income countries. Only recently have more car manufacturers begun to implement standards in high-income countries to ensure that design also protects road users outside of the vehicle (16). The heavy burden of deaths borne by these groups constitutes an issue of equity, as income and social status become social determinants of road traffic deaths and injury (17).

1 The distribution of deaths among road user categories is based on data reported by countries. In some countries, these data are not available or are incomplete, which contributes to the large percentage of those identified as 'others' or 'unspecified'.

Figure 6: Distribution of deaths by road user type by WHO Region

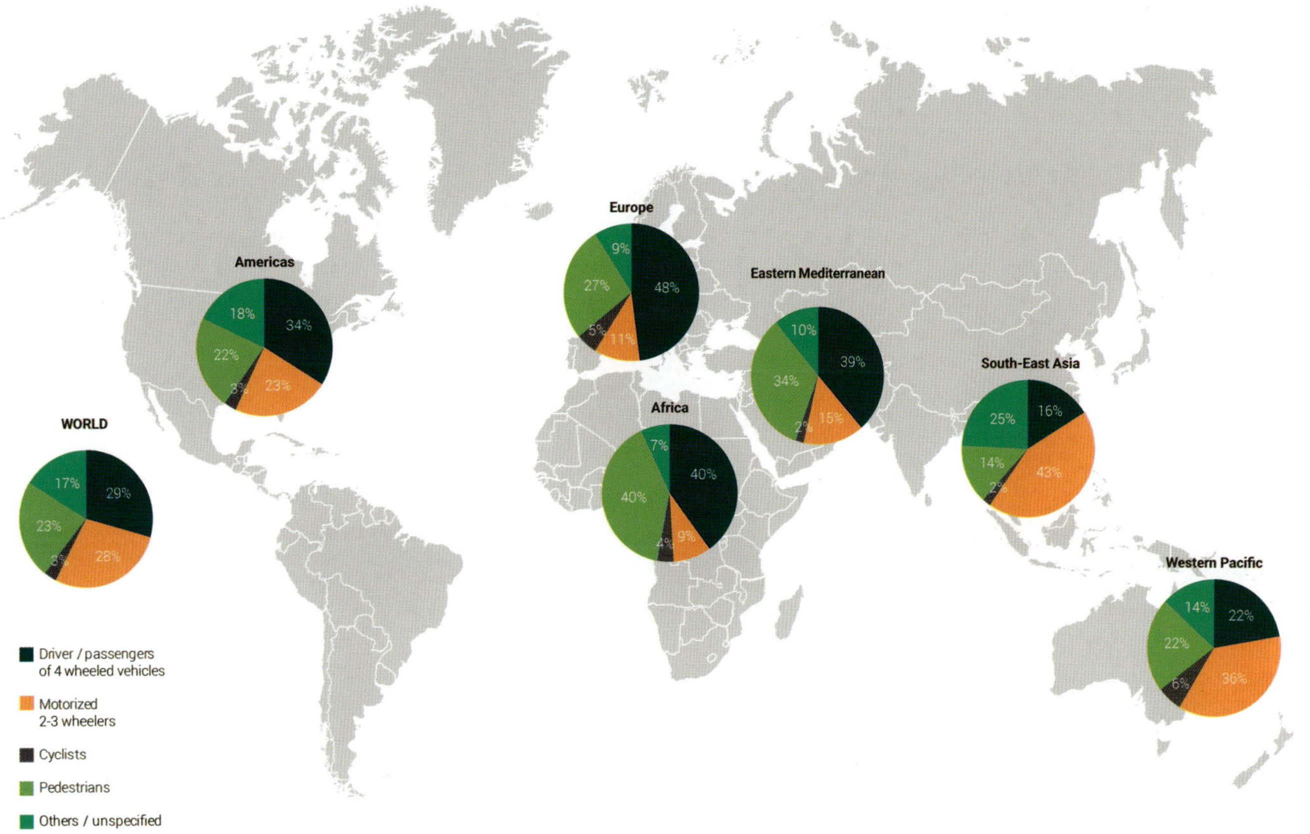

Box 1: Integrating road safety and urban mobility strategies in Bogotá, Colombia

Bogotá reduced the number of traffic deaths by 50% between 1996 and 2006, by implementing an integrated approach to road safety and urban mobility:

- Strong mayoral leadership was present, which allowed integrated institutional, financial and regulatory reforms, combined with messages that resonated with citizens.
- New investment was undertaken in city infrastructure of around US$ 2 billion between 1997 and 2006 in over 80 km of Bus Rapid Transport (BRT), nearly 300 km of bikeways and 60,000 m^2 of improved pedestrian infrastructure. The investment was enabled by institutional and tax reform and a sustainable mobility-oriented response to public demand for improved commuting options.
- Road safety improvements included safer public transport, improved sidewalks and cycle lanes, regulations and their enforcement of seat-belt wearing and drink-driving penalties, reform of the police system, public transport improvement reducing the rate of mode shift to private cars and motorcycles and avoiding exposure to risk.
- In December 2017, Bogotá adopted a new Vision Zero plan, based on the safe system approach, comprising further coordinated, integrated action to proactively reduce deaths and serious injury numbers yet further.

Sources:
https://www.odi.org/sites/odi.org.uk/files/resource-documents/12129.pdf
http://www.despacio.org/portfolio/bogota-bicycle-account-2014/https://ascelibrary.org/doi/abs/10.1061/40717%28148%292:

Box 2: Improving the safety of school zones in the Republic of Korea

The Republic of Korea has experienced the 3rd largest decline in the traffic fatality rates among OECD countries since 1972.

A historical focus on transport infrastructure investment and economic development resulted in less emphasis on road safety, particularly on the safety of pedestrians suffering death and injury at the expense of wider, faster roads. To address this problem and with the aim of lowering its high road death rate, the Korean government carried out an analysis of road traffic injury records and the highest risk locations in the network.

A new national strategy was adopted to improve road safety through investments in school zone programmes, improving the regulation of school buses, increasing fines for violations within school zones, clamping down on unregulated school transport, supporting civil society organizations in road safety advocacy and continuously amending and improving road safety legislation. These efforts are reported to have contributed to a 95% reduction in road traffic deaths among children under 14 years of age between 1998 and 2012.

Source: Sul J, Lee J, Kang DS, Lee WY, Shim JI, Myeong M, et al. Korea's 95% Reduction in Child Traffic Fatalities: Policies and Achievements. [Internet]. Goyang-si, Republic of Korea; 2014 [cited 2018 Nov 11]. Available from:https://www.kdevelopedia.org/download.do?timeFile=/mnt/idas/asset/2016/05/02/DOC/PDF/04201605020144393077306.pdf&originFileName=KSP-15.pdf

CHAPTER 2

INSTITUTIONAL MANAGEMENT

Key messages

- Achieving global and national road safety goals and targets requires appropriate management capacity.
- Such capacity should be demonstrated through effective institutional leadership within responsible agencies, multi-sectoral coordination arrangements, sustainable funding and data systems to measure, target and monitor progress.
- The inclusion of two SDG targets focused on road safety represents a major milestone for global road safety, confirming it is an essential element of the health and development agenda.
- 12 recently agreed upon global road safety performance targets will help countries to improve their road safety management and assess progress.

132

countries have national strategies for road safety that are funded

109

countries have national targets for the reduction of road traffic deaths

109 countries have national targets for the reduction of road traffic deaths.

Institutional management provides the foundation for improving road safety (18). The establishment of an appropriately resourced lead agency and coordination arrangements to guide the national road safety effort; the assessment of the state of play and capacity; the setting of goals and targets in road safety strategies; plans and projects; the provision of financial and human resources to address the problem and the monitoring and evaluation of activity are all essential to implementing effective, system-wide interventions (4,18,19).

Among the 175 participating countries, 140 indicated that they have a national strategy for road safety of which 132 reported having strategies that are funded. In addition to having national strategies for road safety, 109 countries reported having a national target for the reduction of road traffic deaths.

Similarly, while most countries (161) reported that they have established lead agency arrangements, only 129 reported that these are funded. While many countries reported having funded lead agencies and strategies, the extent of funding was not assessed. Among those with lead agencies, 159 had lead agencies that assumed responsibility for coordination, 144 had lead agencies that assumed responsibility for monitoring the status of road safety, and 149 had lead agencies that also had responsibility for enacting and revising legislation.

Voluntary global road safety performance targets

Against this background and in addition to the continuing provision of international guidance on a range of issues, several notable global developments have taken place since the last report was published, designed to assist countries in focusing their road safety management initiatives.

149 countries have lead agencies that also assume responsibility for road safety legislation.

In a call to action at the global level in September 2015, the United Nations General Assembly adopted a series of SDGs as part of the 2030 Agenda for Sustainable Development. The SDGs include specific targets related to road safety shown in Box 3 and their setting represents a major milestone for global road safety, confirming road safety as an essential element of the health and development agenda.

In November 2017, Member States, with the support of WHO, the United Nations Economic Commission for Europe, UNICEF, World Bank and other agencies, reached consensus on a set of 12 Voluntary Global Performance Targets for Road Safety Risk Factors and Service Delivery Mechanisms (Box 4). These voluntary targets provide a framework to guide and monitor the implementation of legislation, the establishment of standards and other interventions to prevent crashes, injuries, and deaths that are highlighted in this report.

Box 3: Sustainable Development Goals for Road Safety (September 2015)

3 GOOD HEALTH AND WELL-BEING

By 2020, to halve the number of global deaths and injuries from road traffic crashes.

11 SUSTAINABLE CITIES AND COMMUNITIES

By 2030, to provide access to safe, affordable, accessible and sustainable transport systems for all, improving road safety, notably by expanding public transport, with special attention to the needs of those in vulnerable situations, women, children, persons with disabilities, and older persons.

Box 4: Global Voluntary Performance Targets for Road Safety Risk Factors and Service Delivery Mechanisms, 2017

TARGET 1 – 2020

Target 1: By 2020, all countries establish a comprehensive multisectoral national road safety action plan with time-bound targets.

TARGET 2 – 2030

Target 2: By 2030, all countries accede to one or more of the core road safety-related UN legal instruments.

TARGET 3 – 2030

Target 3: By 2030, all new roads achieve technical standards for all road users that take into account road safety, or meet a three star rating or better.

TARGET 4 – 2030 (75%)

Target 4: By 2030, more than 75% of travel on existing roads is on roads that meet technical standards for all road users that take into account road safety.

TARGET 5 – 2030 (100%)

Target 5: By 2030, 100% of new (defined as produced, sold or imported) and used vehicles meet high quality safety standards, such as the recommended priority UN Regulations, Global Technical Regulations, or equivalent recognized national performance requirements.

TARGET 6 – 2030 (50%)

Target 6: By 2030, halve the proportion of vehicles travelling over the posted speed limit and achieve a reduction in speed-related injuries and fatalities.

TARGET 7 – 2030 (100%)

Target 7: By 2030, increase the proportion of motorcycle riders correctly using standard helmets to close to 100%.

TARGET 8 – 2030 (100%)

Target 8: By 2030, increase the proportion of motor vehicle occupants using safety belts or standard child restraint systems to close to 100%.

TARGET 9 – 2030 (50%)

Target 9: By 2030, halve the number of road traffic injuries and fatalities related to drivers using alcohol, and/or achieve a reduction in those related to other psychoactive substances.

TARGET 10 – 2030

Target 10: By 2030, all countries have national laws to restrict or prohibit the use of mobile phones while driving.

TARGET 11 – 2030

Target 11: By 2030, all countries to enact regulation for driving time and rest periods for professional drivers, and/or accede to international/regional regulation in this area.

TARGET 12 – 2030

Target 12: By 2030, all countries establish and achieve national targets in order to minimize the time interval between road traffic crash and the provision of first professional emergency care.

- PILLAR 1: Road safety management
- PILLAR 2: Safer roads and mobility
- PILLAR 3: Safe vehicles
- PILLAR 4: Safe road users
- PILLAR 5: Post-crash response

Following the request of the United Nations General Assembly, on November 22, 2017 Member States reached consensus on 12 global road safety performance targets. For more information: http://www.who.int/violence_injury_prevention/road_traffic/road-safety-targets/en/

Box 5: Managing by objectives in Sweden

Sweden is a global leader in road safety performance with 2.8 deaths per 100,000 inhabitants. Between 1990 and 2015, the number of road traffic deaths decreased by 66%. Experience in Sweden illustrates how better results can be achieved through long-term, perennial planning of systematic, evidence-based approaches to intervention, supported by a strong institutional delivery including leadership, sustained investment and a focus on achieving ambitious road safety goals and targets across government, business and civil society.

In October 1997 the Swedish Parliament adopted Vision Zero - a new long-term goal and a new strategic framework for road safety, which many countries are now adopting. The goal, supported by interim targets and objectives, follows the public health approach of preventing deaths and serious injury in road traffic crashes. The strategy is to create shared responsibility for the better management of all parts of the road traffic system in order to address known common errors and human vulnerabilities and thus avoid severe crash outcomes.

As with the 12 voluntary global targets set in 2017, the aim is to provide focal points for meaningful, shared, multisectoral activity at national, regional and local levels. The Swedish objectives target progress to 2020 and include safe road infrastructure at national and municipal levels, a higher proportion of undivided roads with an 80 km/h speed limit and median barriers, more municipal roads with footpaths and cycle paths, better compliance with speed limits, sober driving, seat-belt use, helmet use, higher car safety ratings and a higher share of motorcycles equipped with anti-lock braking systems.

Source: Swedish Transport Administration (2015) Analysis of Road Safety Trends 2014 — Management by Objectives for Road Safety Work, Towards the 2020 Interim Targets, Borlange.

CHAPTER 3

LEGISLATION AND ROAD USER BEHAVIOUR

Key messages

- Enacting and enforcing legislation on key risk factors are critical components of an integrated strategy to prevent road traffic deaths and injuries.
- As measured against best practice criteria, 123 countries representing 6 billion people have laws that meet best practice for at least one of the five key behavioural risk factors.
- Despite the progress made in improving legislation across the five key risk factors, enforcement remains a major challenge in most countries.

123
countries have laws that meet best practice for at least one of the five key behavioural risk factors

22
countries made improvements to bring their laws into alignment with best practice on one or more risk factors

46
countries have speed laws that align with best practice

45
countries have drink-driving laws that align with best practice

49
countries have helmet laws that align with best practice

105
countries have seat-belt laws that align with best practice

33
countries have child restraint laws that align with best practice

22 countries representing **1 billion people** amended their laws on one or more risk factors to bring them into alignment with best practice.

Enacting and enforcing legislation on key risk factors including speed, drink-driving, motorcycle helmet use, use of seat-belts and child restraint systems, are critical components of an integrated strategy to prevent road traffic deaths in countries (4,19–24). Legislation, together with standards and compliance regimes for the licensing and disqualification of drivers and riders, needs to be aligned with enforcement, media campaigns and, in some cases, in-vehicle measures such as the availability of seat-belts and fitments, to be effective (25). Police enforcement initiatives need to be swift, frequent and sustained over a long period of time to increase the perceived risk of being caught and punished but also random and widespread to increase the chance of detection. Given the multisectoral nature of road safety, laws and enforcement standards are set by several government agencies, including public health, transport, internal affairs, science and technology, and occupational health and safety, and these require a coordinated effort across sectors (3).

Legislation on key risk factors from participating countries has been reviewed against best practice criteria in order to identify gaps and opportunities for improvement. Currently, 123 countries, representing nearly 6 billion people, have laws that meet best practice for at least one of the five key behavioural risk factors. As shown in Table 2, 45 countries have laws meeting best practice for one risk factor; 31 have laws meeting best practice for two risk factors; 22 have laws meeting best practice on three risk factors; 20 have laws meeting practice on four risk factors; and only five countries have laws that meet best practice for all five key risk factors: speeding, drink-driving, use of motorcycle helmets, use of seat-belts, and use of child restraints.

Table 2: Number of countries and populations covered by laws meeting best practice

Number of risk factors covered by laws	Number of Countries	Total Population covered
1 risk factor	45	1,385,220,916
2 risk factors	31	1,980,475,253
3 risk factors	22	2,131,299,369
4 risk factors	20	347,434,370
5 risk factors	5	144,317,185
Total	123	5,988,747,093

*speeding, drink-driving, use of motorcycle helmets, use of seat-belts, use of child restraints

One-third of countries rated their enforcement as «good» for any of the laws related to the 5 key risk factors.

Since 2014, 22 countries have amended their laws on one or more key risk factors to bring them in line with best practice, covering a potential additional one billion people or 14% of the world's population. As shown in Figure 7, some improvement was made for each of the five behavioural risk factors with the largest improvement found for drink-driving laws (ten countries), followed by motorcycle helmet laws (five countries), child restraints (four countries), and seat-belts (three countries). As a result of one country aligning with best practice and one making changes that brought it out of alignment with best practice, the number of countries with laws aligning with best practice for speed remained the same. Despite the progress made in improving legislation across the five key risk factors, enforcement remains a major challenge in most countries. Only one-third of countries rated their enforcement as "good" (eight or above on a scale of zero to ten, as rated by respondents) for any of the risk factors, indicating that many of these countries are not reaping the full benefit of their legislation.

Figure 7: Countries with laws meeting best practice on 5 risk factors, 2014, 2017

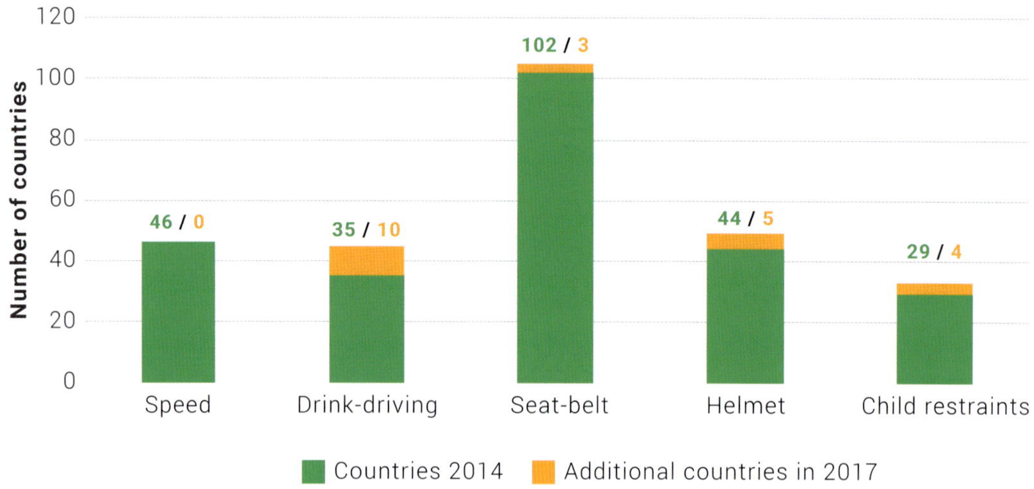

Figure 8: Populations covered by laws meeting best practice, 2014, 2017

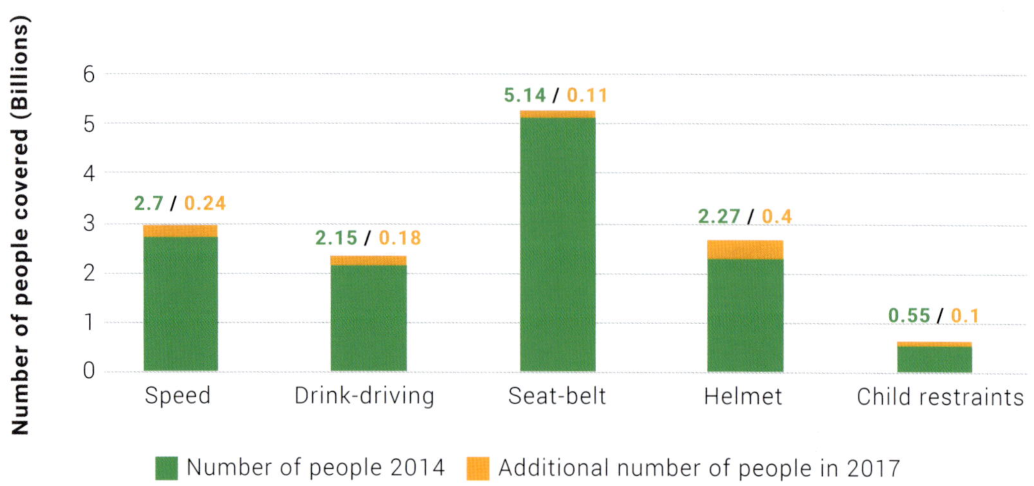

Managing speed

46 countries representing **3 billion people** currently have laws setting speed limits that align with best practice.

The speed at which a vehicle travels directly influences the risk of a crash as well as the severity of injuries, and likelihood of death resulting from that crash (26). Effective speed management is, as such, central to most intervention strategies. The setting and enforcement of speed limits represents a key component of comprehensive speed management as part of an integrated approach involving consideration of the protective quality of roads, roadsides, vehicles and human tolerance thresholds for death and serious injury (3). Even small reductions in speed affect fatal and serious crash risk and the effectiveness of road and vehicle interventions to prevent death and serious injury (19,27).

→ An accepted principle is that every 1% increase in mean speed produces a 4% increase in the fatal crash risk and a 3% increase in the serious crash risk (28).

→ A 5% reduction in average speed can reduce the number of fatalities by 30% (27).

Small reductions in speed also influence thresholds for death and serious injury risk in different crash scenarios:

→ For pedestrians hit by car fronts, the death risk rises rapidly (4.5 times from 50 km/h to 65 km/h) (29).

→ In car-to-car side impacts the fatality risk for car occupants is 85% at 65 km/h (30).

→ For belted occupants in the best designed cars (Euro NCAP 5-star), the threshold for severe and fatal injury have been identified as 70 km/h (travel speed at impact) in head-on car-to-car crashes (30).

Review of speed laws

Three best practice criteria were used in the assessment of legislation on speed laws:

- → presence of a national speed limit law;
- → urban speed limits not exceeding 50 km/h (based on research, lower limits are recommended for urban areas and 30 km/h for residential areas and areas with high pedestrian activity); and
- → local authorities having the power to modify speed limits (to adapt to different contexts).

The presence of best practice laws was found to be more common in high-income countries than in middle- or low-income countries.

The results show that 169 countries (representing 97% of the world's population) have set national speed limit laws, however, only 46 of these countries have laws that meet all three best practice criteria. Since 2014, one additional country aligned its legislation with best practice and one country made changes that resulted in the legislation no longer aligning with best practice on speed management. Among countries with legislation meeting at least one of the three best practice criteria, 95 countries provide for speed limits equal to or under 50 km/h in urban areas, and 84 provide local authorities with the power to modify speed limits in their laws. As shown in Figure 9, the presence of best practice laws was found to be more common among high-income countries (50%) than middle- or low-income countries (37% and 13%, respectively).

Enforcement campaigns play an important role in ensuring respect for and compliance with speed limits (31). Combinations of both manual and automated enforcement methods can increase the probability of detecting violations (31). Automated enforcement (such as fixed camera and mobile in-vehicle fitted devices) systems are highly cost-effective and an important consideration especially for low-resource settings (32). A total of 157 countries reported conducting speed enforcement activities. Despite the fact that 90 of the 157 countries indicated that they do employ some automated methods, for the majority of countries, manual speed enforcement remains the dominant method of enforcement. As such, it is not surprising that only 30 countries rated their enforcement of speed laws as "good" (eight or above on a scale of zero to ten).

Figure 9: Countries with speed laws meeting best practice, 2017

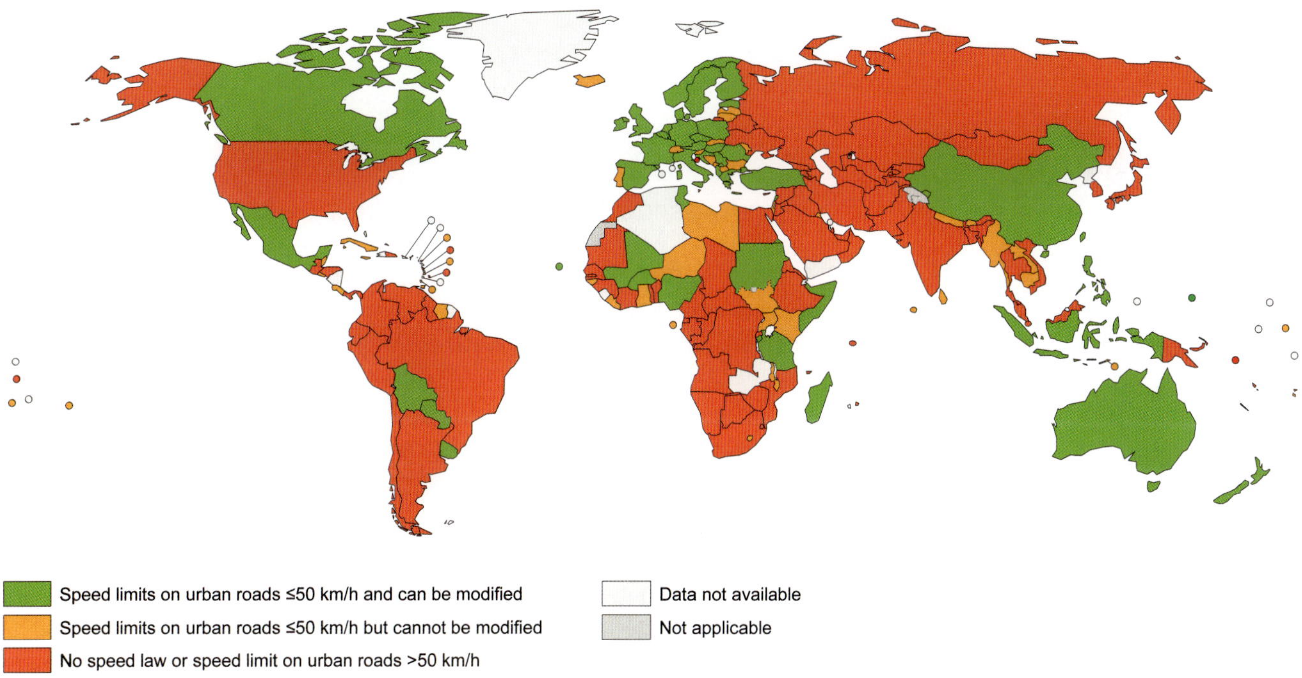

Box 6: Setting urban speed limits in Thailand

Setting speed limits appropriate to road function, layout and design and which take account of the safety needs of all creates a framework for safe road use. Typically, maximum speed limits across the network are set at national level on the initiative of roads and transport authorities.

Thailand's current urban speed law was established in 1979 and sets a maximum speed of 80 km/h for urban areas. The 80 km/h limit on urban roads is far from aligning with current best practice, which recommends a maximum speed limit for urban areas of 50 km/h and lower limits in areas where pedestrian volumes are high, such as residential or city streets.

Since 2015, efforts have been made to amend the national speed legislation but were unsuccessful. In 2015, the focus shifted from changing the national legislation to empowering and encouraging provinces to use the provision in the law to set their own speed limits. Additionally, guidelines have been provided for local governments to set appropriate speed limits.

In 2017, with guidelines in place for setting speed limits in municipalities, provinces have started to set more appropriate speed limits, and by September 2018, half of the 76 provinces have set urban speed limits not exceeding 50 km/h.

This example illustrates the importance of local initiatives in moving towards appropriate urban speed limits, when national speed limit setting fails to move in line with best practice.

Sources:
Ministerial Regulation Number 6 (1979).
Guidelines for Setting Speed Limits in City and Municipality

Reducing drink-driving

45 countries representing **2.3 billion people** currently have drink-driving laws that align with best practice.

It is estimated that between 5% and 35% of all road deaths are reported as alcohol-related (33,34). Driving after drinking alcohol significantly increases the risk of a crash and the severity of that crash (35). Any amount of alcohol has been shown to impair driving behaviour, and there is a rapid and exponential increase in risk for levels exceeding 0.05 g/dl for the general driving population. Reducing blood alcohol concentrations (BAC) from 0.1 g/dl to 0.05 g/dl may contribute to a reduction of 6–18% in alcohol-related road traffic fatalities (36).

While BAC limits provided for in legislation need to be at the core of efforts to address drinking and driving, an integrated approach to intervention involves combined publicity and high visibility police enforcement and the fitment of alcolocks in commercial and public transport vehicles (3,37). It is best practice to set limits of 0.02 g/dl for young and novice drivers in view of their greater susceptibility to impairment by alcohol at lower levels and their disproportionately higher risk of being involved in fatal crashes; though not included as a best practice criteria for this analysis, the setting of a lower limit of 0.02 g/dl has also been considered for commercial drivers due to the fact that they transport passengers and the potential deaths and injuries inflicted by truck collisions is greater than other passenger vehicles (6,38).

Review of drink-driving laws

Three best practice criteria were considered for the assessment of drink-driving laws:

→ presence of a national drink-driving law;

→ BAC limit for the general population not exceeding 0.05 g/dl; and

→ BAC limit for young and novice drivers not exceeding 0.02 g/dl.

While nearly all of the participating countries have national drink-driving laws in place, not all specify a BAC limit which makes it difficult to enforce the law. Of the 174 with laws, 136 countries provide for BAC threshold limits. Among these, 45 countries meet all three best practice criteria for drink-driving laws with specified thresholds for both the general population (0.05 g/dl) as well as for young and novice drivers (0.02 g/dl). Of those countries with laws that meet at least one of the best practice criteria, 89 countries specify the recommended BAC limit of 0.05 g/dl for the general population; 48 specify a BAC limit of 0.02 g/dl for young and novice drivers; while 53 have provisions for reduced limits of 0.02 g/dl among commercial drivers.

Progress has been made since 2014 with an additional ten countries now meeting overall best practice for drink-driving laws, representing coverage of an additional 180 million people. As shown in Figure 10, more high-income countries (58%) have laws that meet overall best practice criteria for drink-driving than middle-income countries or low-income countries (40% and 2%, respectively). Whereas 60% of countries with laws meeting best practice are from the European region only 2% are from the African region.

Enforcement that incorporates random breath testing strategies (as opposed to those that are targeted during certain times and in certain areas) is more effective in increasing both the perceived and actual probability of being caught and so deterring drinking and driving (38). This review showed that more than half of all countries undertake year round random breath testing

Data on drink-driving remains limited in many countries and is necessary to understanding the magnitude of the problem as well as to evaluate the impact of efforts to prevent it. Of those surveyed, 94 countries have data on road traffic deaths, which involve alcohol consumption amongst drivers, mostly high- and middle-income countries and only five low-income. Estimates for many countries are based on data from crash reports that generally underestimate the extent of the problem. 125 countries reported that fatally injured drivers are tested for alcohol of which 72 reported that the testing is routinely carried out for all cases.

Figure 10: Countries with drink-driving laws meeting best practice, 2017

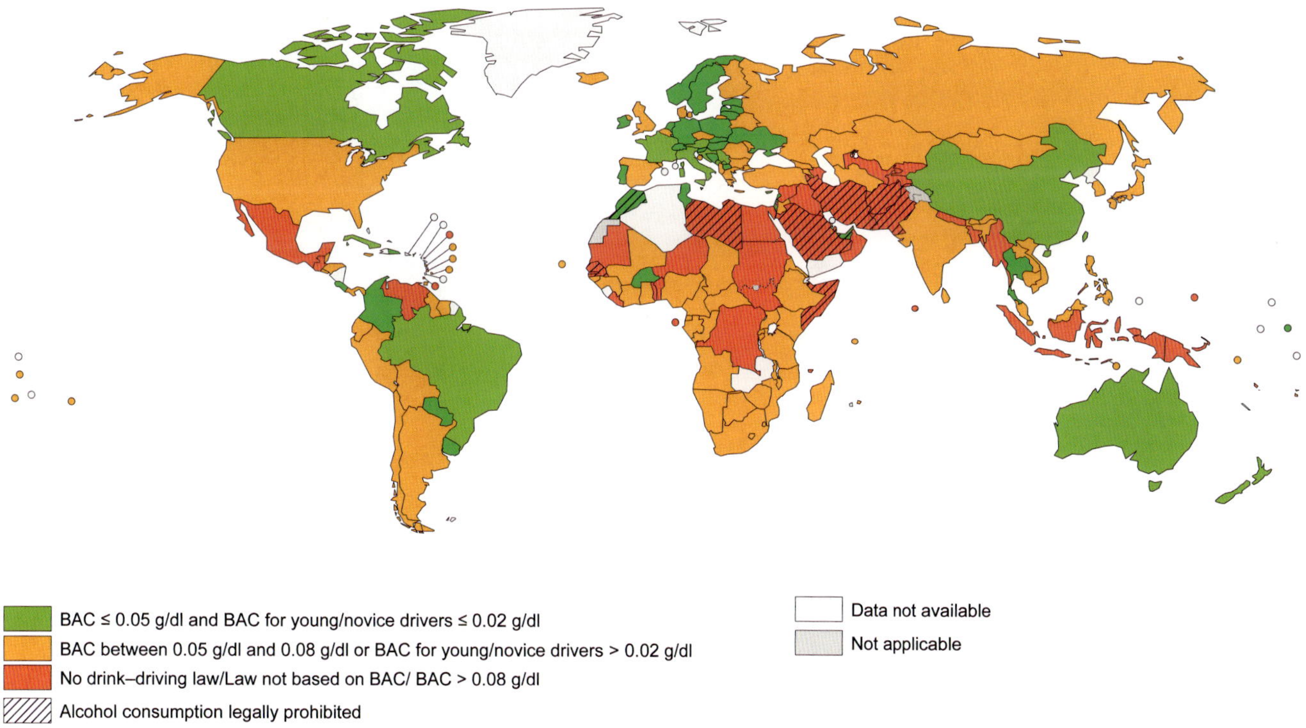

Box 7: Effectiveness of changing legal blood alcohol concentration limits in Brazil

Brazil's first drink-driving law based on BAC limits was enacted in 1998 making it an offence to drive with a BAC in excess of 0.06 g/dl. A study of road fatalities in Sao Paulo, Brazil found that 39% of people killed in road traffic crashes had BAC levels greater than 0.01 g/dl and 42% of drivers presented had BAC levels greater than 0.06 g/dl. In order to tackle this public health threat, the Brazilian government enacted the new "Dry Law" in June 2008, which reduced the legal BAC limit from 0.06 g/dl to 0.02 g/dl.

Monitoring in the capital and State of Sao Paulo between 2001 to 2010 indicated that the new law resulted in significant reductions in injuries and fatalities. The effect was stronger for fatalities (a decrease of −7.2% and −16.0% in the average monthly rate in the State and capital of Sao Paulo, respectively) than for injuries (−1.8% and −2.3%).

While the new law resulted in casualty reduction, barriers to its application remained. Notably, drivers had a right to refuse a BAC test, which made it difficult to impose criminal sanctions related to BAC test levels. The Brazilian government subsequently amended the "Dry Law" in December 2012 to allow police officers to use alternative evidence (e.g. clinical signs or videos) to support a drink-driving offence. The amendment also made it illegal to have any measurable alcohol in the blood and doubled the original 1998 fines.

Sources:
Andreuccetti G, Carvalho HB, Cherpitel CJ, et al. Reducing the legal blood alcohol concentration limit for driving in developing countries: A time for change? Results and implications derived from a time series analysis (2001:10) conducted in Brazil. Addiction. 2011:106(12): 2124-2131.
Moura EC, Malta DC, Morais Neto OL, Penna GO, Temporao JG. Motor vehicle driving after binge drinking, Brazil, 2006 to 2009. Rev Saude Publica. 2009:43(5): 891-894.

49 countries representing **2.7 billion people** currently have laws on motorcycle helmet use that align with best practice.

Increasing motorcycle helmet use

Between 2013 and 2016, the number of two- and three-wheelers in circulation on the world's roads increased by 10%. In the ten countries with the greatest numbers of these vehicles, motorcycles comprise more than 70% of the national vehicle fleet.

Head injuries are the leading cause of death and major trauma for two- and three-wheeled motor vehicle users (40). Correct helmet use can lead to a 42% reduction in the risk of fatal injuries and a 69% reduction in the risk of head injuries (41). The use of helmets is, as such, an important means of preventing road traffic deaths. Legislation should provide for helmet use by all passengers, including children, and should be supported by public awareness campaigns and sustained enforcement. Good helmet design and correct use of standard helmets when riding a motorcycle are highly important (42,43).

Review of motorcycle helmet laws

Five best practice criteria were considered for the assessment of motorcycle helmet laws:

- → presence of a national motorcycle helmet law;
- → law applying to both drivers and passengers;
- → law applying to all road and engine types;
- → law specifying that helmets should be fastened; and
- → law referring to / specifying a standard for helmets.

As shown in Figure 11, of the 167 countries that have mandatory helmet laws for motorcyclists, only 49 (representing 36% of the world

population) have laws that meet all five best practice criteria. Among those with laws that meet at least one best practice criteria, 160 have laws to protect all riders (drivers and passengers); 82 have laws requiring helmets to be fastened; and 93 refer to helmet standards in their laws.

Since 2014, five countries have made amendments to existing legislation to align them with best practice, providing coverage to an additional 397 million people. Despite the prevalence of motorcycles in low-income settings, only 6% of the countries with laws meeting best practice criteria are low-income countries. Only 63 countries, representing 33% of the world's population, restrict child passengers on motorcycles.

Enforcement of helmet-wearing laws are generally weak; only 61 countries rate their enforcement of helmet-wearing laws as "good" (eight or above on a scale of 0 to 10). Similarly, less than half of countries surveyed (75) have data available on helmet-wearing. The majority of these countries are high-income countries; only six low-income countries reported having data on helmet-wearing. Even when it is collected, available data vary largely in terms of quality and methodologies used and very few report on national data.

Figure 11: Countries with helmet laws meeting best practice, 2017

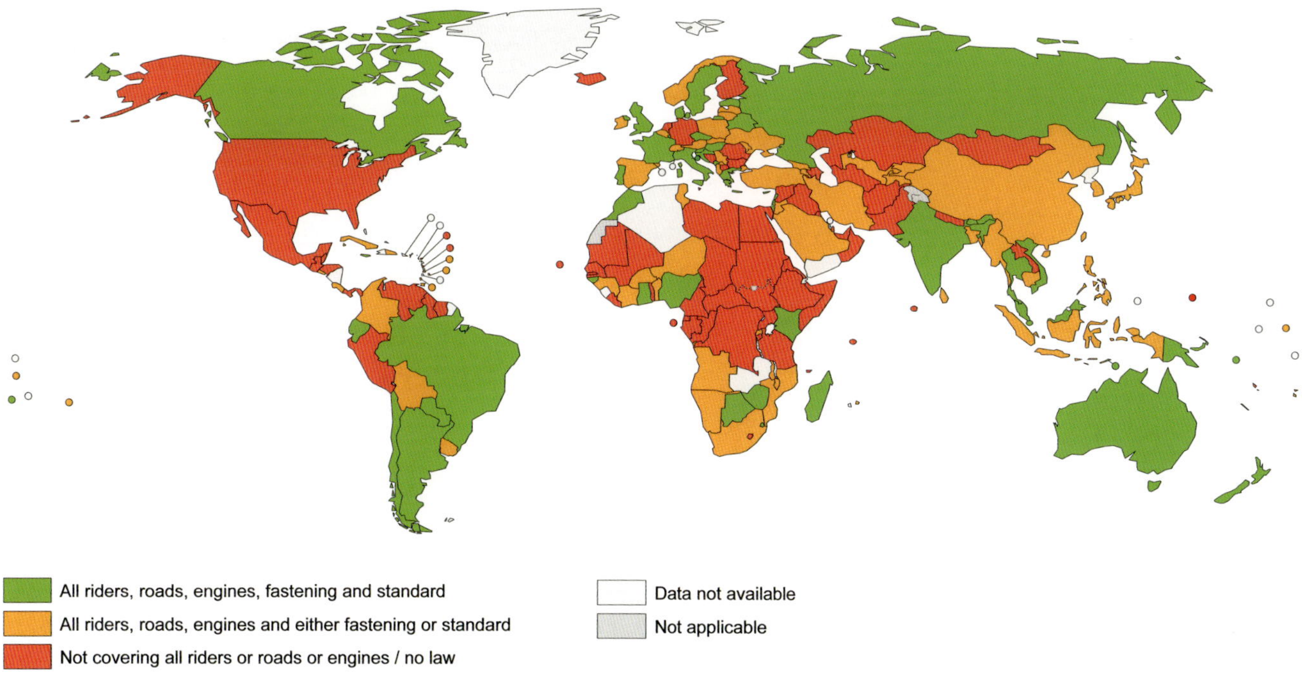

Increasing seat-belt use

105 countries representing **5.3 billion people** currently have laws on seat-belt use that align with best practice.

Wearing a seat-belt reduces the risk of death among drivers and front seat occupants by 45 - 50%, and the risk of death and serious injuries among rear seat occupants by 25% (35). Mandatory seat-belt legislation is highly effective in promoting seat-belt wearing and is a cost-effective means of reducing road traffic deaths and injuries, especially in rapidly motorizing low- and middle-income countries (44). As is the case for other risk factors, increasing seat-belt use requires multisectoral action beyond the setting of appropriate legislation (45). This includes combined publicity and enforcement and the provision of in-vehicle seat-belt reminders, which have been shown to be highly effective in increasing use (45).

Review of seat-belt laws

Two best practice criteria were considered for the assessment of seat-belt legislation:

→ presence of a national seat-belt law; and

→ law applying to front and rear seat occupants.

As shown in Figure 12, of the 161 countries with national seat-belt laws, 105, representing 71% of the world's population, have adopted the best practice of mandating the use of seat-belts by both front and rear seat occupants. Only 7% of countries with seat-belt laws meeting best practice are low-income coutries.

Since 2014, seven countries have made changes to their seat-belt legislation: five additional countries now have laws that meet best practice while two countries have made changes that bring their laws out of alignment with best practice. The net increase of 3 countries accounts for an additional 113 million people covered by best practice seat-belt laws. Enforcement of seat-belt laws is poor with only 40 countries rating their enforcement of seat-belt use laws as "good" (eight or above on a scale of zero to ten). Less than half of countries collect data on seat-belt wearing and the majority of these are high- and middle-income countries.

Figure 12: Countries with seat-belt laws meeting best practice, 2017

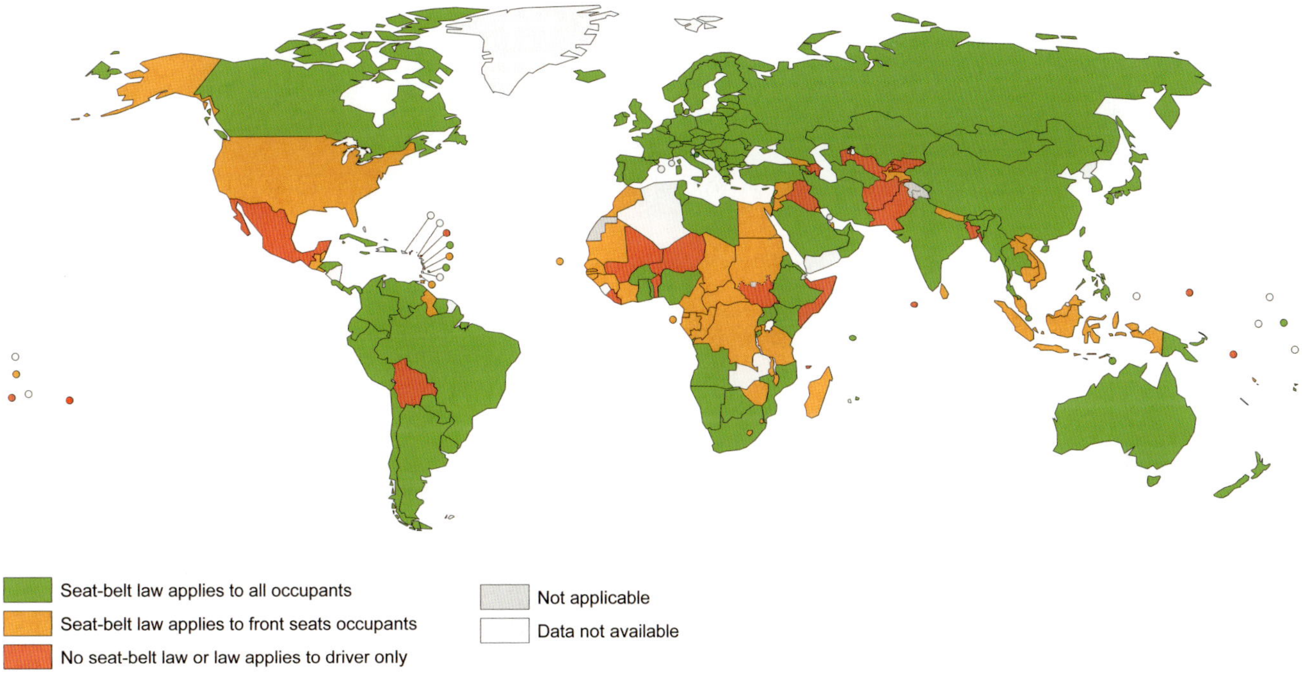

Increasing child restraint use

Child restraints are highly effective in reducing injury and death to child occupants (45–59). The use of child restraints can lead to at least a 60% reduction in deaths (54). The benefits of child restraints have been shown to be greatest for younger children, particularly those under four years of age (49). For children 8-12 years, booster seat use has been associated with a 19% reduction in the odds of injury compared to using a seat-belt alone (48). The position of children in either front or rear seats is also important as a higher risk for injury is associated with the front seating position (59).

33 countries representing **652 million people** currently have laws on the use of child restraints that align with best practice.

Review of child restraint laws

Best practice criteria for child restraints have been further developed since the previous report in view of the additional data collected for this review. Four best practice criteria were considered in the assessment of child restraint laws:

→ presence of a national child restraint law;

→ requirement for children to use a child restraint at least until ten years of age or 135cm in height;

→ restrictions for children under a certain age or height from sitting in the front seat

→ reference to or specification of a standard for child restraints.

As shown in Figure 13, 84 countries have a national child restraint law. Among these, 33 countries, representing 9% of the world population, meet the overall best practice criteria for child restraints. Of those with laws that meet at least one of the best practice criteria, 53 countries refer to a standard for child restraints, 113 restrict seating children in the front seat (including 61 banning front seating) and 41 countries address the age and/or height criteria of ten years of age or 135 cm in height in the legislation.

Since 2014, four countries have made amendments to legislation on the use of child restraints to bring them in line with best practice. Among those with laws meeting best practice, 85% are high-income countries and 15% are middle-income countries. No low-income countries have laws on the use of child restraint systems that meet best practice. Best practice laws are most common among countries in the European region; in all other regions, less than 7% of countries have laws on the use of child restraint systems that align with best practice.

Only 22 countries rate their enforcement of child restraint laws as "good" (eight or above on a scale of zero to ten) and only 35 collect data on child restraint use.

Figure 13: Countries with child restraint laws meeting best practice, 2017

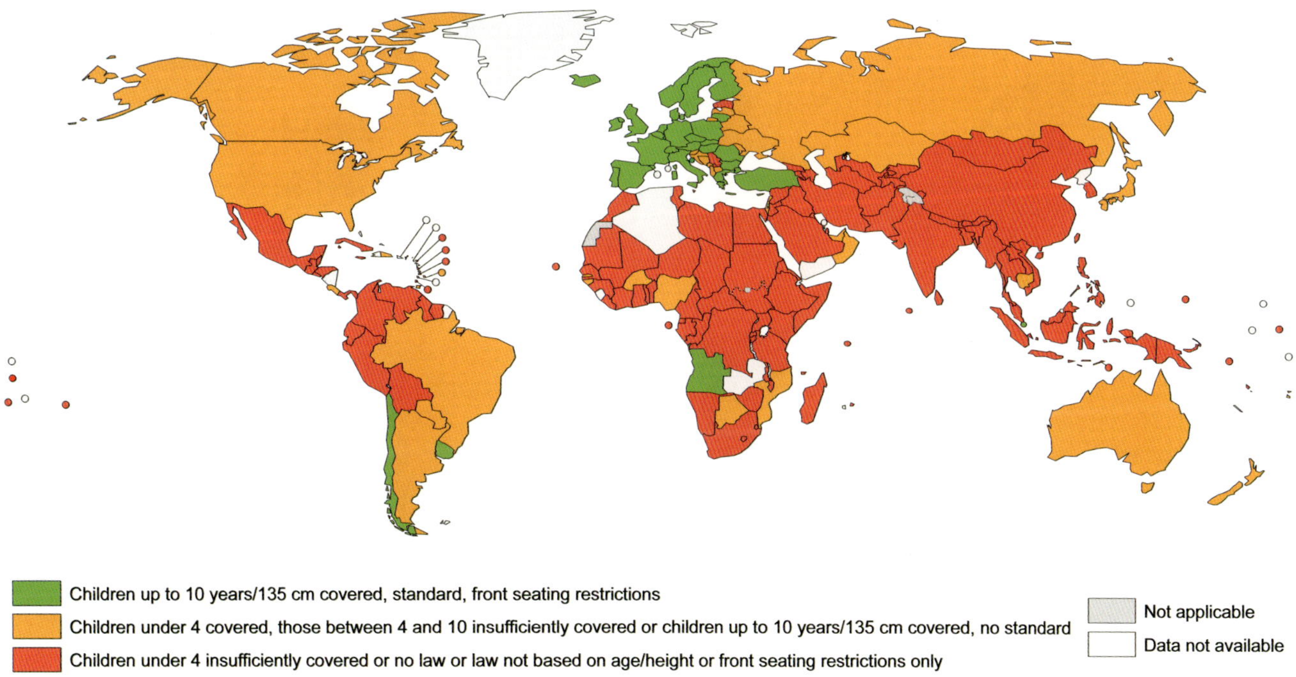

Reducing distracted driving

Distracted driving by mobile devices such as smartphones and/or other in-vehicle devices is a growing risk factor linked to serious negative outcomes (60–62). The use of a mobile phone while driving is widespread amongst young and novice drivers and growing amongst motorcyclists, adding further to the already high risk of crash and death among these groups. Telephone use while driving (whether hand-held or hands-free) increases the likelihood of being involved in a crash by a factor of four, while texting increases crash risk by around 23 times (63). Driver reaction times have also been shown to be 50% slower with telephone use than without. Similarly, in-car telephone conversations impair drivers more than listening to the radio or talking to passengers (64,65). Despite the growing body of evidence on the risks associated with distracted driving, there remains a dearth of evidence on the effectiveness of interventions to reduce distracted driving.

64 countries routinely collect data on distracted driving through police reports and observational studies.

Review of mobile phone laws

There is insufficient evidence on the effectiveness of legislation to limit or prohibit the use of mobile devices while driving to establish best practice criteria. A total of 150 countries have a national mobile phone law in place and most (145) prohibit the use of hand-held mobile phones while driving. In terms of progress made, four additional countries have national mobile phone laws though the impact of this cannot be assessed at this time as there is currently not a best practice for legislation on distracted driving.

Given the difficulty in detecting these behaviours, enforcement and data collection remain challenging. 64 countries routinely collect data on this risk, largely through regular police crash reports with few regular observational studies. An additional 21 countries have some non-routinely collected data from research.

Reducing drug-driving

75 countries reported doing some drug testing among fatally injured drivers.

Though more difficult to quantify than alcohol, the use of illegal drugs and certain prescription medications is increasingly linked to road traffic crashes and deaths, though there are many complexities around testing and establishing the causality of different drugs (66). The concomitant use of drugs and alcohol presents further complexities and risks (66). There is a dearth of data on how frequently drivers use and/or are impaired by drugs and few countries systematically measure the extent of the drug-driving problem. Data from the United States show that among fatally-injured drivers for whom drug test results were available, 43.6% were positive in 2016, an increase from 27.8% in 2006 (67). The risk of crash and death varies depending on the type of psychoactive drug. The use of amphetamines increases the risk for fatal crashes by five times and risk for non-fatal crashes by six times.

Review of drug-driving laws

There is insufficient evidence on the effectiveness of legislation to limit or prohibit drug-driving to establish best practice criteria. The majority of countries surveyed (156) have a national drug-driving law in place. This includes two countries that have adopted laws to prohibit drug-driving since 2014, though the impact of this cannot be assessed at this time as there is currently not a best practice for legislation on drug-driving.

The extent of the drug-driving problem is insufficiently known in many countries. Only 75 reported doing some drug testing among fatally injured drivers.

Distracted
Driving

CHAPTER 4

SAFE ROADS

Key messages

- When safety is taken into consideration during the planning, design and operation of roads, substantial contributions can be made to reducing road traffic deaths and injuries.
- For pedestrians, cyclists and motorcyclists, the lack of specific infrastructure features that can ensure them a safe journey leaves them vulnerable to injury.
- Road safety inspections and the star rating of roads can provide mechanisms to identify failings in infrastructure which can affect a crash likelihood and severity.
- Upgrading high-risk roads and providing access to safe and affordable public transport will reduce road traffic death and injury.

88%
of pedestrian travel is on 1- or 2-star roads

86%
of bicyclist travel is on 1- or 2-star roads

67%
of motorcyclist travel is on 1- or 2-star roads

114 countries currently undertake systematic assessments or star rating of existing roads.

Road infrastructure is strongly linked to fatal and serious injury causation in road collisions, and research has shown that improvements to the road infrastructure are critical to improving overall road safety (69). The aim is to create a safe road environment, rather than placing the main responsibility for safety on users who fail to deal with the intrinsic dangers of the roads. Head-on crashes, for example, occur on undivided roads while the lack of a footpath or a safe crossing presents a major risk for death and injury to pedestrians (3). For cyclists and motorcyclists, the lack of specific infrastructure features that ensure a safe journey like cycle lanes and motorcycle lanes leaves them vulnerable to impact and injury (69). The provision of affordable and safe public transport as well as facilities for safe walking and cycling are highly important.

Review of the use of standards and tools to improve the safety quality of roads

This report has continued to track the status of countries in setting design standards, undertaking audits and/or the star rating of new road infrastructure and inspection/star rating of existing roads. Three new questions in this report involve:

→ ***the use of dedicated funding to upgrade high-risk roads.*** In most countries and cities, more than half of all road deaths and severe injuries happen on less than 10% of the road length (70). The return on investment for improving road infrastructure safety on these high-risk roads is substantial.

→ ***design standards that specifically meet the needs of vulnerable road users.*** Historic road design practice and standards have focussed on meeting the capacity and travel time needs of motorized vehicles whereas the specific needs of vulnerable road users have often been secondary considerations.

- → ***the provision of affordable and safe public transport.*** In urban areas, where an additional two billion people are expected to be living in cities by 2045, the provision of affordable and safe public transport is an essential investment for sustainable mobility.

88% of pedestrian travel occurs on roads that are unsafe.

While design standards exist in most countries, the way in which they are applied to a new road design is influenced by the complexity of the location (urban, rural, utility services, road users present), the priority on safety outcomes and the budgets allocated for the project. This review shows that 112 countries have national design standards for the management of speed. Ninety-two countries have national design standards for separating pedestrians and cyclists road users from motorized traffic. One hundred and thirty-two countries have national design standards for the provision of safe crossings for pedestrians and cyclists.

Road safety inspections and the star rating of existing roads provide a mechanism to identify any existing road design and speed management features that can affect crash likelihood and severity. Systematic risk rate mapping, performance tracking and safety rating

using objective data are carried out by international and national road assessment programmes. (71). Road protection scores assess the level of protection against the risk of death and serious injury in collisions for all main user groups afforded by the road environment. Each road is given a star rating from one to five stars. Minimum star ratings for the infrastructure safety of major roads are increasingly being used in targeted programmes and are recommended, especially where high-quality crash injury data are not yet available or where capacity is still being built for safety engineering (69).

A sample of recent of International Road Assessment Programme (iRAP) assessments from 54 countries, covering 358,000 kilometers of rural and urban roads with over 700 billion vehicle kilometres of travel a year has highlighted that 88% of pedestrian travel is on one- or two-star roads, 86% of bicycle travel is one- or two-star roads, 67% of motorcycle travel is on one- or two-star roads, and 44% of vehicle travel is one- or two-star roads (72). One hundred forty-seven countries reported carrying out road safety audits or star ratings for new roads while 114 countries reported doing safety assessments or star rating on existing roads.

The implementation of a dedicated funding stream and targeted programmes to upgrade high-risk roads and provide access to safe and affordable public transport will help to systematically eliminate the highest-risk roads in a country and reduce death and injury. This review found that 116 countries have a systematic programme in place for targeting and upgrading high-risk locations on existing roads. Additionally, 77 countries reported investing in mass transit while 103 countries reported having formal policies for formal bus/ mini-bus systems.

Table 3: Star rating of roads – what makes a road safe?

Star Rating				
★	No sidewalk, No safe crossing, 60 km/h traffic	No cyclepath, No safe crossings, poor road surface, 70 km/h traffic	No motorcycle lane, undivided road, trees close to road, winding alignment, 90 km/h traffic	Undivided road with narrow centerline, trees close to road, winding alignment, 100 km/h traffic
★★★	Sidewalk present, pedestrian refuge, street lighting, 50 km/h traffic	On-road cycle lane, good road surface, street lighting, 60 km/h traffic	On-road motorcycle lane, undivided road, good road surface, >5m to any roadside hazards, 90 km/h traffic	Wide centerline separating oncoming vehicles, >5m to any roadside hazards, 100 km/h traffic
★★★★★	Sidewalk present, signalized crossing with refuge, street lighting, 40 km/h	Off-road dedicated cycle facility, raised platform crossing of major roads, street lighting	Dedicated separated motorcycle lane, central hatching, no roadside hazards, straight alignment, 80 km/h traffic	Safety barrier separating oncoming vehicles and protecting roadside hazards, straight alignment, 100 km/h traffic

* For details on the full model for all road users and more urban and rural examples see https://www.irap.org//3-star-or-better/what-is-star-rating.

Box 8: 5-star school journey for Lusaka students

Sub-Saharan Africa has the world's highest road traffic injury rates. For students of Justin Kabwe Primary School in Lusaka, Zambia, their journey to school is now much safer, with access roads raised from one- and two-star dangerous to five-star safety excellence, assessed using iRAP's Star Rating for Schools app. Four children were injured on roads around the school before the school was upgraded. 4,700 vehicles pass the entrance, 200 people cross the road and over 900 people walk along the road past the school every peak hour. Crossing the road into school used to be very dangerous.

Thanks to a project completed in November 2017 by the nonprofit Amend and supported by FedEx, infrastructure enhancements have improved safety, assessed using the Star Rating for Schools (SR4S) app powered by iRAP's Pedestrian Star Rating. The improvements included the addition of a raised platform pedestrian crossing, footpaths, fencing and a school zone warning, removal of vehicle parking which blocked sight lines, and reduced operating speeds of passing vehicles.

Four locations with high pedestrian traffic flows were star rated for safety using the SR4S app before and after the infrastructure improvements. The before and after star rating results captured by SR4S reflected a major improvement in safety. The school's main entrance intersection and nearby corner achieved star rating improvements from one to five stars and two to five stars respectively.

Source: iRAP, 2018 https://www.irap.org/media-centre/case-studies/

School Safety
Zone
Slow Down

CHAPTER 5

SAFE VEHICLES

Key messages

- Vehicle safety features such as electronic stability control and advanced braking make a substantial contribution to reducing road traffic deaths and injuries.
- Despite these potential benefits, not all new and used vehicles are required to be equipped with these and other internationally recognized vehicle safety standards.
- New Car Assessment Programmes (NCAPs) have proved highly effective in raising levels of vehicle safety significantly above minimum regulatory requirements.

40

countries implement 7 or 8 of the priority UN vehicle safety standards

124

countries apply 0 or 1 of the 8 priority UN vehicle safety standards

40 countries representing **1 billion people**, have implemented at least 7 or all of the 8 priority UN vehicle safety standards.

Vehicle safety is increasingly critical to the prevention of crashes and has been shown to contribute to substantial reductions in the number of deaths and serious injuries on the roads (6). Features such as electronic stability control and advanced braking are examples of vehicle safety standards that can prevent a crash from occurring or reduce the severity of injuries (74). Despite these potential benefits, not all new and used vehicles are required to be equipped with internationally recognized safety standards (75). Eight UN vehicle safety standards have been prioritized for implementation by countries (Box 9).

Review of take up of key vehicle safety regulations

As shown in Figure 14, progress with uptake of the eight[1] priority UN vehicle safety standards has been very limited since the last review. To-date, only 40 mainly high-income countries have implemented seven or eight of these standards. Eleven countries apply two to six standards, and 124 apply one or none of the standards. Since the last review, one additional country, India, is applying the front and side impact protection standard. One other country, Malaysia, has applied the electronic stability control regulation from 2018.

Figure 14: Countries implementing priority UN safety standards for vehicles, 2018

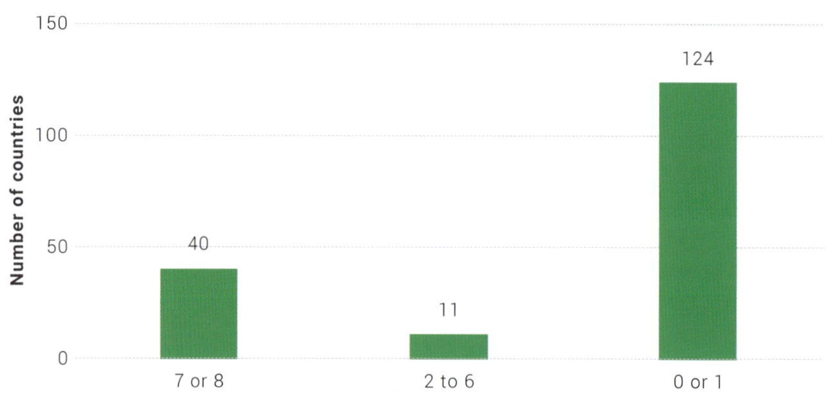

1 In the previous report, 7 priority standards were identified. An additional standard for motorcycle anti-lock braking systems (ABS) has been included in this report.

In relation to the motorcycle anti-lock braking systems (ABS), a number of countries with high usage of motorcycles, are or will be implementing regulations requiring the use of ABS or combined braking systems (CBS) for motorcycles. As shown in Table 4, most of the countries implementing these regulations require ABS systems for vehicles greater than 125cc; China and Brazil only require ABS for vehicles greater than 250cc and 300cc respectively, which means that a large number of motorcycles and e-bikes are excluded from this requirement. With the exception of Brazil, all have provisions to extend the ABS requirements for used motorcycles already in circulation in circulation, requiring them to be retrofitted, as well as for new motorcycles.

Table 4: Motorcycle ABS regulation, 2018

Countries	Motorcycle ABS regulation	Note
EU	YES – for all new types >125cc as of 01/2016 and for all existing types > 125cc as of 01/2017	>50cc can have ABS or CBS fitted
Japan	YES – for all new types >125cc as of 10/2018 and for all existing types > 125cc as of 10/2021	>50cc can have ABS or CBS fitted
India	YES – for all new types >125cc as of 04/2018 and for all existing types > 125cc as of 04/2019	<125cc can have ABS or CBS fitted
China	YES – for all new types >250cc as of 07/2019 and for all existing types >250cc as of 07/2020	>250cc mandatory both front and rear wheel; >150cc and 250cc ABS or CBS
Brazil	YES – for all new types ≥300cc ramp up from 2016-2019	<300cc can have ABS or CBS fitted; off road bikes excluded
Australia	YES – for all new types > 125cc from 11/2019 and for all existing types >125cc from 11/2021	>50cc can have ABS or CBS

Review of consumer information programme progress:

The UN General Assembly has recommended the implementation of new car assessments as a means of improving vehicle safety (76). New Car Assessment Programmes (NCAPs) have proved highly effective in raising levels of vehicle safety significantly above minimum regulatory requirements. NCAPs typically carry out safety ratings for crashworthiness to promote occupant and pedestrian protection and crash avoidance through crash tests and technology assessments (77).

Figure 15: Countries applying UN vehicle safety standards, 2018

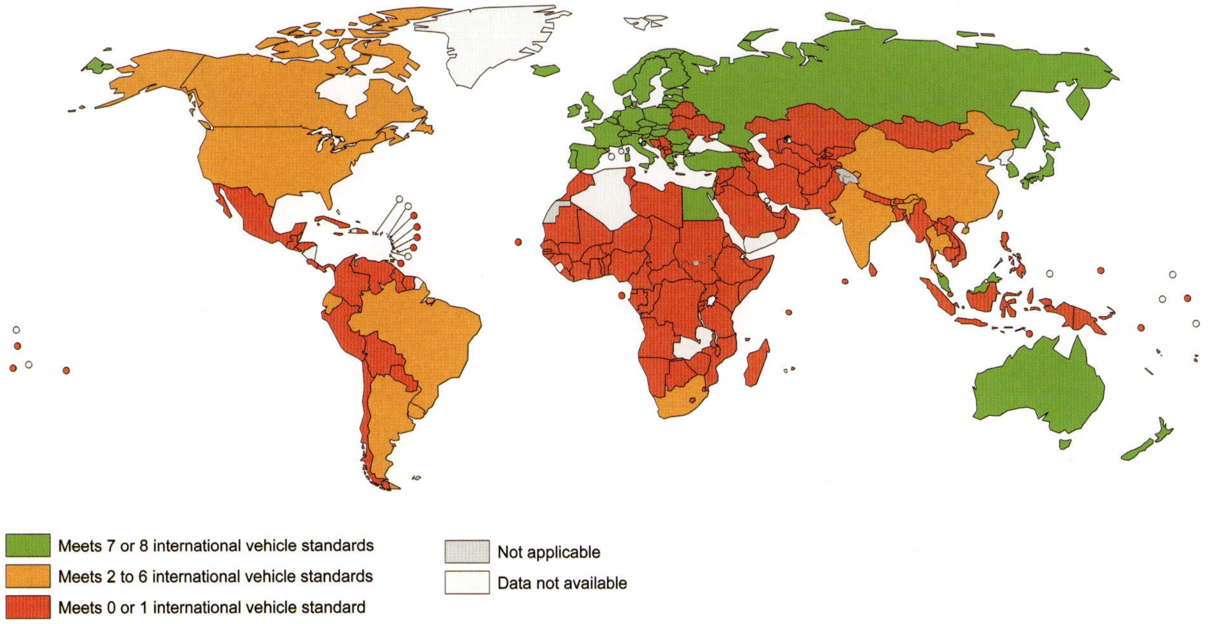

Box 9: Priority UN vehicle safety standards

1–2: Frontal impact protection and side impact protection (R94 and R95): ensure that cars withstand the impacts of a frontal and side impact crash when tested at certain speeds. These crashworthiness regulations help to protect occupants withstand the impact of front and side impact crashes.

3: Electronic stability control (R140): prevents skidding and loss of control in cases of over-steering or understeering and is effective at reducing crashes and saving lives. It is effective in avoiding single car and roll over crashes, reducing both fatal and serious injuries.

4: Pedestrian front protection (R127): provides softer bumpers and modifies the front ends of vehicles (e.g. removes unnecessarily rigid structures) that can reduce the severity of a pedestrian impact with a car.

5–6: Seat-belts and seat-belt anchorages (R14 & R16): ensure that seat-belts are fitted in vehicles when they are manufactured and assembled and that the seat-belt anchor points can withstand the impact incurred during a crash, to minimize the risk of belt slippage and ensure that passengers can be safely removed from their seats if there is a crash.

7: Child restraints (R129): ensure that the child seat is in place with the adult seat-belt and that ISOFIX child restraint anchorage points are fitted to secure the restraint.

8: Motorcycle anti-lock braking systems (R78): help the rider maintain control during an emergency braking situation and reduce the likelihood of a road traffic crash and subsequent injury.

Box 10: Establishing new e-bike standards in China

China, like many other countries, is seeing a surge in the use of e-bikes – some estimates indicate that there are 200 million such vehicles in use nationally, three million of which can be found in Beijing. As the nature of e-bikes has evolved, the existing standards established in 1999 are no longer relevant and as a result, e-bikes sold and used in China are not standardized.

Without an appropriate standard, many vehicles are being manufactured and sold as 'e-bikes' when they are essentially motorcycles that are capable of going 40 km/h or faster. However, they are all treated as bicycles and thus helmet requirements and speed limits are not imposed. As such, they use bike lanes and footpaths designed for and used by non-motorised users.

In May 2018 a new standard was issued aiming to improve the regulation of e-bikes and putting an end to the practice of motorcycles passing for e-bikes. This standard is being phased in (commencing in April 2019). Any vehicle that meets the new standard (which is aligned with international practice with a speed limit of 25 km/h) will be considered a bicycle and not subject to registration, licensing or helmet requirements. Those e-bikes not meeting that standard will be treated as motorcycles and subject to helmet laws and licensing requirements. As the majority of e-bikes in circulation are likely to be non-standard, this standard closes a loophole that allowed millions of motorcycle riders to not wear a helmet.

Source: Electric Bicycles-General Technical Requirements GB17761-1999; Electric Bicycles-General Technical Requirements GB17761-2018

Box 11: Vehicle safety standards in India

India is the fourth largest vehicle producer in the world and now applies new vehicle safety standards to passenger cars and motorcycles. In 2014, independent crash tests carried out by Global NCAP's 'Safer Cars for India' initiative revealed that some of India's top selling models would fail the UN's frontal impact crash test. Further Global NCAP tests at a higher speed also resulted in zero-star ratings indicating a high risk of fatal or serious injury.

In 2015 the Indian government announced the application of new regulations consistent with the UN standards for front and side impact and also pedestrian protection. For new car models, the use of front and side crash tests came into force from October 2017 and will apply to all new cars from October 2019. The pedestrian protection regulation for new models came into force from October 2018 and will apply to all new cars from October 2020. In addition, new cars are required to have air bags fitted as standard and to have a speed warning device above 80 km/h.

The combination of the new regulations and the Safer Cars for India project is raising consumer demand for key features such as airbags and acting as a strong catalyst for improved safety design by the automobile industry. New models are now on the market that not only comply with the new standards but also achieve good scores – including a model that achieved four stars in Global NCAP tests that are more stringent. The production of older designs of cars that cannot pass the new crash tests, such as the Tata Nano, which received zero stars in Global NCAP's first round of tests in 2014, is being phased out. The next challenge for India is to accelerate use of electronic stability control which is currently fitted in over 70% of new passenger cars worldwide but to less than 10% of new cars in India.

CHAPTER 6

POST-CRASH CARE

Key messages

- Simple and affordable post-crash care interventions save lives.
- Effective care for the injured requires timely care at the scene, prompt transport to appropriate emergency and surgical care at hospital, and early access to rehabilitation services.
- The proportion of patients who die before reaching a hospital in low-income countries is over twice that in high-income countries.
- Bystanders contribute by activating the emergency care system and taking simple, potentially life-saving actions until professional help is available.

109
countries have a telephone number with national coverage to activate the emergency care

55%
of countries have a formal process to train and certify prehospital providers

45%
of countries have national or subnational trauma registries

A broad and integrated approach to post-crash care can save millions of lives and mitigate the short- and long-term effects of experiencing a crash to help survivors return to function and independence at home and at work (45, 46). Key elements of post-crash care identified in the Decade of Action include structures to allow timely delivery of health services, data to inform policy and support quality care delivery, and legislation to ensure access to emergency care without regard to ability to pay (4).

Building systems to ensure timely care for the injured

Countries should set up lead agencies to set standards and coordinate care for those injured in road traffic crashes.

Emergency care is at the core of the post-crash response. There is a series of time sensitive actions that are essential to provide effective care for the injured, beginning with activation of the emergency care system and continuing with care at the scene, transport, and facility-based emergency care. Rehabilitation – both in hospital and beyond, is essential to maximise the impact of emergency and surgical care and to limit the physical and psychological impact of injuries (18). Ideally, countries should designate a lead government agency with the authority to set system-wide standards and to coordinate prehospital and hospital-based care for the injured.

Role of bystanders in the emergency care system

Even the most sophisticated emergency care system is ineffective if bystanders fail to recognize a serious injury or do not know how to call for help. Bystanders contribute by activating the emergency care system and taking simple, potentially life-saving actions until professional help is available (80–82). To facilitate the important contribution of bystanders it is important that there is legislation in place to protect those who assist the injured. WHO's Emergency Care System Assessments, carried out in over 30 countries worldwide, found that many countries have no bystander protection laws or limited enforcement, and many countries report that those who assist the injured experience a range of serious financial, legal and social consequences.

55% of countries have a formal process to train and certify prehospital care providers.

To activate the emergency care system, ideally there should be a single telephone number that is valid throughout the country, easy to remember and available as a free call (6,80,83). This current report found that 109 countries have a telephone number with full national coverage. Among the countries that have conducted the WHO Emergency Care System Assessment, several report that less than half the population know the emergency care access number by memory.

Care at the scene

The proportion of patients who die before reaching a hospital in middle-income countries is over twice that in high-income countries (84). Despite the enormous potential impact of prehospital care, the current report shows that 55% of countries have a formal process to train and certify prehospital providers. In addition, the WHO Emergency Care System Assessments data show that most countries report either no ambulances available to travel to the scene of the crash or that the number of ambulances available is grossly inadequate to meet population needs. It is important to recognise that while the optimal system may be one that can quickly dispatch equipped ambulances with trained providers to the scene of the injury, there are many ways to improve care at the scene of a crash (3,80). For example, simple systems using mobile phones and targeted training of key lay groups (e.g. community leaders, police, and professional drivers) to provide basic interventions can bridge to professional care and improve outcomes (3,80).

Less than 25% of people have access to a staffed operating theatre within two hours of a road traffic crash.

Hospital-based emergency care for the injured

Even short delays to care for the injured can mean lives lost. The WHO Emergency Care System Assessments have found that first-level hospitals in many countries lack dedicated emergency units altogether. Where these units exist, many lack essential equipment for diagnosis and treatment of injuries, and few have the protocols and checklists needed to ensure a systematic approach to every injured patient. They are often staffed only by providers working on a rotational basis who may or may not have the benefit of dedicated training in the care of emergencies: indeed, this report found that just more than half (54%) of countries have speciality training pathways in emergency medicine and trauma surgery.

Beyond a staffed and equipped emergency unit, any facility that is certified to care for the seriously injured should have 24-hour access to operative and critical care services. However, most countries who have conducted the Emergency Care System Assessment report that less than a quarter of the population overall would be able to access a staffed operating theatre within two hours of serious injury. In addition, all assessed countries report inadequate numbers of qualified rehabilitation providers and long delays in accessing community-based rehabilitation services.

Data and information to guide post-crash response

Systematic hospital-based data collection is critical to both clinical quality improvement activities and targeted planning and prevention initiatives. Trauma registries are case-based databases that gather information on injury epidemiology, clinical interventions and health outcomes in order to identify and address specific gaps in care. In both high- and limited-resource settings, registries have been shown to improve the quality of care and clinical outcomes, as well as allow for the identification of high-yield targets for prevention.

Overall, the current report found that fewer than half (45%) of countries had national or subnational trauma registries in place. Over half of the world's countries either have registries only in a few scattered facilities or no registry at all. To address this gap, WHO has recently established a Global Registry for Emergency and Trauma Care, and implementation has been initiated in a number of middle-income countries. In addition, it is essential for countries to establish policies that ensure effective crash investigation and equitable access to information for survivors and their families.

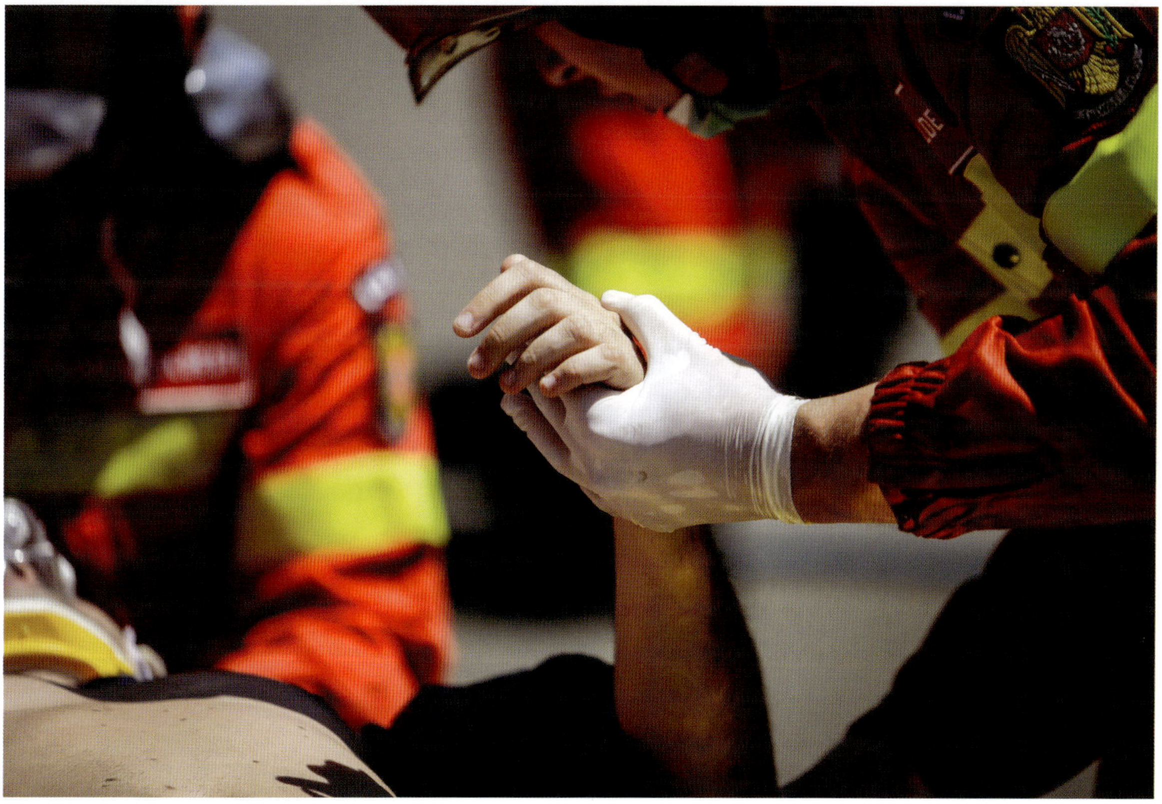

Box 12: A simple low-cost emergency care package in Uganda

Emergency care in health facilities across Uganda is improving following a Ministry of Health scale-up of a WHO pilot intervention that halved the number of hospital deaths from emergency conditions (road traffic injuries, childhood diarrhoea, pneumonia, asthma and postpartum haemorrhage). Executed at a cost of US$ 3500 per hospital, this pilot included WHO basic emergency care training for hospital staff, the introduction of simple WHO emergency unit protocols (including checklists and triage) and identifying and organizing a simple resuscitation area with existing resources. In addition, Uganda has undertaken pilot implementation of the WHO Global Registry for Emergency and Trauma Care at regional hospitals around the country. The registry's automated reporting functions allow data to be used to improve the quality of clinical care as well as to inform policy and planning.

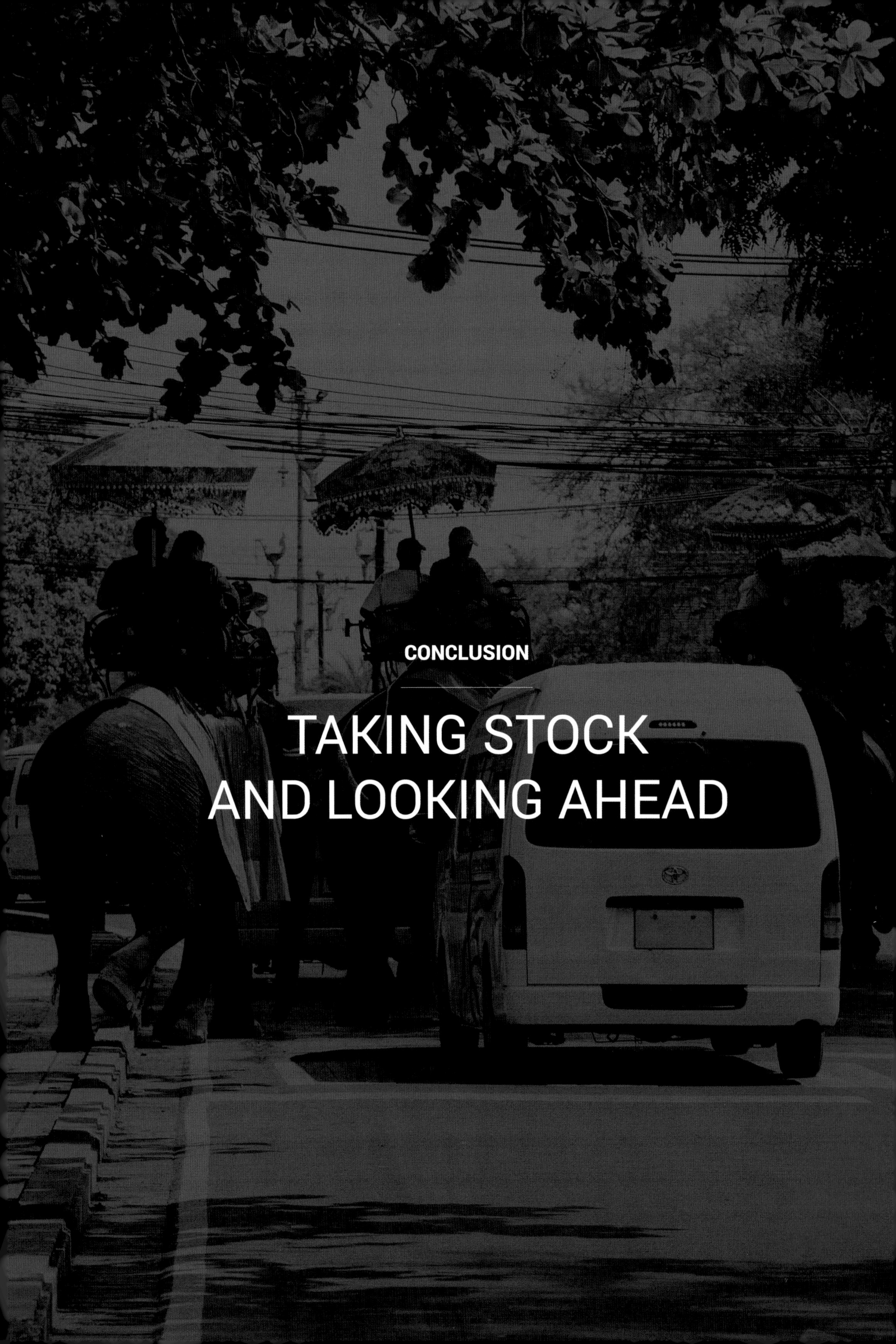

CONCLUSION

TAKING STOCK AND LOOKING AHEAD

Key messages

- The Decade of Action for Road Safety 2011-2020 has led to a remarkable increase in global attention, investments and efforts to reduce deaths and injuries on the world's roads.
- While progress has been made by countries in strengthening road traffic laws, improving the safety of roads and vehicles, and enhancing post-crash care, the number of road traffic deaths and injuries remains unacceptably high.
- The progress that has been achieved has not occurred at a pace fast enough to achieve the SDG target 3.6 to reduce road traffic deaths by 50% by 2020.
- Above all, accelerating progress will require increased political will and commitment at the highest level of government.

1.35
million deaths each year

123
countries have road traffic laws that meet best practice for at least one of the key behavioural risk factors

88%
of pedestrian travel is on 1- or 2-star roads

40
countries have implemented 7 or 8 of the priority UN vehicle safety standards

109
countries have a telephone number with national coverage to activate the emergency care system

Summary of progress to date

The number of road traffic deaths continues to climb, reaching 1.35 million in 2016, while the rate of death relative to the size of the world's population has stabilized in recent years. The progress that has been achieved has not occurred at a pace fast enough to compensate for the rising population and rapid motorization of transport taking place in many parts of the world. At this rate, the SDG target 3.6 to halve road traffic deaths by 2020 will not be met. This review of key risk factors does show, however, that progress is being made in improving key road safety laws, infrastructure, adoption of vehicles standards and improving access to the post-crash care.

As countries work over time to create sustainably safe environments for road use through improved planning, design, operation and investment in the safety quality of roads, vehicles and post-crash care, the combined publicity and enforcement of key safety legislation

presents opportunities to achieve immediate and substantial road safety results. The review has found that the progress has been made across countries to bring laws into line with best practice with ten additional countries (45 in total) aligning with best practices on addressing drink-driving, five additional countries (49 in total) aligning with best practices on motorcycle helmet use, four additional countries (33 in total) aligning with best practices on the use of child restraint systems, and three additional countries (105 in total) aligning with best practices on the use of seat-belts. The number of countries with laws in line with best practices for speed management has not changed (46 in total). As a result of these interventions, an additional one billion people are now covered by road traffic laws that meet best practice.

The Decade of Action has led to an increase in global attention, investments, and efforts to reduce deaths and injuries on roads.

Progress is evident in the planning, design and operation of roads and roadsides, addressing high-risk sections and areas and in the take-up of a range of tools. Vehicle safety measures continue to make a substantial and efficient contribution to reducing death and serious injuries amongst car occupants. Despite the fact that only 40 countries have implemented seven or eight of the priority UN vehicle safety standards, there are signs of progress with countries such as India producing its first four-star vehicle. There are also signs that access to post-crash care is improving.

There has also been significant progress in advancing the global road safety agenda. The Decade of Action has led to a remarkable increase in global attention, investments, and efforts to reduce deaths and injuries on the world's roads. The increased recognition and political support for road safety have fostered an enabling environment for targeted actions and are exemplified by several important developments. Examples of these include:

→ SDG targets 3.6 and 11.2 addressing road safety;

- 12 voluntary global road safety performance targets in support of the SDGs and new linkages between road safety and other public health and societal goals;
- United Nations Road Safety Trust Fund to catalyse investments in road safety in countries;
- regional data observatories to facilitate better reporting of road traffic deaths; and
- networks of legislators in Africa and the Eastern Mediterranean to facilitate the implementation of road safety legislation that meet best practice.

Investments of government, financiers and private foundations, have laid the foundation for future efforts.

These outcomes are not directly captured by this report, but they contribute in critical ways to strengthening the field. Along with the investments of governments, financiers and private foundations, they have laid the foundation for future efforts and are indicative of the momentum generated in recent years.

Remaining challenges

The results presented in this report, and the developments highlighted above indicate significant moves forward have been made on road safety over the past decade. Further progress will depend upon future success in addressing the range of significant challenges which remain.

Increasing political will

Despite a better understanding of the problem and its solutions, political will to carry out the necessary actions is often lacking. Too many countries still lack funded strategies, lead agencies and good laws that are enforced.

Ensuring accountability

Improving the safety of roads requires clear responsibility and accountability that cuts across sectors. Those who plan, design, operate and use the road system share responsibility for creating a road system in which crashes do not result in death or serious injury. This responsibility is shared across government, business, media and civil society, requiring alignment with a range of societal goals, careful governmental leadership and an effective safety performance framework. However, there needs to be clear responsibility for progress on the system as well as for each component. The establishment of lead agencies with appropriate capacity and related multisectoral coordination arrangements amongst the responsible agencies are a prerequisite for effective action.

Strengthening data collection

Robust data are a critical component for the attainment of any future target. Without the ability to assess progress and the effectiveness of efforts to reduce fatalities and injuries, countries will not be able to identify gaps in the system and deliver tailored improvements. As a result of the differences in definitions, reporting, and coding practices adopted by health, police, and insurance, the individual sources of data often provide an incomplete view of the actual situation.

Building capacity

Many countries are still struggling to establish capacity for sustainable safety management and the leadership, coordination and funding arrangements, which underpin better performance. Silo approaches to intervention persist and while there are examples of multisectoral activity and shared responsibility, these are atypical.

Looking Ahead

While many key elements of the road safety response are now well articulated, there is a failure of implementation and scale of response in most countries. Current action is insufficient to meet the targets and a large burden of unnecessary death and injury, particularly to the young, will remain without a change in political will, clear responsibilities and accountability, good data and capacity to act.

Experience shows that sustained gains in road safety only happen when a more integrated approach is taken. Going forward, it will be important to learn from experiences to date and address the factors noted above that hinder success. There is an urgent need for governments to scale up their road safety efforts in order to live up to their commitments made in the Sustainable Development Agenda 2030. The upcoming Third Global Ministerial Conference on Road Safety in Sweden in February 2020 will be a key opportunity to take a strategic view and set a road safety agenda for the next decade, including by setting a new global target on fatalities.

REFERENCES

1. World Health Organization. Projections of mortality and causes of death, 2015 and 2030 [Internet]. World Health Organization; 2013 [cited 2018 Oct 29]. Available from: http://www.who.int/healthinfo/global_burden_disease/projections2015_2030/en/

2. Foreman KJ, Marquez N, Dolgert A, Fukutaki K, Mcgaughey M, Pletcher MA, et al. Forecasting life expectancy, years of life lost, all-cause and cause-specific mortality for 250 causes of death: reference and alternative scenarios 2016–2040 for 195 countries and territories. Lancet. 2018;392:2052–90.

3. World Health Organization. Save LIVES: a road safety technical package [Internet]. 2017 [cited 2018 Nov 1]. Available from: http://iris.paho.org/xmlui/bitstream/handle/123456789/34980/9789275320013-por.pdf?sequence=1&isAllowed=y

4. Global Plan for the Decade of Action for Road Safety 2011-2020 [Internet]. World Health Organization; 2011 [cited 2018 Oct 29]. Available from: http://www.who.int/roadsafety/decade_of_action/plan/en/

5. Hyder AA, Paichadze N, Toroyan T, Peden MM. Monitoring the Decade of Action for Global Road Safety 2011-2020: An update. Glob Public Health. 2017 Dec 2;12(12):1492–505.

6. World Health Organization. Global status report on road safety 2015 [Internet]. 2015 [cited 2018 Nov 1]. Available from: http://www.who.int/violence_injury_prevention/road_safety_status/2015/en/

7. World Health Organization. Global Health Expenditure Database [Internet]. 2018 [cited 2018 Oct 31]. Available from: http://apps.who.int/nha/database

8. United Nations General Assembly. Transforming our world: the 2030 Agenda for Sustainable Development [Internet]. 2015 [cited 2018 May 16]. Available from: https://sustainabledevelopment.un.org/post2015/transformingourworld

9. United Nations General Assembly. 64/255. Improving global road safety [Internet]. 2010 [cited 2018 May 16]. Available from: http://www.who.int/violence_injury_prevention/publications/road_traffic/UN_GA_resolution-54-255-en.pdf?ua=1

10. World Health Organization. Global Health Estimates [Internet]. World Health Organization; 2018 [cited 2018 Oct 29]. Available from: http://www.who.int/healthinfo/global_burden_disease/en/

11. World Health Organization. Disease, injury and causes of death country estimates, 2000–2015 [Internet]. World Health Organization; 2017 [cited 2018 Oct 29]. Available from: http://www.who.int/healthinfo/global_burden_disease/estimates_country_2000_2015/en/

12. Addy CL, Wilson DK, Kirtland KA, Ainsworth BE, Sharpe P, Kimsey D. Associations of perceived social and physical environmental supports with physical activity and walking behavior. Am J Public Health. 2004 Mar;94(3):440–3.

13. Nantulya VM, Reich MR. The neglected epidemic: road traffic injuries in developing countries. BMJ. 2002 May 11;324(7346):1139–41.

14. Road traffic injuries among vulnerable road users [Internet]. [cited 2018 Nov 11]. Available from: http://www.euro.who.int/__data/assets/pdf_file/0004/98779/polbrief_road_injuries.pdf

15. Reynolds CCO, Harris MA, Teschke K, Cripton PA, Winters M. The impact of transportation infrastructure on bicycling injuries and crashes: a review of the literature. Environ Heal. 2009 Oct 21;8(47).

16. Crandall JR, Bhalla KS, Madeley NJ. Designing road vehicles for pedestrian protection. BMJ. 2002 May 11;324(7346):1145–8.

17. Borowy I. Road traffic injuries: social change and development. Med Hist. 2013 Jan;57(1):108–38.

18. Peden M, Scurfield R, Sleet D, Mohan D, Hyder AA, Jarawan E, et al. World report on road traffic injury prevention [Internet]. 2004 [cited 2018 Nov 1]. Available from: http://www.who.int/violence_injury_prevention/publications/road_traffic/world_report/en/

19. Bachani A, Zia N, Hung Y, Adetunji R, Cuong V, Faried A, et al. Speeding in urban South East Asia: Results from a multi-site observational study. J Australas Coll Road Saf. 2017;28(2):27–35.

20. Moulton AD, Mercer SL, Popovic T, Briss PA, Goodman RA, Thombley ML, et al. The scientific basis for law as a public health tool. Am J Public Health. 2009 Jan;99(1):17–24.

21. Goodman RA, Moulton A, Matthews G, Shaw F, Kocher P, Mensah G, et al. Law and public health at CDC. MMWR Suppl. 2006 Dec 22;55(2):29–33.

22. Magnusson R, Patterson D. Role of law in global response to non-communicable diseases. Lancet. 2011 Sep 3;378(9794):859–60.

23. Miller TR, Levy DT, Swedler DI. Lives saved by laws and regulations that resulted from the Bloomberg road safety program. Accid Anal Prev. 2018 Apr;113:131–6.

24. Magnusson R. Advancing the right to health: The vital role of law [Internet]. Geneva; 2017 [cited 2018 Nov 1]. Available from: http://www.who.int/healthsystems/topics/health-law/health_law-report/en/

25. Sheng R, Zhong S, Barnett AG, Weiner BJ, Xu J, Li H, et al. Effect of traffic legislation on road traffic deaths in Ningbo, China. Ann Epidemiol. 2018 Aug;28(8):576–81.

26. Vadeby A, Forsman Å. Traffic safety effects of new speed limits in Sweden. Accid Anal Prev. 2018 May;114:34–9.

27. World Health Organization. Managing speed [Internet]. 2017 [cited 2018 Nov 1]. Available from: http://www.who.int/violence_injury_prevention/publications/road_traffic/managing-speed/en/

28. Finch DJ, Kompfner P, Lockwood CR, Maycock G. Speed, speed limits and accidents (Project Report 58) [Internet]. Crowthorne, United Kingdom; 1994 [cited 2018 Nov 1]. Available from: https://trl.co.uk/sites/default/files/PR058.pdf

29. Martin J-L, Wu D. Pedestrian fatality and impact speed squared: Cloglog modeling from French national data. Traffic Inj Prev. 2018 Jan 2;19(1):94–101.

30. Jurewicz C, Sobhani A, Woolley J, Dutschke J, Corben B. Exploration of vehicle impact speed-injury severity relationships for application in safer road design. Transp Res Procedia. 2016;14:4247–4256.

31. Wali B, Ahmed A, Iqbal S, Hussain A. Effectiveness of enforcement levels of speed limit and drink driving laws and associated factors—Exploratory empirical analysis using a bivariate ordered probit model. J Traffic Transp Eng. 2017;4(3):272–279.

32. Rahim SASM, Jamil HM, Musa M, Isah N, Voon WS. Impact studies of automated enforcement system implementation [Internet]. Kajang, Malaysia; 2014 [cited 2018 Nov 11]. Available from: https://www.miros.gov.my/1/dl.php?filename=MRR_AES Evaluation Report.pdf

33. Vissers L, Houwing S, Wegman F. Alcohol-related road casualties in official crash statistics [Internet]. 2018 [cited 2018 Nov 11]. Available from: https://www.itf-oecd.org/sites/default/files/docs/alcohol-related-road-casualties-official-crash-statistics.pdf

34. Global status report on alcohol and health 2018 [Internet]. Geneva; 2018 [cited 2018 Nov 11]. Available from: https://www.who.int/substance_abuse/publications/global_alcohol_report/en/

35. Elvik R, Høye A, Vaa T, Sørensen M, editors. The Handbook of Road Safety Measures. 2nd ed. Bingley, UK: Emerald Group Publishing Limited; 2009.

36. Fell JC, Voas RB. The effectiveness of reducing illegal blood alcohol concentration (BAC) limits for driving: Evidence for lowering the limit to .05 BAC. J Safety Res. 2006 Jan;37(3):233–43.

37. Bachani AM, Risko CB, Gnim C, Coelho S, Hyder AA. Knowledge, attitudes, and practices around drinking and driving in Cambodia: 2010-2012. Public Health. 2017 Mar;144S:S32–8.

38. Shults RA, Elder RW, Sleet DA, Nichols JL, Alao MO, Carande-Kulis VG, et al. Reviews of evidence regarding interventions to reduce alcohol-impaired driving. Am J Prev Med. 2001 Nov;21(4 Suppl):66–88.

39. Purssell R, Solomon R, Chamberlain E. Random breath testing: a needed and effective measure to prevent impaired driving fatalities. B C Med J. 2009;51(10):446.

40. MacLeod JBA, DiGiacomo JC, Tinkoff G. An evidence-based review: helmet efficacy to reduce head Injury and mortality in motorcycle crashes: EAST practice management guidelines. J Trauma. 2010 Nov;69(5):1101–11.

41. Liu BC, Ivers R, Norton R, Boufous S, Blows S, Lo SK. Helmets for preventing injury in motorcycle riders. Cochrane Database Syst Rev. 2008 Jan 23;(1):CD004333.

42. Passmore JW, Nguyen LH, Nguyen NP, Olivé J-M. The formulation and implementation of a national helmet law: a case study from Viet Nam. Bull World Health Organ [Internet]. 2010 Oct 1 [cited 2018 Oct 29];88(10):783–7. Available from: http://www.who.int/bulletin/volumes/88/10/09-071662.pdf

43. Road Traffic Injuries Research Network Multicenter Study Collaborators, Ackaah W, Afukaar F, Agyemang W, Thuy Anh T, Hejar AR, et al. The use of non-standard motorcycle helmets in low- and middle-income countries: a multicentre study. Inj Prev [Internet]. 2013 Jun [cited 2018 Oct 29];19(3):158–63. Available from: http://injuryprevention.bmj.com/lookup/doi/10.1136/injuryprev-2012-040348

44. Stevenson M, Yu J, Hendrie D, Li L-P, Ivers R, Zhou Y, et al. Reducing the burden of road traffic injury: translating high-income country interventions to middle-income and low-income countries. Inj Prev [Internet]. 2008 Oct 1 [cited 2018 Oct 29];14(5):284–9. Available from: http://injuryprevention.bmj.com/cgi/doi/10.1136/ip.2008.018820

45. Farmer CM, Wells JK. Effect of enhanced seat belt reminders on driver fatality risk. J Safety Res. 2010 Feb;41(1):53–7.

46. Durbin DR, Elliott MR, Winston FK. Belt-positioning booster seats and reduction in risk of injury among children in vehicle crashes. JAMA. 2003 Jun 4;289(21):2835–2840.

47. Ma X, Griffin R, McGwin G, Allison DB, Heymsfield SB, He W, et al. Effectiveness of booster seats compared with no restraint or seat belt alone for crash injury prevention. Acad Emerg Med. 2013 Sep;20(9):880–7.

48. Anderson DM, Carlson LL, Rees DI. Booster seat effectiveness among older children: evidence from Washington State. Am J Prev Med. 2017 Aug;53(2):210–5.

49. Nazif-Munoz JI, Blank-Gommel A, Shor E. Effectiveness of child restraints and booster legislation in Israel. Inj Prev. 2017 Oct 10;

50. Asbridge M, Ogilvie R, Wilson M, Hayden J. The impact of booster seat use on child injury and mortality: Systematic review and meta-analysis of observational studies of booster seat effectiveness. Accid Anal Prev. 2018 Oct;119:50–7.

51. Nazif-Munoz JI, Nikolic N. The effectiveness of child restraint and seat belt legislation in reducing child injuries: The case of Serbia. Traffic Inj Prev. 2018 Feb 28;19(sup1):S7–14.

52. Arbogast KB, Durbin DR, Cornejo RA, Kallan MJ, Winston FK. An evaluation of the effectiveness of forward facing child restraint systems. Accid Anal Prev. 2004 Jul;36(4):585–9.

53. Arbogast KB, Kallan MJ, Durbin DR. Effectiveness of high back and backless belt-positioning booster seats in side impact crashes. Annu proceedings Assoc Adv Automot Med. 2005;49:201–13.

54. Jakobsson L, Isaksson-Hellman I, Lundell B. Safety for the growing child—experiences from Swedish accident data. 2005.

55. Zaloshnja E, Miller TR, Hendrie D. Effectiveness of child safety seats vs safety belts for children aged 2 to 3 years. Arch Pediatr Adolesc Med. 2007 Jan 1;161(1):65.

56. Rice TM, Anderson CL. The effectiveness of child restraint systems for children aged 3 years or younger during motor vehicle collisions: 1996 to 2005. Am J Public Health. 2009 Feb;99(2):252–7.

57. Rice TM, Anderson CL, Lee AS. The association between booster seat use and risk of death among motor vehicle occupants aged 4-8: a matched cohort study. Inj Prev. 2009 Dec 1;15(6):379–83.

58. House DR, Huffman G, Walthall JDH. Emergency department transport rates of children from the scene of motor vehicle collisions: do booster seats make a difference? Pediatr Emerg Care. 2012 Nov;28(11):1211–4.

59. Ma X, Layde P, Zhu S. Association between child restraint systems use and injury in motor vehicle crashes. Acad Emerg Med. 2012 Aug;19(8):916–23.

60. Lipovac K, Đerić M, Tešić M, Andrić Z, Marić B. Mobile phone use while driving—literary review. Transp Res Part F Traffic Psychol Behav. 2017;47:132–42.

61. Caird JK, Willness CR, Steel P, Scialfa C. A meta-analysis of the effects of cell phones on driver performance. Accid Anal Prev. 2008 Jul;40(4):1282–93.

62. Horrey WJ, Wickens CD. Examining the impact of cell phone conversations on driving using meta-analytic techniques. Hum Factors. 2006 Mar 6;48(1):196–205.

63. Farmer CM, Braitman KA, Lund AK. Cell phone use while driving and attribuTable crash risk. Traffic Injury Prevention. 2010 Oct; 11(5):466-70.

64. Drews FA, Pasupathi M, Strayer DL. Passenger and cell phone conversations in simulated driving. J Exp Psychol Appl. 2008 Dec;14(4):392–400.

65. Née M, Contrand B, Orriols L, Gil-Jardiné C, Galéra C, Lagarde E. Road safety and distraction, results from a responsibility case-control study among a sample of road users interviewed at the emergency room. Accid Anal Prev. 2018 Oct;122:19–24.

66. Brown T, Milavetz G, Murry DJ. Alcohol, drugs and driving: implications for evaluating driver impairment. Ann Adv Automot Med Assoc Adv Automot Med. 2013;57:23–32.

67. Drug-impaired driving: marijuana and opioids raise critical issues for States [Internet]. 2018 [cited 2018 Nov 11]. Available from: https://www.ghsa.org/resources/publications?issues=1

68. Elvik R. Risk of road accident associated with the use of drugs: a systematic review and meta-analysis of evidence from epidemiological studies. Accid Anal Prev. 2013 Nov;60:254–67.

69. World Road Association. Road safety manual: a manual for practitioners and decision makers on implementing safe system infrastructure [Internet]. Paris; 2015 [cited 2018 Nov 1]. Available from: https://roadsafety.piarc.org/en

70. Vaccines for roads. 2nd ed. [Internet]. Basingstoke, United Kingdom; 2012 [cited 2018 Nov 11]. Available from: https://www.globalfueleconomy.org/media/45121/vaccines-for-roads-second-edition.pdf

71. International Road Assessment Programme. 3 Star or better [Internet]. 2018 [cited 2018 Oct 29]. Available from: https://www.irap.org/3-star-or-better/

72. International Road Assessment Programme. How Safe Are The Worlds Roads? – Vaccines For Roads [Internet]. 2018 [cited 2018 Oct 29]. Available from: https://www.vaccinesforroads.org/how-safe-are-the-worlds-roads/

73. Programme IRA. iRAP Big Data Tool [Internet]. 2018 [cited 2018 Oct 30]. Available from: https://www.vaccinesforroads.org/irap-big-data-tool/

74. Erke A. Effects of electronic stability control (ESC) on accidents: A review of empirical evidence. Accid Anal Prev. 2008 Jan;40(1):167–73.

75. United Nations Economic Commission for Europe. Vehicle Regulations [Internet]. 2018 [cited 2018 Oct 31]. Available from: https://www.unece.org/trans/main/welcwp29.html

76. United Nations General Assembly. 66/260. Improving global road safety [Internet]. 2012 [cited 2018 Nov 1]. Available from: http://repository.un.org/bitstream/handle/11176/295228/A_RES_66_260-EN.pdf?sequence=3&isAllowed=y

77. Global New Car Assessment Programme [Internet]. 2017 [cited 2018 Oct 31]. Available from: http://www.globalncap.org/

78. Mock C, Joshipura M, Arreola-Risa C, Quansah R. An estimate of the number of lives that could be saved through improvements in trauma care globally. World J Surg. 2012 May 15;36(5):959–63.

79. Kotagal M, Agarwal-Harding KJ, Mock C, Quansah R, Arreola-Risa C, Meara JG. Health and economic benefits of improved injury prevention and trauma care worldwide. PLoS One. 2014 Mar 13;9(3):e91862.

80. World Health Organization. Prehospital trauma care systems [Internet]. Geneva; 2005 [cited 2018 Nov 1]. Available from: http://www.who.int/violence_injury_prevention/publications/services/39162_oms_new.pdf

81. World Health Organization. Post-crash response: Supporting those affected by road traffic crashes [Internet]. Geneva; 2016 [cited 2018 Nov 1]. Available from: http://www.who.int/violence_injury_prevention/publications/road_traffic/post-crash-response/en/

82. Balhara KS, Bustamante ND, Selvam A, Winders WT, Coker A, Trehan I, et al. Bystander assistance for trauma victims in low- and middle-income countries: a systematic review of prevalence and training interventions. Prehospital Emerg Care. 2018 Sep 25;1–22.

83. Bachani AM, Botchey I, Paruk F, Wako D, Saidi H, Aliwa B, et al. Nine-point plan to improve care of the injured patient: A case study from Kenya. Surgery. 2017 Dec;162(6S):S32–44.

84. Mock CN, Jurkovich GJ, nii-Amon-Kotei D, Arreola-Risa C, Maier R V. Trauma mortality patterns in three nations at different economic levels: implications for global trauma system development. J Trauma. 1998 May;44(5):804-12; discussion 812-4.

SECTION 2

Afghanistan

Population: 34 656 032 | Income group: Low | Gross national income per capita: US$ 580

INSTITUTIONAL FRAMEWORK

Lead agency	No
Funded in national budget	–
National road safety strategy	No
Funding to implement strategy	–
Fatality reduction target	–

SAFER ROADS AND MOBILITY

Audits or star rating required for new road infrastructure	Partial
Design standards for the safety of pedestrians / cyclists	Partial
Inspections / star rating of existing roads	–
Investments to upgrade high risk locations	Yes
Policies & investment in urban public transport	Yes

SAFER VEHICLES

Total registered vehicles for 2013	655 357
Cars and 4-wheeled light vehicles	407 608
Motorized 2- and 3-wheelers	68 090
Heavy trucks	81 416
Buses	20 589
Other	77 654
Vehicle standards applied (UNECE WP.29)	
Frontal impact standard	No
Electronic stability control	No
Pedestrian protection	No
Motorcycle anti-lock braking system	No

POST-CRASH CARE

National emergency care access number	National, single number
Trauma registry	None
Formal certification for prehospital providers	No
National assessment of emergency care systems	No

DATA

Reported road traffic fatalities (2016)	1 565[a] (63% M, 10% F)
WHO estimated road traffic fatalities (2016)	5 230 (95% CI 4 502 - 5 958)
WHO estimated rate per 100 000 population (2016)	15.1

[a] Traffic Police Department. Unlimited time period following crash

SAFER ROAD USERS

National speed limit law	Yes
Max urban speed limit	90 km/h[b]
Max rural speed limit	90 km/h[b]
Max motorway speed limit	90 km/h[b]
Local authorities can modify limits	No
Enforcement	0 1 2 3 ④ 5 6 7 8 9 10
Predominant type of enforcement	–
National drink-driving law	Yes[c]
BAC limit – general population	–
BAC limit – young or novice drivers	–
Random breath testing carried out	Yes
Testing carried out in case of fatal crash	All drivers tested
Enforcement	0 1 2 3 4 5 ⑥ 7 8 9 10
% road traffic deaths involving alcohol	–
National motorcycle helmet law	No
Applies to drivers and passengers	–
Helmet fastening required	–
Helmet standard referred to and/or specified	–
Children passengers on motorcycles	Not restricted
Enforcement	–
Helmet wearing rate	–
National seat-belt law	No
Applies to front and rear seat occupants	–
Enforcement	–
Seat-belt wearing rate	–
National child restraint law	No
Children seated in front seat	Not restricted
Child restraint required	–
Child restraint standard referred to and/or specified	–
Enforcement	–
% children using child restraints	–
National law on mobile phone use while driving	No
Ban on hand-held mobile phone use	–
Ban on hands-free mobile phone use	–
National drug-driving law	Yes

[b] Speed limit set per vehicle type with a maximum speed limit of 90 km/h for fast moving vehicles, decreased by 20 km/h in mountain paths

[c] Not based on BAC. Alcohol consumption legally prohibited

Deaths by road user category

Trends in reported road traffic deaths

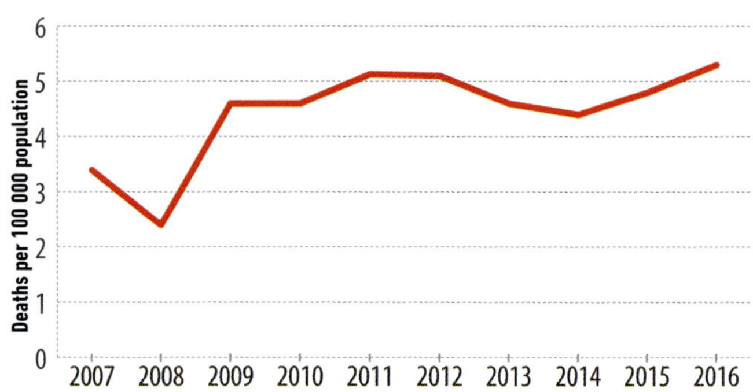

Source: Traffic Police Department

Legislative review conducted by WHO. Vehicle safety data from UNECE WP29. Other data collected by questionnaire and cleared by Ministry of Public Health.

Albania

Population: 2 926 348 | Income group: Middle | Gross national income per capita: US$ 4 250

INSTITUTIONAL FRAMEWORK	
Lead agency	Inter-ministerial Committee for Road Safety, Ministry of Transport and Infrastructure
Funded in national budget	Yes
National road safety strategy	Yes
Funding to implement strategy	Partially funded
Fatality reduction target	50% (2009-2020)

SAFER ROADS AND MOBILITY	
Audits or star rating required for new road infrastructure	Yes
Design standards for the safety of pedestrians / cyclists	Partial
Inspections / star rating of existing roads	No
Investments to upgrade high risk locations	Yes
Policies & investment in urban public transport	Yes

SAFER VEHICLES	
Total registered vehicles for 2016	563 106
Cars and 4-wheeled light vehicles	436 013
Motorized 2- and 3-wheelers	36 096
Heavy trucks	17 670
Buses	7 050
Other	66 277
Vehicle standards applied (UNECE WP.29)	
Frontal impact standard	No
Electronic stability control	No
Pedestrian protection	No
Motorcycle anti-lock braking system	No

POST-CRASH CARE	
National emergency care access number	National, single number
Trauma registry	Subnational
Formal certification for prehospital providers	Yes
National assessment of emergency care systems	No

DATA	
Reported road traffic fatalities (2016)	269[a] (81% M, 19% F)
WHO estimated road traffic fatalities (2016)	399 (95% CI 369 - 428)
WHO estimated rate per 100 000 population (2016)	13.6

[a] Directorate of Road Traffic Police. Died within 30 days of crash

SAFER ROAD USERS	
National speed limit law	Yes
Max urban speed limit	40 km/h
Max rural speed limit	80 km/h
Max motorway speed limit	110 km/h
Local authorities can modify limits	Yes
Enforcement	0 1 2 3 (4) 5 6 7 8 9 10
Predominant type of enforcement	Manual and automated
National drink-driving law	Yes
BAC limit – general population	≤ 0.05 g/dl
BAC limit – young or novice drivers	≤ 0.05 g/dl
Random breath testing carried out	Yes
Testing carried out in case of fatal crash	Some drivers tested
Enforcement	0 1 2 3 4 5 (6) 7 8 9 10
% road traffic deaths involving alcohol	5%[b]
National motorcycle helmet law	Yes
Applies to drivers and passengers	Yes
Helmet fastening required	No
Helmet standard referred to and/or specified	Yes
Children passengers on motorcycles	Not restricted
Enforcement	0 1 2 3 4 5 (6) 7 8 9 10
Helmet wearing rate	75% Drivers[c], 60% Passengers[c]
National seat-belt law	Yes
Applies to front and rear seat occupants	Yes
Enforcement	0 1 2 3 4 5 6 7 (8) 9 10
Seat-belt wearing rate	85% Front seats[c], 80% Rear seats[c]
National child restraint law	Yes
Children seated in front seat	Allowed in a child restraint[d]
Child restraint required	Up to 4 yrs
Child restraint standard referred to and/or specified	Yes
Enforcement	0 1 2 3 4 5 (6) 7 8 9 10
% children using child restraints	–
National law on mobile phone use while driving	Yes
Ban on hand-held mobile phone use	Yes
Ban on hands-free mobile phone use	No
National drug-driving law	Yes

[b] 2016, Directorate of Road Traffic Police, Accidents Information System (AIS)
[c] 2016, Directorate of Road Traffic Police
[d] Children under 12 years can travel in the front if placed in an appropriate restraining device (with airbag deactivated for rear-facing restraint)

Deaths by road user category

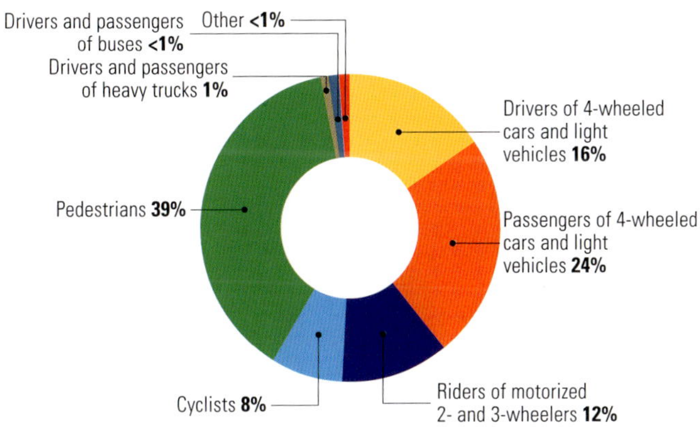

Source: 2016, Directorate of Road Traffic Police, Accidents Information System (AIS)

Trends in reported road traffic deaths

Source: Directorate of Road Traffic Police, Accidents Information System (AIS)

Angola

Population: 28 813 464 | Income group: Middle | Gross national income per capita: US$ 3 440

INSTITUTIONAL FRAMEWORK

Lead agency	**National Council of Road Traffic Planning (CNVOT)**
Funded in national budget	No
National road safety strategy	**Yes**
Funding to implement strategy	Partially funded
Fatality reduction target	–

SAFER ROADS AND MOBILITY

Audits or star rating required for new road infrastructure	No
Design standards for the safety of pedestrians / cyclists	Partial
Inspections / star rating of existing roads	No
Investments to upgrade high risk locations	Yes
Policies & investment in urban public transport	Yes

SAFER VEHICLES

Total registered vehicles	**–**
Cars and 4-wheeled light vehicles	–
Motorized 2- and 3-wheelers	–
Heavy trucks	–
Buses	–
Other	–
Vehicle standards applied (UNECE WP.29)	
Frontal impact standard	No
Electronic stability control	No
Pedestrian protection	No
Motorcycle anti-lock braking system	No

POST-CRASH CARE

National emergency care access number	National, multiple numbers
Trauma registry	National
Formal certification for prehospital providers	Yes
National assessment of emergency care systems	Yes

DATA

Reported road traffic fatalities (2016)	2 845[a] (71% M, 29% F)
WHO estimated road traffic fatalities (2016)	6 797 (95% CI 5 304 - 8 289)
WHO estimated rate per 100 000 population (2016)	23.6

[a] National Police and Ministry of Health. Died within 72 hours of crash

SAFER ROAD USERS

National speed limit law	**Yes**
Max urban speed limit	60 km/h
Max rural speed limit	90 km/h
Max motorway speed limit	120 km/h
Local authorities can modify limits	No
Enforcement	0 1 2 3 4 ⑤ 6 7 8 9 10
Predominant type of enforcement	Manual
National drink-driving law	**Yes**
BAC limit – general population	≤ 0.06 g/dl
BAC limit – young or novice drivers	≤ 0.06 g/dl
Random breath testing carried out	Yes
Testing carried out in case of fatal crash	Some drivers tested
Enforcement	0 1 2 3 4 ⑤ 6 7 8 9 10
% road traffic deaths involving alcohol	–
National motorcycle helmet law	**Yes**
Applies to drivers and passengers	Yes
Helmet fastening required	Yes
Helmet standard referred to and/or specified	No
Children passengers on motorcycles	Prohibited under 7 yrs
Enforcement	0 1 2 3 4 5 6 ⑦ 8 9 10
Helmet wearing rate	40% Drivers[b], 15% Passengers[b]
National seat-belt law	**Yes**
Applies to front and rear seat occupants	Yes
Enforcement	0 1 2 3 4 5 ⑥ 7 8 9 10
Seat-belt wearing rate	40% Front seats[b], 10% Rear seats[b]
National child restraint law	**Yes**
Children seated in front seat	Prohibited under 12 yrs/150cm
Child restraint required	Up to 12 yrs/36 kg/150 cm
Child restraint standard referred to and/or specified	Yes
Enforcement	0 1 2 3 4 ⑤ 6 7 8 9 10
% children using child restraints	–
National law on mobile phone use while driving	**Yes**
Ban on hand-held mobile phone use	Yes
Ban on hands-free mobile phone use	No
National drug-driving law	**Yes**

[b] 2016, National Police

Deaths by road user category

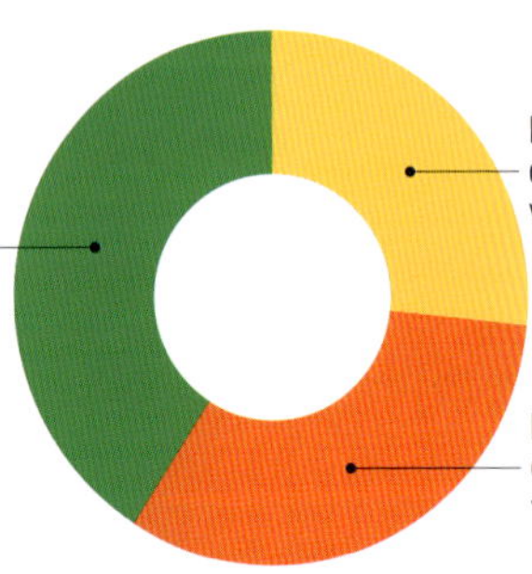

Source: 2016, National Police

Trends in reported road traffic deaths

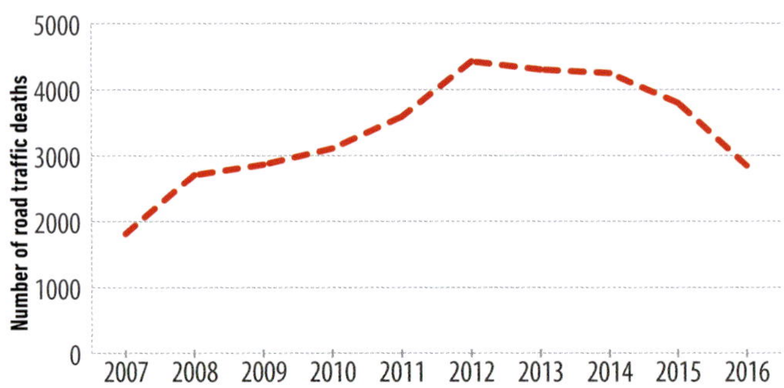

Source: National Police

Antigua and Barbuda

Population: 100 963 | Income group: High | Gross national income per capita: US$ 13 400

INSTITUTIONAL FRAMEWORK

Lead agency	Antigua & Barbuda Transport Board
Funded in national budget	No
National road safety strategy	No
Funding to implement strategy	–
Fatality reduction target	–

SAFER ROADS AND MOBILITY

Audits or star rating required for new road infrastructure	Partial
Design standards for the safety of pedestrians / cyclists	Partial
Inspections / star rating of existing roads	No
Investments to upgrade high risk locations	No
Policies & investment in urban public transport	No

SAFER VEHICLES

Total registered vehicles for 2016	36 030
Cars and 4-wheeled light vehicles	32 828
Motorized 2- and 3-wheelers	180
Heavy trucks	1 272
Buses	1 630
Other	120
Vehicle standards applied (UNECE WP.29)	
Frontal impact standard	No
Electronic stability control	No
Pedestrian protection	No
Motorcycle anti-lock braking system	No

POST-CRASH CARE

National emergency care access number	National, single number
Trauma registry	–
Formal certification for prehospital providers	No
National assessment of emergency care systems	No

DATA

Reported road traffic fatalities (2016)	8[a] (88% M, 13% F)
WHO estimated road traffic fatalities (2016)	8
WHO estimated rate per 100 000 population (2016)	7.9

[a] Police Traffic Department Records. Unlimited time period following crash

SAFER ROAD USERS

National speed limit law	Yes
Max urban speed limit	~ 32 km/h[b]
Max rural speed limit	~ 64 km/h
Max motorway speed limit	No
Local authorities can modify limits	No
Enforcement	0 1 2 3 4 (5) 6 7 8 9 10
Predominant type of enforcement	Manual
National drink-driving law	Yes[c]
BAC limit – general population	–
BAC limit – young or novice drivers	–
Random breath testing carried out	No
Testing carried out in case of fatal crash	Some drivers tested
Enforcement	0 1 2 3 (4) 5 6 7 8 9 10
% road traffic deaths involving alcohol	<1%[d]
National motorcycle helmet law	No
Applies to drivers and passengers	–
Helmet fastening required	–
Helmet standard referred to and/or specified	–
Children passengers on motorcycles	Not restricted
Enforcement	–
Helmet wearing rate	–
National seat-belt law	No
Applies to front and rear seat occupants	–
Enforcement	–
Seat-belt wearing rate	–
National child restraint law	No
Children seated in front seat	Not restricted
Child restraint required	–
Child restraint standard referred to and/or specified	–
Enforcement	–
% children using child restraints	–
National law on mobile phone use while driving	No
Ban on hand-held mobile phone use	–
Ban on hands-free mobile phone use	–
National drug-driving law	Yes

[b] Applies in the City of Saint John's and in designated "speed limit areas"
[c] Not based on BAC
[d] 2011, Police Traffic Department Report

Deaths by road user category

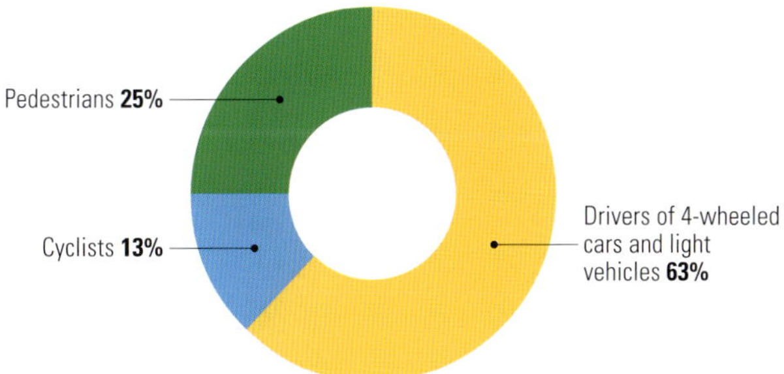

Source: 2016, Police Traffic Department Records

Trends in reported road traffic deaths

Source: Police Traffic Department Records

Legislative review conducted by WHO. Vehicle safety data from UNECE WP29. Other data collected by questionnaire and cleared by Ministry of Health and the Environment.

Argentina

Population: 43 847 432 | Income group: Middle | Gross national income per capita: US$ 11 960

INSTITUTIONAL FRAMEWORK	
Lead agency	National Road Safety Agency (ANSV), Ministry of Transportation
Funded in national budget	Yes
National road safety strategy	Yes
Funding to implement strategy	Fully funded
Fatality reduction target	30% (2016-2026)
SAFER ROADS AND MOBILITY	
Audits or star rating required for new road infrastructure	Partial
Design standards for the safety of pedestrians / cyclists	Yes
Inspections / star rating of existing roads	Yes
Investments to upgrade high risk locations	Yes
Policies & investment in urban public transport	Yes
SAFER VEHICLES	
Total registered vehicles for 2016	21 633 587
Cars and 4-wheeled light vehicles	13 850 936
Motorized 2- and 3-wheelers	7 040 248
Heavy trucks	306 171
Buses	88 307
Other	347 925
Vehicle standards applied (UNECE WP.29)	
Frontal impact standard	Yes [a]
Electronic stability control	No [b]
Pedestrian protection	No
Motorcycle anti-lock braking system	No
POST-CRASH CARE	
National emergency care access number	Partial coverage
Trauma registry	Some facilities
Formal certification for prehospital providers	—
National assessment of emergency care systems	No
DATA	
Reported road traffic fatalities (2016)	5 530 [c] (78% M, 22% F)
WHO estimated road traffic fatalities (2016)	6 119
WHO estimated rate per 100 000 population (2016)	14

[a] Only for new models
[b] Mandatory as from 2018 under voluntray agreement with car makers but postponed to 2022 by the new government following Brazil ESC mandatory date.
[c] Statistical Report 2016 of the National Directorate of Road Observatory, National Road Safety Agency. Died within 30 days of crash

SAFER ROAD USERS	
National speed limit law	Yes
Max urban speed limit	60 km/h
Max rural speed limit	110 km/h
Max motorway speed limit	130 km/h
Local authorities can modify limits	Yes
Enforcement	0 1 2 3 4 (5) 6 7 8 9 10
Predominant type of enforcement	Manual and automated
National drink-driving law	Yes
BAC limit – general population	≤ 0.05 g/dl [d]
BAC limit – young or novice drivers	≤ 0.05 g/dl [d]
Random breath testing carried out	Yes
Testing carried out in case of fatal crash	—
Enforcement	0 1 2 3 4 5 (6) 7 8 9 10
% road traffic deaths involving alcohol	17% [e]
National motorcycle helmet law	Yes
Applies to drivers and passengers	Yes
Helmet fastening required	Yes
Helmet standard referred to and/or specified	Yes
Children passengers on motorcycles	Not restricted
Enforcement	0 1 2 3 (4) 5 6 7 8 9 10
Helmet wearing rate	65% Drivers [f], 44% Passengers [f]
National seat-belt law	Yes
Applies to front and rear seat occupants	Yes
Enforcement	0 1 2 3 4 (5) 6 7 8 9 10
Seat-belt wearing rate	41% Front seats [f], 23% Rear seats [f]
National child restraint law	Yes
Children seated in front seat	Prohibited under 10 yrs
Child restraint required	Up to 4 yrs [g]
Child restraint standard referred to and/or specified	No
Enforcement	—
% children using child restraints	26% [f]
National law on mobile phone use while driving	Yes
Ban on hand-held mobile phone use	Yes
Ban on hands-free mobile phone use	Yes
National drug-driving law	Yes

[d] ≤0.2 g/l for motorcycles drivers.
[e] 2015, OAD/Sedronar. (2017) Mortality related to the consumption of psychoactive substances
[f] 2016, Observational study of road safety behavior, National Directorate of Road Observatory
[g] A 2018 amendment (not covered in the review period ending at December 2017) raised the age for mandatory child restraint use to 10 years old

Deaths by road user category

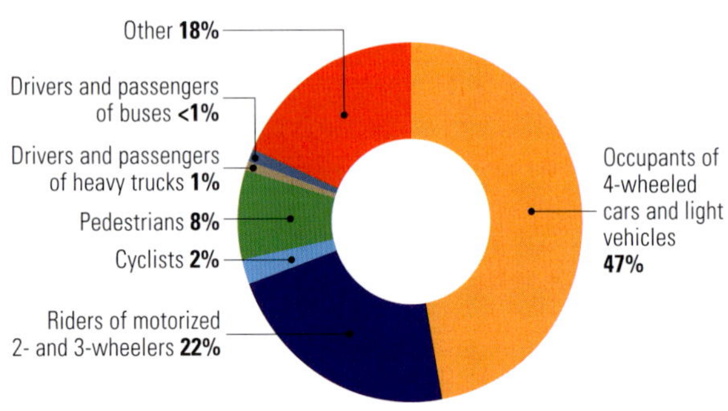

Source: 2014, Ministry of Health of the Nation "Mortality from injuries in traffic accidents" Argentina. Years 2005-2014. Directorate of Health Statistics and Information. Buenos Aires December 2016. Series 12 N ° 7

Trends in reported road traffic deaths

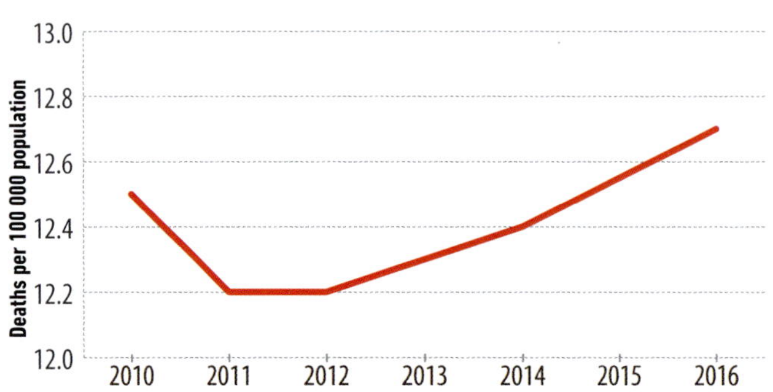

Source: National Directorate of Road Observatory, National Road Safety Agency.

Legislative review conducted by WHO. Vehicle safety data from UNECE WP29. Other data collected by questionnaire and cleared by Ministry of the Interior and Transport

Armenia

Population: 2 924 816 | Income group: Middle | Gross national income per capita: US$ 3 760

INSTITUTIONAL FRAMEWORK	
Lead agency	National Road Safety Council
Funded in national budget	Yes
National road safety strategy	No
Funding to implement strategy	–
Fatality reduction target	–
SAFER ROADS AND MOBILITY	
Audits or star rating required for new road infrastructure	Yes
Design standards for the safety of pedestrians / cyclists	Partial
Inspections / star rating of existing roads	Yes
Investments to upgrade high risk locations	Yes
Policies & investment in urban public transport	Yes
SAFER VEHICLES	
Total registered vehicles	–
Cars and 4-wheeled light vehicles	–
Motorized 2- and 3-wheelers	–
Heavy trucks	–
Buses	–
Other	–
Vehicle standards applied (UNECE WP.29)	
Frontal impact standard	No
Electronic stability control	No
Pedestrian protection	No
Motorcycle anti-lock braking system	No
POST-CRASH CARE	
National emergency care access number	National, single number
Trauma registry	National
Formal certification for prehospital providers	Yes
National assessment of emergency care systems	No
DATA	
Reported road traffic fatalities (2016)	267 [a] (81% M, 19% F)
WHO estimated road traffic fatalities (2016)	499 (95% CI 469 - 530)
WHO estimated rate per 100 000 population (2016)	17.1

[a] Annual statistics report, based on death compiled by provincial vital statistics authorities. Died within 30 days of crash

SAFER ROAD USERS	
National speed limit law	Yes
Max urban speed limit	90 km/h [b]
Max rural speed limit	90 km/h
Max motorway speed limit	110 km/h
Local authorities can modify limits	No
Enforcement	0 1 2 3 4 5 6 7 (8) 9 10
Predominant type of enforcement	Automated
National drink-driving law	Yes
BAC limit – general population	≤ 0.04 g/dl
BAC limit – young or novice drivers	≤ 0.04 g/dl
Random breath testing carried out	Yes [c]
Testing carried out in case of fatal crash	All drivers tested
Enforcement	0 1 2 3 4 5 (6) 7 8 9 10
% road traffic deaths involving alcohol	2% [d]
National motorcycle helmet law	Yes
Applies to drivers and passengers	Yes
Helmet fastening required	Yes
Helmet standard referred to and/or specified	No
Children passengers on motorcycles	Prohibited under 12 yrs
Enforcement	0 1 2 3 4 5 6 7 8 (9) 10
Helmet wearing rate	95% Drivers [d], 90% Passengers [d]
National seat-belt law	Yes
Applies to front and rear seat occupants	Yes
Enforcement	0 1 2 3 4 5 6 7 (8) 9 10
Seat-belt wearing rate	70% Drivers [d], 70% Front seats [d]
National child restraint law	No
Children seated in front seat	Allowed in a child restraint [e]
Child restraint required	–
Child restraint standard referred to and/or specified	–
Enforcement	–
% children using child restraints	–
National law on mobile phone use while driving	Yes
Ban on hand-held mobile phone use	Yes
Ban on hands-free mobile phone use	No
National drug-driving law	Yes

[b] The limit in residential area is reduced to 60 km/h
[c] Legislation requires probable cause to test drivers
[d] 2016, Road police data
[e] Transport of children under 12 years in the front seat shall be made in a "child protecting device"

Deaths by road user category

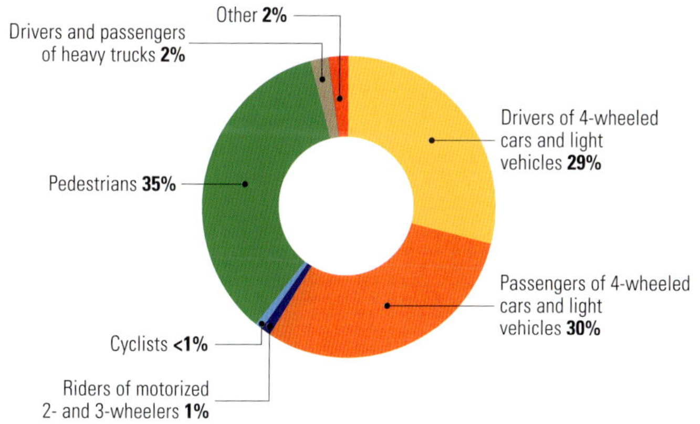

Source: 2016, Road police data

Trends in reported road traffic deaths

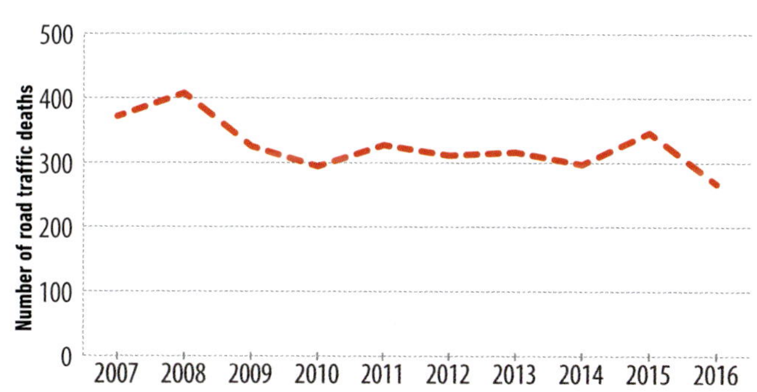

Source: Road police and vital registration data

Australia

Population: 24 125 848 | Income group: High | Gross national income per capita: US$ 54 420

INSTITUTIONAL FRAMEWORK	
Lead agency	Department of Infrastructure and Regional Development
Funded in national budget	Yes
National road safety strategy	Yes
Funding to implement strategy	Not funded
Fatality reduction target	30% annually (2011-2020)

SAFER ROADS AND MOBILITY	
Audits or star rating required for new road infrastructure	Yes
Design standards for the safety of pedestrians / cyclists	Yes
Inspections / star rating of existing roads	Yes
Investments to upgrade high risk locations	Yes
Policies & investment in urban public transport	No

SAFER VEHICLES	
Total registered vehicles for 2016	18 326 236
Cars and 4-wheeled light vehicles	16 946 125
Motorized 2- and 3-wheelers	828 965
Heavy trucks	430 997
Buses	96 582
Other	23 567
Vehicle standards applied (UNECE WP.29)	
Frontal impact standard	Yes
Electronic stability control	Yes
Pedestrian protection	Yes [a]
Motorcycle anti-lock braking system	Yes

POST-CRASH CARE	
National emergency care access number	National, single number
Trauma registry	National
Formal certification for prehospital providers	Yes
National assessment of emergency care systems	No

DATA	
Reported road traffic fatalities (2016)	1 296 [b] (74% M, 26% F)
WHO estimated road traffic fatalities (2016)	1 351
WHO estimated rate per 100 000 population (2016)	5.6

[a] Australia has signed the UN127 for Pedestrian Protection as a Contracting Party but is not enforcing it

[b] National Crash Database, Department of Infrastructure and Regional Development. Died within 30 days of crash

SAFER ROAD USERS	
National speed limit law	Yes
Max urban speed limit	50 km/h
Max rural speed limit	100 - 130 km/h
Max motorway speed limit	100 - 130 km/h
Local authorities can modify limits	Yes
Enforcement	0 1 2 3 4 5 6 7 (8) 9 10
Predominant type of enforcement	Manual and automated
National drink-driving law	Yes
BAC limit – general population	< 0.05 g/dl
BAC limit – young or novice drivers	0.00 g/dl
Random breath testing carried out	Yes
Testing carried out in case of fatal crash	All drivers tested
Enforcement	0 1 2 3 4 5 6 7 (8) 9 10
% road traffic deaths involving alcohol	17% [c]
National motorcycle helmet law	Yes
Applies to drivers and passengers	Yes
Helmet fastening required	Yes
Helmet standard referred to and/or specified	Yes
Children passengers on motorcycles	Prohibited under 8 yrs
Enforcement	0 1 2 3 4 5 6 7 (8) 9 10
Helmet wearing rate	99% Drivers [d]
National seat-belt law	Yes
Applies to front and rear seat occupants	Yes
Enforcement	0 1 2 3 4 5 6 (7) 8 9 10
Seat-belt wearing rate	97% Front seats [e], 96% Rear seats [e]
National child restraint law	Yes
Children seated in front seat	Prohibited under 7 yrs [f]
Child restraint required	Up to 7 yrs
Child restraint standard referred to and/or specified	Yes
Enforcement	0 1 2 3 4 5 6 (7) 8 9 10
% children using child restraints	—
National law on mobile phone use while driving	Yes
Ban on hand-held mobile phone use	Yes
Ban on hands-free mobile phone use	No
National drug-driving law	Yes

[c] 2015, National Crash Database, Department of Infrastructure and Regional Development

[d] 1997, Haworth N et al, Case-Control Study of Motorcycle Crashes

[e] 2013, Petroulias T, Community Attitudes to Road Safety: 2013 survey report

[f] In no circumstances are children under 4 years allowed to sit in the front. Children from 4-7 years can sit in the front only if there is no room for them in the back due to the back seats being occupied by other children under 7 years

Deaths by road user category

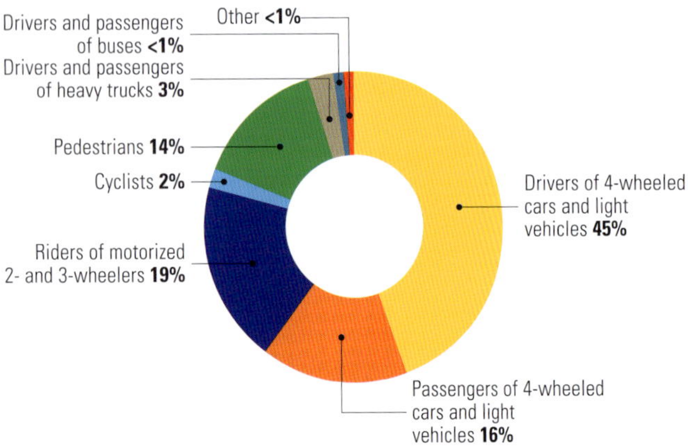

Source: 2016, Australian Road Deaths Database and National Crash Database

Trends in reported road traffic deaths

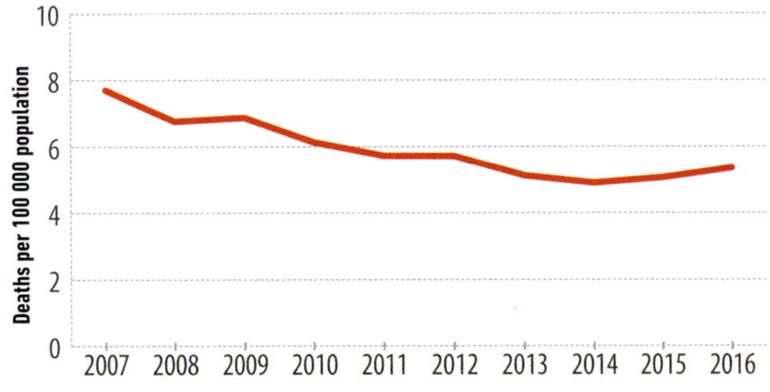

Source: Australian Road Deaths Database and National Crash Database

Legislative review conducted by WHO. Vehicle safety data from UNECE WP29. Other data collected by questionnaire and cleared by Department of Infrastructure & Regional Development.

Austria

Population: 8 712 137 | Income group: High | Gross national income per capita: US$ 45 230

INSTITUTIONAL FRAMEWORK	
Lead agency	BMVIT - Federal Ministry for Transport, Innovation and Technology
Funded in national budget	Yes
National road safety strategy	Yes
Funding to implement strategy	Partially funded
Fatality reduction target	50% (2011-2020)

SAFER ROADS AND MOBILITY	
Audits or star rating required for new road infrastructure	Yes
Design standards for the safety of pedestrians / cyclists	Yes
Inspections / star rating of existing roads	Yes
Investments to upgrade high risk locations	Yes
Policies & investment in urban public transport	Yes

SAFER VEHICLES	
Total registered vehicles for 2016	7 421 647
Cars and 4-wheeled light vehicles	4 821 557
Motorized 2- and 3-wheelers	816 477
Heavy trucks	440 368
Buses	9 825
Other	1 333 420
Vehicle standards applied (UNECE WP.29)	
Frontal impact standard	Yes
Electronic stability control	Yes
Pedestrian protection	Yes
Motorcycle anti-lock braking system	Yes

POST-CRASH CARE	
National emergency care access number	National, single number
Trauma registry	National
Formal certification for prehospital providers	Yes
National assessment of emergency care systems	No

DATA	
Reported road traffic fatalities (2016)	432 [a] (72% M, 28% F)
WHO estimated road traffic fatalities (2016)	452
WHO estimated rate per 100 000 population (2016)	5.2

[a] Statistics Austria (online). Died within 30 days of crash

SAFER ROAD USERS	
National speed limit law	Yes
Max urban speed limit	50 km/h
Max rural speed limit	100 km/h
Max motorway speed limit	130 km/h
Local authorities can modify limits	Yes
Enforcement	–
Predominant type of enforcement	Automated
National drink-driving law	Yes
BAC limit – general population	< 0.05 g/dl
BAC limit – young or novice drivers	< 0.01 g/dl
Random breath testing carried out	Yes
Testing carried out in case of fatal crash	All drivers tested
Enforcement	–
% road traffic deaths involving alcohol	5% [b]
National motorcycle helmet law	Yes
Applies to drivers and passengers	Yes
Helmet fastening required	No
Helmet standard referred to and/or specified	Yes
Children passengers on motorcycles	Prohibited under 12 yrs [c]
Enforcement	–
Helmet wearing rate	100% All riders [d]
National seat-belt law	Yes
Applies to front and rear seat occupants	Yes
Enforcement	–
Seat-belt wearing rate	95% Front seats [d], 93% Rear seats [d]
National child restraint law	Yes
Children seated in front seat	Allowed in a child restraint
Child restraint required	Up to 14 yrs/150 cm
Child restraint standard referred to and/or specified	Yes
Enforcement	–
% children using child restraints	97% Rear seats [d]
National law on mobile phone use while driving	Yes
Ban on hand-held mobile phone use	Yes
Ban on hands-free mobile phone use	No
National drug-driving law	Yes

[b] 2016, Statistics Austria (online)
[c] Or until footrests can be reached
[d] 2016, IRTAD Road Safety Annual Report 2016

Deaths by road user category

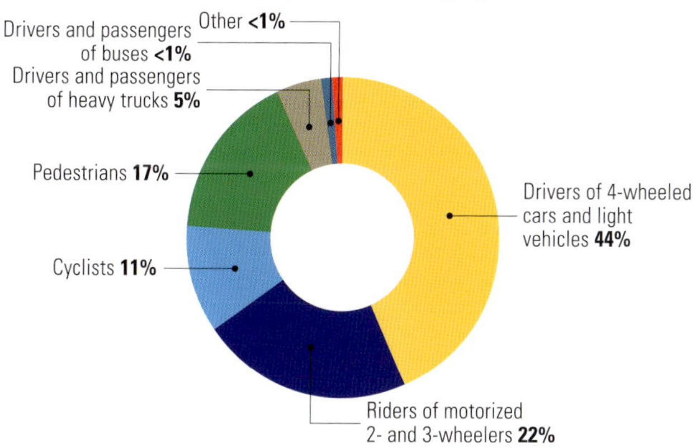

Source: Statistics Austria (online)

Trends in reported road traffic deaths

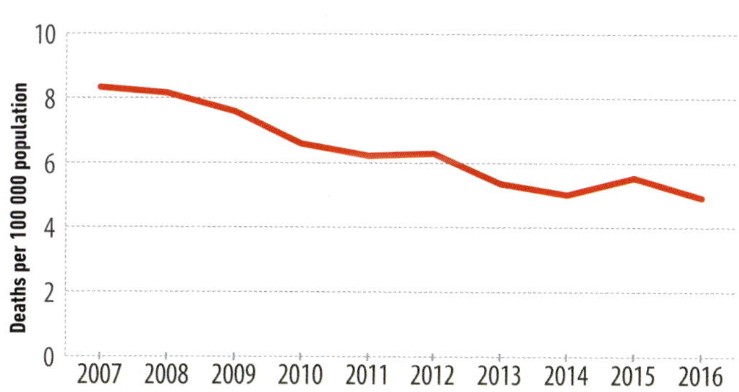

Source: Statistics Austria (online)

Legislative review conducted by WHO. Vehicle safety data from UNECE WP.29. Other data collected by questionnaire and cleared by Ministry of Transport, Innovation and Technology.

Azerbaijan

Population: 9 725 376 | Income group: Middle | Gross national income per capita: US$ 4 760

INSTITUTIONAL FRAMEWORK	
Lead agency	State Road Police
Funded in national budget	Yes
National road safety strategy	No
Funding to implement strategy	–
Fatality reduction target	–
SAFER ROADS AND MOBILITY	
Audits or star rating required for new road infrastructure	Partial
Design standards for the safety of pedestrians / cyclists	Partial
Inspections / star rating of existing roads	Yes
Investments to upgrade high risk locations	No
Policies & investment in urban public transport	Yes
SAFER VEHICLES	
Total registered vehicles for 2016	1 330 551
Cars and 4-wheeled light vehicles	1 136 983
Motorized 2- and 3-wheelers	3 290
Heavy trucks	141 525
Buses	30 958
Other	17 795
Vehicle standards applied (UNECE WP.29)	
Frontal impact standard	No
Electronic stability control	No
Pedestrian protection	No
Motorcycle anti-lock braking system	No
POST-CRASH CARE	
National emergency care access number	National, single number
Trauma registry	National
Formal certification for prehospital providers	No
National assessment of emergency care systems	No
DATA	
Reported road traffic fatalities (2016)	759[a] (77% M, 23% F)
WHO estimated road traffic fatalities (2016)	845
WHO estimated rate per 100 000 population (2016)	8.7

[a] State Statistical Committee and State Road Police. Died within 7 days of crash

SAFER ROAD USERS	
National speed limit law	Yes
Max urban speed limit	60 km/h
Max rural speed limit	90km/h
Max motorway speed limit	110 km/h
Local authorities can modify limits	No
Enforcement	0 1 2 3 4 5 6 7 ⑧ 9 10
Predominant type of enforcement	Automated
National drink-driving law	Yes[b]
BAC limit – general population	–
BAC limit – young or novice drivers	–
Random breath testing carried out	Yes
Testing carried out in case of fatal crash	All drivers tested
Enforcement	0 1 2 3 4 5 6 7 8 ⑨ 10
% road traffic deaths involving alcohol	15%[c]
National motorcycle helmet law	Yes
Applies to drivers and passengers	Yes
Helmet fastening required	No
Helmet standard referred to and/or specified	No
Children passengers on motorcycles	Prohibited under 12 yrs
Enforcement	0 1 2 3 4 5 ⑥ 7 8 9 10
Helmet wearing rate	–
National seat-belt law	Yes
Applies to front and rear seat occupants	No[d]
Enforcement	0 1 2 3 4 5 6 ⑦ 8 9 10
Seat-belt wearing rate	40% Front seats[c], 20% Rear seats[c]
National child restraint law	No[e]
Children seated in front seat	Allowed in a child restraint[e]
Child restraint required	–
Child restraint standard referred to and/or specified	–
Enforcement	–
% children using child restraints	–
National law on mobile phone use while driving	Yes
Ban on hand-held mobile phone use	Yes
Ban on hands-free mobile phone use	No
National drug-driving law	Yes

[b] Law not based on BAC/BrAC
[c] 2016, Internal statistical data of State Road Police
[d] The obligation to use seat belt does not apply in residential areas nor for children under 12 years
[e] Child restraint systems are only required for children under 12 years seated in the front

Deaths by road user category

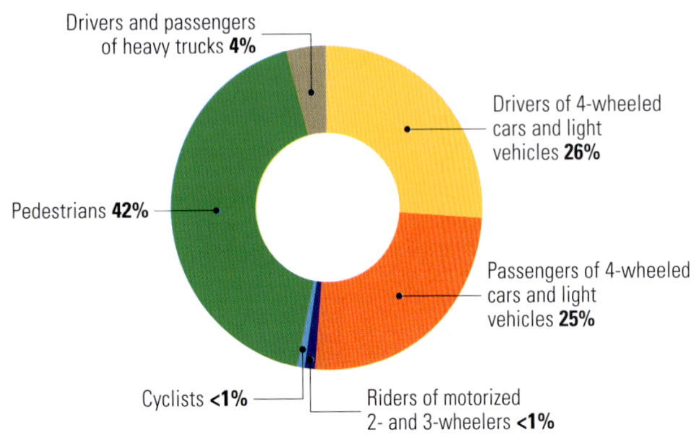

Source: 2016, Internal statistical data of State Road Police

Trends in reported road traffic deaths

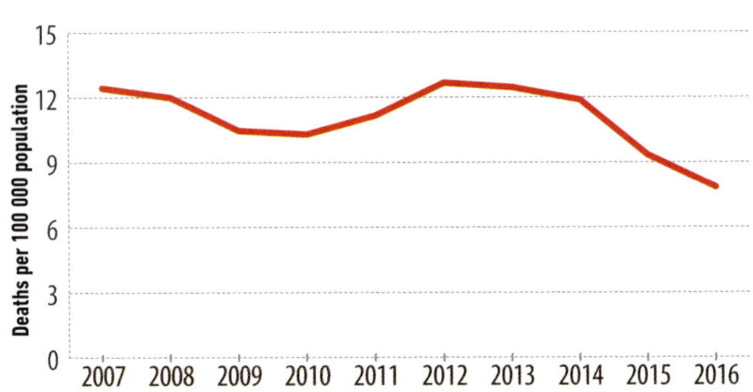

Source: Azerbaijan national statistics (online)

Bangladesh

Population: 162 951 552 | Income group: Middle | Gross national income per capita: US$ 1 330

INSTITUTIONAL FRAMEWORK	
Lead agency	National Road Safety Council (NRSC), Ministry of Road Transport and Bridges
Funded in national budget	No
National road safety strategy	Yes
Funding to implement strategy	Partially funded
Fatality reduction target	50% (2011-2020)
SAFER ROADS AND MOBILITY	
Audits or star rating required for new road infrastructure	Partial
Design standards for the safety of pedestrians / cyclists	Yes
Inspections / star rating of existing roads	Yes
Investments to upgrade high risk locations	Yes
Policies & investment in urban public transport	Yes
SAFER VEHICLES	
Total registered vehicles for 2016	2 879 708
Cars and 4-wheeled light vehicles	613 149
Motorized 2- and 3-wheelers	1 980 246
Heavy trucks	158 379
Buses	64 608
Other	63 326
Vehicle standards applied (UNECE WP.29)	
Frontal impact standard	No
Electronic stability control	No
Pedestrian protection	No
Motorcycle anti-lock braking system	No
POST-CRASH CARE	
National emergency care access number	Partial coverage
Trauma registry	None
Formal certification for prehospital providers	No
National assessment of emergency care systems	No
DATA	
Reported road traffic fatalities (2015)	2 376 [a]
WHO estimated road traffic fatalities (2016)	24 954 (95% CI 20 730 - 29 177)
WHO estimated rate per 100 000 population (2016)	15.3

[a] Bangladesh Police. Died at scene of crash

SAFER ROAD USERS	
National speed limit law	Yes
Max urban speed limit	~ 112 km/h [b]
Max rural speed limit	~ 112 km/h [b]
Max motorway speed limit	~ 112 km/h [b]
Local authorities can modify limits	No
Enforcement	0 1 2 3 4 (5) 6 7 8 9 10
Predominant type of enforcement	Manual
National drink-driving law	Yes [c]
BAC limit – general population	–
BAC limit – young or novice drivers	–
Random breath testing carried out	Yes
Testing carried out in case of fatal crash	Some drivers tested
Enforcement	0 1 (2) 3 4 5 6 7 8 9 10
% road traffic deaths involving alcohol	–
National motorcycle helmet law	Yes
Applies to drivers and passengers	Yes
Helmet fastening required	No
Helmet standard referred to and/or specified	Yes
Children passengers on motorcycles	Not restricted
Enforcement	0 1 2 3 4 5 (6) 7 8 9 10
Helmet wearing rate	–
National seat-belt law	No
Applies to front and rear seat occupants	–
Enforcement	–
Seat-belt wearing rate	–
National child restraint law	No
Children seated in front seat	Not restricted
Child restraint required	–
Child restraint standard referred to and/or specified	–
Enforcement	–
% children using child restraints	–
National law on mobile phone use while driving	No
Ban on hand-held mobile phone use	–
Ban on hands-free mobile phone use	–
National drug-driving law	Yes

[b] Speed limit set per vehicle type with a maximum speed limit of 70 miles per hour (112 km/h) for light vehicles

[c] Not based on BAC

Deaths by road user category

Trends in reported road traffic deaths

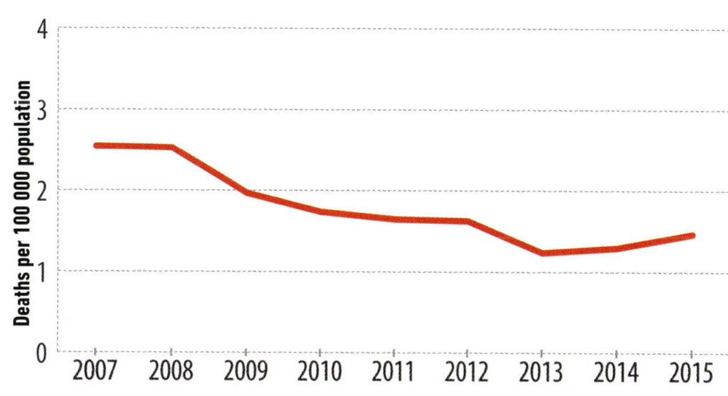

Source: Bangladesh Police (fatality data), World Bank (population data)

Legislative review conducted by WHO. Vehicle safety data from UNECE WP29. Other data collected by questionnaire.

Barbados

Population: 284 996 | Income group: High | Gross national income per capita: US$ 14 830

INSTITUTIONAL FRAMEWORK	
Lead agency	Barbados National Road Safety Council, Ministry of Transport and Works
Funded in national budget	No
National road safety strategy	No
Funding to implement strategy	–
Fatality reduction target	–

SAFER ROADS AND MOBILITY	
Audits or star rating required for new road infrastructure	No
Design standards for the safety of pedestrians / cyclists	Partial
Inspections / star rating of existing roads	Yes
Investments to upgrade high risk locations	No
Policies & investment in urban public transport	Yes

SAFER VEHICLES	
Total registered vehicles for 2015	117 104
Cars and 4-wheeled light vehicles	108 502
Motorized 2- and 3-wheelers	2 154
Heavy trucks	5 530
Buses	816
Other	102
Vehicle standards applied (UNECE WP.29)	
Frontal impact standard	No
Electronic stability control	No
Pedestrian protection	No
Motorcycle anti-lock braking system	No

POST-CRASH CARE	
National emergency care access number	National, multiple numbers
Trauma registry	National
Formal certification for prehospital providers	Yes
National assessment of emergency care systems	No

DATA	
Reported road traffic fatalities (2016)	9[a] (89% M, 11% F)
WHO estimated road traffic fatalities (2016)	16
WHO estimated rate per 100 000 population (2016)	5.6

[a] Royal Barbados Police force. Defined as died within one year and one day of crash

SAFER ROAD USERS	
National speed limit law	Yes
Max urban speed limit	80 km/h[b]
Max rural speed limit	80 km/h[b]
Max motorway speed limit	80 km/h[b]
Local authorities can modify limits	No
Enforcement	0 1 2 3 (4) 5 6 7 8 9 10
Predominant type of enforcement	Manual
National drink-driving law	Yes
BAC limit – general population	≤ 0.08 g/dl
BAC limit – young or novice drivers	≤ 0.08 g/dl
Random breath testing carried out	Yes[c]
Testing carried out in case of fatal crash	All drivers tested
Enforcement	0 1 (2) 3 4 5 6 7 8 9 10
% road traffic deaths involving alcohol	–
National motorcycle helmet law	Yes
Applies to drivers and passengers	Yes
Helmet fastening required	No
Helmet standard referred to and/or specified	Yes
Children passengers on motorcycles	Not restricted
Enforcement	0 1 2 3 4 5 6 7 8 (9) 10
Helmet wearing rate	–
National seat-belt law	Yes
Applies to front and rear seat occupants	Yes
Enforcement	0 1 2 3 4 5 6 (7) 8 9 10
Seat-belt wearing rate	–
National child restraint law	Yes
Children seated in front seat	Prohibited under 4 yrs
Child restraint required	Up to 4 yrs
Child restraint standard referred to and/or specified	Yes
Enforcement	0 1 2 3 (4) 5 6 7 8 9 10
% children using child restraints	–
National law on mobile phone use while driving	Yes
Ban on hand-held mobile phone use	Yes
Ban on hands-free mobile phone use	No
National drug-driving law	Yes

[b] Speed limit set per vehicle type with a maximum speed limit of 80 km/h for specified vehicles including private motor cars
[c] Legislation requires probable cause to test drivers or commission of a traffic offence

Deaths by road user category

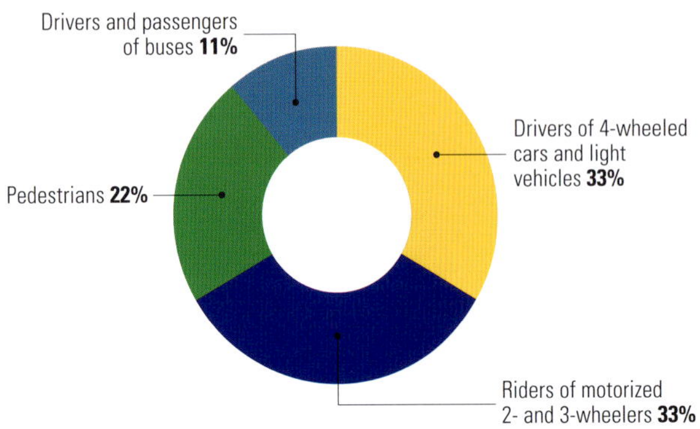

Source: 2016, Royal Barbados Police Force

Trends in reported road traffic deaths

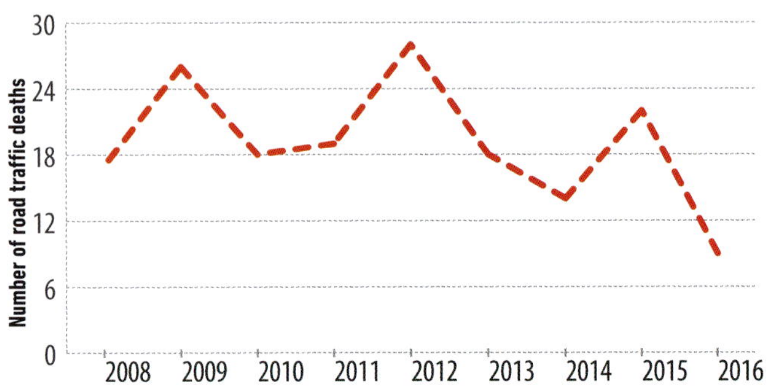

Source: Royal Barbados Police Force

Belarus

Population: 9 480 042 | Income group: Middle | Gross national income per capita: US$ 5 600

INSTITUTIONAL FRAMEWORK

Lead agency	The Permanent Commission of the Ensuring Traffic Safety under the Council of Ministers of the Republic of Belarus
Funded in national budget	Yes
National road safety strategy	Yes
Funding to implement strategy	Partially funded
Fatality reduction target	20% (2016-2020)

SAFER ROADS AND MOBILITY

Audits or star rating required for new road infrastructure	No
Design standards for the safety of pedestrians / cyclists	Yes
Inspections / star rating of existing roads	Yes
Investments to upgrade high risk locations	Yes
Policies & investment in urban public transport	Yes

SAFER VEHICLES

Total registered vehicles for 01.01.2017	4 192 291
Cars and 4-wheeled light vehicles	3 067 501
Motorized 2- and 3-wheelers	415 761
Heavy trucks	414 364
Buses	43 602
Other	251 063
Vehicle standards applied (UNECE WP.29)	
Frontal impact standard	No
Electronic stability control	No
Pedestrian protection	No
Motorcycle anti-lock braking system	No

POST-CRASH CARE

National emergency care access number	National, single number
Trauma registry	None
Formal certification for prehospital providers	No
National assessment of emergency care systems	No

DATA

Reported road traffic fatalities (2016)	588[a] (69% M, 31% F)
WHO estimated road traffic fatalities (2016)	841
WHO estimated rate per 100 000 population (2016)	8.9

[a] Ministry of Internal Affairs, State Automobile Inspection Department. Died within 30 days of crash

SAFER ROAD USERS

National speed limit law	Yes
Max urban speed limit	60 km/h
Max rural speed limit	90 km/h
Max motorway speed limit	110 km/h
Local authorities can modify limits	No
Enforcement	0 1 2 3 4 5 6 ⑦ 8 9 10
Predominant type of enforcement	Manual and automated
National drink-driving law	Yes
BAC limit – general population	< 0.03 g/dl
BAC limit – young or novice drivers	< 0.03 g/dl
Random breath testing carried out	Yes[b]
Testing carried out in case of fatal crash	All drivers tested
Enforcement	0 1 2 3 4 5 6 7 ⑧ 9 10
% road traffic deaths involving alcohol	14% (Drivers)[c]
National motorcycle helmet law	Yes
Applies to drivers and passengers	Yes
Helmet fastening required	Yes
Helmet standard referred to and/or specified	Yes
Children passengers on motorcycles	Prohibited under 12 yrs
Enforcement	0 1 2 3 4 5 6 7 ⑧ 9 10
Helmet wearing rate	–
National seat-belt law	Yes
Applies to front and rear seat occupants	Yes
Enforcement	0 1 2 3 4 5 6 7 ⑧ 9 10
Seat-belt wearing rate	–
National child restraint law	Yes
Children seated in front seat	Allowed in a child restraint[d]
Child restraint required	Up to 5 yrs[e]
Child restraint standard referred to and/or specified	Yes
Enforcement	0 1 2 3 4 5 6 7 ⑧ 9 10
% children using child restraints	–
National law on mobile phone use while driving	Yes
Ban on hand-held mobile phone use	Yes
Ban on hands-free mobile phone use	No
National drug-driving law	Yes

[b] Legislation requires probable cause to test drivers
[c] 2016, Ministry of Internal Affairs, State Automobile Inspection Department
[d] If rear-facing child restraints, airbag shall be deactivated
[e] For children aged 5-12 years, either CRS or "other means" (than CRS) can be used to secure the child using the seat belt

Deaths by road user category

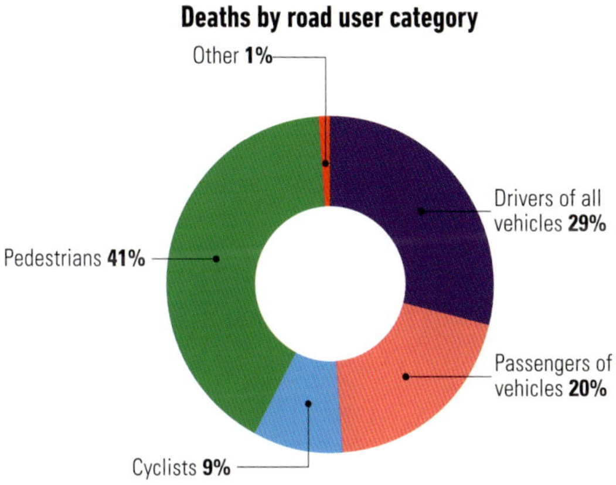

Source: 2016, Information about the State of of Road Traffic Accidents in the Republic of Belarus in 2016

Trends in reported road traffic deaths

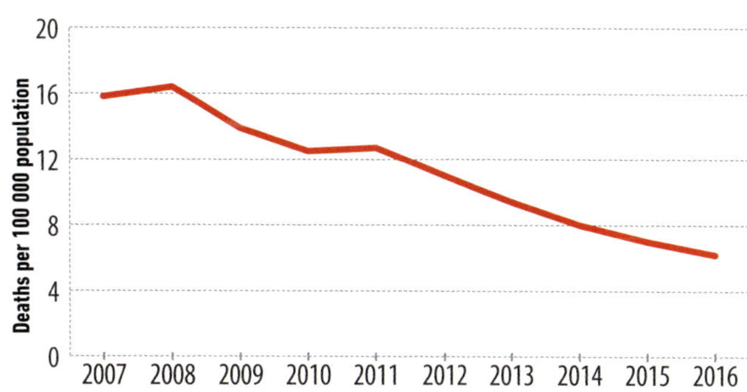

Source: Information about the State of of Road Traffic Accidents in the Republic of Belarus in 2016

Belgium

Population: 11 358 379 | Income group: High | Gross national income per capita: US$ 41 860

INSTITUTIONAL FRAMEWORK

Lead agency	**No**
Funded in national budget	–
National road safety strategy	**Yes**
Funding to implement strategy	Partially funded
Fatality reduction target	50% (2010-2020)

SAFER ROADS AND MOBILITY

Audits or star rating required for new road infrastructure	Yes
Design standards for the safety of pedestrians / cyclists	Yes
Inspections / star rating of existing roads	Yes
Investments to upgrade high risk locations	Yes
Policies & investment in urban public transport	Yes

SAFER VEHICLES

Total registered vehicles for 2016	**7 330 718**
Cars and 4-wheeled light vehicles	6 440 811
Motorized 2- and 3-wheelers	471 766
Heavy trucks	143 554
Buses	15 970
Other	258 617
Vehicle standards applied (UNECE WP.29)	
Frontal impact standard	Yes
Electronic stability control	Yes
Pedestrian protection	Yes
Motorcycle anti-lock braking system	Yes

POST-CRASH CARE

National emergency care access number	National, single number
Trauma registry	National
Formal certification for prehospital providers	Yes
National assessment of emergency care systems	No

DATA

Reported road traffic fatalities (2016)	637[a] (76% M, 24% F)
WHO estimated road traffic fatalities (2016)	657
WHO estimated rate per 100 000 population (2016)	5.8

[a] Statistics Belgium. Died within 30 days of crash

SAFER ROAD USERS

National speed limit law	**Yes**
Max urban speed limit	50 km/h
Max rural speed limit	90 km/h[b]
Max motorway speed limit	120 km/h
Local authorities can modify limits	Yes
Enforcement	0 1 2 3 4 5 6 (7) 8 9 10
Predominant type of enforcement	Manual and automated
National drink-driving law	**Yes**
BAC limit – general population	< 0.05 g/dl
BAC limit – young or novice drivers	< 0.05 g/dl
Random breath testing carried out	Yes
Testing carried out in case of fatal crash	Some drivers tested
Enforcement	0 1 2 3 4 5 (6) 7 8 9 10
% road traffic deaths involving alcohol	–
National motorcycle helmet law	**Yes**
Applies to drivers and passengers	Yes
Helmet fastening required	No
Helmet standard referred to and/or specified	Yes
Children passengers on motorcycles	Prohibited for 3 or 8 yrs[c]
Enforcement	0 1 2 3 4 5 6 8 (9) 10
Helmet wearing rate	99% Drivers[d], 100% Passengers[d]
National seat-belt law	**Yes**
Applies to front and rear seat occupants	Yes
Enforcement	0 1 2 3 4 5 6 (7) 8 9 10
Seat-belt wearing rate	92% Front seats[e], 86% Rear seats[e]
National child restraint law	**Yes**
Children seated in front seat	Allowed in a child restraint[f]
Child restraint required	Up to 18 yrs/135 cm
Child restraint standard referred to and/or specified	Yes[g]
Enforcement	0 1 2 3 4 (5) 6 7 8 9 10
% children using child restraints	89%[h]
National law on mobile phone use while driving	**Yes**
Ban on hand-held mobile phone use	Yes
Ban on hands-free mobile phone use	No
National drug-driving law	**Yes**

[b] The 90 km/h speed limit applies on rural areas in Brussels capital region and Wallon region while there is a 70 km/h speed limit in the Flemish region
[c] Restrictions vary depending on the type of motorcycles: children under 3 years are not allowed on mopeds and motorcycles, children under 8 years are not allowed on motorcycles over 125cc
[d] 2013, Belgian Road Safety Institute
[e] 2015, Belgian Road Safety Institute
[f] Provided that airbag is deactivated if child is in a rear-facing child restraint system
[g] All child restraints sold in Belgium must comply with UNECE regulation
[h] 2014, Roynard, M (2015)

Deaths by road user category

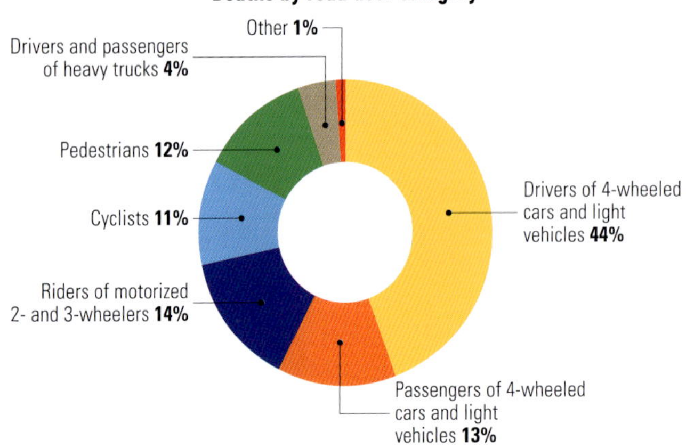

Source: 2016, Statistics Belgium

Trends in reported road traffic deaths

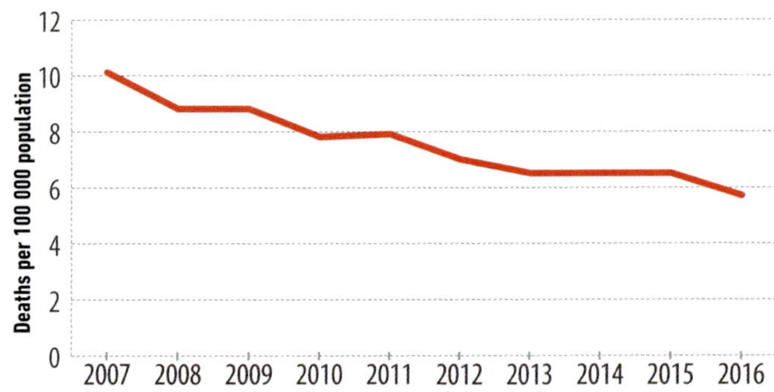

Source: Statistics Belgium

Legislative review conducted by WHO. Vehicle safety data from UNECE WP.29. Other data collected by questionnaire and cleared by National Institute for Road Safety.

Belize

Population: 366 954 | Income group: Middle | Gross national income per capita: US$ 4 410

INSTITUTIONAL FRAMEWORK	
Lead agency	National Road Safety Committee
Funded in national budget	Yes
National road safety strategy	Yes
Funding to implement strategy	Partially funded
Fatality reduction target	0 deaths (2016-2030)
SAFER ROADS AND MOBILITY	
Audits or star rating required for new road infrastructure	Yes
Design standards for the safety of pedestrians / cyclists	Yes
Inspections / star rating of existing roads	Yes
Investments to upgrade high risk locations	No
Policies & investment in urban public transport	No
SAFER VEHICLES	
Total registered vehicles for 2007	56 094
Cars and 4-wheeled light vehicles	45 336
Motorized 2- and 3-wheelers	2 389
Heavy trucks	4 757
Buses	3 612
Other	0
Vehicle standards applied (UNECE WP.29)	
Frontal impact standard	No
Electronic stability control	No
Pedestrian protection	No
Motorcycle anti-lock braking system	No
POST-CRASH CARE	
National emergency care access number	National, single number
Trauma registry	None
Formal certification for prehospital providers	No
National assessment of emergency care systems	No
DATA	
Reported road traffic fatalities (2016)	101[a] (84% M, 16% F)
WHO estimated road traffic fatalities (2016)	104
WHO estimated rate per 100 000 population (2016)	28.3

[a] Ministry of Health Annual RTA Mortality Report. Died within 30 days of crash

SAFER ROAD USERS	
National speed limit law	Yes
Max urban speed limit	~ 40 km/h
Max rural speed limit	~ 88 km/h
Max motorway speed limit	~ 88 km/h
Local authorities can modify limits	No
Enforcement	0 1 2 3 (4) 5 6 7 8 9 10
Predominant type of enforcement	Manual
National drink-driving law	Yes
BAC limit – general population	≤ 0.08 g/dl
BAC limit – young or novice drivers	≤ 0.08 g/dl
Random breath testing carried out	Yes[b]
Testing carried out in case of fatal crash	All drivers tested
Enforcement	0 1 2 3 (4) 5 6 7 8 9 10
% road traffic deaths involving alcohol	–
National motorcycle helmet law	Yes
Applies to drivers and passengers	Yes
Helmet fastening required	Yes
Helmet standard referred to and/or specified	No
Children passengers on motorcycles	Not restricted
Enforcement	0 1 2 3 4 (5) 6 7 8 9 10
Helmet wearing rate	–
National seat-belt law	Yes
Applies to front and rear seat occupants	No
Enforcement	0 1 2 3 4 (5) 6 7 8 9 10
Seat-belt wearing rate	–
National child restraint law	No
Children seated in front seat	Not restricted
Child restraint required	–
Child restraint standard referred to and/or specified	–
Enforcement	–
% children using child restraints	–
National law on mobile phone use while driving	No
Ban on hand-held mobile phone use	–
Ban on hands-free mobile phone use	–
National drug-driving law	Yes

[b] Legislation requires probable cause to test drivers or commission of a traffic offence

Deaths by road user category

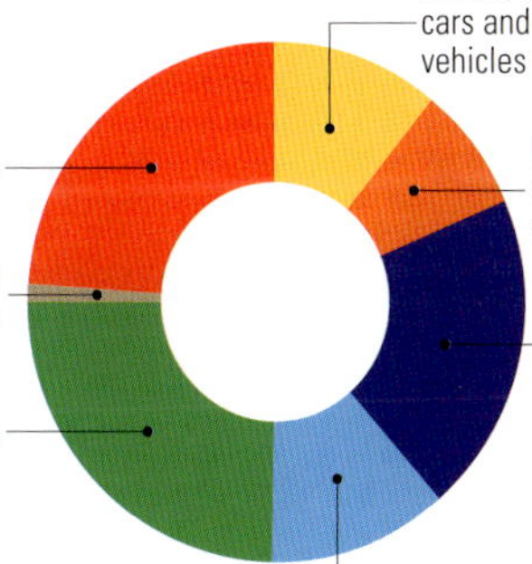

Source: 2016, Ministry of Health Annual RTA Mortality Report

Trends in reported road traffic deaths

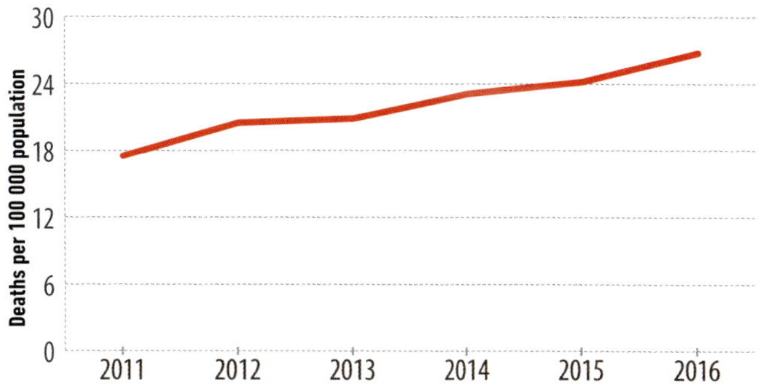

Source: Ministry of Health, Annual RTA Mortality Report based on validated data with JICC

Benin

Population: 10 872 298 | Income group: Low | Gross national income per capita: US$ 820

INSTITUTIONAL FRAMEWORK	
Lead agency	National Centre for Road Safety (CNSR), Ministry of Infrastructure and Transport
Funded in national budget	No
National road safety strategy	No
Funding to implement strategy	–
Fatality reduction target	–
SAFER ROADS AND MOBILITY	
Audits or star rating required for new road infrastructure	Partial
Design standards for the safety of pedestrians / cyclists	Partial
Inspections / star rating of existing roads	No
Investments to upgrade high risk locations	Yes
Policies & investment in urban public transport	No
SAFER VEHICLES	
Total registered vehicles for 2016	469 761
Cars and 4-wheeled light vehicles	238 436
Motorized 2- and 3-wheelers	195 157
Heavy trucks	19 747
Buses	311
Other	16 110
Vehicle standards applied (UNECE WP.29)	
Frontal impact standard	No
Electronic stability control	No
Pedestrian protection	No
Motorcycle anti-lock braking system	No
POST-CRASH CARE	
National emergency care access number	National, single number
Trauma registry	Some facilities
Formal certification for prehospital providers	Yes
National assessment of emergency care systems	No
DATA	
Reported road traffic fatalities (2015)	637[a]
WHO estimated road traffic fatalities (2016)	2 986 (95% CI 2 458 - 3 514)
WHO estimated rate per 100 000 population (2016)	27.5

[a] Republic of Benin, Statistical Yearbook of Accidents 2015. Died within 7 days of crash

SAFER ROAD USERS	
National speed limit law	No
Max urban speed limit	–
Max rural speed limit	–
Max motorway speed limit	–
Local authorities can modify limits	–
Enforcement	–
Predominant type of enforcement	–
National drink-driving law	Yes[b]
BAC limit – general population	–
BAC limit – young or novice drivers	–
Random breath testing carried out	Yes
Testing carried out in case of fatal crash	No
Enforcement	0 ① 2 3 4 5 6 7 8 9 10
% road traffic deaths involving alcohol	–
National motorcycle helmet law	Yes
Applies to drivers and passengers	Yes
Helmet fastening required	Yes
Helmet standard referred to and/or specified	No
Children passengers on motorcycles	Not restricted
Enforcement	0 1 2 ③ 4 5 6 7 8 9 10
Helmet wearing rate	25% Drivers[c], 1% Passengers[c]
National seat-belt law	No
Applies to front and rear seat occupants	–
Enforcement	–
Seat-belt wearing rate	–
National child restraint law	No
Children seated in front seat	Not restricted
Child restraint required	–
Child restraint standard referred to and/or specified	–
Enforcement	–
% children using child restraints	–
National law on mobile phone use while driving	Yes
Ban on hand-held mobile phone use	Yes
Ban on hands-free mobile phone use	Yes
National drug-driving law	No

[b] Not based on BAC
[c] 2016, National Police

Deaths by road user category

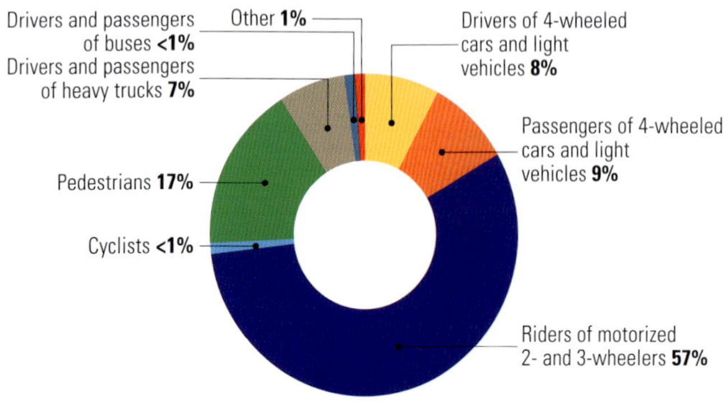

Source: 2015, National Centre for Road Safety (CNSR)

Trends in reported road traffic deaths

Source: National Centre for Road Safety (CNSR)

Bhutan

Population: 797 765 | Income group: Middle | Gross national income per capita: US$ 2 510

INSTITUTIONAL FRAMEWORK	
Lead agency	Road Safety and Transport Authority (RSTA), Ministry of Information and Communications (MoIC)
Funded in national budget	Yes
National road safety strategy	Yes
Funding to implement strategy	Partially funded
Fatality reduction target	<8 deaths per 10 000 vehicles annually (2013-2018)

SAFER ROADS AND MOBILITY	
Audits or star rating required for new road infrastructure	Yes
Design standards for the safety of pedestrians / cyclists	Yes
Inspections / star rating of existing roads	Yes
Investments to upgrade high risk locations	Yes
Policies & investment in urban public transport	Yes

SAFER VEHICLES	
Total registered vehicles for Till 30th April 2017	86 981
Cars and 4-wheeled light vehicles	56 232
Motorized 2- and 3-wheelers	9 786
Heavy trucks	12 891
Buses	681
Other	7 391
Vehicle standards applied (UNECE WP.29)	
Frontal impact standard	No
Electronic stability control	No
Pedestrian protection	No
Motorcycle anti-lock braking system	No

POST-CRASH CARE	
National emergency care access number	National, single number
Trauma registry	None
Formal certification for prehospital providers	Yes
National assessment of emergency care systems	No

DATA	
Reported road traffic fatalities (2016)	125[a] (67% M, 17% F)
WHO estimated road traffic fatalities (2016)	139 (95% CI 121 - 157)
WHO estimated rate per 100 000 population (2016)	17.4

[a] Ministry of Information and Communications (MoIC), Road Safety and Transport Authority (RSTA), Traffic Police and Ministry of Health. Died within 7 days of crash

SAFER ROAD USERS	
National speed limit law	Yes
Max urban speed limit	30 km/h
Max rural speed limit	50 km/h
Max motorway speed limit	50 km/h
Local authorities can modify limits	No
Enforcement	0 1 2 3 4 5 ⑥ 7 8 9 10
Predominant type of enforcement	Manual
National drink-driving law	Yes
BAC limit – general population	≤ 0.08 g/dl
BAC limit – young or novice drivers	0.00 g/dl
Random breath testing carried out	Yes
Testing carried out in case of fatal crash	Some drivers tested
Enforcement	0 1 2 3 4 5 ⑥ 7 8 9 10
% road traffic deaths involving alcohol	–
National motorcycle helmet law	Yes
Applies to drivers and passengers	Yes
Helmet fastening required	Yes
Helmet standard referred to and/or specified	Yes
Children passengers on motorcycles	Not restricted
Enforcement	0 1 2 3 4 5 6 7 8 ⑨ 10
Helmet wearing rate	–
National seat-belt law	Yes
Applies to front and rear seat occupants	Yes
Enforcement	0 1 ② 3 4 5 6 7 8 9 10
Seat-belt wearing rate	–
National child restraint law	No
Children seated in front seat	Not restricted
Child restraint required	–
Child restraint standard referred to and/or specified	–
Enforcement	–
% children using child restraints	–
National law on mobile phone use while driving	Yes
Ban on hand-held mobile phone use	Yes
Ban on hands-free mobile phone use	No
National drug-driving law	Yes

Deaths by road user category

Trends in reported road traffic deaths

Source: Road Safety and Transport Authority (RSTA), Traffic Police, and Ministry of Health (MoH)

Legislative review conducted by WHO. Vehicle safety data from UNECE WP.29. Other data collected by questionnaire and cleared by Ministry of Information and Communications.

Bolivia (Plurinational State of)

Population: 10 887 882 | Income group: Middle | Gross national income per capita: US$ 3 070

INSTITUTIONAL FRAMEWORK	
Lead agency	Vice Ministry of Public Safety, Ministry of Government
Funded in national budget	Yes
National road safety strategy	Yes
Funding to implement strategy	Partially funded
Fatality reduction target	10% (2014-2018)
SAFER ROADS AND MOBILITY	
Audits or star rating required for new road infrastructure	Yes
Design standards for the safety of pedestrians / cyclists	Yes
Inspections / star rating of existing roads	Yes
Investments to upgrade high risk locations	No
Policies & investment in urban public transport	Yes
SAFER VEHICLES	
Total registered vehicles for 2016	1 711 005
Cars and 4-wheeled light vehicles	1 032 581
Motorized 2- and 3-wheelers	391 219
Heavy trucks	146 703
Buses	124 805
Other	15 697
Vehicle standards applied (UNECE WP.29)	
Frontal impact standard	No
Electronic stability control	No
Pedestrian protection	No
Motorcycle anti-lock braking system	No
POST-CRASH CARE	
National emergency care access number	Partial coverage
Trauma registry	Subnational
Formal certification for prehospital providers	No
National assessment of emergency care systems	No
DATA	
Reported road traffic fatalities (2016)	1 259[a] (82% M, 18% F)
WHO estimated road traffic fatalities (2016)	1 687 (95% CI 1 532 - 1 842)
WHO estimated rate per 100 000 population (2016)	15.5

[a] National Observatory of Public Safety, Bolivian Police data. Died at scene of crash

SAFER ROAD USERS	
National speed limit law	Yes
Max urban speed limit	40 km/h[b]
Max rural speed limit	80 km/h[b]
Max motorway speed limit	80 km/h
Local authorities can modify limits	Yes
Enforcement	0 1 2 (3) 4 5 6 7 8 9 10
Predominant type of enforcement	Manual
National drink-driving law	Yes
BAC limit – general population	≤ 0.05 g/dl
BAC limit – young or novice drivers	≤ 0.05 g/dl
Random breath testing carried out	Yes[c]
Testing carried out in case of fatal crash	All drivers tested
Enforcement	0 1 2 3 (4) 5 6 7 8 9 10
% road traffic deaths involving alcohol	6%[d]
National motorcycle helmet law	Yes
Applies to drivers and passengers	Yes
Helmet fastening required	No
Helmet standard referred to and/or specified	Yes
Children passengers on motorcycles	Not restricted
Enforcement	0 1 2 (3) 4 5 6 7 8 9 10
Helmet wearing rate	52% Drivers[e], 3% Passengers[e]
National seat-belt law	Yes
Applies to front and rear seat occupants	No
Enforcement	0 1 (2) 3 4 5 6 7 8 9 10
Seat-belt wearing rate	4% Front seats[e], <1% Rear seats[e]
National child restraint law	No
Children seated in front seat	Not restricted
Child restraint required	–
Child restraint standard referred to and/or specified	–
Enforcement	–
% children using child restraints	–
National law on mobile phone use while driving	No
Ban on hand-held mobile phone use	–
Ban on hands-free mobile phone use	–
National drug-driving law	Yes

[b] Can be increased to an unspecified speed under certain circumstances
[c] Legislation requires probable cause to test drivers
[d] 2016. National observatory of Public safety, Bolivian Police data
[e] 2013, Observational urban field study on the use of seat belts, child restraint systems in private vehicles and the use of helmets on motorcycles and mopeds in the Plurinational State of Bolivia

Deaths by road user category

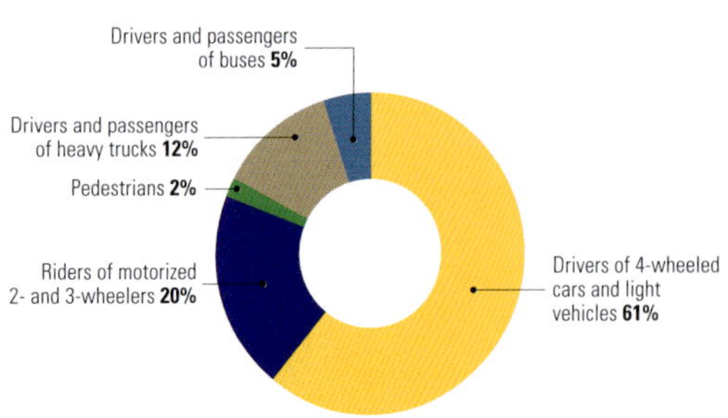

Source: 2016, National Observatory of Public Safety, Bolivian Police data

Trends in reported road traffic deaths

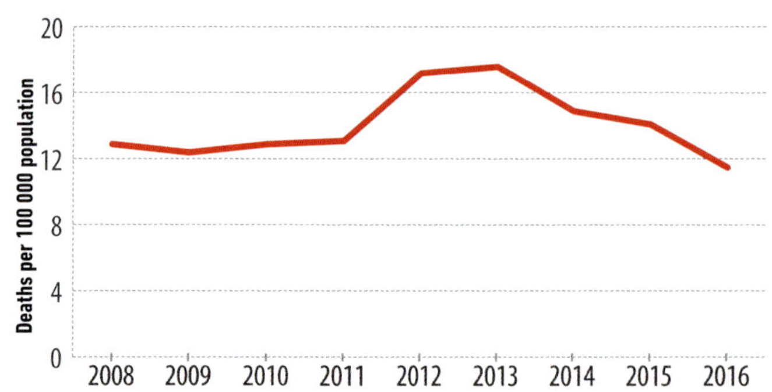

Source: National Observatory of Public Safety, Bolivian Police data and INE

Bosnia and Herzegovina

Population: 3 516 816 | Income group: Middle | Gross national income per capita: US$ 4 880

INSTITUTIONAL FRAMEWORK

Lead agency	Agency for Traffic Safety of the Republic of Srpska, Ministry of Communications and Transport
Funded in national budget	Yes
National road safety strategy	**Yes**
Funding to implement strategy	Partially funded
Fatality reduction target	50% (2013-2022)

SAFER ROADS AND MOBILITY

Audits or star rating required for new road infrastructure	Partial
Design standards for the safety of pedestrians / cyclists	Yes
Inspections / star rating of existing roads	Yes
Investments to upgrade high risk locations	Yes
Policies & investment in urban public transport	No

SAFER VEHICLES

Total registered vehicles for 2016	**978 229**
Cars and 4-wheeled light vehicles	840 280
Motorized 2- and 3-wheelers	14 399
Heavy trucks	79 135
Buses	4 275
Other	40 140
Vehicle standards applied (UNECE WP.29)	
Frontal impact standard	No
Electronic stability control	No
Pedestrian protection	No
Motorcycle anti-lock braking system	No

POST-CRASH CARE

National emergency care access number	National, single number
Trauma registry	None
Formal certification for prehospital providers	Yes
National assessment of emergency care systems	Yes

DATA

Reported road traffic fatalities (2016)	318 [a]
WHO estimated road traffic fatalities (2016)	552 (95% CI 500 - 603)
WHO estimated rate per 100 000 population (2016)	15.7

[a] Combined sources, including Federal Ministry of Interior and Ministry of Interior of Republic of Srpska . Died within 30 days of crash

SAFER ROAD USERS

National speed limit law	**Yes**
Max urban speed limit	50 km/h [b]
Max rural speed limit	80 km/h
Max motorway speed limit	130 km/h
Local authorities can modify limits	No
Enforcement	0 1 2 3 4 5 (6) 7 8 9 10
Predominant type of enforcement	Manual and automated
National drink-driving law	**Yes**
BAC limit – general population	≤ 0.03 g/dl
BAC limit – young or novice drivers	0.00 g/dl
Random breath testing carried out	Yes
Testing carried out in case of fatal crash	All drivers tested
Enforcement	0 1 2 3 4 5 (6) 7 8 9 10
% road traffic deaths involving alcohol	21% [c]
National motorcycle helmet law	**Yes**
Applies to drivers and passengers	Yes
Helmet fastening required	No
Helmet standard referred to and/or specified	No
Children passengers on motorcycles	Prohibited under 12 yrs
Enforcement	0 1 2 3 4 5 6 (7) 8 9 10
Helmet wearing rate	–
National seat-belt law	**Yes**
Applies to front and rear seat occupants	Yes
Enforcement	0 1 2 3 4 (5) 6 7 8 9 10
Seat-belt wearing rate	51% Front seats [d], 11% Rear seats [d]
National child restraint law	**Yes**
Children seated in front seat	Prohibited under 12 yrs [e]
Child restraint required	Up to 12 yrs [f]
Child restraint standard referred to and/or specified	No
Enforcement	0 1 2 3 4 5 6 7 (8) 9 10
% children using child restraints	40% [g]
National law on mobile phone use while driving	**Yes**
Ban on hand-held mobile phone use	Yes
Ban on hands-free mobile phone use	No
National drug-driving law	**Yes**

[b] Can be increased up to an unspecified speed
[c] 2016, Ministry of Interior of Republic of Srpska
[d] 2016, Auto Moto Association of Republic of Srpska
[e] By exception, a child under 2 years can be seated in the front if there is no airbag installed or if the airbag is deactivated when the child is seated in a rear-facing seat
[f] Children aged 5-12 years can be either restrained in a booster seat or in a child restraint
[g] 2016, Auto Moto Association of Republic of Srpska (Data only for Republic of Srpska)

Deaths by road user category

Source: 2016, Annual report for 2016 of Brcko district, B&H traffic police unit and Ministry of Interior of Republic of Srpska

Trends in reported road traffic deaths

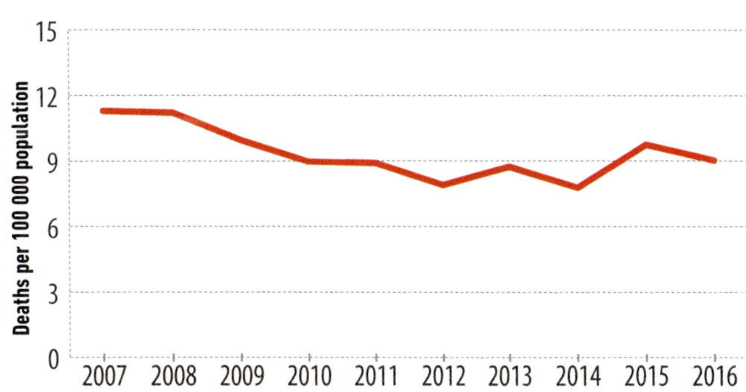

Source: Multiple sources, including Federal Ministry of Internal Affairs and Ministry of Interior of the Republic of Srpska

Legislative review conducted by WHO. Vehicle safety data from UNECE WP29. Other data collected by questionnaire and cleared by Ministry of Civil Affairs.

Botswana

Population: 2 250 260 | Income group: Middle | Gross national income per capita: US$ 6 610

INSTITUTIONAL FRAMEWORK

Lead agency	**National Road Safety Committee (NRSC)**
Funded in national budget	Yes
National road safety strategy	**Yes**
Funding to implement strategy	Fully funded
Fatality reduction target	50% (2011-2020)

SAFER ROADS AND MOBILITY

Audits or star rating required for new road infrastructure	Yes
Design standards for the safety of pedestrians / cyclists	Yes
Inspections / star rating of existing roads	Yes
Investments to upgrade high risk locations	Yes
Policies & investment in urban public transport	No

SAFER VEHICLES

Total registered vehicles for 1995-2016	**653 274**
Cars and 4-wheeled light vehicles	438 224
Motorized 2- and 3-wheelers	2 250
Heavy trucks	28 208
Buses	18 841
Other	165 751
Vehicle standards applied (UNECE WP.29)	
Frontal impact standard	No
Electronic stability control	No
Pedestrian protection	No
Motorcycle anti-lock braking system	No

POST-CRASH CARE

National emergency care access number	National, multiple numbers
Trauma registry	None
Formal certification for prehospital providers	–
National assessment of emergency care systems	No

DATA

Reported road traffic fatalities (2016)	450[a] (72% M, 28% F)
WHO estimated road traffic fatalities (2016)	535 (95% CI 465 - 606)
WHO estimated rate per 100 000 population (2016)	23.8

[a] Botswana Police Service. Died within a year of crash

SAFER ROAD USERS

National speed limit law	**Yes**
Max urban speed limit	60 km/h
Max rural speed limit	80 km/h
Max motorway speed limit	120 km/h
Local authorities can modify limits	Yes
Enforcement	0 1 2 3 4 5 6 7 (8) 9 10
Predominant type of enforcement	Manual
National drink-driving law	**Yes**
BAC limit – general population	≤ 0.05 g/dl
BAC limit – young or novice drivers	≤ 0.05 g/dl
Random breath testing carried out	Yes
Testing carried out in case of fatal crash	Some drivers tested
Enforcement	0 1 2 3 4 5 (6) 7 8 9 10
% road traffic deaths involving alcohol	4%[b]
National motorcycle helmet law	**Yes**
Applies to drivers and passengers	Yes
Helmet fastening required	Yes
Helmet standard referred to and/or specified	Yes
Children passengers on motorcycles	Not restricted
Enforcement	0 1 2 3 4 5 6 7 (8) 9 10
Helmet wearing rate	–
National seat-belt law	**Yes**
Applies to front and rear seat occupants	Yes
Enforcement	0 1 2 3 4 5 6 (7) 8 9 10
Seat-belt wearing rate	–
National child restraint law	**Yes**
Children seated in front seat	Prohibited under 5 yrs
Child restraint required	Up to 5 yrs
Child restraint standard referred to and/or specified	No
Enforcement	0 1 2 3 4 (5) 6 7 8 9 10
% children using child restraints	–
National law on mobile phone use while driving	**Yes**
Ban on hand-held mobile phone use	Yes
Ban on hands-free mobile phone use	No
National drug-driving law	**Yes**

[b] 2016, Botswana Police Service

Deaths by road user category

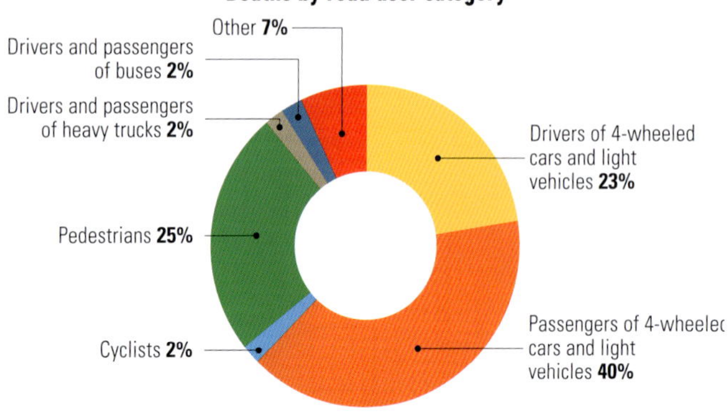

Source: 2016, Botswana Police Service

Trends in reported road traffic deaths

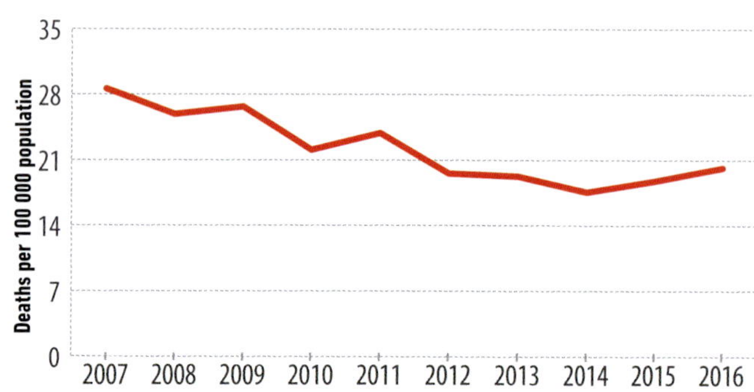

Source: Botswana Police Service

Legislative review conducted by WHO. Vehicle safety data from UNECE WP29. Other data collected by questionnaire and cleared by Ministry of Transport and Communications.

Brazil

Population: 207 652 864 | Income group: Middle | Gross national income per capita: US$ 8 840

INSTITUTIONAL FRAMEWORK

Lead agency	National Traffic Department (DENATRAN), Ministry of Cities
Funded in national budget	Yes
National road safety strategy	Yes
Funding to implement strategy	Partially funded
Fatality reduction target	–

SAFER ROADS AND MOBILITY

Audits or star rating required for new road infrastructure	Yes
Design standards for the safety of pedestrians / cyclists	Partial
Inspections / star rating of existing roads	No
Investments to upgrade high risk locations	Yes
Policies & investment in urban public transport	Yes

SAFER VEHICLES

Total registered vehicles for 2016	93 867 016
Cars and 4-wheeled light vehicles	61 938 226
Motorized 2- and 3-wheelers	25 311 251
Heavy trucks	5 586 558
Buses	984 847
Other	46 134
Vehicle standards applied (UNECE WP.29)	
Frontal impact standard	Yes
Electronic stability control	No
Pedestrian protection	No
Motorcycle anti-lock braking system	Yes

POST-CRASH CARE

National emergency care access number	National, single number
Trauma registry	None
Formal certification for prehospital providers	No
National assessment of emergency care systems	No

DATA

Reported road traffic fatalities (2015)	38 651[a] (82% M, 18% F)
WHO estimated road traffic fatalities (2016)	41 007
WHO estimated rate per 100 000 population (2016)	19.7

[a] Mortality Information System (SIM), Ministry of Health. Unlimited time period following crash

SAFER ROAD USERS

National speed limit law	Yes
Max urban speed limit	80 km/h[b]
Max rural speed limit	60 km/h[c]
Max motorway speed limit	110 km/h
Local authorities can modify limits	Yes
Enforcement	0 1 2 3 4 5 ⑥ 7 8 9 10
Predominant type of enforcement	Automated
National drink-driving law	Yes
BAC limit – general population	0.00 g/dl
BAC limit – young or novice drivers	0.00 g/dl
Random breath testing carried out	Yes
Testing carried out in case of fatal crash	Some drivers tested
Enforcement	0 1 2 3 4 5 ⑥ 7 8 9 10
% road traffic deaths involving alcohol	–
National motorcycle helmet law	Yes
Applies to drivers and passengers	Yes
Helmet fastening required	Yes
Helmet standard referred to and/or specified	Yes
Children passengers on motorcycles	Prohibited under 7 yrs
Enforcement	0 1 2 3 4 5 6 ⑦ 8 9 10
Helmet wearing rate	83% Drivers[d], 80% Passengers[d]
National seat-belt law	Yes
Applies to front and rear seat occupants	Yes
Enforcement	0 1 2 3 4 5 6 ⑦ 8 9 10
Seat-belt wearing rate	79% Front seats[d], 50% Rear seats[d]
National child restraint law	Yes
Children seated in front seat	Prohibited under 10 yrs
Child restraint required	Up to 7.5 yrs
Child restraint standard referred to and/or specified	Yes
Enforcement	0 1 2 3 4 5 6 ⑦ 8 9 10
% children using child restraints	57%[e]
National law on mobile phone use while driving	Yes
Ban on hand-held mobile phone use	Yes
Ban on hands-free mobile phone use	Yes
National drug-driving law	Yes

[b] Can be increased up to an unspecified speed
[c] This limit applies to unpaved roadways while on undivided highway the maximum speed limit is 100 km/h for automobiles, light trucks and motorcycles
[d] 2013, IBGE, Directorate of Research, Coordination of Work and Income, National Health Survey
[e] 2012, Child Restraint Use, Safe Kids

Deaths by road user category

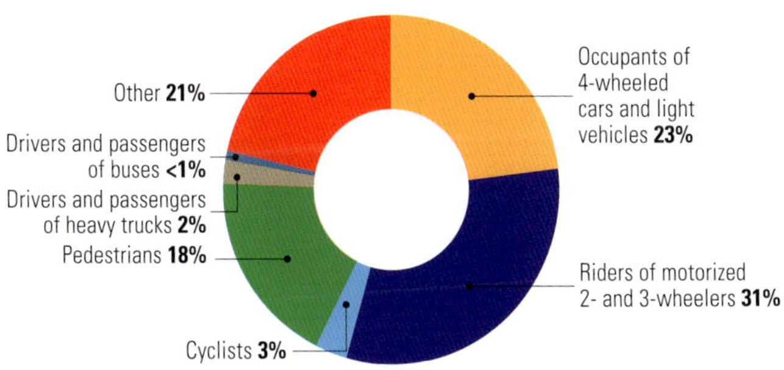

Source: 2015, Mortality Information System (SIM), Ministry of Health

Trends in reported road traffic deaths

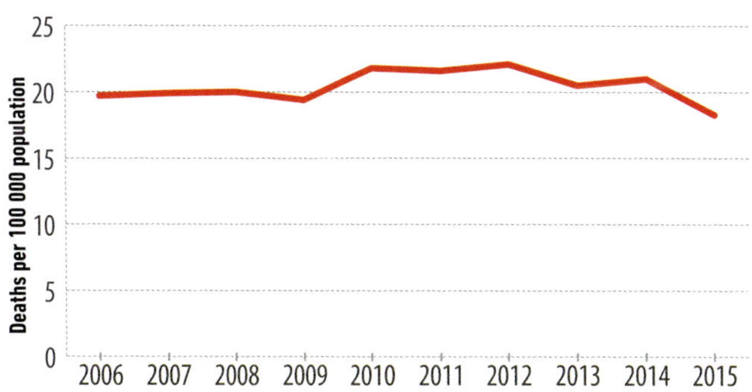

Source: Mortality Information System (SIM), Ministry of Health

Bulgaria

Population: 7 131 494 | Income group: Middle | Gross national income per capita: US$ 7 470

INSTITUTIONAL FRAMEWORK

Lead agency	State-public Consultative Commission on the Problems of Road Safety
Funded in national budget	Yes
National road safety strategy	Yes
Funding to implement strategy	Partially funded
Fatality reduction target	50% (2011-2020)

SAFER ROADS AND MOBILITY

Audits or star rating required for new road infrastructure	Partial
Design standards for the safety of pedestrians / cyclists	Yes
Inspections / star rating of existing roads	No
Investments to upgrade high risk locations	No
Policies & investment in urban public transport	Yes

SAFER VEHICLES

Total registered vehicles for 2016	4 031 748
Cars and 4-wheeled light vehicles	3 637 961
Motorized 2- and 3-wheelers	174 487
Heavy trucks	196 372
Buses	22 928
Other	0
Vehicle standards applied (UNECE WP.29)	
Frontal impact standard	Yes
Electronic stability control	Yes
Pedestrian protection	Yes
Motorcycle anti-lock braking system	Yes

POST-CRASH CARE

National emergency care access number	National, single number
Trauma registry	None
Formal certification for prehospital providers	Yes
National assessment of emergency care systems	No

DATA

Reported road traffic fatalities (2016)	708[a] (78% M, 22% F)
WHO estimated road traffic fatalities (2016)	730
WHO estimated rate per 100 000 population (2016)	10.2

[a] Chief Directorate "National Police", Ministry of Interior; National Statistical Institute. Died within 30 days of crash

SAFER ROAD USERS

National speed limit law	Yes
Max urban speed limit	50 km/h
Max rural speed limit	90 km/h
Max motorway speed limit	140 km/h
Local authorities can modify limits	No
Enforcement	0 1 2 3 4 5 (6) 7 8 9 10
Predominant type of enforcement	Automated
National drink-driving law	Yes
BAC limit – general population	≤ 0.05 g/dl
BAC limit – young or novice drivers	≤ 0.05 g/dl
Random breath testing carried out	Yes
Testing carried out in case of fatal crash	All drivers tested
Enforcement	0 1 2 3 4 (5) 6 7 8 9 10
% road traffic deaths involving alcohol	<1%[b]
National motorcycle helmet law	Yes
Applies to drivers and passengers	Yes
Helmet fastening required	No
Helmet standard referred to and/or specified	No
Children passengers on motorcycles	Prohibited under 12 yrs
Enforcement	0 1 2 3 4 (5) 6 7 8 9 10
Helmet wearing rate	80% Drivers[c], 30% Passengers[c]
National seat-belt law	Yes
Applies to front and rear seat occupants	Yes
Enforcement	0 1 2 3 4 (5) 6 7 8 9 10
Seat-belt wearing rate	80% All occupants[d]
National child restraint law	Yes
Children seated in front seat	Allowed in a child restraint[e]
Child restraint required	Up to 150 cm
Child restraint standard referred to and/or specified	Yes
Enforcement	0 1 2 3 4 5 (6) 7 8 9 10
% children using child restraints	–
National law on mobile phone use while driving	Yes
Ban on hand-held mobile phone use	Yes
Ban on hands-free mobile phone use	No
National drug-driving law	Yes

[b] 2016, Chief Directorate "National Police", Ministry of Interior, National Statistical Institute
[c] 2010, Traffic police monitoring
[d] 2010-2013, Surveys of knowledge and attitudes towards behavioral change and healthy lifestyle skills
[e] Provided that airbag is deactivated if child is in a rear-facing child restraint system

Deaths by road user category

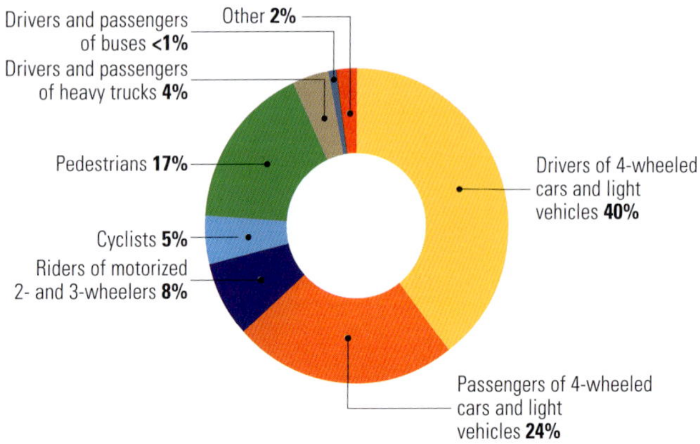

Source: 2016, Chief Directorate "National Police", Ministry of Interior; National Statistical Institute

Trends in reported road traffic deaths

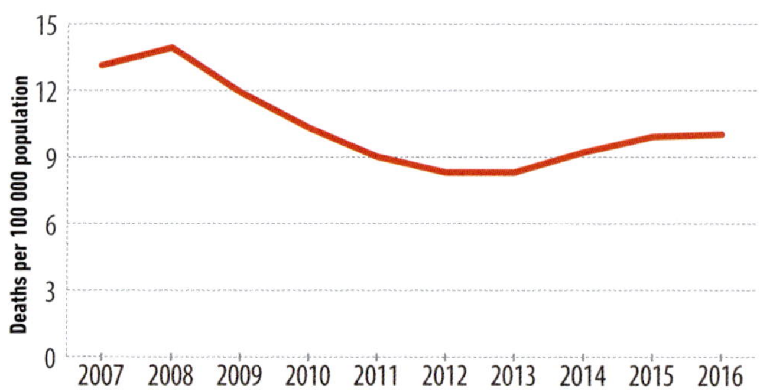

Source: Chief Directorate "National Police", Ministry of Interior and National Statistical Institute

Burkina Faso

Population: 18 646 432 | Income group: Low | Gross national income per capita: US$ 640

INSTITUTIONAL FRAMEWORK	
Lead agency	National Office for Road Safety (ONASER), Ministry of Transport, Urban Mobility and Road Safety (MTMUSR)
Funded in national budget	Yes
National road safety strategy	Yes
Funding to implement strategy	Partially funded
Fatality reduction target	25% (2011-2020)

SAFER ROADS AND MOBILITY	
Audits or star rating required for new road infrastructure	Partial
Design standards for the safety of pedestrians / cyclists	Yes
Inspections / star rating of existing roads	Yes
Investments to upgrade high risk locations	Yes
Policies & investment in urban public transport	No

SAFER VEHICLES	
Total registered vehicles for 2015	2 106 292
Cars and 4-wheeled light vehicles	237 979
Motorized 2- and 3-wheelers	1 789 181
Heavy trucks	28 231
Buses	10 952
Other	39 949
Vehicle standards applied (UNECE WP.29)	
Frontal impact standard	No
Electronic stability control	No
Pedestrian protection	No
Motorcycle anti-lock braking system	No

POST-CRASH CARE	
National emergency care access number	National, single number
Trauma registry	Some facilities
Formal certification for prehospital providers	No
National assessment of emergency care systems	Yes

DATA	
Reported road traffic fatalities (2016)	878[a] (72% M, 28% F)
WHO estimated road traffic fatalities (2016)	5 686 (95% CI 4 499 - 6 872)
WHO estimated rate per 100 000 population (2016)	30.5

[a] National Police and National Gendarmerie. Died within 24 hours of crash

SAFER ROAD USERS	
National speed limit law	Yes
Max urban speed limit	50 km/h
Max rural speed limit	90 km/h
Max motorway speed limit	No
Local authorities can modify limits	Yes
Enforcement	0 1 2 3 4 5 6 (7) 8 9 10
Predominant type of enforcement	Manual
National drink-driving law	Yes
BAC limit – general population	≤ 0.05 g/dl
BAC limit – young or novice drivers	≤ 0.02 g/dl
Random breath testing carried out	Yes
Testing carried out in case of fatal crash	No
Enforcement	(0) 1 2 3 4 5 6 7 8 9 10
% road traffic deaths involving alcohol	–
National motorcycle helmet law	Yes
Applies to drivers and passengers	Yes
Helmet fastening required	No
Helmet standard referred to and/or specified	Yes
Children passengers on motorcycles	Prohibited under 5 yrs
Enforcement	0 1 2 3 (4) 5 6 7 8 9 10
Helmet wearing rate	9% All riders[b]
National seat-belt law	Yes
Applies to front and rear seat occupants	Yes
Enforcement	0 1 2 3 4 5 (6) 7 8 9 10
Seat-belt wearing rate	–
National child restraint law	Yes
Children seated in front seat	Prohibited under 7 yrs
Child restraint required	Up to 8 yrs
Child restraint standard referred to and/or specified	No
Enforcement	(0) 1 2 3 4 5 6 7 8 9 10
% children using child restraints	–
National law on mobile phone use while driving	Yes
Ban on hand-held mobile phone use	Yes
Ban on hands-free mobile phone use	No
National drug-driving law	Yes

[b] 2008, Contextual study on helmet use to develop a national strategy for helmet use in Burkina Faso

Deaths by road user category

Trends in reported road traffic deaths

Source: National Police, National Gendarmerie, and National Institute for Statistics and Demography (INSD)

Legislative review conducted by WHO. Vehicle safety data from UNECE WP.29. Other data collected by questionnaire and cleared by Ministry of Transport, Urban Mobility and Road Safety.

Burundi

Population: 10 524 117 | Income group: Low | Gross national income per capita: US$ 280

INSTITUTIONAL FRAMEWORK	
Lead agency	Traffic and Road Safety Police, Ministry of Public Security
Funded in national budget	Yes
National road safety strategy	No
Funding to implement strategy	–
Fatality reduction target	–

SAFER ROADS AND MOBILITY	
Audits or star rating required for new road infrastructure	Partial
Design standards for the safety of pedestrians / cyclists	No
Inspections / star rating of existing roads	No
Investments to upgrade high risk locations	No
Policies & investment in urban public transport	No

SAFER VEHICLES	
Total registered vehicles for Juin 2017	111 236
Cars and 4-wheeled light vehicles	32 488
Motorized 2- and 3-wheelers	28 269
Heavy trucks	2 876
Buses	2 775
Other	44 828
Vehicle standards applied (UNECE WP.29)	
Frontal impact standard	No
Electronic stability control	No
Pedestrian protection	No
Motorcycle anti-lock braking system	No

POST-CRASH CARE	
National emergency care access number	None
Trauma registry	National
Formal certification for prehospital providers	No
National assessment of emergency care systems	No

DATA	
Reported road traffic fatalities (2015)	112[a] (77% M, 23% F)
WHO estimated road traffic fatalities (2016)	3 651 (95% CI 2 926 - 4 376)
WHO estimated rate per 100 000 population (2016)	34.7

[a] Statistical Yearbook 2015. Died within 30 days of crash

SAFER ROAD USERS	
National speed limit law	Yes
Max urban speed limit	50 km/h
Max rural speed limit	100 km/h
Max motorway speed limit	100 km/h
Local authorities can modify limits	Yes
Enforcement	(0) 1 2 3 4 5 6 7 8 9 10
Predominant type of enforcement	Manual
National drink-driving law	Yes
BAC limit – general population	≤ 0.08 g/dl
BAC limit – young or novice drivers	≤ 0.08 g/dl
Random breath testing carried out	Yes[b]
Testing carried out in case of fatal crash	No
Enforcement	0 (1) 2 3 4 5 6 7 8 9 10
% road traffic deaths involving alcohol	–
National motorcycle helmet law	Yes
Applies to drivers and passengers	Yes
Helmet fastening required	No
Helmet standard referred to and/or specified	No
Children passengers on motorcycles	Not restricted
Enforcement	0 1 2 3 4 (5) 6 7 8 9 10
Helmet wearing rate	–
National seat-belt law	Yes
Applies to front and rear seat occupants	Yes[c]
Enforcement	0 1 2 3 4 5 6 (7) 8 9 10
Seat-belt wearing rate	–
National child restraint law	No
Children seated in front seat	Prohibited under 13 yrs
Child restraint required	–
Child restraint standard referred to and/or specified	–
Enforcement	–
% children using child restraints	–
National law on mobile phone use while driving	Yes
Ban on hand-held mobile phone use	Yes
Ban on hands-free mobile phone use	Yes
National drug-driving law	No

[b] Legislation requires probable cause to test drivers
[c] Legislation requires drivers and passengers "and particularly those sitting in the front" to use a seat belt

Deaths by road user category

Trends in reported road traffic deaths

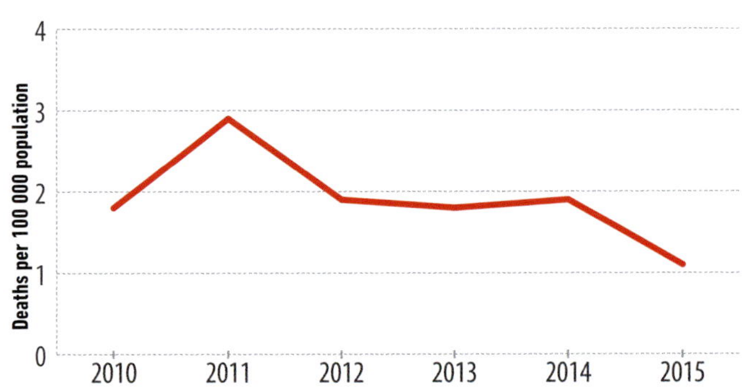

Source: Statistical Yearbooks and National Health Information System, 2010-2015

Legislative review conducted by WHO. Vehicle safety data from UNECE WP29. Other data collected by questionnaire and cleared by Ministry of Public Health

Cabo Verde

Population: 539 560 | Income group: Middle | Gross national income per capita: US$ 2 970

INSTITUTIONAL FRAMEWORK	
Lead agency	General Directorate of Road Transport (DGTR), Ministry of Internal Administration
Funded in national budget	Yes
National road safety strategy	Yes
Funding to implement strategy	Partially funded
Fatality reduction target	50% (2011-2020)

SAFER ROADS AND MOBILITY	
Audits or star rating required for new road infrastructure	Yes
Design standards for the safety of pedestrians / cyclists	Partial
Inspections / star rating of existing roads	Yes
Investments to upgrade high risk locations	Yes
Policies & investment in urban public transport	Yes

SAFER VEHICLES	
Total registered vehicles for 2016	64 955
Cars and 4-wheeled light vehicles	47 354
Motorized 2- and 3-wheelers	7 595
Heavy trucks	10 006
Buses	–
Other	–
Vehicle standards applied (UNECE WP.29)	
Frontal impact standard	No
Electronic stability control	No
Pedestrian protection	No
Motorcycle anti-lock braking system	No

POST-CRASH CARE	
National emergency care access number	National, multiple numbers
Trauma registry	Some facilities
Formal certification for prehospital providers	No
National assessment of emergency care systems	No

DATA	
Reported road traffic fatalities (2016)	41 [a]
WHO estimated road traffic fatalities (2016)	135 (95% CI 118 - 152)
WHO estimated rate per 100 000 population (2016)	25

[a] National Police Office, National Police Report. Died within 30 days of crash

SAFER ROAD USERS	
National speed limit law	Yes
Max urban speed limit	50 km/h
Max rural speed limit	90 km/h
Max motorway speed limit	120 km/h
Local authorities can modify limits	Yes
Enforcement	0 1 2 3 4 **(5)** 6 7 8 9 10
Predominant type of enforcement	Manual
National drink-driving law	Yes
BAC limit – general population	< 0.08 g/dl
BAC limit – young or novice drivers	< 0.08 g/dl
Random breath testing carried out	Yes [b]
Testing carried out in case of fatal crash	No
Enforcement	0 1 2 3 4 **(5)** 6 7 8 9 10
% road traffic deaths involving alcohol	–
National motorcycle helmet law	Yes
Applies to drivers and passengers	Yes
Helmet fastening required	Yes
Helmet standard referred to and/or specified	Yes
Children passengers on motorcycles	Prohibited under 7 yrs
Enforcement	0 1 2 3 4 5 6 7 **(8)** 9 10
Helmet wearing rate	–
National seat-belt law	Yes
Applies to front and rear seat occupants	No
Enforcement	0 1 2 3 4 **(5)** 6 7 8 9 10
Seat-belt wearing rate	–
National child restraint law	No [c]
Children seated in front seat	Allowed in a child restraint [d]
Child restraint required	–
Child restraint standard referred to and/or specified	–
Enforcement	–
% children using child restraints	–
National law on mobile phone use while driving	Yes
Ban on hand-held mobile phone use	Yes
Ban on hands-free mobile phone use	No
National drug-driving law	No

[b] Legislation refers to testing of drivers in case of crash
[c] The legislation refers to the use of either child restraint systems or seat-belts for children
[d] Children under 12 yrs/150cm shall normally sit in the rear except if placed in a suitable child restraint

Deaths by road user category

Trends in reported road traffic deaths

Source: National Police, General Directorate of Road Transport (DGTR), and National Statistics Institute (INE)

Legislative review conducted by WHO. Vehicle safety data from UNECE WP29. Other data collected by questionnaire and cleared by Ministry of Internal Administration.

Cambodia

Population: 15 762 370 | Income group: Middle | Gross national income per capita: US$ 1 140

INSTITUTIONAL FRAMEWORK

Lead agency	National Road Safety Committee (NRSC)
Funded in national budget	Yes
National road safety strategy	Yes
Funding to implement strategy	Partially funded
Fatality reduction target	50% (2011-2020)

SAFER ROADS AND MOBILITY

Audits or star rating required for new road infrastructure	Yes
Design standards for the safety of pedestrians / cyclists	No
Inspections / star rating of existing roads	Yes
Investments to upgrade high risk locations	Yes
Policies & investment in urban public transport	No

SAFER VEHICLES

Total registered vehicles for 2016	3 751 715
Cars and 4-wheeled light vehicles	97 239
Motorized 2- and 3-wheelers	2 714 193
Heavy trucks	57 321
Buses	5 972
Other	876 990
Vehicle standards applied (UNECE WP.29)	
Frontal impact standard	No
Electronic stability control	No
Pedestrian protection	No
Motorcycle anti-lock braking system	No

POST-CRASH CARE

National emergency care access number	National, multiple numbers
Trauma registry	National
Formal certification for prehospital providers	No
National assessment of emergency care systems	No

DATA

Reported road traffic fatalities (2016)	1 852[a] (80% M, 20% F)
WHO estimated road traffic fatalities (2016)	2 803 (95% CI 2 381 - 3 226)
WHO estimated rate per 100 000 population (2016)	17.8

[a] Road Crash and Victim Information System (RCVIS). Died within 30 days of crash

SAFER ROAD USERS

National speed limit law	Yes
Max urban speed limit	40 km/h
Max rural speed limit	90 km/h
Max motorway speed limit	100 km/h
Local authorities can modify limits	No
Enforcement	0 1 2 3 4 (5) 6 7 8 9 10
Predominant type of enforcement	Manual
National drink-driving law	Yes
BAC limit – general population	< 0.05 g/dl
BAC limit – young or novice drivers	< 0.05 g/dl
Random breath testing carried out	Yes
Testing carried out in case of fatal crash	No
Enforcement	0 1 2 3 4 (5) 6 7 8 9 10
% road traffic deaths involving alcohol	13%[b]
National motorcycle helmet law	Yes
Applies to drivers and passengers	Yes
Helmet fastening required	No
Helmet standard referred to and/or specified	Yes
Children passengers on motorcycles	Not restricted
Enforcement	0 1 2 3 4 5 (6) 7 8 9 10
Helmet wearing rate	70% - 43% Drivers[c], 30% - 13% Passengers[c]
National seat-belt law	Yes
Applies to front and rear seat occupants	No[d]
Enforcement	0 1 2 3 4 5 6 (7) 8 9 10
Seat-belt wearing rate	–
National child restraint law	Yes[e]
Children seated in front seat	Prohibited under 10 yrs[f]
Child restraint required	Up to 4 yrs
Child restraint standard referred to and/or specified	No
Enforcement	(0) 1 2 3 4 5 6 7 8 9 10
% children using child restraints	–
National law on mobile phone use while driving	Yes
Ban on hand-held mobile phone use	Yes
Ban on hands-free mobile phone use	No
National drug-driving law	Yes

[b] 2016, Road Crash and Victim Information System (RCVIS)
[c] 2016, Cambodia Helmet Vaccine Initiative (Percentages are for day- and night-time observations, respectively)
[d] Obligation to use seat belts for all passengers only applies outside cities and densely populated areas. Inside cities and densely populated areas, only the driver and front seat passengers are required to wear a seat belt
[e] Enters into force in January 2020
[f] Ban on children under 10 years travelling in the front seat enters into force in January 2020

Deaths by road user category

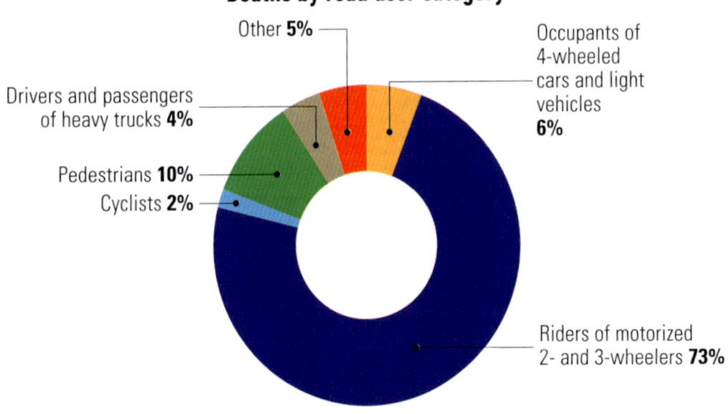

Source: 2016, Road Crash and Victim Information System (RCVIS) annual report

Trends in reported road traffic deaths

Source: Road Crash and Victim Information System (RCVIS)

Legislative review conducted by WHO. Vehicle safety data from UNECE WP29. Other data collected by questionnaire and cleared by Ministry of Health.

Cameroon

Population: 23 439 188 | Income group: Middle | Gross national income per capita: US$ 1 200

INSTITUTIONAL FRAMEWORK	
Lead agency	No
Funded in national budget	–
National road safety strategy	Yes
Funding to implement strategy	Partially funded
Fatality reduction target	–

SAFER ROADS AND MOBILITY	
Audits or star rating required for new road infrastructure	Partial
Design standards for the safety of pedestrians / cyclists	Partial
Inspections / star rating of existing roads	Yes
Investments to upgrade high risk locations	Yes
Policies & investment in urban public transport	Yes

SAFER VEHICLES	
Total registered vehicles for 2007-2016	758 145
Cars and 4-wheeled light vehicles	–
Motorized 2- and 3-wheelers	–
Heavy trucks	–
Buses	–
Other	–
Vehicle standards applied (UNECE WP.29)	
Frontal impact standard	No
Electronic stability control	No
Pedestrian protection	No
Motorcycle anti-lock braking system	No

POST-CRASH CARE	
National emergency care access number	National, single number
Trauma registry	Some facilities
Formal certification for prehospital providers	No
National assessment of emergency care systems	Yes

DATA	
Reported road traffic fatalities (2016)	1 879 [a]
WHO estimated road traffic fatalities (2016)	7 066 (95% CI 5 670 - 8 463)
WHO estimated rate per 100 000 population (2016)	30.1

[a] Ministry of Transport, and Police. Unlimited time period following crash

SAFER ROAD USERS	
National speed limit law	Yes
Max urban speed limit	60 km/h
Max rural speed limit	110 km/h
Max motorway speed limit	No
Local authorities can modify limits	Yes
Enforcement	0 1 2 3 4 (5) 6 7 8 9 10
Predominant type of enforcement	Manual
National drink-driving law	Yes
BAC limit – general population	≤ 0.08 g/dl
BAC limit – young or novice drivers	≤ 0.08 g/dl
Random breath testing carried out	Yes
Testing carried out in case of fatal crash	No
Enforcement	0 1 (2) 3 4 5 6 7 8 9 10
% road traffic deaths involving alcohol	–
National motorcycle helmet law	Yes
Applies to drivers and passengers	Yes
Helmet fastening required	No
Helmet standard referred to and/or specified	No
Children passengers on motorcycles	Prohibited under 5 yrs
Enforcement	0 (1) 2 3 4 5 6 7 8 9 10
Helmet wearing rate	–
National seat-belt law	Yes
Applies to front and rear seat occupants	No
Enforcement	0 1 2 3 4 5 (6) 7 8 9 10
Seat-belt wearing rate	–
National child restraint law	No
Children seated in front seat	Not restricted
Child restraint required	–
Child restraint standard referred to and/or specified	–
Enforcement	–
% children using child restraints	–
National law on mobile phone use while driving	Yes
Ban on hand-held mobile phone use	Yes
Ban on hands-free mobile phone use	Yes
National drug-driving law	No

Deaths by road user category

Trends in reported road traffic deaths

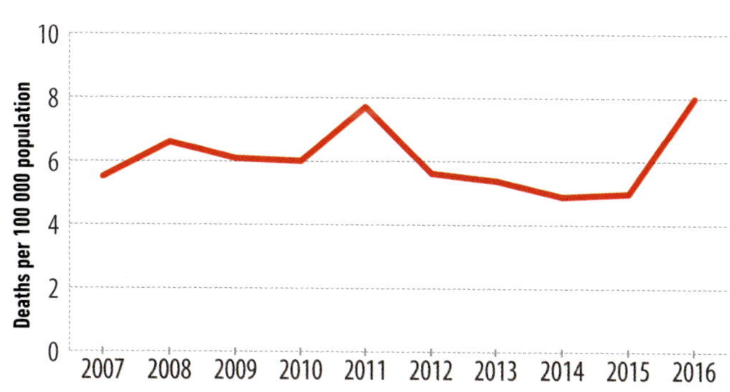

Source: Ministry of Transport, Police, and Gendarmerie

Legislative review conducted by WHO. Vehicle safety data from UNECE WP29. Other data collected by questionnaire and cleared by Ministry of Public Health.

Canada

Population: 36 289 824 | Income group: High | Gross national income per capita: US$ 43 660

INSTITUTIONAL FRAMEWORK

Lead agency	Canadian Council of Motor Transport Administrators, Council of Ministers Responsible for Transportation and Highway Safety
Funded in national budget	No [a]
National road safety strategy	Yes
Funding to implement strategy	Partially funded
Fatality reduction target	Continual downward trend in fatalities over time (2016-2025)

SAFER ROADS AND MOBILITY

Audits or star rating required for new road infrastructure	Partial
Design standards for the safety of pedestrians / cyclists	Yes
Inspections / star rating of existing roads	Yes
Investments to upgrade high risk locations	Yes [b]
Policies & investment in urban public transport	Yes

SAFER VEHICLES

Total registered vehicles for 2015	23 923 806
Cars and 4-wheeled light vehicles	22 067 778
Motorized 2- and 3-wheelers	709 258
Heavy trucks	1 056 219
Buses	90 551
Other	0
Vehicle standards applied (UNECE WP.29)	
Frontal impact standard	Yes
Electronic stability control	Yes
Pedestrian protection	No
Motorcycle anti-lock braking system	No

POST-CRASH CARE

National emergency care access number	Partial coverage
Trauma registry	Subnational
Formal certification for prehospital providers	—
National assessment of emergency care systems	No

DATA

Reported road traffic fatalities (2015)	1 858 [c] (70% M, 30% F)
WHO estimated road traffic fatalities (2016)	2 118
WHO estimated rate per 100 000 population (2016)	5.8

[a] A self-sustaining organization through membership fees and data services
[b] At many provincial and municipal levels of government
[c] Canadian Motor Vehicle Traffic Collision Statistics. Died within 30 days of crash

SAFER ROAD USERS*

National speed limit law	Yes
Max urban speed limit	50 km/h
Max rural speed limit	50 - 100 km/h
Max motorway speed limit	80 - 100 km/h
Local authorities can modify limits	Yes
Enforcement	0 1 2 3 (4) 5 6 7 8 9 10
Predominant type of enforcement	Manual
National drink-driving law	Yes
BAC limit – general population	0.04-0.08 g/dl [d]
BAC limit – young or novice drivers	0.00-0.08 g/dl
Random breath testing carried out	Yes [e]
Testing carried out in case of fatal crash	All drivers tested
Enforcement	0 1 2 3 4 5 6 7 (8) 9 10
% road traffic deaths involving alcohol	30% [f]
National motorcycle helmet law	Yes
Applies to drivers and passengers	Yes
Helmet fastening required	Yes
Helmet standard referred to and/or specified	Yes
Children passengers on motorcycles	Not restricted
Enforcement	0 1 2 3 4 5 6 7 8 9 (10)
Helmet wearing rate	98% Drivers [g], 98% Passengers [g]
National seat-belt law	Yes
Applies to front and rear seat occupants	Yes
Enforcement	0 1 2 3 4 5 (6) 7 8 9 10
Seat-belt wearing rate	95% Front seats [h], 89% Rear seats [h]
National child restraint law	Yes
Children seated in front seat	Allowed in a child restraint
Child restraint required	— [i]
Child restraint standard referred to and/or specified	Yes
Enforcement	0 1 2 3 4 5 6 7 (8) 9 10
% children using child restraints	91% [j]
National law on mobile phone use while driving	Yes
Ban on hand-held mobile phone use	Yes
Ban on hands-free mobile phone use	No
National drug-driving law	Yes

* These data take into consideration subnational laws. A criteria is answered "Yes" if at least 80% of the subnational entities meet the criteria
[d] National BAC limit is set at 0.08 g/dl. However, in practice all subnational entities have provided their own BAC limits that are reflected in the range above.
[e] Legislation requires probable cause to test drivers
[f] 2017, The Alcohol and Drug-Crash Problems in Canada: 2014 Report; The Traffic Injury Research Foundation of Canada
[g] 2016, Police observation
[h] 2010. Result of Transport Canada's Rural and Urban Survey of Seat Belt Use in Canada 2009-2010
[i] Child restraint laws are enacted at subnational level. While all provinces require the use of child restraints, they provide different age / height criteria to specify the period for mandatory use of child restraints / booster seats
[j] 2010. Canada National Survey on Child Restrain Use, Completed for Transport Canada, in partnership with AUTO21

Deaths by road user category

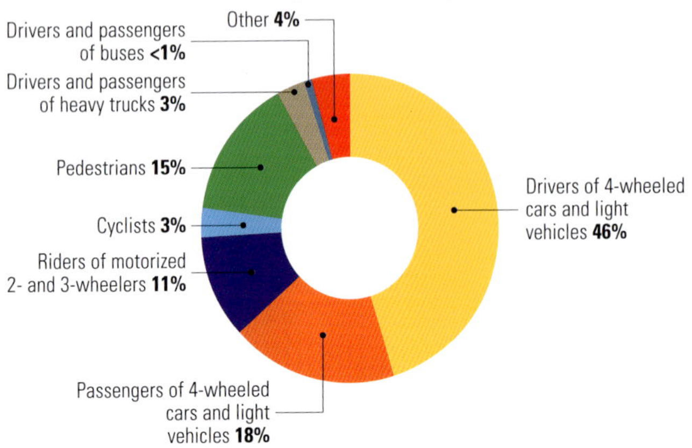

Source: 2015, Canadian Motor Vehicle Traffic Collision Statistics

Trends in reported road traffic deaths

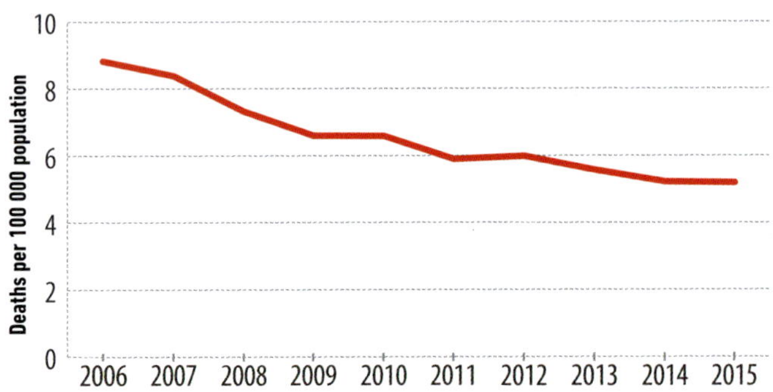

Source: Canadian Motor Vehicle Traffic Collision Statistics

Legislative review conducted by WHO. Vehicle safety data from UNECE WP29. Other data collected by questionnaire and cleared by Transport Canada.

Central African Republic

Population: 4 594 621 | Income group: Low | Gross national income per capita: US$ 370

INSTITUTIONAL FRAMEWORK	
Lead agency	National Committee of Road Safety, Ministry of Transport
Funded in national budget	Yes
National road safety strategy	No
Funding to implement strategy	–
Fatality reduction target	–
SAFER ROADS AND MOBILITY	
Audits or star rating required for new road infrastructure	Partial
Design standards for the safety of pedestrians / cyclists	Partial
Inspections / star rating of existing roads	Yes
Investments to upgrade high risk locations	Yes
Policies & investment in urban public transport	No
SAFER VEHICLES	
Total registered vehicles for 2014	37 475
Cars and 4-wheeled light vehicles	–
Motorized 2- and 3-wheelers	–
Heavy trucks	–
Buses	–
Other	–
Vehicle standards applied (UNECE WP.29)	
Frontal impact standard	No
Electronic stability control	No
Pedestrian protection	No
Motorcycle anti-lock braking system	No
POST-CRASH CARE	
National emergency care access number	–
Trauma registry	Some facilities
Formal certification for prehospital providers	–
National assessment of emergency care systems	No
DATA	
Reported road traffic fatalities (2016)	193[a] (85% M, 15% F)
WHO estimated road traffic fatalities (2016)	1 546 (95% CI 1 209 - 1 884)
WHO estimated rate per 100 000 population (2016)	33.6

[a] Gendarmerie and hospital records. Unlimited time period following crash

SAFER ROAD USERS	
National speed limit law	Yes
Max urban speed limit	60 km/h
Max rural speed limit	110 km/h
Max motorway speed limit	No
Local authorities can modify limits	Yes
Enforcement	(0) 1 2 3 4 5 6 7 8 9 10
Predominant type of enforcement	–
National drink-driving law	Yes
BAC limit – general population	≤ 0.08 g/dl
BAC limit – young or novice drivers	≤ 0.08 g/dl
Random breath testing carried out	No
Testing carried out in case of fatal crash	No
Enforcement	(0) 1 2 3 4 5 6 7 8 9 10
% road traffic deaths involving alcohol	–
National motorcycle helmet law	Yes
Applies to drivers and passengers	Yes
Helmet fastening required	Yes
Helmet standard referred to and/or specified	No
Children passengers on motorcycles	Prohibited under 5 yrs
Enforcement	(0) 1 2 3 4 5 6 7 8 9 10
Helmet wearing rate	–
National seat-belt law	Yes
Applies to front and rear seat occupants	No[b]
Enforcement	(0) 1 2 3 4 5 6 7 8 9 10
Seat-belt wearing rate	–
National child restraint law	No
Children seated in front seat	Not restricted[c]
Child restraint required	–
Child restraint standard referred to and/or specified	–
Enforcement	–
% children using child restraints	–
National law on mobile phone use while driving	Yes
Ban on hand-held mobile phone use	Yes
Ban on hands-free mobile phone use	Yes
National drug-driving law	No

[b] Rear-seated child passengers under 12 years are not subject to the obligation to use a seat belt
[c] Legislation only recommends ("as far as possible") to place children under 12 years in the rear

Deaths by road user category

Trends in reported road traffic deaths

Legislative review conducted by WHO. Vehicle safety data from UNECE WP29. Other data collected by questionnaire and cleared by Ministry of Transport and Civil Aviation.

Chad

Population: 14 452 543 | Income group: Low | Gross national income per capita: US$ 720

INSTITUTIONAL FRAMEWORK	
Lead agency	Ministry of Infrastructure, Transport and Civil Aviation
Funded in national budget	Yes
National road safety strategy	Yes
Funding to implement strategy	Partially funded
Fatality reduction target	From 4.4% to 2% (by 2018)
SAFER ROADS AND MOBILITY	
Audits or star rating required for new road infrastructure	Yes
Design standards for the safety of pedestrians / cyclists	Yes
Inspections / star rating of existing roads	No
Investments to upgrade high risk locations	Yes
Policies & investment in urban public transport	No
SAFER VEHICLES	
Total registered vehicles for 2016	1 124 000
Cars and 4-wheeled light vehicles	–
Motorized 2- and 3-wheelers	–
Heavy trucks	–
Buses	–
Other	–
Vehicle standards applied (UNECE WP.29)	
Frontal impact standard	No
Electronic stability control	No
Pedestrian protection	No
Motorcycle anti-lock braking system	No
POST-CRASH CARE	
National emergency care access number	–
Trauma registry	Some facilities
Formal certification for prehospital providers	Yes
National assessment of emergency care systems	No
DATA	
Reported road traffic fatalities (2016)	1 122 (96% M, 4% F)[a]
WHO estimated road traffic fatalities (2016)	3 990 (95% CI 3 110 - 4 870)
WHO estimated rate per 100 000 population (2016)	27.6

[a] Police Report and Hospital Register. From Jan-Oct 2016. Died within 7 days of crash

SAFER ROAD USERS	
National speed limit law	Yes
Max urban speed limit	60 km/h
Max rural speed limit	110 km/h
Max motorway speed limit	No
Local authorities can modify limits	Yes
Enforcement	0 1 2 (3) 4 5 6 7 8 9 10
Predominant type of enforcement	–
National drink-driving law	Yes
BAC limit – general population	≤ 0.08 g/dl
BAC limit – young or novice drivers	≤ 0.08 g/dl
Random breath testing carried out	No
Testing carried out in case of fatal crash	No
Enforcement	0 (1) 2 3 4 5 6 7 8 9 10
% road traffic deaths involving alcohol	–
National motorcycle helmet law	Yes
Applies to drivers and passengers	Yes
Helmet fastening required	No
Helmet standard referred to and/or specified	No
Children passengers on motorcycles	Prohibited under 5 yrs
Enforcement	0 1 2 3 4 (5) 6 7 8 9 10
Helmet wearing rate	–
National seat-belt law	Yes
Applies to front and rear seat occupants	No
Enforcement	0 1 2 3 (4) 5 6 7 8 9 10
Seat-belt wearing rate	–
National child restraint law	No
Children seated in front seat	Not restricted
Child restraint required	–
Child restraint standard referred to and/or specified	–
Enforcement	–
% children using child restraints	–
National law on mobile phone use while driving	Yes
Ban on hand-held mobile phone use	Yes
Ban on hands-free mobile phone use	Yes
National drug-driving law	No

Deaths by road user category

Trends in reported road traffic deaths

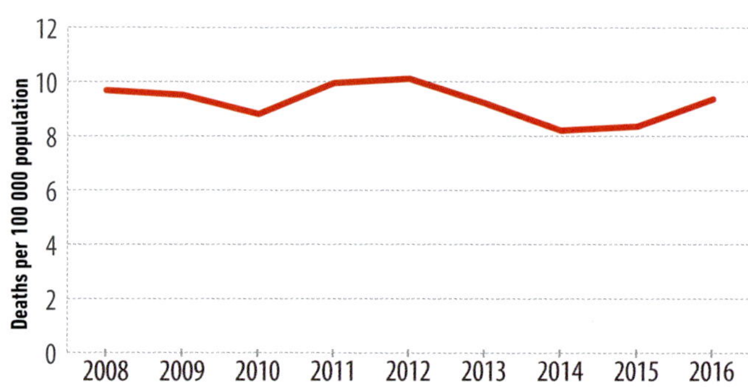

Source: National police (2016 data from Jan-Oct 2016)

Legislative review conducted by WHO. Vehicle safety data from UNECE WP29. Other data collected by questionnaire and cleared by Ministry of Public Health.

Chile

Population: 17 909 754 | Income group: High | Gross national income per capita: US$ 13 530

INSTITUTIONAL FRAMEWORK	
Lead agency	**National Traffic Safety Commission (CONASET)**
Funded in national budget	No
National road safety strategy	**Yes**
Funding to implement strategy	Partially funded
Fatality reduction target	–

SAFER ROADS AND MOBILITY	
Audits or star rating required for new road infrastructure	No
Design standards for the safety of pedestrians / cyclists	Partial
Inspections / star rating of existing roads	No
Investments to upgrade high risk locations	No
Policies & investment in urban public transport	Yes

SAFER VEHICLES	
Total registered vehicles for 2016	**4 960 945**
Cars and 4-wheeled light vehicles	4 366 131
Motorized 2- and 3-wheelers	175 019
Heavy trucks	298 347
Buses	121 448
Other	0
Vehicle standards applied (UNECE WP.29)	
Frontal impact standard	No
Electronic stability control	No
Pedestrian protection	No
Motorcycle anti-lock braking system	No

POST-CRASH CARE	
National emergency care access number	National, single number
Trauma registry	National
Formal certification for prehospital providers	No
National assessment of emergency care systems	No

DATA	
Reported road traffic fatalities (2016)	1 675[a] (78% M, 22% F)
WHO estimated road traffic fatalities (2016)	2 245
WHO estimated rate per 100 000 population (2016)	12.5

[a] Integrated Statistical System of the Chilean Police (SIEC2). Died within 24 hours of crash

SAFER ROAD USERS	
National speed limit law	**Yes**
Max urban speed limit	60 km/h[b]
Max rural speed limit	100 km/h
Max motorway speed limit	120 km/h
Local authorities can modify limits	Yes
Enforcement	0 1 2 3 4 (5) 6 7 8 9 10
Predominant type of enforcement	Manual
National drink-driving law	**Yes**
BAC limit – general population	≤ 0.03 g/dl
BAC limit – young or novice drivers	≤ 0.03 g/dl
Random breath testing carried out	Yes
Testing carried out in case of fatal crash	All drivers tested
Enforcement	0 1 2 3 4 5 (6) 7 8 9 10
% road traffic deaths involving alcohol	13%[c]
National motorcycle helmet law	**Yes**
Applies to drivers and passengers	Yes
Helmet fastening required	Yes
Helmet standard referred to and/or specified	Yes
Children passengers on motorcycles	Not restricted
Enforcement	0 1 2 3 4 5 6 7 8 (9) 10
Helmet wearing rate	99% Drivers[d], 98% Passengers[d]
National seat-belt law	**Yes**
Applies to front and rear seat occupants	Yes
Enforcement	0 1 2 3 4 5 (6) 7 8 9 10
Seat-belt wearing rate	59% Front seats[d], 14% Rear seats[d]
National child restraint law	**Yes**
Children seated in front seat	Prohibited under 12 yrs
Child restraint required	Up to 8 yrs/135 cm
Child restraint standard referred to and/or specified	Yes
Enforcement	0 1 2 3 (4) 5 6 7 8 9 10
% children using child restraints	73%[e]
National law on mobile phone use while driving	**Yes**
Ban on hand-held mobile phone use	Yes
Ban on hands-free mobile phone use	No
National drug-driving law	**Yes**

[b] Can be increased up to an unspecified limit under certain circumstances.
[c] Integrated Statistical System of the Chilean Police (SIEC2), includes driver, passenger and pedestrian deaths caused by alcohol.
[d] 2015, Observation study of use of child restraint systems, helmet, and distracting driving and motorcycles, CONASET
[e] 2015, Observation study of use of child restraint systems, helmet, and distracting driving and motorcycles, CONASET

Deaths by road user category

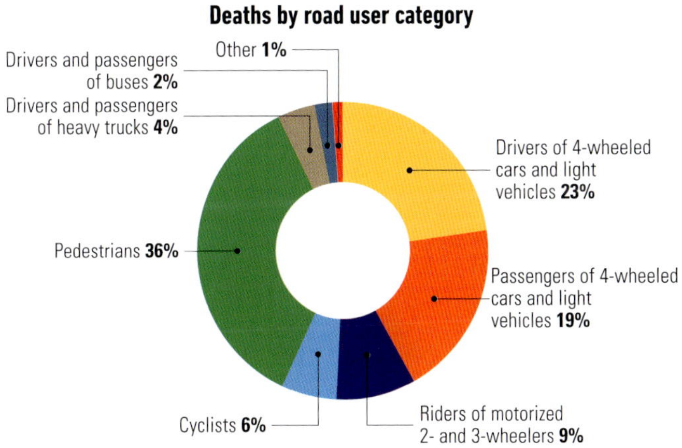

Source: 2016, Integrated Statistical System of the Chilean Police (SIEC2)

Trends in reported road traffic deaths

Source: Integrated Statistical System of the Chilean Police (SIEC2)

Legislative review conducted by WHO. Vehicle safety data from UNECE WP29. Other data collected by questionnaire and cleared by Ministry of Transportation and Telecomunication.

China

Population: 1 411 415 375 | Income group: Middle | Gross national income per capita: US$ 8 260

INSTITUTIONAL FRAMEWORK

Lead agency	Inter-ministerial Convention on Road Traffic Safety
Funded in national budget	Yes
National road safety strategy	Yes
Funding to implement strategy	Partially funded
Fatality reduction target	6% reduction in mortality rate per 10 000 vehicles (2016-2020)

SAFER ROADS AND MOBILITY

Audits or star rating required for new road infrastructure	Yes
Design standards for the safety of pedestrians / cyclists	Yes
Inspections / star rating of existing roads	Yes
Investments to upgrade high risk locations	Yes
Policies & investment in urban public transport	Yes

SAFER VEHICLES

Total registered vehicles for 2016	294 694 457
Cars and 4-wheeled light vehicles	–
Motorized 2- and 3-wheelers	–
Heavy trucks	–
Buses	–
Other	–
Vehicle standards applied (UNECE WP.29)	
Frontal impact standard	Yes
Electronic stability control	No[a]
Pedestrian protection	No
Motorcycle anti-lock braking system	No

POST-CRASH CARE

National emergency care access number	National, single number
Trauma registry	National
Formal certification for prehospital providers	Yes
National assessment of emergency care systems	Yes

DATA

Reported road traffic fatalities (2015)	58 022[b] (94% M, 6% F)
WHO estimated road traffic fatalities (2016)	256 180
WHO estimated rate per 100 000 population (2016)	18.2

[a] However top 12 car makers (more than 70% of sales volume) committed to ESC standard as from 2018
[b] National road traffic accident situation in 2015, Traffic Management Bureau of the Public Security Ministry. Died within 7 days of crash

SAFER ROAD USERS

National speed limit law	Yes
Max urban speed limit	50 km/h
Max rural speed limit	70 km/h
Max motorway speed limit	120 km/h
Local authorities can modify limits	Yes
Enforcement	0 1 2 3 4 5 6 7 (8) 9 10
Predominant type of enforcement	Automated
National drink-driving law	Yes[c]
BAC limit – general population	< 0.02 g/dl
BAC limit – young or novice drivers	< 0.02 g/dl
Random breath testing carried out	Yes
Testing carried out in case of fatal crash	All drivers tested
Enforcement	0 1 2 3 4 5 6 7 8 (9) 10
% road traffic deaths involving alcohol	<1%[d]
National motorcycle helmet law	Yes
Applies to drivers and passengers	Yes
Helmet fastening required	No
Helmet standard referred to and/or specified	Yes
Children passengers on motorcycles	Prohibited under 12 yrs
Enforcement	0 1 2 3 4 5 (6) 7 8 9 10
Helmet wearing rate	20% All riders[e]
National seat-belt law	Yes
Applies to front and rear seat occupants	Yes
Enforcement	0 1 2 3 4 5 6 (7) 8 9 10
Seat-belt wearing rate	37% Drivers[e]
National child restraint law	No
Children seated in front seat	Not restricted
Child restraint required	–
Child restraint standard referred to and/or specified	–
Enforcement	–
% children using child restraints	–
National law on mobile phone use while driving	Yes
Ban on hand-held mobile phone use	Yes
Ban on hands-free mobile phone use	No
National drug-driving law	Yes

[c] Legislation requires probable cause to test drivers
[d] 2015, Chinese annual statistics report on road traffic accidents
[e] 2010, Study on behavioral risk factors of road traffic injury in Chinese adults

Deaths by road user category

Trends in reported road traffic deaths

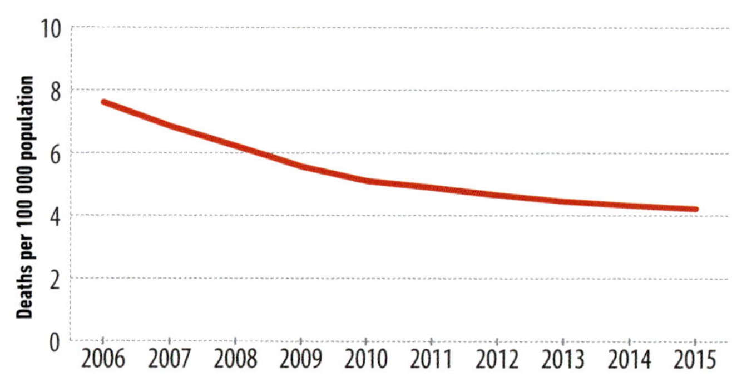

Source: Chinese annual statistics report on road traffic accidents in 2015

Legislative review conducted by WHO. Vehicle safety data from UNECE WP29. Other data collected by questionnaire and cleared by National Health and Family Planning Commission.

Colombia

Population: 48 653 420 | Income group: Middle | Gross national income per capita: US$ 6 320

INSTITUTIONAL FRAMEWORK	
Lead agency	National Road Safety Agency
Funded in national budget	No
National road safety strategy	Yes
Funding to implement strategy	Partially funded
Fatality reduction target	26% (2011-2021)
SAFER ROADS AND MOBILITY	
Audits or star rating required for new road infrastructure	Partial
Design standards for the safety of pedestrians / cyclists	No
Inspections / star rating of existing roads	No
Investments to upgrade high risk locations	No
Policies & investment in urban public transport	Yes
SAFER VEHICLES	
Total registered vehicles for 2017	13 477 996
Cars and 4-wheeled light vehicles	5 388 100
Motorized 2- and 3-wheelers	7 512 036
Heavy trucks	414 836
Buses	147 921
Other	15 103
Vehicle standards applied (UNECE WP.29)	
Frontal impact standard	No
Electronic stability control	No
Pedestrian protection	No
Motorcycle anti-lock braking system	No
POST-CRASH CARE	
National emergency care access number	Partial coverage
Trauma registry	National
Formal certification for prehospital providers	Yes
National assessment of emergency care systems	No
DATA	
Reported road traffic fatalities (2016)	7 158[a] (81% M, 19% F)
WHO estimated road traffic fatalities (2016)	8 987
WHO estimated rate per 100 000 population (2016)	18.5

[a] National Observatory of Road Safety (ONSV/ANSV), Based on Information from the National Institute of Legal Medicine And Forensic Sciences (INMLCF). Died within a year of crash

SAFER ROAD USERS	
National speed limit law	Yes
Max urban speed limit	80 km/h
Max rural speed limit	120 km/h
Max motorway speed limit	120 km/h
Local authorities can modify limits	Yes
Enforcement	0 1 2 3 4 (5) 6 7 8 9 10
Predominant type of enforcement	Manual and automated
National drink-driving law	Yes
BAC limit – general population	< 0.02 g/dl
BAC limit – young or novice drivers	< 0.02 g/dl
Random breath testing carried out	Yes
Testing carried out in case of fatal crash	All drivers tested
Enforcement	0 1 2 3 4 (5) 6 7 8 9 10
% road traffic deaths involving alcohol	–
National motorcycle helmet law	Yes
Applies to drivers and passengers	Yes
Helmet fastening required	No
Helmet standard referred to and/or specified	Yes
Children passengers on motorcycles	Not restricted
Enforcement	0 1 2 3 (4) 5 6 7 8 9 10
Helmet wearing rate	96% Drivers[b], 80% Passengers[b]
National seat-belt law	Yes
Applies to front and rear seat occupants	Yes
Enforcement	0 1 2 3 4 (5) 6 7 8 9 10
Seat-belt wearing rate	64% Front seats[b], 2% Rear seats[b]
National child restraint law	No[c]
Children seated in front seat	Prohibited under 10 yrs
Child restraint required	–
Child restraint standard referred to and/or specified	–
Enforcement	–
% children using child restraints	7.11%[d]
National law on mobile phone use while driving	Yes
Ban on hand-held mobile phone use	Yes
Ban on hands-free mobile phone use	No
National drug-driving law	Yes

[b] 2016, Observational study of road behavior in Colombia, Iberoamerican Road Safety Observatory (OISEVI)
[c] A child under 2 years travelling with a driver only shall be placed in a child restraint. If there is an adult passenger, the child can be held by the adult instead of being placed in a child restraint.
[d] 2016, Use of seat belt and child restraint system in Colombia, OISEVI

Deaths by road user category

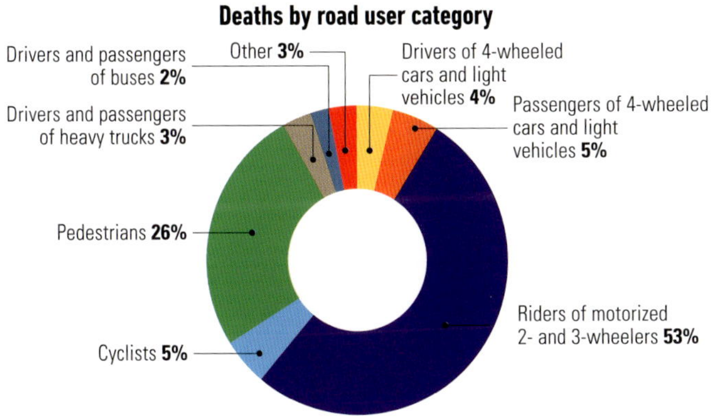

Source: 2016, National Observatory of Road Safety (ONSV/ANSV), Based on Information from the National Institute of Legal Medicine And Forensic Sciences (INMLCF)

Trends in reported road traffic deaths

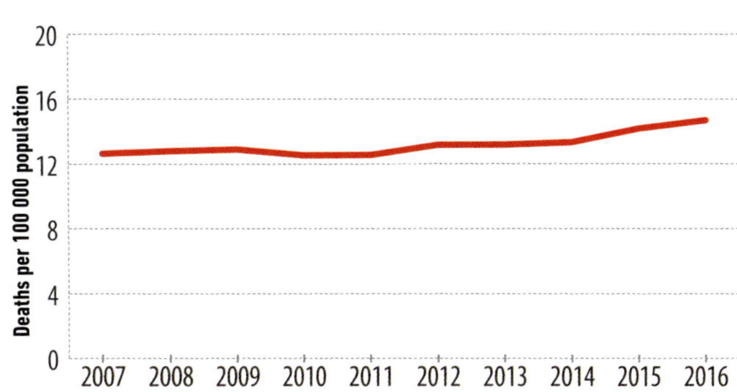

Source: National Observatory of Road Safety (ONSV/ANSV), Based on Information from the National Institute of Legal Medicine And Forensic Sciences (INMLCF)

Legislative review conducted by WHO. Vehicle safety data from UNECE WP.29. Other data collected by questionnaire and cleared by the National Road Safety Agency.

Comoros

Population: 795 601 | Income group: Low | Gross national income per capita: US$ 760

INSTITUTIONAL FRAMEWORK	
Lead agency	National Multi-sectoral Committee on Road Safety
Funded in national budget	No
National road safety strategy	No
Funding to implement strategy	–
Fatality reduction target	–
SAFER ROADS AND MOBILITY	
Audits or star rating required for new road infrastructure	No
Design standards for the safety of pedestrians / cyclists	No
Inspections / star rating of existing roads	No
Investments to upgrade high risk locations	Yes
Policies & investment in urban public transport	No
SAFER VEHICLES	
Total registered vehicles for 2016	34 898
Cars and 4-wheeled light vehicles	–
Motorized 2- and 3-wheelers	–
Heavy trucks	–
Buses	–
Other	–
Vehicle standards applied (UNECE WP.29)	
Frontal impact standard	No
Electronic stability control	No
Pedestrian protection	No
Motorcycle anti-lock braking system	No
POST-CRASH CARE	
National emergency care access number	None
Trauma registry	None
Formal certification for prehospital providers	No
National assessment of emergency care systems	No
DATA	
Reported road traffic fatalities (2016)	23[a] (96% M, 4% F)
WHO estimated road traffic fatalities (2016)	211 (95% CI 177 - 245)
WHO estimated rate per 100 000 population (2016)	26.5

[a] Annual statistics of the National Gendarmerie. Died within 30 days of crash

SAFER ROAD USERS	
National speed limit law	Yes[b]
Max urban speed limit	–
Max rural speed limit	–
Max motorway speed limit	–
Local authorities can modify limits	–
Enforcement	0 1 2 (3) 4 5 6 7 8 9 10
Predominant type of enforcement	Manual
National drink-driving law	Yes[c]
BAC limit – general population	–
BAC limit – young or novice drivers	–
Random breath testing carried out	No
Testing carried out in case of fatal crash	No
Enforcement	0 1 (2) 3 4 5 6 7 8 9 10
% road traffic deaths involving alcohol	–
National motorcycle helmet law	No
Applies to drivers and passengers	–
Helmet fastening required	–
Helmet standard referred to and/or specified	–
Children passengers on motorcycles	Not restricted
Enforcement	–
Helmet wearing rate	–
National seat-belt law	No
Applies to front and rear seat occupants	–
Enforcement	–
Seat-belt wearing rate	–
National child restraint law	No
Children seated in front seat	Not restricted
Child restraint required	–
Child restraint standard referred to and/or specified	–
Enforcement	–
% children using child restraints	–
National law on mobile phone use while driving	No
Ban on hand-held mobile phone use	–
Ban on hands-free mobile phone use	–
National drug-driving law	Yes

[b] Traffic code refers to regulations to set maximum speed limits, regulations not available
[c] Not based on BAC

Deaths by road user category

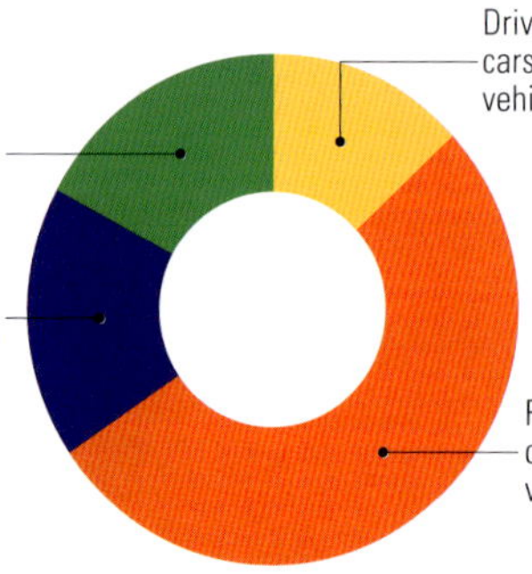

Source: 2016, Annual statistics of the National Gendarmerie

Trends in reported road traffic deaths

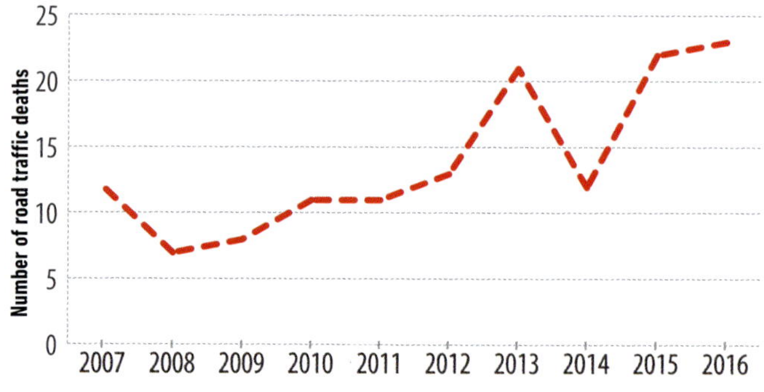

Source: Annual statistics of the National Gendarmerie

Legislative review conducted by WHO. Vehicle safety data from UNECE WP29. Other data collected by questionnaire and cleared by Ministry of Interior, Information, and Decentralization.

Congo

Population: 5 125 821 | Income group: Middle | Gross national income per capita: US$ 1 710

INSTITUTIONAL FRAMEWORK

Lead agency	General Directorate of Land Transport (DGTT)
Funded in national budget	No
National road safety strategy	Yes
Funding to implement strategy	Partially funded
Fatality reduction target	20% (2017-2018)

SAFER ROADS AND MOBILITY

Audits or star rating required for new road infrastructure	Yes
Design standards for the safety of pedestrians / cyclists	Partial
Inspections / star rating of existing roads	No
Investments to upgrade high risk locations	No
Policies & investment in urban public transport	No

SAFER VEHICLES

Total registered vehicles	–
Cars and 4-wheeled light vehicles	–
Motorized 2- and 3-wheelers	–
Heavy trucks	–
Buses	–
Other	–
Vehicle standards applied (UNECE WP.29)	
Frontal impact standard	No
Electronic stability control	No
Pedestrian protection	No
Motorcycle anti-lock braking system	No

POST-CRASH CARE

National emergency care access number	Partial coverage
Trauma registry	None
Formal certification for prehospital providers	No
National assessment of emergency care systems	No

DATA

Reported road traffic fatalities (2016)	308[a] (56% M, 19% F)
WHO estimated road traffic fatalities (2016)	1 405 (95% CI 1 124 - 1 687)
WHO estimated rate per 100 000 population (2016)	27.4

[a] General Directorate of Land Transport (DGTT) Activity Report. Died within 30 days of crash

SAFER ROAD USERS

National speed limit law	Yes
Max urban speed limit	60 km/h
Max rural speed limit	110 km/h
Max motorway speed limit	No
Local authorities can modify limits	Yes
Enforcement	0 1 2 3 (4) 5 6 7 8 9 10
Predominant type of enforcement	–
National drink-driving law	Yes
BAC limit – general population	≤ 0.08 g/dl
BAC limit – young or novice drivers	≤ 0.08 g/dl
Random breath testing carried out	Yes
Testing carried out in case of fatal crash	No
Enforcement	0 1 (2) 3 4 5 6 7 8 9 10
% road traffic deaths involving alcohol	–
National motorcycle helmet law	Yes
Applies to drivers and passengers	Yes
Helmet fastening required	No
Helmet standard referred to and/or specified	No
Children passengers on motorcycles	Prohibited under 5 yrs
Enforcement	0 1 2 (3) 4 5 6 7 8 9 10
Helmet wearing rate	27% All riders[b]
National seat-belt law	Yes
Applies to front and rear seat occupants	No
Enforcement	0 1 (2) 3 4 5 6 7 8 9 10
Seat-belt wearing rate	4% Front seats[b], 4% Rear seats[b]
National child restraint law	No
Children seated in front seat	Not restricted
Child restraint required	–
Child restraint standard referred to and/or specified	–
Enforcement	–
% children using child restraints	–
National law on mobile phone use while driving	Yes
Ban on hand-held mobile phone use	Yes
Ban on hands-free mobile phone use	Yes
National drug-driving law	No

[b] 2015, General Directorate of Land Transport (DGTT) Investigation Report

Deaths by road user category

Trends in reported road traffic deaths

Source: General Directorate of Land Transport (DGTT) Activity Report

Legislative review conducted by WHO. Vehicle safety data from UNECE WP29. Other data collected by questionnaire and cleared by Ministry of Transport, Civil Aviation and Merchant Navy.

Cook Islands

Population: 17 379 | Income group: High | Gross national income per capita: US$ –

INSTITUTIONAL FRAMEWORK

Lead agency	Road Safety Steering Committee
Funded in national budget	Yes
National road safety strategy	Yes
Funding to implement strategy	Partially funded
Fatality reduction target	Zero crash-related deaths (2016-2020)

SAFER ROADS AND MOBILITY

Audits or star rating required for new road infrastructure	Partial
Design standards for the safety of pedestrians / cyclists	Partial
Inspections / star rating of existing roads	Yes
Investments to upgrade high risk locations	Yes
Policies & investment in urban public transport	No

SAFER VEHICLES

Total registered vehicles for July 2013-June 2014	12 453
Cars and 4-wheeled light vehicles	5 085
Motorized 2- and 3-wheelers	6 846
Heavy trucks	491
Buses	31
Other	0
Vehicle standards applied (UNECE WP.29)	
Frontal impact standard	No
Electronic stability control	No
Pedestrian protection	No
Motorcycle anti-lock braking system	No

POST-CRASH CARE

National emergency care access number	National, single number
Trauma registry	National
Formal certification for prehospital providers	No
National assessment of emergency care systems	No

DATA

Reported road traffic fatalities (2015)	5 [a] (40% M, 60% F)
WHO estimated road traffic fatalities (2016)	3
WHO estimated rate per 100 000 population (2016)	17.3

[a] Cook Islands health information bulletin 2015. Unlimited time period following crash

SAFER ROAD USERS

National speed limit law	Yes
Max urban speed limit	50 km/h
Max rural speed limit	50 km/h
Max motorway speed limit	50 km/h
Local authorities can modify limits	No
Enforcement	0 1 2 3 4 5 (6) 7 8 9 10
Predominant type of enforcement	Manual
National drink-driving law	Yes
BAC limit – general population	≤ 0.08 g/dl
BAC limit – young or novice drivers	≤ 0.08 g/dl
Random breath testing carried out	Yes
Testing carried out in case of fatal crash	All drivers tested
Enforcement	0 1 2 3 4 5 (6) 7 8 9 10
% road traffic deaths involving alcohol	39% [b]
National motorcycle helmet law	Yes [c]
Applies to drivers and passengers	Yes
Helmet fastening required	No
Helmet standard referred to and/or specified	Yes
Children passengers on motorcycles	Not restricted
Enforcement	0 1 2 3 4 (5) 6 7 8 9 10
Helmet wearing rate	–
National seat-belt law	No
Applies to front and rear seat occupants	–
Enforcement	–
Seat-belt wearing rate	–
National child restraint law	No
Children seated in front seat	Not restricted
Child restraint required	–
Child restraint standard referred to and/or specified	–
Enforcement	–
% children using child restraints	–
National law on mobile phone use while driving	No
Ban on hand-held mobile phone use	–
Ban on hands-free mobile phone use	–
National drug-driving law	Yes

[b] 2015, Cook Islands health information bulletin

[c] Obligation to use a helmet only applies to those riding on a motorcycle travelling above 40 km/h (except for specific provisions in Rarotonga - persons between 16 and 25 and visitors required to wear helmet at all speeds)

Deaths by road user category

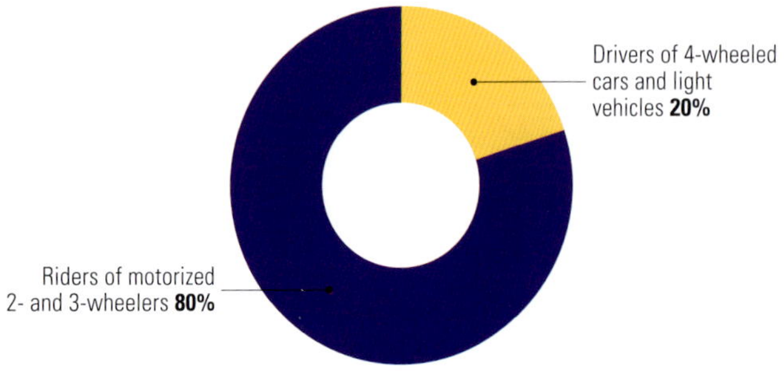

Source: 2015, Cook Islands health information bulletin

Trends in reported road traffic deaths

Source: Cook Islands health information bulletin

Costa Rica

Population: 4 857 274 | Income group: Middle | Gross national income per capita: US$ 10 840

INSTITUTIONAL FRAMEWORK	
Lead agency	Road Safety Council (COSEVI), Ministry of Public Works and Transportation
Funded in national budget	No
National road safety strategy	Yes
Funding to implement strategy	Fully funded
Fatality reduction target	20% (2015-2020)
SAFER ROADS AND MOBILITY	
Audits or star rating required for new road infrastructure	No
Design standards for the safety of pedestrians / cyclists	No
Inspections / star rating of existing roads	–
Investments to upgrade high risk locations	No
Policies & investment in urban public transport	Yes
SAFER VEHICLES	
Total registered vehicles for 2015	1 991 398
Cars and 4-wheeled light vehicles	1 362 737
Motorized 2- and 3-wheelers	5 778
Heavy trucks	44 764
Buses	28 846
Other	549 273
Vehicle standards applied (UNECE WP.29)	
Frontal impact standard	No
Electronic stability control	No
Pedestrian protection	No
Motorcycle anti-lock braking system	No
POST-CRASH CARE	
National emergency care access number	National, single number
Trauma registry	Some facilities
Formal certification for prehospital providers	Yes
National assessment of emergency care systems	No
DATA	
Reported road traffic fatalities (2015)	795[a] (87% M, 13% F)
WHO estimated road traffic fatalities (2016)	812
WHO estimated rate per 100 000 population (2016)	16.7

[a] Judicial Power, Planning Directorate. Died within a year of crash

SAFER ROAD USERS	
National speed limit law	Yes
Max urban speed limit	50 km/h
Max rural speed limit	60 km/h
Max motorway speed limit	No
Local authorities can modify limits	No
Enforcement	0 1 2 3 (4) 5 6 7 8 9 10
Predominant type of enforcement	Manual
National drink-driving law	Yes
BAC limit – general population	≤ 0.05 g/dl
BAC limit – young or novice drivers	≤ 0.02 g/dl
Random breath testing carried out	Yes
Testing carried out in case of fatal crash	All drivers tested
Enforcement	0 1 2 3 (4) 5 6 7 8 9 10
% road traffic deaths involving alcohol	31%[b]
National motorcycle helmet law	Yes
Applies to drivers and passengers	Yes
Helmet fastening required	No
Helmet standard referred to and/or specified	Yes
Children passengers on motorcycles	Prohibited under 5 yrs
Enforcement	0 1 2 3 4 (5) 6 7 8 9 10
Helmet wearing rate	98% Drivers[c], 92% Passengers[c]
National seat-belt law	Yes
Applies to front and rear seat occupants	Yes
Enforcement	0 1 2 3 (4) 5 6 7 8 9 10
Seat-belt wearing rate	75% Front seats[c], 36% Rear seats[c]
National child restraint law	Yes
Children seated in front seat	Prohibited under 12 yrs/145 cm
Child restraint required	Up to 12 yrs/145 cm
Child restraint standard referred to and/or specified	No
Enforcement	0 1 2 3 4 (5) 6 7 8 9 10
% children using child restraints	–
National law on mobile phone use while driving	Yes
Ban on hand-held mobile phone use	Yes
Ban on hands-free mobile phone use	No
National drug-driving law	Yes

[b] 2015, Judicial Power, Judicial Morgue (extraction of physical files)
[c] 2016, Seat belt and helmet study, Road Safety Council, Ministry of Public Works and Transportation (COSEVI)

Deaths by road user category

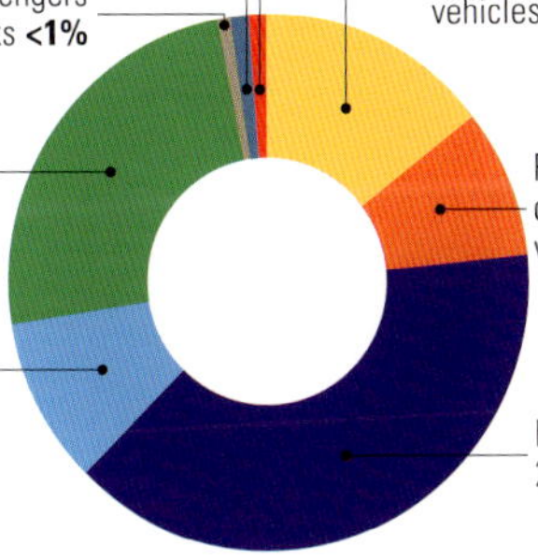

Source: 2015, Judicial Power, Planning Directorate

Trends in reported road traffic deaths

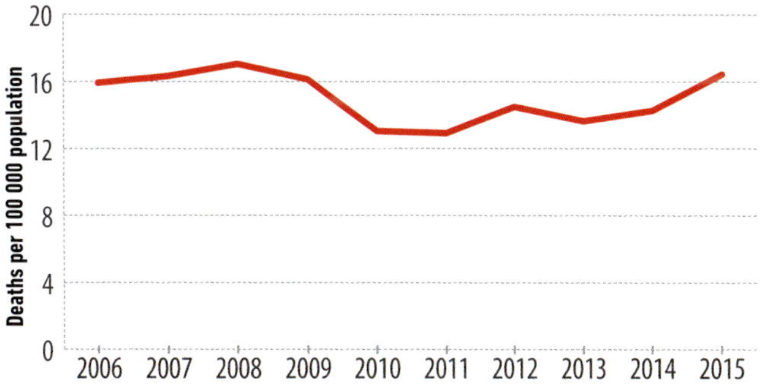

Source: Judicial Power, Planning Directorate

Legislative review conducted by WHO. Vehicle safety data from UNECE WP.29. Other data collected by questionnaire.

Côte d'Ivoire

Population: 23 695 920 | Income group: Middle | Gross national income per capita: US$ 1 520

INSTITUTIONAL FRAMEWORK	
Lead agency	Road Safety Office (OSER), Ministry of Transport
Funded in national budget	Yes
National road safety strategy	Yes
Funding to implement strategy	Fully funded
Fatality reduction target	50 % (2016-2020)
SAFER ROADS AND MOBILITY	
Audits or star rating required for new road infrastructure	Partial
Design standards for the safety of pedestrians / cyclists	Partial
Inspections / star rating of existing roads	No
Investments to upgrade high risk locations	Yes
Policies & investment in urban public transport	Yes
SAFER VEHICLES	
Total registered vehicles for 2016	905 537
Cars and 4-wheeled light vehicles	624 820
Motorized 2- and 3-wheelers	162 996
Heavy trucks	90 554
Buses	27 166
Other	1
Vehicle standards applied (UNECE WP.29)	
Frontal impact standard	No
Electronic stability control	No
Pedestrian protection	No
Motorcycle anti-lock braking system	No
POST-CRASH CARE	
National emergency care access number	Partial coverage
Trauma registry	Some facilities
Formal certification for prehospital providers	Yes
National assessment of emergency care systems	No
DATA	
Reported road traffic fatalities (2016)	991[a] (76% M, 12% F)
WHO estimated road traffic fatalities (2016)	5 582 (95% CI 4 635 - 6 529)
WHO estimated rate per 100 000 population (2016)	23.6

[a] Road Safety Office (OSER). Died within 30 days of crash

SAFER ROAD USERS	
National speed limit law	Yes
Max urban speed limit	60 km/h
Max rural speed limit	110 km/h
Max motorway speed limit	120 km/h
Local authorities can modify limits	No
Enforcement	0 1 2 3 4 (5) 6 7 8 9 10
Predominant type of enforcement	Manual
National drink-driving law	Yes
BAC limit – general population	< 0.08 g/dl
BAC limit – young or novice drivers	< 0.08 g/dl
Random breath testing carried out	Yes
Testing carried out in case of fatal crash	No
Enforcement	0 1 2 (3) 4 5 6 7 8 9 10
% road traffic deaths involving alcohol	–
National motorcycle helmet law	Yes
Applies to drivers and passengers	Yes
Helmet fastening required	No
Helmet standard referred to and/or specified	Yes
Children passengers on motorcycles	Not restricted
Enforcement	0 1 2 3 (4) 5 6 7 8 9 10
Helmet wearing rate	–
National seat-belt law	Yes
Applies to front and rear seat occupants	No
Enforcement	0 1 2 3 (4) 5 6 7 8 9 10
Seat-belt wearing rate	–
National child restraint law	No
Children seated in front seat	Not restricted
Child restraint required	–
Child restraint standard referred to and/or specified	–
Enforcement	–
% children using child restraints	–
National law on mobile phone use while driving	Yes
Ban on hand-held mobile phone use	Yes
Ban on hands-free mobile phone use	Yes
National drug-driving law	No

Deaths by road user category

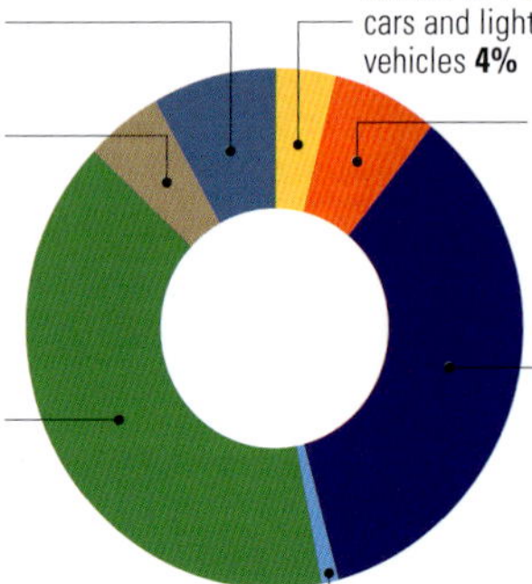

Source: 2016, Road Safety Office (OSER)

Trends in reported road traffic deaths

Source: Road Safety Office (OSER) and National Institute of Statistics (INS)

Legislative review conducted by WHO. Vehicle safety data from UNECE WP29. Other data collected by questionnaire and cleared by Ministry of Transport.

Croatia

Population: 4 213 265 | Income group: Middle | Gross national income per capita: US$ 12 110

INSTITUTIONAL FRAMEWORK	
Lead agency	No
Funded in national budget	–
National road safety strategy	Yes
Funding to implement strategy	Fully funded
Fatality reduction target	50% (2011-2020)
SAFER ROADS AND MOBILITY	
Audits or star rating required for new road infrastructure	Partial
Design standards for the safety of pedestrians / cyclists	Yes
Inspections / star rating of existing roads	Yes
Investments to upgrade high risk locations	Yes
Policies & investment in urban public transport	Yes
SAFER VEHICLES	
Total registered vehicles for 2016	1 996 056
Cars and 4-wheeled light vehicles	1 551 819
Motorized 2- and 3-wheelers	150 478
Heavy trucks	159 542
Buses	5 514
Other	128 703
Vehicle standards applied (UNECE WP.29)	
Frontal impact standard	Yes
Electronic stability control	Yes
Pedestrian protection	Yes
Motorcycle anti-lock braking system	Yes
POST-CRASH CARE	
National emergency care access number	National, single number
Trauma registry	None
Formal certification for prehospital providers	Yes
National assessment of emergency care systems	No
DATA	
Reported road traffic fatalities (2016)	307[a] (79% M, 21% F)
WHO estimated road traffic fatalities (2016)	340
WHO estimated rate per 100 000 population (2016)	8.1

[a] Ministry of Interior. Died within 30 days of crash

SAFER ROAD USERS	
National speed limit law	Yes
Max urban speed limit	50 km/h[b]
Max rural speed limit	90 km/h
Max motorway speed limit	130 km/h
Local authorities can modify limits	Yes
Enforcement	0 1 2 3 4 5 6 (7) 8 9 10
Predominant type of enforcement	Manual and automated
National drink-driving law	Yes
BAC limit – general population	≤ 0.05 g/dl
BAC limit – young or novice drivers	0.00 g/dl
Random breath testing carried out	Yes
Testing carried out in case of fatal crash	Some drivers tested
Enforcement	0 1 2 3 4 5 6 7 (8) 9 10
% road traffic deaths involving alcohol	24%[c]
National motorcycle helmet law	Yes
Applies to drivers and passengers	Yes
Helmet fastening required	Yes
Helmet standard referred to and/or specified	Yes
Children passengers on motorcycles	Prohibited under 12 yrs
Enforcement	0 1 2 3 4 5 6 7 8 (9) 10
Helmet wearing rate	95% Drivers[d], 95% Passengers[d]
National seat-belt law	Yes
Applies to front and rear seat occupants	Yes
Enforcement	0 1 2 3 4 5 (6) 7 8 9 10
Seat-belt wearing rate	62% Front seats[d], 14% Rear seats[d]
National child restraint law	Yes
Children seated in front seat	Prohibited under 150 cm
Child restraint required	Up to 135/150 cm[e]
Child restraint standard referred to and/or specified	No
Enforcement	0 1 2 3 4 (5) 6 7 8 9 10
% children using child restraints	–
National law on mobile phone use while driving	Yes
Ban on hand-held mobile phone use	Yes
Ban on hands-free mobile phone use	No
National drug-driving law	Yes

[b] Can be increased up to 80 km/h
[c] 2016, Ministry of Interior
[d] 2015, Faculty of Transort and Traffic Sciences, University of Zagreb
[e] A child of height 135-150 cm can be restrained with an adult seat belt only provided that this child sits in the rear of the car

Deaths by road user category

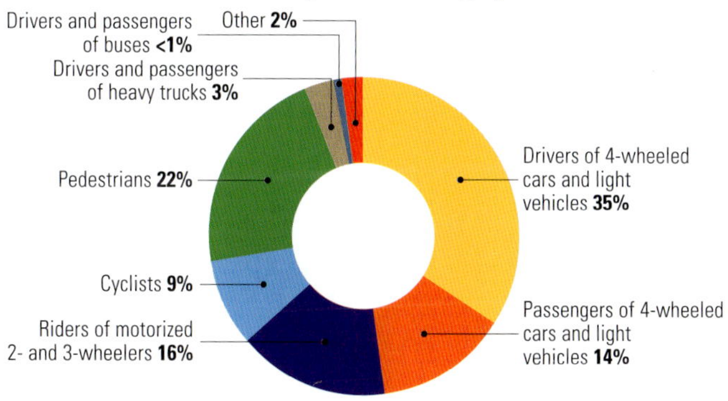

Source: 2016, Ministry of Interior

Trends in reported road traffic deaths

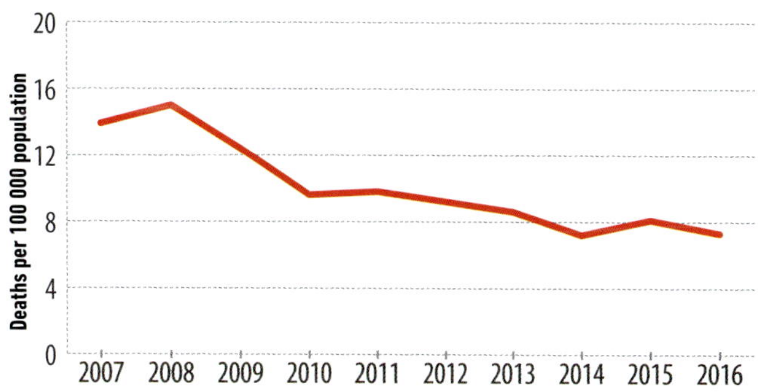

Source: Ministry of Interior

Cuba

Population: 11 475 982 | Income group: Middle | Gross national income per capita: US$ 6 570[a]

INSTITUTIONAL FRAMEWORK	
Lead agency	National Road Safety Commission (CNSV)
Funded in national budget	Yes
National road safety strategy	Yes
Funding to implement strategy	Fully funded
Fatality reduction target	5 deaths per 100 000 population (2010-2025)
SAFER ROADS AND MOBILITY	
Audits or star rating required for new road infrastructure	No
Design standards for the safety of pedestrians / cyclists	Partial
Inspections / star rating of existing roads	Yes
Investments to upgrade high risk locations	Yes
Policies & investment in urban public transport	Yes
SAFER VEHICLES	
Total registered vehicles for 2016	633 369
Cars and 4-wheeled light vehicles	236 006
Motorized 2- and 3-wheelers	217 223
Heavy trucks	65 542
Buses	19 842
Other	94 756
Vehicle standards applied (UNECE WP.29)	
Frontal impact standard	No
Electronic stability control	No
Pedestrian protection	No
Motorcycle anti-lock braking system	No
POST-CRASH CARE	
National emergency care access number	National, single number
Trauma registry	National
Formal certification for prehospital providers	Yes
National assessment of emergency care systems	No
DATA	
Reported road traffic fatalities (2016)	750[b] (80% M, 20% F)
WHO estimated road traffic fatalities (2016)	975
WHO estimated rate per 100 000 population (2016)	8.5

[a] Data available only for 2013
[b] Traffic Accident Registry. Died within 30 days of crash

SAFER ROAD USERS	
National speed limit law	Yes
Max urban speed limit	50 km/h
Max rural speed limit	90 km/h
Max motorway speed limit	100 km/h
Local authorities can modify limits	No
Enforcement	0 1 2 3 4 5 6 (7) 8 9 10
Predominant type of enforcement	Manual
National drink-driving law	Yes
BAC limit – general population	≤ 0.01 g/dl
BAC limit – young or novice drivers	0.00 g/dl
Random breath testing carried out	Yes[c]
Testing carried out in case of fatal crash	All drivers tested
Enforcement	0 1 2 3 4 5 (6) 7 8 9 10
% road traffic deaths involving alcohol	33%[d]
National motorcycle helmet law	Yes
Applies to drivers and passengers	Yes
Helmet fastening required	Yes
Helmet standard referred to and/or specified	No
Children passengers on motorcycles	Prohibited under 7 yrs
Enforcement	0 1 2 3 4 5 6 7 (8) 9 10
Helmet wearing rate	95% Drivers[e], 90% Passengers[e]
National seat-belt law	Yes
Applies to front and rear seat occupants	Yes
Enforcement	0 1 2 3 4 (5) 6 7 8 9 10
Seat-belt wearing rate	35% Drivers[e], 30% Front seats[e]
National child restraint law	No[f]
Children seated in front seat	Prohibited under 12 yrs
Child restraint required	–
Child restraint standard referred to and/or specified	–
Enforcement	–
% children using child restraints	–
National law on mobile phone use while driving	Yes
Ban on hand-held mobile phone use	Yes
Ban on hands-free mobile phone use	Yes
National drug-driving law	Yes

[c] Random breath testing not addressed in the law
[d] Systematic studies carried out since 1985, Institute of Legal Medicine
[e] 2016, National Transit Office
[f] Children under 2 years shall be either accompanied by adults or restrained with special accessories

Deaths by road user category

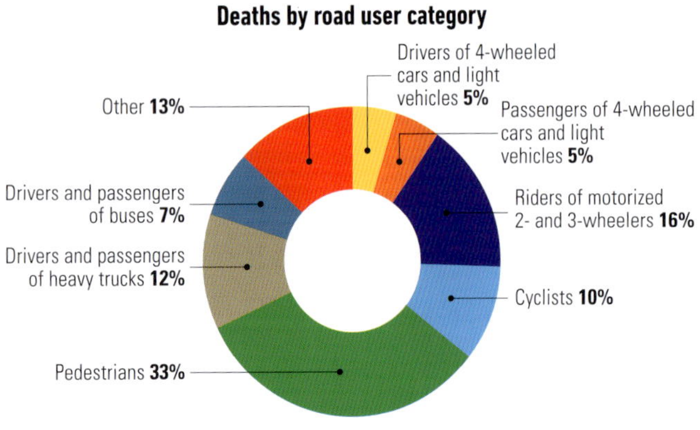

Source: 2016, Traffic Accident Registry

Trends in reported road traffic deaths

Source: Traffic Accident Registry

Legislative review conducted by WHO. Vehicle safety data from UNECE WP29. Other data collected by questionnaire and cleared by Ministry of Public Health

Cyprus

Population: 1 170 125 | Income group: High | Gross national income per capita: US$ 23 680

INSTITUTIONAL FRAMEWORK	
Lead agency	Road Safety Unit, Ministry of Transport, Communications and Works
Funded in national budget	Yes
National road safety strategy	Yes
Funding to implement strategy	Partially funded
Fatality reduction target	50% (2012-2020)
SAFER ROADS AND MOBILITY	
Audits or star rating required for new road infrastructure	Partial
Design standards for the safety of pedestrians / cyclists	Yes
Inspections / star rating of existing roads	Yes
Investments to upgrade high risk locations	Yes
Policies & investment in urban public transport	Yes
SAFER VEHICLES	
Total registered vehicles for 2015	650 805
Cars and 4-wheeled light vehicles	487 692
Motorized 2- and 3-wheelers	39 282
Heavy trucks	121 119
Buses	2 712
Other	0
Vehicle standards applied (UNECE WP.29)	
Frontal impact standard	Yes
Electronic stability control	Yes
Pedestrian protection	Yes
Motorcycle anti-lock braking system	Yes
POST-CRASH CARE	
National emergency care access number	National, multiple numbers
Trauma registry	Subnational
Formal certification for prehospital providers	Yes
National assessment of emergency care systems	Yes
DATA	
Reported road traffic fatalities (2016)	46[a] (78% M, 22% F)
WHO estimated road traffic fatalities (2016)	60
WHO estimated rate per 100 000 population (2016)	5.1

[a] Cyprus Police. Died within 30 days of crash

SAFER ROAD USERS	
National speed limit law	Yes
Max urban speed limit	65 km/h
Max rural speed limit	No
Max motorway speed limit	100 km/h
Local authorities can modify limits	Yes
Enforcement	0 1 2 3 4 5 (6) 7 8 9 10
Predominant type of enforcement	Manual
National drink-driving law	Yes
BAC limit – general population	≤ 0.05 g/dl
BAC limit – young or novice drivers	≤ 0.02 g/dl
Random breath testing carried out	Yes
Testing carried out in case of fatal crash	All drivers tested
Enforcement	0 1 2 3 4 5 6 (7) 8 9 10
% road traffic deaths involving alcohol	17%[b]
National motorcycle helmet law	Yes
Applies to drivers and passengers	Yes
Helmet fastening required	Yes
Helmet standard referred to and/or specified	Yes
Children passengers on motorcycles	Prohibited under 12 yrs
Enforcement	0 1 2 3 4 5 6 (7) 8 9 10
Helmet wearing rate	75% Drivers[c], 68% Passengers[c]
National seat-belt law	Yes
Applies to front and rear seat occupants	Yes
Enforcement	0 1 2 3 4 5 (6) 7 8 9 10
Seat-belt wearing rate	–
National child restraint law	Yes
Children seated in front seat	Allowed in a child restraint[d]
Child restraint required	Up to 135/150 cm[e]
Child restraint standard referred to and/or specified	Yes
Enforcement	0 1 2 3 4 5 (6) 7 8 9 10
% children using child restraints	–
National law on mobile phone use while driving	Yes
Ban on hand-held mobile phone use	Yes
Ban on hands-free mobile phone use	No
National drug-driving law	Yes

[b] 2016, Cyprus Police
[c] 2010, Cyprus Police
[d] Provided that airbag is deactivated if child is in a rear-facing child restraint system
[e] A child of height 135-150 cm can be restrained with an adult seat belt only provided that this child sits in the rear of the car

Deaths by road user category

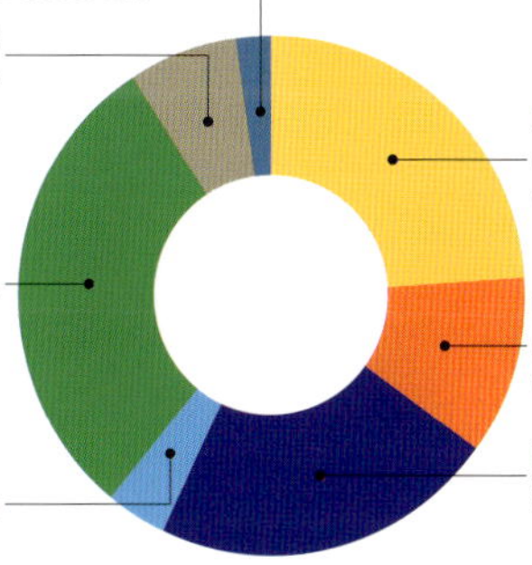

Source: 2016, Cyprus Police

Trends in reported road traffic deaths

Source: Cyprus Police and Cyprus Statistical Service

Czechia

Population: 10 610 947 | Income group: High | Gross national income per capita: US$ 17 570

INSTITUTIONAL FRAMEWORK	
Lead agency	The Council of the Government of the Czech Republic for Road Safety
Funded in national budget	Yes
National road safety strategy	Yes
Funding to implement strategy	Partially funded
Fatality reduction target	60% (2011-2020)
SAFER ROADS AND MOBILITY	
Audits or star rating required for new road infrastructure	Partial
Design standards for the safety of pedestrians / cyclists	Yes
Inspections / star rating of existing roads	Yes
Investments to upgrade high risk locations	No
Policies & investment in urban public transport	Yes
SAFER VEHICLES	
Total registered vehicles for 2015	7 325 789
Cars and 4-wheeled light vehicles	5 115 316
Motorized 2- and 3-wheelers	1 046 467
Heavy trucks	646 792
Buses	19 950
Other	497 264
Vehicle standards applied (UNECE WP.29)	
Frontal impact standard	Yes
Electronic stability control	Yes
Pedestrian protection	Yes
Motorcycle anti-lock braking system	Yes
POST-CRASH CARE	
National emergency care access number	National, single number
Trauma registry	National
Formal certification for prehospital providers	Yes
National assessment of emergency care systems	Yes
DATA	
Reported road traffic fatalities (2016)	611[a] (76% M, 24% F)
WHO estimated road traffic fatalities (2016)	630
WHO estimated rate per 100 000 population (2016)	5.9

[a] Ranking EU Progress on Road Safety. Died within 30 days of crash

SAFER ROAD USERS	
National speed limit law	Yes
Max urban speed limit	50 km/h[b]
Max rural speed limit	90 km/h
Max motorway speed limit	130 km/h
Local authorities can modify limits	Yes
Enforcement	0 1 2 3 4 ⑤ 6 7 8 9 10
Predominant type of enforcement	Manual
National drink-driving law	Yes
BAC limit – general population	≤ 0.03 g/dl
BAC limit – young or novice drivers	≤ 0.03 g/dl
Random breath testing carried out	Yes
Testing carried out in case of fatal crash	All drivers tested
Enforcement	0 1 2 3 4 5 6 ⑦ 8 9 10
% road traffic deaths involving alcohol	10%[c]
National motorcycle helmet law	Yes
Applies to drivers and passengers	Yes
Helmet fastening required	Yes
Helmet standard referred to and/or specified	Yes
Children passengers on motorcycles	Prohibited under 12 yrs
Enforcement	0 1 2 3 4 5 6 7 8 ⑨ 10
Helmet wearing rate	–
National seat-belt law	Yes
Applies to front and rear seat occupants	Yes
Enforcement	0 1 2 3 4 5 6 7 ⑧ 9 10
Seat-belt wearing rate	98% Front seats[d], 72% Rear seats[d]
National child restraint law	Yes
Children seated in front seat	Allowed in a child restraint[e]
Child restraint required	Up to 36 kg/150 cm
Child restraint standard referred to and/or specified	Yes
Enforcement	0 1 2 3 4 5 6 7 ⑧ 9 10
% children using child restraints	–
National law on mobile phone use while driving	Yes
Ban on hand-held mobile phone use	Yes
Ban on hands-free mobile phone use	No
National drug-driving law	Yes

[b] Can be increased up to 80 km/h
[c] 2016, Directorate of Traffic Police Service, Traffic accident statistics
[d] 2016, Center for Transport Research, Public Research Institute
[e] Provided that airbag is deactivated if child is in a rear-facing child restraint system

Deaths by road user category

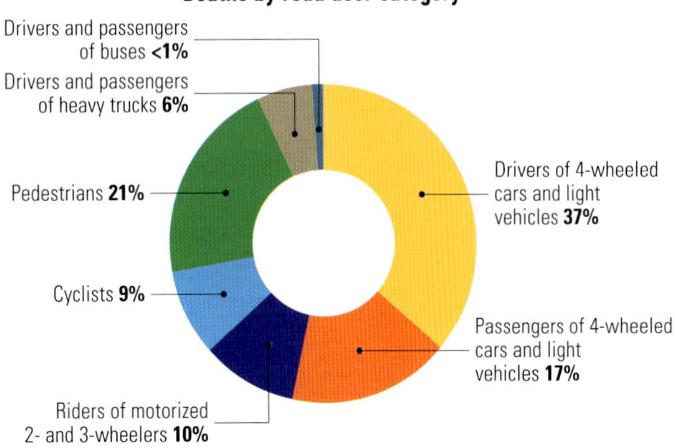

Source: 2016, Directorate of Traffic Police Service, Traffic accident statistics

Trends in reported road traffic deaths

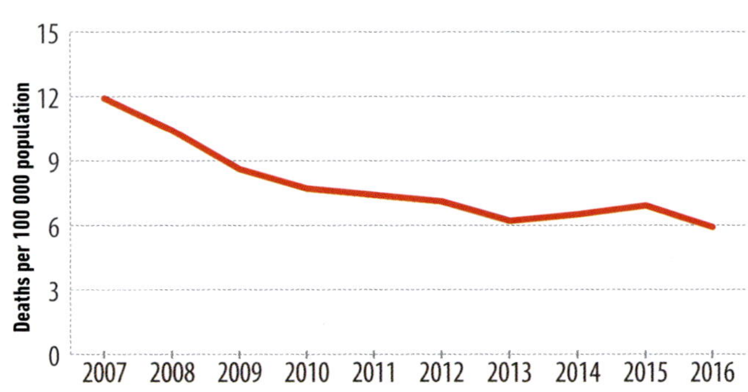

Source: Directorate of Traffic Police Service, Traffic accident statistics

Democratic Republic of the Congo

Population: 78 736 152 | Income group: Low | Gross national income per capita: US$ 420

INSTITUTIONAL FRAMEWORK	
Lead agency	National Program for Road Safety (CNPR), Ministry of Transport and Communication Channels
Funded in national budget	Yes
National road safety strategy	Yes
Funding to implement strategy	Partially funded
Fatality reduction target	–

SAFER ROADS AND MOBILITY	
Audits or star rating required for new road infrastructure	–
Design standards for the safety of pedestrians / cyclists	Partial
Inspections / star rating of existing roads	No
Investments to upgrade high risk locations	No
Policies & investment in urban public transport	No

SAFER VEHICLES	
Total registered vehicles	–
Cars and 4-wheeled light vehicles	–
Motorized 2- and 3-wheelers	–
Heavy trucks	–
Buses	–
Other	–
Vehicle standards applied (UNECE WP.29)	
Frontal impact standard	No
Electronic stability control	No
Pedestrian protection	No
Motorcycle anti-lock braking system	No

POST-CRASH CARE	
National emergency care access number	Partial coverage
Trauma registry	Some facilities
Formal certification for prehospital providers	No
National assessment of emergency care systems	Yes

DATA	
Reported road traffic fatalities (2016)	385[a] (81% M, 19% F)
WHO estimated road traffic fatalities (2016)	26 529 (95% CI 21 142 - 31 915)
WHO estimated rate per 100 000 population (2016)	33.7

[a] National Program for Road Safety (CNPR), Kinshasa city. Died at scene of crash

SAFER ROAD USERS	
National speed limit law	Yes
Max urban speed limit	60 km/h[b]
Max rural speed limit	90 km/h
Max motorway speed limit	120 km/h
Local authorities can modify limits	No
Enforcement	0 1 2 (3) 4 5 6 7 8 9 10
Predominant type of enforcement	–
National drink-driving law	Yes
BAC limit – general population	< 0.10 g/dl
BAC limit – young or novice drivers	< 0.10 g/dl
Random breath testing carried out	Yes[c]
Testing carried out in case of fatal crash	No
Enforcement	0 1 (2) 3 4 5 6 7 8 9 10
% road traffic deaths involving alcohol	–
National motorcycle helmet law	Yes
Applies to drivers and passengers	Yes
Helmet fastening required	No
Helmet standard referred to and/or specified	No
Children passengers on motorcycles	Not restricted
Enforcement	0 1 2 3 (4) 5 6 7 8 9 10
Helmet wearing rate	–
National seat-belt law	Yes
Applies to front and rear seat occupants	No
Enforcement	0 1 2 3 4 (5) 6 7 8 9 10
Seat-belt wearing rate	–
National child restraint law	No
Children seated in front seat	Prohibited under 12 yrs
Child restraint required	–
Child restraint standard referred to and/or specified	–
Enforcement	–
% children using child restraints	–
National law on mobile phone use while driving	No
Ban on hand-held mobile phone use	–
Ban on hands-free mobile phone use	–
National drug-driving law	No

[b] Traffic signs may on certain public highways provide for a higher speed limit not exceeding 80 km/h
[c] Legislation requires probable cause to test drivers

Deaths by road user category

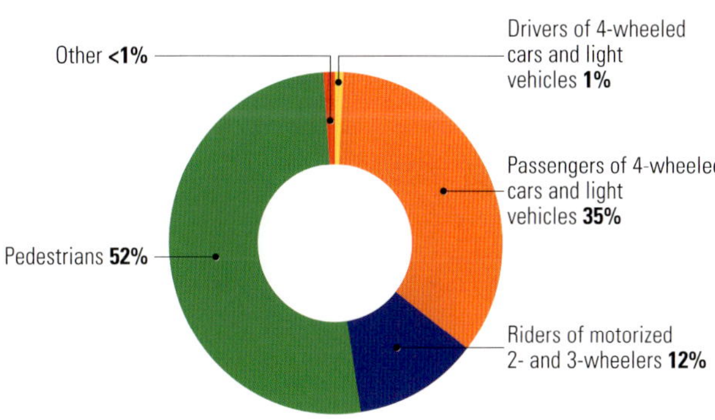

Source: 2016, Road Traffic Police (PCR)

Trends in reported road traffic deaths

Source: Road Traffic Police (PCR)

Legislative review conducted by WHO. Vehicle safety data from UNECE WP29. Other data collected by questionnaire.

Denmark

Population: 5 711 870 | Income group: High | Gross national income per capita: US$ 56 730

INSTITUTIONAL FRAMEWORK

Lead agency	**No**
Funded in national budget	–
National road safety strategy	**Yes**
Funding to implement strategy	Partially funded
Fatality reduction target	≤120 fatalities by 2020 (2013-2020)

SAFER ROADS AND MOBILITY

Audits or star rating required for new road infrastructure	Partial
Design standards for the safety of pedestrians / cyclists	Yes
Inspections / star rating of existing roads	Yes
Investments to upgrade high risk locations	Yes
Policies & investment in urban public transport	Yes

SAFER VEHICLES

Total registered vehicles for 2016	**3 131 673**
Cars and 4-wheeled light vehicles	2 786 472
Motorized 2- and 3-wheelers	198 035
Heavy trucks	41 436
Buses	13 383
Other	92 347
Vehicle standards applied (UNECE WP.29)	
Frontal impact standard	Yes
Electronic stability control	Yes
Pedestrian protection	Yes
Motorcycle anti-lock braking system	Yes

POST-CRASH CARE

National emergency care access number	National, single number
Trauma registry	National
Formal certification for prehospital providers	–
National assessment of emergency care systems	Yes

DATA

Reported road traffic fatalities (2016)	211[a] (73% M, 27% F)
WHO estimated road traffic fatalities (2016)	227
WHO estimated rate per 100 000 population (2016)	4

[a] Road Directorate, Traffic accidents for the year 2016. Died within 30 days of crash

SAFER ROAD USERS

National speed limit law	**Yes**
Max urban speed limit	50 km/h
Max rural speed limit	80 km/h
Max motorway speed limit	130 km/h
Local authorities can modify limits	Yes[b]
Enforcement	–
Predominant type of enforcement	Automated
National drink-driving law	**Yes**
BAC limit – general population	≤ 0.05 g/dl
BAC limit – young or novice drivers	≤ 0.05 g/dl
Random breath testing carried out	Yes
Testing carried out in case of fatal crash	Some drivers tested
Enforcement	–
% road traffic deaths involving alcohol	–
National motorcycle helmet law	**Yes**
Applies to drivers and passengers	Yes
Helmet fastening required	Yes
Helmet standard referred to and/or specified	Yes
Children passengers on motorcycles	Prohibited under 5 yrs / 135 cm
Enforcement	–
Helmet wearing rate	98% Drivers[c]
National seat-belt law	**Yes**
Applies to front and rear seat occupants	Yes
Enforcement	–
Seat-belt wearing rate	96% Front seats[c], 91% Rear seats[c]
National child restraint law	**Yes**
Children seated in front seat	Allowed in a child restraint[d]
Child restraint required	Up to 135 cm
Child restraint standard referred to and/or specified	Yes
Enforcement	–
% children using child restraints	97%[e]
National law on mobile phone use while driving	**Yes**
Ban on hand-held mobile phone use	Yes
Ban on hands-free mobile phone use	No
National drug-driving law	**Yes**

[b] Speed limits can be modified at local level by the road authorities and the police
[c] 2016, Danish Road Safety Council
[d] Provided that airbag is deactivated if a rear-facing restraint is used
[e] 2012, The Danish Road Traffic Investigation Board, Christian Skov

Deaths by road user category

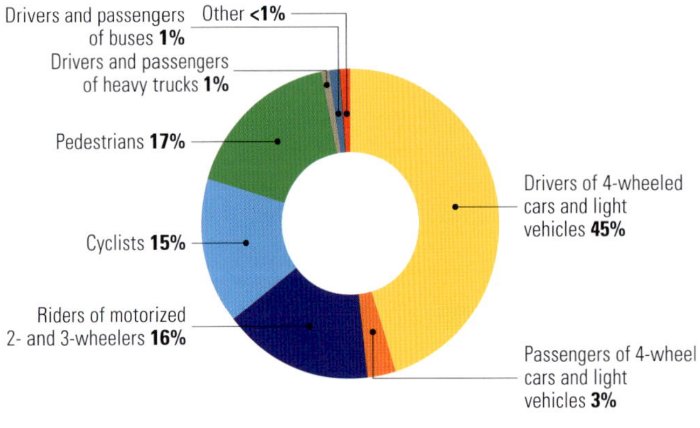

Source: 2016, Danish Road Directorate statistics (based on police data)

Trends in reported road traffic deaths

Source: Danish Road Directorate statistics (based on police data), National statistics (Statistics Denmark)

Legislative review conducted by WHO. Vehicle safety data from UNECE WP29. Other data collected by questionnaire and cleared by Danish Road Directorate.

Dominica

Population: 73 543 | Income group: Middle | Gross national income per capita: US$ 6 750

INSTITUTIONAL FRAMEWORK	
Lead agency	Transport Board, Ministry of Justice, Immigration and National Security
Funded in national budget	No
National road safety strategy	No
Funding to implement strategy	–
Fatality reduction target	–

SAFER ROADS AND MOBILITY	
Audits or star rating required for new road infrastructure	–
Design standards for the safety of pedestrians / cyclists	Partial
Inspections / star rating of existing roads	No
Investments to upgrade high risk locations	No
Policies & investment in urban public transport	No

SAFER VEHICLES	
Total registered vehicles for 2016	35 796
Cars and 4-wheeled light vehicles	25 812
Motorized 2- and 3-wheelers	2 747
Heavy trucks	4 834
Buses	2 403
Other	0
Vehicle standards applied (UNECE WP.29)	
Frontal impact standard	No
Electronic stability control	No
Pedestrian protection	No
Motorcycle anti-lock braking system	No

POST-CRASH CARE	
National emergency care access number	National, single number
Trauma registry	None
Formal certification for prehospital providers	No
National assessment of emergency care systems	No

DATA	
Reported road traffic fatalities (2015)	10[a] (70% M, 30% F)
WHO estimated road traffic fatalities (2016)	8
WHO estimated rate per 100 000 population (2016)	10.9

[a] Death Registry. Unlimited time period following crash

SAFER ROAD USERS	
National speed limit law	No
Max urban speed limit	–
Max rural speed limit	–
Max motorway speed limit	–
Local authorities can modify limits	No
Enforcement	–
Predominant type of enforcement	–
National drink-driving law	Yes
BAC limit – general population	≤ 0.08 g/dl
BAC limit – young or novice drivers	≤ 0.08 g/dl
Random breath testing carried out	No
Testing carried out in case of fatal crash	No
Enforcement	0 (1) 2 3 4 5 6 7 8 9 10
% road traffic deaths involving alcohol	–
National motorcycle helmet law	No
Applies to drivers and passengers	–
Helmet fastening required	–
Helmet standard referred to and/or specified	–
Children passengers on motorcycles	Not restricted
Enforcement	–
Helmet wearing rate	–
National seat-belt law	Yes
Applies to front and rear seat occupants	Yes
Enforcement	0 (1) 2 3 4 5 6 7 8 9 10
Seat-belt wearing rate	–
National child restraint law	No
Children seated in front seat	Not restricted
Child restraint required	–
Child restraint standard referred to and/or specified	–
Enforcement	–
% children using child restraints	–
National law on mobile phone use while driving	No
Ban on hand-held mobile phone use	–
Ban on hands-free mobile phone use	–
National drug-driving law	Yes

Deaths by road user category

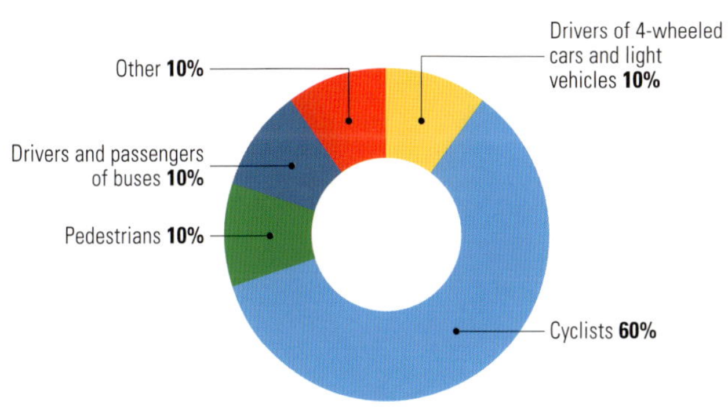

Source: 2015, Vital registration,Verified Police Records and Health Facilities Record

Trends in reported road traffic deaths

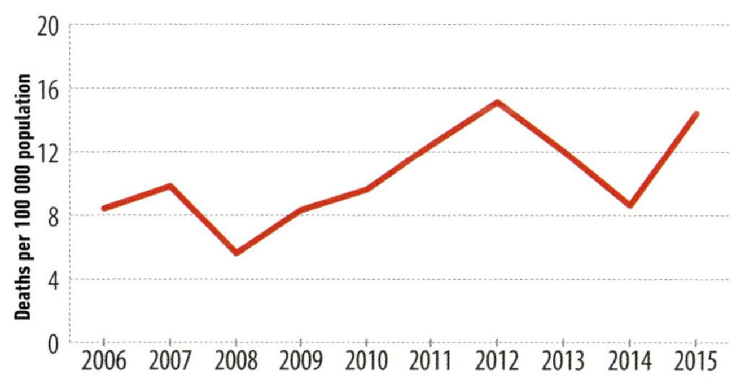

Source: Death Registry

Legislative review conducted by WHO. Vehicle safety data from UNECE WP29. Other data collected by questionnaire.

Dominican Republic

Population: 10 648 791 | Income group: Middle | Gross national income per capita: US$ 6 390

INSTITUTIONAL FRAMEWORK	
Lead agency	Presidential Commission for Road Safety and National Institute of Traffic and Land Transport (INTRANT)
Funded in national budget	Yes
National road safety strategy	Yes
Funding to implement strategy	Partially funded
Fatality reduction target	30% (2017-2020)
SAFER ROADS AND MOBILITY	
Audits or star rating required for new road infrastructure	Yes
Design standards for the safety of pedestrians / cyclists	Partial
Inspections / star rating of existing roads	No
Investments to upgrade high risk locations	Yes
Policies & investment in urban public transport	Yes
SAFER VEHICLES	
Total registered vehicles for 2016	3 854 038
Cars and 4-wheeled light vehicles	1 203 176
Motorized 2- and 3-wheelers	2 096 196
Heavy trucks	41 385
Buses	92 144
Other	421 137
Vehicle standards applied (UNECE WP.29)	
Frontal impact standard	No
Electronic stability control	No
Pedestrian protection	No
Motorcycle anti-lock braking system	No
POST-CRASH CARE	
National emergency care access number	Partial coverage
Trauma registry	National
Formal certification for prehospital providers	Yes
National assessment of emergency care systems	Yes
DATA	
Reported road traffic fatalities (2016)	3 118[a] (88% M, 12% F)
WHO estimated road traffic fatalities (2016)	3 684
WHO estimated rate per 100 000 population (2016)	34.6

[a] Combined sources. Died within 30 days of crash

SAFER ROAD USERS	
National speed limit law	Yes
Max urban speed limit	60 km/h
Max rural speed limit	60 km/h
Max motorway speed limit	120 km/h
Local authorities can modify limits	No
Enforcement	0 1 2 3 4 5 (6) 7 8 9 10
Predominant type of enforcement	Manual
National drink-driving law	Yes
BAC limit – general population	≤ 0.05 g/dl
BAC limit – young or novice drivers	0.00 g/dl
Random breath testing carried out	Yes
Testing carried out in case of fatal crash	Some drivers tested
Enforcement	0 1 2 (3) 4 5 6 7 8 9 10
% road traffic deaths involving alcohol	–
National motorcycle helmet law	Yes
Applies to drivers and passengers	Yes
Helmet fastening required	No
Helmet standard referred to and/or specified	Yes
Children passengers on motorcycles	Prohibited under 8 yrs
Enforcement	0 1 2 3 4 (5) 6 7 8 9 10
Helmet wearing rate	27% Drivers[b], 2% Passengers[b]
National seat-belt law	Yes
Applies to front and rear seat occupants	Yes
Enforcement	0 1 2 3 4 5 6 7 (8) 9 10
Seat-belt wearing rate	18% Front seats[b], 5% Rear seats[b]
National child restraint law	Yes
Children seated in front seat	Prohibited under 12 yrs
Child restraint required	Up to 6 yrs[c]
Child restraint standard referred to and/or specified	Yes
Enforcement	0 1 2 3 (4) 5 6 7 8 9 10
% children using child restraints	–
National law on mobile phone use while driving	Yes
Ban on hand-held mobile phone use	Yes
Ban on hands-free mobile phone use	No
National drug-driving law	Yes

[b] 2014, Metropolitan Transportation Authority (AMET)
[c] Children aged 6-12 years shall be placed in a booster seat

Deaths by road user category

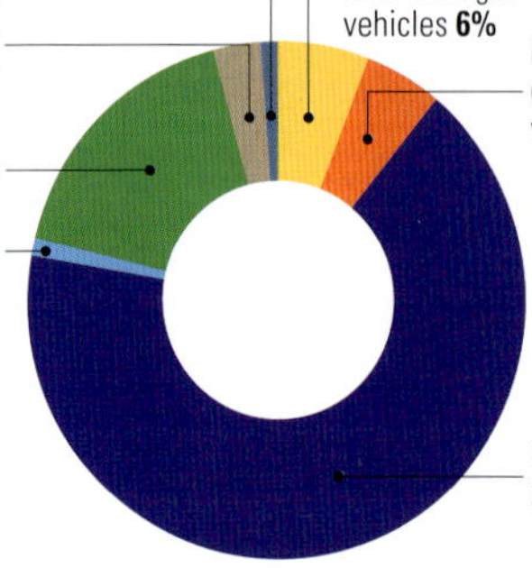

Source: 2016, Metropolitan Transportation Authority (AMET)

Trends in reported road traffic deaths

Source: Metropolitan Transportation Authority (AMET)

Legislative review conducted by WHO. Vehicle safety data from UNECE WP.29. Other data collected by questionnaire and cleared by INTRANT.

Ecuador

Population: 16 385 068 | Income group: Middle | Gross national income per capita: US$ 5 820

INSTITUTIONAL FRAMEWORK

Lead agency	National Traffic Agency, Ministry of Transport and Public Works
Funded in national budget	Yes
National road safety strategy	Yes
Funding to implement strategy	Partially funded
Fatality reduction target	40% (2015 - 2020)

SAFER ROADS AND MOBILITY

Audits or star rating required for new road infrastructure	Yes
Design standards for the safety of pedestrians / cyclists	Partial
Inspections / star rating of existing roads	Yes
Investments to upgrade high risk locations	No
Policies & investment in urban public transport	Yes

SAFER VEHICLES

Total registered vehicles for 2015	1 925 368
Cars and 4-wheeled light vehicles	1 358 713
Motorized 2- and 3-wheelers	431 215
Heavy trucks	111 608
Buses	17 826
Other	6 006
Vehicle standards applied (UNECE WP.29)	
Frontal impact standard	Yes
Electronic stability control	Yes
Pedestrian protection	No
Motorcycle anti-lock braking system	No

POST-CRASH CARE

National emergency care access number	National, single number
Trauma registry	National
Formal certification for prehospital providers	Yes
National assessment of emergency care systems	Yes

DATA

Reported road traffic fatalities (2016)	2 894[a] (81% M, 19% F)
WHO estimated road traffic fatalities (2016)	3 490
WHO estimated rate per 100 000 population (2016)	21.3

[a] National Institute of Statistics and Census. Died within 30 days of crash

SAFER ROAD USERS

National speed limit law	Yes
Max urban speed limit	60 km/h
Max rural speed limit	120 km/h
Max motorway speed limit	135 km/h
Local authorities can modify limits	Yes
Enforcement	0 1 2 3 4 5 6 ⑦ 8 9 10
Predominant type of enforcement	Manual and automated
National drink-driving law	Yes
BAC limit – general population	≤ 0.03 g/dl
BAC limit – young or novice drivers	≤ 0.03 g/dl
Random breath testing carried out	Yes[b]
Testing carried out in case of fatal crash	All drivers tested
Enforcement	0 1 2 3 4 5 6 ⑦ 8 9 10
% road traffic deaths involving alcohol	7%[c]
National motorcycle helmet law	Yes
Applies to drivers and passengers	Yes
Helmet fastening required	Yes
Helmet standard referred to and/or specified	Yes
Children passengers on motorcycles	Prohibited under 7 yrs
Enforcement	0 1 2 3 4 5 6 7 ⑧ 9 10
Helmet wearing rate	90% Drivers[c], 12-52% Passengers[d]
National seat-belt law	Yes
Applies to front and rear seat occupants	Yes
Enforcement	0 1 2 3 4 5 6 7 ⑧ 9 10
Seat-belt wearing rate	26% Front seats[e], 2% Rear seats[e]
National child restraint law	Yes[f]
Children seated in front seat	Prohibited under 12 yrs
Child restraint required	—[f]
Child restraint standard referred to and/or specified	No
Enforcement	0 1 2 3 4 ⑤ 6 7 8 9 10
% children using child restraints	15%[e]
National law on mobile phone use while driving	Yes
Ban on hand-held mobile phone use	Yes
Ban on hands-free mobile phone use	No
National drug-driving law	Yes

[b] Legislation requires probable cause to test drivers
[c] 2015, National Traffic Agency
[d] 52% wear helmet if it is only one more passenger, 12% when there is more than 2 passengers
[e] 2016, National Traffic Agency
[f] The legislation refers to seat belt or child restraints for children under 12 years but does not yet specify a minimum age/height/weight under which only child restraint systems can be used

Deaths by road user category

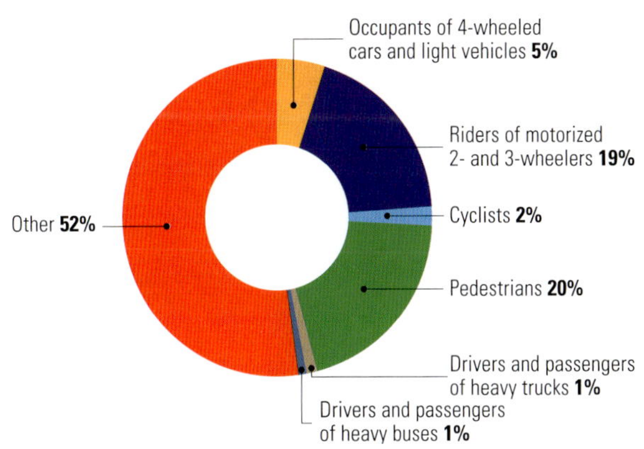

Source: 2015, National Institute of Statistics and Census

Trends in reported road traffic deaths

Source: Statistical Registry of General Deaths and the National Traffic Agency

Legislative review conducted by WHO. Vehicle safety data from UNECE WP29. Other data collected by questionnaire and cleared by National Transit Agency.

Egypt

Population: 95 688 680 | Income group: Middle | Gross national income per capita: US$ 3 460

INSTITUTIONAL FRAMEWORK

Lead agency	National Council for Road Safety, Ministry of Interior
Funded in national budget	No
National road safety strategy	Yes
Funding to implement strategy	Partially funded
Fatality reduction target	2-5 % (2011-2020)

SAFER ROADS AND MOBILITY

Audits or star rating required for new road infrastructure	Yes
Design standards for the safety of pedestrians / cyclists	Partial
Inspections / star rating of existing roads	Yes
Investments to upgrade high risk locations	Yes
Policies & investment in urban public transport	Yes

SAFER VEHICLES

Total registered vehicles for 2016	8 412 673
Cars and 4-wheeled light vehicles	4 966 129
Motorized 2- and 3-wheelers	2 967 829
Heavy trucks	380 980
Buses	97 735
Other	0
Vehicle standards applied (UNECE WP.29)	
Frontal impact standard	Yes
Electronic stability control	Yes
Pedestrian protection	Yes
Motorcycle anti-lock braking system	No

POST-CRASH CARE

National emergency care access number	National, single number
Trauma registry	National
Formal certification for prehospital providers	Yes
National assessment of emergency care systems	Yes

DATA

Reported road traffic fatalities (2016)	8 211 [a] (82% M, 18% F)
WHO estimated road traffic fatalities (2016)	9 287
WHO estimated rate per 100 000 population (2016)	9.7

[a] Central Agency for Public Mobilization and Statistics (CAPMAS) and Ministry of Health. Died within 30 days of crash

SAFER ROAD USERS

National speed limit law	Yes
Max urban speed limit	60 km/h
Max rural speed limit	90 km/h
Max motorway speed limit	100 km/h
Local authorities can modify limits	Yes
Enforcement	0 1 2 3 4 5 6 7 (8) 9 10
Predominant type of enforcement	Manual and automated
National drink-driving law	Yes [b]
BAC limit – general population	–
BAC limit – young or novice drivers	–
Random breath testing carried out	No
Testing carried out in case of fatal crash	Some drivers tested
Enforcement	0 1 2 3 4 5 6 7 (8) 9 10
% road traffic deaths involving alcohol	–
National motorcycle helmet law	Yes
Applies to drivers and passengers	Yes
Helmet fastening required	No
Helmet standard referred to and/or specified	No
Children passengers on motorcycles	Not restricted
Enforcement	0 1 2 (3) 4 5 6 7 8 9 10
Helmet wearing rate	–
National seat-belt law	Yes
Applies to front and rear seat occupants	No
Enforcement	0 1 2 3 4 5 6 (7) 8 9 10
Seat-belt wearing rate	–
National child restraint law	No
Children seated in front seat	Prohibited under 7 yrs
Child restraint required	–
Child restraint standard referred to and/or specified	–
Enforcement	–
% children using child restraints	–
National law on mobile phone use while driving	Yes
Ban on hand-held mobile phone use	Yes
Ban on hands-free mobile phone use	No
National drug-driving law	Yes

[b] Not based on BAC

Deaths by road user category

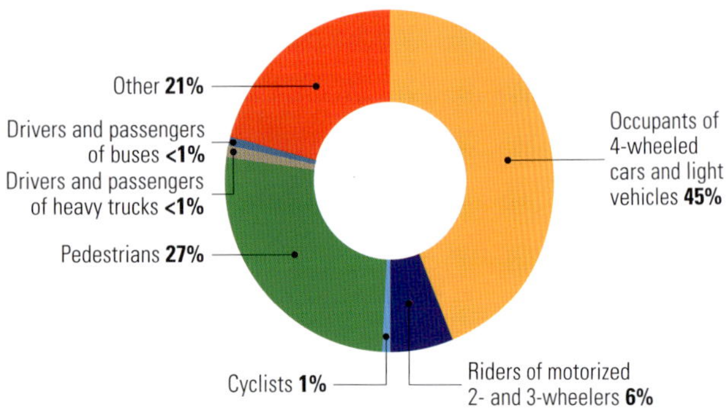

Source: 2016, Ministry of Health

Trends in reported road traffic deaths

Source: Central Agency for Public Mobilization and Statistics (CAPMAS) & Ministry of Interior

Legislative review conducted by WHO. Vehicle safety data from UNECE WP29. Other data collected by questionnaire.

El Salvador

Population: 6 344 722 | Income group: Middle | Gross national income per capita: US$ 3 920

INSTITUTIONAL FRAMEWORK	
Lead agency	Vice Ministry of Transport
Funded in national budget	Yes
National road safety strategy	Yes
Funding to implement strategy	Partially funded
Fatality reduction target	50% (2011-2020)
SAFER ROADS AND MOBILITY	
Audits or star rating required for new road infrastructure	Partial
Design standards for the safety of pedestrians / cyclists	Partial
Inspections / star rating of existing roads	No
Investments to upgrade high risk locations	No
Policies & investment in urban public transport	Yes
SAFER VEHICLES	
Total registered vehicles for 2016	1 008 080
Cars and 4-wheeled light vehicles	727 412
Motorized 2- and 3-wheelers	209 214
Heavy trucks	60 320
Buses	11 134
Other	0
Vehicle standards applied (UNECE WP.29)	
Frontal impact standard	No
Electronic stability control	No
Pedestrian protection	No
Motorcycle anti-lock braking system	No
POST-CRASH CARE	
National emergency care access number	National, multiple numbers
Trauma registry	National
Formal certification for prehospital providers	No
National assessment of emergency care systems	Yes
DATA	
Reported road traffic fatalities (2016)	1 215[a] (84% M, 16% F)
WHO estimated road traffic fatalities (2016)	1 411
WHO estimated rate per 100 000 population (2016)	22.2

[a] Civil National Police. Define as unlimited time period following crash

SAFER ROAD USERS	
National speed limit law	Yes
Max urban speed limit	50 km/h
Max rural speed limit	90 km/h
Max motorway speed limit	No
Local authorities can modify limits	No
Enforcement	0 1 2 3 4 5 ⑥ 7 8 9 10
Predominant type of enforcement	Manual
National drink-driving law	Yes
BAC limit – general population	< 0.05 g/dl
BAC limit – young or novice drivers	< 0.05 g/dl
Random breath testing carried out	Yes
Testing carried out in case of fatal crash	Some drivers tested
Enforcement	0 1 2 3 4 5 6 ⑦ 8 9 10
% road traffic deaths involving alcohol	–
National motorcycle helmet law	Yes
Applies to drivers and passengers	Yes
Helmet fastening required	Yes
Helmet standard referred to and/or specified	No
Children passengers on motorcycles	Not restricted
Enforcement	0 1 2 3 4 5 6 ⑦ 8 9 10
Helmet wearing rate	–
National seat-belt law	Yes
Applies to front and rear seat occupants	No
Enforcement	0 1 2 3 4 5 6 ⑦ 8 9 10
Seat-belt wearing rate	–
National child restraint law	Yes
Children seated in front seat	Not restricted[b]
Child restraint required	Up to 2 yrs/15 kg
Child restraint standard referred to and/or specified	No
Enforcement	–
% children using child restraints	–
National law on mobile phone use while driving	Yes
Ban on hand-held mobile phone use	Yes
Ban on hands-free mobile phone use	Yes
National drug-driving law	Yes

[b] Except for children under 2 yrs or 15 kg who are required to be transported in a child restraint

Deaths by road user category

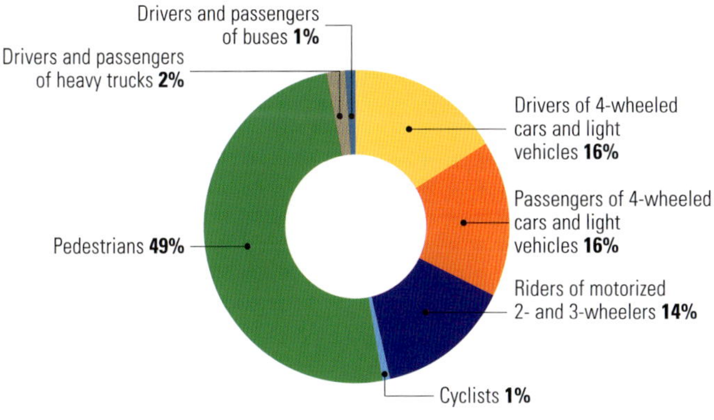

Source: 2016, Civil National Police

Trends in reported road traffic deaths

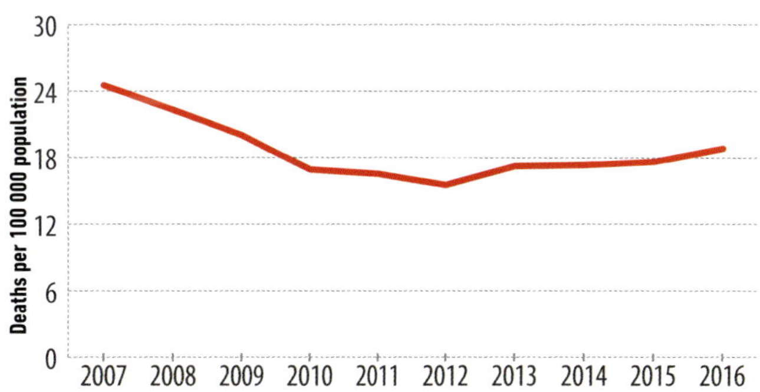

Source: Civil National Police and Institute of Legal Medicine

Equatorial Guinea

Population: 1 221 490 | Income group: Middle | Gross national income per capita: US$ 6 550

INSTITUTIONAL FRAMEWORK

Lead agency	General Directorate of Traffic and Road Safety, Ministry of the Interior and Local Corporations
Funded in national budget	Yes
National road safety strategy	No
Funding to implement strategy	–
Fatality reduction target	–

SAFER ROADS AND MOBILITY

Audits or star rating required for new road infrastructure	No
Design standards for the safety of pedestrians / cyclists	No
Inspections / star rating of existing roads	–
Investments to upgrade high risk locations	–
Policies & investment in urban public transport	No

SAFER VEHICLES

Total registered vehicles	143 000
Cars and 4-wheeled light vehicles	–
Motorized 2- and 3-wheelers	–
Heavy trucks	–
Buses	–
Other	–
Vehicle standards applied (UNECE WP.29)	
Frontal impact standard	No
Electronic stability control	No
Pedestrian protection	No
Motorcycle anti-lock braking system	No

POST-CRASH CARE

National emergency care access number	National, multiple numbers
Trauma registry	National
Formal certification for prehospital providers	Yes
National assessment of emergency care systems	Yes

DATA

Reported road traffic fatalities (2011)	41[a]
WHO estimated road traffic fatalities (2016)	300 (95% CI 221 - 379)
WHO estimated rate per 100 000 population (2016)	24.6

[a] General Directorate of Traffic and Road Safety. Died at scene of crash

SAFER ROAD USERS

National speed limit law	Yes
Max urban speed limit	60 km/h
Max rural speed limit	110 km/h
Max motorway speed limit	No
Local authorities can modify limits	Yes
Enforcement	⓪ 1 2 3 4 5 6 7 8 9 10
Predominant type of enforcement	–
National drink-driving law	Yes
BAC limit – general population	≤ 0.08 g/dl
BAC limit – young or novice drivers	≤ 0.08 g/dl
Random breath testing carried out	No
Testing carried out in case of fatal crash	–
Enforcement	–
% road traffic deaths involving alcohol	–
National motorcycle helmet law	Yes
Applies to drivers and passengers	Yes
Helmet fastening required	No
Helmet standard referred to and/or specified	No
Children passengers on motorcycles	Prohibited under 5 yrs
Enforcement	⓪ 1 2 3 4 5 6 7 8 9 10
Helmet wearing rate	–
National seat-belt law	Yes
Applies to front and rear seat occupants	No
Enforcement	0 1 ② 3 4 5 6 7 8 9 10
Seat-belt wearing rate	–
National child restraint law	No
Children seated in front seat	Not restricted
Child restraint required	–
Child restraint standard referred to and/or specified	–
Enforcement	–
% children using child restraints	–
National law on mobile phone use while driving	Yes
Ban on hand-held mobile phone use	Yes
Ban on hands-free mobile phone use	Yes
National drug-driving law	No

Deaths by road user category

Trends in reported road traffic deaths

Legislative review conducted by WHO. Vehicle safety data from UNECE WP29. Other data collected by questionnaire and cleared by Ministry of the Interior and Local Corporations.

Eritrea

Population: 4 954 645 | Income group: Low | Gross national income per capita: US$ 520[a]

INSTITUTIONAL FRAMEWORK	
Lead agency	Land Transport Authority, Ministry of Transport and Communication
Funded in national budget	Yes
National road safety strategy	Yes
Funding to implement strategy	Partially funded
Fatality reduction target	5% (2012-2016)
SAFER ROADS AND MOBILITY	
Audits or star rating required for new road infrastructure	Partial
Design standards for the safety of pedestrians / cyclists	Yes
Inspections / star rating of existing roads	Yes
Investments to upgrade high risk locations	Yes
Policies & investment in urban public transport	Yes
SAFER VEHICLES	
Total registered vehicles for 2016	72 405
Cars and 4-wheeled light vehicles	42 468
Motorized 2- and 3-wheelers	4 035
Heavy trucks	21 137
Buses	4 765
Other	0
Vehicle standards applied (UNECE WP.29)	
Frontal impact standard	No
Electronic stability control	No
Pedestrian protection	No
Motorcycle anti-lock braking system	No
POST-CRASH CARE	
National emergency care access number	Partial coverage
Trauma registry	Some facilities
Formal certification for prehospital providers	No
National assessment of emergency care systems	No
DATA	
Reported road traffic fatalities (2016)	130[b] (81% M, 19% F)
WHO estimated road traffic fatalities (2016)	1 255 (95% CI 1 025 - 1 485)
WHO estimated rate per 100 000 population (2016)	25.3

[a] Data available only for 2011
[b] Eritrean Police 2016 Annual report. Died within 30 days of crash

SAFER ROAD USERS	
National speed limit law	Yes
Max urban speed limit	60 km/h
Max rural speed limit	100 km/h
Max motorway speed limit	No
Local authorities can modify limits	No
Enforcement	0 1 2 3 4 5 (6) 7 8 9 10
Predominant type of enforcement	Manual
National drink-driving law	Yes
BAC limit – general population	≤ 0.05 g/dl
BAC limit – young or novice drivers	≤ 0.05 g/dl
Random breath testing carried out	Yes[c]
Testing carried out in case of fatal crash	No
Enforcement	0 1 2 3 4 5 6 (7) 8 9 10
% road traffic deaths involving alcohol	–
National motorcycle helmet law	Yes
Applies to drivers and passengers	Yes
Helmet fastening required	No
Helmet standard referred to and/or specified	No
Children passengers on motorcycles	Not restricted
Enforcement	0 1 2 3 4 5 6 7 (8) 9 10
Helmet wearing rate	95% Drivers[d], 95% Passengers[d]
National seat-belt law	Yes
Applies to front and rear seat occupants	Yes
Enforcement	0 1 2 3 4 5 6 7 (8) 9 10
Seat-belt wearing rate	80% Drivers[d], 80% Front seats[d]
National child restraint law	No[e]
Children seated in front seat	Prohibited under 9 yrs[f]
Child restraint required	–
Child restraint standard referred to and/or specified	–
Enforcement	–
% children using child restraints	–
National law on mobile phone use while driving	Yes
Ban on hand-held mobile phone use	Yes
Ban on hands-free mobile phone use	No
National drug-driving law	Yes

[c] Legislation requires probable cause to test drivers
[d] 2016, Eritrean Police
[e] Legislation refers to the use of child restraint or seat belts for "children over 9" while children under 3 years are required to be placed in a restraint only while seated in the front
[f] Except for an infant under 3 years fitted in a proper restraint

Deaths by road user category

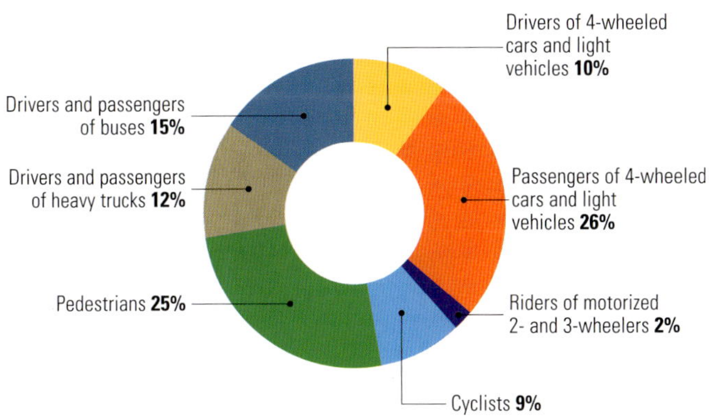

Source: 2016, Eritrean Police 2016 Annual Report

Trends in reported road traffic deaths

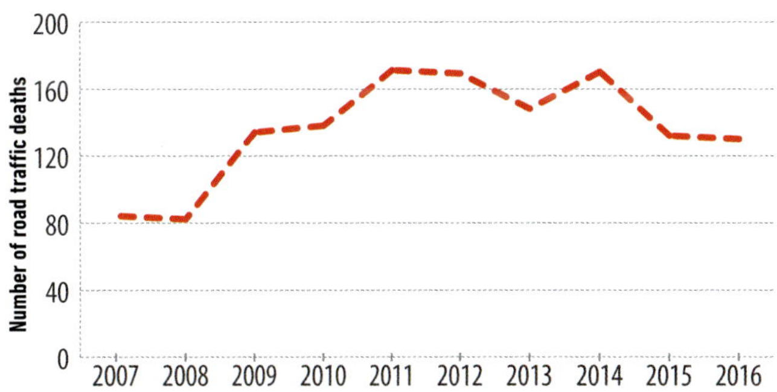

Source: Eritrean Police 2016 Annual Report

Estonia

Population: 1 312 442 | Income group: High | Gross national income per capita: US$ 17 750

INSTITUTIONAL FRAMEWORK

Lead agency	**Governmental Committee of Traffic Safety, Traffic Safety Department**
Funded in national budget	Yes
National road safety strategy	**Yes**
Funding to implement strategy	Partially funded
Fatality reduction target	51% (2015-2025)

SAFER ROADS AND MOBILITY

Audits or star rating required for new road infrastructure	Partial
Design standards for the safety of pedestrians / cyclists	Yes
Inspections / star rating of existing roads	Yes
Investments to upgrade high risk locations	Yes
Policies & investment in urban public transport	No

SAFER VEHICLES

Total registered vehicles for 2016	**865 040**
Cars and 4-wheeled light vehicles	703 151
Motorized 2- and 3-wheelers	48 834
Heavy trucks	108 217
Buses	4 838
Other	0
Vehicle standards applied (UNECE WP.29)	
Frontal impact standard	Yes
Electronic stability control	Yes
Pedestrian protection	Yes
Motorcycle anti-lock braking system	Yes

POST-CRASH CARE

National emergency care access number	National, single number
Trauma registry	None
Formal certification for prehospital providers	No
National assessment of emergency care systems	No

DATA

Reported road traffic fatalities (2016)	71[a] (70% M, 30% F)
WHO estimated road traffic fatalities (2016)	80
WHO estimated rate per 100 000 population (2016)	6.1

[a] Police and Border Guard Board's analysis and data warehouse information system. Died within 30 days of crash

SAFER ROAD USERS

National speed limit law	**Yes**
Max urban speed limit	50 km/h[b]
Max rural speed limit	90 km/h
Max motorway speed limit	No[c]
Local authorities can modify limits	Yes
Enforcement	0 1 2 3 4 5 6 ⑦ 8 9 10
Predominant type of enforcement	Automated
National drink-driving law	**Yes**
BAC limit – general population	< 0.02 g/dl
BAC limit – young or novice drivers	< 0.02 g/dl
Random breath testing carried out	Yes
Testing carried out in case of fatal crash	All drivers tested
Enforcement	0 1 2 3 4 5 6 7 ⑧ 9 10
% road traffic deaths involving alcohol	10%[d]
National motorcycle helmet law	**Yes**
Applies to drivers and passengers	Yes
Helmet fastening required	Yes
Helmet standard referred to and/or specified	Yes
Children passengers on motorcycles	Prohibited under 12 yrs
Enforcement	0 1 2 3 4 5 6 7 8 ⑨ 10
Helmet wearing rate	98% Drivers[e]
National seat-belt law	**Yes**
Applies to front and rear seat occupants	Yes
Enforcement	0 1 2 3 4 5 6 ⑦ 8 9 10
Seat-belt wearing rate	97 Front seats[f], 82% Rear seats[f]
National child restraint law	**Yes[g]**
Children seated in front seat	Not restricted
Child restraint required	—[g]
Child restraint standard referred to and/or specified	No
Enforcement	0 1 2 3 4 5 6 7 ⑧ 9 10
% children using child restraints	98%[f]
National law on mobile phone use while driving	**Yes**
Ban on hand-held mobile phone use	Yes
Ban on hands-free mobile phone use	No
National drug-driving law	**Yes**

[b] Can be increased up to 90 km/h on certain conditions
[c] No motorways in the country
[d] 2016, Police and Border Guard Board's analysis and data warehouse information system
[e] 2015, Motorcyclist's travel, driving and safety habits
[f] 2016, Traffic Behavior Monitoring 2016
[g] The legislation generally states that children not tall enough to wear a seat belt must be secured by a safety device corresponding to the height and weight of the child but does not specify age/height/weight group covered

Deaths by road user category

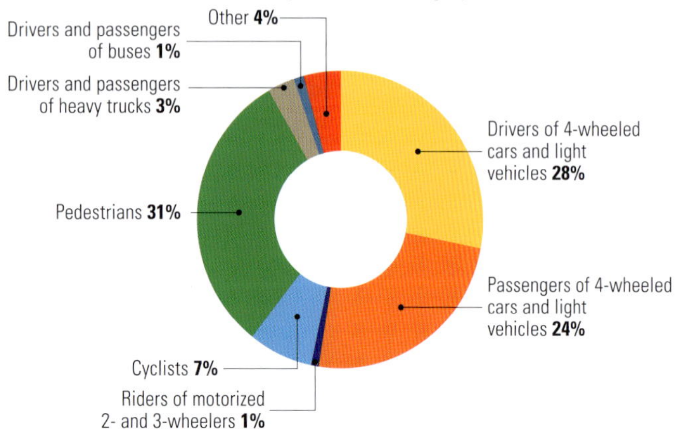

Source: 2016, Police and Border Guard Board's analysis and data warehouse information system

Trends in reported road traffic deaths

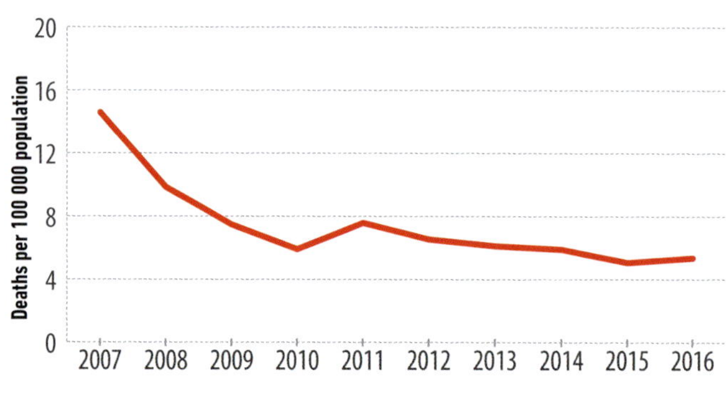

Source: Police and Border Guard Board's analysis and data warehouse information system and Statistics Estonia

Legislative review conducted by WHO. Vehicle safety data from UNECE WP.29. Other data collected by questionnaire and cleared by Estonian Road Administration.

Eswatini

Population: 1 343 098 | Income group: Middle | Gross national income per capita: US$ 2 830

INSTITUTIONAL FRAMEWORK	
Lead agency	Road Safety Council, Ministry of Works and Transport
Funded in national budget	Yes
National road safety strategy	No
Funding to implement strategy	–
Fatality reduction target	–
SAFER ROADS AND MOBILITY	
Audits or star rating required for new road infrastructure	Yes
Design standards for the safety of pedestrians / cyclists	Partial
Inspections / star rating of existing roads	Yes
Investments to upgrade high risk locations	No
Policies & investment in urban public transport	Yes
SAFER VEHICLES	
Total registered vehicles for 2016	99 830
Cars and 4-wheeled light vehicles	–
Motorized 2- and 3-wheelers	–
Heavy trucks	–
Buses	–
Other	–
Vehicle standards applied (UNECE WP.29)	
Frontal impact standard	No
Electronic stability control	No
Pedestrian protection	No
Motorcycle anti-lock braking system	No
POST-CRASH CARE	
National emergency care access number	National, multiple numbers
Trauma registry	None
Formal certification for prehospital providers	Yes
National assessment of emergency care systems	No
DATA	
Reported road traffic fatalities (2016)	203[a] (71% M, 29% F)
WHO estimated road traffic fatalities (2016)	361 (95% CI 296 - 427)
WHO estimated rate per 100 000 population (2016)	26.9

[a] Royal Swaziland Police Annual Report. Unlimited time period following crash

SAFER ROAD USERS	
National speed limit law	Yes
Max urban speed limit	100 km/h[b]
Max rural speed limit	100 km/h[b]
Max motorway speed limit	100 km/h[b]
Local authorities can modify limits	Yes
Enforcement	0 1 2 3 4 5 **6** 7 8 9 10
Predominant type of enforcement	Manual
National drink-driving law	Yes
BAC limit – general population	< 0.05 g/dl
BAC limit – young or novice drivers	< 0.05 g/dl
Random breath testing carried out	Yes[c]
Testing carried out in case of fatal crash	No
Enforcement	0 1 2 3 4 5 6 7 8 **9** 10
% road traffic deaths involving alcohol	–
National motorcycle helmet law	Yes
Applies to drivers and passengers	Yes
Helmet fastening required	Yes
Helmet standard referred to and/or specified	Yes
Children passengers on motorcycles	Not restricted
Enforcement	0 1 2 3 4 **5** 6 7 8 9 10
Helmet wearing rate	–
National seat-belt law	Yes
Applies to front and rear seat occupants	No
Enforcement	0 1 2 3 4 5 6 7 8 **9** 10
Seat-belt wearing rate	–
National child restraint law	No
Children seated in front seat	Not restricted
Child restraint required	–
Child restraint standard referred to and/or specified	–
Enforcement	–
% children using child restraints	–
National law on mobile phone use while driving	Yes
Ban on hand-held mobile phone use	Yes
Ban on hands-free mobile phone use	No
National drug-driving law	Yes

[b] Speed limit for public roads is 100 km/h for a road with a surface of concrete, bitumen or tar and 80 km/h for other roads

[c] Legislation requires probable cause to test drivers

Deaths by road user category

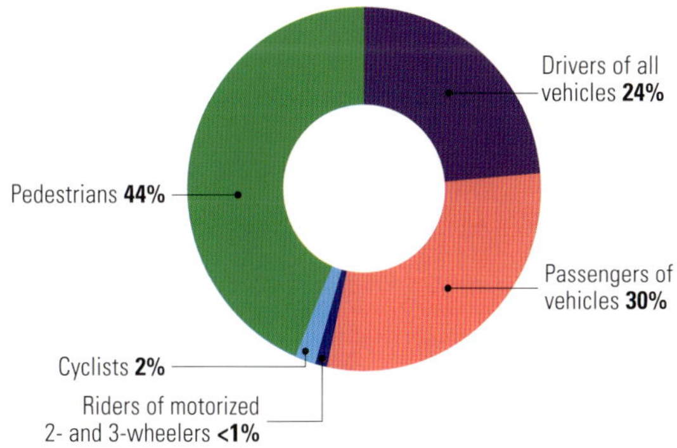

Source: 2016, Royal Swaziland Police Annual Report

Trends in reported road traffic deaths

Source: Central Statistics Office

Ethiopia

Population: 102 403 200 | Income group: Low | Gross national income per capita: US$ 660

INSTITUTIONAL FRAMEWORK

Lead agency	Ministry of Transport
Funded in national budget	Yes
National road safety strategy	Yes
Funding to implement strategy	Partially funded
Fatality reduction target	50% (2011-2020)

SAFER ROADS AND MOBILITY

Audits or star rating required for new road infrastructure	No
Design standards for the safety of pedestrians / cyclists	Partial
Inspections / star rating of existing roads	No
Investments to upgrade high risk locations	No
Policies & investment in urban public transport	Yes

SAFER VEHICLES

Total registered vehicles for 2015/2016	708 416
Cars and 4-wheeled light vehicles	–
Motorized 2- and 3-wheelers	–
Heavy trucks	–
Buses	–
Other	–
Vehicle standards applied (UNECE WP.29)	
Frontal impact standard	No
Electronic stability control	No
Pedestrian protection	No
Motorcycle anti-lock braking system	No

POST-CRASH CARE

National emergency care access number	National, single number
Trauma registry	Some facilities
Formal certification for prehospital providers	Yes
National assessment of emergency care systems	No

DATA

Reported road traffic fatalities (2015/2016)	4 352[a] (78% M, 22% F)
WHO estimated road traffic fatalities (2016)	27 326 (95% CI 21 494 - 33 159)
WHO estimated rate per 100 000 population (2016)	26.7

[a] Federal Police Commission. Died within 30 days of crash

SAFER ROAD USERS

National speed limit law	Yes
Max urban speed limit	60 km/h
Max rural speed limit	70 km/h
Max motorway speed limit	100 km/h
Local authorities can modify limits	Yes
Enforcement	0 1 (2) 3 4 5 6 7 8 9 10
Predominant type of enforcement	Manual
National drink-driving law	Yes
BAC limit – general population	≤ 0.08 g/dl
BAC limit – young or novice drivers	≤ 0.08 g/dl
Random breath testing carried out	Yes[b]
Testing carried out in case of fatal crash	All drivers tested
Enforcement	0 1 (2) 3 4 5 6 7 8 9 10
% road traffic deaths involving alcohol	4%[c]
National motorcycle helmet law	Yes
Applies to drivers and passengers	Yes
Helmet fastening required	No
Helmet standard referred to and/or specified	No
Children passengers on motorcycles	Not restricted
Enforcement	0 1 (2) 3 4 5 6 7 8 9 10
Helmet wearing rate	–
National seat-belt law	Yes
Applies to front and rear seat occupants	Yes
Enforcement	0 1 2 3 4 (5) 6 7 8 9 10
Seat-belt wearing rate	<1% All occupants[d]
National child restraint law	No[e]
Children seated in front seat	Prohibited under 13 yrs
Child restraint required	–
Child restraint standard referred to and/or specified	–
Enforcement	–
% children using child restraints	–
National law on mobile phone use while driving	Yes
Ban on hand-held mobile phone use	Yes
Ban on hands-free mobile phone use	Yes
National drug-driving law	Yes

[b] Legislation requires probable cause to test drivers
[c] 2012/2013, Ethiopian Federal Police Commission
[d] 2013/2014, Ethiopian Federal Police Commission
[e] Legislation requires that children under 7 years be either accompanied by an adult or "hugged by an instrument made for safety purpose"

Deaths by road user category

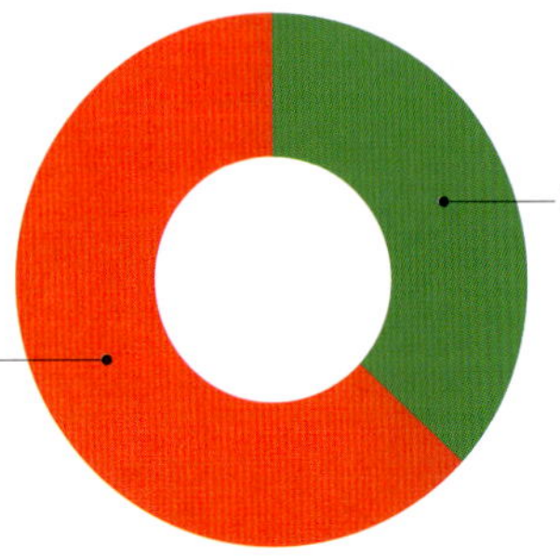

Trends in reported road traffic deaths

Source: Ministry of Transport

Fiji

Population: 898 760 | Income group: Middle | Gross national income per capita: US$ 4 840

INSTITUTIONAL FRAMEWORK	
Lead agency	Land Transport Authority
Funded in national budget	Yes
National road safety strategy	Yes
Funding to implement strategy	Partially funded
Fatality reduction target	50% (2011-2020)
SAFER ROADS AND MOBILITY	
Audits or star rating required for new road infrastructure	Yes
Design standards for the safety of pedestrians / cyclists	Partial
Inspections / star rating of existing roads	Yes
Investments to upgrade high risk locations	Yes
Policies & investment in urban public transport	Yes
SAFER VEHICLES	
Total registered vehicles for 2016	110 763
Cars and 4-wheeled light vehicles	–
Motorized 2- and 3-wheelers	–
Heavy trucks	–
Buses	–
Other	–
Vehicle standards applied (UNECE WP.29)	
Frontal impact standard	No
Electronic stability control	No
Pedestrian protection	No
Motorcycle anti-lock braking system	No
POST-CRASH CARE	
National emergency care access number	National, multiple numbers
Trauma registry	None
Formal certification for prehospital providers	No
National assessment of emergency care systems	No
DATA	
Reported road traffic fatalities (2016)	60[a] (75% M, 25% F)
WHO estimated road traffic fatalities (2016)	86
WHO estimated rate per 100 000 population (2016)	9.6

[a] Fiji Police Force, Road Traffic Accidents Annual Report 2016. Died within 30 days of crash

SAFER ROAD USERS	
National speed limit law	Yes
Max urban speed limit	50 km/h
Max rural speed limit	80 km/h
Max motorway speed limit	–[b]
Local authorities can modify limits	No
Enforcement	0 1 2 3 4 5 6 (7) 8 9 10
Predominant type of enforcement	Manual and automated
National drink-driving law	Yes
BAC limit – general population	≤ 0.08 g/dl
BAC limit – young or novice drivers	0.00 g/dl
Random breath testing carried out	Yes
Testing carried out in case of fatal crash	Some drivers tested
Enforcement	0 1 2 3 4 5 (6) 7 8 9 10
% road traffic deaths involving alcohol	5%[c]
National motorcycle helmet law	Yes
Applies to drivers and passengers	Yes
Helmet fastening required	Yes
Helmet standard referred to and/or specified	No
Children passengers on motorcycles	Prohibited under 8 yrs[d]
Enforcement	0 1 2 3 4 5 6 7 (8) 9 10
Helmet wearing rate	80% Drivers[e], 80% Passengers[e]
National seat-belt law	Yes
Applies to front and rear seat occupants	Yes
Enforcement	0 1 2 3 4 5 6 (7) 8 9 10
Seat-belt wearing rate	75% Front seats[f], 5% Rear seats[f]
National child restraint law	Yes[g]
Children seated in front seat	Allowed in a child restraint
Child restraint required	Up to 8 yrs
Child restraint standard referred to and/or specified	No
Enforcement	0 1 2 (3) 4 5 6 7 8 9 10
% children using child restraints	–
National law on mobile phone use while driving	Yes
Ban on hand-held mobile phone use	Yes
Ban on hands-free mobile phone use	Yes
National drug-driving law	Yes

[b] No motorways in the country
[c] 2016, Fiji Police Force, Road Traffic Accidents Annual Report
[d] Except if motorcycle is fitted with one additional seat designed to transport children
[e] 2016, Observation by Land Transport Authority (LTA) and Police enforcement officers
[f] 2016, Fiji Police Annual Booking Report
[g] The obligation to use a child restraint for children under 8 years sitting in the rear is subject to the availability of a restraint system in the car

Deaths by road user category

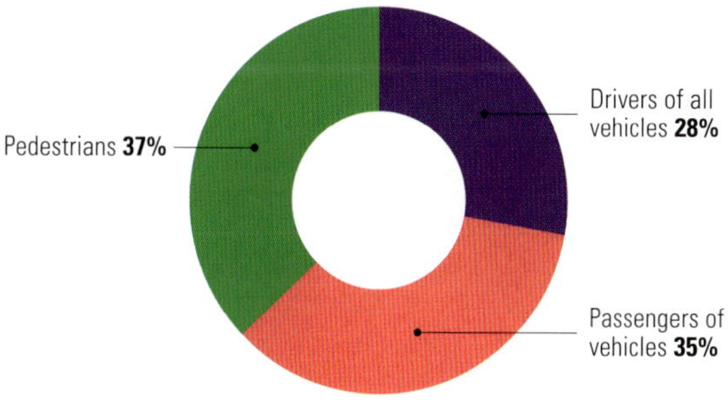

Source: 2016, Fiji Police Force, Road Traffic Accidents Annual Report

Trends in reported road traffic deaths

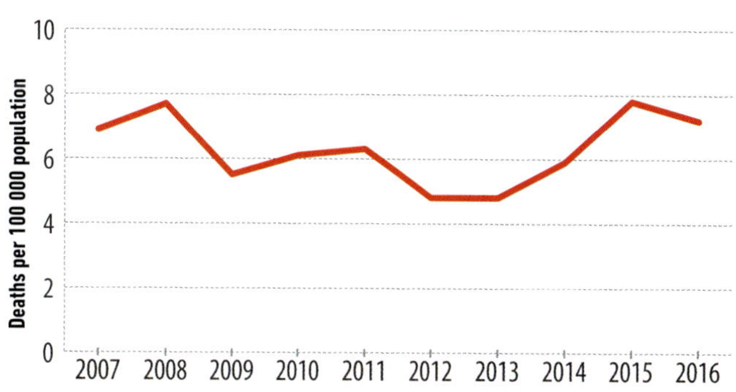

Source: Land Transport Authority, "Factsheet 4: Ratios - Population & Vehicle Registration Ratios over 10 Year Period"

Legislative review conducted by WHO. Vehicle safety data from UNECE WP29. Other data collected by questionnaire and cleared by the Land Transport Authority.

Finland

Population: 5 503 132 | Income group: High | Gross national income per capita: US$ 44 730

INSTITUTIONAL FRAMEWORK

Lead agency	Ministry of Transport and Communications
Funded in national budget	Yes
National road safety strategy	Yes
Funding to implement strategy	Partially funded
Fatality reduction target	< 136 fatalities by 2020 (2010-2020)

SAFER ROADS AND MOBILITY

Audits or star rating required for new road infrastructure	Yes
Design standards for the safety of pedestrians / cyclists	Yes
Inspections / star rating of existing roads	Yes
Investments to upgrade high risk locations	Yes
Policies & investment in urban public transport	Yes

SAFER VEHICLES

Total registered vehicles for 2016	5 217 850
Cars and 4-wheeled light vehicles	3 781 441
Motorized 2- and 3-wheelers	592 960
Heavy trucks	146 624
Buses	17 536
Other	679 289
Vehicle standards applied (UNECE WP.29)	
Frontal impact standard	Yes
Electronic stability control	Yes
Pedestrian protection	Yes
Motorcycle anti-lock braking system	Yes

POST-CRASH CARE

National emergency care access number	National, single number
Trauma registry	National
Formal certification for prehospital providers	Yes
National assessment of emergency care systems	Yes

DATA

Reported road traffic fatalities (2016)	252[a] (81% M, 19% F)
WHO estimated road traffic fatalities (2016)	260
WHO estimated rate per 100 000 population (2016)	4.7

[a] Statistics Finland. Died within 30 days of crash

SAFER ROAD USERS

National speed limit law	Yes
Max urban speed limit	50 km/h
Max rural speed limit	80 km/h
Max motorway speed limit	120 km/h
Local authorities can modify limits	Yes
Enforcement	0 1 2 3 4 5 6 7 ⑧ 9 10
Predominant type of enforcement	Manual and automated
National drink-driving law	Yes
BAC limit – general population	< 0.05 g/dl
BAC limit – young or novice drivers	< 0.05 g/dl
Random breath testing carried out	Yes
Testing carried out in case of fatal crash	All drivers tested
Enforcement	0 1 2 3 4 5 6 7 8 ⑨ 10
% road traffic deaths involving alcohol	24%[b]
National motorcycle helmet law	Yes
Applies to drivers and passengers	Yes
Helmet fastening required	No
Helmet standard referred to and/or specified	No
Children passengers on motorcycles	Not restricted
Enforcement	0 1 2 3 4 5 6 7 8 ⑨ 10
Helmet wearing rate	98% All riders[c]
National seat-belt law	Yes
Applies to front and rear seat occupants	Yes
Enforcement	0 1 2 3 4 5 6 7 ⑧ 9 10
Seat-belt wearing rate	95% Front seats[d], 85% Rear seats[d]
National child restraint law	Yes
Children seated in front seat	Allowed in a child restraint[e]
Child restraint required	Up to 135 cm
Child restraint standard referred to and/or specified	Yes
Enforcement	0 1 2 3 4 5 6 7 ⑧ 9 10
% children using child restraints	97%[d]
National law on mobile phone use while driving	Yes
Ban on hand-held mobile phone use	Yes
Ban on hands-free mobile phone use	No
National drug-driving law	Yes

[b] 2016, Statistics Finland
[c] 2011, Finnish Road Safety Council, Research survey on moped drivers among students
[d] 2016, Finnish Road Safety Council
[e] Provided that airbag is deactivated if child is in a rear-facing child restraint system

Deaths by road user category

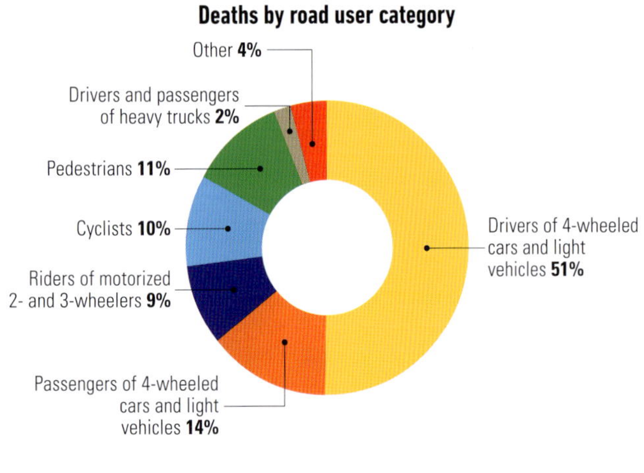

Source: 2016, Statistics Finland

Trends in reported road traffic deaths

Source: Statistics Finland

Legislative review conducted by WHO. Vehicle safety data from UNECE WP29. Other data collected by questionnaire and cleared by Finnish Transport Safety Agency

France

Population: 64 720 688 | Income group: High | Gross national income per capita: US$ 38 950

INSTITUTIONAL FRAMEWORK	
Lead agency	Inter-ministerial Delegation for Road Safety, Ministry of Interior
Funded in national budget	Yes
National road safety strategy	Yes
Funding to implement strategy	Fully funded
Fatality reduction target	50% (2010-2020)
SAFER ROADS AND MOBILITY	
Audits or star rating required for new road infrastructure	Partial
Design standards for the safety of pedestrians / cyclists	Yes
Inspections / star rating of existing roads	Yes
Investments to upgrade high risk locations	Yes
Policies & investment in urban public transport	Yes
SAFER VEHICLES	
Total registered vehicles for 2015	42 363 000
Cars and 4-wheeled light vehicles	37 920 000
Motorized 2- and 3-wheelers	3 800 000
Heavy trucks	550 000
Buses	93 000
Other	0
Vehicle standards applied (UNECE WP.29)	
Frontal impact standard	Yes
Electronic stability control	Yes
Pedestrian protection	Yes
Motorcycle anti-lock braking system	Yes
POST-CRASH CARE	
National emergency care access number	National, single number
Trauma registry	Subnational
Formal certification for prehospital providers	–
National assessment of emergency care systems	No
DATA	
Reported road traffic fatalities (2016)	3 477 [a] (76% M, 24% F)
WHO estimated road traffic fatalities (2016)	3 585
WHO estimated rate per 100 000 population (2016)	5.5

[a] National Interdepartmental Observatory of Road Safety (ONISR). Died within 30 days of crash

SAFER ROAD USERS	
National speed limit law	Yes
Max urban speed limit	50 km/h
Max rural speed limit	90 km/h
Max motorway speed limit	130 km/h
Local authorities can modify limits	Yes
Enforcement	0 1 2 3 4 5 6 7 ⑧ 9 10
Predominant type of enforcement	Automated
National drink-driving law	Yes
BAC limit – general population	< 0.05 g/dl
BAC limit – young or novice drivers	< 0.02 g/dl
Random breath testing carried out	Yes
Testing carried out in case of fatal crash	All drivers tested
Enforcement	0 1 2 3 4 5 6 ⑦ 8 9 10
% road traffic deaths involving alcohol	29% [b]
National motorcycle helmet law	Yes
Applies to drivers and passengers	Yes
Helmet fastening required	Yes
Helmet standard referred to and/or specified	Yes
Children passengers on motorcycles	Not restricted
Enforcement	0 1 2 3 4 5 6 7 8 ⑨ 10
Helmet wearing rate	98% All riders [b]
National seat-belt law	Yes
Applies to front and rear seat occupants	Yes
Enforcement	0 1 2 3 4 5 6 7 ⑧ 9 10
Seat-belt wearing rate	98% Front seats [b], 88% Rear seats [b]
National child restraint law	Yes
Children seated in front seat	Prohibited under 10 yrs [c]
Child restraint required	Up to 10 yrs
Child restraint standard referred to and/or specified	Yes
Enforcement	0 1 2 3 4 5 6 7 8 ⑨ 10
% children using child restraints	–
National law on mobile phone use while driving	Yes
Ban on hand-held mobile phone use	Yes
Ban on hands-free mobile phone use	No
National drug-driving law	Yes

[b] 2016, National Interdepartmental Observatory of Road Safety (ONISR).

[c] By exception, children under 10 years can sit in the front if placed in a rear-facing child restraint (if front airbag is deactivated) or if there are no available rear seats

Deaths by road user category

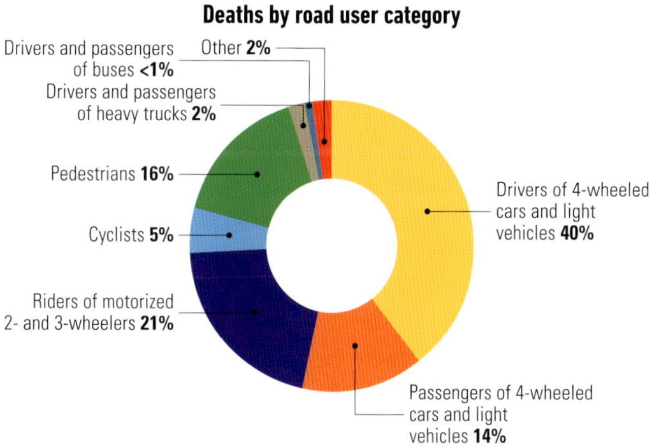

Source: 2016, National Interdepartmental Observatory of Road Safety (ONISR)

Trends in reported road traffic deaths

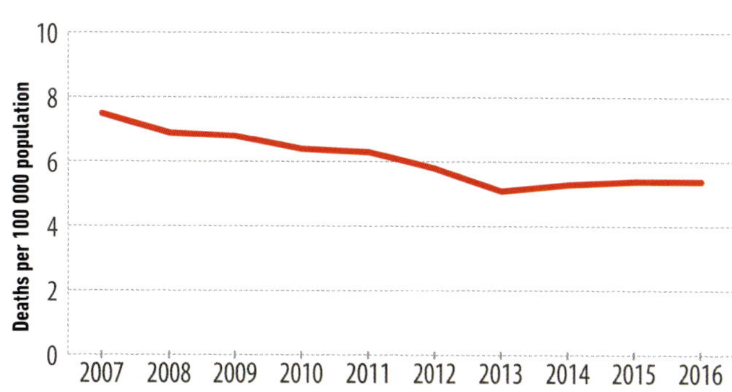

Source: National Interdepartmental Observatory of Road Safety (ONISR, fatality data)

Legislative review conducted by WHO. Vehicle safety data from UNECE WP29. Other data collected by questionnaire and cleared by Ministry of the Interior.

Gabon

Population: 1 979 786 | Income group: Middle | Gross national income per capita: US$ 7 210

INSTITUTIONAL FRAMEWORK	
Lead agency	General Directorate of Road Safety (DGSR), Ministry of Transport and Logistics
Funded in national budget	Yes
National road safety strategy	Yes
Funding to implement strategy	Not funded
Fatality reduction target	–
SAFER ROADS AND MOBILITY	
Audits or star rating required for new road infrastructure	–
Design standards for the safety of pedestrians / cyclists	No
Inspections / star rating of existing roads	–
Investments to upgrade high risk locations	Yes
Policies & investment in urban public transport	Yes
SAFER VEHICLES	
Total registered vehicles	–
Cars and 4-wheeled light vehicles	–
Motorized 2- and 3-wheelers	–
Heavy trucks	–
Buses	–
Other	–
Vehicle standards applied (UNECE WP.29)	
Frontal impact standard	No
Electronic stability control	No
Pedestrian protection	No
Motorcycle anti-lock braking system	No
POST-CRASH CARE	
National emergency care access number	Partial coverage
Trauma registry	Some facilities
Formal certification for prehospital providers	Yes
National assessment of emergency care systems	No
DATA	
Reported road traffic fatalities (2016)	54[a]
WHO estimated road traffic fatalities (2016)	460 (95% CI 382 - 538)
WHO estimated rate per 100 000 population (2016)	23.2

[a] National Police Force (data for Libreville). Died within 30 days of crash

SAFER ROAD USERS	
National speed limit law	Yes
Max urban speed limit	60 km/h
Max rural speed limit	110 km/h
Max motorway speed limit	No
Local authorities can modify limits	Yes
Enforcement	0 ① 2 3 4 5 6 7 8 9 10
Predominant type of enforcement	–
National drink-driving law	Yes
BAC limit – general population	≤ 0.08 g/dl
BAC limit – young or novice drivers	≤ 0.08 g/dl
Random breath testing carried out	Yes
Testing carried out in case of fatal crash	No
Enforcement	0 ① 2 3 4 5 6 7 8 9 10
% road traffic deaths involving alcohol	–
National motorcycle helmet law	Yes
Applies to drivers and passengers	Yes
Helmet fastening required	No
Helmet standard referred to and/or specified	No
Children passengers on motorcycles	Prohibited under 5 yrs
Enforcement	0 1 2 3 4 ⑤ 6 7 8 9 10
Helmet wearing rate	–
National seat-belt law	Yes
Applies to front and rear seat occupants	No
Enforcement	0 1 2 3 4 5 6 ⑦ 8 9 10
Seat-belt wearing rate	–
National child restraint law	No
Children seated in front seat	Not restricted
Child restraint required	–
Child restraint standard referred to and/or specified	–
Enforcement	–
% children using child restraints	–
National law on mobile phone use while driving	Yes
Ban on hand-held mobile phone use	Yes
Ban on hands-free mobile phone use	Yes
National drug-driving law	No

Deaths by road user category

Trends in reported road traffic deaths

Source: General Directorate of Road Safety (DGSR)

Gambia

Population: 2 038 501 | Income group: Low | Gross national income per capita: US$ 440

INSTITUTIONAL FRAMEWORK	
Lead agency	Directorate of Planning, Ministry of Transport, Works and Infrastructure
Funded in national budget	Yes
National road safety strategy	No
Funding to implement strategy	–
Fatality reduction target	–

SAFER ROADS AND MOBILITY	
Audits or star rating required for new road infrastructure	Partial
Design standards for the safety of pedestrians / cyclists	Partial
Inspections / star rating of existing roads	No
Investments to upgrade high risk locations	Yes
Policies & investment in urban public transport	No

SAFER VEHICLES	
Total registered vehicles for 2005-2016	84 963
Cars and 4-wheeled light vehicles	33 734
Motorized 2- and 3-wheelers	28 118
Heavy trucks	3 940
Buses	6 947
Other	12 224
Vehicle standards applied (UNECE WP.29)	
Frontal impact standard	No
Electronic stability control	No
Pedestrian protection	No
Motorcycle anti-lock braking system	No

POST-CRASH CARE	
National emergency care access number	None
Trauma registry	Subnational
Formal certification for prehospital providers	No
National assessment of emergency care systems	No

DATA	
Reported road traffic fatalities (2016)	139 [a]
WHO estimated road traffic fatalities (2016)	605 (95% CI 484 - 726)
WHO estimated rate per 100 000 population (2016)	29.7

[a] Gambia Police Force. Time period following a crash not defined in legislation

SAFER ROAD USERS	
National speed limit law	Yes
Max urban speed limit	No
Max rural speed limit	No
Max motorway speed limit	No
Local authorities can modify limits	Yes
Enforcement	0 1 2 (3) 4 5 6 7 8 9 10
Predominant type of enforcement	Manual
National drink-driving law	Yes [b]
BAC limit – general population	–
BAC limit – young or novice drivers	–
Random breath testing carried out	No
Testing carried out in case of fatal crash	No
Enforcement	0 (1) 2 3 4 5 6 7 8 9 10
% road traffic deaths involving alcohol	2% [c]
National motorcycle helmet law	Yes
Applies to drivers and passengers	Yes
Helmet fastening required	No
Helmet standard referred to and/or specified	No
Children passengers on motorcycles	Not restricted
Enforcement	0 1 2 3 (4) 5 6 7 8 9 10
Helmet wearing rate	–
National seat-belt law	Yes
Applies to front and rear seat occupants	No
Enforcement	0 1 2 3 4 5 (6) 7 8 9 10
Seat-belt wearing rate	–
National child restraint law	Yes
Children seated in front seat	Allowed in a child restraint
Child restraint required	Up to 5 yrs
Child restraint standard referred to and/or specified	No
Enforcement	–
% children using child restraints	–
National law on mobile phone use while driving	Yes
Ban on hand-held mobile phone use	Yes
Ban on hands-free mobile phone use	No
National drug-driving law	Yes

[b] Not based on BAC
[c] 2013, The Gambia Police Accident Statistics Unit

Deaths by road user category

Trends in reported road traffic deaths

Source: : Gambia Police Force and Gambia Bureau of Statistics

Legislative review conducted by WHO. Vehicle safety data from UNECE WP29. Other data collected by questionnaire and cleared by Ministry of Transport, Works and Infrastructure.

Georgia

Population: 3 925 405 | Income group: Middle | Gross national income per capita: US$ 3 810

INSTITUTIONAL FRAMEWORK

Lead agency	Ministry of Economy and Sustainable Development of Georgia
Funded in national budget	Yes
National road safety strategy	Yes
Funding to implement strategy	Partially funded
Fatality reduction target	25% (2016-2020)

SAFER ROADS AND MOBILITY

Audits or star rating required for new road infrastructure	Yes
Design standards for the safety of pedestrians / cyclists	Partial
Inspections / star rating of existing roads	No
Investments to upgrade high risk locations	Yes
Policies & investment in urban public transport	Yes

SAFER VEHICLES

Total registered vehicles for 2016	1 126 470
Cars and 4-wheeled light vehicles	919 199
Motorized 2- and 3-wheelers	63 083
Heavy trucks	93 497
Buses	50 691
Other	0
Vehicle standards applied (UNECE WP.29)	
Frontal impact standard	No
Electronic stability control	No
Pedestrian protection	No
Motorcycle anti-lock braking system	No

POST-CRASH CARE

National emergency care access number	National, single number
Trauma registry	None
Formal certification for prehospital providers	Yes
National assessment of emergency care systems	No

DATA

Reported road traffic fatalities (2016)	581[a] (54% M, 20% F)
WHO estimated road traffic fatalities (2016)	599
WHO estimated rate per 100 000 population (2016)	15.3

[a] Ministry of Interior Affairs. Unlimited time period following crash

SAFER ROAD USERS

National speed limit law	Yes
Max urban speed limit	60 km/h
Max rural speed limit	90 km/h
Max motorway speed limit	110 km/h
Local authorities can modify limits	No
Enforcement	0 1 2 3 4 5 ⑥ 7 8 9 10
Predominant type of enforcement	Automated
National drink-driving law	Yes
BAC limit – general population	≤ 0.03 g/dl
BAC limit – young or novice drivers	≤ 0.03 g/dl
Random breath testing carried out	Yes[b]
Testing carried out in case of fatal crash	All drivers tested
Enforcement	0 1 2 3 4 5 6 ⑦ 8 9 10
% road traffic deaths involving alcohol	9%[c]
National motorcycle helmet law	Yes
Applies to drivers and passengers	Yes
Helmet fastening required	Yes
Helmet standard referred to and/or specified	No
Children passengers on motorcycles	Prohibited under 12 yrs
Enforcement	0 1 2 3 4 5 6 ⑦ 8 9 10
Helmet wearing rate	–
National seat-belt law	Yes
Applies to front and rear seat occupants	No
Enforcement	0 1 2 3 4 5 6 7 ⑧ 9 10
Seat-belt wearing rate	70% Drivers[d], 60% Front seats[d]
National child restraint law	No
Children seated in front seat	Prohibited under 12 yrs
Child restraint required	–
Child restraint standard referred to and/or specified	–
Enforcement	–
% children using child restraints	–
National law on mobile phone use while driving	Yes
Ban on hand-held mobile phone use	Yes
Ban on hands-free mobile phone use	No
National drug-driving law	Yes

[b] Legislation requires probable cause to test drivers
[c] 2016, Ministry of Interior Affairs (Patrol police)
[d] 2006, World Bank Survey on Seat Belt in Tbilisi

Deaths by road user category

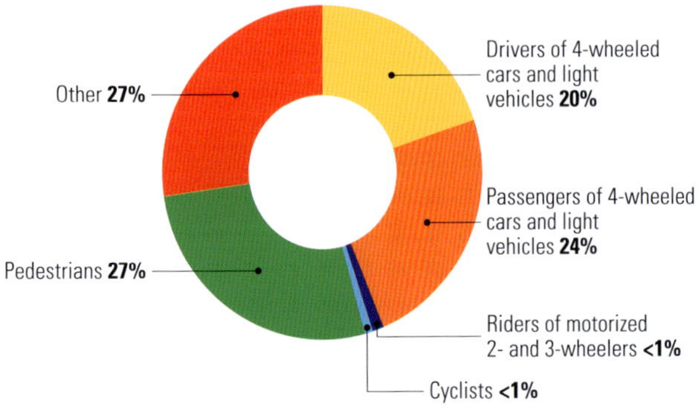

Source: 2016, Patrol police of the Ministry of Interior Affairs

Trends in reported road traffic deaths

Source: Ministry of Interior Affairs of Georgia

Legislative review conducted by WHO. Vehicle safety data from UNECE WP29. Other data collected by questionnaire and cleared by National Center for Disease Control and Public Health.

Germany

Population: 81 914 672 | Income group: High | Gross national income per capita: US$ 43 660

INSTITUTIONAL FRAMEWORK	
Lead agency	Federal Ministry of Transport and Digital Infrastructure (BMVI)
Funded in national budget	Yes
National road safety strategy	Yes
Funding to implement strategy	Partially funded
Fatality reduction target	40% (2011-2020)

SAFER ROADS AND MOBILITY	
Audits or star rating required for new road infrastructure	Yes
Design standards for the safety of pedestrians / cyclists	Yes
Inspections / star rating of existing roads	Yes
Investments to upgrade high risk locations	Yes
Policies & investment in urban public transport	No

SAFER VEHICLES	
Total registered vehicles for 2016	56 622 000
Cars and 4-wheeled light vehicles	45 071 000
Motorized 2- and 3-wheelers	6 248 000
Heavy trucks	4 942 000
Buses	78 000
Other	283 000
Vehicle standards applied (UNECE WP.29)	
Frontal impact standard	Yes
Electronic stability control	Yes
Pedestrian protection	Yes
Motorcycle anti-lock braking system	Yes

POST-CRASH CARE	
National emergency care access number	National, single number
Trauma registry	Some facilities
Formal certification for prehospital providers	Yes
National assessment of emergency care systems	Yes

DATA	
Reported road traffic fatalities (2016)	3 206 [a] (73% M, 27% F)
WHO estimated road traffic fatalities (2016)	3 327
WHO estimated rate per 100 000 population (2016)	4.1

[a] Federal Statistical Office. Died within 30 days of crash

SAFER ROAD USERS	
National speed limit law	Yes
Max urban speed limit	50 km/h
Max rural speed limit	100 km/h
Max motorway speed limit	No [b]
Local authorities can modify limits	Yes
Enforcement	–
Predominant type of enforcement	–
National drink-driving law	Yes
BAC limit – general population	< 0.05 g/dl
BAC limit – young or novice drivers	0.00 g/dl
Random breath testing carried out	Yes
Testing carried out in case of fatal crash	Some drivers tested
Enforcement	–
% road traffic deaths involving alcohol	7% [c]
National motorcycle helmet law	Yes
Applies to drivers and passengers	Yes
Helmet fastening required	No
Helmet standard referred to and/or specified	No
Children passengers on motorcycles	Not restricted
Enforcement	–
Helmet wearing rate	99% Drivers [d], 100% Passengers [d]
National seat-belt law	Yes
Applies to front and rear seat occupants	Yes
Enforcement	–
Seat-belt wearing rate	98% Front seats [d], 99% Rear seats [d]
National child restraint law	Yes
Children seated in front seat	Allowed in a child restraint
Child restraint required	Up to 12 yrs/150 cm
Child restraint standard referred to and/or specified	Yes
Enforcement	–
% children using child restraints	97-99% [d]
National law on mobile phone use while driving	Yes
Ban on hand-held mobile phone use	Yes
Ban on hands-free mobile phone use	No
National drug-driving law	Yes

[b] There is no maximum speed limit on motorways
[c] 2016, Federal Statistical Office
[d] 2015, Federal Highway Research Institute (BASt)

Deaths by road user category

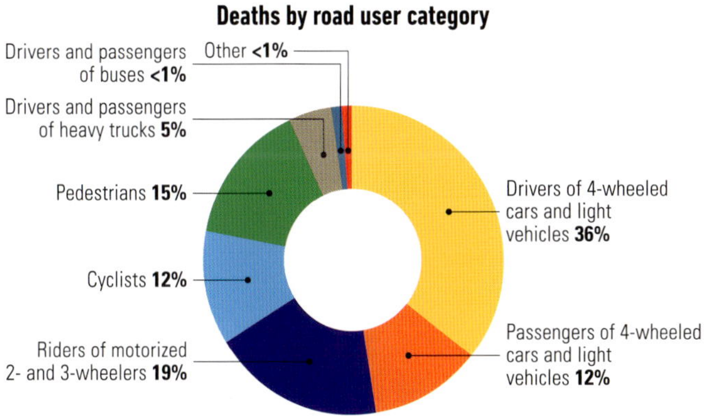

Source: 2016, Federal Statistical Office

Trends in reported road traffic deaths

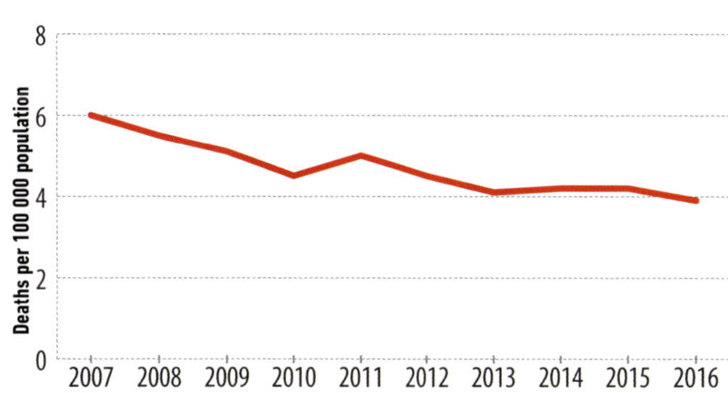

Source: Federal Statistical Office

Legislative review conducted by WHO. Vehicle safety data from UNECE WP.29. Other data collected by questionnaire and cleared by Federal Highway Research Institute (BASt).

Ghana

Population: 28 206 728 | Income group: Middle | Gross national income per capita: US$ 1 380

INSTITUTIONAL FRAMEWORK	
Lead agency	National Road Safety Commission (NRSC), Ministry of Transport
Funded in national budget	Yes
National road safety strategy	Yes
Funding to implement strategy	Partially funded
Fatality reduction target	50% (2011-2020)

SAFER ROADS AND MOBILITY	
Audits or star rating required for new road infrastructure	Yes
Design standards for the safety of pedestrians / cyclists	Yes
Inspections / star rating of existing roads	Yes
Investments to upgrade high risk locations	Yes
Policies & investment in urban public transport	Yes

SAFER VEHICLES	
Total registered vehicles for 2016	2 066 943
Cars and 4-wheeled light vehicles	1 171 169
Motorized 2- and 3-wheelers	515 507
Heavy trucks	153 923
Buses	210 997
Other	15 347
Vehicle standards applied (UNECE WP.29)	
Frontal impact standard	No
Electronic stability control	No
Pedestrian protection	No
Motorcycle anti-lock braking system	No

POST-CRASH CARE	
National emergency care access number	National, single number
Trauma registry	Some facilities
Formal certification for prehospital providers	Yes
National assessment of emergency care systems	Yes

DATA	
Reported road traffic fatalities (2015)	1 802[a] (79% M, 21% F)
WHO estimated road traffic fatalities (2016)	7 018 (95% CI 6 056 - 7 980)
WHO estimated rate per 100 000 population (2016)	24.9

[a] National Road Safety Commission (NRSC), National Accident Statistics 2015. Died within 30 days of crash

SAFER ROAD USERS	
National speed limit law	Yes
Max urban speed limit	50 km/h
Max rural speed limit	90 km/h
Max motorway speed limit	100 km/h
Local authorities can modify limits	No
Enforcement	0 1 2 3 (4) 5 6 7 8 9 10
Predominant type of enforcement	Manual
National drink-driving law	Yes
BAC limit – general population	≤ 0.08 g/dl
BAC limit – young or novice drivers	≤ 0.08 g/dl
Random breath testing carried out	Yes[b]
Testing carried out in case of fatal crash	Some drivers tested
Enforcement	0 1 2 (3) 4 5 6 7 8 9 10
% road traffic deaths involving alcohol	–
National motorcycle helmet law	Yes
Applies to drivers and passengers	Yes
Helmet fastening required	Yes
Helmet standard referred to and/or specified	Yes
Children passengers on motorcycles	Not restricted
Enforcement	0 1 2 3 4 (5) 6 7 8 9 10
Helmet wearing rate	42% Drivers[c], 17% Passengers[c]
National seat-belt law	Yes
Applies to front and rear seat occupants	Yes
Enforcement	0 1 2 (3) 4 5 6 7 8 9 10
Seat-belt wearing rate	18% Front seats[c], 4% Rear seats[c]
National child restraint law	No
Children seated in front seat	Prohibited under 5 yrs[d]
Child restraint required	–
Child restraint standard referred to and/or specified	–
Enforcement	–
% children using child restraints	–
National law on mobile phone use while driving	Yes
Ban on hand-held mobile phone use	Yes
Ban on hands-free mobile phone use	No
National drug-driving law	Yes

[b] Legislation requires probable cause to test drivers or commission of a traffic offence
[c] 2015, National seatbelt and crash helmet usage survey
[d] Under the road traffic act, children aged 5 years and below shall not sit in the front, while under the road traffic regulations they can sit in the front if placed in a child restraint

Deaths by road user category

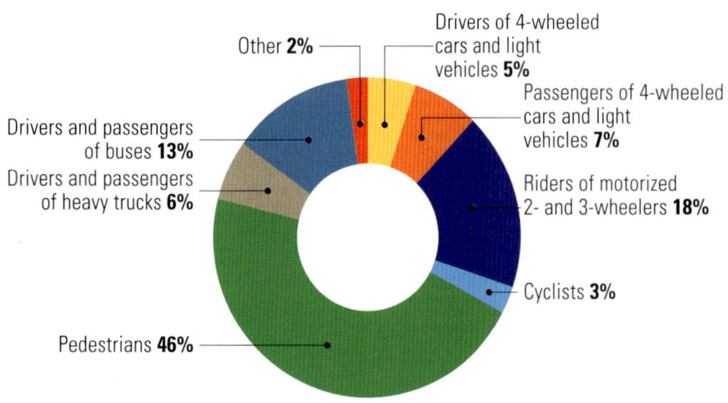

Source: 2015, National Road Safety Commission (NRSC), National Accident Statistics 2015

Trends in reported road traffic deaths

Source: National Road Safety Commission (NRSC), National Accident Statistics 2015

Legislative review conducted by WHO. Vehicle safety data from UNECE WP29. Other data collected by questionnaire and cleared by National Road Safety Commission.

Greece

Population: 11 183 716 | Income group: High | Gross national income per capita: US$ 18 960

INSTITUTIONAL FRAMEWORK	
Lead agency	Inter-Ministerial Road Safety Committee
Funded in national budget	No
National road safety strategy	Yes
Funding to implement strategy	Partially funded
Fatality reduction target	< 640 fatalities (2010-2020)
SAFER ROADS AND MOBILITY	
Audits or star rating required for new road infrastructure	Partial
Design standards for the safety of pedestrians / cyclists	Partial
Inspections / star rating of existing roads	Yes
Investments to upgrade high risk locations	Yes
Policies & investment in urban public transport	Yes
SAFER VEHICLES	
Total registered vehicles for 2016	9 489 299
Cars and 4-wheeled light vehicles	5 160 056
Motorized 2- and 3-wheelers	2 969 879
Heavy trucks	1 332 823
Buses	26 541
Other	0
Vehicle standards applied (UNECE WP.29)	
Frontal impact standard	Yes
Electronic stability control	Yes
Pedestrian protection	Yes
Motorcycle anti-lock braking system	Yes
POST-CRASH CARE	
National emergency care access number	National, single number
Trauma registry	Some facilities
Formal certification for prehospital providers	Yes
National assessment of emergency care systems	No
DATA	
Reported road traffic fatalities (2016)	824[a] (80% M, 20% F)
WHO estimated road traffic fatalities (2016)	1 026
WHO estimated rate per 100 000 population (2016)	9.2

[a] Hellenic Statistical Authority (ELSTAT). Died within 30 days of crash

SAFER ROAD USERS	
National speed limit law	Yes
Max urban speed limit	50 km/h
Max rural speed limit	90 km/h
Max motorway speed limit	130 km/h
Local authorities can modify limits	Yes
Enforcement	0 1 2 ③ 4 5 6 7 8 9 10
Predominant type of enforcement	Manual
National drink-driving law	Yes
BAC limit – general population	< 0.05 g/dl
BAC limit – young or novice drivers	< 0.05 g/dl
Random breath testing carried out	Yes
Testing carried out in case of fatal crash	All drivers tested
Enforcement	0 1 2 3 ④ 5 6 7 8 9 10
% road traffic deaths involving alcohol	25%[b]
National motorcycle helmet law	Yes
Applies to drivers and passengers	Yes
Helmet fastening required	Yes
Helmet standard referred to and/or specified	Yes
Children passengers on motorcycles	Prohibited under 5 yrs[c]
Enforcement	0 1 2 3 ④ 5 6 7 8 9 10
Helmet wearing rate	75% Drivers[d], 46% Passengers[d]
National seat-belt law	Yes
Applies to front and rear seat occupants	Yes
Enforcement	0 1 2 3 ④ 5 6 7 8 9 10
Seat-belt wearing rate	74% Front seats[d], 23% Rear seats[d]
National child restraint law	Yes
Children seated in front seat	Allowed in a child restraint
Child restraint required	135-150 cm[e]
Child restraint standard referred to and/or specified	Yes
Enforcement	0 1 ② 3 4 5 6 7 8 9 10
% children using child restraints	67%[d]
National law on mobile phone use while driving	Yes
Ban on hand-held mobile phone use	Yes
Ban on hands-free mobile phone use	No
National drug-driving law	Yes

[b] 2015, Hellenic Statistical Authority (ELSTAT), National Technical University of Athens
[c] Unless placed in an appropriate child restraint
[d] 2009, National Technical University of Athens
[e] The use of seat belt is allowed for children of height 135-150 cm sitting in the rear

Deaths by road user category

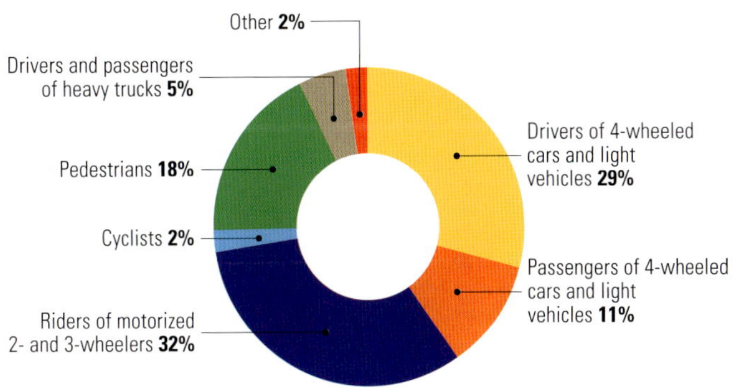

Source: 2016, Hellenic Statistical Authority (ELSTAT)

Trends in reported road traffic deaths

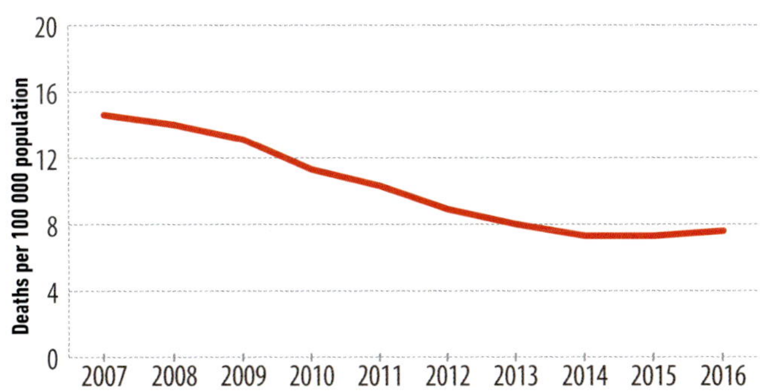

Source: Hellenic Statistical Authority (ELSTAT)

Legislative review conducted by WHO. Vehicle safety data from UNECE WP.29. Other data collected by questionnaire and cleared by Department of Transportation Planning and Engineering.

Grenada

Population: 107 317 | Income group: Middle | Gross national income per capita: US$ 8 830

INSTITUTIONAL FRAMEWORK

Lead agency	National Transport Board, Ministry of Works
Funded in national budget	Yes
National road safety strategy	No
Funding to implement strategy	–
Fatality reduction target	–

SAFER ROADS AND MOBILITY

Audits or star rating required for new road infrastructure	Partial
Design standards for the safety of pedestrians / cyclists	Partial
Inspections / star rating of existing roads	Yes
Investments to upgrade high risk locations	Yes
Policies & investment in urban public transport	No

SAFER VEHICLES

Total registered vehicles for 2016	27 266
Cars and 4-wheeled light vehicles	–
Motorized 2- and 3-wheelers	–
Heavy trucks	–
Buses	–
Other	–
Vehicle standards applied (UNECE WP.29)	
Frontal impact standard	No
Electronic stability control	No
Pedestrian protection	No
Motorcycle anti-lock braking system	No

POST-CRASH CARE

National emergency care access number	National, single number
Trauma registry	None
Formal certification for prehospital providers	No
National assessment of emergency care systems	No

DATA

Reported road traffic fatalities (2016)	10 [a] (100% M, 0% F)
WHO estimated road traffic fatalities (2016)	10
WHO estimated rate per 100 000 population (2016)	9.3

[a] Royal Grenada Police Force Traffic Department and death certificates from the Epidemiology and Information Unit of the Ministry of Health. Time period for deaths not defined

SAFER ROAD USERS

National speed limit law	Yes
Max urban speed limit	~ 32 km/h
Max rural speed limit	~ 64 km/h
Max motorway speed limit	No
Local authorities can modify limits	No
Enforcement	0 1 2 3 4 5 (6) 7 8 9 10
Predominant type of enforcement	Manual
National drink-driving law	Yes [b]
BAC limit – general population	–
BAC limit – young or novice drivers	–
Random breath testing carried out	No
Testing carried out in case of fatal crash	No
Enforcement	0 (1) 2 3 4 5 6 7 8 9 10
% road traffic deaths involving alcohol	–
National motorcycle helmet law	Yes
Applies to drivers and passengers	Yes
Helmet fastening required	No
Helmet standard referred to and/or specified	Yes
Children passengers on motorcycles	Not restricted
Enforcement	0 (1) 2 3 4 5 6 7 8 9 10
Helmet wearing rate	–
National seat-belt law	Yes
Applies to front and rear seat occupants	No
Enforcement	0 1 2 3 4 5 6 7 (8) 9 10
Seat-belt wearing rate	–
National child restraint law	No
Children seated in front seat	Not restricted
Child restraint required	–
Child restraint standard referred to and/or specified	–
Enforcement	–
% children using child restraints	–
National law on mobile phone use while driving	No
Ban on hand-held mobile phone use	–
Ban on hands-free mobile phone use	–
National drug-driving law	Yes

[b] Not based on BAC

Deaths by road user category

Trends in reported road traffic deaths

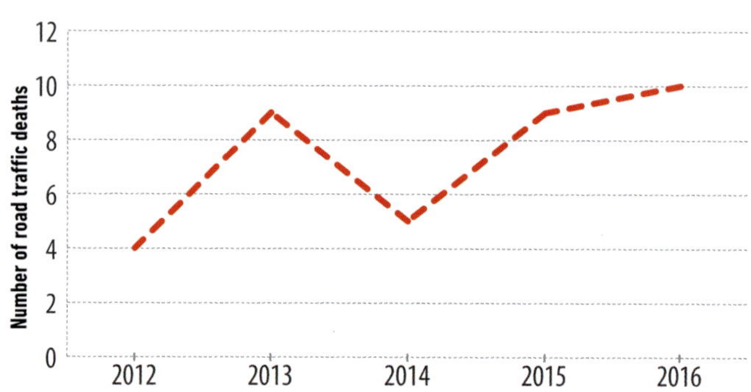

Source: Royal Grenada Police Force Traffic Department and death certificates from the Epidemiology and Information Unit of the Ministry of Health

Guatemala

Population: 16 582 469 | Income group: Middle | Gross national income per capita: US$ 3 790

INSTITUTIONAL FRAMEWORK	
Lead agency	Transit Department, Ministry of Government
Funded in national budget	Yes
National road safety strategy	Yes
Funding to implement strategy	Partially funded
Fatality reduction target	5.5% deaths per 100 000 population (2017-2020)

SAFER ROADS AND MOBILITY	
Audits or star rating required for new road infrastructure	Partial
Design standards for the safety of pedestrians / cyclists	Partial
Inspections / star rating of existing roads	No
Investments to upgrade high risk locations	Yes
Policies & investment in urban public transport	Yes

SAFER VEHICLES	
Total registered vehicles for 2016	3 250 194
Cars and 4-wheeled light vehicles	1 706 275
Motorized 2- and 3-wheelers	1 227 879
Heavy trucks	154 473
Buses	113 448
Other	48 119
Vehicle standards applied (UNECE WP.29)	
Frontal impact standard	No
Electronic stability control	No
Pedestrian protection	No
Motorcycle anti-lock braking system	No

POST-CRASH CARE	
National emergency care access number	National, multiple numbers
Trauma registry	Some facilities
Formal certification for prehospital providers	Yes
National assessment of emergency care systems	No

DATA	
Reported road traffic fatalities (2016)	2 058[a] (84% M, 16% F)
WHO estimated road traffic fatalities (2016)	2 758
WHO estimated rate per 100 000 population (2016)	16.6

[a] National Observatory of Traffic Safety (ONSET), Bulletin 37, 2016. Died at scene of crash

SAFER ROAD USERS	
National speed limit law	Yes
Max urban speed limit	60 km/h
Max rural speed limit	80 km/h
Max motorway speed limit	100 km/h
Local authorities can modify limits	Yes
Enforcement	0 1 2 3 (4) 5 6 7 8 9 10
Predominant type of enforcement	Manual
National drink-driving law	Yes[b]
BAC limit – general population	–
BAC limit – young or novice drivers	–
Random breath testing carried out	Yes
Testing carried out in case of fatal crash	Some drivers tested
Enforcement	0 1 2 3 (4) 5 6 7 8 9 10
% road traffic deaths involving alcohol	–
National motorcycle helmet law	Yes
Applies to drivers and passengers	Yes
Helmet fastening required	No
Helmet standard referred to and/or specified	No
Children passengers on motorcycles	Not restricted
Enforcement	0 1 2 3 (4) 5 6 7 8 9 10
Helmet wearing rate	36% Drivers[c], 11% Passengers[c]
National seat-belt law	Yes
Applies to front and rear seat occupants	No
Enforcement	0 1 2 3 (4) 5 6 7 8 9 10
Seat-belt wearing rate	–
National child restraint law	No
Children seated in front seat	Not restricted
Child restraint required	–
Child restraint standard referred to and/or specified	–
Enforcement	–
% children using child restraints	–
National law on mobile phone use while driving	Yes
Ban on hand-held mobile phone use	Yes
Ban on hands-free mobile phone use	No
National drug-driving law	Yes

[b] Not based on BAC

[c] 2016, Observational study of helmet and vest, National Observatory of Traffic Safety.

Deaths by road user category

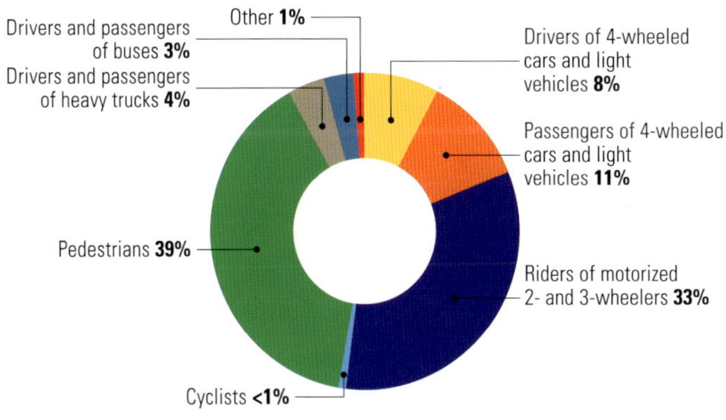

Source: 2016, Traffic accidents database, National Civil Police.

Trends in reported road traffic deaths

Source: Traffic accidents database, National Civil Police.

Legislative review conducted by WHO. Vehicle safety data from UNECE WP29. Other data collected by questionnaire and cleared by the Transit Department.

Guinea

Population: 12 395 924 | Income group: Low | Gross national income per capita: US$ 490

INSTITUTIONAL FRAMEWORK

Lead agency	**National Program to Combat Trauma and Violence**
Funded in national budget	–
National road safety strategy	**No**
Funding to implement strategy	–
Fatality reduction target	–

SAFER ROADS AND MOBILITY

Audits or star rating required for new road infrastructure	Yes
Design standards for the safety of pedestrians / cyclists	No
Inspections / star rating of existing roads	No
Investments to upgrade high risk locations	No
Policies & investment in urban public transport	Yes

SAFER VEHICLES

Total registered vehicles for 2016	**259 731**
Cars and 4-wheeled light vehicles	187 165
Motorized 2- and 3-wheelers	72 566
Heavy trucks	–
Buses	–
Other	–
Vehicle standards applied (UNECE WP.29)	
Frontal impact standard	No
Electronic stability control	No
Pedestrian protection	No
Motorcycle anti-lock braking system	No

POST-CRASH CARE

National emergency care access number	None
Trauma registry	Subnational
Formal certification for prehospital providers	No
National assessment of emergency care systems	No

DATA

Reported road traffic fatalities (2016)	458[a] (72% M, 22% F)
WHO estimated road traffic fatalities (2016)	3 490 (95% CI 2 903 - 4 077)
WHO estimated rate per 100 000 population (2016)	28.2

[a] Police and Gendarmerie. Died at scene of crash

SAFER ROAD USERS

National speed limit law	**No**
Max urban speed limit	–
Max rural speed limit	–
Max motorway speed limit	–
Local authorities can modify limits	–
Enforcement	–
Predominant type of enforcement	Manual
National drink-driving law	**Yes**
BAC limit – general population	< 0.08 g/dl
BAC limit – young or novice drivers	< 0.08 g/dl
Random breath testing carried out	No
Testing carried out in case of fatal crash	No
Enforcement	0 1 (2) 3 4 5 6 7 8 9 10
% road traffic deaths involving alcohol	–
National motorcycle helmet law	**Yes**
Applies to drivers and passengers	Yes
Helmet fastening required	No
Helmet standard referred to and/or specified	Yes
Children passengers on motorcycles	Not restricted
Enforcement	0 1 2 3 (4) 5 6 7 8 9 10
Helmet wearing rate	–
National seat-belt law	**Yes**
Applies to front and rear seat occupants	No
Enforcement	–
Seat-belt wearing rate	–
National child restraint law	**Yes**
Children seated in front seat	Prohibited under 10 yrs
Child restraint required	Up to 18 mths[b]
Child restraint standard referred to and/or specified	No
Enforcement	–
% children using child restraints	–
National law on mobile phone use while driving	**Yes**
Ban on hand-held mobile phone use	Yes
Ban on hands-free mobile phone use	No
National drug-driving law	**No**

[b] The legislation refers to homologated seats for children under 18 months and to cribs and hammocs for children under 10 years

Deaths by road user category

Trends in reported road traffic deaths

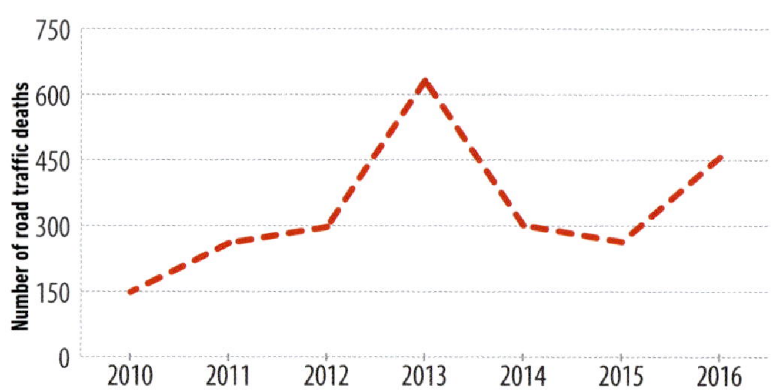

Source: Police and Gendarmerie, Statistical Directory on Transport of the Republic of Guinea, 2nd Edition

Guinea-Bissau

Population: 1 815 698 | Income group: Low | Gross national income per capita: US$ 620

INSTITUTIONAL FRAMEWORK	
Lead agency	No
Funded in national budget	–
National road safety strategy	No
Funding to implement strategy	–
Fatality reduction target	–
SAFER ROADS AND MOBILITY	
Audits or star rating required for new road infrastructure	No
Design standards for the safety of pedestrians / cyclists	No
Inspections / star rating of existing roads	No
Investments to upgrade high risk locations	No
Policies & investment in urban public transport	No
SAFER VEHICLES	
Total registered vehicles for 2016	62 239
Cars and 4-wheeled light vehicles	–
Motorized 2- and 3-wheelers	–
Heavy trucks	–
Buses	–
Other	–
Vehicle standards applied (UNECE WP.29)	
Frontal impact standard	No
Electronic stability control	No
Pedestrian protection	No
Motorcycle anti-lock braking system	No
POST-CRASH CARE	
National emergency care access number	National, single number
Trauma registry	Some facilities
Formal certification for prehospital providers	No
National assessment of emergency care systems	No
DATA	
Reported road traffic fatalities (2016)	122[a]
WHO estimated road traffic fatalities (2016)	565 (95% CI 465 - 664)
WHO estimated rate per 100 000 population (2016)	31.1

[a] National Transit Group. Time period following a crash not defined

SAFER ROAD USERS	
National speed limit law	Yes
Max urban speed limit	50 km/h
Max rural speed limit	80 km/h
Max motorway speed limit	100 km/h
Local authorities can modify limits	No
Enforcement	0 ① 2 3 4 5 6 7 8 9 10
Predominant type of enforcement	Manual
National drink-driving law	Yes
BAC limit – general population	≤ 0.05 g/dl
BAC limit – young or novice drivers	≤ 0.05 g/dl
Random breath testing carried out	No
Testing carried out in case of fatal crash	Some drivers tested
Enforcement	0 ① 2 3 4 5 6 7 8 9 10
% road traffic deaths involving alcohol	–
National motorcycle helmet law	Yes
Applies to drivers and passengers	Yes
Helmet fastening required	Yes
Helmet standard referred to and/or specified	Yes
Children passengers on motorcycles	Prohibited under 6 yrs
Enforcement	0 1 2 3 ④ 5 6 7 8 9 10
Helmet wearing rate	–
National seat-belt law	Yes
Applies to front and rear seat occupants	No
Enforcement	0 ① 2 3 4 5 6 7 8 9 10
Seat-belt wearing rate	–
National child restraint law	Yes
Children seated in front seat	Prohibited under 12 yrs/135 cm
Child restraint required	Up to 12 yrs/135 cm
Child restraint standard referred to and/or specified	No
Enforcement	⓪ 1 2 3 4 5 6 7 8 9 10
% children using child restraints	–
National law on mobile phone use while driving	Yes
Ban on hand-held mobile phone use	Yes
Ban on hands-free mobile phone use	No
National drug-driving law	Yes

Deaths by road user category

Trends in reported road traffic deaths

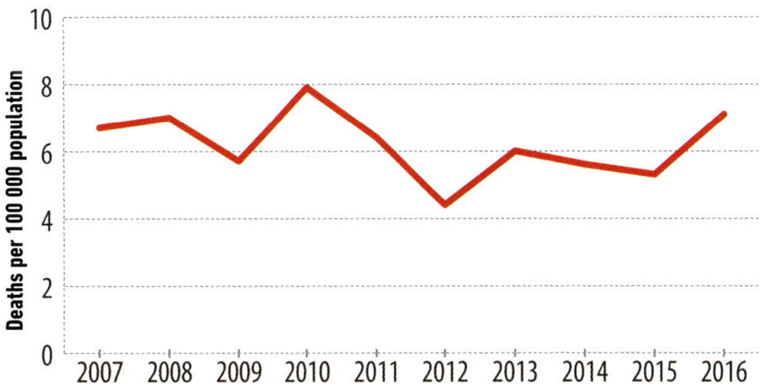

Source: National Transit Group

Legislative review conducted by WHO. Vehicle safety data from UNECE WP29. Other data collected by questionnaire and cleared by Ministry of Public Health.

Guyana

Population: 773 303 | Income group: Middle | Gross national income per capita: US$ 4 250

INSTITUTIONAL FRAMEWORK

Lead agency	**Ministry of Public Security**
Funded in national budget	Yes
National road safety strategy	**Yes**
Funding to implement strategy	Partially funded
Fatality reduction target	50% (2011-2020)

SAFER ROADS AND MOBILITY

Audits or star rating required for new road infrastructure	Yes
Design standards for the safety of pedestrians / cyclists	Partial
Inspections / star rating of existing roads	No
Investments to upgrade high risk locations	No
Policies & investment in urban public transport	No

SAFER VEHICLES

Total registered vehicles for 2013	**15 694**
Cars and 4-wheeled light vehicles	8 846
Motorized 2- and 3-wheelers	3 505
Heavy trucks	1 356
Buses	785
Other	1 202
Vehicle standards applied (UNECE WP.29)	
Frontal impact standard	No
Electronic stability control	No
Pedestrian protection	No
Motorcycle anti-lock braking system	No

POST-CRASH CARE

National emergency care access number	Partial coverage
Trauma registry	None
Formal certification for prehospital providers	Yes
National assessment of emergency care systems	No

DATA

Reported road traffic fatalities (2016)	128[a] (77% M, 23% F)
WHO estimated road traffic fatalities (2016)	190
WHO estimated rate per 100 000 population (2016)	24.6

[a] Guyana Police Force. Died within a year of crash

SAFER ROAD USERS

National speed limit law	**Yes[b]**
Max urban speed limit	~ 64 km/h
Max rural speed limit	~ 64 km/h
Max motorway speed limit	No
Local authorities can modify limits	No
Enforcement	0 1 2 3 4 5 6 ⑦ 8 9 10
Predominant type of enforcement	Manual
National drink-driving law	**Yes**
BAC limit – general population	≤ 0.08 g/dl
BAC limit – young or novice drivers	≤ 0.08 g/dl
Random breath testing carried out	Yes[c]
Testing carried out in case of fatal crash	No
Enforcement	0 1 2 3 4 5 6 ⑦ 8 9 10
% road traffic deaths involving alcohol	17%[d]
National motorcycle helmet law	**No**
Applies to drivers and passengers	–
Helmet fastening required	–
Helmet standard referred to and/or specified	–
Children passengers on motorcycles	Not restricted
Enforcement	–
Helmet wearing rate	50% Drivers[d], 20% Passengers[d]
National seat-belt law	**Yes**
Applies to front and rear seat occupants	No
Enforcement	0 1 2 3 4 5 6 7 ⑧ 9 10
Seat-belt wearing rate	95% Drivers[d], 95% Front seats[d]
National child restraint law	**Yes[e]**
Children seated in front seat	Not restricted
Child restraint required	–[e]
Child restraint standard referred to and/or specified	No
Enforcement	⓪ 1 2 3 4 5 6 7 8 9 10
% children using child restraints	–
National law on mobile phone use while driving	**Yes**
Ban on hand-held mobile phone use	Yes
Ban on hands-free mobile phone use	No
National drug-driving law	**Yes**

[b] Speed limits set per vehicle type and road type - for motor cars, speed limits are: 30 mph (48 km/h) on restricted roads, 60 mph (96 km/h) on Timehri/Linden Highway and 40 mph (64 km/h) elsewhere
[c] Legislation requires probable cause to test drivers
[d] 2016, Guyana Police Force
[e] The legislation refers to child restraint sytem for children but does not specify the age/height group covered by this obligation

Deaths by road user category

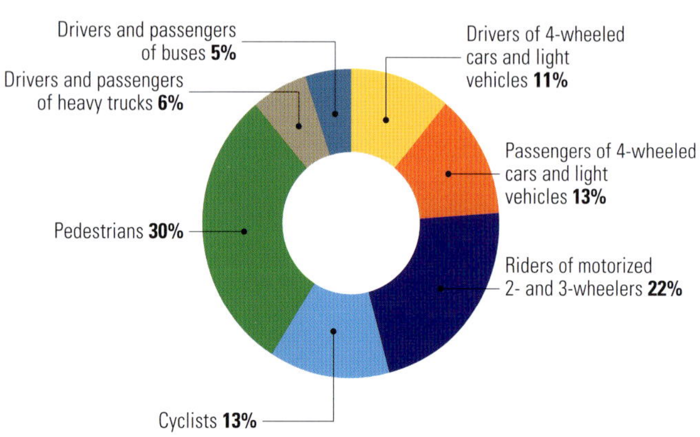

Source: 2016, Guyana Police Force

Trends in reported road traffic deaths

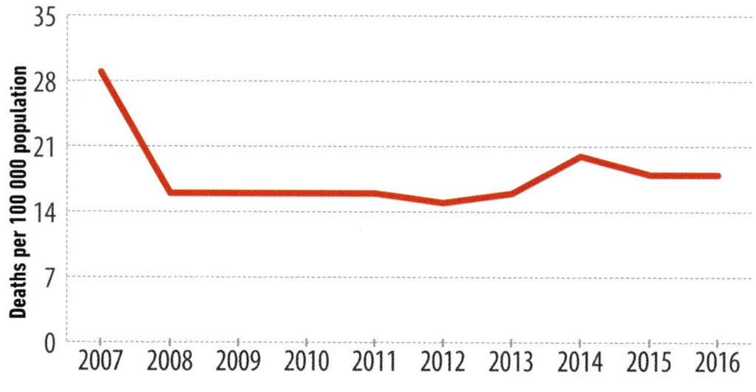

Source: Guyana Police Force

Legislative review conducted by WHO. Vehicle safety data from UNECE WP.29. Other data collected by questionnaire and cleared by Ministry of Public Security.

Honduras

Population: 9 112 867 | Income group: Middle | Gross national income per capita: US$ 2 150

INSTITUTIONAL FRAMEWORK

Lead agency	National Directorate of Roads and Transportation, Secretariat for Security
Funded in national budget	Yes
National road safety strategy	Yes
Funding to implement strategy	Partially funded
Fatality reduction target	–

SAFER ROADS AND MOBILITY

Audits or star rating required for new road infrastructure	Yes
Design standards for the safety of pedestrians / cyclists	Yes
Inspections / star rating of existing roads	No
Investments to upgrade high risk locations	Yes
Policies & investment in urban public transport	No

SAFER VEHICLES

Total registered vehicles for 2016	1 694 504
Cars and 4-wheeled light vehicles	987 829
Motorized 2- and 3-wheelers	602 837
Heavy trucks	63 094
Buses	40 744
Other	0
Vehicle standards applied (UNECE WP.29)	
Frontal impact standard	No
Electronic stability control	No
Pedestrian protection	No
Motorcycle anti-lock braking system	No

POST-CRASH CARE

National emergency care access number	National, single number
Trauma registry	Some facilities
Formal certification for prehospital providers	Yes
National assessment of emergency care systems	No

DATA

Reported road traffic fatalities (2016)	1 407[a] (83% M, 17% F)
WHO estimated road traffic fatalities (2016)	1 525 (95% CI 1 388 - 1 661)
WHO estimated rate per 100 000 population (2016)	16.7

[a] Combined sources: National Observatory of Road Safety, Police Statistical System, and National Observatory of Violence. Unlimited time period following crash

SAFER ROAD USERS

National speed limit law	Yes[b]
Max urban speed limit	–
Max rural speed limit	–
Max motorway speed limit	–
Local authorities can modify limits	No
Enforcement	0 1 2 3 4 5 (6) 7 8 9 10
Predominant type of enforcement	Manual
National drink-driving law	Yes
BAC limit – general population	< 0.07 g/dl
BAC limit – young or novice drivers	< 0.07 g/dl
Random breath testing carried out	Yes[c]
Testing carried out in case of fatal crash	All drivers tested
Enforcement	0 1 2 3 4 5 6 7 (8) 9 10
% road traffic deaths involving alcohol	7%[d]
National motorcycle helmet law	Yes
Applies to drivers and passengers	Yes
Helmet fastening required	No
Helmet standard referred to and/or specified	No
Children passengers on motorcycles	Not restricted
Enforcement	0 1 2 3 (4) 5 6 7 8 9 10
Helmet wearing rate	–
National seat-belt law	Yes
Applies to front and rear seat occupants	Yes
Enforcement	0 1 2 3 4 5 (6) 7 8 9 10
Seat-belt wearing rate	–
National child restraint law	No[e]
Children seated in front seat	Prohibited under 12 yrs
Child restraint required	–
Child restraint standard referred to and/or specified	–
Enforcement	–
% children using child restraints	–
National law on mobile phone use while driving	Yes
Ban on hand-held mobile phone use	Yes
Ban on hands-free mobile phone use	Yes
National drug-driving law	Yes

[b] Legislation refers to regulations to set maximum speed limits, regulations not available
[c] Legislation requires probable cause to test drivers
[d] National Observatory of Road Safety, Statistical Police System (ONASEVIH/SEPOL)
[e] Legislation refers to the protection of children under 5 years but does not specify which form this protection takes

Deaths by road user category

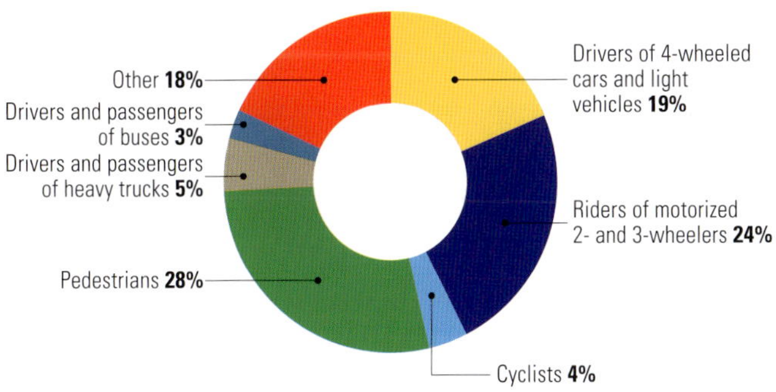

Source: 2016, Summary of Accidents, National Observatory of Road Safety, Statistical Police System (ONASEVIH/SEPOL)

Trends in reported road traffic deaths

Source: National Observatory of Road Safety, Statistical Police System and National Observatory of Violence

Legislative review conducted by WHO. Vehicle safety data from UNECE WP29. Other data collected by questionnaire and cleared by State Secretariat of Security.

Hungary

Population: 9 753 281 | Income group: High | Gross national income per capita: US$ 12 570

INSTITUTIONAL FRAMEWORK	
Lead agency	No
Funded in national budget	–
National road safety strategy	Yes
Funding to implement strategy	Partially funded
Fatality reduction target	50% (2017-2020)
SAFER ROADS AND MOBILITY	
Audits or star rating required for new road infrastructure	Yes
Design standards for the safety of pedestrians / cyclists	Yes
Inspections / star rating of existing roads	Yes
Investments to upgrade high risk locations	No
Policies & investment in urban public transport	No
SAFER VEHICLES	
Total registered vehicles for 2016	4 022 798
Cars and 4-wheeled light vehicles	3 313 206
Motorized 2- and 3-wheelers	162 148
Heavy trucks	528 962
Buses	18 482
Other	0
Vehicle standards applied (UNECE WP.29)	
Frontal impact standard	Yes
Electronic stability control	Yes
Pedestrian protection	Yes
Motorcycle anti-lock braking system	Yes
POST-CRASH CARE	
National emergency care access number	National, single number
Trauma registry	None
Formal certification for prehospital providers	Yes
National assessment of emergency care systems	No
DATA	
Reported road traffic fatalities (2016)	607 [a] (76% M, 24% F)
WHO estimated road traffic fatalities (2016)	756
WHO estimated rate per 100 000 population (2016)	7.8

[a] Hungarian Central Statistical Office: Data collection No. 1009. Died within 30 days of crash

SAFER ROAD USERS	
National speed limit law	Yes
Max urban speed limit	50 km/h
Max rural speed limit	90 km/h
Max motorway speed limit	130 km/h
Local authorities can modify limits	Yes
Enforcement	0 1 2 3 4 5 (6) 7 8 9 10
Predominant type of enforcement	Manual and automated
National drink-driving law	Yes [b]
BAC limit – general population	0.00 g/dl
BAC limit – young or novice drivers	0.00 g/dl
Random breath testing carried out	Yes [c]
Testing carried out in case of fatal crash	All drivers tested
Enforcement	0 1 2 3 4 (5) 6 7 8 9 10
% road traffic deaths involving alcohol	7% [d]
National motorcycle helmet law	Yes
Applies to drivers and passengers	Yes
Helmet fastening required	Yes
Helmet standard referred to and/or specified	Yes
Children passengers on motorcycles	Not restricted
Enforcement	0 1 2 3 4 5 6 7 (8) 9 10
Helmet wearing rate	100% Budapest, 92% Country road [e]
National seat-belt law	Yes
Applies to front and rear seat occupants	Yes
Enforcement	0 1 2 3 4 5 6 (7) 8 9 10
Seat-belt wearing rate	83% Front seats [f], 39% Rear seats [f]
National child restraint law	Yes
Children seated in front seat	Allowed in a child restraint
Child restraint required	135-150 cm [g]
Child restraint standard referred to and/or specified	Yes
Enforcement	0 1 2 3 4 5 6 (7) 8 9 10
% children using child restraints	67% [h]
National law on mobile phone use while driving	Yes
Ban on hand-held mobile phone use	Yes
Ban on hands-free mobile phone use	No
National drug-driving law	Yes

[b] Any presence of alcohol in the body is prohibited
[c] Legislation requires probable cause to test drivers
[d] 2016, Hungarian Central Statistical Office
[e] 2017, Institute for Transport Sciences
[f] 2015, Institute for Transport Sciences
[g] Children of height 135-150 cm can be restrained with seat belt only if they sit in the back
[h] 2015, Institute for Transport Sciences, Roadside survey

Deaths by road user category

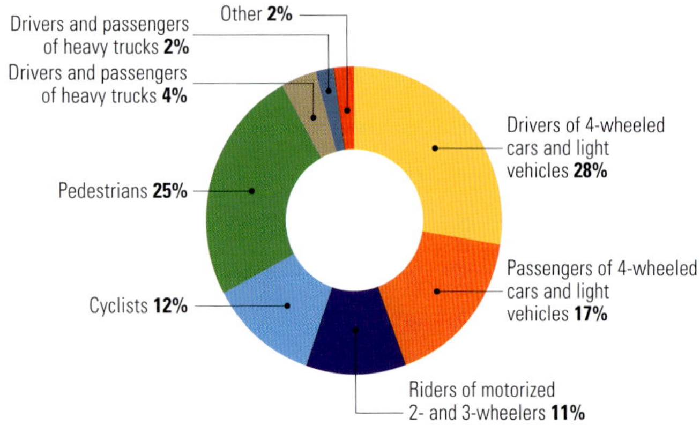

Source: 2016, Hungarian Central Statistical Office: Data collection No. 1009

Trends in reported road traffic deaths

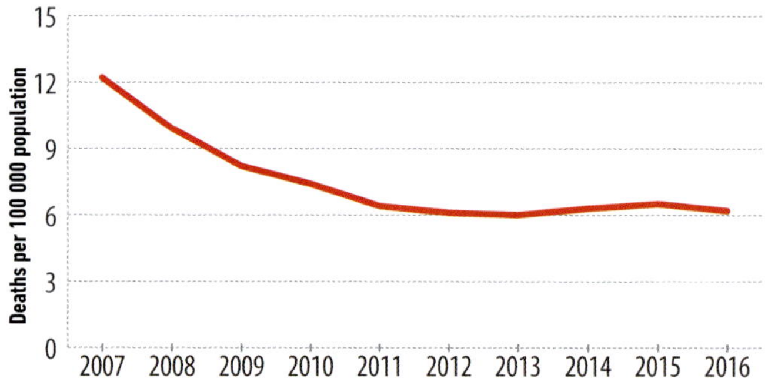

Source: Hungarian Central Statistical Office: Data collection No. 1009

Legislative review conducted by WHO. Vehicle safety data from UNECE WP29. Other data collected by questionnaire and cleared by Ministry of Human Capacities.

Iceland

Population: 332 474 | Income group: High | Gross national income per capita: US$ 56 990

INSTITUTIONAL FRAMEWORK	
Lead agency	The Icelandic Transport Authority (Samgöngustofa)
Funded in national budget	Yes
National road safety strategy	Yes
Funding to implement strategy	Partially funded
Fatality reduction target	–

SAFER ROADS AND MOBILITY	
Audits or star rating required for new road infrastructure	Yes
Design standards for the safety of pedestrians / cyclists	Partial
Inspections / star rating of existing roads	Yes
Investments to upgrade high risk locations	Yes
Policies & investment in urban public transport	Yes

SAFER VEHICLES	
Total registered vehicles for 2016	289 501
Cars and 4-wheeled light vehicles	264 998
Motorized 2- and 3-wheelers	10 573
Heavy trucks	11 068
Buses	2 862
Other	0
Vehicle standards applied (UNECE WP.29)	
Frontal impact standard	Yes
Electronic stability control	Yes
Pedestrian protection	Yes
Motorcycle anti-lock braking system	Yes

POST-CRASH CARE	
National emergency care access number	National, single number
Trauma registry	National
Formal certification for prehospital providers	Yes
National assessment of emergency care systems	No

DATA	
Reported road traffic fatalities (2016)	18[a] (72% M, 28% F)
WHO estimated road traffic fatalities (2016)	22
WHO estimated rate per 100 000 population (2016)	6.6

[a] Road Traffic Accident Report 2016, The Icelandic Transport Authority. Died within 30 days of crash

SAFER ROAD USERS	
National speed limit law	Yes
Max urban speed limit	50 km/h
Max rural speed limit	90 km/h
Max motorway speed limit	100 km/h
Local authorities can modify limits	No
Enforcement	0 1 2 3 4 5 6 (7) 8 9 10
Predominant type of enforcement	Automated
National drink-driving law	Yes
BAC limit – general population	< 0.05 g/dl
BAC limit – young or novice drivers	< 0.05 g/dl
Random breath testing carried out	Yes
Testing carried out in case of fatal crash	All drivers tested
Enforcement	0 1 2 3 4 5 6 (7) 8 9 10
% road traffic deaths involving alcohol	14%[b]
National motorcycle helmet law	Yes
Applies to drivers and passengers	Yes
Helmet fastening required	No
Helmet standard referred to and/or specified	No
Children passengers on motorcycles	Not restricted[c]
Enforcement	0 1 2 3 4 5 6 7 8 (9) 10
Helmet wearing rate	–
National seat-belt law	Yes
Applies to front and rear seat occupants	Yes
Enforcement	0 1 2 3 4 5 6 7 8 (9) 10
Seat-belt wearing rate	93% Front seats[d], 86% Rear seats[d]
National child restraint law	Yes
Children seated in front seat	Allowed in a child restraint[e]
Child restraint required	Up to 135 cm
Child restraint standard referred to and/or specified	Yes
Enforcement	0 1 2 3 4 5 6 7 8 (9) 10
% children using child restraints	93%[f]
National law on mobile phone use while driving	Yes
Ban on hand-held mobile phone use	Yes
Ban on hands-free mobile phone use	No
National drug-driving law	Yes

[b] 2007-2016, The IceTrA accident database
[c] Children who are 7 years or younger shall be placed in an appropriate child seat while children older than 7 years shall be able to have their feet reaching the pedals
[d] Survey on attitudes and behaviour in traffic 2016
[e] Seating of children under 150cm allowed in the front only if front airbag deactivated
[f] 2015, Transport Authority

Deaths by road user category

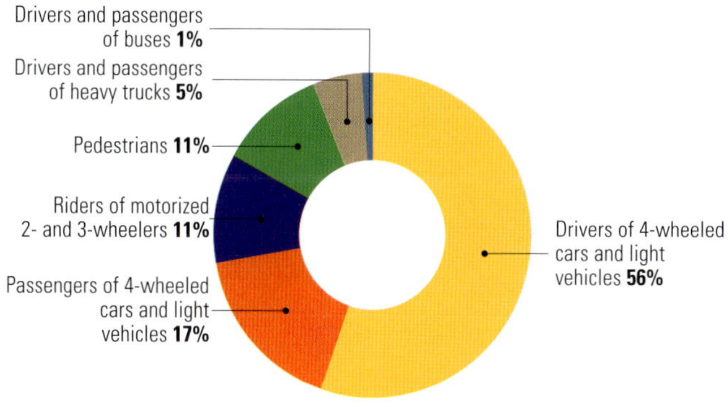

Source: The Icelandic Transport Authority, Road Traffic Accident Report 2016

Trends in reported road traffic deaths

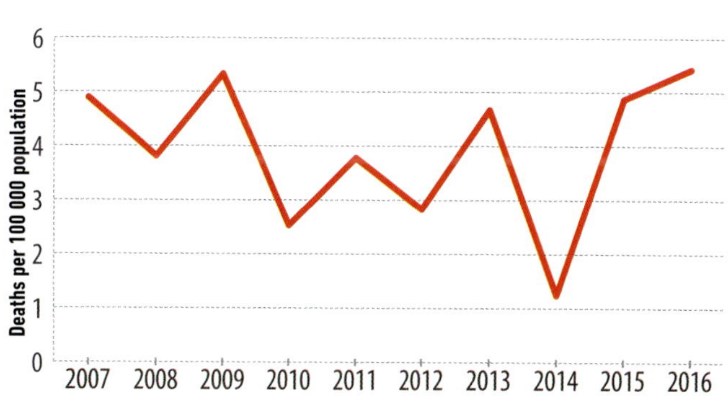

Source: The Icelandic Transport Authority, Road Traffic Accident Report 2016

Legislative review conducted by WHO. Vehicle safety data from UNECE WP29. Other data collected by questionnaire and cleared by Icelandic Transport Authority.

India

Population: 1 324 171 392 | Income group: Middle | Gross national income per capita: US$ 1 680

INSTITUTIONAL FRAMEWORK

Lead agency	**Ministry of Road Transport and Highways**
Funded in national budget	Yes
National road safety strategy	**Yes**
Funding to implement strategy	Partially funded
Fatality reduction target	50% (2011-2020)

SAFER ROADS AND MOBILITY

Audits or star rating required for new road infrastructure	Partial
Design standards for the safety of pedestrians / cyclists	Yes
Inspections / star rating of existing roads	Yes
Investments to upgrade high risk locations	Yes
Policies & investment in urban public transport	Yes

SAFER VEHICLES

Total registered vehicles for 2015	**210 023 289**
Cars and 4-wheeled light vehicles	38 523 053
Motorized 2- and 3-wheelers	154 297 746
Heavy trucks	4 461 059
Buses	1 970 786
Other	10 770 645
Vehicle standards applied (UNECE WP.29)	
Frontal impact standard	Yes
Electronic stability control	No
Pedestrian protection	Yes[a]
Motorcycle anti-lock braking system	Yes

POST-CRASH CARE

National emergency care access number	Partial coverage
Trauma registry	Some facilities
Formal certification for prehospital providers	Yes
National assessment of emergency care systems	No

DATA

Reported road traffic fatalities (2016)	150 785[b] (85% M, 15% F)
WHO estimated road traffic fatalities (2016)	299 091
WHO estimated rate per 100 000 population (2016)	22.6

[a] Mandatory from October 2018
[b] Ministry of Road Transport and Highways, Road Accidents in India 2016. Died within 30 days of crash

SAFER ROAD USERS

National speed limit law	**Yes**
Max urban speed limit	100 km/h[c]
Max rural speed limit	100 km/h[c]
Max motorway speed limit	100 km/h[c]
Local authorities can modify limits	Yes
Enforcement	0 1 2 ③ 4 5 6 7 8 9 10
Predominant type of enforcement	Manual
National drink-driving law	**Yes**
BAC limit – general population	≤ 0.03 g/dl
BAC limit – young or novice drivers	≤ 0.03 g/dl
Random breath testing carried out	Yes[d]
Testing carried out in case of fatal crash	Some drivers tested
Enforcement	0 1 2 3 ④ 5 6 7 8 9 10
% road traffic deaths involving alcohol	4%[e]
National motorcycle helmet law	**Yes**
Applies to drivers and passengers	Yes
Helmet fastening required	Yes
Helmet standard referred to and/or specified	Yes
Children passengers on motorcycles	Not restricted
Enforcement	0 1 2 3 ④ 5 6 7 8 9 10
Helmet wearing rate	30% Drivers[f], <10% Passengers[f]
National seat-belt law	**Yes**
Applies to front and rear seat occupants	Yes
Enforcement	0 1 2 ③ 4 5 6 7 8 9 10
Seat-belt wearing rate	14-40% Drivers[g], 4-11% Front seats[g]
National child restraint law	**No**
Children seated in front seat	Not restricted
Child restraint required	–
Child restraint standard referred to and/or specified	–
Enforcement	–
% children using child restraints	–
National law on mobile phone use while driving	**Yes**
Ban on hand-held mobile phone use	Yes
Ban on hands-free mobile phone use	Yes
National drug-driving law	**Yes**

[c] Speed limit set per vehicle type with a maximum speed limit of 100 km/h for passengers cars comprising not more than eight seats in addition to the driver's seat
[d] Legislation requires probable cause to test drivers
[e] 2016, Ministry of Road Transport and Highways, Road Accidents in India 2016
[f] 2015, The validity of self-reported helmet use among motorcyclists in India, Wadhwaniya et al
[g] 2000-2015, Various journal articles and reports

Deaths by road user category

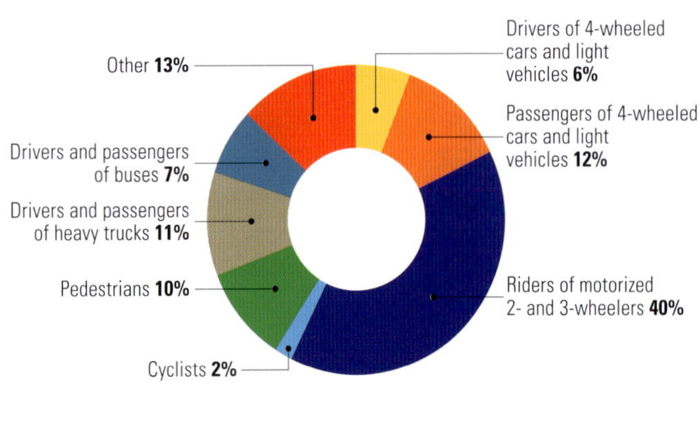

Source: Ministry of Road Transport and Highways, Road Accidents in India 2016

Trends in reported road traffic deaths

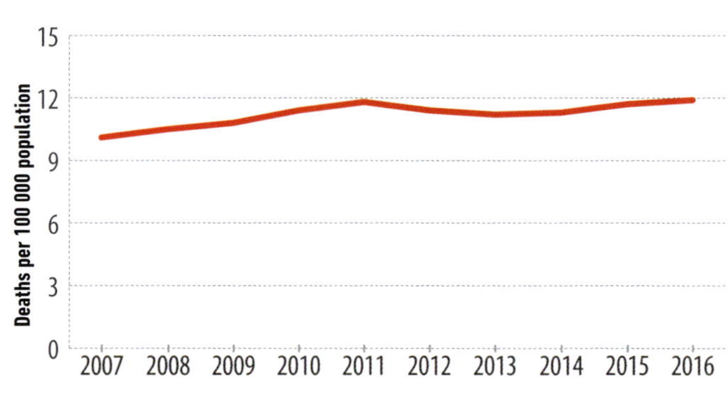

Source: Ministry of Road Transport and Highways, Road Accidents in India 2016

Legislative review conducted by WHO. Vehicle safety data from UNECE WP29. Other data collected by questionnaire and cleared by Ministry of Road Transport and Highways.

Indonesia

Population: 261 115 456 | Income group: Middle | Gross national income per capita: US$ 3 400

INSTITUTIONAL FRAMEWORK

Lead agency	National Planning Agency (Badan Perencanaan Pembangunan Nasional - BAPPENAS)
Funded in national budget	Yes
National road safety strategy	Yes
Funding to implement strategy	Partially funded
Fatality reduction target	50% (2011-2020)

SAFER ROADS AND MOBILITY

Audits or star rating required for new road infrastructure	Yes
Design standards for the safety of pedestrians / cyclists	Yes
Inspections / star rating of existing roads	Yes
Investments to upgrade high risk locations	Yes
Policies & investment in urban public transport	Yes

SAFER VEHICLES

Total registered vehicles for 2016	128 398 594
Cars and 4-wheeled light vehicles	–
Motorized 2- and 3-wheelers	–
Heavy trucks	–
Buses	–
Other	–
Vehicle standards applied (UNECE WP.29)	
Frontal impact standard	No
Electronic stability control	No
Pedestrian protection	No
Motorcycle anti-lock braking system	No

POST-CRASH CARE

National emergency care access number	Partial coverage
Trauma registry	None
Formal certification for prehospital providers	Yes
National assessment of emergency care systems	No

DATA

Reported road traffic fatalities (2016)	31 282[a] (76% M, 22% F)
WHO estimated road traffic fatalities (2016)	31 726 (95% CI 27 277 - 36 176)
WHO estimated rate per 100 000 population (2016)	12.2

[a] IRSMS Korlantas Polri. Died within 30 days of crash

SAFER ROAD USERS

National speed limit law	Yes
Max urban speed limit	50 km/h
Max rural speed limit	80 km/h
Max motorway speed limit	100 km/h
Local authorities can modify limits	Yes
Enforcement	0 1 2 3 4 5 6 7 ⑧ 9 10
Predominant type of enforcement	Manual
National drink-driving law	Yes[b]
BAC limit – general population	–
BAC limit – young or novice drivers	–
Random breath testing carried out	Yes
Testing carried out in case of fatal crash	All drivers tested
Enforcement	0 1 2 3 4 5 6 7 8 ⑨ 10
% road traffic deaths involving alcohol	–
National motorcycle helmet law	Yes
Applies to drivers and passengers	Yes
Helmet fastening required	No
Helmet standard referred to and/or specified	Yes
Children passengers on motorcycles	Not restricted
Enforcement	0 1 2 3 4 5 6 7 8 ⑨ 10
Helmet wearing rate	71% All riders[c]
National seat-belt law	Yes
Applies to front and rear seat occupants	No
Enforcement	0 1 2 3 4 5 6 7 ⑧ 9 10
Seat-belt wearing rate	69% All occupants[c]
National child restraint law	No
Children seated in front seat	Not restricted
Child restraint required	–
Child restraint standard referred to and/or specified	–
Enforcement	–
% children using child restraints	–
National law on mobile phone use while driving	Yes
Ban on hand-held mobile phone use	No
Ban on hands-free mobile phone use	No
National drug-driving law	Yes

[b] Not based on BAC
[c] 2013, Average helmet and safety belt compliance across 42 cities enrolled in Wahana Tata Nugraha annual traffic and transport award

Deaths by road user category

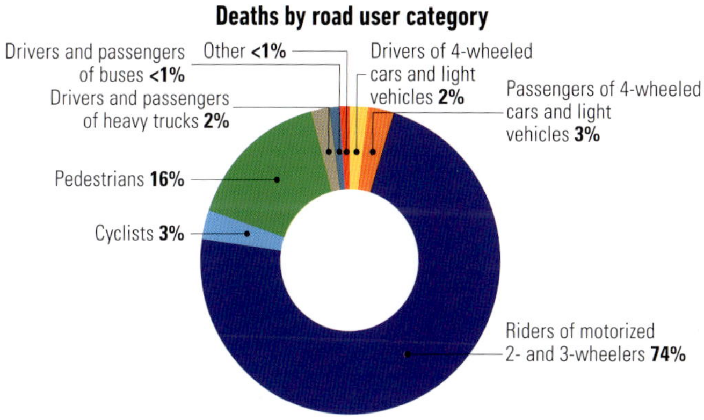

Source: 2016, Indonesia National Police

Trends in reported road traffic deaths

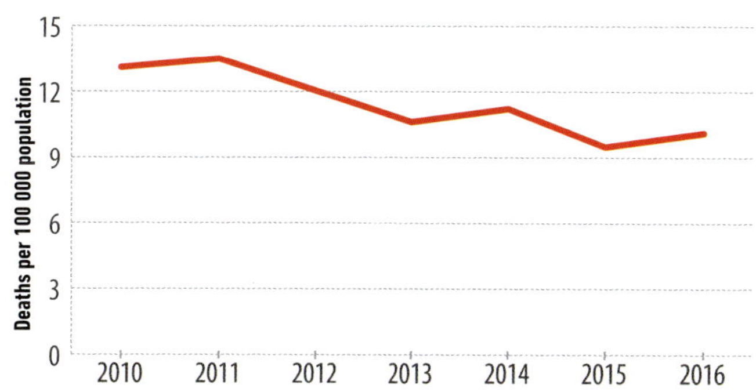

Source: IRSMS Korlantas Polri

Legislative review conducted by WHO. Vehicle safety data from UNECE WP.29. Other data collected by questionnaire and cleared by Ministry of Transportation.

Iran (Islamic Republic of)

Population: 80 277 424 | Income group: Middle | Gross national income per capita: US$ 6 530[a]

INSTITUTIONAL FRAMEWORK

Lead agency	Road Safety Commission, Ministry of Road and Urban Development
Funded in national budget	No
National road safety strategy	Yes
Funding to implement strategy	Partially funded
Fatality reduction target	10% annually (2011-2020)

SAFER ROADS AND MOBILITY

Audits or star rating required for new road infrastructure	Yes
Design standards for the safety of pedestrians / cyclists	Partial
Inspections / star rating of existing roads	Yes
Investments to upgrade high risk locations	Yes
Policies & investment in urban public transport	Yes

SAFER VEHICLES

Total registered vehicles for 2016-2017[b]	30 377 065
Cars and 4-wheeled light vehicles	17 588 666
Motorized 2- and 3-wheelers	11 576 219
Heavy trucks	1 079 127
Buses	133 053
Other	0
Vehicle standards applied (UNECE WP.29)	
Frontal impact standard	No
Electronic stability control	No
Pedestrian protection	No
Motorcycle anti-lock braking system	No

POST-CRASH CARE

National emergency care access number	National, single number
Trauma registry	Subnational
Formal certification for prehospital providers	Yes
National assessment of emergency care systems	Yes

DATA

Reported road traffic fatalities (2016)	15 932[c] (78% M, 22% F)
WHO estimated road traffic fatalities (2016)	16 426
WHO estimated rate per 100 000 population (2016)	20.5

[a] Data available only for 2014
[b] Based on Iranian calendar from 21 March 2016 to 20 March 2017
[c] Legal Medicine Organization. Died within 30 days of crash

SAFER ROAD USERS

National speed limit law	Yes
Max urban speed limit	60 km/h
Max rural speed limit	95 km/h
Max motorway speed limit	120 km/h
Local authorities can modify limits	No
Enforcement	0 1 2 3 4 5 6 (7) 8 9 10
Predominant type of enforcement	Manual and automated
National drink-driving law	Yes[d]
BAC limit – general population	–
BAC limit – young or novice drivers	–
Random breath testing carried out	Yes[e]
Testing carried out in case of fatal crash	Some drivers tested
Enforcement	0 1 2 3 4 5 6 (7) 8 9 10
% road traffic deaths involving alcohol	2%[f]
National motorcycle helmet law	Yes
Applies to drivers and passengers	Yes
Helmet fastening required	No
Helmet standard referred to and/or specified	Yes
Children passengers on motorcycles	Not restricted
Enforcement	0 1 2 3 4 (5) 6 7 8 9 10
Helmet wearing rate	59% Drivers[g], 20% Passengers[g]
National seat-belt law	Yes
Applies to front and rear seat occupants	Yes
Enforcement	0 1 2 3 4 5 6 7 (8) 9 10
Seat-belt wearing rate	93% Front seats[g], 15% Rear seats[g]
National child restraint law	No
Children seated in front seat	Prohibited under 12 yrs
Child restraint required	–
Child restraint standard referred to and/or specified	–
Enforcement	–
% children using child restraints	–
National law on mobile phone use while driving	Yes
Ban on hand-held mobile phone use	Yes
Ban on hands-free mobile phone use	Yes
National drug-driving law	Yes

[d] Not based on BAC. Alcohol consumption is legally prohibited
[e] Legislation requires probable cause to test drivers
[f] 21 March 2016 - 20 March 2017 (Iranian Calendar), Traffic Police
[g] 21 March 2016 - 20 March 2017 (Iranian Calendar), Traffic Police Field Surveys

Deaths by road user category

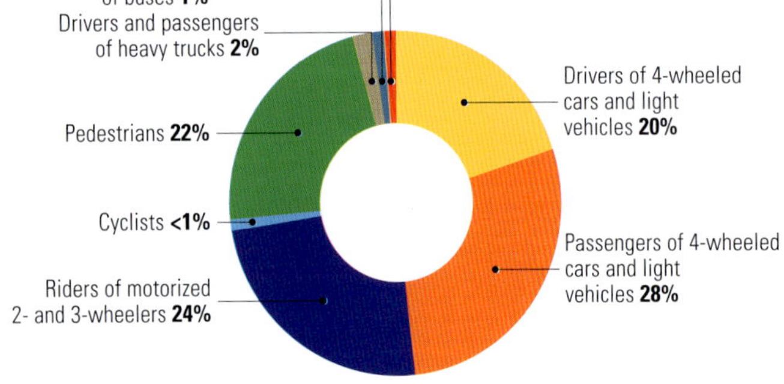

Source: 21 March 2016 - 20 March 2017 (Iranian Calendar), Legal Medicine Organization and Traffic Police

Trends in reported road traffic deaths

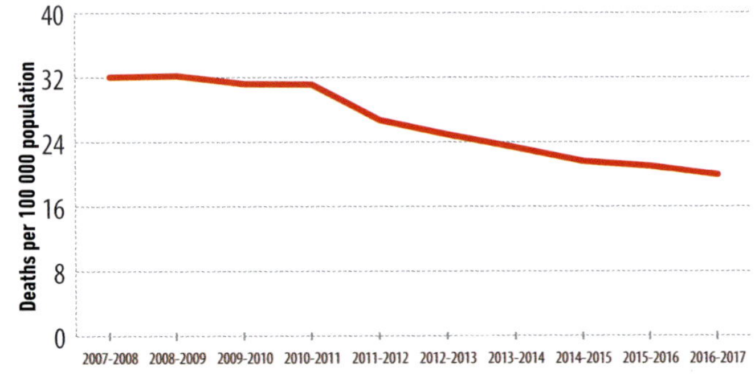

Source: Legal Medicine Organization and National Statistics Center

Legislative review conducted by WHO. Vehicle safety data from UNECE WP29. Other data collected by questionnaire and cleared by Ministry of Health and Medical Education.

Iraq

Population: 37 202 572 | Income group: Middle | Gross national income per capita: US$ 5 430

INSTITUTIONAL FRAMEWORK	
Lead agency	Supreme Council for Road Safety, Ministry of Interior
Funded in national budget	No
National road safety strategy	Yes
Funding to implement strategy	Not funded
Fatality reduction target	–
SAFER ROADS AND MOBILITY	
Audits or star rating required for new road infrastructure	Partial
Design standards for the safety of pedestrians / cyclists	Partial
Inspections / star rating of existing roads	No
Investments to upgrade high risk locations	No
Policies & investment in urban public transport	Yes
SAFER VEHICLES	
Total registered vehicles for 2015	5 775 777
Cars and 4-wheeled light vehicles	5 483 711[a]
Motorized 2- and 3-wheelers	159 736
Heavy trucks	97 553
Buses	34 777
Other	–
Vehicle standards applied (UNECE WP.29)	
Frontal impact standard	No
Electronic stability control	No
Pedestrian protection	No
Motorcycle anti-lock braking system	No
POST-CRASH CARE	
National emergency care access number	National, single number
Trauma registry	Some facilities
Formal certification for prehospital providers	Yes
National assessment of emergency care systems	Yes
DATA	
Reported road traffic fatalities (2016)	4 134[b] (78% M, 22% F)
WHO estimated road traffic fatalities (2016)	7 686 (95% CI 6 548 - 8 824)
WHO estimated rate per 100 000 population (2016)	20.7

[a] Including Kurdistan
[b] Combined sources including hospital and forensic medicine data. Unlimited time period following crash

SAFER ROAD USERS	
National speed limit law	Yes
Max urban speed limit	60 km/h
Max rural speed limit	100 km/h
Max motorway speed limit	120 km/h
Local authorities can modify limits	No
Enforcement	0 1 (2) 3 4 5 6 7 8 9 10
Predominant type of enforcement	Manual
National drink-driving law	Yes[c]
BAC limit – general population	–
BAC limit – young or novice drivers	–
Random breath testing carried out	Yes
Testing carried out in case of fatal crash	Some drivers tested
Enforcement	0 1 (2) 3 4 5 6 7 8 9 10
% road traffic deaths involving alcohol	–
National motorcycle helmet law	Yes
Applies to drivers and passengers	No
Helmet fastening required	No
Helmet standard referred to and/or specified	No
Children passengers on motorcycles	Not restricted
Enforcement	0 1 2 3 4 (5) 6 7 8 9 10
Helmet wearing rate	–
National seat-belt law	Yes
Applies to front and rear seat occupants	No
Enforcement	0 1 2 3 4 (5) 6 7 8 9 10
Seat-belt wearing rate	–
National child restraint law	No
Children seated in front seat	Prohibited[d]
Child restraint required	–
Child restraint standard referred to and/or specified	–
Enforcement	–
% children using child restraints	–
National law on mobile phone use while driving	Yes
Ban on hand-held mobile phone use	Yes
Ban on hands-free mobile phone use	Yes
National drug-driving law	Yes

[c] Not based on BAC
[d] The law prohibits children to sit in the front but does not specify the age, size or weight of children concerned

Deaths by road user category

Trends in reported road traffic deaths

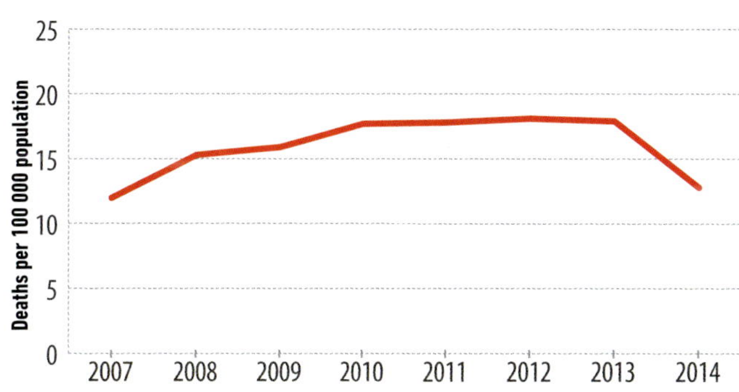

Source: Ministry of Health

Legislative review conducted by WHO. Vehicle safety data from UNECE WP.29. Other data collected by questionnaire and cleared by Ministry of Health.

Ireland

Population: 4 726 078 | Income group: High | Gross national income per capita: US$ 52 560

INSTITUTIONAL FRAMEWORK

Lead agency	The Road Safety Authority (RSA)
Funded in national budget	No
National road safety strategy	Yes
Funding to implement strategy	Fully funded
Fatality reduction target	25 deaths per million population by 2020 (2012-2020)

SAFER ROADS AND MOBILITY

Audits or star rating required for new road infrastructure	Partial
Design standards for the safety of pedestrians / cyclists	Yes
Inspections / star rating of existing roads	Yes
Investments to upgrade high risk locations	Yes
Policies & investment in urban public transport	Yes

SAFER VEHICLES

Total registered vehicles for 2015	2 573 961
Cars and 4-wheeled light vehicles	1 985 130
Motorized 2- and 3-wheelers	36 974
Heavy trucks	330 541
Buses	31 236
Other	190 080
Vehicle standards applied (UNECE WP.29)	
Frontal impact standard	Yes
Electronic stability control	Yes
Pedestrian protection	Yes
Motorcycle anti-lock braking system	Yes

POST-CRASH CARE

National emergency care access number	National, single number
Trauma registry	National
Formal certification for prehospital providers	Yes
National assessment of emergency care systems	Yes

DATA

Reported road traffic fatalities (2016)	188[a] (74% M, 26% F)
WHO estimated road traffic fatalities (2016)	194
WHO estimated rate per 100 000 population (2016)	4.1

[a] Road Safety Authority Collision Database, 2017. Died within 30 days of crash

SAFER ROAD USERS

National speed limit law	Yes
Max urban speed limit	50 km/h
Max rural speed limit	100 km/h
Max motorway speed limit	120 km/h
Local authorities can modify limits	Yes
Enforcement	0 1 2 3 4 5 6 7 8 9 **10**
Predominant type of enforcement	Automated
National drink-driving law	Yes
BAC limit – general population	≤ 0.05 g/dl
BAC limit – young or novice drivers	≤ 0.02 g/dl
Random breath testing carried out	Yes
Testing carried out in case of fatal crash	All drivers tested
Enforcement	0 1 2 3 4 5 6 7 8 9 **10**
% road traffic deaths involving alcohol	39%[b]
National motorcycle helmet law	Yes
Applies to drivers and passengers	Yes
Helmet fastening required	No
Helmet standard referred to and/or specified	Yes
Children passengers on motorcycles	Not restricted
Enforcement	0 1 2 3 4 5 6 7 8 9 **10**
Helmet wearing rate	99% Drivers[c]
National seat-belt law	Yes
Applies to front and rear seat occupants	Yes
Enforcement	0 1 2 3 4 5 6 7 8 9 **10**
Seat-belt wearing rate	94% Front seats[d], 74% Rear seats[d]
National child restraint law	Yes
Children seated in front seat	Allowed in a child restraint[e]
Child restraint required	Up to 36 kg/150 cm
Child restraint standard referred to and/or specified	Yes
Enforcement	0 1 2 3 4 5 6 7 8 9 **10**
% children using child restraints	–
National law on mobile phone use while driving	Yes
Ban on hand-held mobile phone use	Yes
Ban on hands-free mobile phone use	No
National drug-driving law	Yes

[b] 2008-2012, Fatal Collisions 2008-2012, Alcohol as a Factor, 2016
[c] 2016, 2016 Observational Report on High Visibility and Helmet Wearing rates (only motorcycle drivers)
[d] 2016, Mobile Phone and Seatbelt Observational Study 2016
[e] Provided that airbag is deactivated if child is in a rear-facing child restraint system

Deaths by road user category

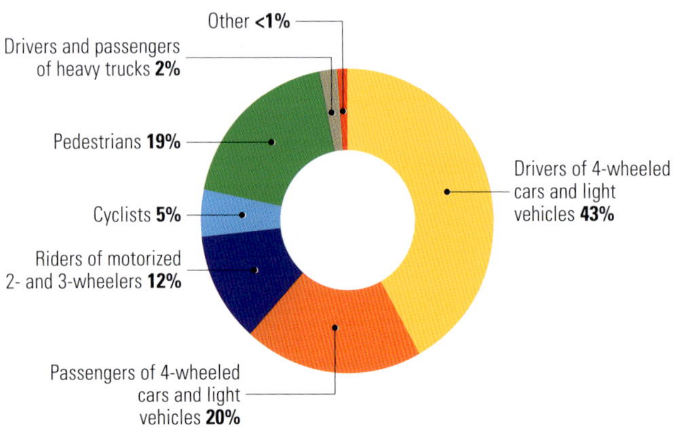

Source: 2016, Road Safety Authority Collision Database, 2017

Trends in reported road traffic deaths

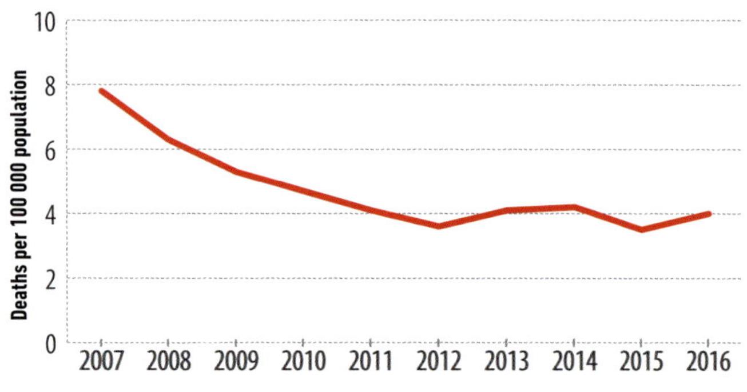

Source: Road Safety Authority Collision Database 2017 and CSO website

Legislative review conducted by WHO. Vehicle safety data from UNECE WP.29. Other data collected by questionnaire and cleared by Department for Transport, Tourism and Sport.

Israel

Population: 8 191 828 | Income group: High | Gross national income per capita: US$ 36 190

INSTITUTIONAL FRAMEWORK	
Lead agency	Israel National Road Safety Authority (RSA)
Funded in national budget	Yes
National road safety strategy	Yes
Funding to implement strategy	Fully funded
Fatality reduction target	–
SAFER ROADS AND MOBILITY	
Audits or star rating required for new road infrastructure	Yes
Design standards for the safety of pedestrians / cyclists	Partial
Inspections / star rating of existing roads	Yes
Investments to upgrade high risk locations	Yes
Policies & investment in urban public transport	Yes
SAFER VEHICLES	
Total registered vehicles for 2016	3 239 305
Cars and 4-wheeled light vehicles	2 726 835
Motorized 2- and 3-wheelers	130 442
Heavy trucks	92 817
Buses	20 212
Other	268 999
Vehicle standards applied (UNECE WP.29)	
Frontal impact standard	Yes[a]
Electronic stability control	Yes[a]
Pedestrian protection	No
Motorcycle anti-lock braking system	No
POST-CRASH CARE	
National emergency care access number	National, single number
Trauma registry	National
Formal certification for prehospital providers	Yes
National assessment of emergency care systems	No
DATA	
Reported road traffic fatalities (2016)	335[b] (76% M, 24% F)
WHO estimated road traffic fatalities (2016)	345
WHO estimated rate per 100 000 population (2016)	4.2

[a] Required for cars made under US regulations - for European cars, no requirements further than ESC
[b] Central Bureau of Statistic, Jerusalem, Israel. Died within 30 days of crash

SAFER ROAD USERS	
National speed limit law	Yes
Max urban speed limit	50 km/h
Max rural speed limit	80 km/h
Max motorway speed limit	110 km/h
Local authorities can modify limits	No
Enforcement	0 1 2 3 4 (5) 6 7 8 9 10
Predominant type of enforcement	Automated
National drink-driving law	Yes
BAC limit – general population	≤ 0.05 g/dl
BAC limit – young or novice drivers	≤ 0.01 g/dl
Random breath testing carried out	Yes
Testing carried out in case of fatal crash	All drivers tested
Enforcement	0 1 2 3 4 5 6 (7) 8 9 10
% road traffic deaths involving alcohol	4%[c]
National motorcycle helmet law	Yes
Applies to drivers and passengers	Yes
Helmet fastening required	Yes
Helmet standard referred to and/or specified	Yes
Children passengers on motorcycles	Not restricted
Enforcement	0 1 2 3 4 5 6 7 8 (9) 10
Helmet wearing rate	98% Drivers[d], 98% Passengers[d]
National seat-belt law	Yes
Applies to front and rear seat occupants	Yes
Enforcement	0 1 2 3 4 5 6 (7) 8 9 10
Seat-belt wearing rate	89% Front seats[e], 70% Rear seats[e]
National child restraint law	Yes
Children seated in front seat	Allowed in a child restraint
Child restraint required	Up to 8 yrs[f]
Child restraint standard referred to and/or specified	Yes
Enforcement	0 1 2 3 4 5 (6) 7 8 9 10
% children using child restraints	52%[g]
National law on mobile phone use while driving	Yes
Ban on hand-held mobile phone use	Yes
Ban on hands-free mobile phone use	No
National drug-driving law	Yes

[c] 2016, Israeli police
[d] 2011, Israel National Road Safety authority
[e] 2016, Israel National Road Safety Authority
[f] For children under 3 years, a child restraint is required (and a rear-facing child restraint for children under one year) while for children aged 3-8 years the legislation refers either to child restraint or booster seat use
[g] Observational survey (Figure for children aged 0-15 years buckled in accordance with the law)

Deaths by road user category

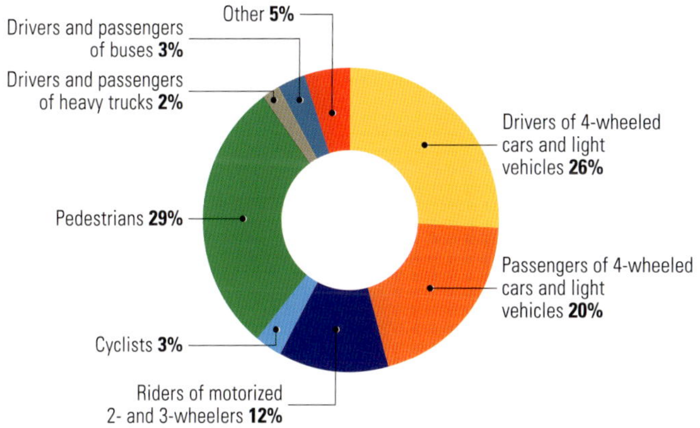

Source: 2016, Central Bureau of Statistics, Jerusalem, Israel and Israeli Police data

Trends in reported road traffic deaths

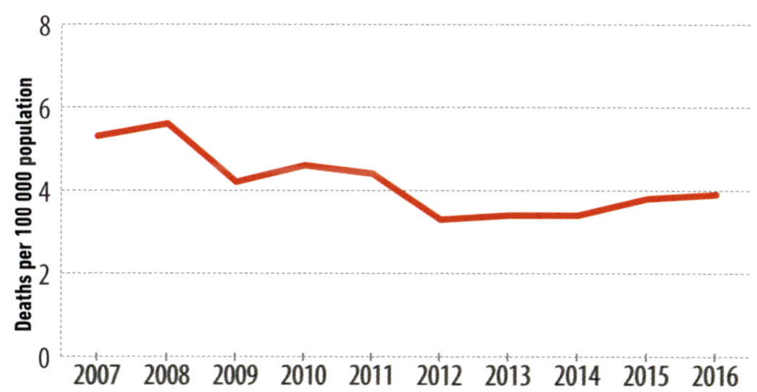

Source: Central Bureau of Statistics, Jerusalem, Israel

Italy

Population: 59 429 936 | Income group: High | Gross national income per capita: US$ 31 590

INSTITUTIONAL FRAMEWORK	
Lead agency	Ministry of Transport, Directorate General Road Safety
Funded in national budget	Yes
National road safety strategy	Yes
Funding to implement strategy	Partially funded
Fatality reduction target	50% (2010-2020)
SAFER ROADS AND MOBILITY	
Audits or star rating required for new road infrastructure	Yes
Design standards for the safety of pedestrians / cyclists	Yes
Inspections / star rating of existing roads	Yes
Investments to upgrade high risk locations	No
Policies & investment in urban public transport	Yes
SAFER VEHICLES	
Total registered vehicles for 2016	52 581 575
Cars and 4-wheeled light vehicles	41 322 370
Motorized 2- and 3-wheelers	9 354 428
Heavy trucks	885 513
Buses	97 817
Other	921 447
Vehicle standards applied (UNECE WP.29)	
Frontal impact standard	Yes
Electronic stability control	Yes
Pedestrian protection	Yes
Motorcycle anti-lock braking system	Yes
POST-CRASH CARE	
National emergency care access number	National, single number
Trauma registry	Subnational
Formal certification for prehospital providers	Yes
National assessment of emergency care systems	No
DATA	
Reported road traffic fatalities (2015)	3 428[a] (80% M, 20% F)
WHO estimated road traffic fatalities (2016)	3 333
WHO estimated rate per 100 000 population (2016)	5.6

[a] Italian National Institute of Statistics (ISTAT) and Automobile Club of Italy (ACI) Survey on road accidents resulting in death or injury. Died within 30 days of crash

SAFER ROAD USERS	
National speed limit law	Yes
Max urban speed limit	50 km/h
Max rural speed limit	110 km/h[b]
Max motorway speed limit	150 km/h
Local authorities can modify limits	Yes
Enforcement	0 1 2 3 4 5 6 7 (8) 9 10
Predominant type of enforcement	Automated
National drink-driving law	Yes
BAC limit – general population	≤ 0.05 g/dl
BAC limit – young or novice drivers	0.00 g/dl
Random breath testing carried out	Yes
Testing carried out in case of fatal crash	Some drivers tested
Enforcement	0 1 2 3 4 5 6 (7) 8 9 10
% road traffic deaths involving alcohol	20-25%[c]
National motorcycle helmet law	Yes
Applies to drivers and passengers	Yes
Helmet fastening required	Yes
Helmet standard referred to and/or specified	Yes
Children passengers on motorcycles	Prohibited under 5 yrs
Enforcement	0 1 2 3 4 5 6 7 8 (9) 10
Helmet wearing rate	98% All riders[d]
National seat-belt law	Yes
Applies to front and rear seat occupants	Yes
Enforcement	0 1 2 3 4 5 6 (7) 8 9 10
Seat-belt wearing rate	62% Front seats[d], 15% Rear seats[d]
National child restraint law	Yes
Children seated in front seat	Allowed in a child restraint[e]
Child restraint required	Up to 150 cm
Child restraint standard referred to and/or specified	Yes
Enforcement	0 1 2 3 4 5 (6) 7 8 9 10
% children using child restraints	38%[d]
National law on mobile phone use while driving	Yes
Ban on hand-held mobile phone use	Yes
Ban on hands-free mobile phone use	No
National drug-driving law	Yes

[b] 110 km/h for main suburban roads, 90 km/h for secondary suburban roads
[c] 2010, DRUID project on prevalence of alcohol and other psychoactive substances in drivers killed and injured (Isalberti et al., 2011)
[d] 2015, Italian National Institute of Health
[e] Provided that airbag is deactivated

Deaths by road user category

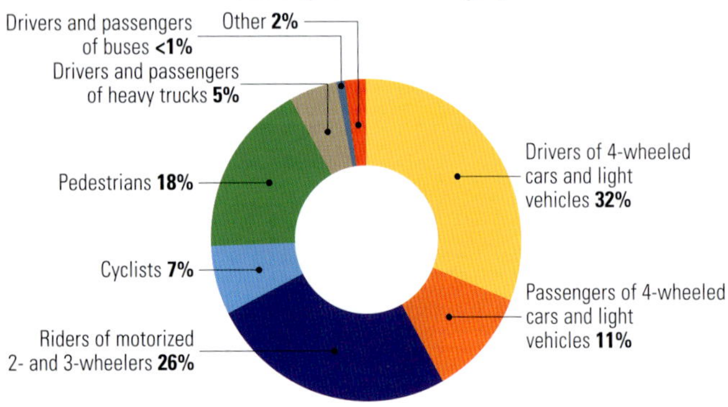

Source: 2015, Italian National Institute of Statistics (ISTAT) and Automobile Club of Italy (ACI) Survey on road accidents resulting in death or injury

Trends in reported road traffic deaths

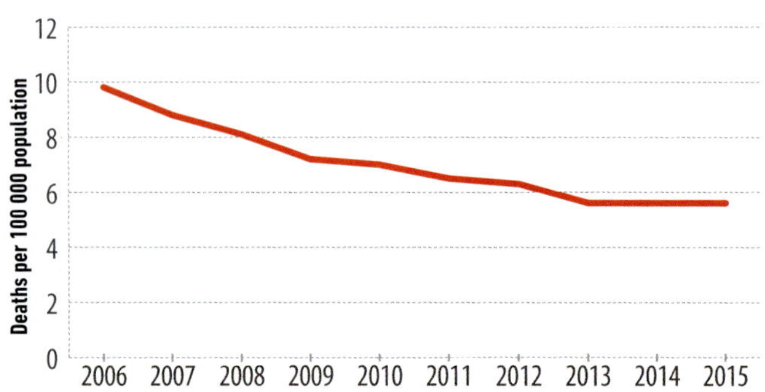

Source: Italian National Institute of Statistics (ISTAT) and Automobile Club of Italy (ACI) Survey on road accidents resulting in death or injury

Jamaica

Population: 2 881 355 | Income group: Middle | Gross national income per capita: US$ 4 660

INSTITUTIONAL FRAMEWORK	
Lead agency	National Road Safety Council (NRSC)
Funded in national budget	Yes
National road safety strategy	Yes
Funding to implement strategy	Partially funded
Fatality reduction target	< 300 deaths (By 2020)
SAFER ROADS AND MOBILITY	
Audits or star rating required for new road infrastructure	Yes
Design standards for the safety of pedestrians / cyclists	Partial
Inspections / star rating of existing roads	Yes
Investments to upgrade high risk locations	No
Policies & investment in urban public transport	Yes
SAFER VEHICLES	
Total registered vehicles for 2016	541 316
Cars and 4-wheeled light vehicles	418 945
Motorized 2- and 3-wheelers	14 090
Heavy trucks	107 815
Buses	—[a]
Other	466
Vehicle standards applied (UNECE WP.29)	
Frontal impact standard	No
Electronic stability control	No
Pedestrian protection	No
Motorcycle anti-lock braking system	No
POST-CRASH CARE	
National emergency care access number	National, single number
Trauma registry	Some facilities
Formal certification for prehospital providers	No
National assessment of emergency care systems	No
DATA	
Reported road traffic fatalities (2016)	379[b] (84% M, 16% F)
WHO estimated road traffic fatalities (2016)	391
WHO estimated rate per 100 000 population (2016)	13.6

[a] Buses are included under heavy trucks
[b] Jamaica Constabulary Force (JCF). Died within 30 days of crash

SAFER ROAD USERS	
National speed limit law	Yes
Max urban speed limit	~ 48 km/h
Max rural speed limit	~ 80 km/h
Max motorway speed limit	No
Local authorities can modify limits	No
Enforcement	0 1 2 3 ④ 5 6 7 8 9 10
Predominant type of enforcement	Manual
National drink-driving law	Yes
BAC limit – general population	≤ 0.08 g/dl
BAC limit – young or novice drivers	≤ 0.08 g/dl
Random breath testing carried out	Yes[c]
Testing carried out in case of fatal crash	Some drivers tested
Enforcement	0 1 ② 3 4 5 6 7 8 9 10
% road traffic deaths involving alcohol	—
National motorcycle helmet law	Yes
Applies to drivers and passengers	Yes
Helmet fastening required	Yes
Helmet standard referred to and/or specified	Yes
Children passengers on motorcycles	Not restricted
Enforcement	0 1 ② 3 4 5 6 7 8 9 10
Helmet wearing rate	6% Drivers, 2% Passengers[d]
National seat-belt law	Yes
Applies to front and rear seat occupants	Yes
Enforcement	0 1 2 ③ 4 5 6 7 8 9 10
Seat-belt wearing rate	54% Front seats[d], 4% Rear seats[d]
National child restraint law	Yes[e]
Children seated in front seat	Not restricted
Child restraint required	—[e]
Child restraint standard referred to and/or specified	Yes
Enforcement	0 1 ② 3 4 5 6 7 8 9 10
% children using child restraints	—
National law on mobile phone use while driving	No
Ban on hand-held mobile phone use	—
Ban on hands-free mobile phone use	—
National drug-driving law	Yes

[c] Legislation requires probable cause to test drivers or commission of a traffic offence
[d] 2008, Jamaica Health and Lifestyle Survey (refers to use always or most times)
[e] The legislation refers to child restraint system for children but does not specify the age/height group covered by this obligation

Deaths by road user category

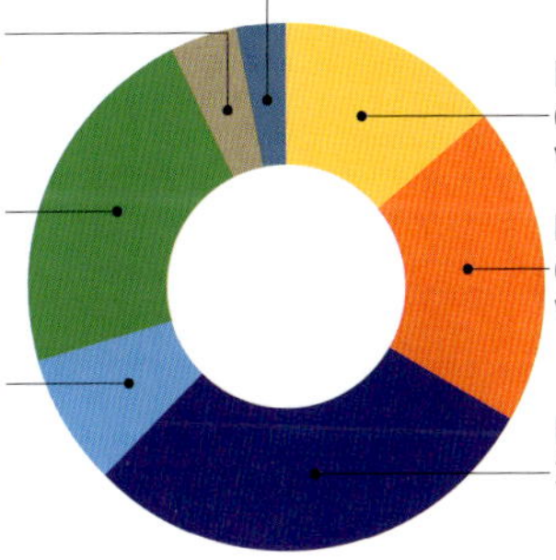

Source: 2016, Jamaica Constabulary Force

Trends in reported road traffic deaths

Source: Jamaica Constabulary Force (death data) and Statistical Institute of Jamaica (population data).

Japan

Population: 127 748 512 | Income group: High | Gross national income per capita: US$ 38 000

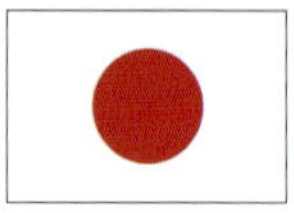

INSTITUTIONAL FRAMEWORK

Lead agency	Central Traffic Safety Policy Council
Funded in national budget	Yes
National road safety strategy	Yes
Funding to implement strategy	Fully funded
Fatality reduction target	<2 500 deaths (within 24hrs) per year (2016-2020)

SAFER ROADS AND MOBILITY

Audits or star rating required for new road infrastructure	Yes
Design standards for the safety of pedestrians / cyclists	Yes
Inspections / star rating of existing roads	Yes
Investments to upgrade high risk locations	Yes
Policies & investment in urban public transport	Yes

SAFER VEHICLES

Total registered vehicles for 2016	81 602 046
Cars and 4-wheeled light vehicles	–
Motorized 2- and 3-wheelers	–
Heavy trucks	–
Buses	–
Other	–
Vehicle standards applied (UNECE WP.29)	
Frontal impact standard	Yes
Electronic stability control	Yes
Pedestrian protection	Yes
Motorcycle anti-lock braking system	Yes

POST-CRASH CARE

National emergency care access number	National, single number
Trauma registry	National
Formal certification for prehospital providers	Yes
National assessment of emergency care systems	No

DATA

Reported road traffic fatalities (2016)	4 682[a] (68% M, 32% F)
WHO estimated road traffic fatalities (2016)	5 224
WHO estimated rate per 100 000 population (2016)	4.1

[a] National Police Agency. Died within 30 days of crash

SAFER ROAD USERS

National speed limit law	Yes
Max urban speed limit	60 km/h
Max rural speed limit	60 km/h
Max motorway speed limit	100 km/h
Local authorities can modify limits	Yes
Enforcement	0 1 2 3 4 5 6 (7) 8 9 10
Predominant type of enforcement	Manual
National drink-driving law	Yes
BAC limit – general population	< 0.03 g/dl
BAC limit – young or novice drivers	< 0.03 g/dl
Random breath testing carried out	Yes[b]
Testing carried out in case of fatal crash	Some drivers tested
Enforcement	0 1 2 3 4 5 6 7 8 (9) 10
% road traffic deaths involving alcohol	6%[c]
National motorcycle helmet law	Yes
Applies to drivers and passengers	Yes
Helmet fastening required	No
Helmet standard referred to and/or specified	Yes
Children passengers on motorcycles	Not restricted
Enforcement	0 1 2 3 4 5 6 7 8 (9) 10
Helmet wearing rate	–
National seat-belt law	Yes
Applies to front and rear seat occupants	Yes
Enforcement	0 1 2 3 4 5 6 (7) 8 9 10
Seat-belt wearing rate	98/95% Front seats[d], 72/36% Rear seats[d]
National child restraint law	Yes
Children seated in front seat	Allowed in a child restraint
Child restraint required	Up to 6 yrs
Child restraint standard referred to and/or specified	Yes
Enforcement	0 1 2 3 4 5 6 (7) 8 9 10
% children using child restraints	64%[e]
National law on mobile phone use while driving	Yes
Ban on hand-held mobile phone use	Yes
Ban on hands-free mobile phone use	No
National drug-driving law	Yes

[b] Legislation requires probable cause to test drivers
[c] 2016, National Police Agency
[d] 2016, Joint study by Japan Automobile Federation (JAF) and National Police Agency. Percentages are for expressways and other roads, respectively
[e] Joint study by Japan Automobile Federation (JAF) and National Police Agency.

Deaths by road user category

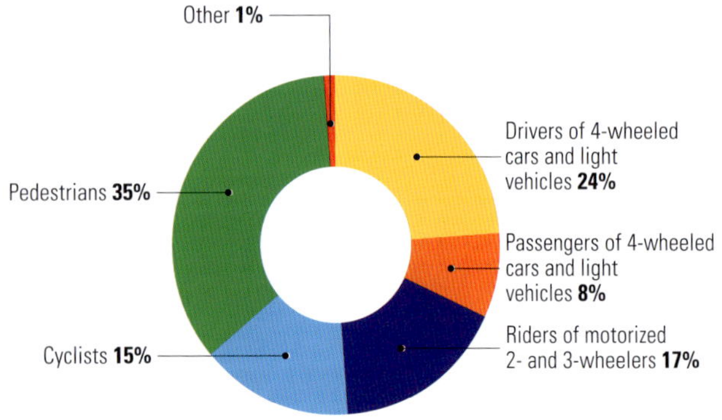

Source: 2016, National Police Agency

Trends in reported road traffic deaths

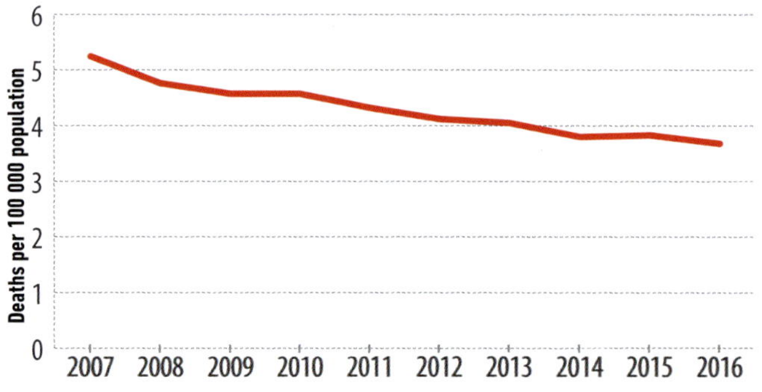

Source: National Police Agency

Legislative review conducted by WHO. Vehicle safety data from UNECE WP29. Other data collected by questionnaire and cleared by Ministry of Health, Labour and Welfare.

Jordan

Population: 9 455 802 | Income group: Middle | Gross national income per capita: US$ 3 920

INSTITUTIONAL FRAMEWORK	
Lead agency	No
Funded in national budget	–
National road safety strategy	No
Funding to implement strategy	–
Fatality reduction target	–
SAFER ROADS AND MOBILITY	
Audits or star rating required for new road infrastructure	Yes
Design standards for the safety of pedestrians / cyclists	Partial
Inspections / star rating of existing roads	Yes
Investments to upgrade high risk locations	Yes
Policies & investment in urban public transport	Yes
SAFER VEHICLES	
Total registered vehicles for 2016	1 502 420
Cars and 4-wheeled light vehicles	–
Motorized 2- and 3-wheelers	–
Heavy trucks	–
Buses	–
Other	–
Vehicle standards applied (UNECE WP.29)	
Frontal impact standard	No
Electronic stability control	No
Pedestrian protection	No
Motorcycle anti-lock braking system	No
POST-CRASH CARE	
National emergency care access number	National, single number
Trauma registry	None
Formal certification for prehospital providers	Yes
National assessment of emergency care systems	No
DATA	
Reported road traffic fatalities (2016)	750[a] (79% M, 21% F)
WHO estimated road traffic fatalities (2016)	2 306 (95% CI 1 926 - 2 686)
WHO estimated rate per 100 000 population (2016)	24.4

[a] Public Security Directorate (Jordan Police), 2016 Traffic Accidents Report. Died within 30 days of crash

SAFER ROAD USERS	
National speed limit law	Yes
Max urban speed limit	90 km/h
Max rural speed limit	120 km/h
Max motorway speed limit	120 km/h
Local authorities can modify limits	Yes
Enforcement	0 1 2 3 4 5 6 (7) 8 9 10
Predominant type of enforcement	Manual and automated
National drink-driving law	Yes
BAC limit – general population	< 0.08 g/dl
BAC limit – young or novice drivers	< 0.08 g/dl
Random breath testing carried out	Yes[b]
Testing carried out in case of fatal crash	Some drivers tested
Enforcement	0 1 2 (3) 4 5 6 7 8 9 10
% road traffic deaths involving alcohol	–
National motorcycle helmet law	Yes
Applies to drivers and passengers	Yes
Helmet fastening required	No
Helmet standard referred to and/or specified	Yes
Children passengers on motorcycles	Not restricted
Enforcement	0 1 2 3 4 5 6 (7) 8 9 10
Helmet wearing rate	–
National seat-belt law	Yes
Applies to front and rear seat occupants	No
Enforcement	0 1 2 3 4 5 (6) 7 8 9 10
Seat-belt wearing rate	–
National child restraint law	No
Children seated in front seat	Prohibited under 10 yrs
Child restraint required	–
Child restraint standard referred to and/or specified	–
Enforcement	–
% children using child restraints	–
National law on mobile phone use while driving	Yes
Ban on hand-held mobile phone use	Yes
Ban on hands-free mobile phone use	No
National drug-driving law	Yes

[b] Legislation refers to alcohol testing in the case of reckless driving or in the case of a crash

Deaths by road user category

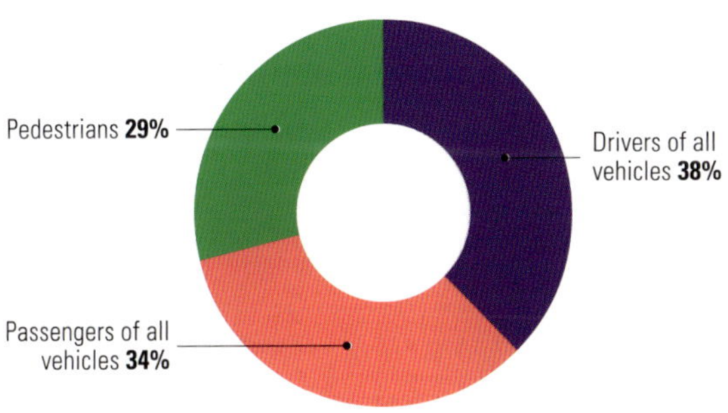

Trends in reported road traffic deaths

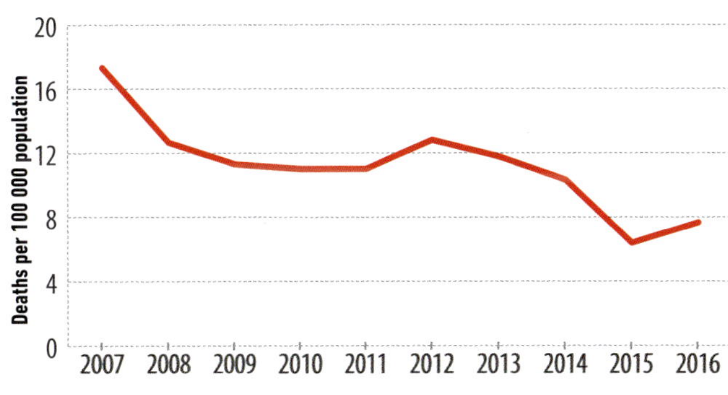

Source: Directorate of General Security, Annual Reports of Traffic Accidents in Jordan

Legislative review conducted by WHO. Vehicle safety data from UNECE WP29. Other data collected by questionnaire and cleared by Jordan Traffic Institute.

Kazakhstan

Population: 17 987 736 | Income group: Middle | Gross national income per capita: US$ 8 710

INSTITUTIONAL FRAMEWORK

Lead agency	Internal Affairs Ministry of the Republic of Kazakhstan
Funded in national budget	Yes
National road safety strategy	Yes
Funding to implement strategy	Partially funded
Fatality reduction target	≤ 12 fatalities per 100 000 population by 2020 (2011-2020)

SAFER ROADS AND MOBILITY

Audits or star rating required for new road infrastructure	Yes
Design standards for the safety of pedestrians / cyclists	Yes
Inspections / star rating of existing roads	Yes
Investments to upgrade high risk locations	Yes
Policies & investment in urban public transport	Yes

SAFER VEHICLES

Total registered vehicles for 2016	4 383 120
Cars and 4-wheeled light vehicles	3 835 609
Motorized 2- and 3-wheelers	9 692
Heavy trucks	439 167
Buses	98 652
Other	0
Vehicle standards applied (UNECE WP.29)	
Frontal impact standard	No
Electronic stability control	No
Pedestrian protection	No
Motorcycle anti-lock braking system	No

POST-CRASH CARE

National emergency care access number	National, single number
Trauma registry	National
Formal certification for prehospital providers	Yes
National assessment of emergency care systems	No

DATA

Reported road traffic fatalities (2016)	2 625[a] (74% M, 26% F)
WHO estimated road traffic fatalities (2016)	3 158
WHO estimated rate per 100 000 population (2016)	17.6

[a] Combined sources, including Committee on Statistics of the Ministry of National Economy of the Republic of Kazakhstan. Died within 30 days of crash

SAFER ROAD USERS

National speed limit law	Yes
Max urban speed limit	60 km/h[b]
Max rural speed limit	110 km/h
Max motorway speed limit	140 km/h
Local authorities can modify limits	No
Enforcement	0 1 2 3 4 5 6 (7) 8 9 10
Predominant type of enforcement	Automated
National drink-driving law	Yes
BAC limit – general population	< 0.05 g/dl[c]
BAC limit – young or novice drivers	< 0.05 g/dl[c]
Random breath testing carried out	No
Testing carried out in case of fatal crash	All drivers tested
Enforcement	0 1 2 3 4 5 6 (7) 8 9 10
% road traffic deaths involving alcohol	<1%[d]
National motorcycle helmet law	Yes
Applies to drivers and passengers	Yes
Helmet fastening required	Yes
Helmet standard referred to and/or specified	No
Children passengers on motorcycles	Prohibited under 12 yrs
Enforcement	0 1 2 3 4 5 6 (7) 8 9 10
Helmet wearing rate	–
National seat-belt law	Yes
Applies to front and rear seat occupants	Yes
Enforcement	0 1 2 3 4 5 6 (7) 8 9 10
Seat-belt wearing rate	–
National child restraint law	Yes
Children seated in front seat	Allowed in a child restraint
Child restraint required	–[e]
Child restraint standard referred to and/or specified	Yes[e]
Enforcement	0 1 2 3 4 5 6 (7) 8 9 10
% children using child restraints	–
National law on mobile phone use while driving	Yes
Ban on hand-held mobile phone use	Yes
Ban on hands-free mobile phone use	No
National drug-driving law	Yes

[b] Can be increased up to 90 km/h

[c] Different ranges are provided to characterize the degree of intoxication with the 0.05 to <0.15g/dl range corresponding to light intoxication

[d] 2016, Committee on Statistics of the Ministry of National Economy of the Republic of Kazakhstan

[e] The legislation requires that children under 12 years be placed in a child restraint or "other means" used in conjunction with a seat belt

Deaths by road user category

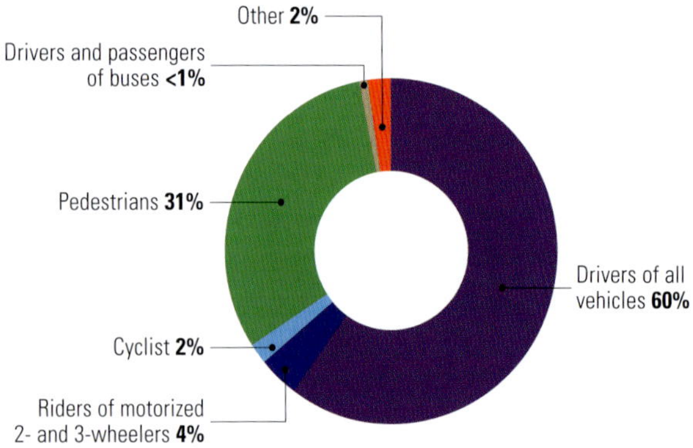

Source: 2016, Committee on Statistics of the Ministry of National Economy of the Republic of Kazakhstan

Trends in reported road traffic deaths

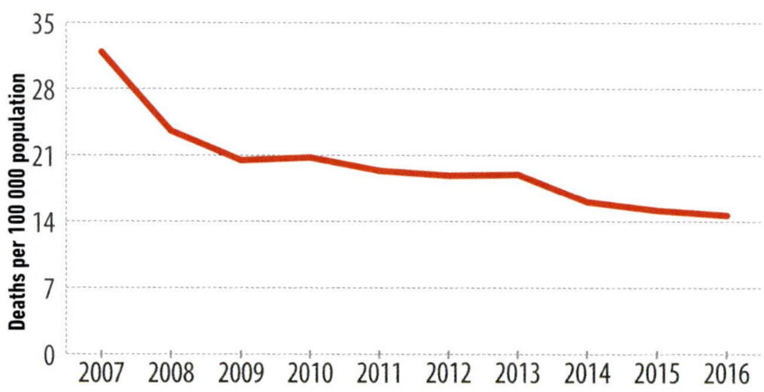

Source: Committee on Statistics of the Ministry of National Economy of the Republic of Kazakhstan

Kenya

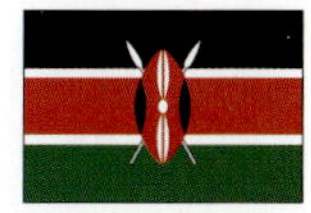

Population: 48 461 568 | Income group: Middle | Gross national income per capita: US$ 1 380

INSTITUTIONAL FRAMEWORK	
Lead agency	National Transport and Safety Authority, Ministry of Transport, Infrastructure, Housing and Urban Development
Funded in national budget	Yes
National road safety strategy	No
Funding to implement strategy	–
Fatality reduction target	–
SAFER ROADS AND MOBILITY	
Audits or star rating required for new road infrastructure	Partial
Design standards for the safety of pedestrians / cyclists	Partial
Inspections / star rating of existing roads	No
Investments to upgrade high risk locations	Yes
Policies & investment in urban public transport	Yes
SAFER VEHICLES	
Total registered vehicles for 2016	2 979 910
Cars and 4-wheeled light vehicles	–
Motorized 2- and 3-wheelers	–
Heavy trucks	–
Buses	–
Other	–
Vehicle standards applied (UNECE WP.29)	
Frontal impact standard	No
Electronic stability control	No
Pedestrian protection	No
Motorcycle anti-lock braking system	No
POST-CRASH CARE	
National emergency care access number	National, single number
Trauma registry	Some facilities
Formal certification for prehospital providers	No
National assessment of emergency care systems	No
DATA	
Reported road traffic fatalities (2016)	2 965[a] (83% M, 17% F)
WHO estimated road traffic fatalities (2016)	13 463 (95% CI 11 486 - 15 440)
WHO estimated rate per 100 000 population (2016)	27.8

[a] National Transport and Safety Authority, 2016 Road Safety Status Report. Died at scene of crash

SAFER ROAD USERS	
National speed limit law	Yes
Max urban speed limit	50 km/h
Max rural speed limit	100 km/h
Max motorway speed limit	110 km/h
Local authorities can modify limits	No
Enforcement	0 1 2 3 ④ 5 6 7 8 9 10
Predominant type of enforcement	Manual
National drink-driving law	Yes
BAC limit – general population	≤ 0.08 g/dl
BAC limit – young or novice drivers	≤ 0.08 g/dl
Random breath testing carried out	Yes[b]
Testing carried out in case of fatal crash	No
Enforcement	0 1 2 3 4 ⑤ 6 7 8 9 10
% road traffic deaths involving alcohol	–
National motorcycle helmet law	Yes
Applies to drivers and passengers	Yes
Helmet fastening required	Yes
Helmet standard referred to and/or specified	Yes
Children passengers on motorcycles	Not restricted
Enforcement	0 1 2 ③ 4 5 6 7 8 9 10
Helmet wearing rate	35% Drivers[c], 3% Passengers[c]
National seat-belt law	Yes
Applies to front and rear seat occupants	Yes
Enforcement	0 1 2 3 ④ 5 6 7 8 9 10
Seat-belt wearing rate	–
National child restraint law	No
Children seated in front seat	Not restricted
Child restraint required	–
Child restraint standard referred to and/or specified	–
Enforcement	–
% children using child restraints	–
National law on mobile phone use while driving	Yes
Ban on hand-held mobile phone use	Yes
Ban on hands-free mobile phone use	No
National drug-driving law	Yes

[b] Legislation requires probable cause to test drivers or commission of a traffic offence
[c] 2010, Helmet wearing in Kenya, Bachani et al

Deaths by road user category

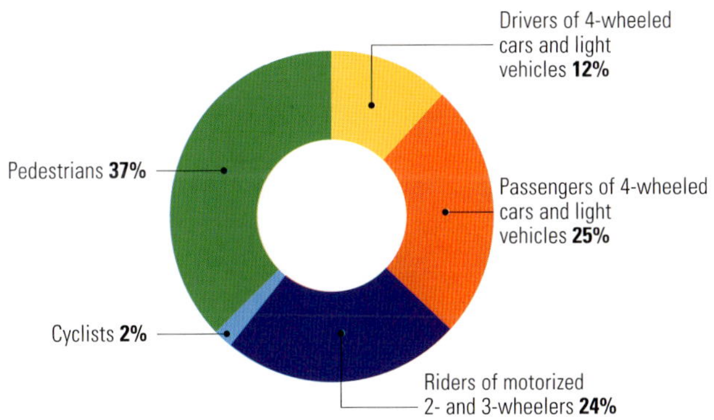

Source: National Transport and Safety Authority, 2016 Road Safety Status Report

Trends in reported road traffic deaths

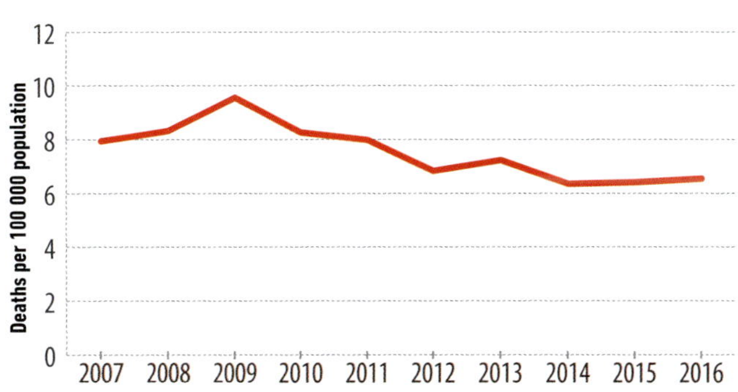

Source: National Transport and Safety Authority, World Bank, and Kenya National Bureau of Statistics

Kiribati

Population: 114 395 | Income group: Middle | Gross national income per capita: US$ 2 380

INSTITUTIONAL FRAMEWORK	
Lead agency	No
Funded in national budget	–
National road safety strategy	Yes
Funding to implement strategy	Partially funded
Fatality reduction target	Zero deaths by 2019 (2016 - 2019)

SAFER ROADS AND MOBILITY	
Audits or star rating required for new road infrastructure	Yes
Design standards for the safety of pedestrians / cyclists	Partial
Inspections / star rating of existing roads	No
Investments to upgrade high risk locations	Yes
Policies & investment in urban public transport	Yes

SAFER VEHICLES	
Total registered vehicles for June 2016 - August 2017	3 706
Cars and 4-wheeled light vehicles	2 547
Motorized 2- and 3-wheelers	757
Heavy trucks	4
Buses	398
Other	0
Vehicle standards applied (UNECE WP.29)	
Frontal impact standard	No
Electronic stability control	No
Pedestrian protection	No
Motorcycle anti-lock braking system	No

POST-CRASH CARE	
National emergency care access number	National, multiple numbers
Trauma registry	National
Formal certification for prehospital providers	Yes
National assessment of emergency care systems	No

DATA	
Reported road traffic fatalities (2016)	5[a] (60% M, 40% F)
WHO estimated road traffic fatalities (2016)	5
WHO estimated rate per 100 000 population (2016)	4.4

[a] Health & Police. Died within 24 hours of crash

SAFER ROAD USERS	
National speed limit law	Yes
Max urban speed limit	40 km/h
Max rural speed limit	60 km/h
Max motorway speed limit	60 km/h
Local authorities can modify limits	No
Enforcement	0 1 2 3 4 (5) 6 7 8 9 10
Predominant type of enforcement	Manual
National drink-driving law	Yes
BAC limit – general population	≤ 0.05 g/dl[b]
BAC limit – young or novice drivers	0.00 g/dl[b]
Random breath testing carried out	Yes
Testing carried out in case of fatal crash	No
Enforcement	0 1 2 3 (4) 5 6 7 8 9 10
% road traffic deaths involving alcohol	–
National motorcycle helmet law	Yes[c]
Applies to drivers and passengers	Yes
Helmet fastening required	No
Helmet standard referred to and/or specified	Yes
Children passengers on motorcycles	Not restricted
Enforcement	–
Helmet wearing rate	–
National seat-belt law	Yes
Applies to front and rear seat occupants	Yes
Enforcement	(0) 1 2 3 4 5 6 7 8 9 10
Seat-belt wearing rate	–
National child restraint law	No[d]
Children seated in front seat	Not restricted
Child restraint required	–
Child restraint standard referred to and/or specified	–
Enforcement	–
% children using child restraints	–
National law on mobile phone use while driving	Yes
Ban on hand-held mobile phone use	Yes
Ban on hands-free mobile phone use	No
National drug-driving law	Yes

[b] Reduced BAC limits introduced by the Traffic Act 2017, at December 2017, the notice of commencment had not yet been signed

[c] Helmet provisions introduced by the Traffic Act 2017, at December 2017, the notice of commencment had not yet been signed

[d] The Traffic Act 2017 requires children aged 1-16 years to be either seated in the back with a seat belt or restrained by passenger over 16 years

Deaths by road user category

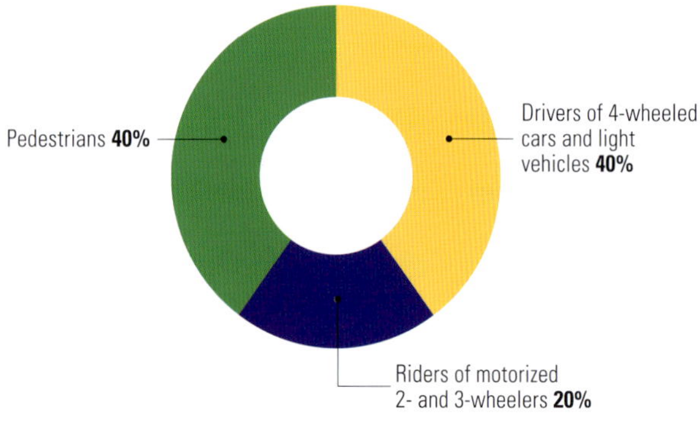

Source: 2016, Health & Police

Trends in reported road traffic deaths

Source: Health & Police

Legislative review conducted by WHO. Vehicle safety data from UNECE WP29. Other data collected by questionnaire and cleared by Ministry of Health and Medical Services.

Kuwait

Population: 4 052 584 | Income group: High | Gross national income per capita: US$ 41 680[a]

INSTITUTIONAL FRAMEWORK	
Lead agency	General Directorate of Traffic, Ministry of Interior
Funded in national budget	Yes
National road safety strategy	No
Funding to implement strategy	–
Fatality reduction target	–
SAFER ROADS AND MOBILITY	
Audits or star rating required for new road infrastructure	Yes
Design standards for the safety of pedestrians / cyclists	No
Inspections / star rating of existing roads	–
Investments to upgrade high risk locations	No
Policies & investment in urban public transport	No
SAFER VEHICLES	
Total registered vehicles for 2016	2 001 940
Cars and 4-wheeled light vehicles	1 628 834
Motorized 2- and 3-wheelers	19 193
Heavy trucks	264 567
Buses	54 633
Other	34 713
Vehicle standards applied (UNECE WP.29)	
Frontal impact standard	No
Electronic stability control	No
Pedestrian protection	No
Motorcycle anti-lock braking system	No
POST-CRASH CARE	
National emergency care access number	National, single number
Trauma registry	None
Formal certification for prehospital providers	Yes
National assessment of emergency care systems	No
DATA	
Reported road traffic fatalities (2016)	424[b] (88% M, 13% F)
WHO estimated road traffic fatalities (2016)	715
WHO estimated rate per 100 000 population (2016)	17.6

[a] Data available only for 2015
[b] Traffic department, Ministry of Interior. Died within 30 days of crash

SAFER ROAD USERS	
National speed limit law	Yes
Max urban speed limit	45 km/h
Max rural speed limit	80 km/h
Max motorway speed limit	80 km/h
Local authorities can modify limits	No
Enforcement	0 1 2 (3) 4 5 6 7 8 9 10
Predominant type of enforcement	Automated
National drink-driving law	Yes[c]
BAC limit – general population	–
BAC limit – young or novice drivers	–
Random breath testing carried out	No
Testing carried out in case of fatal crash	No
Enforcement	0 1 2 3 4 (5) 6 7 8 9 10
% road traffic deaths involving alcohol	–
National motorcycle helmet law	Yes
Applies to drivers and passengers	Yes
Helmet fastening required	No
Helmet standard referred to and/or specified	No
Children passengers on motorcycles	Not restricted
Enforcement	0 1 2 (3) 4 5 6 7 8 9 10
Helmet wearing rate	–
National seat-belt law	Yes
Applies to front and rear seat occupants	No
Enforcement	0 1 2 3 4 (5) 6 7 8 9 10
Seat-belt wearing rate	–
National child restraint law	No
Children seated in front seat	Prohibited under 10 yrs
Child restraint required	–
Child restraint standard referred to and/or specified	–
Enforcement	–
% children using child restraints	–
National law on mobile phone use while driving	Yes
Ban on hand-held mobile phone use	Yes
Ban on hands-free mobile phone use	No
National drug-driving law	Yes

[c] Not based on BAC. Alcohol consumption legally prohibited

Deaths by road user category

Trends in reported road traffic deaths

Source: Ministry of Interior

Legislative review conducted by WHO. Vehicle safety data from UNECE WP29. Other data collected by questionnaire and cleared by Ministry of Health.

Kyrgyzstan

Population: 5 955 734 | Income group: Middle | Gross national income per capita: US$ 1 100

INSTITUTIONAL FRAMEWORK	
Lead agency	Commission for Road Safety, under leadership of the Prime Minister
Funded in national budget	Yes
National road safety strategy	Yes
Funding to implement strategy	Partially funded
Fatality reduction target	Decrease mortality by 156 (2007-2016)

SAFER ROADS AND MOBILITY	
Audits or star rating required for new road infrastructure	Yes
Design standards for the safety of pedestrians / cyclists	Partial
Inspections / star rating of existing roads	No
Investments to upgrade high risk locations	Yes
Policies & investment in urban public transport	Yes

SAFER VEHICLES	
Total registered vehicles for 2015	993 000
Cars and 4-wheeled light vehicles	–
Motorized 2- and 3-wheelers	–
Heavy trucks	–
Buses	–
Other	–
Vehicle standards applied (UNECE WP.29)	
Frontal impact standard	No
Electronic stability control	No
Pedestrian protection	No
Motorcycle anti-lock braking system	No

POST-CRASH CARE	
National emergency care access number	National, single number
Trauma registry	None
Formal certification for prehospital providers	Yes
National assessment of emergency care systems	Yes

DATA	
Reported road traffic fatalities (2016)	812[a] (74% M, 26% F)
WHO estimated road traffic fatalities (2016)	916
WHO estimated rate per 100 000 population (2016)	15.4

[a] National Statistical Committee. Died within a year of crash

SAFER ROAD USERS	
National speed limit law	Yes
Max urban speed limit	60 km/h
Max rural speed limit	90 km/h
Max motorway speed limit	110 km/h
Local authorities can modify limits	No
Enforcement	0 1 2 3 4 ⑤ 6 7 8 9 10
Predominant type of enforcement	Manual and automated
National drink-driving law	Yes[b]
BAC limit – general population	–
BAC limit – young or novice drivers	–
Random breath testing carried out	Yes
Testing carried out in case of fatal crash	All drivers tested
Enforcement	0 1 2 3 4 ⑤ 6 7 8 9 10
% road traffic deaths involving alcohol	–
National motorcycle helmet law	Yes
Applies to drivers and passengers	Yes
Helmet fastening required	Yes
Helmet standard referred to and/or specified	No
Children passengers on motorcycles	Prohibited under 12 yrs
Enforcement	0 1 2 3 4 ⑤ 6 7 8 9 10
Helmet wearing rate	–
National seat-belt law	Yes
Applies to front and rear seat occupants	No[c]
Enforcement	0 1 2 3 4 5 6 ⑦ 8 9 10
Seat-belt wearing rate	–
National child restraint law	No
Children seated in front seat	Allowed in a child restraint[d]
Child restraint required	–[e]
Child restraint standard referred to and/or specified	–
Enforcement	–
% children using child restraints	–
National law on mobile phone use while driving	Yes
Ban on hand-held mobile phone use	Yes
Ban on hands-free mobile phone use	No
National drug-driving law	Yes

[b] Not based on BAC
[c] The obligation to use seat belt does not apply in residential areas nor for children under 12 years
[d] Children under 12 years travelling in the front of a car must be placed in a child restraint
[e] Legislation only refers to the use of child restraints for children under 12 years travelling in the front

Deaths by road user category

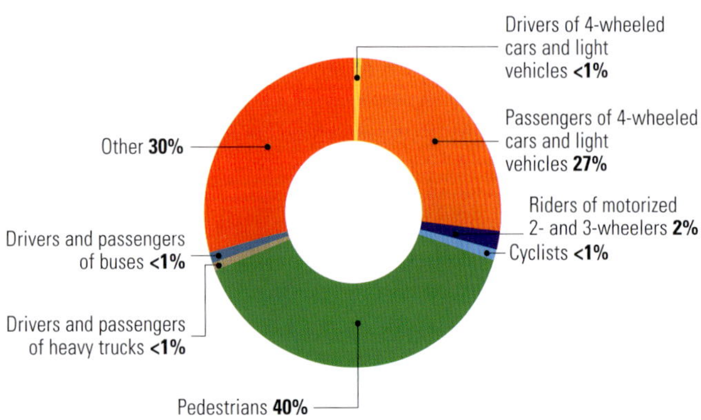

Source: 2016, National Statistical Committee

Trends in reported road traffic deaths

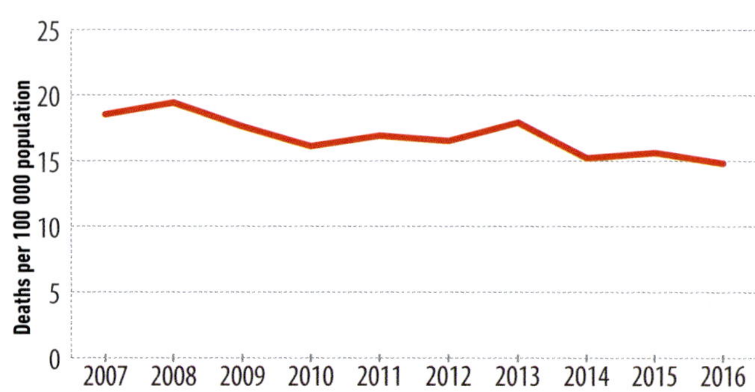

Source: National Statistical Committee

Lao People's Democratic Republic

Population: 6 758 353 | Income group: Middle | Gross national income per capita: US$ 2 150

INSTITUTIONAL FRAMEWORK	
Lead agency	National Road Safety Committee (NRSC)
Funded in national budget	Yes
National road safety strategy	Yes
Funding to implement strategy	Partially funded
Fatality reduction target	50% (2011-2020)
SAFER ROADS AND MOBILITY	
Audits or star rating required for new road infrastructure	Partial
Design standards for the safety of pedestrians / cyclists	Partial
Inspections / star rating of existing roads	No
Investments to upgrade high risk locations	Yes
Policies & investment in urban public transport	No
SAFER VEHICLES	
Total registered vehicles for 2016	1 850 020
Cars and 4-wheeled light vehicles	370 043
Motorized 2- and 3-wheelers	1 422 869
Heavy trucks	52 443
Buses	4 665
Other	0
Vehicle standards applied (UNECE WP.29)	
Frontal impact standard	No
Electronic stability control	No
Pedestrian protection	No
Motorcycle anti-lock braking system	No
POST-CRASH CARE	
National emergency care access number	Partial coverage
Trauma registry	None
Formal certification for prehospital providers	Yes
National assessment of emergency care systems	No
DATA	
Reported road traffic fatalities (2016)	1 086[a] (86% M, 14% F)
WHO estimated road traffic fatalities (2016)	1 120 (95% CI 946 - 1 294)
WHO estimated rate per 100 000 population (2016)	16.6

[a] Department of Traffic Police. Died within 30 days of crash

SAFER ROAD USERS	
National speed limit law	Yes
Max urban speed limit	40 km/h
Max rural speed limit	90 km/h
Max motorway speed limit	—[b]
Local authorities can modify limits	No
Enforcement	0 1 2 3 4 ⑤ 6 7 8 9 10
Predominant type of enforcement	Manual
National drink-driving law	Yes
BAC limit – general population	≤ 0.05 g/dl
BAC limit – young or novice drivers	≤ 0.05 g/dl
Random breath testing carried out	Yes
Testing carried out in case of fatal crash	No
Enforcement	0 1 2 ③ 4 5 6 7 8 9 10
% road traffic deaths involving alcohol	—
National motorcycle helmet law	Yes
Applies to drivers and passengers	Yes
Helmet fastening required	No
Helmet standard referred to and/or specified	No
Children passengers on motorcycles	Not restricted
Enforcement	0 1 2 3 4 5 6 ⑦ 8 9 10
Helmet wearing rate	—
National seat-belt law	Yes
Applies to front and rear seat occupants	No
Enforcement	0 1 ② 3 4 5 6 7 8 9 10
Seat-belt wearing rate	—
National child restraint law	Yes[c]
Children seated in front seat	Not restricted
Child restraint required	Yes[c]
Child restraint standard referred to and/or specified	No
Enforcement	0 ① 2 3 4 5 6 7 8 9 10
% children using child restraints	—
National law on mobile phone use while driving	Yes
Ban on hand-held mobile phone use	Yes
Ban on hands-free mobile phone use	Yes
National drug-driving law	No[d]

[b] No motorways in the country
[c] The law states that children unable to wear normal seat belts must be placed in a child restraint seat but no specific age / weight / height is specified
[d] Legislation banning drug driving only applies to bus and truck drivers

Deaths by road user category

Trends in reported road traffic deaths

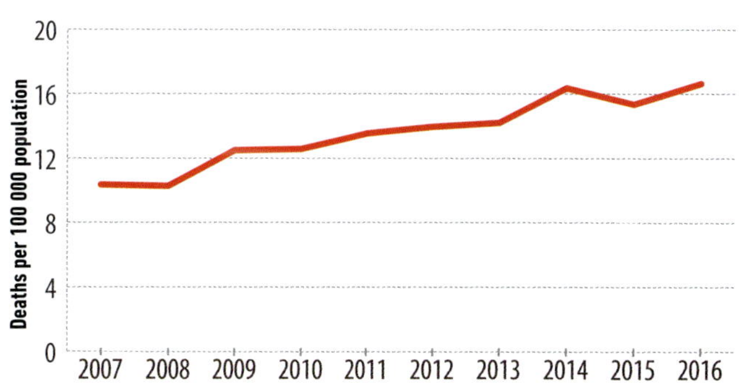

Source: Secretariat to National Road Safety Committee (NRSC)

Legislative review conducted by WHO. Vehicle safety data from UNECE WP29. Other data collected by questionnaire and cleared by Ministry of Public Works and Transport.

Latvia

Population: 1 970 530 | Income group: High | Gross national income per capita: US$ 14 630

INSTITUTIONAL FRAMEWORK

Lead agency	**No**
Funded in national budget	–
National road safety strategy	**Yes**
Funding to implement strategy	Not funded
Fatality reduction target	50% (2010-2020)

SAFER ROADS AND MOBILITY

Audits or star rating required for new road infrastructure	Yes
Design standards for the safety of pedestrians / cyclists	Yes
Inspections / star rating of existing roads	Yes
Investments to upgrade high risk locations	Yes
Policies & investment in urban public transport	No

SAFER VEHICLES

Total registered vehicles for on 01.01.2017	**803 628**
Cars and 4-wheeled light vehicles	665 284
Motorized 2- and 3-wheelers	49 581
Heavy trucks	84 067
Buses	4 696
Other	0
Vehicle standards applied (UNECE WP.29)	
Frontal impact standard	Yes
Electronic stability control	Yes
Pedestrian protection	Yes
Motorcycle anti-lock braking system	Yes

POST-CRASH CARE

National emergency care access number	National, single number
Trauma registry	National
Formal certification for prehospital providers	Yes
National assessment of emergency care systems	Yes

DATA

Reported road traffic fatalities (2016)	158[a] (78% M, 22% F)
WHO estimated road traffic fatalities (2016)	184
WHO estimated rate per 100 000 population (2016)	9.3

[a] Road traffic safety directorate. Died within 30 days of crash

SAFER ROAD USERS

National speed limit law	**Yes**
Max urban speed limit	50 km/h
Max rural speed limit	90 km/h
Max motorway speed limit	No
Local authorities can modify limits	No
Enforcement	0 1 2 3 4 5 6 (7) 8 9 10
Predominant type of enforcement	Manual and automated
National drink-driving law	**Yes**
BAC limit – general population	≤ 0.05 g/dl
BAC limit – young or novice drivers	≤ 0.02 g/dl
Random breath testing carried out	Yes[b]
Testing carried out in case of fatal crash	All drivers tested
Enforcement	0 1 2 3 4 5 6 (7) 8 9 10
% road traffic deaths involving alcohol	11%[c]
National motorcycle helmet law	**Yes**
Applies to drivers and passengers	Yes
Helmet fastening required	Yes
Helmet standard referred to and/or specified	No
Children passengers on motorcycles	Prohibited under 150 cm[d]
Enforcement	0 1 2 3 4 5 6 (7) 8 9 10
Helmet wearing rate	–
National seat-belt law	**Yes**
Applies to front and rear seat occupants	Yes
Enforcement	0 1 2 3 4 5 6 (7) 8 9 10
Seat-belt wearing rate	85% Front seats[e], 53% Rear seats[e]
National child restraint law	**Yes**
Children seated in front seat	Allowed in a child restraint[f]
Child restraint required	Up to 150 cm
Child restraint standard referred to and/or specified	No
Enforcement	0 1 2 3 4 5 6 (7) 8 9 10
% children using child restraints	–
National law on mobile phone use while driving	**Yes**
Ban on hand-held mobile phone use	Yes
Ban on hands-free mobile phone use	No
National drug-driving law	**Yes**

[b] Legislation requires probable cause to test drivers
[c] 2016, Road traffic safety directorate
[d] Or until the child can hold the balance and reach feet support or is sitting on a seat corresponding to its age and weight
[e] 2016, Health behaviour among Latvian adult population, 2016
[f] Except if no seat belt is fitted in the vehicle, in which case children under 150cm shall be travelling in the rear

Deaths by road user category

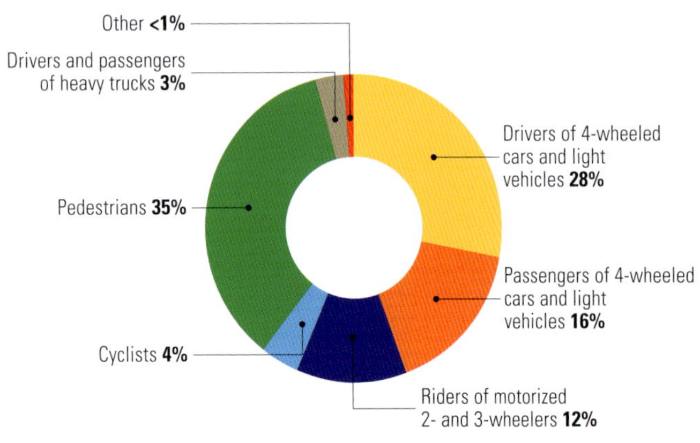

Source: 2016, Road traffic safety directorate

Trends in reported road traffic deaths

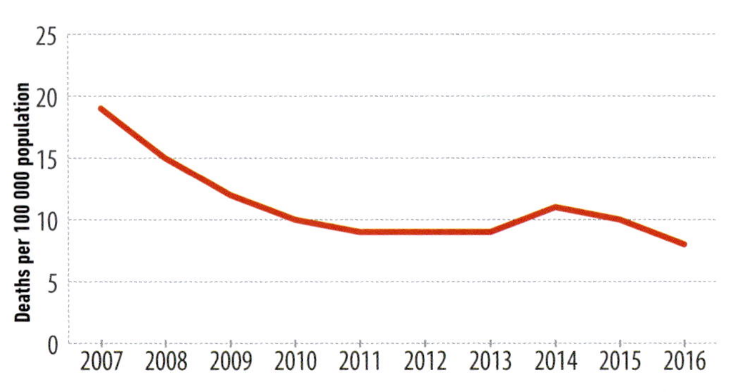

Source: Central Statistical Bureau of Latvia

Legislative review conducted by WHO. Vehicle safety data from UNECE WP29. Other data collected by questionnaire and cleared by Centre for Disease Prevention and Control of the Republic of Latvia

Lebanon

Population: 6 006 668 | Income group: Middle | Gross national income per capita: US$ 7 680

INSTITUTIONAL FRAMEWORK	
Lead agency	National Road Safety Council
Funded in national budget	Yes
National road safety strategy	No
Funding to implement strategy	–
Fatality reduction target	–
SAFER ROADS AND MOBILITY	
Audits or star rating required for new road infrastructure	Partial
Design standards for the safety of pedestrians / cyclists	Partial
Inspections / star rating of existing roads	–
Investments to upgrade high risk locations	No
Policies & investment in urban public transport	No
SAFER VEHICLES	
Total registered vehicles for 2016	1 866 407
Cars and 4-wheeled light vehicles	1 696 444
Motorized 2- and 3-wheelers	124 348
Heavy trucks	19 037
Buses	15 703
Other	10 875
Vehicle standards applied (UNECE WP.29)	
Frontal impact standard	No
Electronic stability control	No
Pedestrian protection	No
Motorcycle anti-lock braking system	No
POST-CRASH CARE	
National emergency care access number	National, multiple numbers
Trauma registry	None
Formal certification for prehospital providers	No
National assessment of emergency care systems	No
DATA	
Reported road traffic fatalities (2015)	576[a] (78% M, 22% F)
WHO estimated road traffic fatalities (2016)	1 090 (95% CI 837 - 1 396)
WHO estimated rate per 100 000 population (2016)	18.1

[a] General Directorate of the Internal Security Forces. Unlimited time period following crash

SAFER ROAD USERS	
National speed limit law	Yes
Max urban speed limit	50 km/h
Max rural speed limit	70 km/h
Max motorway speed limit	100 km/h
Local authorities can modify limits	Yes
Enforcement	0 1 2 3 4 (5) 6 7 8 9 10
Predominant type of enforcement	Manual
National drink-driving law	Yes
BAC limit – general population	≤ 0.05 g/dl
BAC limit – young or novice drivers	0.00 g/dl
Random breath testing carried out	Yes
Testing carried out in case of fatal crash	Some drivers tested
Enforcement	0 1 2 (3) 4 5 6 7 8 9 10
% road traffic deaths involving alcohol	–
National motorcycle helmet law	Yes
Applies to drivers and passengers	Yes
Helmet fastening required	Yes
Helmet standard referred to and/or specified	Yes
Children passengers on motorcycles	Prohibited under 10 yrs
Enforcement	0 1 2 3 4 (5) 6 7 8 9 10
Helmet wearing rate	–
National seat-belt law	Yes
Applies to front and rear seat occupants	Yes
Enforcement	0 1 2 3 (4) 5 6 7 8 9 10
Seat-belt wearing rate	–
National child restraint law	Yes
Children seated in front seat	Prohibited under 10 yrs
Child restraint required	Up to 5 yrs[b]
Child restraint standard referred to and/or specified	No
Enforcement	0 1 2 (3) 4 5 6 7 8 9 10
% children using child restraints	–
National law on mobile phone use while driving	Yes
Ban on hand-held mobile phone use	Yes
Ban on hands-free mobile phone use	Yes
National drug-driving law	Yes

[b] Legislation refers to regulations to further specify the child restraint rules

Deaths by road user category

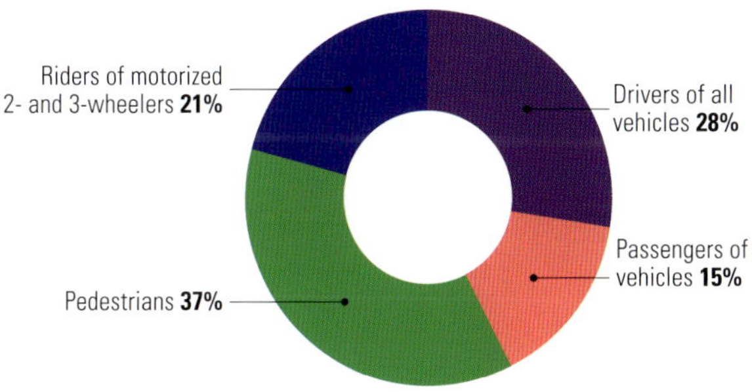

Trends in reported road traffic deaths

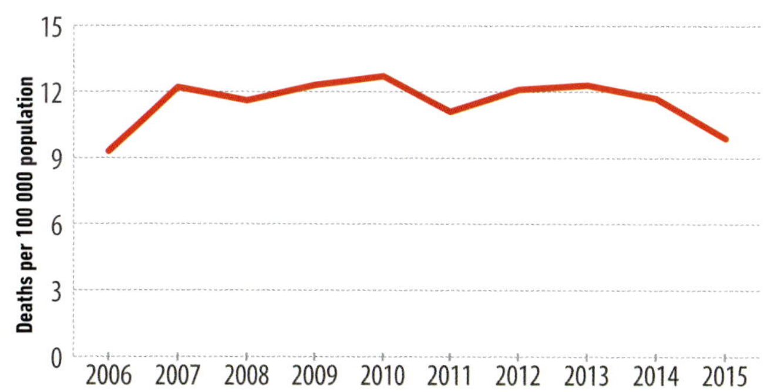

Source: General Directorate of the Internal Security Forces (death data) and World Bank (population data)

Legislative review conducted by WHO. Vehicle safety data from UNECE WP.29. Other data collected by questionnaire and cleared by National Road Safety Council.

Lesotho

Population: 2 203 821 | Income group: Middle | Gross national income per capita: US$ 1 210

INSTITUTIONAL FRAMEWORK

Lead agency	Department of Road Safety
Funded in national budget	Yes
National road safety strategy	No
Funding to implement strategy	–
Fatality reduction target	–

SAFER ROADS AND MOBILITY

Audits or star rating required for new road infrastructure	Yes
Design standards for the safety of pedestrians / cyclists	No
Inspections / star rating of existing roads	Yes
Investments to upgrade high risk locations	No
Policies & investment in urban public transport	No

SAFER VEHICLES

Total registered vehicles	–
Cars and 4-wheeled light vehicles	–
Motorized 2- and 3-wheelers	–
Heavy trucks	–
Buses	–
Other	–
Vehicle standards applied (UNECE WP.29)	
Frontal impact standard	No
Electronic stability control	No
Pedestrian protection	No
Motorcycle anti-lock braking system	No

POST-CRASH CARE

National emergency care access number	None
Trauma registry	None
Formal certification for prehospital providers	Yes
National assessment of emergency care systems	No

DATA

Reported road traffic fatalities (2016)	318[a] (63% M, 37% F)
WHO estimated road traffic fatalities (2016)	638 (95% CI 544 - 733)
WHO estimated rate per 100 000 population (2016)	28.9

[a] Police records. Unlimited time period following crash

SAFER ROAD USERS

National speed limit law	Yes
Max urban speed limit	50 km/h
Max rural speed limit	80 km/h
Max motorway speed limit	No
Local authorities can modify limits	No
Enforcement	0 1 ② 3 4 5 6 7 8 9 10
Predominant type of enforcement	Manual
National drink-driving law	Yes
BAC limit – general population	≤ 0.08 g/dl
BAC limit – young or novice drivers	≤ 0.08 g/dl
Random breath testing carried out	Yes
Testing carried out in case of fatal crash	No
Enforcement	0 1 ② 3 4 5 6 7 8 9 10
% road traffic deaths involving alcohol	60%[b]
National motorcycle helmet law	Yes
Applies to drivers and passengers	Yes
Helmet fastening required	No
Helmet standard referred to and/or specified	No
Children passengers on motorcycles	Not restricted
Enforcement	0 1 2 3 4 5 6 7 ⑧ 9 10
Helmet wearing rate	75% Drivers[b], 3% Passengers[b]
National seat-belt law	Yes
Applies to front and rear seat occupants	No
Enforcement	0 1 2 3 4 5 6 ⑦ 8 9 10
Seat-belt wearing rate	–
National child restraint law	No
Children seated in front seat	Not restricted
Child restraint required	–
Child restraint standard referred to and/or specified	–
Enforcement	–
% children using child restraints	–
National law on mobile phone use while driving	No
Ban on hand-held mobile phone use	–
Ban on hands-free mobile phone use	–
National drug-driving law	Yes

[b] 2016, Police records

Deaths by road user category

Trends in reported road traffic deaths

Source: Police records

Liberia

Population: 4 613 823 | Income group: Low | Gross national income per capita: US$ 370

INSTITUTIONAL FRAMEWORK	
Lead agency	No
Funded in national budget	–
National road safety strategy	No
Funding to implement strategy	–
Fatality reduction target	–
SAFER ROADS AND MOBILITY	
Audits or star rating required for new road infrastructure	Yes
Design standards for the safety of pedestrians / cyclists	Partial
Inspections / star rating of existing roads	Yes
Investments to upgrade high risk locations	No
Policies & investment in urban public transport	Yes
SAFER VEHICLES	
Total registered vehicles for 2012	1 085 075
Cars and 4-wheeled light vehicles	1 073 438
Motorized 2- and 3-wheelers	3 780
Heavy trucks	396
Buses	7 461
Other	0
Vehicle standards applied (UNECE WP.29)	
Frontal impact standard	No
Electronic stability control	No
Pedestrian protection	No
Motorcycle anti-lock braking system	No
POST-CRASH CARE	
National emergency care access number	National, single number
Trauma registry	None
Formal certification for prehospital providers	–
National assessment of emergency care systems	No
DATA	
Reported road traffic fatalities (2016)	175[a]
WHO estimated road traffic fatalities (2016)	1 657 (95% CI 1 299 - 2 015)
WHO estimated rate per 100 000 population (2016)	35.9

[a] Liberia National Police. Died at scene of crash

SAFER ROAD USERS	
National speed limit law	Yes
Max urban speed limit	~40 km/h
Max rural speed limit	~56 km/h
Max motorway speed limit	~72 km/h
Local authorities can modify limits	No
Enforcement	(0) 1 2 3 4 5 6 7 8 9 10
Predominant type of enforcement	Manual
National drink-driving law	Yes
BAC limit – general population	< 0.15 g/dl[b]
BAC limit – young or novice drivers	< 0.15 g/dl[b]
Random breath testing carried out	No
Testing carried out in case of fatal crash	All drivers tested
Enforcement	(0) 1 2 3 4 5 6 7 8 9 10
% road traffic deaths involving alcohol	–
National motorcycle helmet law	Yes
Applies to drivers and passengers	Yes
Helmet fastening required	No
Helmet standard referred to and/or specified	No
Children passengers on motorcycles	Prohibited under 13 yrs
Enforcement	0 (1) 2 3 4 5 6 7 8 9 10
Helmet wearing rate	–
National seat-belt law	No
Applies to front and rear seat occupants	–
Enforcement	–
Seat-belt wearing rate	–
National child restraint law	No
Children seated in front seat	Not restricted
Child restraint required	–
Child restraint standard referred to and/or specified	–
Enforcement	–
% children using child restraints	–
National law on mobile phone use while driving	No
Ban on hand-held mobile phone use	–
Ban on hands-free mobile phone use	–
National drug-driving law	Yes

[b] Over this limit there is a presumption of alcohol impairement (from 0.05 to 0.15 no presumption established but the alcohol concentration can be used to decide on the guilt or innocence of the driver)

Deaths by road user category

Trends in reported road traffic deaths

Legislative review conducted by WHO. Vehicle safety data from UNECE WP29. Other data collected by questionnaire and cleared by Ministry of Health and Social Welfare.

Libya

Population: 6 293 253 | Income group: Middle | Gross national income per capita: US$ 4 730[a]

INSTITUTIONAL FRAMEWORK	
Lead agency	Department of Traffic and Licenses, Ministry of Interior
Funded in national budget	No
National road safety strategy	Yes
Funding to implement strategy	Not funded
Fatality reduction target	3-5 % (2008 -2010, renewable every 3 years)
SAFER ROADS AND MOBILITY	
Audits or star rating required for new road infrastructure	Yes
Design standards for the safety of pedestrians / cyclists	Partial
Inspections / star rating of existing roads	No
Investments to upgrade high risk locations	Yes
Policies & investment in urban public transport	Yes
SAFER VEHICLES	
Total registered vehicles for 2013	3 553 497
Cars and 4-wheeled light vehicles	2 821 285
Motorized 2- and 3-wheelers	1 828
Heavy trucks	624 243
Buses	8 248
Other	97 893
Vehicle standards applied (UNECE WP.29)	
Frontal impact standard	No
Electronic stability control	No
Pedestrian protection	No
Motorcycle anti-lock braking system	No
POST-CRASH CARE	
National emergency care access number	National, single number
Trauma registry	National
Formal certification for prehospital providers	Yes
National assessment of emergency care systems	Yes
DATA	
Reported road traffic fatalities (2016)	2 414[b] (86% M, 14% F)
WHO estimated road traffic fatalities (2016)	1 645 (95% CI 1 234 - 2 171)
WHO estimated rate per 100 000 population (2016)	26.1

[a] Data available only for 2011
[b] Department of Traffic and Licenses, Statistical report for road traffic crashes 2016

SAFER ROAD USERS	
National speed limit law	Yes
Max urban speed limit	50 km/h
Max rural speed limit	85 km/h
Max motorway speed limit	100 km/h
Local authorities can modify limits	No
Enforcement	0 1 ② 3 4 5 6 7 8 9 10
Predominant type of enforcement	Manual and automated
National drink-driving law	Yes[c]
BAC limit – general population	–
BAC limit – young or novice drivers	–
Random breath testing carried out	No
Testing carried out in case of fatal crash	Some drivers tested
Enforcement	0 1 2 3 4 5 6 ⑦ 8 9 10
% road traffic deaths involving alcohol	1%[d]
National motorcycle helmet law	Yes
Applies to drivers and passengers	No
Helmet fastening required	No
Helmet standard referred to and/or specified	No
Children passengers on motorcycles	Not restricted
Enforcement	0 ① 2 3 4 5 6 7 8 9 10
Helmet wearing rate	–
National seat-belt law	Yes
Applies to front and rear seat occupants	Yes
Enforcement	0 1 2 3 4 5 6 ⑦ 8 9 10
Seat-belt wearing rate	–
National child restraint law	No
Children seated in front seat	Not restricted
Child restraint required	–
Child restraint standard referred to and/or specified	–
Enforcement	–
% children using child restraints	–
National law on mobile phone use while driving	Yes
Ban on hand-held mobile phone use	No
Ban on hands-free mobile phone use	No
National drug-driving law	Yes

[c] Not based on BAC. Alcohol consumption legally prohibited
[d] 2016, Department of Traffic and Licenses, Statistical report for road traffic crashes 2016

Deaths by road user category

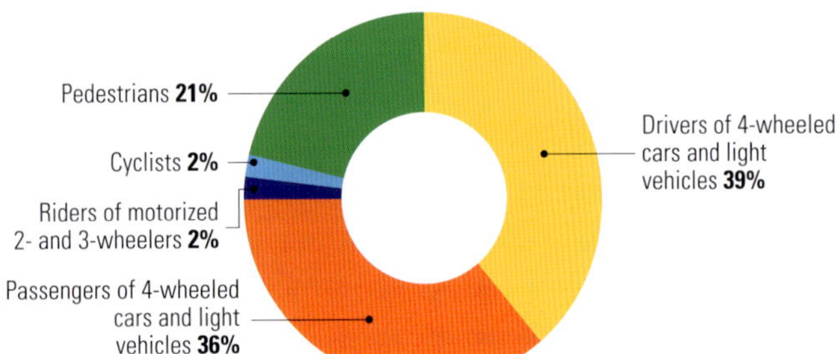

Source: 2016, Department of Traffic and Licenses, Statistical report for road traffic crashes 2016

Trends in reported road traffic deaths

Source: Department of Traffic and Licenses, Statistical report for road traffic crashes 2016

Legislative review conducted by WHO. Vehicle safety data from UNECE WP29. Other data collected by questionnaire and cleared by Ministry of Health.

Lithuania

Population: 2 908 249 | Income group: High | Gross national income per capita: US$ 14 770

INSTITUTIONAL FRAMEWORK

Lead agency	State Traffic Safety Commission, Ministry of Transport and Communications
Funded in national budget	Yes
National road safety strategy	Yes
Funding to implement strategy	Partially funded
Fatality reduction target	35%, from 92 to 60 deaths per 1 million population (2011–2017)

SAFER ROADS AND MOBILITY

Audits or star rating required for new road infrastructure	Partial
Design standards for the safety of pedestrians / cyclists	Yes
Inspections / star rating of existing roads	Yes
Investments to upgrade high risk locations	Yes
Policies & investment in urban public transport	Yes

SAFER VEHICLES

Total registered vehicles for 2015	1 391 568
Cars and 4-wheeled light vehicles	1 295 018
Motorized 2- and 3-wheelers	37 753
Heavy trucks	51 941
Buses	6 856
Other	0
Vehicle standards applied (UNECE WP.29)	
Frontal impact standard	Yes
Electronic stability control	Yes
Pedestrian protection	Yes
Motorcycle anti-lock braking system	Yes

POST-CRASH CARE

National emergency care access number	National, single number
Trauma registry	National
Formal certification for prehospital providers	No
National assessment of emergency care systems	No

DATA

Reported road traffic fatalities (2016)	192[a] (74% M, 26% F)
WHO estimated road traffic fatalities (2016)	234
WHO estimated rate per 100 000 population (2016)	8

[a] Police Department, Ministry of Interior. Died within 30 days of crash

SAFER ROAD USERS

National speed limit law	Yes
Max urban speed limit	50 km/h[b]
Max rural speed limit	90 km/h
Max motorway speed limit	130 km/h
Local authorities can modify limits	No
Enforcement	0 1 2 3 4 5 6 ⑦ 8 9 10
Predominant type of enforcement	Automated
National drink-driving law	Yes
BAC limit – general population	≤ 0.04 g/dl
BAC limit – young or novice drivers	0.00 g/dl
Random breath testing carried out	Yes
Testing carried out in case of fatal crash	All drivers tested
Enforcement	0 1 2 3 4 5 6 7 ⑧ 9 10
% road traffic deaths involving alcohol	10%[c]
National motorcycle helmet law	Yes
Applies to drivers and passengers	Yes
Helmet fastening required	Yes
Helmet standard referred to and/or specified	No
Children passengers on motorcycles	Prohibited under 12 yrs
Enforcement	0 1 2 3 4 5 6 7 8 ⑨ 10
Helmet wearing rate	–
National seat-belt law	Yes
Applies to front and rear seat occupants	Yes
Enforcement	0 1 2 3 4 5 6 ⑦ 8 9 10
Seat-belt wearing rate	97% Front seats[d], 30% Rear seats[d]
National child restraint law	Yes
Children seated in front seat	Allowed in a child restraint[e]
Child restraint required	Up to 135 cm
Child restraint standard referred to and/or specified	Yes
Enforcement	0 1 2 3 4 5 6 7 ⑧ 9 10
% children using child restraints	–
National law on mobile phone use while driving	Yes
Ban on hand-held mobile phone use	Yes
Ban on hands-free mobile phone use	No
National drug-driving law	Yes

[b] Can be increased or decreased to an unspecified speed under certain circumstances
[c] 2016, Lithuanian Traffic Police Service, Ministry of Interior
[d] 2016, Road and Transport Research Institute
[e] If transported in rear-facing restraints, airbag must be deactivated

Deaths by road user category

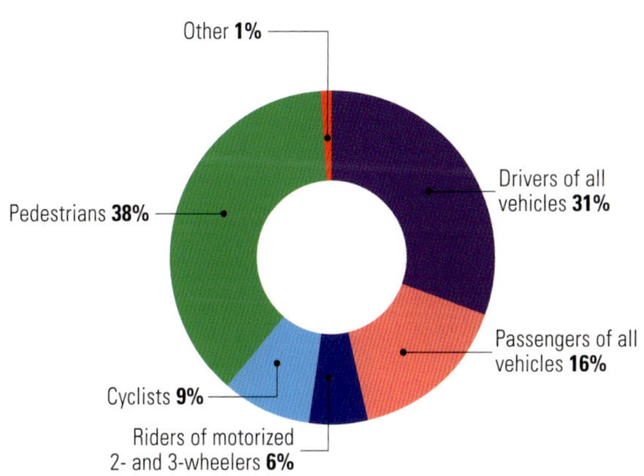

Source: 2016, Lithuania Traffic Police Service report

Trends in reported road traffic deaths

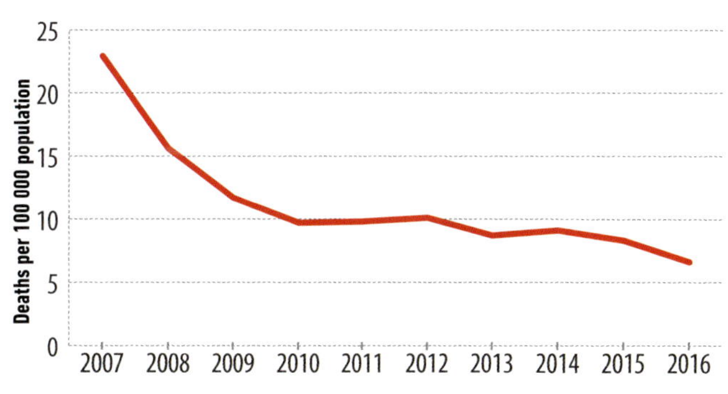

Source: Police records and Statistics Lithuania

Legislative review conducted by WHO. Vehicle safety data from UNECE WP.29. Other data collected by questionnaire and cleared by Centre for Health Education and Diseases Prevention.

Luxembourg

Population: 575 747 | Income group: High | Gross national income per capita: US$ 76 660

INSTITUTIONAL FRAMEWORK

Lead agency	Ministry of Sustainable Development and Infrastructure, Department of Transport
Funded in national budget	Yes
National road safety strategy	Yes
Funding to implement strategy	Partially funded
Fatality reduction target	50% (2011-2020)

SAFER ROADS AND MOBILITY

Audits or star rating required for new road infrastructure	Partial
Design standards for the safety of pedestrians / cyclists	Yes
Inspections / star rating of existing roads	Yes
Investments to upgrade high risk locations	Yes
Policies & investment in urban public transport	Yes

SAFER VEHICLES

Total registered vehicles for 01.01.2017	466 472
Cars and 4-wheeled light vehicles	422 073
Motorized 2- and 3-wheelers	29 253
Heavy trucks	13 242
Buses	1 904
Other	0
Vehicle standards applied (UNECE WP.29)	
Frontal impact standard	Yes
Electronic stability control	Yes
Pedestrian protection	Yes
Motorcycle anti-lock braking system	Yes

POST-CRASH CARE

National emergency care access number	National, single number
Trauma registry	Some facilities
Formal certification for prehospital providers	No
National assessment of emergency care systems	No

DATA

Reported road traffic fatalities (2016)	32[a] (66% M, 34% F)
WHO estimated road traffic fatalities (2016)	36
WHO estimated rate per 100 000 population (2016)	6.3

[a] National Institute of Statistics and Economic Studies (STATEC), Police Grand-Ducale. Died within 30 days of crash

SAFER ROAD USERS

National speed limit law	Yes
Max urban speed limit	50 km/h
Max rural speed limit	90 km/h
Max motorway speed limit	130 km/h
Local authorities can modify limits	Yes
Enforcement	0 1 2 3 4 5 6 **(7)** 8 9 10
Predominant type of enforcement	Automated
National drink-driving law	Yes
BAC limit – general population	< 0.05 g/dl
BAC limit – young or novice drivers	< 0.02 g/dl
Random breath testing carried out	Yes
Testing carried out in case of fatal crash	All drivers tested
Enforcement	0 1 2 3 4 5 **(6)** 7 8 9 10
% road traffic deaths involving alcohol	14%[b]
National motorcycle helmet law	Yes
Applies to drivers and passengers	Yes
Helmet fastening required	Yes
Helmet standard referred to and/or specified	Yes
Children passengers on motorcycles	Prohibited under 12 yrs[c]
Enforcement	0 1 2 3 4 5 6 7 8 9 **(10)**
Helmet wearing rate	–
National seat-belt law	Yes
Applies to front and rear seat occupants	Yes
Enforcement	0 1 2 3 4 5 6 **(7)** 8 9 10
Seat-belt wearing rate	90% Front seats[d], 76% Rear seats[d]
National child restraint law	Yes
Children seated in front seat	Allowed in a child restraint[e]
Child restraint required	Up to 17 yrs/150 cm
Child restraint standard referred to and/or specified	Yes
Enforcement	0 1 2 3 4 5 6 7 **(8)** 9 10
% children using child restraints	–
National law on mobile phone use while driving	Yes
Ban on hand-held mobile phone use	Yes
Ban on hands-free mobile phone use	No
National drug-driving law	Yes

[b] 2016, National Institute of Statistics and Economic Studies (STATEC), Police Grand-Ducale
[c] And until the child is tall enough to adequately use the foot pegs
[d] 2015, TNS ILRES/MDDI
[e] Provided that airbag is deactivated if child is in a rear-facing child restraint system

Deaths by road user category

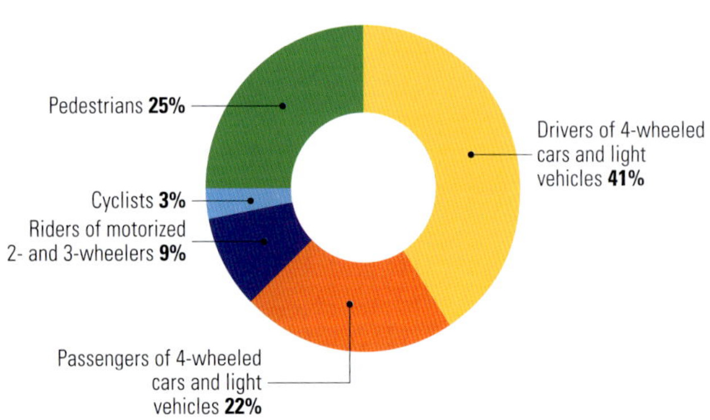

Source: 2016, National Institute of Statistics and Economic Studies (STATEC), Police Grand-Ducale

Trends in reported road traffic deaths

Source: National Institute of Statistics and Economic Studies (STATEC), Police Grand-Ducale

Legislative review conducted by WHO. Vehicle safety data from UNECE WP29. Other data collected by questionnaire and cleared by Minsitry of Health.

Madagascar

Population: 24 894 552 | Income group: Low | Gross national income per capita: US$ 400

INSTITUTIONAL FRAMEWORK	
Lead agency	Intersectoral Committee for Road Safety (CISR), Ministry of Transport and Meteorology
Funded in national budget	Yes
National road safety strategy	Yes
Funding to implement strategy	Partially funded
Fatality reduction target	5% (2015-2017)
SAFER ROADS AND MOBILITY	
Audits or star rating required for new road infrastructure	Yes
Design standards for the safety of pedestrians / cyclists	Partial
Inspections / star rating of existing roads	Yes
Investments to upgrade high risk locations	No
Policies & investment in urban public transport	No
SAFER VEHICLES	
Total registered vehicles for 2015	236 979
Cars and 4-wheeled light vehicles	136 508
Motorized 2- and 3-wheelers	42 835
Heavy trucks	24 912
Buses	32 724
Other	0
Vehicle standards applied (UNECE WP.29)	
Frontal impact standard	No
Electronic stability control	No
Pedestrian protection	No
Motorcycle anti-lock braking system	No
POST-CRASH CARE	
National emergency care access number	None
Trauma registry	None
Formal certification for prehospital providers	No
National assessment of emergency care systems	No
DATA	
Reported road traffic fatalities (2016)	340[a]
WHO estimated road traffic fatalities (2016)	7 108 (95% CI 5 895 - 8 321)
WHO estimated rate per 100 000 population (2016)	28.6

[a] National Gendarmerie. Died within 24 hours of crash

SAFER ROAD USERS	
National speed limit law	Yes
Max urban speed limit	50 km/h[b]
Max rural speed limit	No
Max motorway speed limit	No
Local authorities can modify limits	Yes
Enforcement	0 1 2 3 (4) 5 6 7 8 9 10
Predominant type of enforcement	–
National drink-driving law	Yes
BAC limit – general population	< 0.08 g/dl
BAC limit – young or novice drivers	< 0.08 g/dl
Random breath testing carried out	Yes
Testing carried out in case of fatal crash	Some drivers tested
Enforcement	0 1 (2) 3 4 5 6 7 8 9 10
% road traffic deaths involving alcohol	–
National motorcycle helmet law	Yes
Applies to drivers and passengers	Yes
Helmet fastening required	Yes
Helmet standard referred to and/or specified	Yes
Children passengers on motorcycles	Not restricted
Enforcement	0 1 (2) 3 4 5 6 7 8 9 10
Helmet wearing rate	–
National seat-belt law	Yes
Applies to front and rear seat occupants	No
Enforcement	0 1 2 3 4 (5) 6 7 8 9 10
Seat-belt wearing rate	–
National child restraint law	No
Children seated in front seat	Prohibited under 5 yrs
Child restraint required	–
Child restraint standard referred to and/or specified	–
Enforcement	–
% children using child restraints	–
National law on mobile phone use while driving	Yes
Ban on hand-held mobile phone use	Yes
Ban on hands-free mobile phone use	No
National drug-driving law	Yes

[b] Can be modified up to 80 km/h

Deaths by road user category

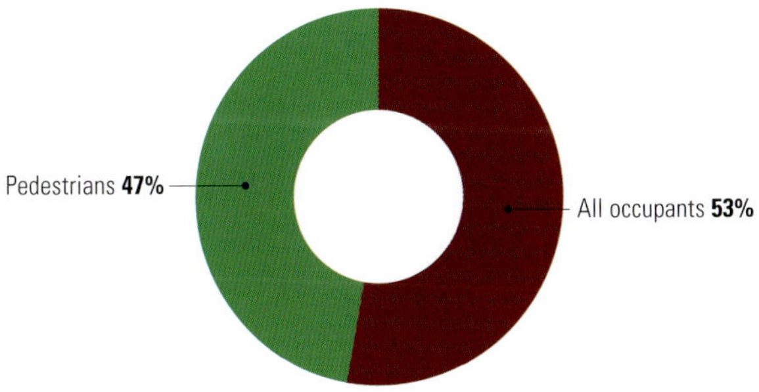

Source: 2016, Insurance Companies Committee (CEAM)

Trends in reported road traffic deaths

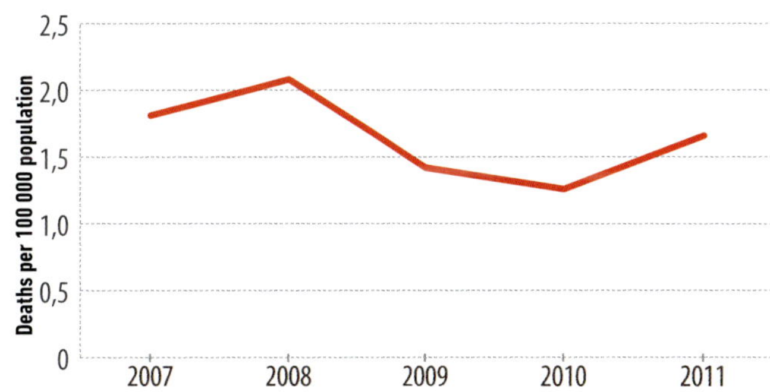

Source: National Gendarmerie

Legislative review conducted by WHO. Vehicle safety data from UNECE WP29. Other data collected by questionnaire and cleared by Ministry of Public Health.

Malawi

Population: 18 091 576 | Income group: Low | Gross national income per capita: US$ 320

INSTITUTIONAL FRAMEWORK

Lead agency	Directorate of Road Traffic and Safety Services, Ministry of Transport and Public Works
Funded in national budget	Yes
National road safety strategy	Yes
Funding to implement strategy	Partially funded
Fatality reduction target	20% (2015-2020)

SAFER ROADS AND MOBILITY

Audits or star rating required for new road infrastructure	Partial
Design standards for the safety of pedestrians / cyclists	Yes
Inspections / star rating of existing roads	No
Investments to upgrade high risk locations	No
Policies & investment in urban public transport	No

SAFER VEHICLES

Total registered vehicles	–
Cars and 4-wheeled light vehicles	–
Motorized 2- and 3-wheelers	–
Heavy trucks	–
Buses	–
Other	–
Vehicle standards applied (UNECE WP.29)	
Frontal impact standard	No
Electronic stability control	No
Pedestrian protection	No
Motorcycle anti-lock braking system	No

POST-CRASH CARE

National emergency care access number	Partial coverage
Trauma registry	Some facilities
Formal certification for prehospital providers	No
National assessment of emergency care systems	No

DATA

Reported road traffic fatalities (2016)	1 122[a] (82% M, 18% F)
WHO estimated road traffic fatalities (2016)	5 601 (95% CI 4 590 - 6 612)
WHO estimated rate per 100 000 population (2016)	31

[a] Road Safety Database. Died within 30 days of crash

SAFER ROAD USERS

National speed limit law	Yes
Max urban speed limit	50 km/h
Max rural speed limit	80 km/h
Max motorway speed limit	100 km/h
Local authorities can modify limits	No
Enforcement	0 1 2 3 (4) 5 6 7 8 9 10
Predominant type of enforcement	Manual
National drink-driving law	Yes
BAC limit – general population	< 0.08 g/dl
BAC limit – young or novice drivers	< 0.08 g/dl
Random breath testing carried out	Yes
Testing carried out in case of fatal crash	No
Enforcement	0 1 2 3 (4) 5 6 7 8 9 10
% road traffic deaths involving alcohol	–
National motorcycle helmet law	Yes
Applies to drivers and passengers	Yes
Helmet fastening required	Yes
Helmet standard referred to and/or specified	No
Children passengers on motorcycles	Not restricted
Enforcement	0 1 (2) 3 4 5 6 7 8 9 10
Helmet wearing rate	–
National seat-belt law	Yes
Applies to front and rear seat occupants	No
Enforcement	0 1 2 (3) 4 5 6 7 8 9 10
Seat-belt wearing rate	26% Drivers[b], 21% Front seats[b]
National child restraint law	No
Children seated in front seat	Not restricted
Child restraint required	–
Child restraint standard referred to and/or specified	–
Enforcement	–
% children using child restraints	–
National law on mobile phone use while driving	Yes
Ban on hand-held mobile phone use	Yes
Ban on hands-free mobile phone use	No
National drug-driving law	Yes

[b] 2016, 2016 Seat-belt wearing and mobile phone use baseline survey

Deaths by road user category

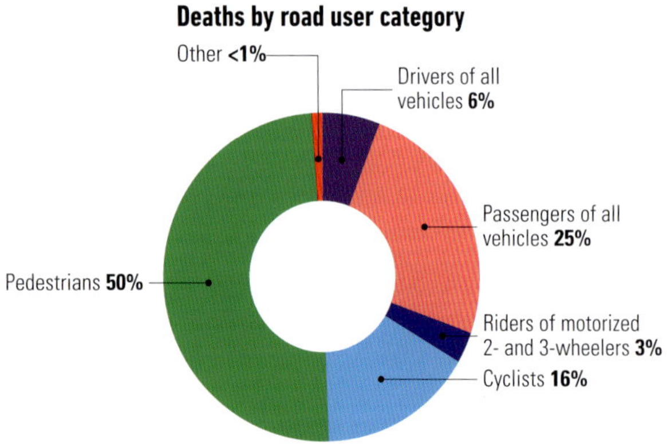

Source: 2016, Annual Traffic Accidents Report

Trends in reported road traffic deaths

Source: Road Safety Database

Malaysia

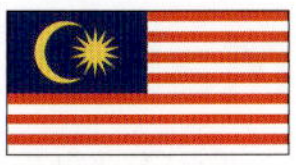

Population: 31 187 264 | Income group: Middle | Gross national income per capita: US$ 9 850

INSTITUTIONAL FRAMEWORK	
Lead agency	Road Safety Department, Ministry of Transport
Funded in national budget	Yes
National road safety strategy	Yes
Funding to implement strategy	Partially funded
Fatality reduction target	50% (2014-2020)
SAFER ROADS AND MOBILITY	
Audits or star rating required for new road infrastructure	Yes
Design standards for the safety of pedestrians / cyclists	Yes
Inspections / star rating of existing roads	Yes
Investments to upgrade high risk locations	Yes
Policies & investment in urban public transport	Yes
SAFER VEHICLES	
Total registered vehicles for 2016	27 613 120
Cars and 4-wheeled light vehicles	13 123 638
Motorized 2- and 3-wheelers	12 677 041
Heavy trucks	1 191 310
Buses	59 977
Other	561 154
Vehicle standards applied (UNECE WP.29)	
Frontal impact standard	Yes
Electronic stability control	Yes
Pedestrian protection	Yes
Motorcycle anti-lock braking system	No
POST-CRASH CARE	
National emergency care access number	National, single number
Trauma registry	None
Formal certification for prehospital providers	Yes
National assessment of emergency care systems	No
DATA	
Reported road traffic fatalities (2016)	7 152[a] (87% M, 13% F)
WHO estimated road traffic fatalities (2016)	7 374 (95% CI 6 482 - 8 266)
WHO estimated rate per 100 000 population (2016)	23.6

[a] Traffic Investigations and Enforcement Department, The Royal Malaysia Police (RMP). Died within 30 days of crash

SAFER ROAD USERS	
National speed limit law	Yes[b]
Max urban speed limit	90 km/h
Max rural speed limit	90 km/h
Max motorway speed limit	110 km/h
Local authorities can modify limits	Yes
Enforcement	0 1 2 3 4 5 (6) 7 8 9 10
Predominant type of enforcement	Manual
National drink-driving law	Yes
BAC limit – general population	≤ 0.08 g/dl
BAC limit – young or novice drivers	≤ 0.08 g/dl
Random breath testing carried out	Yes[c]
Testing carried out in case of fatal crash	All drivers tested
Enforcement	0 1 2 3 (4) 5 6 7 8 9 10
% road traffic deaths involving alcohol	<1%[d]
National motorcycle helmet law	Yes
Applies to drivers and passengers	Yes
Helmet fastening required	Yes
Helmet standard referred to and/or specified	Yes
Children passengers on motorcycles	Not restricted
Enforcement	0 1 2 3 4 5 6 7 (8) 9 10
Helmet wearing rate	91% Drivers[e], 87% Passengers[e]
National seat-belt law	Yes
Applies to front and rear seat occupants	No
Enforcement	0 1 2 3 (4) 5 6 7 8 9 10
Seat-belt wearing rate	74% Front seats[f], 10% Rear seats[f]
National child restraint law	No
Children seated in front seat	Not restricted
Child restraint required	–
Child restraint standard referred to and/or specified	–
Enforcement	–
% children using child restraints	–
National law on mobile phone use while driving	Yes
Ban on hand-held mobile phone use	Yes
Ban on hands-free mobile phone use	No
National drug-driving law	No

[b] Speed limit set per vehicle and road type with a maximum speed limit for passenger cars of 110 km/h on highways and 90 km/h on other roads
[c] Legislation requires probable cause to test drivers or commission of a traffic offence
[d] 2016, The Royal Malaysia Police
[e] 2016, Malaysian Institute of Road Safety Research (MIROS)
[f] 2015, Malaysian Institute of Road Safety Research (MIROS)

Deaths by road user category

Trends in reported road traffic deaths

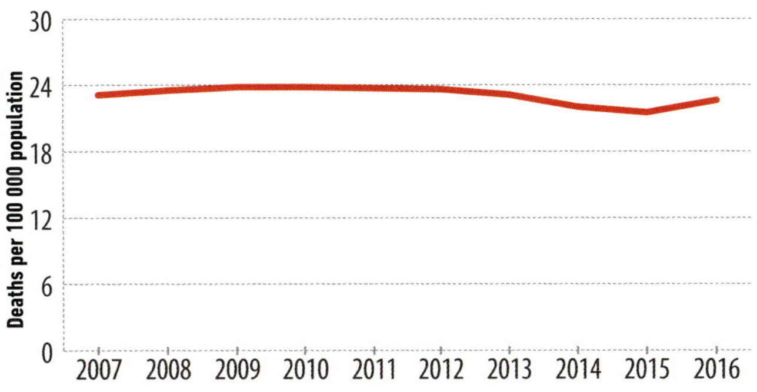

Source: The Royal Malaysia Police

Maldives

Population: 427 756 | Income group: Middle | Gross national income per capita: US$ 7 430

INSTITUTIONAL FRAMEWORK	
Lead agency	Transport Authority, Ministry of Economic Development
Funded in national budget	Yes
National road safety strategy	Yes
Funding to implement strategy	Not funded
Fatality reduction target	–
SAFER ROADS AND MOBILITY	
Audits or star rating required for new road infrastructure	No
Design standards for the safety of pedestrians / cyclists	Partial
Inspections / star rating of existing roads	Yes
Investments to upgrade high risk locations	No
Policies & investment in urban public transport	Yes
SAFER VEHICLES	
Total registered vehicles for 2016	92 983
Cars and 4-wheeled light vehicles	14 314
Motorized 2- and 3-wheelers	75 053
Heavy trucks	3 438
Buses	178
Other	0
Vehicle standards applied (UNECE WP.29)	
Frontal impact standard	No
Electronic stability control	No
Pedestrian protection	No
Motorcycle anti-lock braking system	No
POST-CRASH CARE	
National emergency care access number	Partial coverage
Trauma registry	None
Formal certification for prehospital providers	No
National assessment of emergency care systems	No
DATA	
Reported road traffic fatalities (2016)	4 [a] (50% M, 50% F)
WHO estimated road traffic fatalities (2016)	4
WHO estimated rate per 100 000 population (2016)	0.9

[a] Maldives Police Service. Unlimited time period following crash

SAFER ROAD USERS	
National speed limit law	Yes
Max urban speed limit	30 km/h [b]
Max rural speed limit	30 km/h [b]
Max motorway speed limit	No
Local authorities can modify limits	No
Enforcement	0 1 2 (3) 4 5 6 7 8 9 10
Predominant type of enforcement	Manual
National drink-driving law	No [c]
BAC limit – general population	–
BAC limit – young or novice drivers	–
Random breath testing carried out	No
Testing carried out in case of fatal crash	No
Enforcement	–
% road traffic deaths involving alcohol	–
National motorcycle helmet law	Yes
Applies to drivers and passengers	No [d]
Helmet fastening required	No
Helmet standard referred to and/or specified	No
Children passengers on motorcycles	Not restricted
Enforcement	0 1 2 3 4 (5) 6 7 8 9 10
Helmet wearing rate	–
National seat-belt law	Yes
Applies to front and rear seat occupants	No [d]
Enforcement	0 1 2 3 4 (5) 6 7 8 9 10
Seat-belt wearing rate	–
National child restraint law	No
Children seated in front seat	Not restricted
Child restraint required	–
Child restraint standard referred to and/or specified	–
Enforcement	–
% children using child restraints	–
National law on mobile phone use while driving	Yes
Ban on hand-held mobile phone use	Yes
Ban on hands-free mobile phone use	No
National drug-driving law	No

[b] Speed limit set per vehicle type with a maximum speed limit of 30 km/h for specified vehicles, except in designated areas with higher speeds
[c] Alcohol consumption legally prohibited
[d] Only required on roads where vehicles may be driven at a speed higher than the normal limit

Deaths by road user category

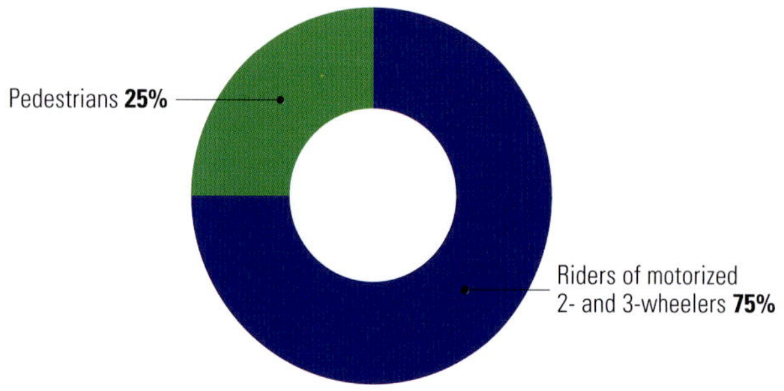

Source: 2016, Maldives Police Service

Trends in reported road traffic deaths

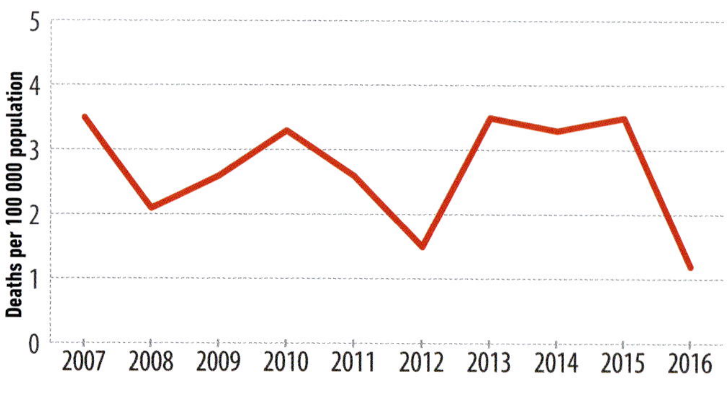

Source: Maldives Police Service

Legislative review conducted by WHO. Vehicle safety data from UNECE WP29. Other data collected by questionnaire and cleared by Ministry of Health.

Mali

Population: 17 994 836 | Income group: Low | Gross national income per capita: US$ 750

INSTITUTIONAL FRAMEWORK

Lead agency	National Agency for Road Safety (ANASER), Ministry of Transport
Funded in national budget	Yes
National road safety strategy	Yes
Funding to implement strategy	Partially funded
Fatality reduction target	50% (2011-2020)

SAFER ROADS AND MOBILITY

Audits or star rating required for new road infrastructure	Yes
Design standards for the safety of pedestrians / cyclists	Partial
Inspections / star rating of existing roads	Yes
Investments to upgrade high risk locations	Yes
Policies & investment in urban public transport	No

SAFER VEHICLES

Total registered vehicles for 2015	344 345
Cars and 4-wheeled light vehicles	197 660
Motorized 2- and 3-wheelers	54 952
Heavy trucks	22 073
Buses	–
Other	69 660
Vehicle standards applied (UNECE WP.29)	
Frontal impact standard	No
Electronic stability control	No
Pedestrian protection	No
Motorcycle anti-lock braking system	No

POST-CRASH CARE

National emergency care access number	Partial coverage
Trauma registry	Some facilities
Formal certification for prehospital providers	No
National assessment of emergency care systems	No

DATA

Reported road traffic fatalities (2016)	541[a] (88% M, 12% F)
WHO estimated road traffic fatalities (2016)	4 159 (95% CI 3 404 - 4 914)
WHO estimated rate per 100 000 population (2016)	23.1

[a] National Agency for Road Safety (ANASER). Died within 30 days of crash

SAFER ROAD USERS

National speed limit law	Yes
Max urban speed limit	50 km/h
Max rural speed limit	90 km/h
Max motorway speed limit	110 km/h
Local authorities can modify limits	Yes
Enforcement	0 1 2 3 **4** 5 6 7 8 9 10
Predominant type of enforcement	Manual
National drink-driving law	Yes
BAC limit – general population	< 0.03 g/dl
BAC limit – young or novice drivers	< 0.03 g/dl
Random breath testing carried out	Yes
Testing carried out in case of fatal crash	No
Enforcement	0 1 2 **3** 4 5 6 7 8 9 10
% road traffic deaths involving alcohol	<1%[b]
National motorcycle helmet law	Yes
Applies to drivers and passengers	Yes
Helmet fastening required	Yes
Helmet standard referred to and/or specified	Yes
Children passengers on motorcycles	Not restricted[c]
Enforcement	0 1 2 **3** 4 5 6 7 8 9 10
Helmet wearing rate	6% Drivers[d], <1% Passengers[d]
National seat-belt law	Yes[e]
Applies to front and rear seat occupants	No[e]
Enforcement	0 1 2 3 **4** 5 6 7 8 9 10
Seat-belt wearing rate	20% Drivers[d]
National child restraint law	No[f]
Children seated in front seat	Prohibited under 10 yrs
Child restraint required	–
Child restraint standard referred to and/or specified	–
Enforcement	–
% children using child restraints	–
National law on mobile phone use while driving	Yes
Ban on hand-held mobile phone use	Yes
Ban on hands-free mobile phone use	No
National drug-driving law	Yes

[b] 2016, National Agency for Road Safety (ANASER)
[c] Children under 5 years traveling on motorcycles must be placed in a seat with tether belts
[d] 2015, Spirit Survey Report
[e] Seat belts are only required outside cities
[f] Children under 13 years can be restrained either by a child restraint system or a seat belt

Deaths by road user category

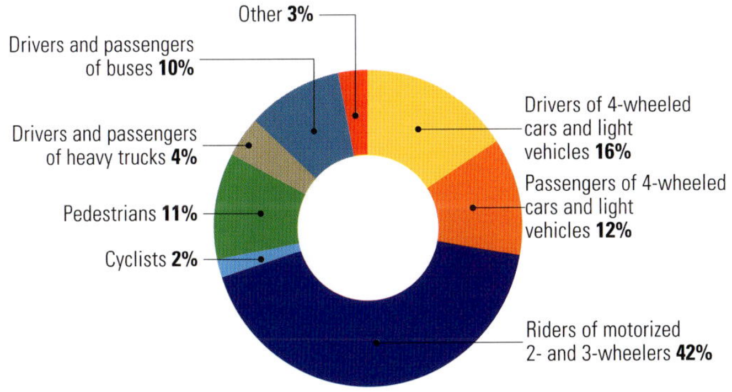

Source: 2016, National Agency for Road Safety (ANASER)

Trends in reported road traffic deaths

Source: National Agency for Road Safety (ANASER), DNT, Police, and Gendarmerie

Legislative review conducted by WHO. Vehicle safety data from UNECE WP.29. Other data collected by questionnaire and cleared by Ministry of Transport.

Malta

Population: 429 362 | Income group: High | Gross national income per capita: US$ 24 140

INSTITUTIONAL FRAMEWORK	
Lead agency	Transport Malta
Funded in national budget	Yes
National road safety strategy	Yes
Funding to implement strategy	Fully funded
Fatality reduction target	50% (2014-2020)

SAFER ROADS AND MOBILITY	
Audits or star rating required for new road infrastructure	Partial
Design standards for the safety of pedestrians / cyclists	Partial
Inspections / star rating of existing roads	Yes
Investments to upgrade high risk locations	No
Policies & investment in urban public transport	Yes

SAFER VEHICLES	
Total registered vehicles for 2016	358 947
Cars and 4-wheeled light vehicles	—
Motorized 2- and 3-wheelers	—
Heavy trucks	—
Buses	—
Other	—
Vehicle standards applied (UNECE WP.29)	
Frontal impact standard	Yes
Electronic stability control	Yes
Pedestrian protection	Yes
Motorcycle anti-lock braking system	Yes

POST-CRASH CARE	
National emergency care access number	National, single number
Trauma registry	National
Formal certification for prehospital providers	Yes
National assessment of emergency care systems	Yes

DATA	
Reported road traffic fatalities (2016)	22[a] (77% M, 23% F)
WHO estimated road traffic fatalities (2016)	26
WHO estimated rate per 100 000 population (2016)	6.1

[a] Vital registration data (mortality registry). Died within a year of crash

SAFER ROAD USERS	
National speed limit law	Yes
Max urban speed limit	50 km/h
Max rural speed limit	80 km/h
Max motorway speed limit	No
Local authorities can modify limits	No
Enforcement	0 1 2 3 (4) 5 6 7 8 9 10
Predominant type of enforcement	Automated
National drink-driving law	Yes
BAC limit – general population	≤ 0.05 g/dl
BAC limit – young or novice drivers	≤ 0.02 g/dl
Random breath testing carried out	Yes[b]
Testing carried out in case of fatal crash	All drivers tested
Enforcement	0 1 2 3 (4) 5 6 7 8 9 10
% road traffic deaths involving alcohol	—
National motorcycle helmet law	Yes
Applies to drivers and passengers	Yes
Helmet fastening required	No
Helmet standard referred to and/or specified	No
Children passengers on motorcycles	Not restricted
Enforcement	0 1 2 3 4 5 6 7 8 (9) 10
Helmet wearing rate	—
National seat-belt law	Yes
Applies to front and rear seat occupants	Yes
Enforcement	0 1 2 3 4 5 (6) 7 8 9 10
Seat-belt wearing rate	—
National child restraint law	Yes
Children seated in front seat	Allowed in a child restraint
Child restraint required	Up to 3 yrs[c]
Child restraint standard referred to and/or specified	Yes
Enforcement	0 1 2 (3) 4 5 6 7 8 9 10
% children using child restraints	—
National law on mobile phone use while driving	Yes
Ban on hand-held mobile phone use	Yes
Ban on hands-free mobile phone use	No
National drug-driving law	Yes

[b] Legislation requires probable cause to test drivers

[c] Legislation refers to child restraint use for children up to 12 yrs / 150cm but allows children aged 3 years and over, in the absence of an available restraint, to travel in the rear without a restraint. For children under 3 years, a child restraint shall be mandatorily used

Deaths by road user category

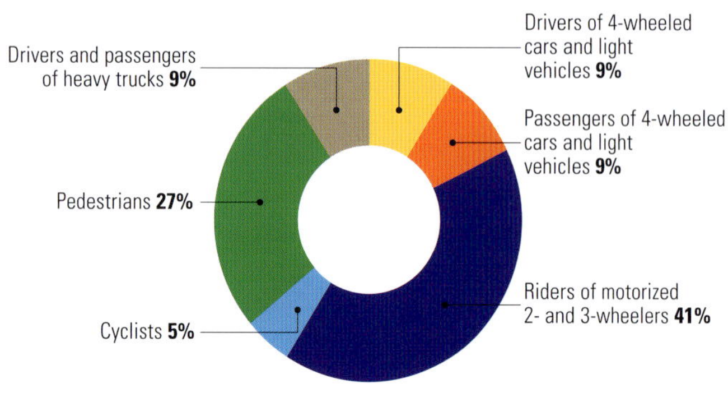

Source: 2016, Malta National Mortality Register, Directorate for Health Information and Research

Trends in reported road traffic deaths

Source: National Statistics Office

Legislative review conducted by WHO. Vehicle safety data from UNECE WP29. Other data collected by questionnaire and cleared by Ministry for Health

Mauritania

Population: 4 301 018 | Income group: Middle | Gross national income per capita: US$ 1 120

INSTITUTIONAL FRAMEWORK	
Lead agency	Directorate of Road Safety, General Directorate of Land Transport (DGTT)
Funded in national budget	Yes
National road safety strategy	Yes
Funding to implement strategy	Partially funded
Fatality reduction target	25% (2012-2016)
SAFER ROADS AND MOBILITY	
Audits or star rating required for new road infrastructure	No
Design standards for the safety of pedestrians / cyclists	No
Inspections / star rating of existing roads	No
Investments to upgrade high risk locations	Yes
Policies & investment in urban public transport	No
SAFER VEHICLES	
Total registered vehicles	–
Cars and 4-wheeled light vehicles	–
Motorized 2- and 3-wheelers	–
Heavy trucks	–
Buses	–
Other	–
Vehicle standards applied (UNECE WP.29)	
Frontal impact standard	No
Electronic stability control	No
Pedestrian protection	No
Motorcycle anti-lock braking system	No
POST-CRASH CARE	
National emergency care access number	–
Trauma registry	None
Formal certification for prehospital providers	No
National assessment of emergency care systems	No
DATA	
Reported road traffic fatalities (2016)	184 [a] (60% M, 40% F)
WHO estimated road traffic fatalities (2016)	1 064 (95% CI 891 - 1 236)
WHO estimated rate per 100 000 population (2016)	24.7

[a] Directorate of Road Safety (DGTT). Died within 30 days of crash

SAFER ROAD USERS	
National speed limit law	Yes
Max urban speed limit	80 km/h
Max rural speed limit	100 km/h
Max motorway speed limit	100 km/h
Local authorities can modify limits	Yes
Enforcement	0 1 2 3 ④ 5 6 7 8 9 10
Predominant type of enforcement	Manual
National drink-driving law	Yes [b]
BAC limit – general population	–
BAC limit – young or novice drivers	–
Random breath testing carried out	No
Testing carried out in case of fatal crash	No
Enforcement	0 1 2 3 4 5 6 7 ⑧ 9 10
% road traffic deaths involving alcohol	–
National motorcycle helmet law	Yes
Applies to drivers and passengers	Yes
Helmet fastening required	No
Helmet standard referred to and/or specified	No
Children passengers on motorcycles	Not restricted
Enforcement	0 1 2 ③ 4 5 6 7 8 9 10
Helmet wearing rate	–
National seat-belt law	Yes
Applies to front and rear seat occupants	No [c]
Enforcement	0 1 2 ③ 4 5 6 7 8 9 10
Seat-belt wearing rate	–
National child restraint law	No
Children seated in front seat	Prohibited under 10 yrs
Child restraint required	–
Child restraint standard referred to and/or specified	–
Enforcement	–
% children using child restraints	–
National law on mobile phone use while driving	Yes
Ban on hand-held mobile phone use	Yes
Ban on hands-free mobile phone use	Yes
National drug-driving law	Yes

[b] Not based on BAC
[c] The use of seat belt for rear seat passengers is only required outside urban areas

Deaths by road user category

Trends in reported road traffic deaths

Source: Directorate of Road Safety (DGTT)

Mauritius

Population: 1 262 132 | Income group: Middle | Gross national income per capita: US$ 9 760

INSTITUTIONAL FRAMEWORK

Lead agency	**Traffic Management and Road Safety Unit, Ministry of Public Infrastructure and Land Transport**
Funded in national budget	Yes
National road safety strategy	**Yes**
Funding to implement strategy	Fully funded
Fatality reduction target	50% (2016-2025)

SAFER ROADS AND MOBILITY

Audits or star rating required for new road infrastructure	Yes
Design standards for the safety of pedestrians / cyclists	Partial
Inspections / star rating of existing roads	Yes
Investments to upgrade high risk locations	Yes
Policies & investment in urban public transport	Yes

SAFER VEHICLES

Total registered vehicles for 2016	**507 676**
Cars and 4-wheeled light vehicles	282 855
Motorized 2- and 3-wheelers	199 399
Heavy trucks	14 645
Buses	3 107
Other	7 670
Vehicle standards applied (UNECE WP.29)	
Frontal impact standard	No
Electronic stability control	No
Pedestrian protection	No
Motorcycle anti-lock braking system	No

POST-CRASH CARE

National emergency care access number	National, single number
Trauma registry	Subnational
Formal certification for prehospital providers	Yes
National assessment of emergency care systems	Yes

DATA

Reported road traffic fatalities (2016)	144[a] (94% M, 6% F)
WHO estimated road traffic fatalities (2016)	173
WHO estimated rate per 100 000 population (2016)	13.7

[a] Statistics Mauritius, Economic and Social Indicators on Road Transport and Road Traffic Accident Statistics, March 2017. Died within 30 days of crash

SAFER ROAD USERS

National speed limit law	**Yes**
Max urban speed limit	90 km/h
Max rural speed limit	90 km/h
Max motorway speed limit	110 km/h
Local authorities can modify limits	No
Enforcement	0 1 2 3 4 5 (6) 7 8 9 10
Predominant type of enforcement	Manual and automated
National drink-driving law	**Yes**
BAC limit – general population	≤ 0.05 g/dl
BAC limit – young or novice drivers	≤ 0.05 g/dl
Random breath testing carried out	Yes[b]
Testing carried out in case of fatal crash	All drivers tested
Enforcement	0 1 2 3 4 5 6 (7) 8 9 10
% road traffic deaths involving alcohol	24%[c]
National motorcycle helmet law	**Yes**
Applies to drivers and passengers	Yes
Helmet fastening required	No
Helmet standard referred to and/or specified	Yes[d]
Children passengers on motorcycles	Not restricted
Enforcement	0 1 2 3 4 5 6 7 8 9 (10)
Helmet wearing rate	–
National seat-belt law	**Yes**
Applies to front and rear seat occupants	Yes
Enforcement	0 1 2 3 4 (5) 6 7 8 9 10
Seat-belt wearing rate	97% Front seats[e], <1% Rear seats[e]
National child restraint law	**No**
Children seated in front seat	Prohibited under 10 yrs
Child restraint required	–
Child restraint standard referred to and/or specified	–
Enforcement	–
% children using child restraints	–
National law on mobile phone use while driving	**Yes**
Ban on hand-held mobile phone use	Yes
Ban on hands-free mobile phone use	Yes
National drug-driving law	**Yes**

[b] Legislation requires probable cause to test drivers
[c] 2016, Forensic Scientific Laboratory
[d] Reference is made to regulations to specify the types, shape and construction of helmets
[e] 2011, Traffic Management and Road Safety Unit

Deaths by road user category

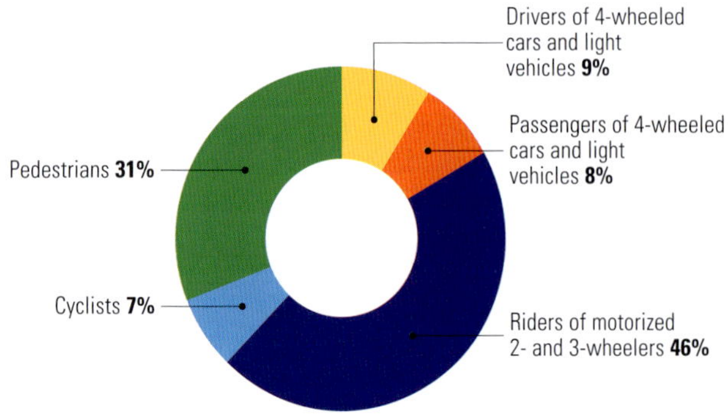

Source: 2016, Statistics Mauritius, Economic and Social Indicators on Road Transport and Road Traffic Accident Statistics, March 2017

Trends in reported road traffic deaths

Source: Statistics Mauritius, Economic and Social Indicators on Road Transport and Road Traffic Accident Statistics, March 2017

Legislative review conducted by WHO. Vehicle safety data from UNECE WP29. Other data collected by questionnaire and cleared by Ministry of Public Infrastructure.

Mexico

Population: 127 540 424 | Income group: Middle | Gross national income per capita: US$ 9 040

INSTITUTIONAL FRAMEWORK	
Lead agency	National Council for Accident Prevention through its Secretariat (STCONAPRA)
Funded in national budget	Yes
National road safety strategy	Yes
Funding to implement strategy	Partially funded
Fatality reduction target	50% (2011-2020)

SAFER ROADS AND MOBILITY	
Audits or star rating required for new road infrastructure	No
Design standards for the safety of pedestrians / cyclists	Yes
Inspections / star rating of existing roads	Yes
Investments to upgrade high risk locations	Yes
Policies & investment in urban public transport	Yes

SAFER VEHICLES	
Total registered vehicles for 2015	40 205 671
Cars and 4-wheeled light vehicles	27 171 560
Motorized 2- and 3-wheelers	2 608 659
Heavy trucks	10 067 394
Buses	358 058
Other	0
Vehicle standards applied (UNECE WP.29)	
Frontal impact standard	No
Electronic stability control	No
Pedestrian protection	No
Motorcycle anti-lock braking system	No

POST-CRASH CARE	
National emergency care access number	National, single number
Trauma registry	National
Formal certification for prehospital providers	Yes
National assessment of emergency care systems	Yes

DATA	
Reported road traffic fatalities (2015)	16 039[a] (79% M, 21% F)
WHO estimated road traffic fatalities (2016)	16 725
WHO estimated rate per 100 000 population (2016)	13.1

[a] Mortality Statistics, National Institute of Statistics, Geography and Informatics (INEGI). Unlimited time period following crash

SAFER ROAD USERS[*]	
National speed limit law	Yes
Max urban speed limit	20 -70 km/h
Max rural speed limit	20-90 km/h
Max motorway speed limit	45-110 km/h
Local authorities can modify limits	Yes
Enforcement	0 1 2 3 ④ 5 6 7 8 9 10
Predominant type of enforcement	Manual and automated
National drink-driving law	Yes[b]
BAC limit – general population	–
BAC limit – young or novice drivers	–
Random breath testing carried out	Yes
Testing carried out in case of fatal crash	Some drivers tested
Enforcement	0 1 2 3 4 5 6 ⑦ 8 9 10
% road traffic deaths involving alcohol	20%[c]
National motorcycle helmet law	No
Applies to drivers and passengers	No
Helmet fastening required	No
Helmet standard referred to and/or specified	No
Children passengers on motorcycles	Not restricted
Enforcement	0 1 2 3 ④ 5 6 7 8 9 10
Helmet wearing rate	83% Drivers[d], 55% Passengers[d]
National seat-belt law	No
Applies to front and rear seat occupants	No
Enforcement	–
Seat-belt wearing rate	49% Front seats[d], 6% Rear seats[d]
National child restraint law	No
Children seated in front seat	Not restricted
Child restraint required	–
Child restraint standard referred to and/or specified	–
Enforcement	–
% children using child restraints	14%[e]
National law on mobile phone use while driving	No
Ban on hand-held mobile phone use	No
Ban on hands-free mobile phone use	No
National drug-driving law	Yes

[*] These data take into consideration subnational laws. A criteria is answered "Yes" if at least 80% of the subnational entities meet the criteria
[b] Not based on BAC in 19 out of 32 states
[c] 2010-2013, Estimating the Drink-Driving attributable fraction of road traffic deaths in Mexico (Santoyo-Castillo et al, manuscript under peer-review)
[d] 2016, Use of helmet, cell phone and speeding when driving: prevalence and associated factors in four Mexican cities (Hidalgo-Solórzano & Gómez-García)
[e] 2014, Estimated use of child restraint in 2 Mexican States, STCONAPRA

Deaths by road user category

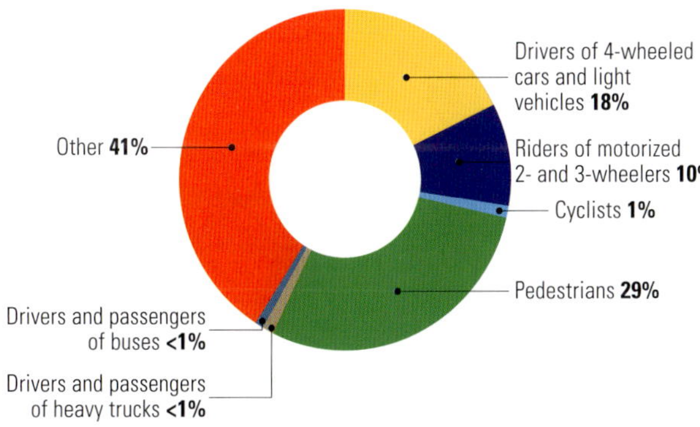

Source: 2015, Mortality Statistics, National Institute of Statistics, Geography and Informatics (INEGI)

Trends in reported road traffic deaths

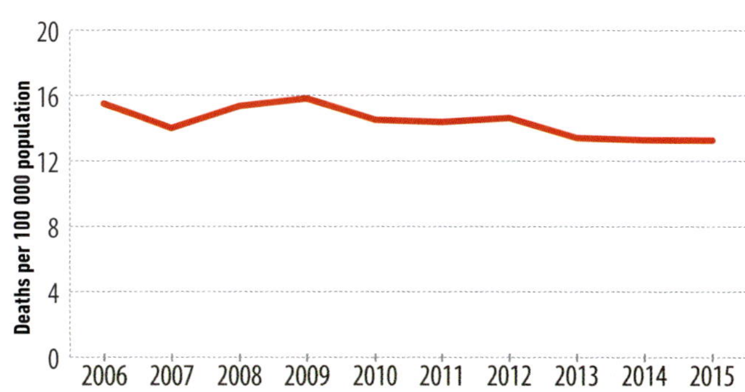

Source: 2015, Mortality Statistics, National Institute of Statistics, Geography and Informatics (INEGI) and National Council of Population (latter for population data)

Legislative review conducted by WHO. Vehicle safety data from UNECE WP29. Other data collected by questionnaire and cleared by Secretariat of Health.

Micronesia (Federated States of)

Population: 104 937 | Income group: Middle | Gross national income per capita: US$ 3 680

INSTITUTIONAL FRAMEWORK	
Lead agency	**No**
Funded in national budget	–
National road safety strategy	**No**
Funding to implement strategy	–
Fatality reduction target	–

SAFER ROADS AND MOBILITY	
Audits or star rating required for new road infrastructure	Partial
Design standards for the safety of pedestrians / cyclists	Partial
Inspections / star rating of existing roads	Yes
Investments to upgrade high risk locations	No
Policies & investment in urban public transport	No

SAFER VEHICLES[a]	
Total registered vehicles for 2016	**5 673**
Cars and 4-wheeled light vehicles	5 436
Motorized 2- and 3-wheelers	25
Heavy trucks	55
Buses	62
Other	95
Vehicle standards applied (UNECE WP.29)	
Frontal impact standard	No
Electronic stability control	No
Pedestrian protection	No
Motorcycle anti-lock braking system	No

POST-CRASH CARE	
National emergency care access number	National, multiple numbers
Trauma registry	None
Formal certification for prehospital providers	No
National assessment of emergency care systems	No

DATA	
Reported road traffic fatalities (2016)[a]	2[b] (100% M, 0% F)
WHO estimated road traffic fatalities (2016)	2
WHO estimated rate per 100 000 population (2016)	1.9

[a] Data for Pohnpei only
[b] Pohnpei State Department of Public Safety and FSM Department of Health & Social Affairs. Died within 24 hours of crash

SAFER ROAD USERS[c]	
National speed limit law	**Yes[d]**
Max urban speed limit	~ 40 km/h
Max rural speed limit	~ 40 km/h
Max motorway speed limit	~ 40 km/h
Local authorities can modify limits	Yes
Enforcement	0 1 2 (3) 4 5 6 7 8 9 10
Predominant type of enforcement	Manual
National drink-driving law	**Yes[e]**
BAC limit – general population	–
BAC limit – young or novice drivers	–
Random breath testing carried out	No
Testing carried out in case of fatal crash	No
Enforcement	0 1 2 3 4 (5) 6 7 8 9 10
% road traffic deaths involving alcohol	100%[f]
National motorcycle helmet law	**Yes**
Applies to drivers and passengers	Yes
Helmet fastening required	No
Helmet standard referred to and/or specified	No
Children passengers on motorcycles	Not restricted
Enforcement	0 1 2 3 4 5 6 (7) 8 9 10
Helmet wearing rate	–
National seat-belt law	**No**
Applies to front and rear seat occupants	–
Enforcement	–
Seat-belt wearing rate	–
National child restraint law	**No**
Children seated in front seat	Not restricted
Child restraint required	–
Child restraint standard referred to and/or specified	–
Enforcement	–
% children using child restraints	–
National law on mobile phone use while driving	**No**
Ban on hand-held mobile phone use	–
Ban on hands-free mobile phone use	–
National drug-driving law	**Yes**

[c] Legislation analysis takes into consideration subnational laws from Kosrae, Pohnpei and Yap (no data was available for Chuuk). A criteria is answered Yes if at least 75% of the subnational entities meet this criteria
[d] Speed limits may be increased by the Governor (Kosrae and Yap) or by the Director of the Department of Public Safety (Pohnpei)
[e] In Yap, a BAC limit is provided in the law. In Kosrae and Pohnpei, the law is not based on a BAC limit. No data is available for Chuuk.
[f] 2016, Pohnpei State Department of Public Safety

Deaths by road user category

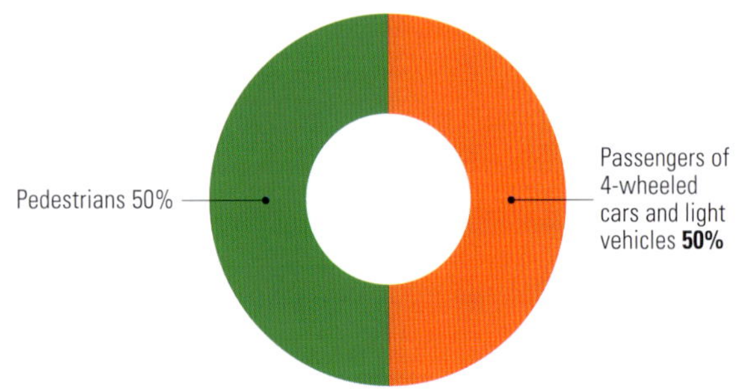

Source: 2016, Pohnpei Department of Public Safety

Trends in reported road traffic deaths

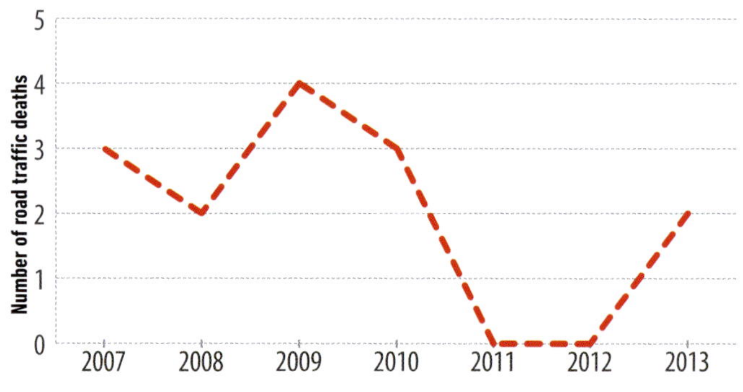

Source: Department of Health and Social Affairs (HIS) - 3rd Global Status Report for Road Safety

Legislative review conducted by WHO. Vehicle safety data from UNECE WP29. Other data collected by questionnaire and cleared by Department of Health and Social Affairs

Mongolia

Population: 3 027 398 | Income group: Middle | Gross national income per capita: US$ 3 550

INSTITUTIONAL FRAMEWORK	
Lead agency	Ministry of Road and Transport Development, The National Committee
Funded in national budget	Yes
National road safety strategy	Yes
Funding to implement strategy	Partially funded
Fatality reduction target	50% (2012-2020)

SAFER ROADS AND MOBILITY	
Audits or star rating required for new road infrastructure	Yes
Design standards for the safety of pedestrians / cyclists	Partial
Inspections / star rating of existing roads	No
Investments to upgrade high risk locations	No
Policies & investment in urban public transport	Yes

SAFER VEHICLES	
Total registered vehicles for 2016	841 537
Cars and 4-wheeled light vehicles	547 299
Motorized 2- and 3-wheelers	42 751
Heavy trucks	175 648
Buses	6 823
Other	69 016
Vehicle standards applied (UNECE WP.29)	
Frontal impact standard	No
Electronic stability control	No
Pedestrian protection	No
Motorcycle anti-lock braking system	No

POST-CRASH CARE	
National emergency care access number	National, single number
Trauma registry	National
Formal certification for prehospital providers	No
National assessment of emergency care systems	No

DATA	
Reported road traffic fatalities (2016)	484[a] (75% M, 25% F)
WHO estimated road traffic fatalities (2016)	499 (95% CI 471 - 527)
WHO estimated rate per 100 000 population (2016)	16.5

[a] Health icators 2016, Center for Health Development. Died within 30 days of crash

SAFER ROAD USERS	
National speed limit law	Yes
Max urban speed limit	60 km/h
Max rural speed limit	80 km/h
Max motorway speed limit	100 km/h
Local authorities can modify limits	No
Enforcement	0 1 2 3 4 (5) 6 7 8 9 10
Predominant type of enforcement	Manual and automated
National drink-driving law	Yes
BAC limit – general population	< 0.04 g/dl[b]
BAC limit – young or novice drivers	< 0.04 g/dl[b]
Random breath testing carried out	Yes[c]
Testing carried out in case of fatal crash	All drivers tested
Enforcement	0 1 2 3 4 5 6 7 (8) 9 10
% road traffic deaths involving alcohol	25%[d]
National motorcycle helmet law	Yes
Applies to drivers and passengers	Yes
Helmet fastening required	No
Helmet standard referred to and/or specified	No
Children passengers on motorcycles	Not restricted[e]
Enforcement	0 (1) 2 3 4 5 6 7 8 9 10
Helmet wearing rate	–
National seat-belt law	Yes
Applies to front and rear seat occupants	Yes
Enforcement	0 1 2 3 4 (5) 6 7 8 9 10
Seat-belt wearing rate	–
National child restraint law	No
Children seated in front seat	Not restricted
Child restraint required	–
Child restraint standard referred to and/or specified	–
Enforcement	–
% children using child restraints	–
National law on mobile phone use while driving	Yes
Ban on hand-held mobile phone use	Yes
Ban on hands-free mobile phone use	No
National drug-driving law	Yes

[b] Law based on breath alcohol concentration, values converted to BAC
[c] Legislation requires probable cause to test drivers or commission of a traffic offence
[d] 2016, General Police Department, "Statistics on road traffic injury and violation"
[e] Children under 12 years can be transported on a motorcycle provided that there is a special support installed in the rear seat

Deaths by road user category

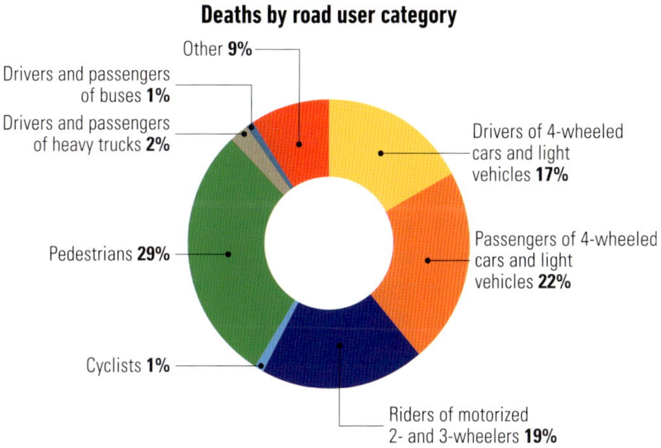

Source: 2016, General Police Department, "Statistics on road traffic injury and violation"

Trends in reported road traffic deaths

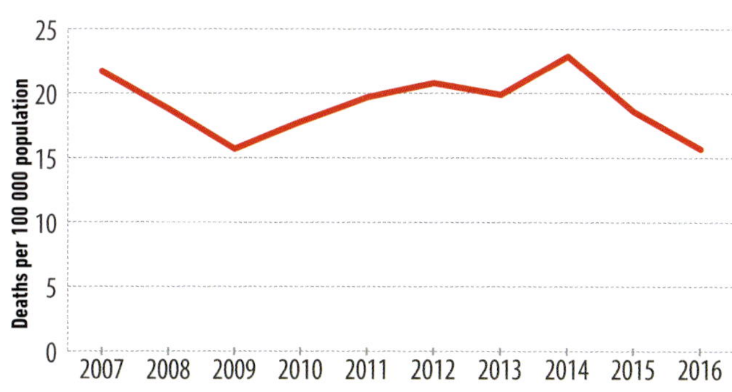

Source: Center for Health Development, Health Indicators 2016

Legislative review conducted by WHO. Vehicle safety data from UNECE WP29. Other data collected by questionnaire.

Montenegro

Population: 628 615 | Income group: Middle | Gross national income per capita: US$ 6 970

INSTITUTIONAL FRAMEWORK	
Lead agency	Coordination Body for monitoring the implementation of Strategy for the improvement of Road Safety
Funded in national budget	Yes
National road safety strategy	Yes
Funding to implement strategy	Partially funded
Fatality reduction target	50% (2010-2019)
SAFER ROADS AND MOBILITY	
Audits or star rating required for new road infrastructure	Yes
Design standards for the safety of pedestrians / cyclists	Yes
Inspections / star rating of existing roads	Yes
Investments to upgrade high risk locations	Yes
Policies & investment in urban public transport	No
SAFER VEHICLES	
Total registered vehicles for 2016	211 219
Cars and 4-wheeled light vehicles	184 623
Motorized 2- and 3-wheelers	4 362
Heavy trucks	13 445
Buses	1 308
Other	7 481
Vehicle standards applied (UNECE WP.29)	
Frontal impact standard	No
Electronic stability control	No
Pedestrian protection	No
Motorcycle anti-lock braking system	No
POST-CRASH CARE	
National emergency care access number	National, single number
Trauma registry	National
Formal certification for prehospital providers	Yes
National assessment of emergency care systems	Yes
DATA	
Reported road traffic fatalities (2016)	65[a] (80% M, 20% F)
WHO estimated road traffic fatalities (2016)	67
WHO estimated rate per 100 000 population (2016)	10.7

[a] Statistical office of Montenegro (MONSTAT). Died within 30 days of crash

SAFER ROAD USERS	
National speed limit law	Yes
Max urban speed limit	50 km/h
Max rural speed limit	80 km/h
Max motorway speed limit	130 km/h
Local authorities can modify limits	No
Enforcement	0 1 2 3 4 5 6 ⑦ 8 9 10
Predominant type of enforcement	Manual
National drink-driving law	Yes
BAC limit – general population	≤ 0.03 g/dl
BAC limit – young or novice drivers	0.00 g/dl
Random breath testing carried out	Yes
Testing carried out in case of fatal crash	All drivers tested
Enforcement	0 1 2 3 4 5 6 ⑦ 8 9 10
% road traffic deaths involving alcohol	–
National motorcycle helmet law	Yes
Applies to drivers and passengers	Yes
Helmet fastening required	Yes
Helmet standard referred to and/or specified	Yes[b]
Children passengers on motorcycles	Prohibited under 12 yrs
Enforcement	0 1 2 3 4 5 ⑥ 7 8 9 10
Helmet wearing rate	70% Drivers[c], 30% Passengers[c]
National seat-belt law	Yes
Applies to front and rear seat occupants	Yes
Enforcement	0 1 2 3 4 5 ⑥ 7 8 9 10
Seat-belt wearing rate	40% Front seats[c], 5% Rear seats[c]
National child restraint law	Yes
Children seated in front seat	Prohibited under 12 yrs[d]
Child restraint required	Up to 5 yrs
Child restraint standard referred to and/or specified	No
Enforcement	0 1 2 3 ④ 5 6 7 8 9 10
% children using child restraints	–
National law on mobile phone use while driving	Yes
Ban on hand-held mobile phone use	Yes
Ban on hands-free mobile phone use	Yes
National drug-driving law	Yes

[b] As prescribed by the responsible state administration
[c] 2016, Police Directorate
[d] By exception, a child under 3 years can be transported in the front of the vehicle if placed in a rear-facing restraint provided that the airbag is deactivated

Deaths by road user category

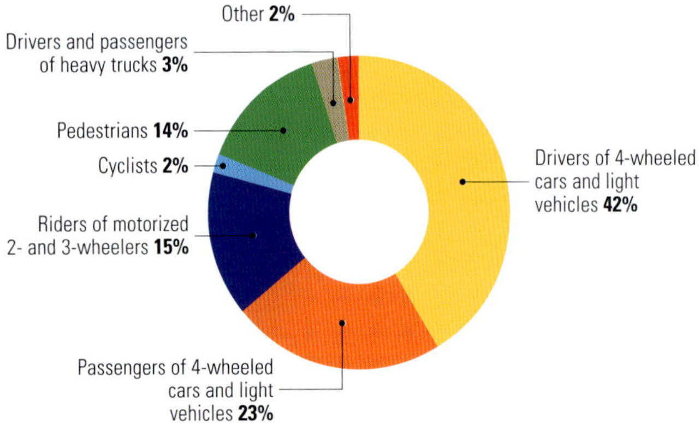

Source: 2016, Police Directorate

Trends in reported road traffic deaths

Source: Statistical office of Montenegro (MONSTAT)

Morocco

Population: 35 276 784 | Income group: Middle | Gross national income per capita: US$ 2 850

INSTITUTIONAL FRAMEWORK	
Lead agency	Directorate of Road Transport and Road Safety, Ministry of Equipment, Transport, Logistics and Water
Funded in national budget	Yes
National road safety strategy	Yes
Funding to implement strategy	Fully funded
Fatality reduction target	20% / 50% (2017-2020 / 2017-2026)

SAFER ROADS AND MOBILITY	
Audits or star rating required for new road infrastructure	Partial
Design standards for the safety of pedestrians / cyclists	No
Inspections / star rating of existing roads	Yes
Investments to upgrade high risk locations	Yes
Policies & investment in urban public transport	Yes

SAFER VEHICLES	
Total registered vehicles for 2016	3 791 469
Cars and 4-wheeled light vehicles	3 413 980
Motorized 2- and 3-wheelers	55 517
Heavy trucks	196 066
Buses	13 329
Other	112 557
Vehicle standards applied (UNECE WP.29)	
Frontal impact standard	No
Electronic stability control	No
Pedestrian protection	No
Motorcycle anti-lock braking system	No

POST-CRASH CARE	
National emergency care access number	National, single number
Trauma registry	None
Formal certification for prehospital providers	No
National assessment of emergency care systems	No

DATA	
Reported road traffic fatalities (2016)	3 785 [a] (83% M, 16% F)
WHO estimated road traffic fatalities (2016)	6 917 (95% CI 6 109 - 7 726)
WHO estimated rate per 100 000 population (2016)	19.6

[a] Directorate of Roads. Died within 30 days of crash

SAFER ROAD USERS	
National speed limit law	Yes
Max urban speed limit	60 km/h
Max rural speed limit	100 km/h
Max motorway speed limit	120 km/h
Local authorities can modify limits	Yes
Enforcement	0 1 2 3 4 5 6 ⑦ 8 9 10
Predominant type of enforcement	Manual and automated
National drink-driving law	Yes [b]
BAC limit – general population	< 0.02 g/dl
BAC limit – young or novice drivers	< 0.02 g/dl
Random breath testing carried out	Yes
Testing carried out in case of fatal crash	No
Enforcement	0 1 2 3 4 ⑤ 6 7 8 9 10
% road traffic deaths involving alcohol	4% [c]
National motorcycle helmet law	Yes
Applies to drivers and passengers	Yes
Helmet fastening required	Yes
Helmet standard referred to and/or specified	Yes
Children passengers on motorcycles	Not restricted
Enforcement	0 1 2 3 4 5 6 ⑦ 8 9 10
Helmet wearing rate	64% Drivers [d], 31% Passengers [d]
National seat-belt law	Yes
Applies to front and rear seat occupants	No [e]
Enforcement	0 1 2 3 4 5 6 7 ⑧ 9 10
Seat-belt wearing rate	63% Front seats [d], 22% Rear seats [d]
National child restraint law	No
Children seated in front seat	Prohibited under 10 yrs
Child restraint required	–
Child restraint standard referred to and/or specified	–
Enforcement	–
% children using child restraints	–
National law on mobile phone use while driving	Yes
Ban on hand-held mobile phone use	Yes
Ban on hands-free mobile phone use	No
National drug-driving law	Yes

[b] Alcohol consumption legally prohibited.
[c] 2014, Directorate of Roads
[d] 2016, National Committee for Road Accidents Prevention, Study on the measurement of behavioural indicators of road users
[e] For rear seat passengers, seat belt required only outside cities

Legislative review conducted by WHO. Vehicle safety data from UNECE WP29. Other data collected by questionnaire and cleared by Ministry of Equipment, Transport and Logistics.

Deaths by road user category

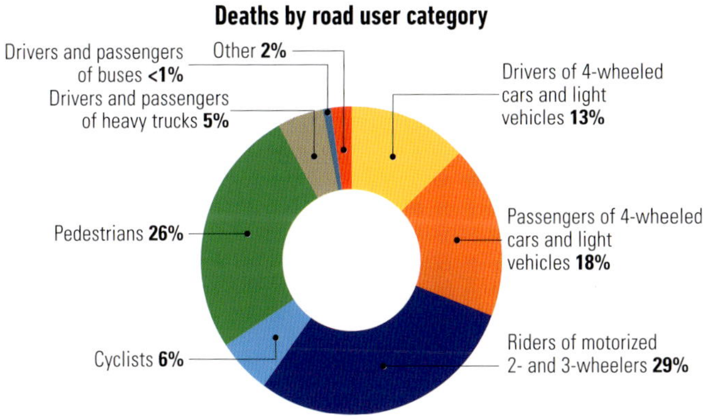

Source: 2016, Directorate of Roads

Trends in reported road traffic deaths

Source: Directorate of Roads (death data) and High-Commission for Planning (population data)

Mozambique

Population: 28 829 476 | Income group: Low | Gross national income per capita: US$ 480

INSTITUTIONAL FRAMEWORK

Lead agency	National Land Transport Institute (INATTER), Ministry of Transport and Communications
Funded in national budget	Yes
National road safety strategy	Yes
Funding to implement strategy	Partially funded
Fatality reduction target	–

SAFER ROADS AND MOBILITY

Audits or star rating required for new road infrastructure	No
Design standards for the safety of pedestrians / cyclists	Partial
Inspections / star rating of existing roads	No
Investments to upgrade high risk locations	No
Policies & investment in urban public transport	No

SAFER VEHICLES

Total registered vehicles for 2016	698 864
Cars and 4-wheeled light vehicles	–
Motorized 2- and 3-wheelers	–
Heavy trucks	–
Buses	–
Other	–
Vehicle standards applied (UNECE WP.29)	
Frontal impact standard	No
Electronic stability control	No
Pedestrian protection	No
Motorcycle anti-lock braking system	No

POST-CRASH CARE

National emergency care access number	National, multiple numbers
Trauma registry	Some facilities
Formal certification for prehospital providers	No
National assessment of emergency care systems	No

DATA

Reported road traffic fatalities (2016)	1 379 [a] (76% M, 24% F)
WHO estimated road traffic fatalities (2016)	8 665 (95% CI 7 081 - 10 250)
WHO estimated rate per 100 000 population (2016)	30.1

[a] Traffic police department. Died within 30 days of crash

SAFER ROAD USERS

National speed limit law	Yes
Max urban speed limit	60 km/h
Max rural speed limit	120 km/h
Max motorway speed limit	No
Local authorities can modify limits	No
Enforcement	0 1 2 3 4 (5) 6 7 8 9 10
Predominant type of enforcement	Manual
National drink-driving law	Yes
BAC limit – general population	< 0.06 g/dl
BAC limit – young or novice drivers	< 0.06 g/dl
Random breath testing carried out	Yes
Testing carried out in case of fatal crash	Some drivers tested
Enforcement	0 1 2 3 4 5 (6) 7 8 9 10
% road traffic deaths involving alcohol	–
National motorcycle helmet law	Yes
Applies to drivers and passengers	Yes
Helmet fastening required	Yes
Helmet standard referred to and/or specified	No
Children passengers on motorcycles	Prohibited under 7 yrs
Enforcement	0 1 2 3 (4) 5 6 7 8 9 10
Helmet wearing rate	–
National seat-belt law	Yes
Applies to front and rear seat occupants	Yes
Enforcement	0 1 2 3 4 5 (6) 7 8 9 10
Seat-belt wearing rate	–
National child restraint law	Yes
Children seated in front seat	Prohibited under 12 yrs [b]
Child restraint required	Up to 12 yrs
Child restraint standard referred to and/or specified	No
Enforcement	0 1 2 3 (4) 5 6 7 8 9 10
% children using child restraints	–
National law on mobile phone use while driving	Yes
Ban on hand-held mobile phone use	Yes
Ban on hands-free mobile phone use	No
National drug-driving law	Yes

[b] Except for infant under 3 years in a rear-facing child restraint with airbag deactivated

Deaths by road user category

Trends in reported road traffic deaths

Source: National Land Transport Institute (INATTER)

Legislative review conducted by WHO. Vehicle safety data from UNECE WP29. Other data collected by questionnaire and cleared by Ministry of Transport and Communications.

Myanmar

Population: 52 885 224 | Income group: Middle | Gross national income per capita: US$ 1 190[a]

INSTITUTIONAL FRAMEWORK

Lead agency	National Road Safety Council (NRSC), Ministry of Transport and Communications
Funded in national budget	No
National road safety strategy	Yes
Funding to implement strategy	Not funded
Fatality reduction target	50% (2011-2020)

SAFER ROADS AND MOBILITY

Audits or star rating required for new road infrastructure	Yes
Design standards for the safety of pedestrians / cyclists	Yes
Inspections / star rating of existing roads	Yes
Investments to upgrade high risk locations	Yes
Policies & investment in urban public transport	Yes

SAFER VEHICLES

Total registered vehicles for Till April 30,2017	6 381 136
Cars and 4-wheeled light vehicles	516 707
Motorized 2- and 3-wheelers	5 391 505
Heavy trucks	59 680
Buses	28 383
Other	384 861
Vehicle standards applied (UNECE WP.29)	
Frontal impact standard	No
Electronic stability control	No
Pedestrian protection	No
Motorcycle anti-lock braking system	No

POST-CRASH CARE

National emergency care access number	National, multiple numbers
Trauma registry	National
Formal certification for prehospital providers	No
National assessment of emergency care systems	No

DATA

Reported road traffic fatalities (2016)	4 887[b] (82% M, 18% F)
WHO estimated road traffic fatalities (2016)	10 540 (95% CI 8 860 - 12 219)
WHO estimated rate per 100 000 population (2016)	19.9

[a] Data available only for 2015
[b] Traffic Police. Died within 30 days of crash

SAFER ROAD USERS

National speed limit law	Yes
Max urban speed limit	48 km/h
Max rural speed limit	80 km/h
Max motorway speed limit	No
Local authorities can modify limits	No
Enforcement	0 1 2 3 4 5 ⑥ 7 8 9 10
Predominant type of enforcement	Automated
National drink-driving law	Yes[c]
BAC limit – general population	–
BAC limit – young or novice drivers	–
Random breath testing carried out	Yes
Testing carried out in case of fatal crash	Some drivers tested
Enforcement	0 1 2 3 4 5 ⑥ 7 8 9 10
% road traffic deaths involving alcohol	21%[d]
National motorcycle helmet law	Yes
Applies to drivers and passengers	Yes
Helmet fastening required	Yes
Helmet standard referred to and/or specified	No
Children passengers on motorcycles	Prohibited[e]
Enforcement	0 1 2 3 4 5 ⑥ 7 8 9 10
Helmet wearing rate	32% Drivers[d], 27% Passengers[d]
National seat-belt law	Yes
Applies to front and rear seat occupants	Yes
Enforcement	0 1 2 3 4 5 6 ⑦ 8 9 10
Seat-belt wearing rate	7% Drivers[d]
National child restraint law	No
Children seated in front seat	Not restricted
Child restraint required	–
Child restraint standard referred to and/or specified	–
Enforcement	–
% children using child restraints	–
National law on mobile phone use while driving	No
Ban on hand-held mobile phone use	–
Ban on hands-free mobile phone use	–
National drug-driving law	Yes

[c] Not based on BAC
[d] 2016, National Injury Surveillance System (NISS)
[e] Until footrests can be reached

Deaths by road user category

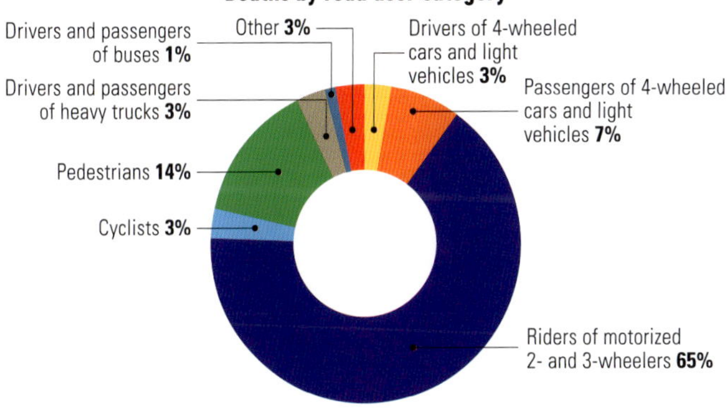

Source: 2016, National Injury Surveillance System (NISS)

Trends in reported road traffic deaths

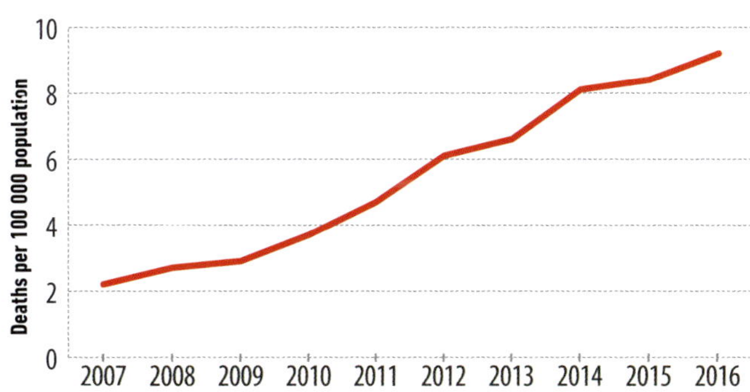

Source: Health Ministry Information System (HMIS)

Legislative review conducted by WHO. Vehicle safety data from UNECE WP29. Other data collected by questionnaire.

Namibia

Population: 2 479 713 | Income group: Middle | Gross national income per capita: US$ 4 620

INSTITUTIONAL FRAMEWORK	
Lead agency	National Road Safety Council (NRSC), Ministry of Works and Transport
Funded in national budget	Yes
National road safety strategy	Yes
Funding to implement strategy	Partially funded
Fatality reduction target	50% (2011-2020)
SAFER ROADS AND MOBILITY	
Audits or star rating required for new road infrastructure	No
Design standards for the safety of pedestrians / cyclists	Partial
Inspections / star rating of existing roads	No
Investments to upgrade high risk locations	Yes
Policies & investment in urban public transport	Yes
SAFER VEHICLES	
Total registered vehicles for 6 March 2017	371 281
Cars and 4-wheeled light vehicles	315 443
Motorized 2- and 3-wheelers	5 431
Heavy trucks	21 439
Buses	9 247
Other	19 721
Vehicle standards applied (UNECE WP.29)	
Frontal impact standard	No
Electronic stability control	No
Pedestrian protection	No
Motorcycle anti-lock braking system	No
POST-CRASH CARE	
National emergency care access number	National, multiple numbers
Trauma registry	National
Formal certification for prehospital providers	Yes
National assessment of emergency care systems	Yes
DATA	
Reported road traffic fatalities (2016)	731 [a] (72% M, 27% F)
WHO estimated road traffic fatalities (2016)	754 (95% CI 633 - 875)
WHO estimated rate per 100 000 population (2016)	30.4

[a] Combined sources, including MVA Fund crash and claim data. Died within 30 days of crash

SAFER ROAD USERS	
National speed limit law	Yes
Max urban speed limit	60 km/h
Max rural speed limit	120 km/h
Max motorway speed limit	120 km/h
Local authorities can modify limits	No
Enforcement	0 1 2 3 ④ 5 6 7 8 9 10
Predominant type of enforcement	Manual
National drink-driving law	Yes
BAC limit – general population	≤ 0.079 g/dl
BAC limit – young or novice drivers	≤ 0.079 g/dl
Random breath testing carried out	Yes
Testing carried out in case of fatal crash	Some drivers tested
Enforcement	0 1 2 3 ④ 5 6 7 8 9 10
% road traffic deaths involving alcohol	4% [b]
National motorcycle helmet law	Yes
Applies to drivers and passengers	Yes
Helmet fastening required	Yes
Helmet standard referred to and/or specified	No
Children passengers on motorcycles	Not restricted
Enforcement	0 1 2 3 4 5 6 ⑦ 8 9 10
Helmet wearing rate	–
National seat-belt law	Yes
Applies to front and rear seat occupants	Yes
Enforcement	0 1 2 3 4 5 6 ⑦ 8 9 10
Seat-belt wearing rate	–
National child restraint law	No [c]
Children seated in front seat	Not restricted
Child restraint required	–
Child restraint standard referred to and/or specified	–
Enforcement	–
% children using child restraints	–
National law on mobile phone use while driving	Yes
Ban on hand-held mobile phone use	Yes
Ban on hands-free mobile phone use	No
National drug-driving law	Yes

[b] 2011-2013, NRSC Alcohol Study Report 2016

[c] The law requires the use of child restraints for children (defined as people aged between 3-14 years) if available or the use of a seat belt if a child restraint is not available and an unoccupied seat fitted with a seat-belt is available

Deaths by road user category

Trends in reported road traffic deaths

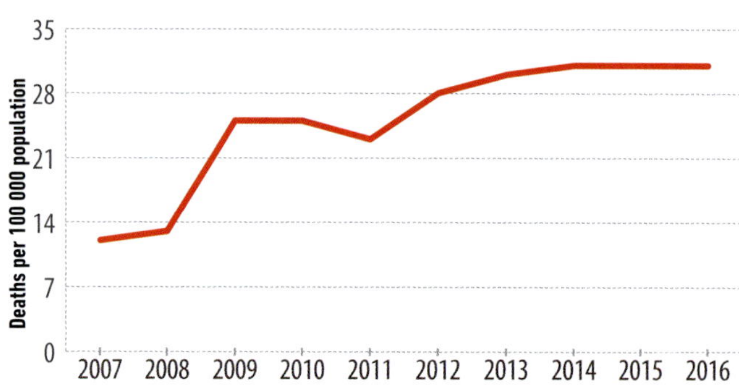

Source: MVA Fund crash and claim data (fatalities) and National Census Report (population and projections)

Legislative review conducted by WHO. Vehicle safety data from UNECE WP29. Other data collected by questionnaire and cleared by National Road Safety Council.

Nepal

Population: 28 982 772 | Income group: Low | Gross national income per capita: US$ 730

INSTITUTIONAL FRAMEWORK

Lead agency	Ministry of Physical Infrastructure and Transport
Funded in national budget	Yes
National road safety strategy	Yes
Funding to implement strategy	Partially funded
Fatality reduction target	–

SAFER ROADS AND MOBILITY

Audits or star rating required for new road infrastructure	Partial
Design standards for the safety of pedestrians / cyclists	Partial
Inspections / star rating of existing roads	Yes
Investments to upgrade high risk locations	No
Policies & investment in urban public transport	Yes

SAFER VEHICLES

Total registered vehicles for 2014/2015	2 339 169
Cars and 4-wheeled light vehicles	187 014
Motorized 2- and 3-wheelers	1 547 312
Heavy trucks	56 250
Buses	52 388
Other	496 205
Vehicle standards applied (UNECE WP.29)	
Frontal impact standard	No
Electronic stability control	No
Pedestrian protection	No
Motorcycle anti-lock braking system	No

POST-CRASH CARE

National emergency care access number	Partial coverage
Trauma registry	Some facilities
Formal certification for prehospital providers	No
National assessment of emergency care systems	No

DATA

Reported road traffic fatalities (2015)	2 006[a] (80% M, 20% F)
WHO estimated road traffic fatalities (2016)	4 622 (95% CI 3 928 - 5 317)
WHO estimated rate per 100 000 population (2016)	15.9

[a] Nepal Police. Died within 30 days of crash

SAFER ROAD USERS

National speed limit law	Yes
Max urban speed limit	40 km/h[b]
Max rural speed limit	80 km/h[b]
Max motorway speed limit	80 km/h[b]
Local authorities can modify limits	No
Enforcement	0 1 ② 3 4 5 6 7 8 9 10
Predominant type of enforcement	Manual
National drink-driving law	Yes[c]
BAC limit – general population	–
BAC limit – young or novice drivers	–
Random breath testing carried out	Yes
Testing carried out in case of fatal crash	Some drivers tested
Enforcement	0 1 2 3 4 5 6 7 ⑧ 9 10
% road traffic deaths involving alcohol	–
National motorcycle helmet law	Yes
Applies to drivers and passengers	Yes
Helmet fastening required	No
Helmet standard referred to and/or specified	No
Children passengers on motorcycles	Not restricted
Enforcement	0 1 2 3 4 5 6 7 ⑧ 9 10
Helmet wearing rate	–
National seat-belt law	Yes
Applies to front and rear seat occupants	No
Enforcement	0 1 2 3 4 ⑤ 6 7 8 9 10
Seat-belt wearing rate	–
National child restraint law	No
Children seated in front seat	Not restricted
Child restraint required	–
Child restraint standard referred to and/or specified	–
Enforcement	–
% children using child restraints	–
National law on mobile phone use while driving	No
Ban on hand-held mobile phone use	–
Ban on hands-free mobile phone use	–
National drug-driving law	Yes

[b] Speed limit set per vehicle type with a maximum speed limit of 80 km/h for specified vehicles including cars, and a maximum limit of 40 km/h in an area with dense settlement

[c] Not based on BAC

Deaths by road user category

Trends in reported road traffic deaths

Source: Nepal Police

Legislative review conducted by WHO. Vehicle safety data from UNECE WP29. Other data collected by questionnaire and cleared by Ministry of Health.

Netherlands

Population: 16 987 330 | Income group: High | Gross national income per capita: US$ 46 310

INSTITUTIONAL FRAMEWORK

Lead agency	Ministry of Infrastructure and the Environment, Directorate-general for Mobility and Transport (DGB)
Funded in national budget	Yes
National road safety strategy	Yes
Funding to implement strategy	Partially funded
Fatality reduction target	≤140 fatalities (2010-2020)

SAFER ROADS AND MOBILITY

Audits or star rating required for new road infrastructure	Yes
Design standards for the safety of pedestrians / cyclists	Yes
Inspections / star rating of existing roads	Yes
Investments to upgrade high risk locations	Yes
Policies & investment in urban public transport	Yes

SAFER VEHICLES

Total registered vehicles for 2015	10 757 655
Cars and 4-wheeled light vehicles	8 794 037
Motorized 2- and 3-wheelers	652 336
Heavy trucks	133 889
Buses	9 597
Other	1 167 796
Vehicle standards applied (UNECE WP.29)	
Frontal impact standard	Yes
Electronic stability control	Yes
Pedestrian protection	Yes
Motorcycle anti-lock braking system	Yes

POST-CRASH CARE

National emergency care access number	National, single number
Trauma registry	National
Formal certification for prehospital providers	No
National assessment of emergency care systems	No

DATA

Reported road traffic fatalities (2015)	621[a] (74% M, 26% F)
WHO estimated road traffic fatalities (2016)	648
WHO estimated rate per 100 000 population (2016)	3.8

[a] Dutch Statistics, Vital Statistics. Died within 30 days of crash

SAFER ROAD USERS

National speed limit law	Yes
Max urban speed limit	50 km/h
Max rural speed limit	80 km/h
Max motorway speed limit	130 km/h
Local authorities can modify limits	Yes
Enforcement	0 1 2 3 4 5 (6) 7 8 9 10
Predominant type of enforcement	Manual and automated
National drink-driving law	Yes
BAC limit – general population	≤ 0.05 g/dl
BAC limit – young or novice drivers	≤ 0.02 g/dl
Random breath testing carried out	Yes
Testing carried out in case of fatal crash	No
Enforcement	0 1 2 3 4 5 (6) 7 8 9 10
% road traffic deaths involving alcohol	11-24%[b]
National motorcycle helmet law	Yes
Applies to drivers and passengers	Yes
Helmet fastening required	Yes
Helmet standard referred to and/or specified	Yes
Children passengers on motorcycles	Not restricted
Enforcement	0 1 2 3 4 (5) 6 7 8 9 10
Helmet wearing rate	100% Drivers[c], 84% Passengers[d]
National seat-belt law	Yes
Applies to front and rear seat occupants	Yes
Enforcement	0 1 2 3 4 5 (6) 7 8 9 10
Seat-belt wearing rate	97% Front seats[e], 82% Rear seats[e]
National child restraint law	Yes
Children seated in front seat	Allowed in a child restraint[f]
Child restraint required	Up to 18 yrs/135 cm
Child restraint standard referred to and/or specified	Yes
Enforcement	0 1 2 3 4 5 (6) 7 8 9 10
% children using child restraints	–
National law on mobile phone use while driving	Yes
Ban on hand-held mobile phone use	Yes
Ban on hands-free mobile phone use	No
National drug-driving law	Yes

[b] 2013-2015, SWOV factsheet DUI
[c] 2012, PROV final report
[d] 2008, BVOM, 'Monitoring Bromfietshelmen 2008'
[e] 2010, BIA report
[f] Provided that the airbag is deactivated if child is in a rear-facing child restraint

Deaths by road user category

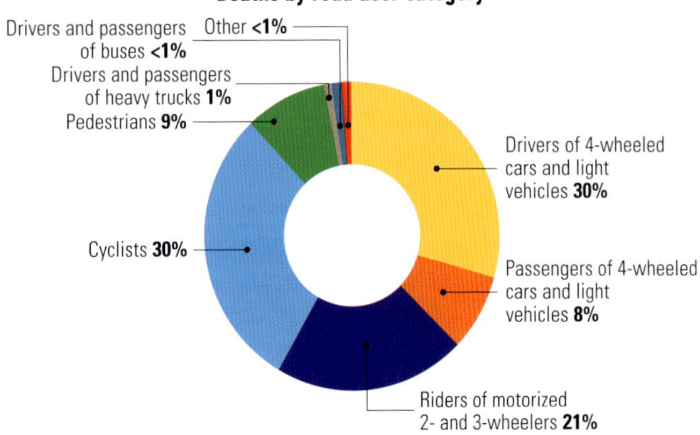

Source: 2015, Dutch Statistics

Trends in reported road traffic deaths

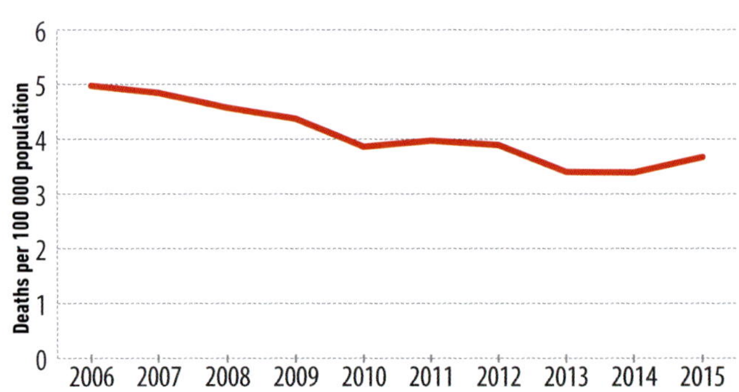

Source: Dutch Statistics

Legislative review conducted by WHO. Vehicle safety data from UNECE WP29. Other data collected by questionnaire and cleared by Ministry of Infrastructure and the Environment.

New Zealand

Population: 4 660 833 | Income group: High | Gross national income per capita: US$ 39 070

INSTITUTIONAL FRAMEWORK	
Lead agency	Land Transport Safety Team, Ministry of Transport
Funded in national budget	Yes
National road safety strategy	Yes
Funding to implement strategy	Fully funded
Fatality reduction target	Multiple (2010-2020)[a]
SAFER ROADS AND MOBILITY	
Audits or star rating required for new road infrastructure	Yes
Design standards for the safety of pedestrians / cyclists	Yes
Inspections / star rating of existing roads	Yes
Investments to upgrade high risk locations	Yes
Policies & investment in urban public transport	Yes
SAFER VEHICLES	
Total registered vehicles for 2016	3 656 300
Cars and 4-wheeled light vehicles	–
Motorized 2- and 3-wheelers	–
Heavy trucks	–
Buses	–
Other	–
Vehicle standards applied (UNECE WP.29)	
Frontal impact standard	Yes
Electronic stability control	Yes[b]
Pedestrian protection	Yes
Motorcycle anti-lock braking system	No
POST-CRASH CARE	
National emergency care access number	National, single number
Trauma registry	National
Formal certification for prehospital providers	Yes
National assessment of emergency care systems	No
DATA	
Reported road traffic fatalities (2016)	327[c] (69% M, 30% F)
WHO estimated road traffic fatalities (2016)	364
WHO estimated rate per 100 000 population (2016)	7.8

[a] Targets vary for specific groups. See New Zealand Road Safety Strategy 2010 - 2020
[b] For new models as from 2018
[c] 2016, Motor Vehicle Crashes in New Zealand. Died within 30 days of crash

SAFER ROAD USERS	
National speed limit law	Yes
Max urban speed limit	50 km/h
Max rural speed limit	100 km/h
Max motorway speed limit	100 km/h
Local authorities can modify limits	Yes
Enforcement	0 1 2 3 4 5 6 (7) 8 9 10
Predominant type of enforcement	Manual and automated
National drink-driving law	Yes
BAC limit – general population	≤ 0.05 g/dl
BAC limit – young or novice drivers	0.00 g/dl
Random breath testing carried out	Yes
Testing carried out in case of fatal crash	Some drivers tested
Enforcement	0 1 2 3 4 5 6 (7) 8 9 10
% road traffic deaths involving alcohol	27%[d]
National motorcycle helmet law	Yes
Applies to drivers and passengers	Yes
Helmet fastening required	Yes
Helmet standard referred to and/or specified	Yes
Children passengers on motorcycles	Not restricted
Enforcement	0 1 2 3 4 5 6 7 8 (9) 10
Helmet wearing rate	–
National seat-belt law	Yes
Applies to front and rear seat occupants	Yes
Enforcement	0 1 2 3 4 5 6 (7) 8 9 10
Seat-belt wearing rate	97% Front seats[e], 92% Rear seats[f]
National child restraint law	Yes
Children seated in front seat	Allowed in a child restraint
Child restraint required	Up to 7 yrs
Child restraint standard referred to and/or specified	No
Enforcement	0 1 2 3 4 5 6 7 (8) 9 10
% children using child restraints	93%[g] and 95%[h]
National law on mobile phone use while driving	Yes
Ban on hand-held mobile phone use	Yes
Ban on hands-free mobile phone use	No
National drug-driving law	Yes

[d] 2016, Motor Vehicle Crashes in New Zealand (Percentages are for 0-4 years and 5-9 years, respectively)
[e] 2016, National Survey of Seatbelts in New Zealand
[f] 2014, National Survey of Seatbelts in New Zealand.
[g] 2016, Ministry of Transport, Child restraint use by children under 5 years
[h] 2016, Ministry of Transport, Child restraint use by children aged 5-9 years

Deaths by road user category

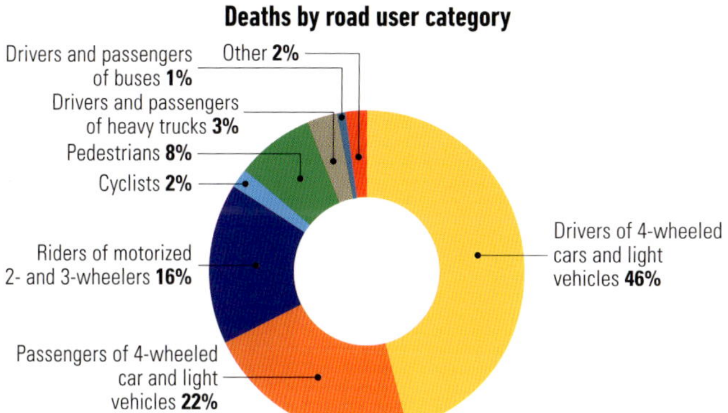

Source: 2016, Motor Vehicle Crashes in New Zealand

Trends in reported road traffic deaths

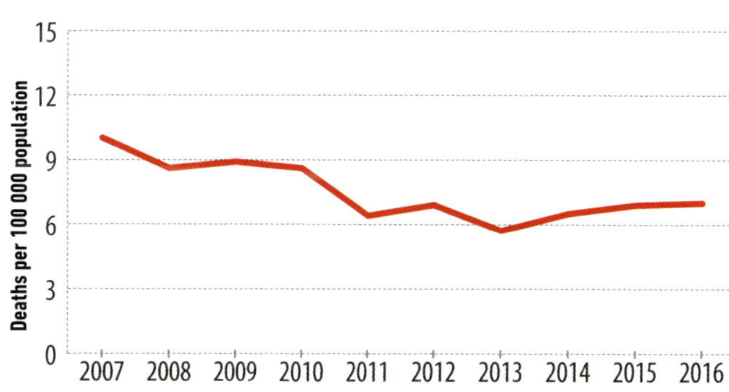

Source: Motor Vehicle Crashes in New Zealand

Legislative review conducted by WHO. Vehicle safety data from UNECE WP29. Other data collected by questionnaire and cleared by Ministry of Transport.

Niger

Population: 20 672 988 | Income group: Low | Gross national income per capita: US$ 370

INSTITUTIONAL FRAMEWORK

Lead agency	**Directorate of Traffic and Road Safety (DC/SR), Ministry of Transport**
Funded in national budget	Yes
National road safety strategy	**Yes**
Funding to implement strategy	Partially funded
Fatality reduction target	–

SAFER ROADS AND MOBILITY

Audits or star rating required for new road infrastructure	Partial
Design standards for the safety of pedestrians / cyclists	Yes
Inspections / star rating of existing roads	No
Investments to upgrade high risk locations	No
Policies & investment in urban public transport	No

SAFER VEHICLES

Total registered vehicles for 2016	**436 420**
Cars and 4-wheeled light vehicles	231 740
Motorized 2- and 3-wheelers	–
Heavy trucks	11 389
Buses	10 676
Other	182 615
Vehicle standards applied (UNECE WP.29)	
Frontal impact standard	No
Electronic stability control	No
Pedestrian protection	No
Motorcycle anti-lock braking system	No

POST-CRASH CARE

National emergency care access number	National, single number
Trauma registry	Some facilities
Formal certification for prehospital providers	Yes
National assessment of emergency care systems	No

DATA

Reported road traffic fatalities (2016)	978[a] (39% M, 61% F)
WHO estimated road traffic fatalities (2016)	5 414 (95% CI 4 273 - 6 554)
WHO estimated rate per 100 000 population (2016)	26.2

[a] Ministry of Transport, 2012-2016 Statistics Yearbook. Died at scene of crash

SAFER ROAD USERS

National speed limit law	**Yes**
Max urban speed limit	50 km/h
Max rural speed limit	No
Max motorway speed limit	No
Local authorities can modify limits	No
Enforcement	0 1 2 (3) 4 5 6 7 8 9 10
Predominant type of enforcement	Manual
National drink-driving law	**Yes[b]**
BAC limit – general population	–
BAC limit – young or novice drivers	–
Random breath testing carried out	No
Testing carried out in case of fatal crash	No
Enforcement	0 1 2 3 4 5 (6) 7 8 9 10
% road traffic deaths involving alcohol	–
National motorcycle helmet law	**Yes**
Applies to drivers and passengers	Yes
Helmet fastening required	No
Helmet standard referred to and/or specified	Yes
Children passengers on motorcycles	Not restricted
Enforcement	0 1 2 3 4 (5) 6 7 8 9 10
Helmet wearing rate	–
National seat-belt law	**No**
Applies to front and rear seat occupants	–
Enforcement	–
Seat-belt wearing rate	–
National child restraint law	**No**
Children seated in front seat	Not restricted
Child restraint required	–
Child restraint standard referred to and/or specified	–
Enforcement	–
% children using child restraints	–
National law on mobile phone use while driving	**Yes**
Ban on hand-held mobile phone use	Yes
Ban on hands-free mobile phone use	Yes
National drug-driving law	**Yes**

[b] Not based on BAC

Deaths by road user category

Trends in reported road traffic deaths

Source: Directorate of Traffic and Road Safety (DC/SR)

Legislative review conducted by WHO. Vehicle safety data from UNECE WP29. Other data collected by questionnaire and cleared by Ministry of Transport.

Nigeria

Population: 185 989 632 | Income group: Middle | Gross national income per capita: US$ 2 450

INSTITUTIONAL FRAMEWORK	
Lead agency	Federal Road Safety Corps
Funded in national budget	Yes
National road safety strategy	Yes
Funding to implement strategy	Fully funded
Fatality reduction target	25% Annually (2014-2018)
SAFER ROADS AND MOBILITY	
Audits or star rating required for new road infrastructure	Yes
Design standards for the safety of pedestrians / cyclists	Partial
Inspections / star rating of existing roads	Yes
Investments to upgrade high risk locations	Yes
Policies & investment in urban public transport	Yes
SAFER VEHICLES	
Total registered vehicles for 2016	11 733 425
Cars and 4-wheeled light vehicles	6 732 639
Motorized 2- and 3-wheelers	1 302 410
Heavy trucks[a]	1 325 877
Buses	2 372 499
Other	–
Vehicle standards applied (UNECE WP.29)	
Frontal impact standard	No
Electronic stability control	No
Pedestrian protection	No
Motorcycle anti-lock braking system	No
POST-CRASH CARE	
National emergency care access number	National, single number
Trauma registry	Some facilities
Formal certification for prehospital providers	Yes
National assessment of emergency care systems	No
DATA	
Reported road traffic fatalities (2016)	5 053[b] (79% M, 21% F)
WHO estimated road traffic fatalities (2016)	39 802 (95% CI 32 076 - 47 529)
WHO estimated rate per 100 000 population (2016)	21.4

[a] All trucks included
[b] Federal Road Safety Corps. Died within 30 days of crash

SAFER ROAD USERS	
National speed limit law	Yes
Max urban speed limit	50 km/h
Max rural speed limit	80 km/h
Max motorway speed limit	100 km/h
Local authorities can modify limits	Yes
Enforcement	0 1 2 3 4 5 ⑥ 7 8 9 10
Predominant type of enforcement	Manual
National drink-driving law	Yes
BAC limit – general population	≤ 0.05[c]
BAC limit – young or novice drivers	≤ 0.002[d]
Random breath testing carried out	Yes
Testing carried out in case of fatal crash	No
Enforcement	0 1 2 3 ④ 5 6 7 8 9 10
% road traffic deaths involving alcohol	<1%[e]
National motorcycle helmet law	Yes
Applies to drivers and passengers	Yes
Helmet fastening required	Yes
Helmet standard referred to and/or specified	Yes
Children passengers on motorcycles	Not restricted
Enforcement	0 1 2 3 ④ 5 6 7 8 9 10
Helmet wearing rate	–
National seat-belt law	Yes
Applies to front and rear seat occupants	Yes
Enforcement	0 1 2 3 4 5 6 7 8 ⑨ 10
Seat-belt wearing rate	–
National child restraint law	Yes
Children seated in front seat	Prohibited under 7 yrs
Child restraint required	Up to 7 yrs
Child restraint standard referred to and/or specified	No
Enforcement	0 1 2 ③ 4 5 6 7 8 9 10
% children using child restraints	–
National law on mobile phone use while driving	Yes
Ban on hand-held mobile phone use	Yes
Ban on hands-free mobile phone use	Yes
National drug-driving law	Yes

[c] The legislation, as amended in 2016, refers to an alcohol legal limit of "0.05" for the general population but does not specify the unit to consider
[d] The legislation, as amended in 2016, refers to an alcohol legal limit of "0.002" for young or novice drivers but does not specify the unit to consider
[e] 2016, Federal Road Safety Corps

Deaths by road user category

Trends in reported road traffic deaths

Source: Federal Road Safety Corps

Legislative review conducted by WHO. Vehicle safety data from UNECE WP.29. Other data collected by questionnaire and cleared by Federal Road Safety Corps (FRSC).

Norway

Population: 5 254 694 | Income group: High | Gross national income per capita: US$ 82 330

INSTITUTIONAL FRAMEWORK

Lead agency	The Norwegian Public Road Administration
Funded in national budget	Yes
National road safety strategy	Yes
Funding to implement strategy	Fully funded
Fatality reduction target	Deaths and serious injuries ≤500 (2014-2023)

SAFER ROADS AND MOBILITY

Audits or star rating required for new road infrastructure	Yes
Design standards for the safety of pedestrians / cyclists	Partial
Inspections / star rating of existing roads	Yes
Investments to upgrade high risk locations	Yes
Policies & investment in urban public transport	Yes

SAFER VEHICLES

Total registered vehicles for 2016	3 969 612
Cars and 4-wheeled light vehicles	3 147 101
Motorized 2- and 3-wheelers	305 265
Heavy trucks	74 622
Buses	16 258
Other	426 366
Vehicle standards applied (UNECE WP.29)	
Frontal impact standard	Yes
Electronic stability control	Yes
Pedestrian protection	Yes
Motorcycle anti-lock braking system	Yes

POST-CRASH CARE

National emergency care access number	National, single number
Trauma registry	National
Formal certification for prehospital providers	Yes
National assessment of emergency care systems	Yes

DATA

Reported road traffic fatalities (2016)	135[a] (82% M, 18% F)
WHO estimated road traffic fatalities (2016)	143
WHO estimated rate per 100 000 population (2016)	2.7

[a] Statistics Norway. Died within 30 days of crash

SAFER ROAD USERS

National speed limit law	Yes
Max urban speed limit	50 km/h
Max rural speed limit	80 km/h
Max motorway speed limit	100 km/h
Local authorities can modify limits	Yes
Enforcement	0 1 2 3 4 5 6 7 8 9 **10**
Predominant type of enforcement	Manual and automated
National drink-driving law	Yes
BAC limit – general population	≤ 0.02 g/dl
BAC limit – young or novice drivers	≤ 0.02 g/dl
Random breath testing carried out	Yes
Testing carried out in case of fatal crash	Some drivers tested
Enforcement	0 1 2 3 4 5 6 7 8 9 **10**
% road traffic deaths involving alcohol	13%[b]
National motorcycle helmet law	Yes
Applies to drivers and passengers	Yes
Helmet fastening required	No
Helmet standard referred to and/or specified	Yes
Children passengers on motorcycles	Not restricted
Enforcement	0 1 2 3 4 5 6 7 8 9 **10**
Helmet wearing rate	99% Drivers[c], 99% Passengers[c]
National seat-belt law	Yes
Applies to front and rear seat occupants	Yes
Enforcement	0 1 2 3 4 5 6 7 8 9 **10**
Seat-belt wearing rate	96-98% Drivers[d], 95-96% Front seats[d]
National child restraint law	Yes
Children seated in front seat	Allowed in a child restraint[e]
Child restraint required	135-150 cm[f]
Child restraint standard referred to and/or specified	Yes
Enforcement	0 1 2 3 4 5 6 7 8 9 **10**
% children using child restraints	–
National law on mobile phone use while driving	Yes
Ban on hand-held mobile phone use	Yes
Ban on hands-free mobile phone use	No
National drug-driving law	Yes

[b] 2015, Road safety, environmental and technology department, 2015 state of road safety report
[c] 2010, Statistics Norway
[d] 2016, The Norwegian Public Road Administration (Percentages reflect "urban" and "outside urban" areas, respectively)
[e] Provided that the airbag is deactivated if child is in a rear-facing child restraint
[f] Child restraints are required for children under 150 cm. By exception, children of height 135-150 cm can be restrained with a seat belt only if sitting in the rear

Deaths by road user category

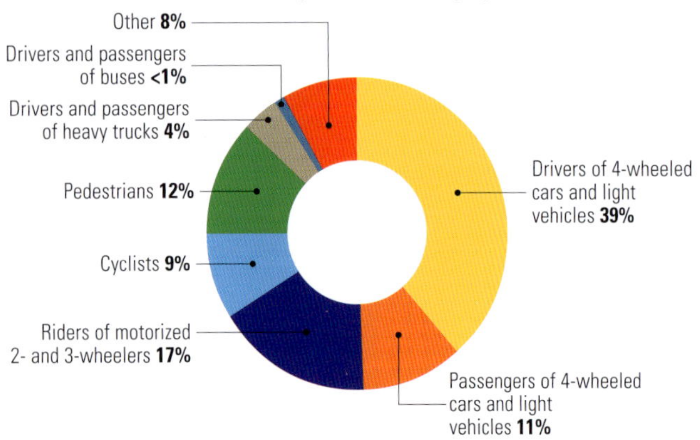

Source: 2016, Norwegian Public Roads database (STRAKS)

Trends in reported road traffic deaths

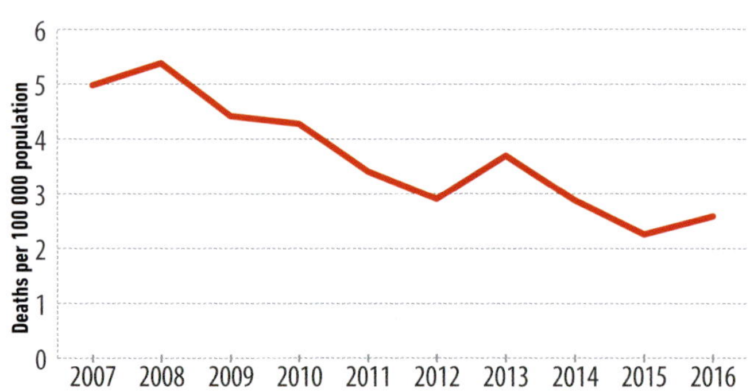

Source: Statistics Norway

Legislative review conducted by WHO. Vehicle safety data from UNECE WP29. Other data collected by questionnaire and cleared by Norwegian Public Road Administration.

Oman

Population: 4 424 762 | Income group: High | Gross national income per capita: US$ 18 080[a]

INSTITUTIONAL FRAMEWORK	
Lead agency	National Committee for Road Safety
Funded in national budget	Yes
National road safety strategy	Yes
Funding to implement strategy	Fully funded
Fatality reduction target	25% (2011-2020)
SAFER ROADS AND MOBILITY	
Audits or star rating required for new road infrastructure	Yes
Design standards for the safety of pedestrians / cyclists	Yes
Inspections / star rating of existing roads	Yes
Investments to upgrade high risk locations	Yes
Policies & investment in urban public transport	Yes
SAFER VEHICLES	
Total registered vehicles for 2016	1 370 913
Cars and 4-wheeled light vehicles	1 162 446
Motorized 2- and 3-wheelers	7 337
Heavy trucks	159 778
Buses	41 352
Other	0
Vehicle standards applied (UNECE WP.29)	
Frontal impact standard	No
Electronic stability control	No
Pedestrian protection	No
Motorcycle anti-lock braking system	No
POST-CRASH CARE	
National emergency care access number	National, single number
Trauma registry	Some facilities
Formal certification for prehospital providers	Yes
National assessment of emergency care systems	No
DATA	
Reported road traffic fatalities (2016)	692[b] (86% M, 14% F)
WHO estimated road traffic fatalities (2016)	713
WHO estimated rate per 100 000 population (2016)	16.1

[a] Data available only for 2015
[b] Royal Oman Police. Died within 30 days of crash

SAFER ROAD USERS	
National speed limit law	Yes
Max urban speed limit	–
Max rural speed limit	–
Max motorway speed limit	–
Local authorities can modify limits	No
Enforcement	0 1 2 3 4 5 6 7 8 9 (10)
Predominant type of enforcement	Manual and automated
National drink-driving law	Yes[c]
BAC limit – general population	–
BAC limit – young or novice drivers	–
Random breath testing carried out	Yes
Testing carried out in case of fatal crash	All drivers tested
Enforcement	0 1 2 3 4 5 6 7 8 9 (10)
% road traffic deaths involving alcohol	<1%[d]
National motorcycle helmet law	Yes
Applies to drivers and passengers	Yes
Helmet fastening required	No
Helmet standard referred to and/or specified	No
Children passengers on motorcycles	Not restricted
Enforcement	0 1 2 3 4 5 6 7 8 9 (10)
Helmet wearing rate	98% Drivers[e], 92% Passengers[e]
National seat-belt law	Yes
Applies to front and rear seat occupants	Yes
Enforcement	0 1 2 3 4 5 6 7 8 9 (10)
Seat-belt wearing rate	98% Drivers[e]
National child restraint law	Yes
Children seated in front seat	Prohibited under 10 yrs
Child restraint required	Up to 4 yrs
Child restraint standard referred to and/or specified	No
Enforcement	0 1 2 3 4 5 6 (7) 8 9 10
% children using child restraints	–
National law on mobile phone use while driving	Yes
Ban on hand-held mobile phone use	Yes
Ban on hands-free mobile phone use	No
National drug-driving law	Yes

[c] Not based on BAC
[d] 2016, Royal Oman Police, Facts and figures
[e] 2016, Royal Oman Police

Deaths by road user category

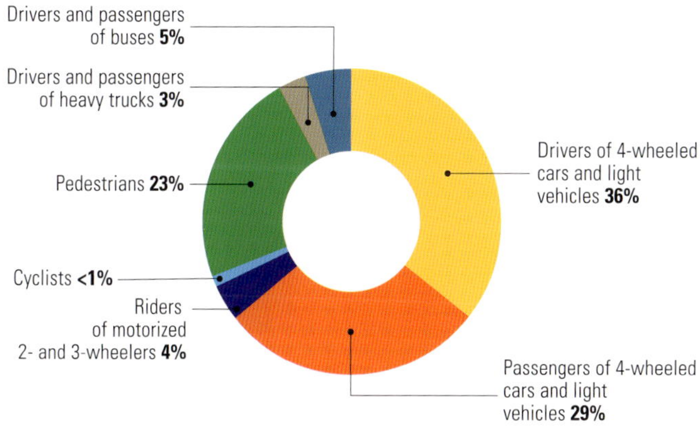

Source: 2016, Royal Oman Police

Trends in reported road traffic deaths

Source: Royal Oman Police and The National Centre for Information and Statistics

Legislative review conducted by WHO. Vehicle safety data from UNECE WP29. Other data collected by questionnaire and cleared by Ministry of Health.

Pakistan

Population: 193 203 472 | Income group: Middle | Gross national income per capita: US$ 1 510

INSTITUTIONAL FRAMEWORK	
Lead agency	Ministry of Communication
Funded in national budget	Yes
National road safety strategy	Yes
Funding to implement strategy	Fully funded
Fatality reduction target	–
SAFER ROADS AND MOBILITY	
Audits or star rating required for new road infrastructure	Yes
Design standards for the safety of pedestrians / cyclists	Partial
Inspections / star rating of existing roads	Yes
Investments to upgrade high risk locations	Yes
Policies & investment in urban public transport	Yes
SAFER VEHICLES	
Total registered vehicles for 2016	18 352 500
Cars and 4-wheeled light vehicles	2 835 400
Motorized 2- and 3-wheelers	13 538 200
Heavy trucks	259 900
Buses	229 200
Other	1 489 800
Vehicle standards applied (UNECE WP.29)	
Frontal impact standard	No
Electronic stability control	No
Pedestrian protection	No
Motorcycle anti-lock braking system	No
POST-CRASH CARE	
National emergency care access number	National, multiple numbers
Trauma registry	Subnational
Formal certification for prehospital providers	No
National assessment of emergency care systems	No
DATA	
Reported road traffic fatalities (2015)	4 448[a]
WHO estimated road traffic fatalities (2016)	27 582 (95% CI 23 243 - 31 920)
WHO estimated rate per 100 000 population (2016)	14.3

[a] Pakistan Bureau of Statistics (Police records of provinces). Died at scene of crash

SAFER ROAD USERS	
National speed limit law	Yes
Max urban speed limit	90 km/h
Max rural speed limit	110 km/h
Max motorway speed limit	130 km/h
Local authorities can modify limits	Yes
Enforcement	0 1 2 3 (4) 5 6 7 8 9 10
Predominant type of enforcement	Manual
National drink-driving law	Yes[b]
BAC limit – general population	–
BAC limit – young or novice drivers	–
Random breath testing carried out	No
Testing carried out in case of fatal crash	No
Enforcement	0 1 2 3 (4) 5 6 7 8 9 10
% road traffic deaths involving alcohol	–
National motorcycle helmet law	Yes
Applies to drivers and passengers	Yes
Helmet fastening required	No
Helmet standard referred to and/or specified	No
Children passengers on motorcycles	Not restricted
Enforcement	0 1 2 (3) 4 5 6 7 8 9 10
Helmet wearing rate	10% All riders[c]
National seat-belt law	Yes
Applies to front and rear seat occupants	No
Enforcement	0 1 2 3 4 5 (6) 7 8 9 10
Seat-belt wearing rate	–
National child restraint law	No
Children seated in front seat	Not restricted
Child restraint required	–
Child restraint standard referred to and/or specified	–
Enforcement	–
% children using child restraints	–
National law on mobile phone use while driving	Yes
Ban on hand-held mobile phone use	Yes
Ban on hands-free mobile phone use	No
National drug-driving law	Yes

[b] Not based on BAC. Alcohol consumption legally prohibited
[c] 2013, Road Traffic Injury Research & Prevention Centre, Karachi

Deaths by road user category

Trends in reported road traffic deaths

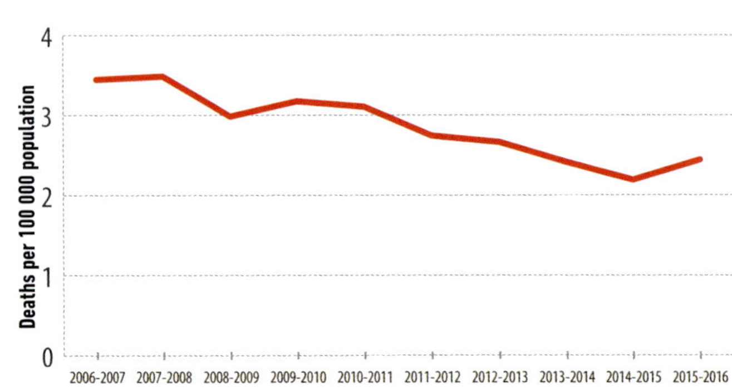

Source: Pakistan Bureau of Statistics (police records of provinces)

Legislative review conducted by WHO. Vehicle safety data from UNECE WP29. Other data collected by questionnaire and cleared by Ministry of National Health Services, Regulations and Coordination

Panama

Population: 4 034 119 | Income group: Middle | Gross national income per capita: US$ 12 140

INSTITUTIONAL FRAMEWORK	
Lead agency	Traffic and Ground Transport Authority (ATTT)
Funded in national budget	Yes
National road safety strategy	Yes
Funding to implement strategy	Partially funded
Fatality reduction target	15% of mortality rate per 100 000 population (2011- 2020)

SAFER ROADS AND MOBILITY	
Audits or star rating required for new road infrastructure	No
Design standards for the safety of pedestrians / cyclists	Partial
Inspections / star rating of existing roads	No
Investments to upgrade high risk locations	No
Policies & investment in urban public transport	Yes

SAFER VEHICLES	
Total registered vehicles for 2016	1 288 573
Cars and 4-wheeled light vehicles	968 516
Motorized 2- and 3-wheelers	62 948
Heavy trucks	107 713
Buses	44 193
Other	105 203
Vehicle standards applied (UNECE WP.29)	
Frontal impact standard	No
Electronic stability control	No
Pedestrian protection	No
Motorcycle anti-lock braking system	No

POST-CRASH CARE	
National emergency care access number	National, single number
Trauma registry	Some facilities
Formal certification for prehospital providers	Yes
National assessment of emergency care systems	No

DATA	
Reported road traffic fatalities (2016)	440[a] (85% M, 15% F)
WHO estimated road traffic fatalities (2016)	575
WHO estimated rate per 100 000 population (2016)	14.3

[a] Traffic Operations Directorate, National Police. Died within 30 days of crash

SAFER ROAD USERS	
National speed limit law	Yes
Max urban speed limit	80 km/h
Max rural speed limit	100 km/h
Max motorway speed limit	120 km/h
Local authorities can modify limits	No
Enforcement	0 1 2 3 (4) 5 6 7 8 9 10
Predominant type of enforcement	Manual
National drink-driving law	Yes
BAC limit – general population	≤ 0.05 g/dl
BAC limit – young or novice drivers	≤ 0.05 g/dl
Random breath testing carried out	Yes
Testing carried out in case of fatal crash	All drivers tested
Enforcement	0 1 2 3 4 (5) 6 7 8 9 10
% road traffic deaths involving alcohol	–
National motorcycle helmet law	Yes
Applies to drivers and passengers	Yes
Helmet fastening required	No
Helmet standard referred to and/or specified	No
Children passengers on motorcycles	Not restricted
Enforcement	0 1 2 3 4 5 (6) 7 8 9 10
Helmet wearing rate	–
National seat-belt law	Yes
Applies to front and rear seat occupants	Yes
Enforcement	0 1 2 3 4 5 6 (7) 8 9 10
Seat-belt wearing rate	–
National child restraint law	No[b]
Children seated in front seat	Prohibited under 5 yrs
Child restraint required	–
Child restraint standard referred to and/or specified	–
Enforcement	–
% children using child restraints	–
National law on mobile phone use while driving	Yes
Ban on hand-held mobile phone use	Yes
Ban on hands-free mobile phone use	Yes
National drug-driving law	Yes

[b] Children under 2 years shall be placed in a child restraint only where there is no other passenger seated in the rear

Deaths by road user category

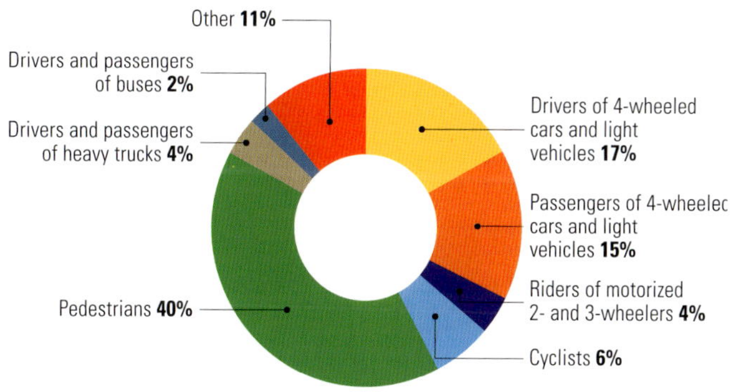

Source: 2015, Comptroller General of the Republic of Panama

Trends in reported road traffic deaths

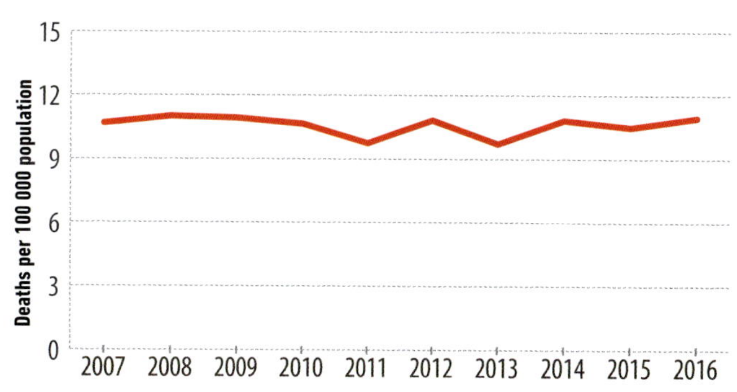

Source: Traffic Operations Directorate, National Police

Papua New Guinea

Population: 8 084 991 | Income group: Middle | Gross national income per capita: US$ 2 160[a]

INSTITUTIONAL FRAMEWORK	
Lead agency	Road Traffic Authority (RTA), Ministry of Transport and Infrastructure
Funded in national budget	Yes
National road safety strategy	Yes
Funding to implement strategy	Partially funded
Fatality reduction target	–

SAFER ROADS AND MOBILITY	
Audits or star rating required for new road infrastructure	Partial
Design standards for the safety of pedestrians / cyclists	Partial
Inspections / star rating of existing roads	Yes
Investments to upgrade high risk locations	No
Policies & investment in urban public transport	No

SAFER VEHICLES	
Total registered vehicles for 2016	100 993
Cars and 4-wheeled light vehicles	66 017
Motorized 2- and 3-wheelers	1 289
Heavy trucks	22 072
Buses	11 615
Other	0
Vehicle standards applied (UNECE WP.29)	
Frontal impact standard	No
Electronic stability control	No
Pedestrian protection	No
Motorcycle anti-lock braking system	No

POST-CRASH CARE	
National emergency care access number	Partial coverage
Trauma registry	Some facilities
Formal certification for prehospital providers	Yes
National assessment of emergency care systems	No

DATA	
Reported road traffic fatalities (2016)	158[b] (79% M, 21% F)
WHO estimated road traffic fatalities (2016)	1 145 (95% CI 991 - 1 298)
WHO estimated rate per 100 000 population (2016)	14.2

[a] Data available only for 2014
[b] Traffic Police. Died within 30 days of crash

SAFER ROAD USERS	
National speed limit law	Yes
Max urban speed limit	60 km/h
Max rural speed limit	75 km/h
Max motorway speed limit	–
Local authorities can modify limits	No
Enforcement	–
Predominant type of enforcement	–
National drink-driving law	Yes[c]
BAC limit – general population	–
BAC limit – young or novice drivers	–
Random breath testing carried out	No
Testing carried out in case of fatal crash	No
Enforcement	–
% road traffic deaths involving alcohol	56%[d]
National motorcycle helmet law	Yes
Applies to drivers and passengers	Yes
Helmet fastening required	Yes
Helmet standard referred to and/or specified	Yes
Children passengers on motorcycles	Not restricted
Enforcement	–
Helmet wearing rate	7.9% All riders
National seat-belt law	Yes
Applies to front and rear seat occupants	Yes
Enforcement	–
Seat-belt wearing rate	–
National child restraint law	No
Children seated in front seat	Not restricted[e]
Child restraint required	–
Child restraint standard referred to and/or specified	–
Enforcement	–
% children using child restraints	–
National law on mobile phone use while driving	No
Ban on hand-held mobile phone use	–
Ban on hands-free mobile phone use	–
National drug-driving law	Yes

[c] Law not based on BAC
[d] 2013, Royal Papua New Guinea Constabulary Police records
[e] Children can sit in the front as long as they are using a seat belt

Deaths by road user category

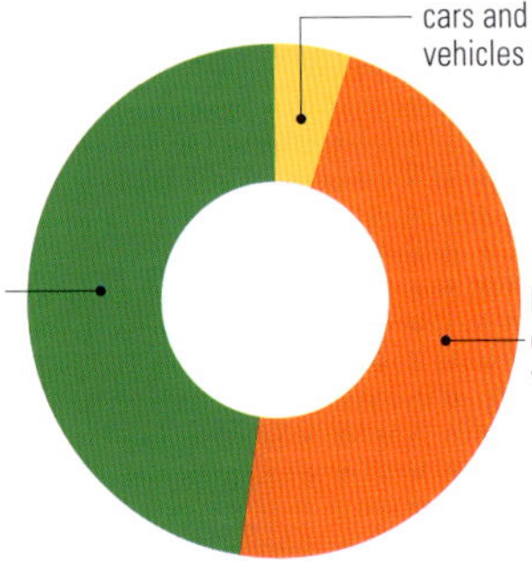

Source: 2016, Traffic Police

Trends in reported road traffic deaths

Source: National Road Safety Council

Other data collected by questionnaire and cleared by Road Traffic Authority

Paraguay

Population: 6 725 308 | Income group: Middle | Gross national income per capita: US$ 4 070

INSTITUTIONAL FRAMEWORK	
Lead agency	National Transit and Road Safety Agency
Funded in national budget	Yes
National road safety strategy	Yes
Funding to implement strategy	Partially funded
Fatality reduction target	20% (2013-2018)
SAFER ROADS AND MOBILITY	
Audits or star rating required for new road infrastructure	Yes
Design standards for the safety of pedestrians / cyclists	Partial
Inspections / star rating of existing roads	Yes
Investments to upgrade high risk locations	No
Policies & investment in urban public transport	Yes
SAFER VEHICLES	
Total registered vehicles for 2016	1 871 947
Cars and 4-wheeled light vehicles	567 388
Motorized 2- and 3-wheelers	624 202
Heavy trucks	75 247
Buses	18 456
Other	586 654
Vehicle standards applied (UNECE WP.29)	
Frontal impact standard	No
Electronic stability control	No
Pedestrian protection	No
Motorcycle anti-lock braking system	No
POST-CRASH CARE	
National emergency care access number	National, single number
Trauma registry	National
Formal certification for prehospital providers	No
National assessment of emergency care systems	No
DATA	
Reported road traffic fatalities (2016)	1 202[a] (83% M, 17% F)
WHO estimated road traffic fatalities (2016)	1 529
WHO estimated rate per 100 000 population (2016)	22.7

[a] General Directorate of Strategic Health Information (DIGIES). Died within 30 days of crash

SAFER ROAD USERS	
National speed limit law	Yes
Max urban speed limit	50 km/h
Max rural speed limit	110 km/h
Max motorway speed limit	110 km/h
Local authorities can modify limits	Yes
Enforcement	0 1 2 3 ④ 5 6 7 8 9 10
Predominant type of enforcement	Manual
National drink-driving law	Yes
BAC limit – general population	0.00 g/dl
BAC limit – young or novice drivers	0.00 g/dl
Random breath testing carried out	Yes
Testing carried out in case of fatal crash	All drivers tested
Enforcement	0 1 2 3 4 5 ⑥ 7 8 9 10
% road traffic deaths involving alcohol	–
National motorcycle helmet law	Yes
Applies to drivers and passengers	Yes
Helmet fastening required	Yes
Helmet standard referred to and/or specified	Yes
Children passengers on motorcycles	Prohibited under 12 yrs
Enforcement	0 1 2 3 4 5 ⑥ 7 8 9 10
Helmet wearing rate	–
National seat-belt law	Yes
Applies to front and rear seat occupants	Yes
Enforcement	0 1 2 3 4 5 ⑥ 7 8 9 10
Seat-belt wearing rate	–
National child restraint law	Yes
Children seated in front seat	Prohibited under 10 yrs
Child restraint required	Up to 5 yrs
Child restraint standard referred to and/or specified	No
Enforcement	0 1 ② 3 4 5 6 7 8 9 10
% children using child restraints	–
National law on mobile phone use while driving	Yes
Ban on hand-held mobile phone use	Yes
Ban on hands-free mobile phone use	Yes
National drug-driving law	Yes

Deaths by road user category

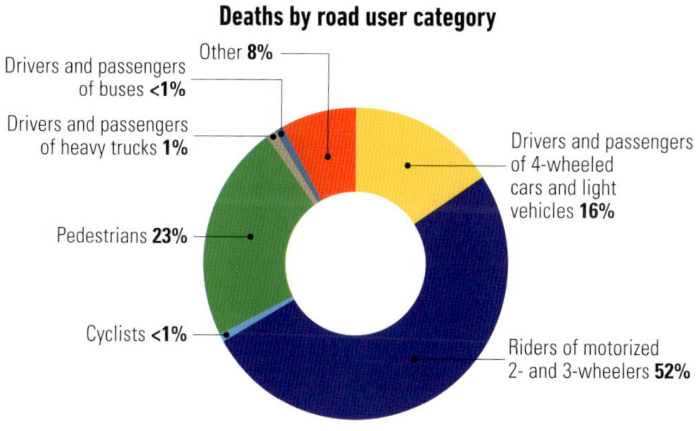

Source: 2016, General Directorate of Strategic Health Information (DIGIES)

Trends in reported road traffic deaths

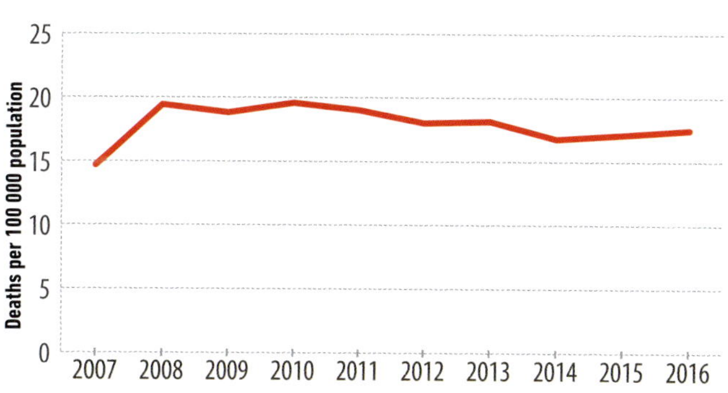

Source: General Directorate of Strategic Health Information (DIGIES)

Legislative review conducted by WHO. Vehicle safety data from UNECE WP29. Other data collected by questionnaire and cleared by National Transit and Road Safety Agency.

Peru

Population: 31 773 840 | Income group: Middle | Gross national income per capita: US$ 5 950

INSTITUTIONAL FRAMEWORK

Lead agency	**National Road Safety Council**
Funded in national budget	Yes
National road safety strategy	**Yes**
Funding to implement strategy	Partially funded
Fatality reduction target	From 10 to 6 deaths per 100 000 population (2016-2021)

SAFER ROADS AND MOBILITY

Audits or star rating required for new road infrastructure	No
Design standards for the safety of pedestrians / cyclists	No
Inspections / star rating of existing roads	–
Investments to upgrade high risk locations	Yes
Policies & investment in urban public transport	No

SAFER VEHICLES

Total registered vehicles for 2016	**5 604 789**
Cars and 4-wheeled light vehicles	2 262 416
Motorized 2- and 3-wheelers	2 943 070
Heavy trucks	319 184
Buses	80 119
Other	0
Vehicle standards applied (UNECE WP.29)	
Frontal impact standard	No
Electronic stability control	No
Pedestrian protection	No
Motorcycle anti-lock braking system	No

POST-CRASH CARE

National emergency care access number	Partial coverage
Trauma registry	National
Formal certification for prehospital providers	No
National assessment of emergency care systems	No

DATA

Reported road traffic fatalities (2016)	2 696[a] (77% M, 23% F)
WHO estimated road traffic fatalities (2016)	4 286 (95% CI 3 898 - 4 674)
WHO estimated rate per 100 000 population (2016)	13.5

[a] Peruvian National Police. Died at scene of crash

SAFER ROAD USERS

National speed limit law	**Yes**
Max urban speed limit	60 km/h
Max rural speed limit	60 km/h
Max motorway speed limit	100 km/h
Local authorities can modify limits	Yes
Enforcement	0 (1) 2 3 4 5 6 7 8 9 10
Predominant type of enforcement	Manual
National drink-driving law	**Yes**
BAC limit – general population	≤ 0.05 g/dl
BAC limit – young or novice drivers	≤ 0.05 g/dl
Random breath testing carried out	Yes
Testing carried out in case of fatal crash	All drivers tested
Enforcement	0 1 (2) 3 4 5 6 7 8 9 10
% road traffic deaths involving alcohol	9%[b]
National motorcycle helmet law	**Yes**
Applies to drivers and passengers	Yes
Helmet fastening required	No
Helmet standard referred to and/or specified	No
Children passengers on motorcycles	Not restricted
Enforcement	0 1 2 3 (4) 5 6 7 8 9 10
Helmet wearing rate	70% Drivers[c], 8% Passengers[c]
National seat-belt law	**Yes**
Applies to front and rear seat occupants	Yes
Enforcement	0 1 2 3 4 (5) 6 7 8 9 10
Seat-belt wearing rate	16% Front seats[d], <1% Rear seats[d]
National child restraint law	**Yes**
Children seated in front seat	Prohibited under 12 yrs
Child restraint required	Up to 3 yrs[e]
Child restraint standard referred to and/or specified	Yes
Enforcement	0 (1) 2 3 4 5 6 7 8 9 10
% children using child restraints	<1[d]
National law on mobile phone use while driving	**Yes**
Ban on hand-held mobile phone use	Yes
Ban on hands-free mobile phone use	No
National drug-driving law	**Yes**

[b] 2016, Peruvian National Police
[c] 2014, Technical Secretariat of Road Safety
[d] 2014, Observational urban study on the use of seat belt and child restraint system
[e] Legislation requires the use of the seat belt for children from 3-12 years old

Deaths by road user category

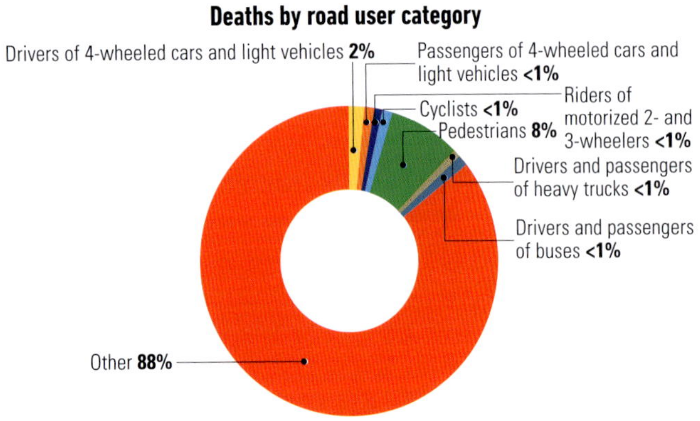

Source: 2013, Ministry of Health, Vital System

Trends in reported road traffic deaths

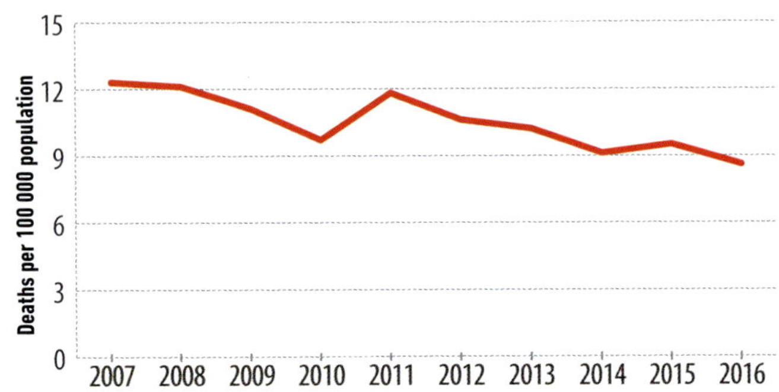

Source: Peruvian National Police

Philippines

Population: 103 320 224 | Income group: Middle | Gross national income per capita: US$ 3 580

INSTITUTIONAL FRAMEWORK	
Lead agency	Department of Transportation (DOTr)
Funded in national budget	Yes
National road safety strategy	Yes
Funding to implement strategy	Fully funded
Fatality reduction target	50% (2011-2020)

SAFER ROADS AND MOBILITY	
Audits or star rating required for new road infrastructure	Yes
Design standards for the safety of pedestrians / cyclists	Partial
Inspections / star rating of existing roads	Yes
Investments to upgrade high risk locations	Yes
Policies & investment in urban public transport	Yes

SAFER VEHICLES	
Total registered vehicles for 2016	9 251 565
Cars and 4-wheeled light vehicles	3 434 329
Motorized 2- and 3-wheelers	5 329 770
Heavy trucks	407 357
Buses	29 794
Other	50 315
Vehicle standards applied (UNECE WP.29)	
Frontal impact standard	No
Electronic stability control	No
Pedestrian protection	No
Motorcycle anti-lock braking system	No

POST-CRASH CARE	
National emergency care access number	National, single number
Trauma registry	National
Formal certification for prehospital providers	No
National assessment of emergency care systems	No

DATA	
Reported road traffic fatalities (2015)	10 012 [a] (81% M, 19% F)
WHO estimated road traffic fatalities (2016)	12 690
WHO estimated rate per 100 000 population (2016)	12.3

[a] Philippine Statistical Authority, Civil Registration and Vital Statistics. Unlimited time period following crash

SAFER ROAD USERS	
National speed limit law	Yes
Max urban speed limit	40 km/h
Max rural speed limit	80 km/h
Max motorway speed limit [b]	No
Local authorities can modify limits	Yes
Enforcement	0 1 2 3 4 (5) 6 7 8 9 10
Predominant type of enforcement	Manual
National drink-driving law	Yes
BAC limit – general population	< 0.05 g/dl
BAC limit – young or novice drivers	< 0.05 g/dl
Random breath testing carried out	Yes [b]
Testing carried out in case of fatal crash	Some drivers tested
Enforcement	0 1 2 3 (4) 5 6 7 8 9 10
% road traffic deaths involving alcohol	–
National motorcycle helmet law	Yes
Applies to drivers and passengers	Yes
Helmet fastening required	No
Helmet standard referred to and/or specified	Yes
Children passengers on motorcycles	Not restricted [c]
Enforcement	0 1 2 3 4 5 (6) 7 8 9 10
Helmet wearing rate	87% Drivers [d], 51% All riders [d]
National seat-belt law	Yes
Applies to front and rear seat occupants	Yes
Enforcement	0 1 2 3 4 5 (6) 7 8 9 10
Seat-belt wearing rate	80% Drivers [e]
National child restraint law	No
Children seated in front seat	Prohibited under 6 yrs [d]
Child restraint required	–
Child restraint standard referred to and/or specified	–
Enforcement	–
% children using child restraints	–
National law on mobile phone use while driving	Yes
Ban on hand-held mobile phone use	Yes
Ban on hands-free mobile phone use	No
National drug-driving law	Yes

[b] Legislation requires probable cause to test drivers
[c] Child passengers on motorcycles are restricted in specific circumstances only (heavy volume of vehicles, high density of fast moving vehicles, speed limit over 60 km/h)
[d] 2010, "Prevalence of Road Traffic Injury Risk Factors in the Province of Guimaras"
[e] Ban on front seating set for children aged 6 years and below

Deaths by road user category

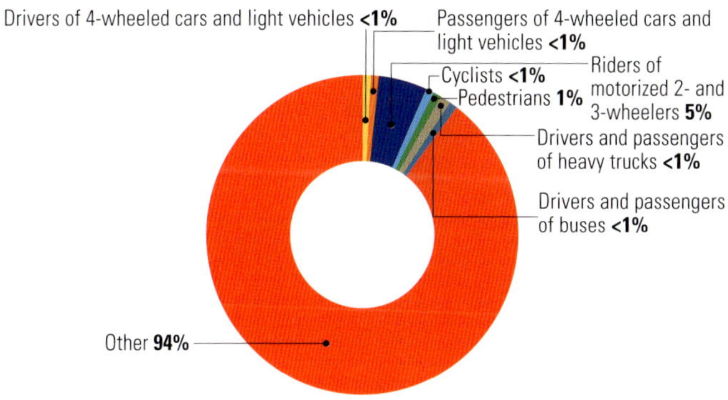

Source: 2015, Philippine Statistical Authority, Civil Registration and Vital Statistics

Trends in reported road traffic deaths

Source: Philippine Statistical Authority, Civil Registration and Vital Statistics

Legislative review conducted by WHO. Vehicle safety data from UNECE WP29. Other data collected by questionnaire and cleared by Department of Health.

Poland

Population: 38 224 408 | Income group: High | Gross national income per capita: US$ 12 680

INSTITUTIONAL FRAMEWORK

Lead agency	National Road Safety Council
Funded in national budget	Yes
National road safety strategy	Yes
Funding to implement strategy	Partially funded
Fatality reduction target	50% (2013-2020)

SAFER ROADS AND MOBILITY

Audits or star rating required for new road infrastructure	Partial
Design standards for the safety of pedestrians / cyclists	Yes
Inspections / star rating of existing roads	Yes
Investments to upgrade high risk locations	Yes
Policies & investment in urban public transport	Yes

SAFER VEHICLES

Total registered vehicles for 2015	27 409 106
Cars and 4-wheeled light vehicles	20 723 423
Motorized 2- and 3-wheelers	2 531 520
Heavy trucks	3 098 376
Buses	109 844
Other	945 943
Vehicle standards applied (UNECE WP.29)	
Frontal impact standard	Yes
Electronic stability control	Yes
Pedestrian protection	Yes
Motorcycle anti-lock braking system	Yes

POST-CRASH CARE

National emergency care access number	National, single number
Trauma registry	None
Formal certification for prehospital providers	No
National assessment of emergency care systems	No

DATA

Reported road traffic fatalities (2016)	3 026[a] (75% M, 25% F)
WHO estimated road traffic fatalities (2016)	3 698
WHO estimated rate per 100 000 population (2016)	9.7

[a] SEWiK Police Database (Traffic accidents and collisions reporting system). Died within 30 days of crash

SAFER ROAD USERS

National speed limit law	Yes
Max urban speed limit	50 km/h[b]
Max rural speed limit	90 km/h
Max motorway speed limit	140 km/h
Local authorities can modify limits	Yes
Enforcement	0 1 2 3 4 5 6 7 ⑧ 9 10
Predominant type of enforcement	Manual
National drink-driving law	Yes
BAC limit – general population	< 0.02 g/dl
BAC limit – young or novice drivers	< 0.02 g/dl
Random breath testing carried out	Yes
Testing carried out in case of fatal crash	All drivers tested
Enforcement	0 1 2 3 4 5 6 7 8 9 ⑩
% road traffic deaths involving alcohol	13%[c]
National motorcycle helmet law	Yes
Applies to drivers and passengers	Yes
Helmet fastening required	No
Helmet standard referred to and/or specified	Yes
Children passengers on motorcycles	Not restricted[d]
Enforcement	0 1 2 3 4 5 6 ⑦ 8 9 10
Helmet wearing rate	99% Drivers[e], 100% Passengers[e]
National seat-belt law	Yes
Applies to front and rear seat occupants	Yes
Enforcement	0 1 2 3 4 5 6 7 ⑧ 9 10
Seat-belt wearing rate	96% Front seats[f], 76% Rear seats[f]
National child restraint law	Yes
Children seated in front seat	Allowed in a child restraint[g]
Child restraint required	135-150 cm[h]
Child restraint standard referred to and/or specified	Yes
Enforcement	0 1 2 3 4 5 6 ⑦ 8 9 10
% children using child restraints	93%[i]
National law on mobile phone use while driving	Yes
Ban on hand-held mobile phone use	Yes
Ban on hands-free mobile phone use	No
National drug-driving law	Yes

[b] 60 km/h from 23:00 - 05:00
[c] 2016, SEWiK Police Database (Traffic accidents and collisions reporting system)
[d] Speed limit for motorcycles transporting a child under 7 years is limited to 40 km/h
[e] 2015, Ministry of Infrastructure and Development, Using of motorcycle helmet in Poland 2015
[f] 2015, Ministry of Infrastructure and Development, Using of seat belts in Poland 2015
[g] Provided that airbag is deactivated if child is in a rear-facing restraint
[h] Child restraints are required for children under 150 cm. By exception, children of height 135-150 cm can be restrained with a seat belt only if sitting in the rear
[i] 2015, Ministry of Infrastructure and Development, Using of child restraints device in Poland 2015a

Deaths by road user category

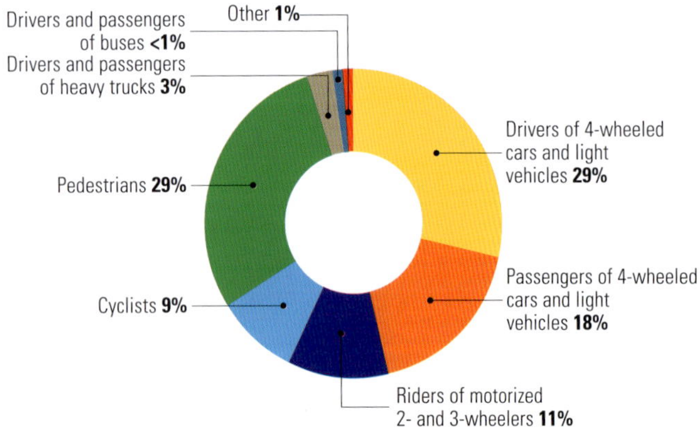

Source: 2016, SEWiK Police Database (Traffic accidents and collisions reporting system)

Trends in reported road traffic deaths

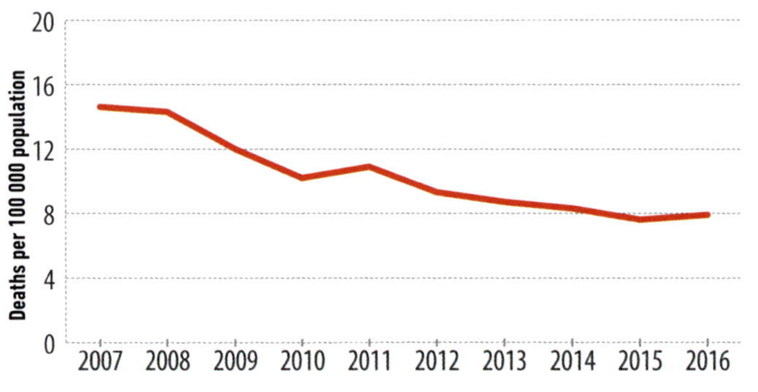

Source: SEWiK Police Database (Traffic accidents and collisions reporting system)

Legislative review conducted by WHO. Vehicle safety data from UNECE WP29. Other data collected by questionnaire.

Portugal

Population: 10 371 627 | Income group: High | Gross national income per capita: US$ 19 850

INSTITUTIONAL FRAMEWORK	
Lead agency	National Authority for Road Safety, Ministry of Internal Administration
Funded in national budget	Yes
National road safety strategy	Yes
Funding to implement strategy	Partially funded
Fatality reduction target	41 deaths per million people (2016-2020)

SAFER ROADS AND MOBILITY	
Audits or star rating required for new road infrastructure	Partial
Design standards for the safety of pedestrians / cyclists	Yes
Inspections / star rating of existing roads	Yes
Investments to upgrade high risk locations	No
Policies & investment in urban public transport	Yes

SAFER VEHICLES	
Total registered vehicles for 2015	6 590 094
Cars and 4-wheeled light vehicles	5 970 710
Motorized 2- and 3-wheelers	506 400
Heavy trucks	98 267
Buses	14 717
Other	0
Vehicle standards applied (UNECE WP.29)	
Frontal impact standard	Yes
Electronic stability control	Yes
Pedestrian protection	Yes
Motorcycle anti-lock braking system	Yes

POST-CRASH CARE	
National emergency care access number	National, single number
Trauma registry	National
Formal certification for prehospital providers	Yes
National assessment of emergency care systems	No

DATA	
Reported road traffic fatalities (2016)	563[a] (77% M, 23% F)
WHO estimated road traffic fatalities (2016)	768
WHO estimated rate per 100 000 population (2016)	7.4

[a] National Authority for Road Safety. Died within 30 days of crash

SAFER ROAD USERS	
National speed limit law	Yes
Max urban speed limit	50 km/h
Max rural speed limit	90 km/h
Max motorway speed limit	120 km/h
Local authorities can modify limits	No
Enforcement	0 1 2 3 4 5 6 (7) 8 9 10
Predominant type of enforcement	Manual
National drink-driving law	Yes
BAC limit – general population	< 0.05 g/dl
BAC limit – young or novice drivers	< 0.02 g/dl
Random breath testing carried out	Yes
Testing carried out in case of fatal crash	All drivers tested
Enforcement	0 1 2 3 4 5 6 (7) 8 9 10
% road traffic deaths involving alcohol	29%[b]
National motorcycle helmet law	Yes
Applies to drivers and passengers	Yes
Helmet fastening required	Yes
Helmet standard referred to and/or specified	Yes
Children passengers on motorcycles	Prohibited under 7 yrs
Enforcement	0 1 2 3 4 5 6 7 8 (9) 10
Helmet wearing rate	98% Drivers[c], 97% Passengers[c]
National seat-belt law	Yes
Applies to front and rear seat occupants	Yes
Enforcement	0 1 2 3 4 5 6 7 (8) 9 10
Seat-belt wearing rate	96% Front seats[c], 77% Rear seats[c]
National child restraint law	Yes
Children seated in front seat	Prohibited under 12 yrs/135 cm[d]
Child restraint required	Up to 12 yrs/135 cm
Child restraint standard referred to and/or specified	Yes
Enforcement	0 1 2 3 4 5 6 7 (8) 9 10
% children using child restraints	91-100%[c]
National law on mobile phone use while driving	Yes
Ban on hand-held mobile phone use	Yes
Ban on hands-free mobile phone use	No
National drug-driving law	Yes

[b] 2015, National Authority for Road Safety and National Institute of Forensic Medicine and Forensic Sciences (INMLCF)
[c] 2012, Portuguese Road Safety (PRP)
[d] Except for children under 3 years in rear-facing child restraint with airbag deactivated

Deaths by road user category

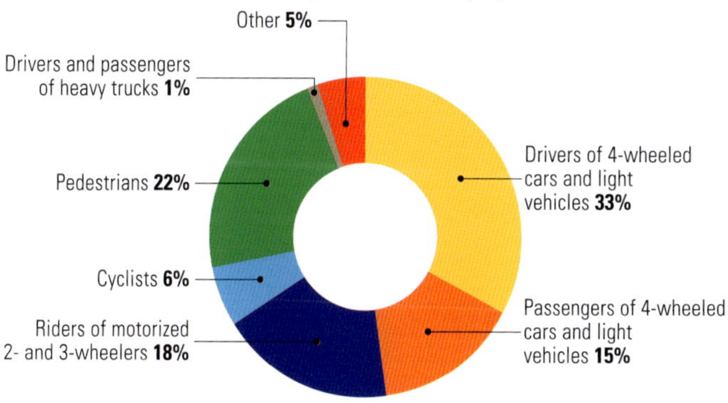

Source: 2016, National Authority for Road Safety, Ministry of Internal Administration

Trends in reported road traffic deaths

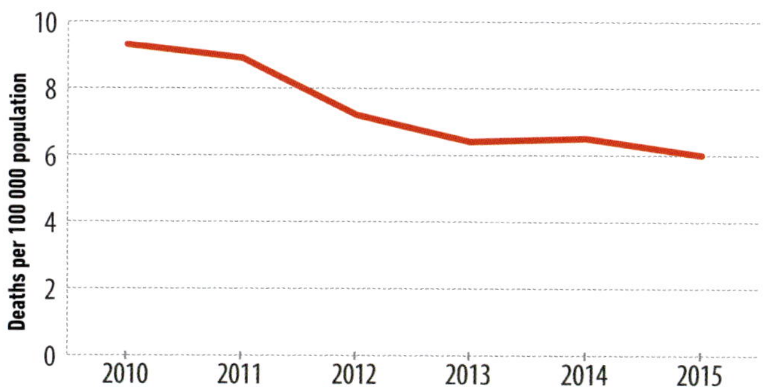

Source: National Authority for Road Safety, Ministry of Internal Administration and National Institute of Statistics

Legislative review conducted by WHO. Vehicle safety data from UNECE WP29. Other data collected by questionnaire.

Qatar

Population: 2 569 804 | Income group: High | Gross national income per capita: US$ 75 660[a]

INSTITUTIONAL FRAMEWORK

Lead agency	National Traffic Safety Committee (NTSC)
Funded in national budget	Yes
National road safety strategy	Yes
Funding to implement strategy	Fully funded
Fatality reduction target	130 deaths by 2022 (2013-2022)

SAFER ROADS AND MOBILITY

Audits or star rating required for new road infrastructure	Yes
Design standards for the safety of pedestrians / cyclists	Yes
Inspections / star rating of existing roads	Yes
Investments to upgrade high risk locations	Yes
Policies & investment in urban public transport	Yes

SAFER VEHICLES

Total registered vehicles for 2016	1 330 487
Cars and 4-wheeled light vehicles	–
Motorized 2- and 3-wheelers	16 479
Heavy trucks	–
Buses	–
Other	1 314 008
Vehicle standards applied (UNECE WP.29)	
Frontal impact standard	No
Electronic stability control	No
Pedestrian protection	No
Motorcycle anti-lock braking system	No

POST-CRASH CARE

National emergency care access number	National, single number
Trauma registry	National
Formal certification for prehospital providers	Yes
National assessment of emergency care systems	Yes

DATA

Reported road traffic fatalities (2016)	178[b] (95% M, 5% F)
WHO estimated road traffic fatalities (2016)	239
WHO estimated rate per 100 000 population (2016)	9.3

[a] Data available only for 2015
[b] Ministry of Interior, General Traffic Directorate . Died within 30 days of crash

SAFER ROAD USERS

National speed limit law	Yes
Max urban speed limit	100 km/h
Max rural speed limit	120 km/h
Max motorway speed limit	120 km/h
Local authorities can modify limits	No
Enforcement	0 1 2 3 4 5 6 (7) 8 9 10
Predominant type of enforcement	Automated
National drink-driving law	Yes[c]
BAC limit – general population	–
BAC limit – young or novice drivers	–
Random breath testing carried out	No
Testing carried out in case of fatal crash	All drivers tested
Enforcement	0 1 2 3 4 5 6 7 8 (9) 10
% road traffic deaths involving alcohol	2%[d]
National motorcycle helmet law	Yes
Applies to drivers and passengers	Yes
Helmet fastening required	No
Helmet standard referred to and/or specified	No
Children passengers on motorcycles	Not restricted
Enforcement	0 1 2 3 4 5 6 7 8 (9) 10
Helmet wearing rate	–
National seat-belt law	Yes
Applies to front and rear seat occupants	No
Enforcement	0 1 2 3 4 5 6 (7) 8 9 10
Seat-belt wearing rate	–
National child restraint law	No
Children seated in front seat	Prohibited under 10 yrs
Child restraint required	–
Child restraint standard referred to and/or specified	–
Enforcement	–
% children using child restraints	72%[e]
National law on mobile phone use while driving	Yes
Ban on hand-held mobile phone use	Yes
Ban on hands-free mobile phone use	No
National drug-driving law	Yes

[c] Not based on BAC. Alcohol consumption legally prohibited
[d] 2016, Ministry of Interior, General Traffic Directorate (data from 2016)
[e] 2015, Roadside observational study

Deaths by road user category

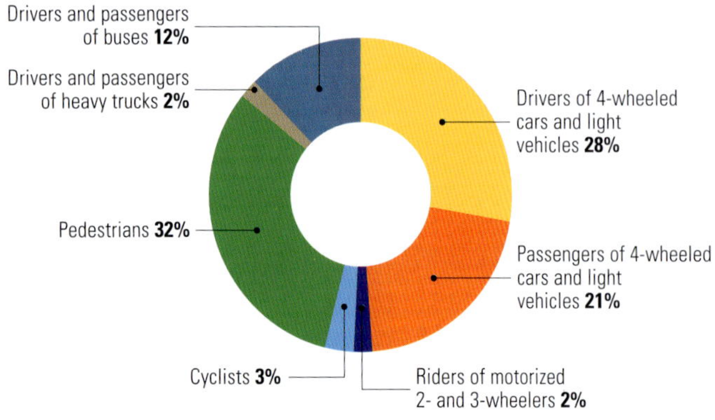

Source: 2016, Ministry of Interior, General Traffic Directorate

Trends in reported road traffic deaths

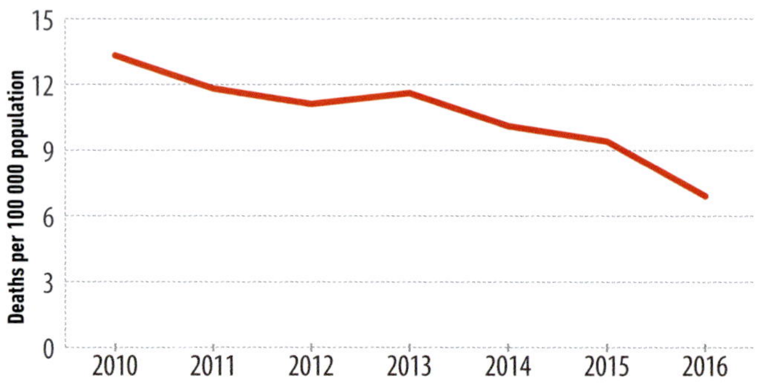

Source: Ministry of Interior, General Traffic Directorate

Legislative review conducted by WHO. Vehicle safety data from UNECE WP29. Other data collected by questionnaire and cleared by Supreme Council of Health.

Republic of Korea

Population: 50 791 920 | Income group: High | Gross national income per capita: US$ 27 600

INSTITUTIONAL FRAMEWORK

Lead agency	Ministry of Land, Infrastructure and Transport
Funded in national budget	Yes
National road safety strategy	Yes
Funding to implement strategy	Partially funded
Fatality reduction target	< 2700 deaths by 2021 (2017-2021)

SAFER ROADS AND MOBILITY

Audits or star rating required for new road infrastructure	Yes
Design standards for the safety of pedestrians / cyclists	Yes
Inspections / star rating of existing roads	Yes
Investments to upgrade high risk locations	Yes
Policies & investment in urban public transport	Yes

SAFER VEHICLES

Total registered vehicles for 2016	25 680 967
Cars and 4-wheeled light vehicles	17 338 160
Motorized 2- and 3-wheelers	2 180 688
Heavy trucks	3 492 173
Buses	892 539
Other	1 777 407
Vehicle standards applied (UNECE WP.29)	
Frontal impact standard	Yes
Electronic stability control	Yes
Pedestrian protection	Yes
Motorcycle anti-lock braking system	No

POST-CRASH CARE

National emergency care access number	National, single number
Trauma registry	Subnational
Formal certification for prehospital providers	Yes
National assessment of emergency care systems	Yes

DATA

Reported road traffic fatalities (2016)	4 292[a] (71% M, 29% F)
WHO estimated road traffic fatalities (2016)	4 990
WHO estimated rate per 100 000 population (2016)	9.8

[a] Korean National Police Agency. Died within 30 days of crash

SAFER ROAD USERS

National speed limit law	Yes
Max urban speed limit	80 km/h
Max rural speed limit	80 km/h
Max motorway speed limit	120 km/h
Local authorities can modify limits	Yes
Enforcement	0 1 2 3 4 5 6 7 (8) 9 10
Predominant type of enforcement	Automated
National drink-driving law	Yes
BAC limit – general population	< 0.05 g/dl
BAC limit – young or novice drivers	< 0.05 g/dl
Random breath testing carried out	Yes[b]
Testing carried out in case of fatal crash	Some drivers tested
Enforcement	0 1 2 3 4 5 6 (7) 8 9 10
% road traffic deaths involving alcohol	11%[c]
National motorcycle helmet law	Yes
Applies to drivers and passengers	Yes
Helmet fastening required	No
Helmet standard referred to and/or specified	Yes
Children passengers on motorcycles	Not restricted
Enforcement	0 1 2 3 4 5 (6) 7 8 9 10
Helmet wearing rate	86% Drivers[d], 40% Passengers[d]
National seat-belt law	Yes
Applies to front and rear seat occupants	Yes
Enforcement	0 1 2 3 4 5 6 7 (8) 9 10
Seat-belt wearing rate	83% Front seats[e], 30% Rear seats[e]
National child restraint law	No[f]
Children seated in front seat	Allowed in a child restraint[g]
Child restraint required	–
Child restraint standard referred to and/or specified	–
Enforcement	–
% children using child restraints	40-42%[h]
National law on mobile phone use while driving	Yes
Ban on hand-held mobile phone use	Yes
Ban on hands-free mobile phone use	No
National drug-driving law	Yes

[b] Legislation requires probable cause to test drivers
[c] 2016, Korean National Police Agency
[d] 2016, Korea Traffic Culture Index, KOTSA (Korea Transportation Safety Authority)
[e] 2016, Korea Traffic Culture Index
[f] Only required for small children (defined as children under 6 years) sitting in the front
[g] Safety seats required for small children (defined as children under 6 years) sitting in the front
[h] 2016, National Survey

Deaths by road user category

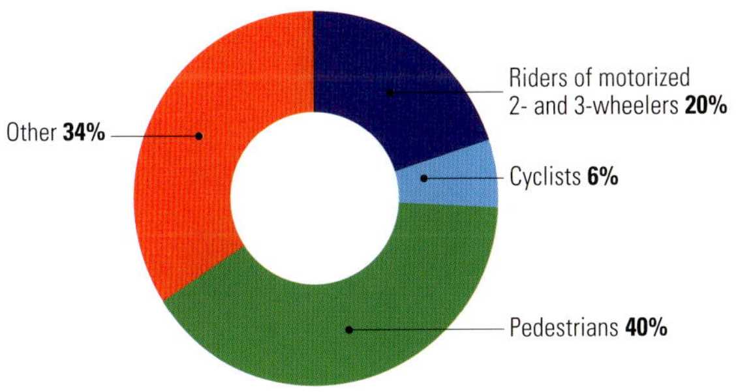

Source: 2016, Korean National Police Agency

Trends in reported road traffic deaths

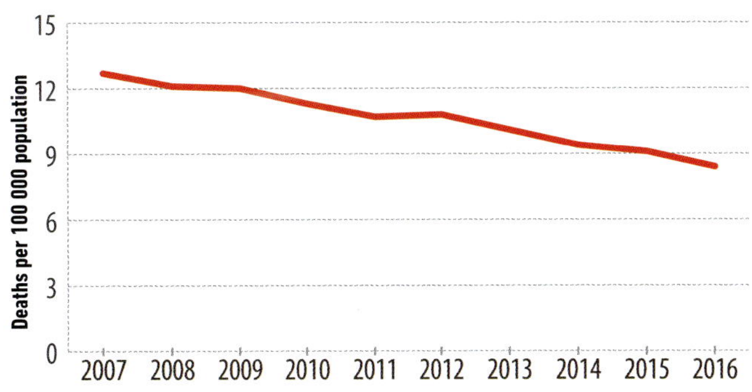

Source: Korean National Police Agency

Legislative review conducted by WHO. Vehicle safety data from UNECE WP29. Other data collected by questionnaire and cleared by Ministry of Land, Infrastructure and Transport.

Republic of Moldova

Population: 4 059 608 | Income group: Middle | Gross national income per capita: US$ 2 120

INSTITUTIONAL FRAMEWORK	
Lead agency	The National Committee on Road safety
Funded in national budget	No
National road safety strategy	Yes
Funding to implement strategy	Partially funded
Fatality reduction target	50% (2011-2020)
SAFER ROADS AND MOBILITY	
Audits or star rating required for new road infrastructure	Yes
Design standards for the safety of pedestrians / cyclists	Yes
Inspections / star rating of existing roads	Yes
Investments to upgrade high risk locations	Yes
Policies & investment in urban public transport	Yes
SAFER VEHICLES	
Total registered vehicles for 2016	894 253
Cars and 4-wheeled light vehicles	547 712
Motorized 2- and 3-wheelers	37 987
Heavy trucks	177 781
Buses	20 971
Other	109 802
Vehicle standards applied (UNECE WP.29)	
Frontal impact standard	No
Electronic stability control	No
Pedestrian protection	No
Motorcycle anti-lock braking system	No
POST-CRASH CARE	
National emergency care access number	National, multiple numbers
Trauma registry	Some facilities
Formal certification for prehospital providers	Yes
National assessment of emergency care systems	No
DATA	
Reported road traffic fatalities (2016)	346[a] (76% M, 24% F)
WHO estimated road traffic fatalities (2016)	394
WHO estimated rate per 100 000 population (2016)	9.7

[a] National Center for Health Management. Died within 30 days of crash

SAFER ROAD USERS	
National speed limit law	Yes
Max urban speed limit	50 km/h
Max rural speed limit	110 km/h
Max motorway speed limit	110 km/h
Local authorities can modify limits	No
Enforcement	0 1 2 3 4 5 6 7 ⑧ 9 10
Predominant type of enforcement	Manual and automated
National drink-driving law	Yes
BAC limit – general population	≤ 0.03 g/dl
BAC limit – young or novice drivers	≤ 0.03 g/dl
Random breath testing carried out	Yes
Testing carried out in case of fatal crash	All drivers tested
Enforcement	0 1 2 3 4 5 6 7 ⑧ 9 10
% road traffic deaths involving alcohol	9%[b]
National motorcycle helmet law	Yes
Applies to drivers and passengers	Yes
Helmet fastening required	Yes
Helmet standard referred to and/or specified	No
Children passengers on motorcycles	Prohibited under 12 yrs
Enforcement	0 1 2 3 4 5 6 7 ⑧ 9 10
Helmet wearing rate	–
National seat-belt law	Yes
Applies to front and rear seat occupants	Yes
Enforcement	0 1 2 3 4 5 6 7 ⑧ 9 10
Seat-belt wearing rate	62% Front seats[c], 18% Rear seats[c]
National child restraint law	Yes
Children seated in front seat	Prohibited under 12 yrs
Child restraint required	–[d]
Child restraint standard referred to and/or specified	No
Enforcement	0 1 2 3 4 5 6 7 ⑧ 9 10
% children using child restraints	50%[c]
National law on mobile phone use while driving	Yes
Ban on hand-held mobile phone use	Yes
Ban on hands-free mobile phone use	No
National drug-driving law	Yes

[b] 2016, Ministry of Internal Affairs statistics
[c] 2012, Joint report on the statistical data and the public's attitude to road safety in Chisinau and Tiraspol
[d] The legislation refers to the use of child restraint systems or other means to transport children under 12 years

Deaths by road user category

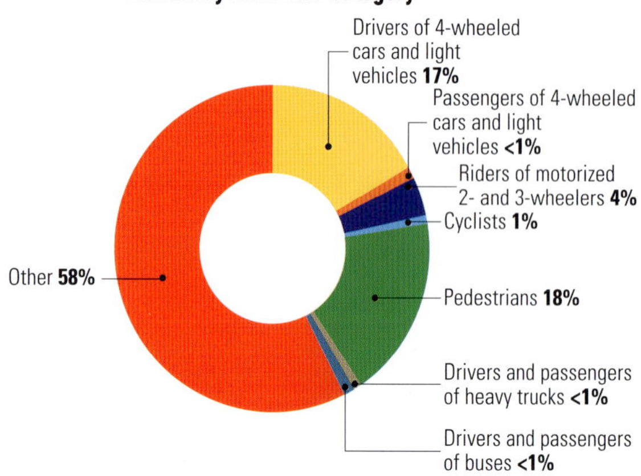

Source: 2016, National Center for Health Management

Trends in reported road traffic deaths

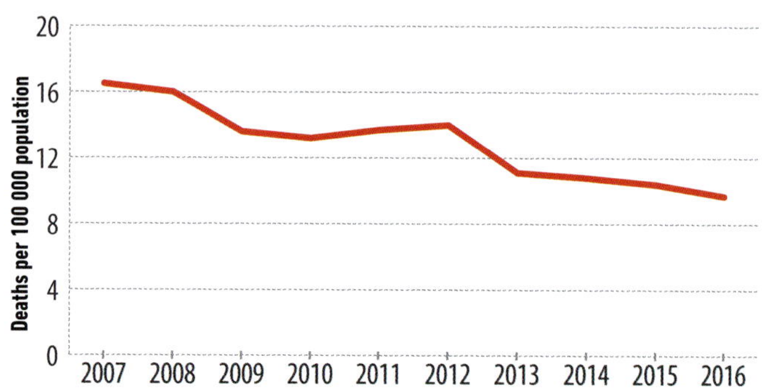

Source: National Center for Health Management

Romania

Population: 19 778 084 | Income group: Middle | Gross national income per capita: US$ 9 470

INSTITUTIONAL FRAMEWORK	
Lead agency	Interministerial Council for Road Safety
Funded in national budget	No
National road safety strategy	Yes
Funding to implement strategy	Partially funded
Fatality reduction target	50% (2011-2020)
SAFER ROADS AND MOBILITY	
Audits or star rating required for new road infrastructure	Yes
Design standards for the safety of pedestrians / cyclists	Yes
Inspections / star rating of existing roads	Yes
Investments to upgrade high risk locations	No
Policies & investment in urban public transport	Yes
SAFER VEHICLES	
Total registered vehicles for 2016	7 014 661
Cars and 4-wheeled light vehicles	5 472 423
Motorized 2- and 3-wheelers	119 534
Heavy trucks	912 790
Buses	48 803
Other	461 111
Vehicle standards applied (UNECE WP.29)	
Frontal impact standard	Yes
Electronic stability control	Yes
Pedestrian protection	Yes
Motorcycle anti-lock braking system	Yes
POST-CRASH CARE	
National emergency care access number	National, single number
Trauma registry	None
Formal certification for prehospital providers	Yes
National assessment of emergency care systems	Yes
DATA	
Reported road traffic fatalities (2016)	1 913[a] (73% M, 27% F)
WHO estimated road traffic fatalities (2016)	2 044
WHO estimated rate per 100 000 population (2016)	10.3

[a] National database (EAC). Died within 30 days of crash

SAFER ROAD USERS	
National speed limit law	Yes
Max urban speed limit	50 km/h
Max rural speed limit	90 km/h
Max motorway speed limit	130 km/h
Local authorities can modify limits	Yes
Enforcement	0 1 2 3 4 5 6 (7) 8 9 10
Predominant type of enforcement	Manual
National drink-driving law	Yes
BAC limit – general population	≤ 0.08 g/dl
BAC limit – young or novice drivers	≤ 0.08 g/dl
Random breath testing carried out	Yes
Testing carried out in case of fatal crash	All drivers tested
Enforcement	0 1 2 3 4 5 6 7 (8) 9 10
% road traffic deaths involving alcohol	6%[b]
National motorcycle helmet law	Yes
Applies to drivers and passengers	Yes
Helmet fastening required	No
Helmet standard referred to and/or specified	No
Children passengers on motorcycles	Prohibited under 14 yrs[c]
Enforcement	0 1 2 3 4 5 6 (7) 8 9 10
Helmet wearing rate	–
National seat-belt law	Yes
Applies to front and rear seat occupants	Yes
Enforcement	0 1 2 3 4 5 6 (7) 8 9 10
Seat-belt wearing rate	–
National child restraint law	Yes
Children seated in front seat	Allowed in a child restraint[d]
Child restraint required	Up to 135 cm
Child restraint standard referred to and/or specified	Yes
Enforcement	0 1 2 3 4 5 6 (7) 8 9 10
% children using child restraints	–
National law on mobile phone use while driving	Yes
Ban on hand-held mobile phone use	Yes
Ban on hands-free mobile phone use	No
National drug-driving law	Yes

[b] 2016, National database (EAC)
[c] Children under 14 years allowed to be transported in the motorcycle sidecar and must be held in the arms under 7 years
[d] If in accordance with the manufacturer's instruction and for rear-facing restraint if airbag is deactivated

Deaths by road user category

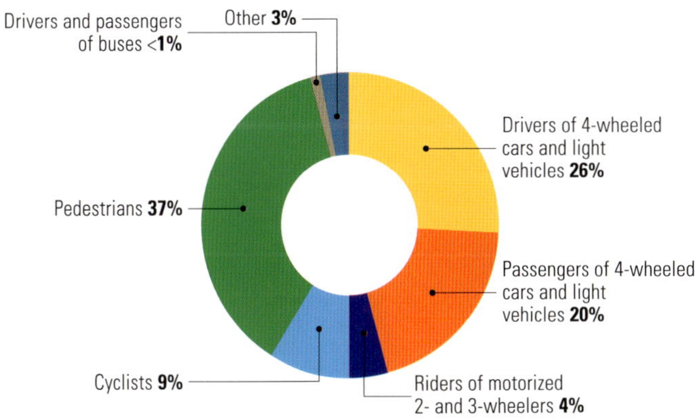

Source: 2016, National database (EAC)

Trends in reported road traffic deaths

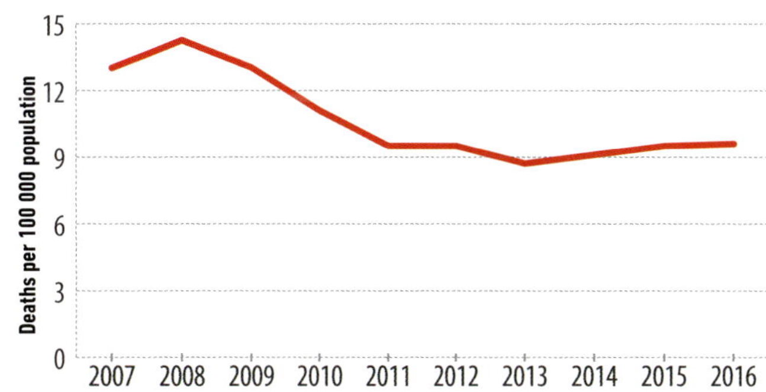

Source: National database (EAC) and National Institute of Statistics (INS)

Legislative review conducted by WHO. Vehicle safety data from UNECE WP29. Other data collected by questionnaire and cleared by Ministry of Internal Affairs.

Russian Federation

Population: 143 964 512 | Income group: Middle | Gross national income per capita: US$ 9 720

INSTITUTIONAL FRAMEWORK

Lead agency	**The Governmental Commission on Road Safety**
Funded in national budget	Yes
National road safety strategy	**Yes**
Funding to implement strategy	Partially funded
Fatality reduction target	Reduce deaths by 8 000 (2012-2020)

SAFER ROADS AND MOBILITY

Audits or star rating required for new road infrastructure	Yes
Design standards for the safety of pedestrians / cyclists	Yes
Inspections / star rating of existing roads	No
Investments to upgrade high risk locations	Yes
Policies & investment in urban public transport	Yes

SAFER VEHICLES

Total registered vehicles for 2016	**54 014 259**
Cars and 4-wheeled light vehicles	44 698 592
Motorized 2- and 3-wheelers	2 237 218
Heavy trucks	3 179 460
Buses	865 897
Other	3 033 092
Vehicle standards applied (UNECE WP.29)	
Frontal impact standard	Yes
Electronic stability control	Yes
Pedestrian protection	Yes
Motorcycle anti-lock braking system	No

POST-CRASH CARE

National emergency care access number	National, single number
Trauma registry	Some facilities
Formal certification for prehospital providers	Yes
National assessment of emergency care systems	No

DATA

Reported road traffic fatalities (2016)	20 308[a] (72% M, 25% F)
WHO estimated road traffic fatalities (2016)	25 969
WHO estimated rate per 100 000 population (2016)	18

[a] Ministry of Internal Affairs of the Russian Federation. Died within 30 days of crash

SAFER ROAD USERS

National speed limit law	**Yes**
Max urban speed limit	60 km/h
Max rural speed limit	90 km/h
Max motorway speed limit	110 km/h
Local authorities can modify limits	Yes[b]
Enforcement	0 1 2 3 4 5 6 7 **8** 9 10
Predominant type of enforcement	Automated
National drink-driving law	**Yes**
BAC limit – general population	≤ 0.03 g/dl[c]
BAC limit – young or novice drivers	≤ 0.03 g/dl[c]
Random breath testing carried out	Yes[d]
Testing carried out in case of fatal crash	All drivers tested
Enforcement	0 1 2 3 4 5 **6** 7 8 9 10
% road traffic deaths involving alcohol	23%[e]
National motorcycle helmet law	**Yes**
Applies to drivers and passengers	Yes
Helmet fastening required	Yes
Helmet standard referred to and/or specified	Yes
Children passengers on motorcycles	Prohibited under 12 yrs
Enforcement	0 1 2 3 **4** 5 6 7 8 9 10
Helmet wearing rate	–
National seat-belt law	**Yes**
Applies to front and rear seat occupants	Yes
Enforcement	0 1 2 3 4 **5** 6 7 8 9 10
Seat-belt wearing rate	66-83% Front seats[f], 20-50% Rear seats[f]
National child restraint law	**Yes[g]**
Children seated in front seat	Allowed in a child restraint[h]
Child restraint required	Up to 7 yrs[i]
Child restraint standard referred to and/or specified	Yes
Enforcement	0 1 2 3 4 5 6 **7** 8 9 10
% children using child restraints	49-52%[f]
National law on mobile phone use while driving	**Yes**
Ban on hand-held mobile phone use	Yes
Ban on hands-free mobile phone use	No
National drug-driving law	**Yes**

[b] Local authorities can modify national speed limits through the posting of speed signs
[c] Law based on breath alcohol concentration, values converted to BAC
[d] Legislation requires probable cause to test drivers
[e] 2016, Ministry of Internal Affairs of the Russian Federation
[f] 2016, Survey performed by the Russian Public Opinion Research Center, 2016
[g] Since 2017, child restraint systems are the only form of restraint allowed for children under 7 years (before the 2017 revision, children under 12 years were to be restrained either in a child restraint or by "other means")
[h] Children up to 11 years (included) while sitting in the front shall be placed in a child restraint, children aged 12 years and more can sit in the front without a child restraint
[i] For children aged 7-11 years old (included) sitting in the rear, child restraint or seat belt can be used

Deaths by road user category

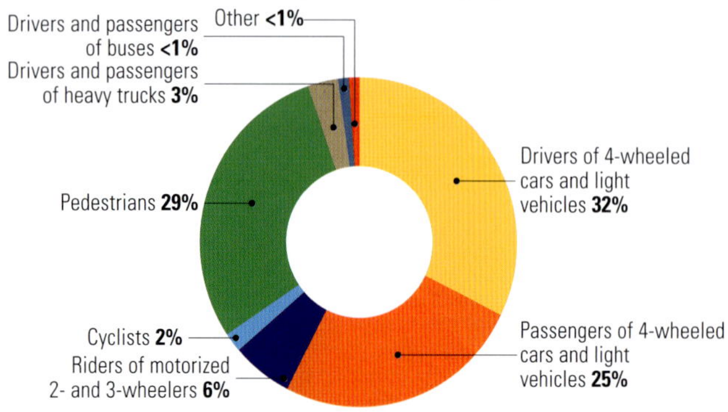

Source: 2016, Ministry of Internal Affairs of the Russian Federation

Trends in reported road traffic deaths

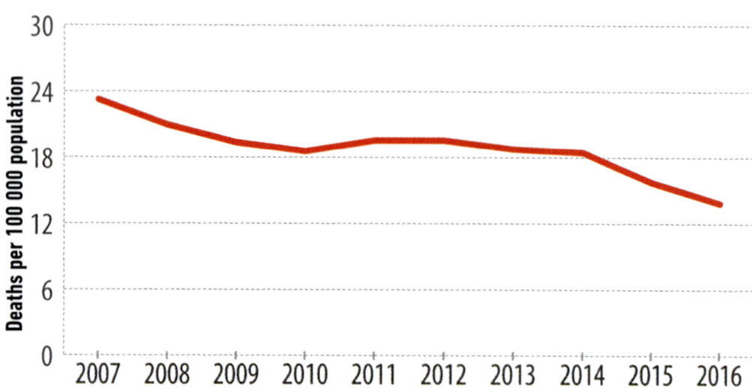

Source: Ministry of Internal Affairs of the Russian Federation

Legislative review conducted by WHO. Vehicle safety data from UNECE WP29. Other data collected by questionnaire and cleared by Ministry of Internal Affairs.

Rwanda

Population: 11 917 508 | Income group: Low | Gross national income per capita: US$ 700

INSTITUTIONAL FRAMEWORK	
Lead agency	**National Road Safety Committee**
Funded in national budget	Yes
National road safety strategy	**Yes**
Funding to implement strategy	Partially funded
Fatality reduction target	–
SAFER ROADS AND MOBILITY	
Audits or star rating required for new road infrastructure	Yes
Design standards for the safety of pedestrians / cyclists	Yes
Inspections / star rating of existing roads	Yes
Investments to upgrade high risk locations	Yes
Policies & investment in urban public transport	Yes
SAFER VEHICLES	
Total registered vehicles for 2016	**180 137**
Cars and 4-wheeled light vehicles	71 394
Motorized 2- and 3-wheelers	91 874
Heavy trucks	5 909
Buses	1 234
Other	9 726
Vehicle standards applied (UNECE WP.29)	
Frontal impact standard	No
Electronic stability control	No
Pedestrian protection	No
Motorcycle anti-lock braking system	No
POST-CRASH CARE	
National emergency care access number	National, single number
Trauma registry	None
Formal certification for prehospital providers	–
National assessment of emergency care systems	No
DATA	
Reported road traffic fatalities (2016)	593 [a]
WHO estimated road traffic fatalities (2016)	3 535 (95% CI 2 690 - 4 380)
WHO estimated rate per 100 000 population (2016)	29.7

[a] Traffic Police. Died within 30 days of crash

SAFER ROAD USERS	
National speed limit law	**Yes**
Max urban speed limit	80 km/h [b]
Max rural speed limit	80 km/h [b]
Max motorway speed limit	80 km/h [b]
Local authorities can modify limits	Yes
Enforcement	0 1 2 3 4 5 6 7 **(8)** 9 10
Predominant type of enforcement	Automated
National drink-driving law	**Yes**
BAC limit – general population	≤ 0.08 g/dl
BAC limit – young or novice drivers	≤ 0.08 g/dl
Random breath testing carried out	Yes [c]
Testing carried out in case of fatal crash	Some drivers tested
Enforcement	0 1 2 3 4 5 6 7 8 **(9)** 10
% road traffic deaths involving alcohol	–
National motorcycle helmet law	**Yes**
Applies to drivers and passengers	Yes
Helmet fastening required	Yes
Helmet standard referred to and/or specified	No
Children passengers on motorcycles	Not restricted
Enforcement	0 1 2 3 4 5 6 7 8 9 **(10)**
Helmet wearing rate	–
National seat-belt law	**Yes**
Applies to front and rear seat occupants	No
Enforcement	0 1 2 3 4 5 6 7 **(8)** 9 10
Seat-belt wearing rate	–
National child restraint law	**No**
Children seated in front seat	Not restricted
Child restraint required	–
Child restraint standard referred to and/or specified	–
Enforcement	–
% children using child restraints	–
National law on mobile phone use while driving	**No**
Ban on hand-held mobile phone use	–
Ban on hands-free mobile phone use	–
National drug-driving law	**No**

[b] Speed limit set per vehicle type with a maximum speed limit of 80 km/h for passenger cars (not exceeding 3500 kg)

[c] Legislation requires probable cause to test drivers or commission of a traffic offence

Deaths by road user category

Trends in reported road traffic deaths

Legislative review conducted by WHO. Vehicle safety data from UNECE WP29. Other data collected by questionnaire.

Saint Lucia

Population: 178 015 | Income group: Middle | Gross national income per capita: US$ 7 670

INSTITUTIONAL FRAMEWORK	
Lead agency	Saint Lucia Road Transport Board
Funded in national budget	Yes
National road safety strategy	No
Funding to implement strategy	–
Fatality reduction target	–
SAFER ROADS AND MOBILITY	
Audits or star rating required for new road infrastructure	No
Design standards for the safety of pedestrians / cyclists	Partial
Inspections / star rating of existing roads	No
Investments to upgrade high risk locations	No
Policies & investment in urban public transport	No
SAFER VEHICLES	
Total registered vehicles for 2016	35 681
Cars and 4-wheeled light vehicles	29 790
Motorized 2- and 3-wheelers	215
Heavy trucks	4 310
Buses	1 120
Other	246
Vehicle standards applied (UNECE WP.29)	
Frontal impact standard	No
Electronic stability control	No
Pedestrian protection	No
Motorcycle anti-lock braking system	No
POST-CRASH CARE	
National emergency care access number	National, single number
Trauma registry	–
Formal certification for prehospital providers	Yes
National assessment of emergency care systems	No
DATA	
Reported road traffic fatalities (2016)	15[a] (73% M, 27% F)
WHO estimated road traffic fatalities (2016)	63
WHO estimated rate per 100 000 population (2016)	35.4

[a] Saint Lucia Royal Police Force (Traffic Department). Unlimited time period following crash

SAFER ROAD USERS	
National speed limit law	Yes
Max urban speed limit	~ 24 km/h
Max rural speed limit	~ 24 km/h
Max motorway speed limit	~ 56 km/h
Local authorities can modify limits	No
Enforcement	⓪ 1 2 3 4 5 6 7 8 9 10
Predominant type of enforcement	–
National drink-driving law	Yes
BAC limit – general population	≤ 0.08 g/dl
BAC limit – young or novice drivers	≤ 0.08 g/dl
Random breath testing carried out	No
Testing carried out in case of fatal crash	All drivers tested
Enforcement	⓪ 1 2 3 4 5 6 7 8 9 10
% road traffic deaths involving alcohol	–
National motorcycle helmet law	Yes
Applies to drivers and passengers	Yes
Helmet fastening required	No
Helmet standard referred to and/or specified	Yes
Children passengers on motorcycles	Not restricted
Enforcement	0 1 ② 3 4 5 6 7 8 9 10
Helmet wearing rate	–
National seat-belt law	Yes
Applies to front and rear seat occupants	No
Enforcement	0 1 2 3 4 5 6 ⑦ 8 9 10
Seat-belt wearing rate	–
National child restraint law	No
Children seated in front seat	Not restricted
Child restraint required	–
Child restraint standard referred to and/or specified	–
Enforcement	–
% children using child restraints	–
National law on mobile phone use while driving	Yes
Ban on hand-held mobile phone use	No
Ban on hands-free mobile phone use	No
National drug-driving law	Yes

Deaths by road user category

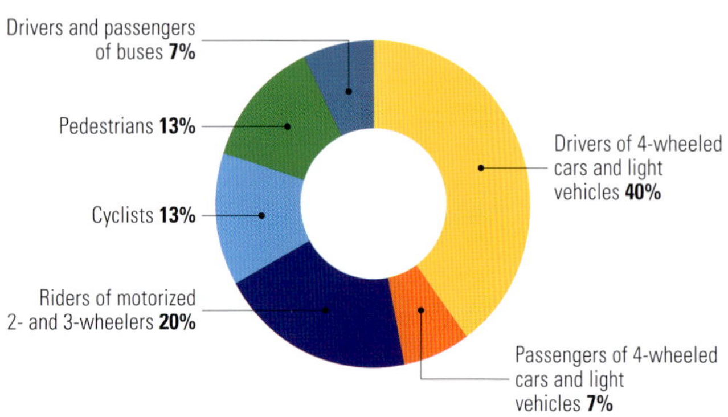

Source: 2016, Saint Lucia Royal Police Force (Traffic Department)

Trends in reported road traffic deaths

Source: Saint Lucia Royal Police Force (Traffic Department)

Legislative review conducted by WHO. Vehicle safety data from UNECE WP29. Other data collected by questionnaire and cleared by Department of Health and Wellness.

Samoa

Population: 195 125 | Income group: Middle | Gross national income per capita: US$ 4 100

INSTITUTIONAL FRAMEWORK	
Lead agency	Ministry of Works, Transport & Infrastructure (MWTI)
Funded in national budget	Yes
National road safety strategy	Yes
Funding to implement strategy	Partially funded
Fatality reduction target	<5 deaths per 10 000 vehicles (2011-2020)

SAFER ROADS AND MOBILITY	
Audits or star rating required for new road infrastructure	Yes
Design standards for the safety of pedestrians / cyclists	Partial
Inspections / star rating of existing roads	Yes
Investments to upgrade high risk locations	Yes
Policies & investment in urban public transport	Yes

SAFER VEHICLES	
Total registered vehicles for 2016	25 235
Cars and 4-wheeled light vehicles	23 557
Motorized 2- and 3-wheelers	95
Heavy trucks	1 184
Buses	326
Other	73
Vehicle standards applied (UNECE WP.29)	
Frontal impact standard	No
Electronic stability control	No
Pedestrian protection	No
Motorcycle anti-lock braking system	No

POST-CRASH CARE	
National emergency care access number	National, multiple numbers
Trauma registry	None
Formal certification for prehospital providers	No
National assessment of emergency care systems	No

DATA	
Reported road traffic fatalities (2015/2016)[a]	17[b] (71% M, 29% F)
WHO estimated road traffic fatalities (2016)	22 (95% CI 20 - 25)
WHO estimated rate per 100 000 population (2016)	11.3

[a] Data collected across fiscal year calendar 2015-2016
[b] Accident Compensation Cooperation (ACC). Unlimited time period following crash

SAFER ROAD USERS	
National speed limit law	Yes
Max urban speed limit	~ 56 km/h
Max rural speed limit	~ 56 km/h
Max motorway speed limit	—[c]
Local authorities can modify limits	No
Enforcement	0 1 2 3 4 5 6 7 8 (9) 10
Predominant type of enforcement	Manual
National drink-driving law	Yes
BAC limit – general population	≤ 0.08 g/dl
BAC limit – young or novice drivers	≤ 0.08 g/dl
Random breath testing carried out	Yes
Testing carried out in case of fatal crash	No
Enforcement	0 1 2 3 4 5 6 7 (8) 9 10
% road traffic deaths involving alcohol	—
National motorcycle helmet law	Yes
Applies to drivers and passengers	Yes
Helmet fastening required	Yes
Helmet standard referred to and/or specified	No
Children passengers on motorcycles	Not restricted
Enforcement	0 1 2 3 4 5 6 7 8 9 (10)
Helmet wearing rate	100% Drivers[d], 100% Passengers[e]
National seat-belt law	Yes
Applies to front and rear seat occupants	No
Enforcement	0 1 2 3 4 5 6 7 8 9 (10)
Seat-belt wearing rate	100% Front seats[f], 100% Rear seats[f]
National child restraint law	No[g]
Children seated in front seat	Not restricted[h]
Child restraint required	—
Child restraint standard referred to and/or specified	—
Enforcement	—
% children using child restraints	—
National law on mobile phone use while driving	Yes
Ban on hand-held mobile phone use	Yes
Ban on hands-free mobile phone use	No
National drug-driving law	Yes

[c] No motorways in the country
[d] 2016, Land Transport Authority Instant Fine Act 2009/Traffic Offence Notice
[e] 2016, Land Transport Authority, Authorized Traffic Officers Report, Traffic Offence Notice
[f] 2016, Traffic Offence Notice
[g] Legislation refers to either child restraint or seat belt to restrain children under 12 years
[h] Except if child restraint or seat belt are available in the front seat

Deaths by road user category

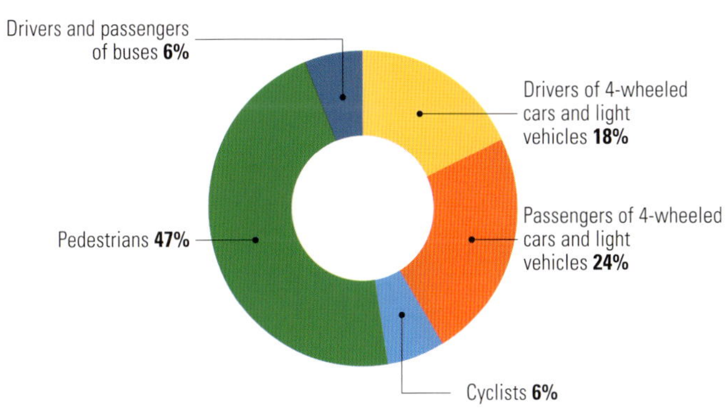

Source: 2015/2016, Accident Compensation Cooperation (ACC)

Trends in reported road traffic deaths

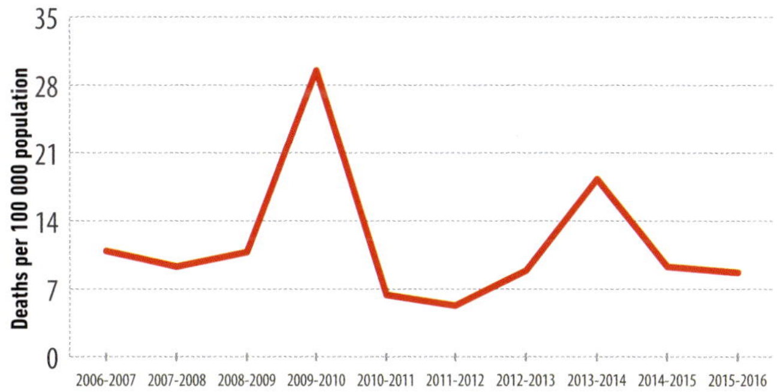

Source: Accident Compensation Cooperation (ACC)

San Marino

Population: 33 203 | Income group: High | Gross national income per capita: US$ 51 810[a]

INSTITUTIONAL FRAMEWORK

Lead agency	Working Group on Road Security
Funded in national budget	No
National road safety strategy	Yes
Funding to implement strategy	Partially funded
Fatality reduction target	–

SAFER ROADS AND MOBILITY

Audits or star rating required for new road infrastructure	Partial
Design standards for the safety of pedestrians / cyclists	Partial
Inspections / star rating of existing roads	No
Investments to upgrade high risk locations	Yes
Policies & investment in urban public transport	Yes

SAFER VEHICLES

Total registered vehicles for 2016	54 956
Cars and 4-wheeled light vehicles	35 369
Motorized 2- and 3-wheelers	13 109
Heavy trucks	548
Buses	76
Other	5 854
Vehicle standards applied (UNECE WP.29)	
Frontal impact standard	Yes
Electronic stability control	Yes
Pedestrian protection	Yes
Motorcycle anti-lock braking system	No

POST-CRASH CARE

National emergency care access number	National, multiple numbers
Trauma registry	None
Formal certification for prehospital providers	Yes
National assessment of emergency care systems	Yes

DATA

Reported road traffic fatalities (2016)	0[b]
WHO estimated road traffic fatalities (2016)	0
WHO estimated rate per 100 000 population (2016)	0

[a] Data available only for 2008
[b] Information Technology, Data and Statistics Office. Died within 30 days of crash

SAFER ROAD USERS

National speed limit law	Yes
Max urban speed limit	70 km/h
Max rural speed limit	70 km/h
Max motorway speed limit	No
Local authorities can modify limits	No
Enforcement	0 1 2 3 4 5 (6) 7 8 9 10
Predominant type of enforcement	Manual and automated
National drink-driving law	Yes
BAC limit – general population	< 0.05 g/dl
BAC limit – young or novice drivers	< 0.05 g/dl
Random breath testing carried out	Yes[c]
Testing carried out in case of fatal crash	All drivers tested
Enforcement	0 1 2 3 4 5 (6) 7 8 9 10
% road traffic deaths involving alcohol	–
National motorcycle helmet law	Yes
Applies to drivers and passengers	Yes
Helmet fastening required	Yes
Helmet standard referred to and/or specified	Yes
Children passengers on motorcycles	Not restricted
Enforcement	0 1 2 3 4 5 6 7 8 9 (10)
Helmet wearing rate	–
National seat-belt law	Yes
Applies to front and rear seat occupants	Yes
Enforcement	0 1 2 3 4 5 6 7 (8) 9 10
Seat-belt wearing rate	–
National child restraint law	Yes
Children seated in front seat	Allowed in a child restraint
Child restraint required	Up to 150 cm
Child restraint standard referred to and/or specified	Yes
Enforcement	0 1 2 3 4 5 6 7 (8) 9 10
% children using child restraints	–
National law on mobile phone use while driving	Yes
Ban on hand-held mobile phone use	Yes
Ban on hands-free mobile phone use	No
National drug-driving law	Yes

[c] Legislation requires probable cause to test drivers

Deaths by road user category

Trends in reported road traffic deaths

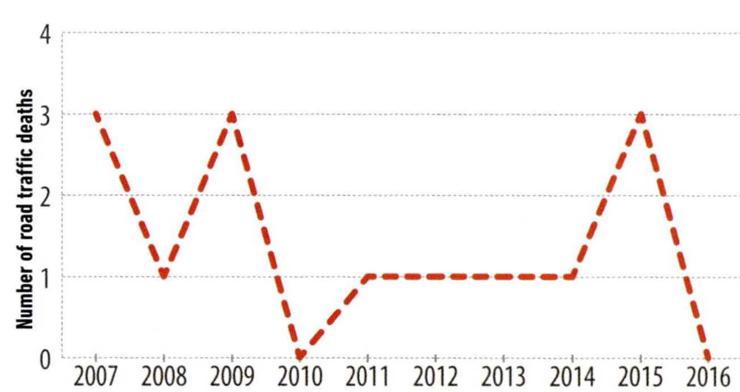

Source: Information Technology, Data and Statistics Office

Sao Tome and Principe

Population: 199 910 | Income group: Middle | Gross national income per capita: US$ 1 730

INSTITUTIONAL FRAMEWORK	
Lead agency	Department of Land Transport, Ministry of Infrastructure, Natural Resources and Environment
Funded in national budget	No
National road safety strategy	No
Funding to implement strategy	–
Fatality reduction target	–

SAFER ROADS AND MOBILITY	
Audits or star rating required for new road infrastructure	No
Design standards for the safety of pedestrians / cyclists	Partial
Inspections / star rating of existing roads	No
Investments to upgrade high risk locations	No
Policies & investment in urban public transport	No

SAFER VEHICLES	
Total registered vehicles for 2017	34 050
Cars and 4-wheeled light vehicles	–
Motorized 2- and 3-wheelers	–
Heavy trucks	–
Buses	–
Other	–
Vehicle standards applied (UNECE WP.29)	
Frontal impact standard	No
Electronic stability control	No
Pedestrian protection	No
Motorcycle anti-lock braking system	No

POST-CRASH CARE	
National emergency care access number	National, single number
Trauma registry	National
Formal certification for prehospital providers	No
National assessment of emergency care systems	No

DATA	
Reported road traffic fatalities (2016)	23 [a]
WHO estimated road traffic fatalities (2016)	55 (95% CI 43 - 68)
WHO estimated rate per 100 000 population (2016)	27.5

[a] Special police transit unit of the national police. Died within 30 days of crash

SAFER ROAD USERS	
National speed limit law	Yes
Max urban speed limit	50 km/h
Max rural speed limit	90 km/h
Max motorway speed limit	120 km/h
Local authorities can modify limits	No
Enforcement	0 1 ② 3 4 5 6 7 8 9 10
Predominant type of enforcement	–
National drink-driving law	Yes
BAC limit – general population	< 0.12 g/dl
BAC limit – young or novice drivers	< 0.12 g/dl
Random breath testing carried out	No
Testing carried out in case of fatal crash	No
Enforcement	0 1 ② 3 4 5 6 7 8 9 10
% road traffic deaths involving alcohol	–
National motorcycle helmet law	Yes
Applies to drivers and passengers	Yes
Helmet fastening required	Yes
Helmet standard referred to and/or specified	Yes
Children passengers on motorcycles	Prohibited under 7 yrs
Enforcement	0 1 2 3 4 5 6 ⑦ 8 9 10
Helmet wearing rate	–
National seat-belt law	Yes
Applies to front and rear seat occupants	No
Enforcement	0 1 ② 3 4 5 6 7 8 9 10
Seat-belt wearing rate	–
National child restraint law	No [b]
Children seated in front seat	Prohibited under 12 yrs/150 cm [c]
Child restraint required	–
Child restraint standard referred to and/or specified	–
Enforcement	–
% children using child restraints	–
National law on mobile phone use while driving	Yes
Ban on hand-held mobile phone use	Yes
Ban on hands-free mobile phone use	No
National drug-driving law	Yes

[b] Legislation refers to either child restraint or seat belt use to transport children
[c] Except if the vehicle does not have rear seats provided and such transportation is made in a child restraint (with airbag deactivated if a rear-facing restraint is being used)

Deaths by road user category

Trends in reported road traffic deaths

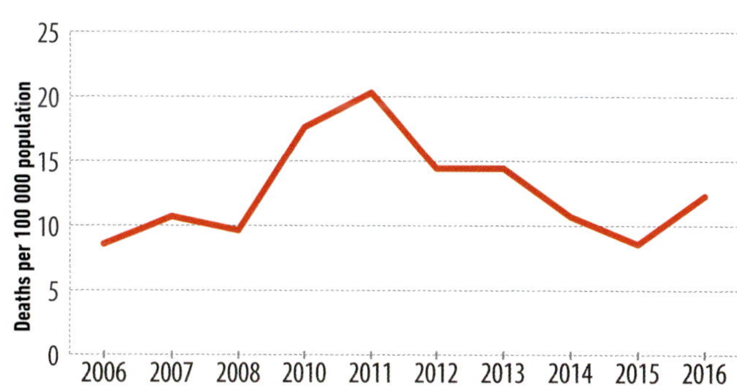

Source: Special Transit Unit of the National Police

Legislative review conducted by WHO. Vehicle safety data from UNECE WP29. Other data collected by questionnaire and cleared by Ministry of Health.

Saudi Arabia

Population: 32 275 688 | Income group: High | Gross national income per capita: US$ 21 750

INSTITUTIONAL FRAMEWORK	
Lead agency	Traffic Department, Ministry of Interior
Funded in national budget	Yes
National road safety strategy	Yes
Funding to implement strategy	Partially funded
Fatality reduction target	–
SAFER ROADS AND MOBILITY	
Audits or star rating required for new road infrastructure	Partial
Design standards for the safety of pedestrians / cyclists	Partial
Inspections / star rating of existing roads	Yes
Investments to upgrade high risk locations	Yes
Policies & investment in urban public transport	Yes
SAFER VEHICLES	
Total registered vehicles for 2016	6 895 799
Cars and 4-wheeled light vehicles	–
Motorized 2- and 3-wheelers	–
Heavy trucks	–
Buses	–
Other	–
Vehicle standards applied (UNECE WP.29)	
Frontal impact standard	No
Electronic stability control	No
Pedestrian protection	No
Motorcycle anti-lock braking system	No
POST-CRASH CARE	
National emergency care access number	National, single number
Trauma registry	Subnational
Formal certification for prehospital providers	Yes
National assessment of emergency care systems	No
DATA	
Reported road traffic fatalities (2016)	9 031 [a] (87% M, 13% F)
WHO estimated road traffic fatalities (2016)	9 311 (95% CI 8 268 - 10 354)
WHO estimated rate per 100 000 population (2016)	28.8

[a] Traffic Department, Annual statistical report. Died within 30 days of crash

SAFER ROAD USERS	
National speed limit law	Yes
Max urban speed limit	80 km/h
Max rural speed limit	120 km/h
Max motorway speed limit	No
Local authorities can modify limits	No
Enforcement	0 1 2 3 4 5 6 (7) 8 9 10
Predominant type of enforcement	Automated
National drink-driving law	Yes [b]
BAC limit – general population	–
BAC limit – young or novice drivers	–
Random breath testing carried out	No
Testing carried out in case of fatal crash	Some drivers tested
Enforcement	0 1 2 3 4 5 6 7 8 (9) 10
% road traffic deaths involving alcohol	–
National motorcycle helmet law	Yes
Applies to drivers and passengers	Yes
Helmet fastening required	Yes
Helmet standard referred to and/or specified	No
Children passengers on motorcycles	Prohibited under 16 yrs
Enforcement	0 1 (2) 3 4 5 6 7 8 9 10
Helmet wearing rate	–
National seat-belt law	Yes
Applies to front and rear seat occupants	Yes
Enforcement	0 1 2 (3) 4 5 6 7 8 9 10
Seat-belt wearing rate	–
National child restraint law	Yes
Children seated in front seat	Prohibited under 10 yrs
Child restraint required	Yes [c]
Child restraint standard referred to and/or specified	No
Enforcement	0 (1) 2 3 4 5 6 7 8 9 10
% children using child restraints	–
National law on mobile phone use while driving	Yes
Ban on hand-held mobile phone use	Yes
Ban on hands-free mobile phone use	No
National drug-driving law	Yes

[b] Not based on BAC. Alcohol consumption legally prohibited
[c] Reference is made to special seats to be used for children with no details as to the specific age/height under which children should be mandatorily placed in them

Deaths by road user category

Trends in reported road traffic deaths

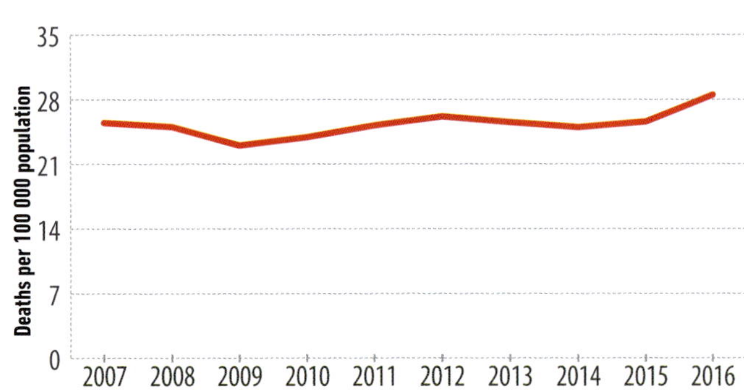

Source: Traffic Department, Annual statistical report

Legislative review conducted by WHO. Vehicle safety data from UNECE WP29. Other data collected by questionnaire and cleared by Ministry of Health

Senegal

Population: 15 411 614 | Income group: Low | Gross national income per capita: US$ 950

INSTITUTIONAL FRAMEWORK	
Lead agency	Directorate of Land Transport
Funded in national budget	Yes
National road safety strategy	Yes
Funding to implement strategy	Partially funded
Fatality reduction target	35% (2011-2020)
SAFER ROADS AND MOBILITY	
Audits or star rating required for new road infrastructure	Yes
Design standards for the safety of pedestrians / cyclists	No
Inspections / star rating of existing roads	Yes
Investments to upgrade high risk locations	No
Policies & investment in urban public transport	Yes
SAFER VEHICLES	
Total registered vehicles for 2015	468 051
Cars and 4-wheeled light vehicles	348 088
Motorized 2- and 3-wheelers	38 879
Heavy trucks	56 631
Buses	17 689
Other	6 764
Vehicle standards applied (UNECE WP.29)	
Frontal impact standard	No
Electronic stability control	No
Pedestrian protection	No
Motorcycle anti-lock braking system	No
POST-CRASH CARE	
National emergency care access number	Partial coverage
Trauma registry	Some facilities
Formal certification for prehospital providers	No
National assessment of emergency care systems	No
DATA	
Reported road traffic fatalities (2016)	604 [a]
WHO estimated road traffic fatalities (2016)	3 609 (95% CI 3 052 - 4 165)
WHO estimated rate per 100 000 population (2016)	23.4

[a] Road Transport Final Report, February 2017. Died within 30 days of crash

SAFER ROAD USERS	
National speed limit law	Yes
Max urban speed limit	No
Max rural speed limit	90 km/h
Max motorway speed limit	110 km/h
Local authorities can modify limits	Yes
Enforcement	0 1 2 3 4 (5) 6 7 8 9 10
Predominant type of enforcement	Manual
National drink-driving law	Yes [b]
BAC limit – general population	–
BAC limit – young or novice drivers	–
Random breath testing carried out	No
Testing carried out in case of fatal crash	No
Enforcement	0 1 2 (3) 4 5 6 7 8 9 10
% road traffic deaths involving alcohol	–
National motorcycle helmet law	Yes
Applies to drivers and passengers	No
Helmet fastening required	No
Helmet standard referred to and/or specified	No
Children passengers on motorcycles	Not restricted
Enforcement	0 1 2 3 4 (5) 6 7 8 9 10
Helmet wearing rate	–
National seat-belt law	Yes
Applies to front and rear seat occupants	No
Enforcement	0 1 2 3 4 5 (6) 7 8 9 10
Seat-belt wearing rate	–
National child restraint law	No
Children seated in front seat	Not restricted
Child restraint required	–
Child restraint standard referred to and/or specified	–
Enforcement	–
% children using child restraints	–
National law on mobile phone use while driving	Yes
Ban on hand-held mobile phone use	Yes
Ban on hands-free mobile phone use	Yes
National drug-driving law	Yes

[b] Not based on BAC

Deaths by road user category

Trends in reported road traffic deaths

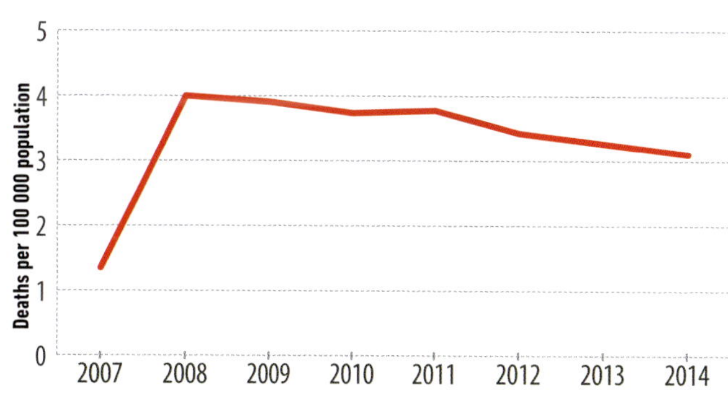

Source: Road Transport Final Report, February 2017

Legislative review conducted by WHO. Vehicle safety data from UNECE WP29. Other data collected by questionnaire and cleared by Ministry of Health and Social Action.

Serbia

Population: 8 820 083 | Income group: Middle | Gross national income per capita: US$ 5 280

INSTITUTIONAL FRAMEWORK	
Lead agency	Coordination Body for Road Traffic Safety
Funded in national budget	Yes
National road safety strategy	Yes
Funding to implement strategy	Partially funded
Fatality reduction target	50% (2011-2020)
SAFER ROADS AND MOBILITY	
Audits or star rating required for new road infrastructure	No
Design standards for the safety of pedestrians / cyclists	Yes
Inspections / star rating of existing roads	No
Investments to upgrade high risk locations	Yes
Policies & investment in urban public transport	Yes
SAFER VEHICLES	
Total registered vehicles for 2016	2 282 401
Cars and 4-wheeled light vehicles	1 908 449
Motorized 2- and 3-wheelers	63 587
Heavy trucks	208 925
Buses	9 709
Other	91 731
Vehicle standards applied (UNECE WP.29)	
Frontal impact standard	No
Electronic stability control	No
Pedestrian protection	No
Motorcycle anti-lock braking system	No
POST-CRASH CARE	
National emergency care access number	National, multiple numbers
Trauma registry	Some facilities
Formal certification for prehospital providers	Yes
National assessment of emergency care systems	Yes
DATA	
Reported road traffic fatalities (2016)	607[a] (82% M, 18% F)
WHO estimated road traffic fatalities (2016)	649
WHO estimated rate per 100 000 population (2016)	7.4

[a] Database of the Ministry of Interior on road traffic accidents. Died within 30 days of crash

SAFER ROAD USERS	
National speed limit law	Yes
Max urban speed limit	50 km/h[b]
Max rural speed limit	100 km/h
Max motorway speed limit	120 km/h
Local authorities can modify limits	Yes
Enforcement	0 1 2 3 4 5 ⑥ 7 8 9 10
Predominant type of enforcement	Manual
National drink-driving law	Yes
BAC limit – general population	≤ 0.03 g/dl
BAC limit – young or novice drivers	0.00 g/dl
Random breath testing carried out	Yes
Testing carried out in case of fatal crash	All drivers tested
Enforcement	0 1 2 3 4 ⑤ 6 7 8 9 10
% road traffic deaths involving alcohol	17%[c]
National motorcycle helmet law	Yes
Applies to drivers and passengers	Yes
Helmet fastening required	Yes
Helmet standard referred to and/or specified	No
Children passengers on motorcycles	Prohibited under 12 yrs
Enforcement	0 1 2 3 4 5 6 7 ⑧ 9 10
Helmet wearing rate	86% Drivers[d], 74-87% Passengers[d]
National seat-belt law	Yes
Applies to front and rear seat occupants	Yes
Enforcement	0 1 2 3 4 5 ⑥ 7 8 9 10
Seat-belt wearing rate	75% Front seats[d], 10% Rear seats[d]
National child restraint law	Yes
Children seated in front seat	Prohibited under 12 yrs[e]
Child restraint required	Up to 3 yrs
Child restraint standard referred to and/or specified	Yes
Enforcement	0 1 2 ③ 4 5 6 7 8 9 10
% children using child restraints	28%[d]
National law on mobile phone use while driving	Yes
Ban on hand-held mobile phone use	Yes
Ban on hands-free mobile phone use	No
National drug-driving law	Yes

[b] Can be increased to 80 km/h
[c] 2016, Database of the Ministry of Interior on road traffic accidents
[d] 2016, Road Traffic Safety Agency of Republic of Serbia (percentages for helmet wearing are for mopeds and motorcycles, respectively)
[e] Except for children under 3 years if airbag is deactivated

Deaths by road user category

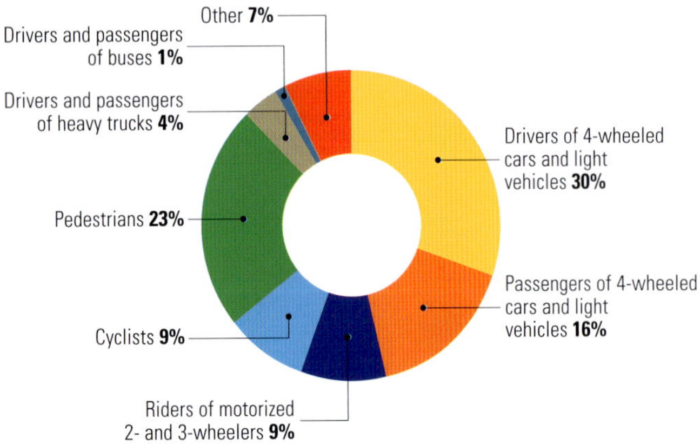

Source: 2016, Database of the Ministry of Interior on road traffic accidents

Trends in reported road traffic deaths

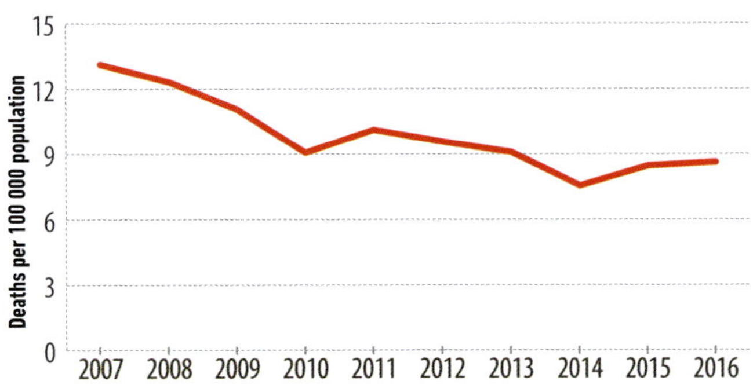

Source: Statistical Office of the Republic of Serbia and Database of the Ministry of Interior on road traffic accidents

Seychelles

Population: 94 228 | Income group: High | Gross national income per capita: US$ 15 410

INSTITUTIONAL FRAMEWORK	
Lead agency	Department of Land Transport
Funded in national budget	Yes
National road safety strategy	Yes
Funding to implement strategy	Partially funded
Fatality reduction target	–
SAFER ROADS AND MOBILITY	
Audits or star rating required for new road infrastructure	Partial
Design standards for the safety of pedestrians / cyclists	Yes
Inspections / star rating of existing roads	Yes
Investments to upgrade high risk locations	Yes
Policies & investment in urban public transport	Yes
SAFER VEHICLES	
Total registered vehicles for 2016	23 076
Cars and 4-wheeled light vehicles	19 469
Motorized 2- and 3-wheelers	799
Heavy trucks	2 211
Buses	597
Other	0
Vehicle standards applied (UNECE WP.29)	
Frontal impact standard	No
Electronic stability control	No
Pedestrian protection	No
Motorcycle anti-lock braking system	No
POST-CRASH CARE	
National emergency care access number	National, single number
Trauma registry	None
Formal certification for prehospital providers	Yes
National assessment of emergency care systems	No
DATA	
Reported road traffic fatalities (2016)	15[a] (87% M, 13% F)
WHO estimated road traffic fatalities (2016)	15
WHO estimated rate per 100 000 population (2016)	15.9

[a] Police and Ministry of Health. Died within 30 days of crash

SAFER ROAD USERS	
National speed limit law	Yes
Max urban speed limit	25-80 km/h[b]
Max rural speed limit	80 km/h[b]
Max motorway speed limit	80 km/h[b]
Local authorities can modify limits	No
Enforcement	0 1 2 3 4 5 ⑥ 7 8 9 10
Predominant type of enforcement	Manual
National drink-driving law	Yes
BAC limit – general population	≤ 0.08 g/dl
BAC limit – young or novice drivers	≤ 0.08 g/dl
Random breath testing carried out	Yes[c]
Testing carried out in case of fatal crash	No
Enforcement	0 1 2 3 4 5 ⑥ 7 8 9 10
% road traffic deaths involving alcohol	–
National motorcycle helmet law	Yes
Applies to drivers and passengers	Yes
Helmet fastening required	No
Helmet standard referred to and/or specified	No[d]
Children passengers on motorcycles	Prohibited under 10 yrs
Enforcement	0 1 2 3 4 5 6 ⑦ 8 9 10
Helmet wearing rate	–
National seat-belt law	Yes
Applies to front and rear seat occupants	Yes
Enforcement	0 1 2 3 4 5 6 ⑦ 8 9 10
Seat-belt wearing rate	–
National child restraint law	Yes[e]
Children seated in front seat	Not restricted
Child restraint required	Yes[f]
Child restraint standard referred to and/or specified	No
Enforcement	0 1 2 3 4 ⑤ 6 7 8 9 10
% children using child restraints	–
National law on mobile phone use while driving	Yes
Ban on hand-held mobile phone use	Yes
Ban on hands-free mobile phone use	No
National drug-driving law	Yes

[b] Speed limits depend on the geographical area considered: the maximum speed limit is 40 km/h on roads in Greater Victoria and 80 km/h on any other roads; the islands of Praslin and La Digue are subject to 65 km/h and 25 km/h, respectively

[c] Legislation requires probable cause to test drivers or commission of a traffic offence

[d] Reference is made to regulations to specify helmet types, in 2017 these regulations were in the process of being developed

[e] The legislation refers to the use of child restraint systems for infant or child passenger but does not refer to a specific age/ height up to which the use of child restraint is mandatory

[f] Obligation not based on age/height or weight

Deaths by road user category

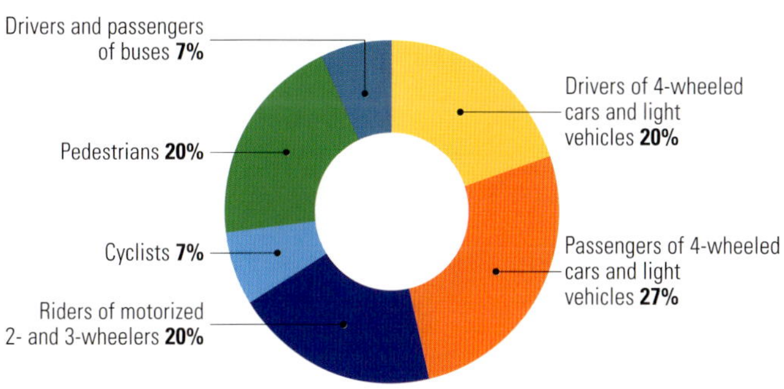

Source: 2016, Police

Trends in reported road traffic deaths

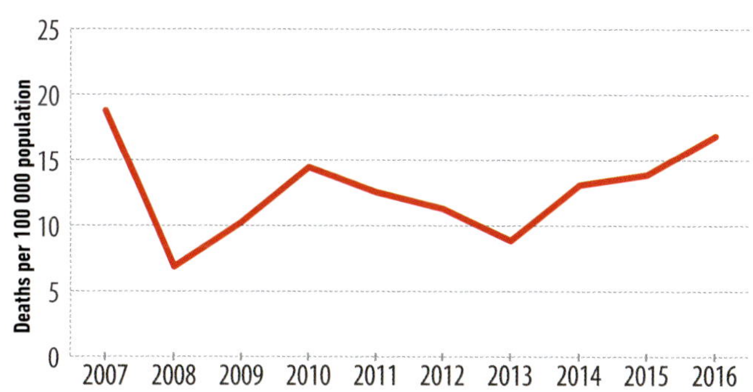

Source: Ministry of Health, National Bureau of Statistics, and Police

Singapore

Population: 5 622 455 | Income group: High | Gross national income per capita: US$ 51 880

INSTITUTIONAL FRAMEWORK	
Lead agency	Traffic Police & Land Transport Authority
Funded in national budget	Yes
National road safety strategy	Yes
Funding to implement strategy	Partially funded
Fatality reduction target	–
SAFER ROADS AND MOBILITY	
Audits or star rating required for new road infrastructure	Yes
Design standards for the safety of pedestrians / cyclists	Yes
Inspections / star rating of existing roads	Yes
Investments to upgrade high risk locations	No
Policies & investment in urban public transport	Yes
SAFER VEHICLES	
Total registered vehicles for 2016	933 534
Cars and 4-wheeled light vehicles	727 533
Motorized 2- and 3-wheelers	142 439
Heavy trucks	45 224
Buses	18 338
Other	0
Vehicle standards applied (UNECE WP.29)	
Frontal impact standard	No
Electronic stability control	No
Pedestrian protection	No
Motorcycle anti-lock braking system	No
POST-CRASH CARE	
National emergency care access number	National, single number
Trauma registry	National
Formal certification for prehospital providers	Yes
National assessment of emergency care systems	No
DATA	
Reported road traffic fatalities (2016)	141[a] (73% M, 27% F)
WHO estimated road traffic fatalities (2016)	155
WHO estimated rate per 100 000 population (2016)	2.8

[a] Singapore Police Force. Died within 30 days of crash

SAFER ROAD USERS	
National speed limit law	Yes
Max urban speed limit	70 km/h[b]
Max rural speed limit	–[c]
Max motorway speed limit	90 km/h
Local authorities can modify limits	No
Enforcement	0 1 2 3 4 5 6 7 (8) 9 10
Predominant type of enforcement	Manual and automated
National drink-driving law	Yes
BAC limit – general population	≤ 0.08 g/dl
BAC limit – young or novice drivers	≤ 0.08 g/dl
Random breath testing carried out	Yes[d]
Testing carried out in case of fatal crash	All drivers tested
Enforcement	0 1 2 3 4 5 6 7 (8) 9 10
% road traffic deaths involving alcohol	6%[e]
National motorcycle helmet law	Yes
Applies to drivers and passengers	Yes
Helmet fastening required	Yes
Helmet standard referred to and/or specified	Yes
Children passengers on motorcycles	Prohibited under 10 yrs
Enforcement	0 1 2 3 4 5 6 7 8 (9) 10
Helmet wearing rate	–
National seat-belt law	Yes
Applies to front and rear seat occupants	Yes
Enforcement	0 1 2 3 4 5 6 7 (8) 9 10
Seat-belt wearing rate	–
National child restraint law	Yes
Children seated in front seat	Allowed in a child restraint
Child restraint required	Up to 135 cm
Child restraint standard referred to and/or specified	Yes
Enforcement	0 1 2 3 4 5 6 7 (8) 9 10
% children using child restraints	–
National law on mobile phone use while driving	Yes
Ban on hand-held mobile phone use	Yes
Ban on hands-free mobile phone use	No
National drug-driving law	Yes

[b] Different speed limits are set in urban areas ranging from 30 km/h to 70km/h
[c] No rural roads in Singapore
[d] Legislation requires probable cause to test drivers or commission of a traffic offence
[e] 2016, Singapore Police Force

Deaths by road user category

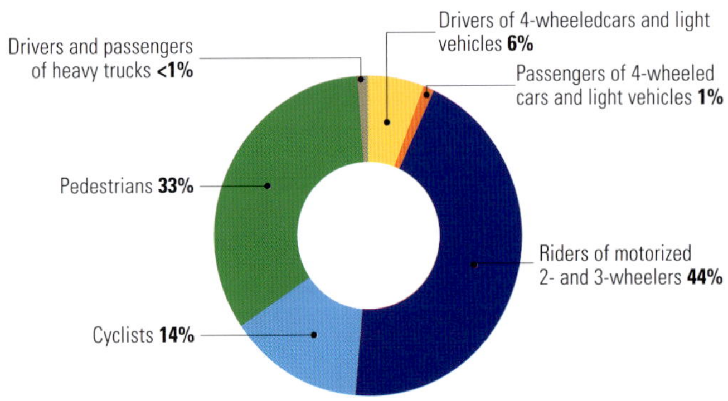

Source: 2016, Singapore Police Force

Trends in reported road traffic deaths

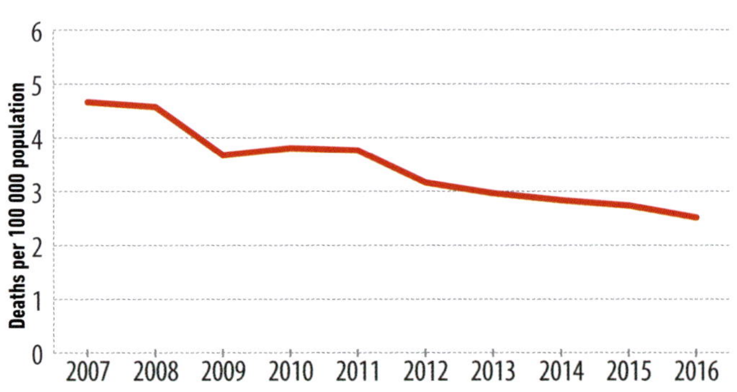

Source: Singapore Police Force

Slovakia

Population: 5 444 218 | Income group: High | Gross national income per capita: US$ 16 810

INSTITUTIONAL FRAMEWORK	
Lead agency	Ministry of transport of the Slovak Republic
Funded in national budget	Yes
National road safety strategy	Yes
Funding to implement strategy	Partially funded
Fatality reduction target	50% (2011-2020)
SAFER ROADS AND MOBILITY	
Audits or star rating required for new road infrastructure	Partial
Design standards for the safety of pedestrians / cyclists	Yes
Inspections / star rating of existing roads	Yes
Investments to upgrade high risk locations	Yes
Policies & investment in urban public transport	Yes
SAFER VEHICLES	
Total registered vehicles for 2016	2 606 412
Cars and 4-wheeled light vehicles	2 388 415
Motorized 2- and 3-wheelers	126 630
Heavy trucks	82 563
Buses	8 804
Other	0
Vehicle standards applied (UNECE WP.29)	
Frontal impact standard	Yes
Electronic stability control	Yes
Pedestrian protection	Yes
Motorcycle anti-lock braking system	Yes
POST-CRASH CARE	
National emergency care access number	National, single number
Trauma registry	None
Formal certification for prehospital providers	Yes
National assessment of emergency care systems	No
DATA	
Reported road traffic fatalities (2016)	275[a] (78% M, 22% F)
WHO estimated road traffic fatalities (2016)	330
WHO estimated rate per 100 000 population (2016)	6.1

[a] Road Accident Database (ISDN). Died within 30 days of crash

SAFER ROAD USERS	
National speed limit law	Yes
Max urban speed limit	50 km/h
Max rural speed limit	90 km/h
Max motorway speed limit	130 km/h
Local authorities can modify limits	No
Enforcement	0 1 2 3 4 5 6 ⑦ 8 9 10
Predominant type of enforcement	Manual
National drink-driving law	Yes[b]
BAC limit – general population	0.00 g/dl[b]
BAC limit – young or novice drivers	0.00 g/dl[b]
Random breath testing carried out	Yes
Testing carried out in case of fatal crash	All drivers tested
Enforcement	0 1 2 3 4 5 6 7 ⑧ 9 10
% road traffic deaths involving alcohol	6%[c]
National motorcycle helmet law	Yes
Applies to drivers and passengers	Yes
Helmet fastening required	Yes
Helmet standard referred to and/or specified	No
Children passengers on motorcycles	Prohibited under 12 yrs
Enforcement	0 1 2 3 4 5 6 7 ⑧ 9 10
Helmet wearing rate	–
National seat-belt law	Yes
Applies to front and rear seat occupants	Yes
Enforcement	0 1 2 3 4 5 6 7 ⑧ 9 10
Seat-belt wearing rate	–
National child restraint law	Yes
Children seated in front seat	Allowed in a child restraint[d]
Child restraint required	Up to 150 cm
Child restraint standard referred to and/or specified	Yes
Enforcement	0 1 2 3 4 5 6 7 ⑧ 9 10
% children using child restraints	–
National law on mobile phone use while driving	Yes
Ban on hand-held mobile phone use	Yes
Ban on hands-free mobile phone use	No
National drug-driving law	Yes

[b] Driving with presence of any alcohol in the body is prohibited
[c] 2016, Road Accident Database (ISDN)
[d] Provided that airbag is deactivated if child is in a rear-facing child restraint system

Deaths by road user category

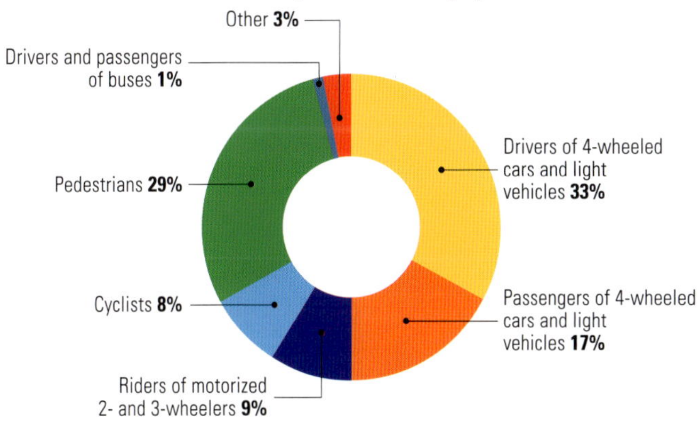

Source: 2016, Road Accident Database (ISDN)

Trends in reported road traffic deaths

Source: Road Accident Database (SEDN) for 2007-2009; Road Accident Database (ISDN) for 2010-2016; and Statistical Bureau of Slovak Republic

Slovenia

Population: 2 077 862 | Income group: High | Gross national income per capita: US$ 21 660

INSTITUTIONAL FRAMEWORK	
Lead agency	Slovenian Traffic Safety Agency
Funded in national budget	Yes
National road safety strategy	Yes
Funding to implement strategy	Partially funded
Fatality reduction target	50% (2013-2022)
SAFER ROADS AND MOBILITY	
Audits or star rating required for new road infrastructure	Partial
Design standards for the safety of pedestrians / cyclists	Yes
Inspections / star rating of existing roads	Yes
Investments to upgrade high risk locations	Yes
Policies & investment in urban public transport	Yes
SAFER VEHICLES	
Total registered vehicles for 2016	1 468 439
Cars and 4-wheeled light vehicles	1 183 476
Motorized 2- and 3-wheelers	97 418
Heavy trucks	31 374
Buses	2 690
Other	153 481
Vehicle standards applied (UNECE WP.29)	
Frontal impact standard	Yes
Electronic stability control	Yes
Pedestrian protection	Yes
Motorcycle anti-lock braking system	Yes
POST-CRASH CARE	
National emergency care access number	National, single number
Trauma registry	National
Formal certification for prehospital providers	Yes
National assessment of emergency care systems	No
DATA	
Reported road traffic fatalities (2016)	130[a] (78% M, 22% F)
WHO estimated road traffic fatalities (2016)	134
WHO estimated rate per 100 000 population (2016)	6.4

[a] Police records. Died within 30 days of crash

SAFER ROAD USERS	
National speed limit law	Yes
Max urban speed limit	50 km/h[b]
Max rural speed limit	90 km/h
Max motorway speed limit	130 km/h
Local authorities can modify limits	No
Enforcement	0 1 2 3 4 5 6 (7) 8 9 10
Predominant type of enforcement	Manual
National drink-driving law	Yes
BAC limit – general population	≤ 0.05 g/dl
BAC limit – young or novice drivers	0.00 g/dl
Random breath testing carried out	Yes
Testing carried out in case of fatal crash	All drivers tested
Enforcement	0 1 2 3 4 5 6 (7) 8 9 10
% road traffic deaths involving alcohol	32%[c]
National motorcycle helmet law	Yes
Applies to drivers and passengers	Yes
Helmet fastening required	Yes
Helmet standard referred to and/or specified	Yes
Children passengers on motorcycles	Prohibited under 12 yrs[d]
Enforcement	0 1 2 3 4 5 6 7 (8) 9 10
Helmet wearing rate	–
National seat-belt law	Yes
Applies to front and rear seat occupants	Yes
Enforcement	0 1 2 3 4 5 6 7 8 (9) 10
Seat-belt wearing rate	92% Front seats[e], 69% Rear seats[e]
National child restraint law	Yes
Children seated in front seat	Allowed in a child restraint[f]
Child restraint required	Up to 150 cm
Child restraint standard referred to and/or specified	No
Enforcement	0 1 2 3 4 5 6 7 8 (9) 10
% children using child restraints	–
National law on mobile phone use while driving	Yes
Ban on hand-held mobile phone use	Yes
Ban on hands-free mobile phone use	No
National drug-driving law	Yes

[b] Can be increased up to 70 km/h
[c] 2016, Police records
[d] Only children older than 12 years are allowed to ride as passengers on motorcycles
[e] 2016, Slovenian Traffic Safety Agency
[f] Provided that airbag is deactivated if child is in a rear-facing child restraint system

Deaths by road user category

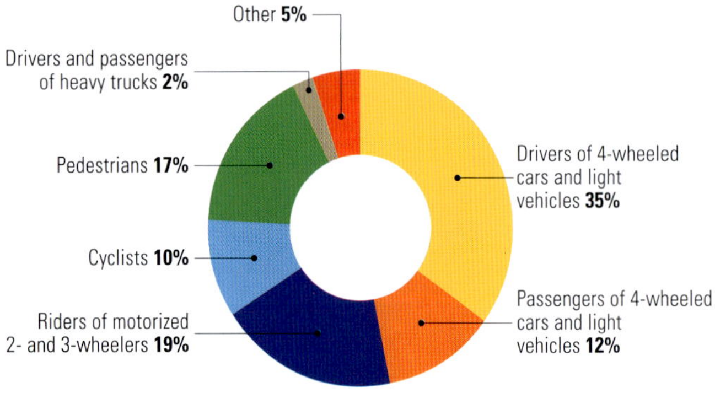

Source: 2016, Police database

Trends in reported road traffic deaths

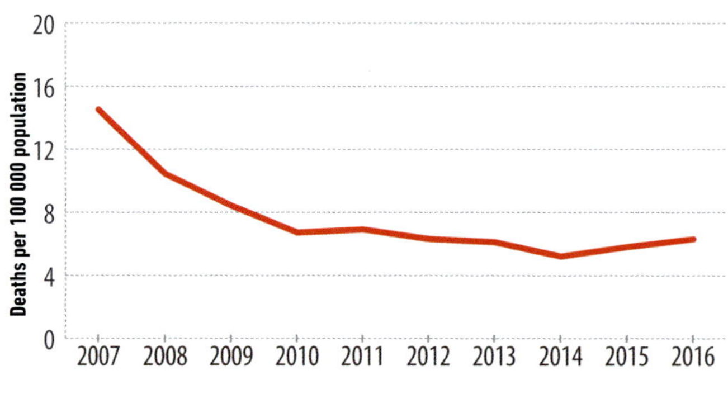

Source: Slovenian Traffic Safety Agency

Legislative review conducted by WHO. Vehicle safety data from UNECE WP29. Other data collected by questionnaire and cleared by Slovenian Traffic Safety Agency.

Solomon Islands

Population: 599 419 | Income group: Middle | Gross national income per capita: US$ 1 880

INSTITUTIONAL FRAMEWORK

Lead agency	Traffic Unit, Ministry of Infrastructure and Development and Ministry of Police & Correctional Services
Funded in national budget	Yes
National road safety strategy	No
Funding to implement strategy	–
Fatality reduction target	–

SAFER ROADS AND MOBILITY

Audits or star rating required for new road infrastructure	Yes
Design standards for the safety of pedestrians / cyclists	Yes
Inspections / star rating of existing roads	Yes
Investments to upgrade high risk locations	No
Policies & investment in urban public transport	Yes

SAFER VEHICLES

Total registered vehicles	–
Cars and 4-wheeled light vehicles	–
Motorized 2- and 3-wheelers	–
Heavy trucks	–
Buses	–
Other	–
Vehicle standards applied (UNECE WP.29)	
Frontal impact standard	No
Electronic stability control	No
Pedestrian protection	No
Motorcycle anti-lock braking system	No

POST-CRASH CARE

National emergency care access number	National, single number
Trauma registry	Some facilities
Formal certification for prehospital providers	No
National assessment of emergency care systems	No

DATA

Reported road traffic fatalities (2016)	11 [a]
WHO estimated road traffic fatalities (2016)	104 (95% CI 94 - 115)
WHO estimated rate per 100 000 population (2016)	17.4

[a] Honiara Traffic Statistics 2016 Report. Died within 24 hours of crash

SAFER ROAD USERS

National speed limit law	Yes [b]
Max urban speed limit	–
Max rural speed limit	–
Max motorway speed limit	–
Local authorities can modify limits	Yes
Enforcement	0 1 2 3 4 (5) 6 7 8 9 10
Predominant type of enforcement	Manual
National drink-driving law	Yes
BAC limit – general population	< 0.05 g/dl
BAC limit – young or novice drivers	< 0.05 g/dl
Random breath testing carried out	Yes
Testing carried out in case of fatal crash	Some drivers tested
Enforcement	0 1 2 3 4 5 6 (7) 8 9 10
% road traffic deaths involving alcohol	–
National motorcycle helmet law	Yes
Applies to drivers and passengers	Yes
Helmet fastening required	Yes
Helmet standard referred to and/or specified	Yes
Children passengers on motorcycles	Not restricted
Enforcement	0 1 2 3 4 5 (6) 7 8 9 10
Helmet wearing rate	–
National seat-belt law	No
Applies to front and rear seat occupants	–
Enforcement	–
Seat-belt wearing rate	–
National child restraint law	No
Children seated in front seat	Not restricted
Child restraint required	–
Child restraint standard referred to and/or specified	–
Enforcement	–
% children using child restraints	–
National law on mobile phone use while driving	No
Ban on hand-held mobile phone use	–
Ban on hands-free mobile phone use	–
National drug-driving law	Yes

[b] Speed limits are established locally per vehicle type and/or per road names or areas

Deaths by road user category

Trends in reported road traffic deaths

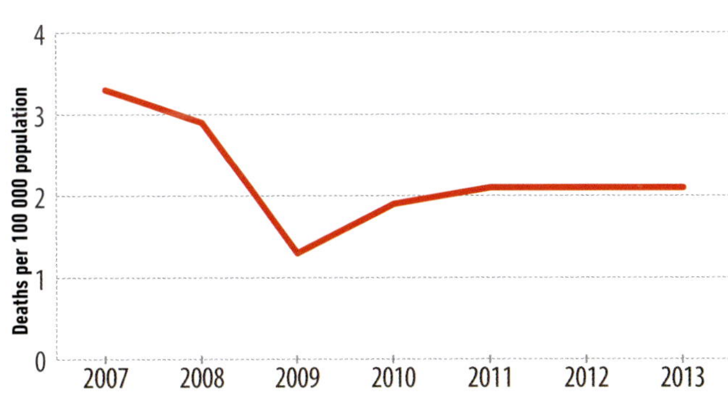

Source: Kukum Traffic Police

Legislative review conducted by WHO. Vehicle safety data from UNECE WP.29. Other data collected by questionnaire and cleared by Police Force.

Somalia[a]

Population: 14 317 996 | Income group: Low | Gross national income per capita: US$ –

[a] The data published herein refers roughly to the following administrative subdivisions of Somalia: Awdal, Marodi Jeeh, Sanaagh, Sool, Togdheer and Woqooyi Galbeed

INSTITUTIONAL FRAMEWORK

Lead agency	**Road Safety Management, Ministry of Public Works, Housing and Transport**
Funded in national budget	Yes
National road safety strategy	**Yes**
Funding to implement strategy	Not funded
Fatality reduction target	–

SAFER ROADS AND MOBILITY

Audits or star rating required for new road infrastructure	No
Design standards for the safety of pedestrians / cyclists	No
Inspections / star rating of existing roads	–
Investments to upgrade high risk locations	No
Policies & investment in urban public transport	No

SAFER VEHICLES

Total registered vehicles for 2014	**59 457**
Cars and 4-wheeled light vehicles	56 000
Motorized 2- and 3-wheelers	760
Heavy trucks	–
Buses	–
Other	2 697
Vehicle standards applied (UNECE WP.29)	
Frontal impact standard	No
Electronic stability control	No
Pedestrian protection	No
Motorcycle anti-lock braking system	No

POST-CRASH CARE

National emergency care access number	None
Trauma registry	None
Formal certification for prehospital providers	No
National assessment of emergency care systems	No

DATA

Reported road traffic fatalities (2016)	165[b]
WHO estimated road traffic fatalities (2016)	3 884 (95% CI 3 023 - 4 745)
WHO estimated rate per 100 000 population (2016)	27.1

[b] Traffic Police. Died at scene of crash

SAFER ROAD USERS

National speed limit law	**Yes**
Max urban speed limit	40 km/h
Max rural speed limit	No
Max motorway speed limit	No
Local authorities can modify limits	Yes
Enforcement	0 ① 2 3 4 5 6 7 8 9 10
Predominant type of enforcement	–
National drink-driving law	**Yes[c]**
BAC limit – general population	–
BAC limit – young or novice drivers	–
Random breath testing carried out	No
Testing carried out in case of fatal crash	No
Enforcement	0 ① 2 3 4 5 6 7 8 9 10
% road traffic deaths involving alcohol	–
National motorcycle helmet law	**No**
Applies to drivers and passengers	–
Helmet fastening required	–
Helmet standard referred to and/or specified	–
Children passengers on motorcycles	Not restricted
Enforcement	–
Helmet wearing rate	–
National seat-belt law	**No**
Applies to front and rear seat occupants	–
Enforcement	–
Seat-belt wearing rate	–
National child restraint law	**No**
Children seated in front seat	Not restricted
Child restraint required	–
Child restraint standard referred to and/or specified	–
Enforcement	–
% children using child restraints	–
National law on mobile phone use while driving	**No**
Ban on hand-held mobile phone use	–
Ban on hands-free mobile phone use	–
National drug-driving law	**Yes**

[c] Not based on BAC. Alcohol consumption legally prohibited

Deaths by road user category

Trends in reported road traffic deaths

Source: Traffic Police

Legislative review conducted by WHO. Vehicle safety data from UNECE WP.29. Other data collected by questionnaire and cleared by Ministry of Health.

South Africa

Population: 56 015 472 | Income group: Middle | Gross national income per capita: US$ 5 480

INSTITUTIONAL FRAMEWORK	
Lead agency	Road Traffic Management Corporation (RTMC), Department of Transport
Funded in national budget	Yes
National road safety strategy	Yes
Funding to implement strategy	Partially funded
Fatality reduction target	50% (2010-2020)
SAFER ROADS AND MOBILITY	
Audits or star rating required for new road infrastructure	Partial
Design standards for the safety of pedestrians / cyclists	Partial
Inspections / star rating of existing roads	Yes
Investments to upgrade high risk locations	Yes
Policies & investment in urban public transport	Yes
SAFER VEHICLES	
Total registered vehicles	–
Cars and 4-wheeled light vehicles	–
Motorized 2- and 3-wheelers	–
Heavy trucks	–
Buses	–
Other	–
Vehicle standards applied (UNECE WP.29)	
Frontal impact standard	No
Electronic stability control	Yes
Pedestrian protection	Yes
Motorcycle anti-lock braking system	No
POST-CRASH CARE	
National emergency care access number	National, multiple numbers
Trauma registry	National
Formal certification for prehospital providers	Yes
National assessment of emergency care systems	No
DATA	
Reported road traffic fatalities (2016)	14 071 [a] (77% M, 23% F)
WHO estimated road traffic fatalities (2016)	14 507
WHO estimated rate per 100 000 population (2016)	25.9

[a] Road Traffic Management Corporation (RTMC), Traffic calendar report 2016. Died within 30 days of crash

SAFER ROAD USERS	
National speed limit law	Yes
Max urban speed limit	60 km/h
Max rural speed limit	100 km/h
Max motorway speed limit	120 km/h
Local authorities can modify limits	Yes
Enforcement	0 1 2 3 4 5 (6) 7 8 9 10
Predominant type of enforcement	Manual and automated
National drink-driving law	Yes
BAC limit – general population	< 0.05 g/dl
BAC limit – young or novice drivers	< 0.05 g/dl
Random breath testing carried out	Yes
Testing carried out in case of fatal crash	Some drivers tested
Enforcement	0 1 2 3 4 (5) 6 7 8 9 10
% road traffic deaths involving alcohol	58% [b]
National motorcycle helmet law	Yes
Applies to drivers and passengers	Yes
Helmet fastening required	Yes
Helmet standard referred to and/or specified	No
Children passengers on motorcycles	Not restricted
Enforcement	0 1 2 3 4 5 6 7 (8) 9 10
Helmet wearing rate	–
National seat-belt law	Yes
Applies to front and rear seat occupants	Yes
Enforcement	0 1 2 3 4 (5) 6 7 8 9 10
Seat-belt wearing rate	33% Drivers [c], 31% Front seats [c]
National child restraint law	Yes
Children seated in front seat	Not restricted [d]
Child restraint required	Up to 3 yrs
Child restraint standard referred to and/or specified	Yes
Enforcement	0 1 2 3 4 (5) 6 7 8 9 10
% children using child restraints	–
National law on mobile phone use while driving	Yes
Ban on hand-held mobile phone use	Yes
Ban on hands-free mobile phone use	No
National drug-driving law	Yes

[b] 2010, National Injury Mortality Surveillance System (NIMSS)
[c] 2010, Road Traffic Management Corporation (RTMC) Traffic Offence Survey 2010
[d] Obligation to place children in the rear only applies in vehicles not fitted with seat belts and having rear seats

Deaths by road user category

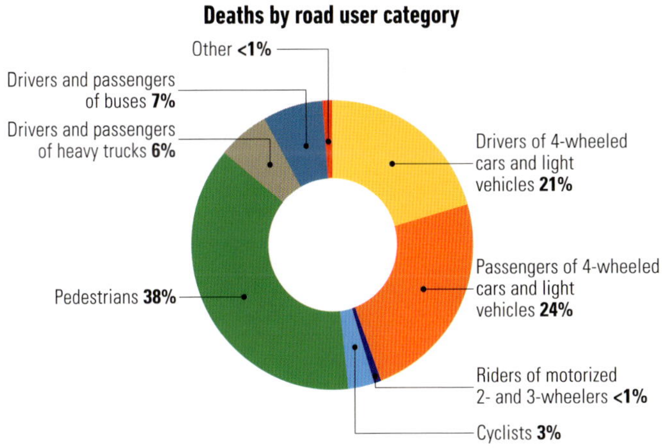

Source: 2016, Road Traffic Management Corporation (RTMC), Traffic calendar report 2016

Trends in reported road traffic deaths

Source: Road Traffic Management Corporation (RTMC), Traffic calendar report 2016

Legislative review conducted by WHO. Vehicle safety data from UNECE WP.29. Other data collected by questionnaire and cleared by Road Traffic Management Corporation.

South Sudan

Population: 12 230 730 | Income group: Low | Gross national income per capita: US$ 820[a]

INSTITUTIONAL FRAMEWORK	
Lead agency	Traffic Police, Ministry of Interior
Funded in national budget	Yes
National road safety strategy	No
Funding to implement strategy	–
Fatality reduction target	–
SAFER ROADS AND MOBILITY	
Audits or star rating required for new road infrastructure	No
Design standards for the safety of pedestrians / cyclists	Partial
Inspections / star rating of existing roads	Yes
Investments to upgrade high risk locations	No
Policies & investment in urban public transport	No
SAFER VEHICLES	
Total registered vehicles for 2012-2016	69 647
Cars and 4-wheeled light vehicles	32 070
Motorized 2- and 3-wheelers	27 250
Heavy trucks	4 830
Buses	5 497
Other	0
Vehicle standards applied (UNECE WP.29)	
Frontal impact standard	No
Electronic stability control	No
Pedestrian protection	No
Motorcycle anti-lock braking system	No
POST-CRASH CARE	
National emergency care access number	National, single number
Trauma registry	Some facilities
Formal certification for prehospital providers	No
National assessment of emergency care systems	No
DATA	
Reported road traffic fatalities (2016)	130[b] (53% M, 47% F)
WHO estimated road traffic fatalities (2016)	3 661 (95% CI 2 976 - 4 346)
WHO estimated rate per 100 000 population (2016)	29.9

[a] Data available only for 2015
[b] Juba Teaching Hospital. Unlimited time period following crash

SAFER ROAD USERS	
National speed limit law	Yes
Max urban speed limit	50 km/h
Max rural speed limit	No
Max motorway speed limit	No
Local authorities can modify limits	No
Enforcement	0 1 2 (3) 4 5 6 7 8 9 10
Predominant type of enforcement	Manual
National drink-driving law	Yes[c]
BAC limit – general population	–
BAC limit – young or novice drivers	–
Random breath testing carried out	No
Testing carried out in case of fatal crash	No
Enforcement	(0) 1 2 3 4 5 6 7 8 9 10
% road traffic deaths involving alcohol	–
National motorcycle helmet law	No
Applies to drivers and passengers	–
Helmet fastening required	–
Helmet standard referred to and/or specified	–
Children passengers on motorcycles	Not restricted
Enforcement	–
Helmet wearing rate	–
National seat-belt law	No
Applies to front and rear seat occupants	–
Enforcement	–
Seat-belt wearing rate	–
National child restraint law	No
Children seated in front seat	Not restricted
Child restraint required	–
Child restraint standard referred to and/or specified	–
Enforcement	–
% children using child restraints	–
National law on mobile phone use while driving	No
Ban on hand-held mobile phone use	–
Ban on hands-free mobile phone use	–
National drug-driving law	Yes

[c] Not based on BAC

Deaths by road user category

Trends in reported road traffic deaths

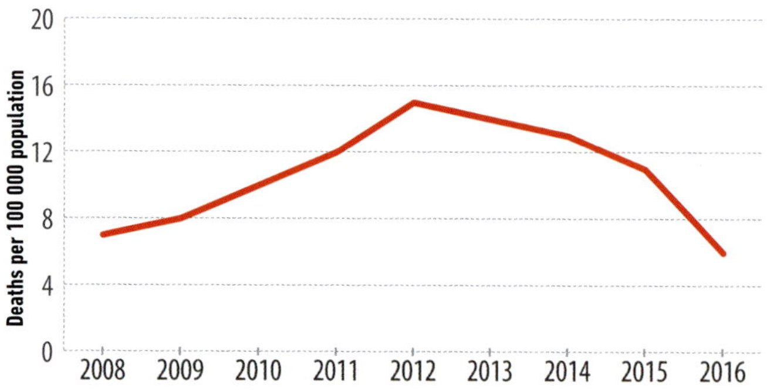

Source: Traffic Police, Statistical yearbook for Southern Sudan 2010 and Population Projection 2015

Spain

Population: 46 347 576 | Income group: High | Gross national income per capita: US$ 27 520

INSTITUTIONAL FRAMEWORK

Lead agency	**Directorate General for Traffic, Ministry of Internal Administration**
Funded in national budget	Yes
National road safety strategy	**Yes**
Funding to implement strategy	Fully funded
Fatality reduction target	<3.7 deaths per 100 000 population (2011-2020)

SAFER ROADS AND MOBILITY

Audits or star rating required for new road infrastructure	Yes
Design standards for the safety of pedestrians / cyclists	Yes
Inspections / star rating of existing roads	Yes
Investments to upgrade high risk locations	Yes
Policies & investment in urban public transport	Yes

SAFER VEHICLES

Total registered vehicles for 2015	**32 986 384**
Cars and 4-wheeled light vehicles	26 876 165
Motorized 2- and 3-wheelers	5 102 674
Heavy trucks	526 559
Buses	60 252
Other	420 734
Vehicle standards applied (UNECE WP.29)	
Frontal impact standard	Yes
Electronic stability control	Yes
Pedestrian protection	Yes
Motorcycle anti-lock braking system	Yes

POST-CRASH CARE

National emergency care access number	National, single number
Trauma registry	Some facilities
Formal certification for prehospital providers	Yes
National assessment of emergency care systems	No

DATA

Reported road traffic fatalities (2016)	1 810[a] (77% M, 23% F)
WHO estimated road traffic fatalities (2016)	1 922
WHO estimated rate per 100 000 population (2016)	4.1

[a] Directorate General of Traffic. Died within 30 days of crash

SAFER ROAD USERS

National speed limit law	**Yes**
Max urban speed limit	50 km/h
Max rural speed limit	90 km/h
Max motorway speed limit	120 km/h
Local authorities can modify limits	Yes[b]
Enforcement	0 1 2 3 4 5 6 7 **8** 9 10
Predominant type of enforcement	Manual and automated
National drink-driving law	**Yes**
BAC limit – general population	≤ 0.05 g/dl
BAC limit – young or novice drivers	≤ 0.03 g/dl
Random breath testing carried out	Yes
Testing carried out in case of fatal crash	Some drivers tested
Enforcement	0 1 2 3 4 5 6 **7** 8 9 10
% road traffic deaths involving alcohol	17% Males, 7% Females[c]
National motorcycle helmet law	**Yes**
Applies to drivers and passengers	Yes
Helmet fastening required	No
Helmet standard referred to and/or specified	Yes
Children passengers on motorcycles	Prohibited under 7/12 yrs[d]
Enforcement	0 1 2 3 4 5 6 7 **8** 9 10
Helmet wearing rate	99% Drivers[e], 93% Passengers[e]
National seat-belt law	**Yes**
Applies to front and rear seat occupants	Yes
Enforcement	0 1 2 3 4 5 6 7 **8** 9 10
Seat-belt wearing rate	91% Front seats[e], 81% Rear seats[e]
National child restraint law	**Yes**
Children seated in front seat	Prohibited under 135 cm[f]
Child restraint required	Up to 135 cm
Child restraint standard referred to and/or specified	Yes
Enforcement	0 1 2 3 4 5 6 7 **8** 9 10
% children using child restraints	88%[g]
National law on mobile phone use while driving	**Yes**
Ban on hand-held mobile phone use	Yes
Ban on hands-free mobile phone use	No
National drug-driving law	**Yes**

[b] Road authorities can decrease speed limits on both urban and rural roads. Speed limits can only be increased on urban highways

[c] 2012, Global Status Report on Alcohol and Health 2014, WHO (percentages for females and males, respectively)

[d] In principle, children under 12 years are not allowed to ride as passenger on motorcycles, by exception the minimum age is lowered to 7 years when the driver is one of the parents, or a person authorized by them

[e] 2012, Directorate General of Traffic

[f] Front seating for children under 135 cm is only allowed as an exception if there are no seats in the back or all other seats are occupied by children

[g] 2012, Directorate General of Traffic.

Deaths by road user category

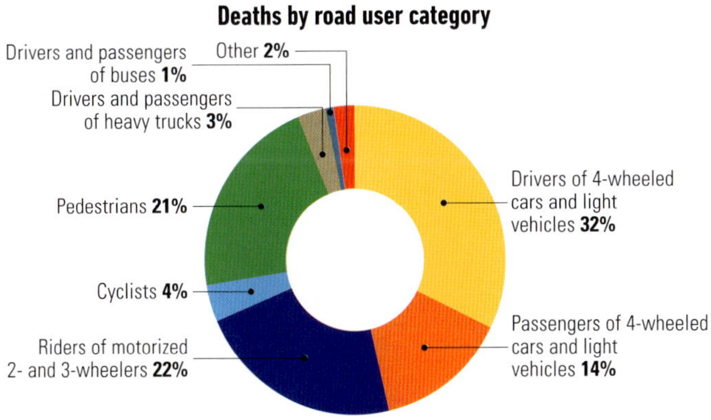

Source: 2015, Directorate General of Traffic

Trends in reported road traffic deaths

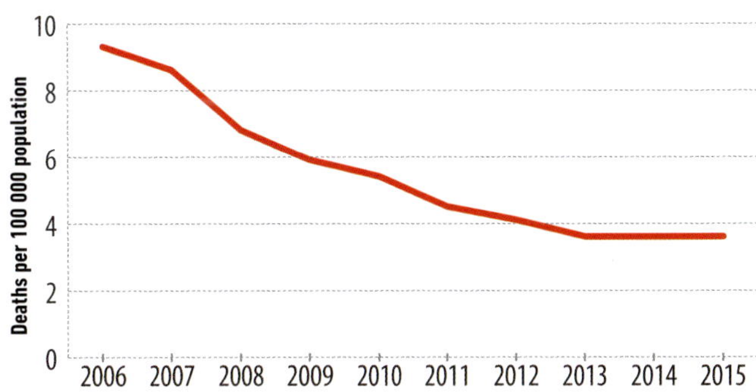

Source: Directorate General of Traffic

Legislative review conducted by WHO. Vehicle safety data from UNECE WP.29. Other data collected by questionnaire and cleared by Ministry of Health, Social Services and Equality.

Sri Lanka

Population: 20 798 492 | Income group: Middle | Gross national income per capita: US$ 3 780

INSTITUTIONAL FRAMEWORK	
Lead agency	National Council for Road Safety (NCRS), Ministry of Transport and Civil Aviation
Funded in national budget	No
National road safety strategy	Yes
Funding to implement strategy	Partially funded
Fatality reduction target	50% (2011-2020)
SAFER ROADS AND MOBILITY	
Audits or star rating required for new road infrastructure	Partial
Design standards for the safety of pedestrians / cyclists	Partial
Inspections / star rating of existing roads	No
Investments to upgrade high risk locations	Yes
Policies & investment in urban public transport	No
SAFER VEHICLES	
Total registered vehicles for 2016	6 795 469
Cars and 4-wheeled light vehicles	717 674
Motorized 2- and 3-wheelers	4 815 617
Heavy trucks	762 912
Buses	104 104
Other	395 162
Vehicle standards applied (UNECE WP.29)	
Frontal impact standard	No
Electronic stability control	No
Pedestrian protection	No
Motorcycle anti-lock braking system	No
POST-CRASH CARE	
National emergency care access number	Partial coverage
Trauma registry	Some facilities
Formal certification for prehospital providers	No
National assessment of emergency care systems	No
DATA	
Reported road traffic fatalities (2016)	3 003[a] (86% M, 14% F)
WHO estimated road traffic fatalities (2016)	3 096 (95% CI 2 777 - 3 415)
WHO estimated rate per 100 000 population (2016)	14.9

[a] Sri Lanka Police, Micro Accident Analysis System (MAAP). Died within 30 days of crash

SAFER ROAD USERS	
National speed limit law	Yes
Max urban speed limit	50 km/h
Max rural speed limit	70 km/h
Max motorway speed limit	100 km/h
Local authorities can modify limits	No
Enforcement	0 1 2 3 4 5 6 7 8 (9) 10
Predominant type of enforcement	Manual
National drink-driving law	Yes
BAC limit – general population	< 0.08 g/dl
BAC limit – young or novice drivers	< 0.08 g/dl
Random breath testing carried out	No
Testing carried out in case of fatal crash	Some drivers tested
Enforcement	0 1 2 3 4 5 6 7 8 (9) 10
% road traffic deaths involving alcohol	–
National motorcycle helmet law	Yes
Applies to drivers and passengers	Yes
Helmet fastening required	No
Helmet standard referred to and/or specified	Yes
Children passengers on motorcycles	Not restricted
Enforcement	0 1 2 3 4 5 6 7 8 (9) 10
Helmet wearing rate	95% All riders[b]
National seat-belt law	Yes
Applies to front and rear seat occupants	No
Enforcement	0 1 2 3 4 5 6 7 (8) 9 10
Seat-belt wearing rate	75% Front seats[b], 75% Rear seats[b]
National child restraint law	No
Children seated in front seat	Not restricted
Child restraint required	–
Child restraint standard referred to and/or specified	–
Enforcement	–
% children using child restraints	–
National law on mobile phone use while driving	Yes
Ban on hand-held mobile phone use	Yes
Ban on hands-free mobile phone use	No
National drug-driving law	Yes

[b] 2016, Sri Lanka Police, Micro Accident Analysis System (MAAP)

Deaths by road user category

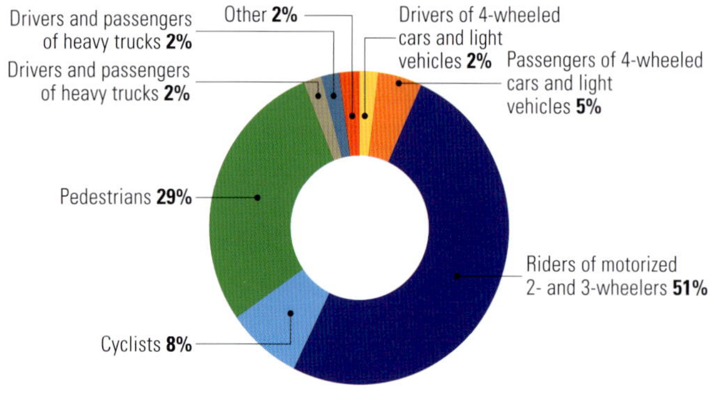

Source: 2016, Sri Lanka Police, Micro Accident Analysis System (MAAP)

Trends in reported road traffic deaths

Source: Sri Lanka Police

Legislative review conducted by WHO. Vehicle safety data from UNECE WP29. Other data collected by questionnaire and cleared by Ministry of Transport and Civil Aviation.

Sudan

Population: 39 578 828 | Income group: Middle | Gross national income per capita: US$ 2 140

INSTITUTIONAL FRAMEWORK	
Lead agency	Road Safety Coordination Council
Funded in national budget	No
National road safety strategy	Yes
Funding to implement strategy	Partially funded
Fatality reduction target	20% (2017-2020)
SAFER ROADS AND MOBILITY	
Audits or star rating required for new road infrastructure	Yes
Design standards for the safety of pedestrians / cyclists	Partial
Inspections / star rating of existing roads	Yes
Investments to upgrade high risk locations	No
Policies & investment in urban public transport	Yes
SAFER VEHICLES	
Total registered vehicles for 2016	1 252 740 [a]
Cars and 4-wheeled light vehicles	935 132
Motorized 2- and 3-wheelers	149 778
Heavy trucks	86 430
Buses	81 400
Other	–
Vehicle standards applied (UNECE WP.29)	
Frontal impact standard	No
Electronic stability control	No
Pedestrian protection	No
Motorcycle anti-lock braking system	No
POST-CRASH CARE	
National emergency care access number	National, multiple numbers
Trauma registry	Subnational
Formal certification for prehospital providers	No
National assessment of emergency care systems	No
DATA	
Reported road traffic fatalities (2016)	2 311 [b] (77% M, 23% F)
WHO estimated road traffic fatalities (2016)	10 178 (95% CI 8 635 - 11 722)
WHO estimated rate per 100 000 population (2016)	25.7

[a] Data includes police, army and national security vehicles, which are not reflected in official records
[b] Traffic police, Annual report for road traffic crashes 2016. Died within 7 days of crash

SAFER ROAD USERS	
National speed limit law	Yes
Max urban speed limit	50 km/h
Max rural speed limit	90 km/h
Max motorway speed limit	No
Local authorities can modify limits	Yes
Enforcement	0 1 2 3 4 5 (6) 7 8 9 10
Predominant type of enforcement	Manual and automated
National drink-driving law	Yes [c]
BAC limit – general population	–
BAC limit – young or novice drivers	–
Random breath testing carried out	Yes
Testing carried out in case of fatal crash	All drivers tested
Enforcement	0 1 2 3 4 5 6 (7) 8 9 10
% road traffic deaths involving alcohol	<1% [d]
National motorcycle helmet law	Yes
Applies to drivers and passengers	Yes
Helmet fastening required	No
Helmet standard referred to and/or specified	No
Children passengers on motorcycles	Not restricted
Enforcement	0 1 2 (3) 4 5 6 7 8 9 10
Helmet wearing rate	–
National seat-belt law	Yes
Applies to front and rear seat occupants	No
Enforcement	0 1 2 3 4 (5) 6 7 8 9 10
Seat-belt wearing rate	–
National child restraint law	No
Children seated in front seat	Prohibited under 10 yrs
Child restraint required	–
Child restraint standard referred to and/or specified	–
Enforcement	–
% children using child restraints	–
National law on mobile phone use while driving	Yes
Ban on hand-held mobile phone use	Yes
Ban on hands-free mobile phone use	Yes
National drug-driving law	Yes

[c] Not based on BAC
[d] 2016, Traffic police, Annual report for road traffic crashes 2016

Deaths by road user category

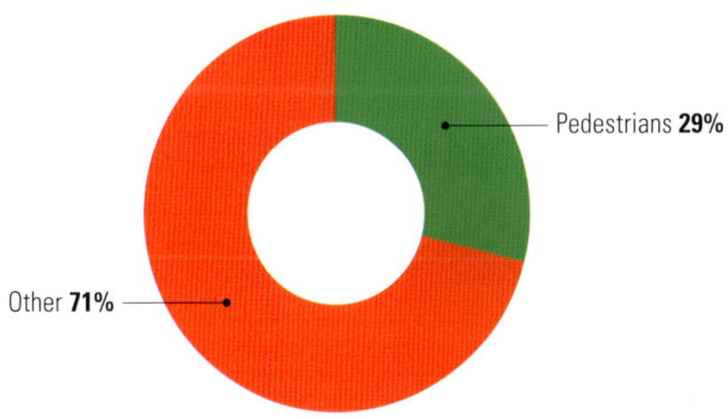

Source: 2016, Traffic police, Annual report for road traffic crashes

Trends in reported road traffic deaths

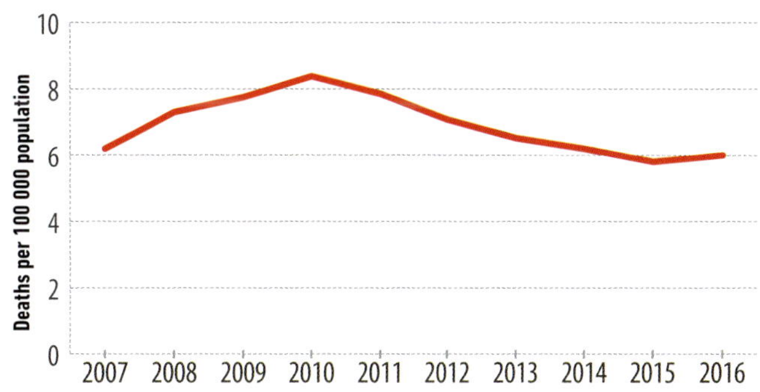

Source: Traffic police, Annual report for road traffic crashes 2013/2016

Legislative review conducted by WHO. Vehicle safety data from UNECE WP.29. Other data collected by questionnaire and cleared by Federal Ministry of Health.

Suriname

Population: 558 368 | Income group: Middle | Gross national income per capita: US$ 7 070

INSTITUTIONAL FRAMEWORK	
Lead agency	**No**
Funded in national budget	–
National road safety strategy	**No**
Funding to implement strategy	–
Fatality reduction target	–
SAFER ROADS AND MOBILITY	
Audits or star rating required for new road infrastructure	No
Design standards for the safety of pedestrians / cyclists	Partial
Inspections / star rating of existing roads	No
Investments to upgrade high risk locations	No
Policies & investment in urban public transport	Yes
SAFER VEHICLES	
Total registered vehicles for 2015	**228 388**
Cars and 4-wheeled light vehicles	146 110
Motorized 2- and 3-wheelers	43 256
Heavy trucks	34 434
Buses	3 608
Other	980
Vehicle standards applied (UNECE WP.29)	
Frontal impact standard	No
Electronic stability control	No
Pedestrian protection	No
Motorcycle anti-lock braking system	No
POST-CRASH CARE	
National emergency care access number	Partial coverage
Trauma registry	Some facilities
Formal certification for prehospital providers	No
National assessment of emergency care systems	No
DATA	
Reported road traffic fatalities (2016)	74[a] (84% M, 16% F)
WHO estimated road traffic fatalities (2016)	81
WHO estimated rate per 100 000 population (2016)	14.5

[a] Combined sources: Traffic Police, Ministry of Justice and Police, and Emergency Medical Department Academic Hospital Paramaribo. Died within 30 days of crash

SAFER ROAD USERS	
National speed limit law	**Yes**
Max urban speed limit	40 km/h
Max rural speed limit	80 km/h
Max motorway speed limit	80 km/h
Local authorities can modify limits	No
Enforcement	0 1 2 3 4 ⑤ 6 7 8 9 10
Predominant type of enforcement	Manual
National drink-driving law	**Yes**
BAC limit – general population	≤ 0.05 g/dl
BAC limit – young or novice drivers	≤ 0.05 g/dl
Random breath testing carried out	Yes
Testing carried out in case of fatal crash	Some drivers tested
Enforcement	0 1 2 3 4 ⑤ 6 7 8 9 10
% road traffic deaths involving alcohol	–
National motorcycle helmet law	**Yes**
Applies to drivers and passengers	Yes
Helmet fastening required	Yes
Helmet standard referred to and/or specified	Yes
Children passengers on motorcycles	Not restricted
Enforcement	0 1 2 3 4 5 6 ⑦ 8 9 10
Helmet wearing rate	95% Drivers[b], 92% Passengers[b]
National seat-belt law	**Yes**
Applies to front and rear seat occupants	Yes
Enforcement	0 1 2 3 4 5 6 ⑦ 8 9 10
Seat-belt wearing rate	75% Front seats[b], 8% Rear seats[b]
National child restraint law	**Yes[c]**
Children seated in front seat	Allowed in a child restraint
Child restraint required	–[c]
Child restraint standard referred to and/or specified	No
Enforcement	0 1 2 3 ④ 5 6 7 8 9 10
% children using child restraints	–
National law on mobile phone use while driving	**Yes**
Ban on hand-held mobile phone use	Yes
Ban on hands-free mobile phone use	No
National drug-driving law	**Yes**

[b] 2016, Traffic Police Suriname, Ministry of Justice and Police
[c] For children under 10 years, the legislation refers to the use of child restraint system (CRS) where available and appropriate, and specifies that in the absence of child restraint, seat belts are to be used

Deaths by road user category

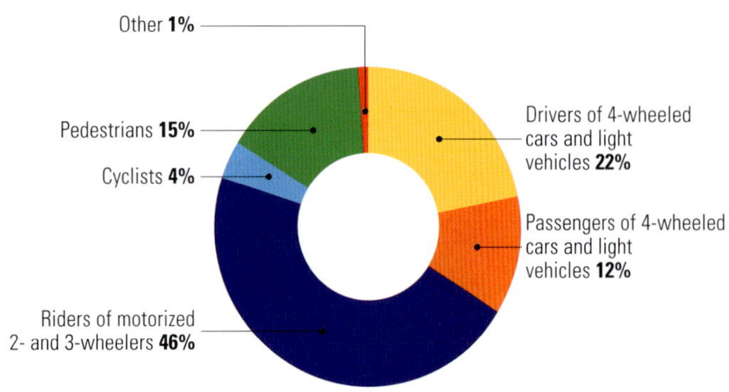

Source: 2016, Traffic Police, Ministry of Justice and Police

Trends in reported road traffic deaths

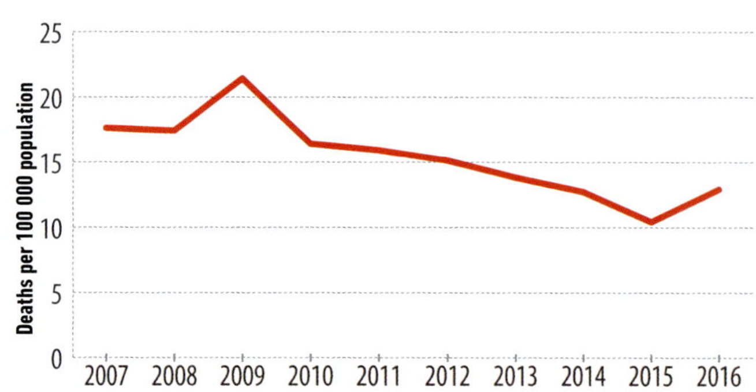

Source: Traffic Police, Ministry of Justice and Police, and General Bureau of Statistics

Sweden

Population: 9 837 533 | Income group: High | Gross national income per capita: US$ 54 630

INSTITUTIONAL FRAMEWORK

Lead agency	Swedish Transport Administration, Ministry of Enterprise and Innovation
Funded in national budget	Yes
National road safety strategy	Yes
Funding to implement strategy	Partially funded
Fatality reduction target	50% (2007-2020)

SAFER ROADS AND MOBILITY

Audits or star rating required for new road infrastructure	Partial
Design standards for the safety of pedestrians / cyclists	Yes
Inspections / star rating of existing roads	Yes
Investments to upgrade high risk locations	Yes
Policies & investment in urban public transport	Yes

SAFER VEHICLES

Total registered vehicles for 2016	6 102 914
Cars and 4-wheeled light vehicles	5 302 808
Motorized 2- and 3-wheelers	375 188
Heavy trucks	81 430
Buses	13 890
Other	329 598
Vehicle standards applied (UNECE WP.29)	
Frontal impact standard	Yes
Electronic stability control	Yes
Pedestrian protection	Yes
Motorcycle anti-lock braking system	Yes

POST-CRASH CARE

National emergency care access number	National, single number
Trauma registry	National
Formal certification for prehospital providers	No
National assessment of emergency care systems	No

DATA

Reported road traffic fatalities (2016)	270[a] (76% M, 24% F)
WHO estimated road traffic fatalities (2016)	278
WHO estimated rate per 100 000 population (2016)	2.8

[a] Official statistics (Swedish Transport Analysis). Died within 30 days of crash

SAFER ROAD USERS

National speed limit law	Yes
Max urban speed limit	50 km/h
Max rural speed limit	110 km/h
Max motorway speed limit	120 km/h
Local authorities can modify limits	Yes
Enforcement	0 1 2 3 4 5 6 7 (8) 9 10
Predominant type of enforcement	Automated
National drink-driving law	Yes
BAC limit – general population	< 0.02 g/dl
BAC limit – young or novice drivers	< 0.02 g/dl
Random breath testing carried out	Yes
Testing carried out in case of fatal crash	All drivers tested
Enforcement	0 1 2 3 4 5 (6) 7 8 9 10
% road traffic deaths involving alcohol	24%[b]
National motorcycle helmet law	Yes
Applies to drivers and passengers	Yes
Helmet fastening required	Yes
Helmet standard referred to and/or specified	Yes
Children passengers on motorcycles	Not restricted
Enforcement	0 1 2 3 4 5 6 7 (8) 9 10
Helmet wearing rate	97-99% All Riders[c]
National seat-belt law	Yes
Applies to front and rear seat occupants	Yes
Enforcement	0 1 2 3 4 5 (6) 7 8 9 10
Seat-belt wearing rate	96% Front seats[d], 90% Rear seats[d]
National child restraint law	Yes
Children seated in front seat	Allowed in a child restraint[e]
Child restraint required	Up to 135 cm
Child restraint standard referred to and/or specified	Yes
Enforcement	0 1 2 3 4 5 (6) 7 8 9 10
% children using child restraints	96%[f]
National law on mobile phone use while driving	Yes
Ban on hand-held mobile phone use	No
Ban on hands-free mobile phone use	No
National drug-driving law	Yes

[b] 2016, In-depth studies of fatal crashes, Swedish Transport Administration
[c] 2016, Travel survey (VTI)
[d] 2016, Swedish Transport Administration, Analysis of road safety development 2016
[e] Provided that airbag is deactivated if child is in a rear-facing child restraint system
[f] 2013, The Sweden National Road and Transport Research Institute (VTI), The use of seat belts in Sweden 2013.

Deaths by road user category

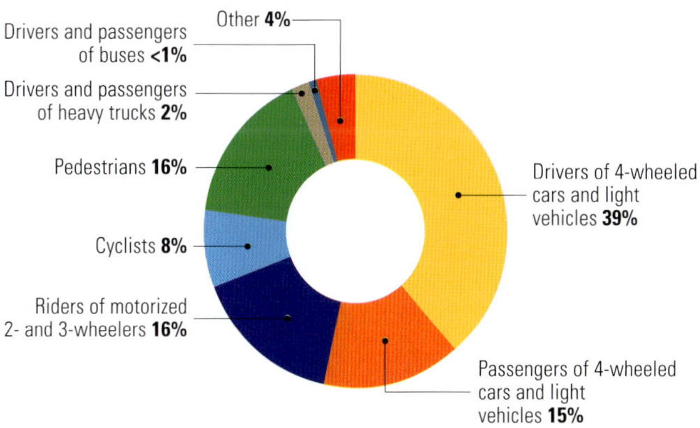

Source: 2016, STRADA (Swedish Traffic Accident Data Acquisition), Swedish Transport Agency

Trends in reported road traffic deaths

Source: Official statistics (Swedish Transport Analysis)

Legislative review conducted by WHO. Vehicle safety data from UNECE WP29. Other data collected by questionnaire and cleared by Swedish Transport Administration.

Switzerland

Population: 8 401 739 | Income group: High | Gross national income per capita: US$ 81 240

INSTITUTIONAL FRAMEWORK	
Lead agency	Federal Roads Office (FEDRO)
Funded in national budget	Yes
National road safety strategy	No
Funding to implement strategy	–
Fatality reduction target	–

SAFER ROADS AND MOBILITY	
Audits or star rating required for new road infrastructure	Partial
Design standards for the safety of pedestrians / cyclists	No
Inspections / star rating of existing roads	Yes
Investments to upgrade high risk locations	Yes
Policies & investment in urban public transport	Yes

SAFER VEHICLES	
Total registered vehicles for 2016	5 980 512
Cars and 4-wheeled light vehicles	4 927 655
Motorized 2- and 3-wheelers	720 381
Heavy trucks	53 094
Buses	14 742
Other	264 640
Vehicle standards applied (UNECE WP.29)	
Frontal impact standard	Yes
Electronic stability control	Yes
Pedestrian protection	Yes
Motorcycle anti-lock braking system	Yes

POST-CRASH CARE	
National emergency care access number	National, single number
Trauma registry	National
Formal certification for prehospital providers	No
National assessment of emergency care systems	No

DATA	
Reported road traffic fatalities (2016)	216[a] (70% M, 30% F)
WHO estimated road traffic fatalities (2016)	223
WHO estimated rate per 100 000 population (2016)	2.7

[a] Federal Roads Office. Died within 30 days of crash

SAFER ROAD USERS	
National speed limit law	Yes
Max urban speed limit	50 km/h
Max rural speed limit	80 km/h
Max motorway speed limit	120 km/h
Local authorities can modify limits	No
Enforcement	0 1 2 3 4 5 6 (7) 8 9 10
Predominant type of enforcement	–
National drink-driving law	Yes
BAC limit – general population	< 0.05 g/dl
BAC limit – young or novice drivers	< 0.01 g/dl
Random breath testing carried out	Yes
Testing carried out in case of fatal crash	Some drivers tested
Enforcement	0 1 2 3 4 5 (6) 7 8 9 10
% road traffic deaths involving alcohol	13%[b]
National motorcycle helmet law	Yes
Applies to drivers and passengers	Yes
Helmet fastening required	No
Helmet standard referred to and/or specified	Yes
Children passengers on motorcycles	Not restricted
Enforcement	0 1 2 3 4 5 6 7 8 (9) 10
Helmet wearing rate	100% Drivers[c]
National seat-belt law	Yes
Applies to front and rear seat occupants	Yes
Enforcement	0 1 2 3 4 5 6 7 (8) 9 10
Seat-belt wearing rate	94% Front seats[c], 86% Rear seats[c]
National child restraint law	Yes
Children seated in front seat	Allowed in a child restraint
Child restraint required	Up to 12 yrs/150 cm[d]
Child restraint standard referred to and/or specified	Yes
Enforcement	0 1 2 3 4 5 6 (7) 8 9 10
% children using child restraints	93%[e]
National law on mobile phone use while driving	Yes
Ban on hand-held mobile phone use	Yes
Ban on hands-free mobile phone use	No
National drug-driving law	Yes

[b] 2016, Federal Roads Office
[c] 2016, Swiss Council for Accident Prevention (BFU)
[d] Children under 12 years and less than 150 cm shall be placed in a child restraint
[e] 2012, Swiss Council for Accident Prevention (BFU)

Deaths by road user category

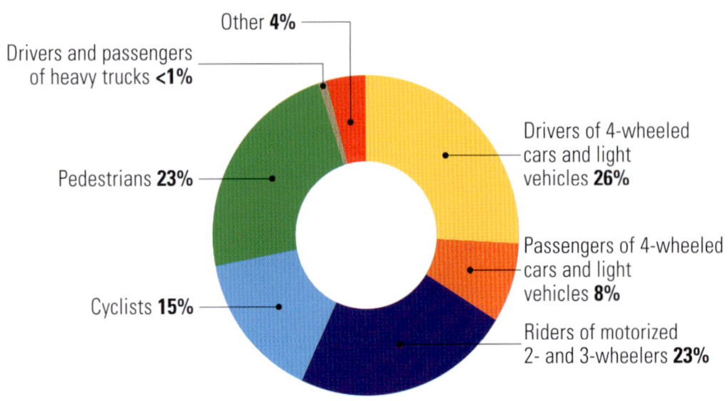

Source: 2016, Federal Roads Office

Trends in reported road traffic deaths

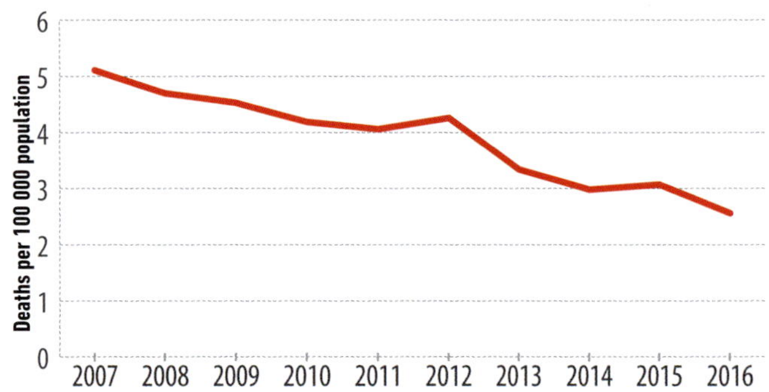

Source: Swiss Federal Statistical Office

Legislative review conducted by WHO. Vehicle safety data from UNECE WP29. Other data collected by questionnaire and cleared by Federal Department of the Environment, Transport, Energy and Communications

Syrian Arab Republic

Population: 18 430 452 | Income group: Middle | Gross national income per capita: US$ 1 840[a]

INSTITUTIONAL FRAMEWORK	
Lead agency	National Committee for Road Safety
Funded in national budget	No
National road safety strategy	Yes
Funding to implement strategy	Partially funded
Fatality reduction target	–
SAFER ROADS AND MOBILITY	
Audits or star rating required for new road infrastructure	Partial
Design standards for the safety of pedestrians / cyclists	Partial
Inspections / star rating of existing roads	Yes
Investments to upgrade high risk locations	Yes
Policies & investment in urban public transport	Yes
SAFER VEHICLES	
Total registered vehicles for 2016	2 396 544
Cars and 4-wheeled light vehicles	1 811 359
Motorized 2- and 3-wheelers	466 205
Heavy trucks	41 647
Buses	77 333
Other	0
Vehicle standards applied (UNECE WP.29)	
Frontal impact standard	No
Electronic stability control	No
Pedestrian protection	No
Motorcycle anti-lock braking system	No
POST-CRASH CARE	
National emergency care access number	Partial coverage
Trauma registry	Subnational
Formal certification for prehospital providers	Yes
National assessment of emergency care systems	No
DATA	
Reported road traffic fatalities (2016)	714[b] (86% M, 14% F)
WHO estimated road traffic fatalities (2016)	4 890 (95% CI 4 009 - 5 772)
WHO estimated rate per 100 000 population (2016)	26.5

[a] Data available only for 2007
[b] Ministry of Interior, Traffic Department. Died within 30 days of crash

SAFER ROAD USERS	
National speed limit law	Yes
Max urban speed limit	–
Max rural speed limit	–
Max motorway speed limit	–
Local authorities can modify limits	Yes
Enforcement	0 1 2 3 4 (5) 6 7 8 9 10
Predominant type of enforcement	Manual and automated
National drink-driving law	Yes[c]
BAC limit – general population	–
BAC limit – young or novice drivers	–
Random breath testing carried out	Yes
Testing carried out in case of fatal crash	Some drivers tested
Enforcement	0 1 2 3 4 5 6 (7) 8 9 10
% road traffic deaths involving alcohol	–
National motorcycle helmet law	Yes
Applies to drivers and passengers	No
Helmet fastening required	No
Helmet standard referred to and/or specified	No
Children passengers on motorcycles	Not restricted
Enforcement	0 1 2 3 4 5 6 (7) 8 9 10
Helmet wearing rate	–
National seat-belt law	Yes
Applies to front and rear seat occupants	No
Enforcement	0 1 2 3 4 5 6 (7) 8 9 10
Seat-belt wearing rate	90% Drivers[d], 90% Front seats[d]
National child restraint law	No
Children seated in front seat	Prohibited under 12 yrs
Child restraint required	–
Child restraint standard referred to and/or specified	–
Enforcement	–
% children using child restraints	–
National law on mobile phone use while driving	Yes
Ban on hand-held mobile phone use	Yes
Ban on hands-free mobile phone use	Yes
National drug-driving law	No

[c] The law refers to regulations to set BAC limit, regulations not available
[d] 2016, Ministry of Interior, Traffic Department

Deaths by road user category

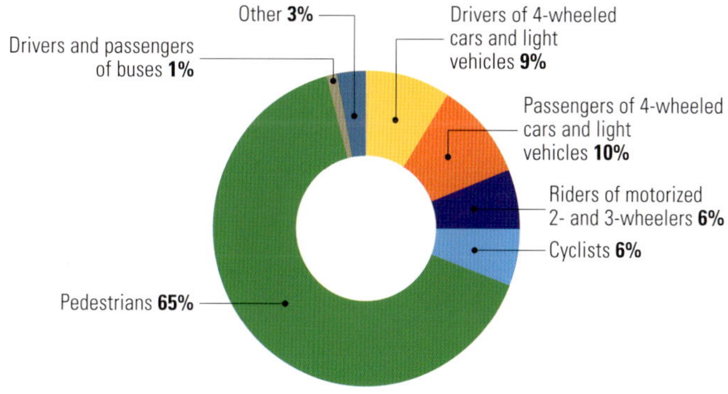

Source: 2016, Ministry of Interior, Traffic Department

Trends in reported road traffic deaths

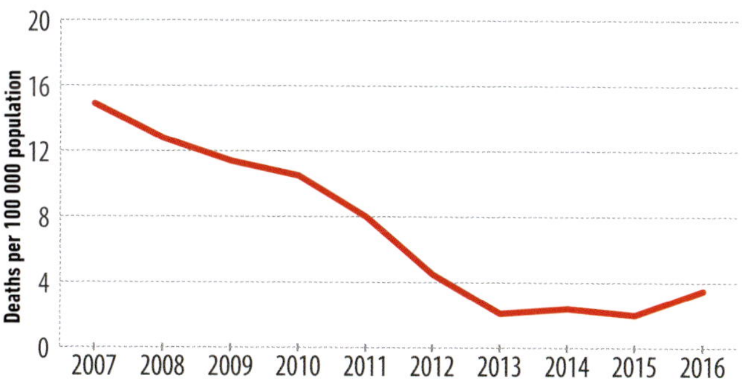

Source: Ministry of Interior, Traffic Department

Legislative review conducted by WHO. Vehicle safety data from UNECE WP.29. Other data collected by questionnaire and cleared by Ministry of Health.

Tajikistan

Population: 8 734 951 | Income group: Middle | Gross national income per capita: US$ 1 110

INSTITUTIONAL FRAMEWORK

Lead agency	Department of the State Automobile Inspection, Ministry of Internal Affairs
Funded in national budget	Yes
National road safety strategy	Yes
Funding to implement strategy	Partially funded
Fatality reduction target	–

SAFER ROADS AND MOBILITY

Audits or star rating required for new road infrastructure	Yes
Design standards for the safety of pedestrians / cyclists	Partial
Inspections / star rating of existing roads	Yes
Investments to upgrade high risk locations	Yes
Policies & investment in urban public transport	Yes

SAFER VEHICLES

Total registered vehicles for 2016	439 972
Cars and 4-wheeled light vehicles	380 496
Motorized 2- and 3-wheelers	4 546
Heavy trucks	39 261
Buses	15 669
Other	0
Vehicle standards applied (UNECE WP.29)	
Frontal impact standard	No
Electronic stability control	No
Pedestrian protection	No
Motorcycle anti-lock braking system	No

POST-CRASH CARE

National emergency care access number	National, single number
Trauma registry	National
Formal certification for prehospital providers	Yes
National assessment of emergency care systems	No

DATA

Reported road traffic fatalities (2016)	427[a] (72% M, 28% F)
WHO estimated road traffic fatalities (2016)	1 577 (95% CI 1 449 - 1 704)
WHO estimated rate per 100 000 population (2016)	18.1

[a] Department of the State Automobile Inspection, Ministry of Internal Affairs. Died within 7 days of crash

SAFER ROAD USERS

National speed limit law	Yes
Max urban speed limit	60 km/h
Max rural speed limit	90 km/h
Max motorway speed limit	110 km/h
Local authorities can modify limits	No
Enforcement	0 1 2 3 4 5 6 7 8 (9) 10
Predominant type of enforcement	Manual
National drink-driving law	Yes[b]
BAC limit – general population	–[b]
BAC limit – young or novice drivers	–[b]
Random breath testing carried out	Yes
Testing carried out in case of fatal crash	All drivers tested
Enforcement	0 1 2 3 4 5 6 7 8 (9) 10
% road traffic deaths involving alcohol	4%[c]
National motorcycle helmet law	Yes
Applies to drivers and passengers	Yes
Helmet fastening required	Yes
Helmet standard referred to and/or specified	No
Children passengers on motorcycles	Prohibited under 12 yrs
Enforcement	0 1 2 3 4 5 (6) 7 8 9 10
Helmet wearing rate	–
National seat-belt law	Yes
Applies to front and rear seat occupants	No
Enforcement	0 1 2 (3) 4 5 6 7 8 9 10
Seat-belt wearing rate	–
National child restraint law	No
Children seated in front seat	Allowed in a child restraint[d]
Child restraint required	–[e]
Child restraint standard referred to and/or specified	–
Enforcement	–
% children using child restraints	–
National law on mobile phone use while driving	Yes
Ban on hand-held mobile phone use	Yes
Ban on hands-free mobile phone use	No
National drug-driving law	Yes

[b] Not based on BAC
[c] 2016, Department of the State Automobile Inspection, Ministry of Internal Affairs.
[d] Front seating of children under 12 years allowed if a child restraint is being used
[e] Legislation refers to child restraints or "other means" to secure children under 12 years but allows the transport of children under 12 years on the knees of an adult passenger seated in the back with the seat belt fastened

Deaths by road user category

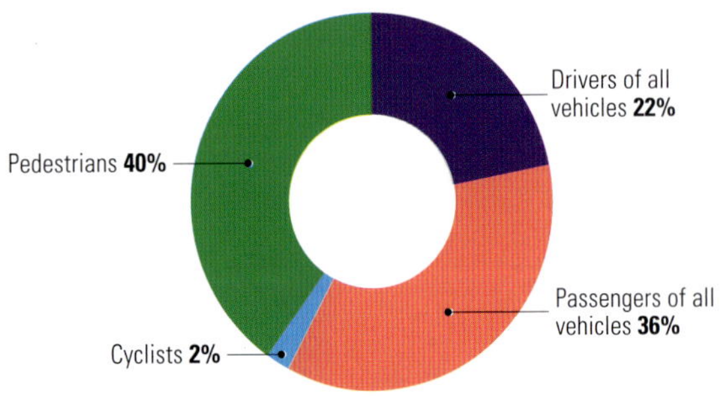

Source: 2016, Department of the State Automobile Inspection, Ministry of Internal Affairs

Trends in reported road traffic deaths

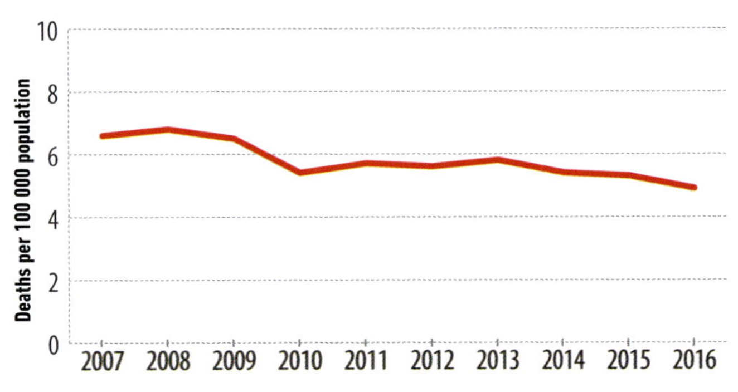

Source: Department of the State Automobile Inspection, Ministry of Internal Affairs.

Legislative review conducted by WHO. Vehicle safety data from UNECE WP29. Other data collected by questionnaire and cleared by Ministry of Health and Social Protection

Thailand

Population: 68 863 512 | Income group: Middle | Gross national income per capita: US$ 5 640

INSTITUTIONAL FRAMEWORK

Lead agency	**Department of Disaster Prevention and Mitigation, Ministry of Interior**
Funded in national budget	Yes
National road safety strategy	**Yes**
Funding to implement strategy	Partially funded
Fatality reduction target	≤ 10 deaths per 100 000 population (2010-2020)

SAFER ROADS AND MOBILITY

Audits or star rating required for new road infrastructure	Partial
Design standards for the safety of pedestrians / cyclists	Partial
Inspections / star rating of existing roads	Yes
Investments to upgrade high risk locations	Yes
Policies & investment in urban public transport	Yes

SAFER VEHICLES

Total registered vehicles for 31 Dec 2016	**37 338 139**
Cars and 4-wheeled light vehicles	15 003 774
Motorized 2- and 3-wheelers	20 497 296
Heavy trucks	1 055 717
Buses	157 799
Other	623 553
Vehicle standards applied (UNECE WP.29)	
Frontal impact standard	No
Electronic stability control	No[a]
Pedestrian protection	Yes
Motorcycle anti-lock braking system	No

POST-CRASH CARE

National emergency care access number	National, single number
Trauma registry	Some facilities
Formal certification for prehospital providers	Yes
National assessment of emergency care systems	Yes

DATA

Reported road traffic fatalities (2016)	21 745[b] (79% M, 21% F)
WHO estimated road traffic fatalities (2016)	22 491 (95% CI 20 265 - 24 717)
WHO estimated rate per 100 000 population (2016)	32.7

[a] Thailand launched an ECO-CAR program with tax incentives to cars with ESC but is not mandatory for all cars

[b] Data Integration: (1) Death registration validated with Medical Certification of Cause of Death from hospitals; (2) Royal Thai Police; (3) Road Accident Victims Protection Company Limited. Unlimited time period following crash

SAFER ROAD USERS

National speed limit law	**Yes**
Max urban speed limit	80 km/h
Max rural speed limit	90 km/h
Max motorway speed limit	120 km/h
Local authorities can modify limits	No
Enforcement	0 1 2 3 4 ⑤ 6 7 8 9 10
Predominant type of enforcement	Manual
National drink-driving law	**Yes**
BAC limit – general population	≤ 0.05 g/dl
BAC limit – young or novice drivers	≤ 0.02 g/dl
Random breath testing carried out	Yes[c]
Testing carried out in case of fatal crash	Some drivers tested
Enforcement	0 1 2 3 4 5 ⑥ 7 8 9 10
% road traffic deaths involving alcohol	14%[d]
National motorcycle helmet law	**Yes**
Applies to drivers and passengers	Yes
Helmet fastening required	Yes
Helmet standard referred to and/or specified	Yes
Children passengers on motorcycles	Not restricted
Enforcement	0 1 2 3 4 5 ⑥ 7 8 9 10
Helmet wearing rate	51% Drivers[e], 20% Passengers[e]
National seat-belt law	**Yes**
Applies to front and rear seat occupants	Yes
Enforcement	0 1 2 3 4 5 ⑥ 7 8 9 10
Seat-belt wearing rate	58% Drivers[f], 40% Front seats[f]
National child restraint law	**No**
Children seated in front seat	Not restricted
Child restraint required	–
Child restraint standard referred to and/or specified	–
Enforcement	–
% children using child restraints	–
National law on mobile phone use while driving	**Yes**
Ban on hand-held mobile phone use	Yes
Ban on hands-free mobile phone use	No
National drug-driving law	**Yes**

[c] Legislation requires probable cause to test drivers

[d] 2016, Injury Surveillance System across 33 hospital sentinel sites

[e] 2015, Survey of ThaiRoads Foundation

[f] 2011, Survey of ThaiRoads Foundation

Deaths by road user category

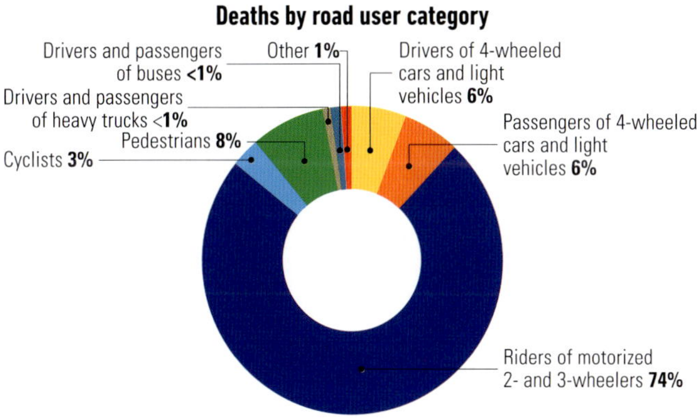

Source: 2016, Injury surveillance system, Bureau of Epidemiology, Department of Disease Control, Ministry of Public Health

Trends in reported road traffic deaths

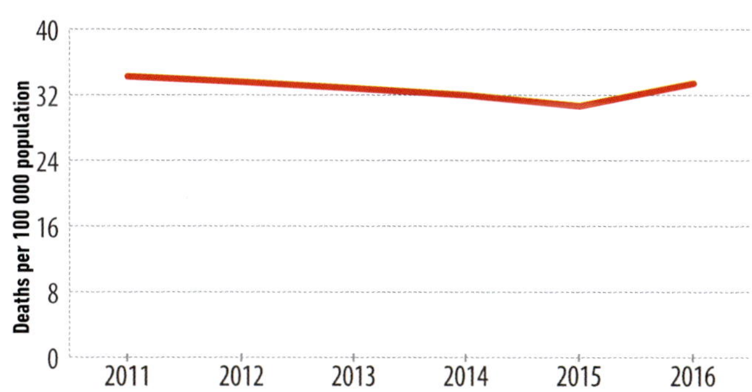

Source: Data Integration: (1) Death registration validated with Medical Certification of Cause of Death from hospitals; (2) Royal Thai Police; (3) Road Accident Victims Protection Company Limited

Legislative review conducted by WHO. Vehicle safety data from UNECE WP29. Other data collected by questionnaire and cleared by Ministry of Public Health.

The former Yugoslav Republic of Macedonia

Population: 2 081 206 | Income group: Middle | Gross national income per capita: US$ 4 980

INSTITUTIONAL FRAMEWORK

Lead agency	Republic Council on Road Traffic Safety and Coordination Body of the Government of Republic of Macedonia
Funded in national budget	Yes
National road safety strategy	Yes
Funding to implement strategy	Partially funded
Fatality reduction target	Reduction of fatalities to EU average, reduction of young driver victims by 30%, and zero child victims (2015 - 2020)

SAFER ROADS AND MOBILITY

Audits or star rating required for new road infrastructure	Partial
Design standards for the safety of pedestrians / cyclists	Yes
Inspections / star rating of existing roads	Yes
Investments to upgrade high risk locations	No
Policies & investment in urban public transport	Yes

SAFER VEHICLES

Total registered vehicles for 2015	442 962
Cars and 4-wheeled light vehicles	383 833
Motorized 2- and 3-wheelers	10 050
Heavy trucks	45 836
Buses	3 243
Other	0
Vehicle standards applied (UNECE WP.29)	
Frontal impact standard	No
Electronic stability control	No
Pedestrian protection	No
Motorcycle anti-lock braking system	No

POST-CRASH CARE

National emergency care access number	National, single number
Trauma registry	National
Formal certification for prehospital providers	Yes
National assessment of emergency care systems	Yes

DATA

Reported road traffic fatalities (2015)	148[a] (80% M, 20% F)
WHO estimated road traffic fatalities (2016)	134
WHO estimated rate per 100 000 population (2016)	6.4

[a] Ministry of Interior and State Statistical Office. Died within 30 days of crash

SAFER ROAD USERS

National speed limit law	Yes
Max urban speed limit	50 km/h[b]
Max rural speed limit	90 km/h
Max motorway speed limit	130 km/h
Local authorities can modify limits	No
Enforcement	0 1 2 3 4 5 (6) 7 8 9 10
Predominant type of enforcement	Manual
National drink-driving law	Yes
BAC limit – general population	≤ 0.05 g/dl
BAC limit – young or novice drivers	< 0.01 g/dl[c]
Random breath testing carried out	Yes
Testing carried out in case of fatal crash	All drivers tested
Enforcement	0 1 2 3 4 (5) 6 7 8 9 10
% road traffic deaths involving alcohol	1%[d]
National motorcycle helmet law	Yes
Applies to drivers and passengers	Yes
Helmet fastening required	No
Helmet standard referred to and/or specified	No
Children passengers on motorcycles	Not restricted
Enforcement	0 1 2 3 4 5 6 (7) 8 9 10
Helmet wearing rate	–
National seat-belt law	Yes
Applies to front and rear seat occupants	Yes
Enforcement	0 1 2 3 4 (5) 6 7 8 9 10
Seat-belt wearing rate	20% Front seats[e], 3% Rear seats[e]
National child restraint law	Yes
Children seated in front seat	Prohibited under 12 yrs[f]
Child restraint required	Up to 5 yrs
Child restraint standard referred to and/or specified	No
Enforcement	0 1 2 3 4 5 6 (7) 8 9 10
% children using child restraints	–
National law on mobile phone use while driving	Yes
Ban on hand-held mobile phone use	Yes
Ban on hands-free mobile phone use	No
National drug-driving law	Yes

[b] Can be increased up to 70 km/h
[c] In the law ≤ 0.009 g/dl
[d] 2015, State Statistical Office and Ministry of Interior
[e] 2015, Survey conducted by the Department for traffic and transport
[f] Except for children under 2 years in a rear-facing child restraint if airbag is deactivated

Deaths by road user category

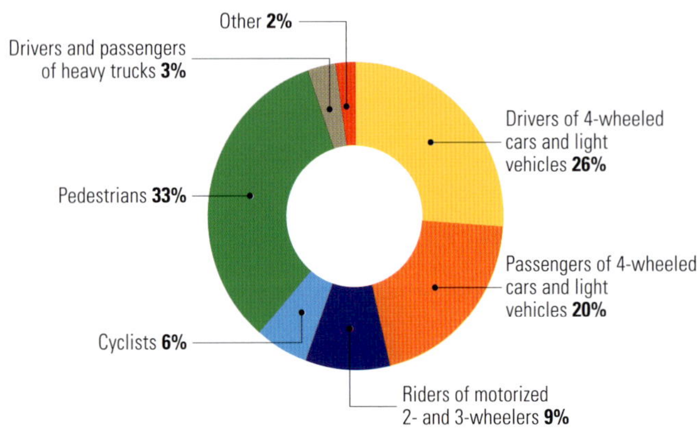

Source: 2015, Ministry of Interior and State Statistical Office

Trends in reported road traffic deaths

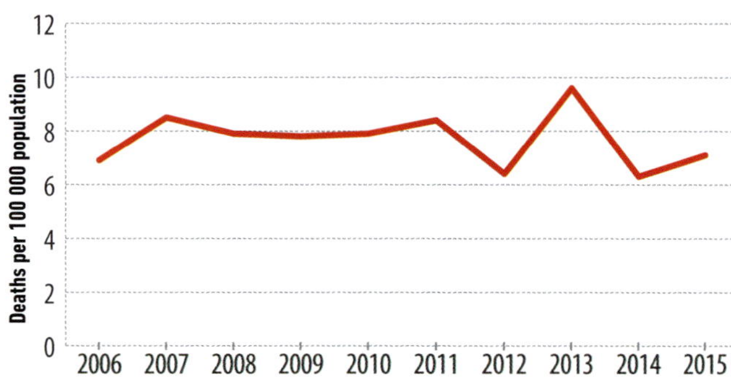

Source: State Statistical Office and Ministry of Interior

Legislative review conducted by WHO. Vehicle safety data from UNECE WP29. Other data collected by questionnaire.

Timor-Leste

Population: 1 268 671 | Income group: Middle | Gross national income per capita: US$ 2 180[a]

INSTITUTIONAL FRAMEWORK	
Lead agency	National Directorate of Transport, Ministry of Interior
Funded in national budget	Yes
National road safety strategy	Yes
Funding to implement strategy	Partially funded
Fatality reduction target	–

SAFER ROADS AND MOBILITY	
Audits or star rating required for new road infrastructure	Partial
Design standards for the safety of pedestrians / cyclists	Yes
Inspections / star rating of existing roads	No
Investments to upgrade high risk locations	No
Policies & investment in urban public transport	Yes

SAFER VEHICLES	
Total registered vehicles for December 2016	146 596
Cars and 4-wheeled light vehicles	24 438
Motorized 2- and 3-wheelers	108 409
Heavy trucks	1 120
Buses	207
Other	12 422
Vehicle standards applied (UNECE WP.29)	
Frontal impact standard	No
Electronic stability control	No
Pedestrian protection	No
Motorcycle anti-lock braking system	No

POST-CRASH CARE	
National emergency care access number	National, single number
Trauma registry	National
Formal certification for prehospital providers	Yes
National assessment of emergency care systems	No

DATA	
Reported road traffic fatalities (2016)	71[b]
WHO estimated road traffic fatalities (2016)	161 (95% CI 138 - 184)
WHO estimated rate per 100 000 population (2016)	12.7

[a] Data available only for 2015
[b] National Police Timor-Leste (PNTL), National Transit Department. Died within 24 hours of crash

SAFER ROAD USERS	
National speed limit law	Yes
Max urban speed limit	50 km/h
Max rural speed limit	90 km/h
Max motorway speed limit	120 km/h
Local authorities can modify limits	No
Enforcement	0 1 2 3 4 ⑤ 6 7 8 9 10
Predominant type of enforcement	Manual
National drink-driving law	Yes
BAC limit – general population	≤ 0.05 g/dl
BAC limit – young or novice drivers	≤ 0.05 g/dl
Random breath testing carried out	No
Testing carried out in case of fatal crash	Some drivers tested
Enforcement	0 1 2 3 ④ 5 6 7 8 9 10
% road traffic deaths involving alcohol	–
National motorcycle helmet law	Yes
Applies to drivers and passengers	Yes
Helmet fastening required	Yes
Helmet standard referred to and/or specified	Yes
Children passengers on motorcycles	Not restricted
Enforcement	0 1 2 3 4 5 6 ⑦ 8 9 10
Helmet wearing rate	–
National seat-belt law	Yes
Applies to front and rear seat occupants	Yes
Enforcement	0 1 ② 3 4 5 6 7 8 9 10
Seat-belt wearing rate	–
National child restraint law	No
Children seated in front seat	Prohibited under 12 yrs[c]
Child restraint required	–
Child restraint standard referred to and/or specified	–
Enforcement	–
% children using child restraints	–
National law on mobile phone use while driving	Yes
Ban on hand-held mobile phone use	Yes
Ban on hands-free mobile phone use	No
National drug-driving law	Yes

[c] Unless the vehicle does not have a back seat and such transportation is carried out by using an approved child restraint, appropriate to the child's size and weight

Legislative review conducted by WHO. Vehicle safety data from UNECE WP29. Other data collected by questionnaire.

Deaths by road user category

Trends in reported road traffic deaths

Source: National Police Timor-Leste (PNTL), National Transit Department (death data), Census 2010 (population data)

Togo

Population: 7 606 374 | Income group: Low | Gross national income per capita: US$ 540

INSTITUTIONAL FRAMEWORK	
Lead agency	National Office of Road Safety (ONSR), Ministry of Infrastructure and Transport (MIT)
Funded in national budget	No
National road safety strategy	No
Funding to implement strategy	–
Fatality reduction target	–

SAFER ROADS AND MOBILITY	
Audits or star rating required for new road infrastructure	Partial
Design standards for the safety of pedestrians / cyclists	Partial
Inspections / star rating of existing roads	No
Investments to upgrade high risk locations	Yes
Policies & investment in urban public transport	Yes

SAFER VEHICLES	
Total registered vehicles for 2016	64 118
Cars and 4-wheeled light vehicles	17 000
Motorized 2- and 3-wheelers	45 341
Heavy trucks	791
Buses	62
Other	924
Vehicle standards applied (UNECE WP.29)	
Frontal impact standard	No
Electronic stability control	No
Pedestrian protection	No
Motorcycle anti-lock braking system	No

POST-CRASH CARE	
National emergency care access number	National, single number
Trauma registry	National
Formal certification for prehospital providers	Yes
National assessment of emergency care systems	No

DATA	
Reported road traffic fatalities (2016)	514[a] (50% M, 22% F)
WHO estimated road traffic fatalities (2016)	2 224 (95% CI 1 800 - 2 649)
WHO estimated rate per 100 000 population (2016)	29.2

[a] Police and Ministry of Security and Civil Protection (MSPC). Died within 30 days of crash

SAFER ROAD USERS	
National speed limit law	No
Max urban speed limit	–
Max rural speed limit	–
Max motorway speed limit	–
Local authorities can modify limits	No
Enforcement	–
Predominant type of enforcement	Manual
National drink-driving law	Yes[b]
BAC limit – general population	–
BAC limit – young or novice drivers	–
Random breath testing carried out	No
Testing carried out in case of fatal crash	No
Enforcement	(0) 1 2 3 4 5 6 7 8 9 10
% road traffic deaths involving alcohol	–
National motorcycle helmet law	Yes
Applies to drivers and passengers	Yes
Helmet fastening required	No
Helmet standard referred to and/or specified	No
Children passengers on motorcycles	Not restricted
Enforcement	0 1 2 3 4 5 6 (7) 8 9 10
Helmet wearing rate	–
National seat-belt law	Yes
Applies to front and rear seat occupants	Yes
Enforcement	0 1 2 3 4 5 (6) 7 8 9 10
Seat-belt wearing rate	–
National child restraint law	No
Children seated in front seat	Not restricted
Child restraint required	–
Child restraint standard referred to and/or specified	–
Enforcement	–
% children using child restraints	–
National law on mobile phone use while driving	Yes
Ban on hand-held mobile phone use	Yes
Ban on hands-free mobile phone use	Yes
National drug-driving law	Yes

[b] Not based on BAC

Deaths by road user category

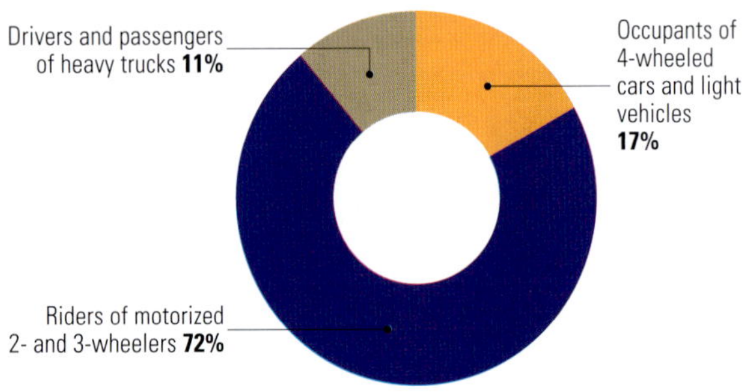

Source: 2016, Ministry of Security and Civil Protection (MSPC), 2008-2016 Annual Report

Trends in reported road traffic deaths

Source: Ministry of Security and Civil Protection (MSPC), 2008-2016 Annual Reports (death data), National Institute of Statistics and Economic and Demographic Studies (population data)

Legislative review conducted by WHO. Vehicle safety data from UNECE WP.29. Other data collected by questionnaire and cleared by Ministry of Security and Civil Protection.

Tonga

Population: 107 122 | Income group: Middle | Gross national income per capita: US$ 4 020

INSTITUTIONAL FRAMEWORK	
Lead agency	Ministry of Police (Department of Traffic) and Ministry of Infrastructure
Funded in national budget	Yes
National road safety strategy	Yes
Funding to implement strategy	Partially funded
Fatality reduction target	50% reduction in rate per 100 000 population (2011-2020)

SAFER ROADS AND MOBILITY	
Audits or star rating required for new road infrastructure	Yes
Design standards for the safety of pedestrians / cyclists	Partial
Inspections / star rating of existing roads	Yes
Investments to upgrade high risk locations	Yes
Policies & investment in urban public transport	No

SAFER VEHICLES	
Total registered vehicles for 2012	8 154
Cars and 4-wheeled light vehicles	6 039
Motorized 2- and 3-wheelers	184
Heavy trucks	1 882
Buses	49
Other	0
Vehicle standards applied (UNECE WP.29)	
Frontal impact standard	No
Electronic stability control	No
Pedestrian protection	No
Motorcycle anti-lock braking system	No

POST-CRASH CARE	
National emergency care access number	National, multiple numbers
Trauma registry	None
Formal certification for prehospital providers	No
National assessment of emergency care systems	No

DATA	
Reported road traffic fatalities (2016)	18[a] (89% M, 11% F)
WHO estimated road traffic fatalities (2016)	18
WHO estimated rate per 100 000 population (2016)	16.8

[a] Road Traffic Accident Registry. Died within 24 hours of crash

SAFER ROAD USERS	
National speed limit law	Yes
Max urban speed limit	50 km/h
Max rural speed limit	70 km/h
Max motorway speed limit	70 km/h
Local authorities can modify limits	No
Enforcement	0 1 2 3 4 5 6 (7) 8 9 10
Predominant type of enforcement	Manual
National drink-driving law	Yes
BAC limit – general population	< 0.03 g/dl[b]
BAC limit – young or novice drivers	< 0.03 g/dl[b]
Random breath testing carried out	Yes
Testing carried out in case of fatal crash	No
Enforcement	0 1 2 3 4 (5) 6 7 8 9 10
% road traffic deaths involving alcohol	77%[c]
National motorcycle helmet law	Yes
Applies to drivers and passengers	Yes
Helmet fastening required	Yes
Helmet standard referred to and/or specified	Yes
Children passengers on motorcycles	Not restricted
Enforcement	0 1 2 3 4 5 6 7 (8) 9 10
Helmet wearing rate	–
National seat-belt law	No
Applies to front and rear seat occupants	–
Enforcement	–
Seat-belt wearing rate	–
National child restraint law	No
Children seated in front seat	Not restricted
Child restraint required	–
Child restraint standard referred to and/or specified	–
Enforcement	–
% children using child restraints	–
National law on mobile phone use while driving	No
Ban on hand-held mobile phone use	–
Ban on hands-free mobile phone use	–
National drug-driving law	No

[b] Law based on breath alcohol concentration, values converted to BAC
[c] 2016, Audit on Major Trauma for the year 2016, Emergency Department, Ministry of Health

Deaths by road user category

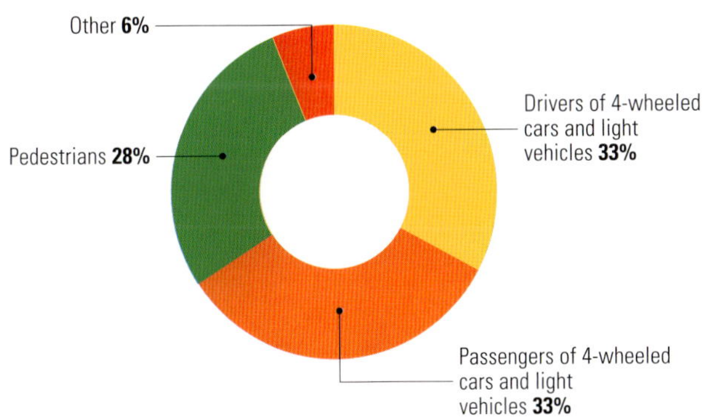

Source: 2016, Road Traffic Accident Registry, Ministry of Police

Trends in reported road traffic deaths

Source: Road Traffic Accident Registry, Ministry of Police

Trinidad and Tobago

Population: 1 364 962 | Income group: High | Gross national income per capita: US$ 15 680

INSTITUTIONAL FRAMEWORK

Lead agency	National Road Safety Council, Ministry of Works and Transport
Funded in national budget	No
National road safety strategy	Yes
Funding to implement strategy	–
Fatality reduction target	–

SAFER ROADS AND MOBILITY

Audits or star rating required for new road infrastructure	Partial
Design standards for the safety of pedestrians / cyclists	Yes
Inspections / star rating of existing roads	–
Investments to upgrade high risk locations	No
Policies & investment in urban public transport	Yes

SAFER VEHICLES

Total registered vehicles for 1996-2015	831 803
Cars and 4-wheeled light vehicles	378 584
Motorized 2- and 3-wheelers	4 736
Heavy trucks	96 612
Buses	431
Other	351 440
Vehicle standards applied (UNECE WP.29)	
Frontal impact standard	No
Electronic stability control	No
Pedestrian protection	No
Motorcycle anti-lock braking system	No

POST-CRASH CARE

National emergency care access number	National, multiple numbers
Trauma registry	Some facilities
Formal certification for prehospital providers	No
National assessment of emergency care systems	No

DATA

Reported road traffic fatalities (2016)	135[a] (76% M, 24% F)
WHO estimated road traffic fatalities (2016)	165
WHO estimated rate per 100 000 population (2016)	12.1

[a] Trinidad and Tobago Police Service. Died within a year of crash

SAFER ROAD USERS

National speed limit law	Yes
Max urban speed limit	50 km/h
Max rural speed limit	80 km/h
Max motorway speed limit	No
Local authorities can modify limits	No
Enforcement	0 1 2 3 4 (5) 6 7 8 9 10
Predominant type of enforcement	Manual
National drink-driving law	Yes
BAC limit – general population	≤ 0.08 g/dl
BAC limit – young or novice drivers	≤ 0.08 g/dl
Random breath testing carried out	Yes[b]
Testing carried out in case of fatal crash	All drivers tested
Enforcement	0 1 2 3 4 5 (6) 7 8 9 10
% road traffic deaths involving alcohol	–
National motorcycle helmet law	Yes
Applies to drivers and passengers	Yes
Helmet fastening required	No
Helmet standard referred to and/or specified	Yes
Children passengers on motorcycles	Not restricted
Enforcement	0 1 2 3 4 5 6 7 8 (9) 10
Helmet wearing rate	–
National seat-belt law	Yes
Applies to front and rear seat occupants	No
Enforcement	0 1 2 3 4 5 6 7 (8) 9 10
Seat-belt wearing rate	–
National child restraint law	Yes
Children seated in front seat	Prohibited under 5 yrs
Child restraint required	Up to 5 yrs
Child restraint standard referred to and/or specified	Yes
Enforcement	0 1 2 (3) 4 5 6 7 8 9 10
% children using child restraints	–
National law on mobile phone use while driving	Yes
Ban on hand-held mobile phone use	Yes
Ban on hands-free mobile phone use	No
National drug-driving law	Yes

[b] Legislation requires probable cause to test drivers

Deaths by road user category

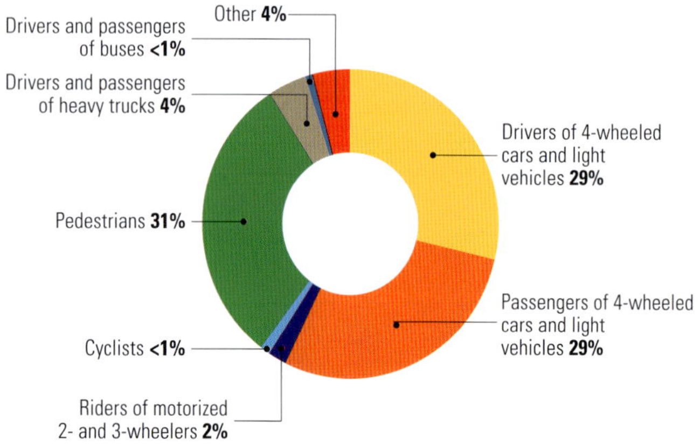

Source: 2016, Trinidad and Tobago Police Service

Trends in reported road traffic deaths

Source: Trinidad and Tobago Police Service

Tunisia

Population: 11 403 248 | Income group: Middle | Gross national income per capita: US$ 3 690

INSTITUTIONAL FRAMEWORK	
Lead agency	National Observatory for Information, Training, Documentation and Studies on Road Safety, Ministry of Interior
Funded in national budget	Yes
National road safety strategy	No
Funding to implement strategy	–
Fatality reduction target	–
SAFER ROADS AND MOBILITY	
Audits or star rating required for new road infrastructure	Partial
Design standards for the safety of pedestrians / cyclists	Partial
Inspections / star rating of existing roads	–
Investments to upgrade high risk locations	Yes
Policies & investment in urban public transport	Yes
SAFER VEHICLES	
Total registered vehicles for 2016	2 015 601
Cars and 4-wheeled light vehicles	1 718 175
Motorized 2- and 3-wheelers	16 306
Heavy trucks	260 369
Buses	20 751
Other	0
Vehicle standards applied (UNECE WP.29)	
Frontal impact standard	No
Electronic stability control	No
Pedestrian protection	No
Motorcycle anti-lock braking system	No
POST-CRASH CARE	
National emergency care access number	National, multiple numbers
Trauma registry	None
Formal certification for prehospital providers	No
National assessment of emergency care systems	Yes
DATA	
Reported road traffic fatalities (2016)	1 443[a] (88% M, 12% F)
WHO estimated road traffic fatalities (2016)	2 595 (95% CI 2 321 - 2 869)
WHO estimated rate per 100 000 population (2016)	22.8

[a] National Traffic Safety Observatory in coordination with the Guard and Traffic Police Departments. Died within 30 days of crash

SAFER ROAD USERS	
National speed limit law	Yes
Max urban speed limit	50 km/h
Max rural speed limit	90 km/h
Max motorway speed limit	110 km/h
Local authorities can modify limits	Yes
Enforcement	0 1 2 3 4 (5) 6 7 8 9 10
Predominant type of enforcement	Manual
National drink-driving law	Yes
BAC limit – general population	< 0.03 g/dl
BAC limit – young or novice drivers	0.00 g/dl
Random breath testing carried out	No
Testing carried out in case of fatal crash	All drivers tested
Enforcement	0 1 2 (3) 4 5 6 7 8 9 10
% road traffic deaths involving alcohol	2%[b]
National motorcycle helmet law	Yes
Applies to drivers and passengers	Yes
Helmet fastening required	No
Helmet standard referred to and/or specified	Yes
Children passengers on motorcycles	Prohibited under 6 yrs[c]
Enforcement	0 1 2 (3) 4 5 6 7 8 9 10
Helmet wearing rate	–
National seat-belt law	Yes
Applies to front and rear seat occupants	Yes
Enforcement	0 1 2 (3) 4 5 6 7 8 9 10
Seat-belt wearing rate	–
National child restraint law	No
Children seated in front seat	Prohibited under 10 yrs
Child restraint required	–
Child restraint standard referred to and/or specified	–
Enforcement	–
% children using child restraints	–
National law on mobile phone use while driving	Yes
Ban on hand-held mobile phone use	Yes
Ban on hands-free mobile phone use	No
National drug-driving law	Yes

[b] 2016, National Traffic Safety Observatory in coordination with the Guard and Traffic Police Departments
[c] The ban includes children aged 6 years

Deaths by road user category

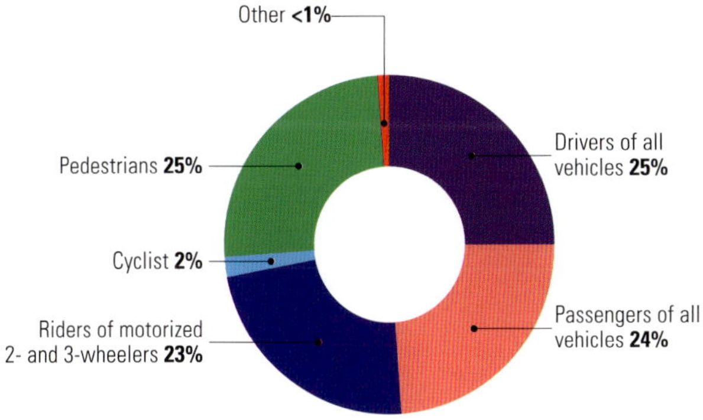

Trends in reported road traffic deaths

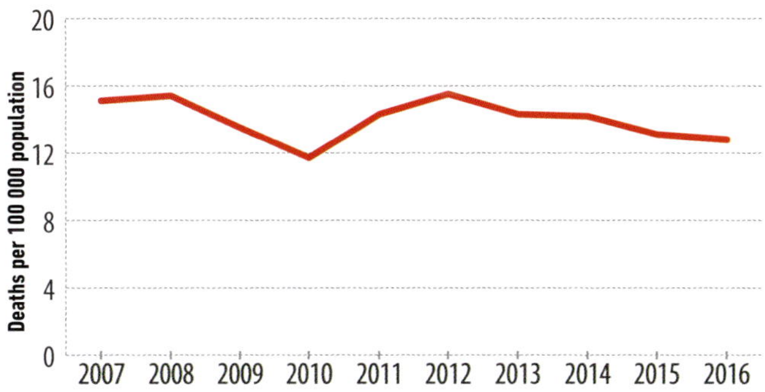

Source: National Traffic Safety Observatory in coordination with the Guard and Traffic Police Departments

Legislative review conducted by WHO. Vehicle safety data from UNECE WP.29. Other data collected by questionnaire and cleared by Ministry of Health.

Turkey

Population: 79 512 424 | Income group: Middle | Gross national income per capita: US$ 11 180

INSTITUTIONAL FRAMEWORK	
Lead agency	Higher Board of Road Safety, Ministry of Interior
Funded in national budget	No
National road safety strategy	Yes
Funding to implement strategy	Fully funded
Fatality reduction target	50% (2011-2020)
SAFER ROADS AND MOBILITY	
Audits or star rating required for new road infrastructure	Partial
Design standards for the safety of pedestrians / cyclists	Yes
Inspections / star rating of existing roads	Yes
Investments to upgrade high risk locations	Yes
Policies & investment in urban public transport	Yes
SAFER VEHICLES	
Total registered vehicles for 2016	21 090 424
Cars and 4-wheeled light vehicles	17 040 996
Motorized 2- and 3-wheelers	3 003 733
Heavy trucks	825 334
Buses	220 361
Other	0
Vehicle standards applied (UNECE WP.29)	
Frontal impact standard	Yes
Electronic stability control	Yes
Pedestrian protection	Yes
Motorcycle anti-lock braking system	No
POST-CRASH CARE	
National emergency care access number	National, single number
Trauma registry	Some facilities
Formal certification for prehospital providers	Yes
National assessment of emergency care systems	Yes
DATA	
Reported road traffic fatalities (2016)	7 300[a] (78% M, 22% F)
WHO estimated road traffic fatalities (2016)	9 782
WHO estimated rate per 100 000 population (2016)	12.3

[a] Directorate General For Security. Died within 30 days of crash

SAFER ROAD USERS	
National speed limit law	Yes
Max urban speed limit	50 km/h
Max rural speed limit	110 km/h[b]
Max motorway speed limit	120 km/h[b]
Local authorities can modify limits	Yes
Enforcement	0 1 2 3 4 5 6 7 8 **9** 10
Predominant type of enforcement	Manual and automated
National drink-driving law	Yes
BAC limit – general population	≤ 0.05 g/dl
BAC limit – young or novice drivers	≤ 0.05 g/dl
Random breath testing carried out	Yes
Testing carried out in case of fatal crash	All drivers tested
Enforcement	0 1 2 3 4 5 6 7 8 **9** 10
% road traffic deaths involving alcohol	3%[c]
National motorcycle helmet law	Yes
Applies to drivers and passengers	Yes
Helmet fastening required	No
Helmet standard referred to and/or specified	Yes
Children passengers on motorcycles	Not restricted
Enforcement	0 1 2 3 4 5 6 7 8 **9** 10
Helmet wearing rate	75% All riders[d]
National seat-belt law	Yes
Applies to front and rear seat occupants	Yes
Enforcement	0 1 2 3 4 5 6 7 8 **9** 10
Seat-belt wearing rate	50% Drivers[e], 41% Front seats[e]
National child restraint law	Yes
Children seated in front seat	Allowed in a child restraint[f]
Child restraint required	Up to 36 kg/135 cm[g]
Child restraint standard referred to and/or specified	Yes
Enforcement	0 1 2 3 4 5 6 7 8 **9** 10
% children using child restraints	—
National law on mobile phone use while driving	Yes
Ban on hand-held mobile phone use	Yes
Ban on hands-free mobile phone use	Yes
National drug-driving law	Yes

[b] Ministry of Interior can increase speed limits by 20 km/h for automobiles
[c] 2012, Turkish National Police
[d] 2016, Directorate General for Security
[e] 2013, 2016 - Turkey Analysis: Follow-up study on driver and front seat-belt use
[f] Provided that airbag is deactivated for children travelling in a rear-facing restraint
[g] Child restraints are required for children under 150cm, by exception children of height 135-150 cm can be restrained by a seat belt only if they sit in the back

Deaths by road user category

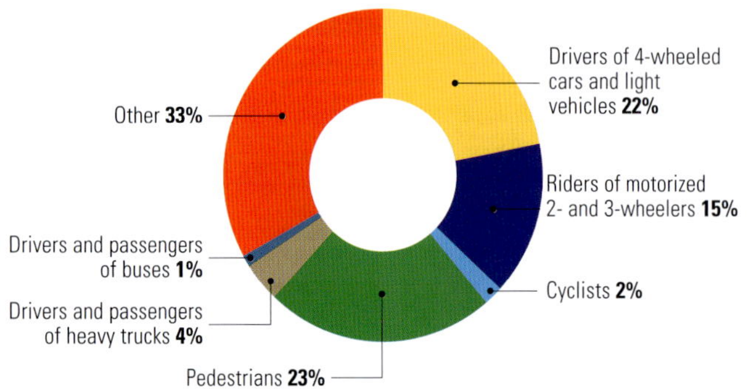

Source: 2016, Accident Reporting Database

Trends in reported road traffic deaths

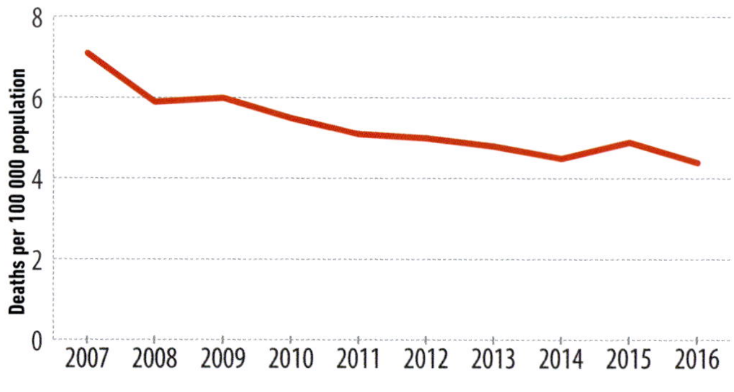

Source: Directorate General for Security

Legislative review conducted by WHO. Vehicle safety data from UNECE WP29. Other data collected by questionnaire.

Turkmenistan

Population: 5 662 544 | Income group: Middle | Gross national income per capita: US$ 6 670

INSTITUTIONAL FRAMEWORK

Lead agency	Ministry of Health and Medical Industry of Turkmenistan
Funded in national budget	Yes
National road safety strategy	Yes
Funding to implement strategy	Fully funded
Fatality reduction target	–

SAFER ROADS AND MOBILITY

Audits or star rating required for new road infrastructure	Yes
Design standards for the safety of pedestrians / cyclists	Partial
Inspections / star rating of existing roads	No
Investments to upgrade high risk locations	Yes
Policies & investment in urban public transport	Yes

SAFER VEHICLES

Total registered vehicles	–
Cars and 4-wheeled light vehicles	–
Motorized 2- and 3-wheelers	–
Heavy trucks	–
Buses	–
Other	–
Vehicle standards applied (UNECE WP.29)	
Frontal impact standard	No
Electronic stability control	No
Pedestrian protection	No
Motorcycle anti-lock braking system	No

POST-CRASH CARE

National emergency care access number	National, single number
Trauma registry	Some facilities
Formal certification for prehospital providers	Yes
National assessment of emergency care systems	No

DATA

Reported road traffic fatalities (2016)	543[a] (66% M, 34% F)
WHO estimated road traffic fatalities (2016)	823 (95% CI 765 - 880)
WHO estimated rate per 100 000 population (2016)	14.5

[a] Statistical report of the State Committee on Statistics. Died within 7 days of crash

SAFER ROAD USERS

National speed limit law	Yes
Max urban speed limit	60 km/h
Max rural speed limit	90 km/h
Max motorway speed limit	110 km/h
Local authorities can modify limits	Yes
Enforcement	0 1 2 3 4 5 6 7 8 9 (10)
Predominant type of enforcement	Manual and automated
National drink-driving law	Yes
BAC limit – general population	< 0.05 g/dl
BAC limit – young or novice drivers	< 0.05 g/dl
Random breath testing carried out	Yes
Testing carried out in case of fatal crash	All drivers tested
Enforcement	0 1 2 3 4 5 6 7 8 9 (10)
% road traffic deaths involving alcohol	–
National motorcycle helmet law	Yes
Applies to drivers and passengers	Yes
Helmet fastening required	No
Helmet standard referred to and/or specified	No
Children passengers on motorcycles	Prohibited under 12 yrs
Enforcement	0 1 2 3 4 5 6 7 8 (9) 10
Helmet wearing rate	–
National seat-belt law	Yes
Applies to front and rear seat occupants	Yes
Enforcement	0 1 2 3 4 5 6 7 8 9 (10)
Seat-belt wearing rate	–
National child restraint law	No
Children seated in front seat	Allowed in a child restraint[b]
Child restraint required	–[c]
Child restraint standard referred to and/or specified	–
Enforcement	–
% children using child restraints	–
National law on mobile phone use while driving	Yes
Ban on hand-held mobile phone use	Yes
Ban on hands-free mobile phone use	Yes
National drug-driving law	No

[b] Law does not specifically refer to child restraint system but to "special seating equipment" for children under 12 years

[c] Special seating equipment for children under 12 years is mentioned only in relation with front seating

Legislative review conducted by WHO. Vehicle safety data from UNECE WP29. Other data collected by questionnaire and cleared by Ministry of Health and Medical Industry.

Deaths by road user category

Trends in reported road traffic deaths

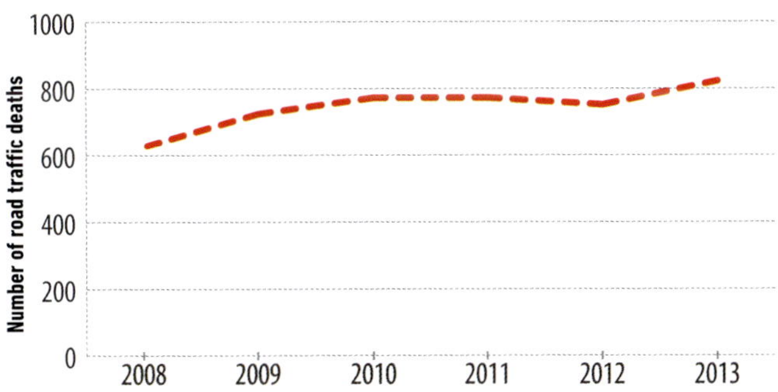

Uganda

Population: 41 487 964 | Income group: Low | Gross national income per capita: US$ 660

INSTITUTIONAL FRAMEWORK	
Lead agency	National Road Safety Council (NRSC), Ministry of Works and Transport
Funded in national budget	Yes
National road safety strategy	Yes
Funding to implement strategy	Partially funded
Fatality reduction target	50% (2014-2022)
SAFER ROADS AND MOBILITY	
Audits or star rating required for new road infrastructure	Yes
Design standards for the safety of pedestrians / cyclists	Partial
Inspections / star rating of existing roads	Yes
Investments to upgrade high risk locations	Yes
Policies & investment in urban public transport	No
SAFER VEHICLES	
Total registered vehicles for 2016	1 594 962
Cars and 4-wheeled light vehicles	–
Motorized 2- and 3-wheelers	946 096
Heavy trucks	–
Buses	3 335
Other	645 531
Vehicle standards applied (UNECE WP.29)	
Frontal impact standard	No
Electronic stability control	No
Pedestrian protection	No
Motorcycle anti-lock braking system	No
POST-CRASH CARE	
National emergency care access number	National, multiple numbers
Trauma registry	Some facilities
Formal certification for prehospital providers	No
National assessment of emergency care systems	Yes
DATA	
Reported road traffic fatalities (2016)	3 503[a] (78% M, 22% F)
WHO estimated road traffic fatalities (2016)	12 036 (95% CI 9 454 - 14 618)
WHO estimated rate per 100 000 population (2016)	29

[a] Police Annual Traffic Report. Died within a year of crash

SAFER ROAD USERS	
National speed limit law	Yes
Max urban speed limit	50 km/h
Max rural speed limit	100 km/h
Max motorway speed limit	No
Local authorities can modify limits	No
Enforcement	0 1 2 3 4 5 6 (7) 8 9 10
Predominant type of enforcement	Manual
National drink-driving law	Yes
BAC limit – general population	≤ 0.08 g/dl
BAC limit – young or novice drivers	≤ 0.08 g/dl
Random breath testing carried out	Yes[b]
Testing carried out in case of fatal crash	Some drivers tested
Enforcement	0 1 2 3 4 5 (6) 7 8 9 10
% road traffic deaths involving alcohol	<1%[c]
National motorcycle helmet law	Yes
Applies to drivers and passengers	Yes
Helmet fastening required	No
Helmet standard referred to and/or specified	No
Children passengers on motorcycles	Not restricted
Enforcement	0 1 2 3 4 (5) 6 7 8 9 10
Helmet wearing rate	49% Drivers[d], 1% Passengers[d]
National seat-belt law	Yes
Applies to front and rear seat occupants	Yes
Enforcement	0 1 2 3 (4) 5 6 7 8 9 10
Seat-belt wearing rate	–
National child restraint law	No
Children seated in front seat	Not restricted
Child restraint required	–
Child restraint standard referred to and/or specified	–
Enforcement	–
% children using child restraints	–
National law on mobile phone use while driving	Yes
Ban on hand-held mobile phone use	Yes
Ban on hands-free mobile phone use	No
National drug-driving law	Yes

[b] Legislation requires probable cause to test drivers or commission of a traffic offence
[c] 2016, Police Annual Traffic Report
[d] 2013, Uganda Helmet Vaccine Initiative 2013

Deaths by road user category

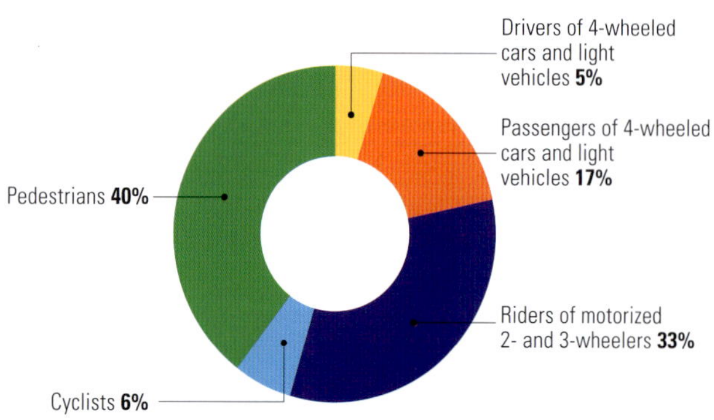

Source: 2016, Police Annual Traffic Report

Trends in reported road traffic deaths

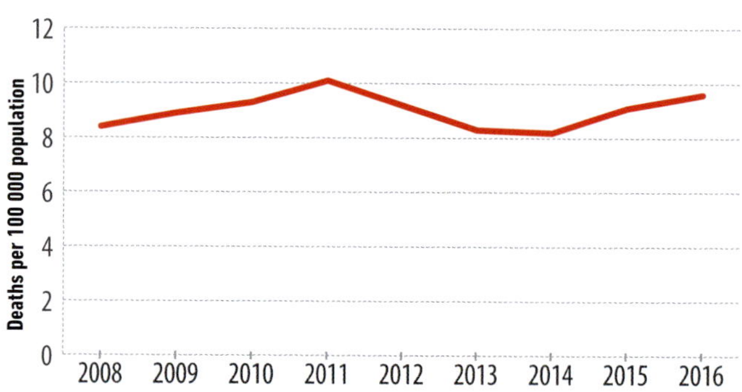

Source: Police Annual Traffic Reports and Uganda Bureau of Statistics

Ukraine

Population: 44 438 624 | Income group: Middle | Gross national income per capita: US$ 2 310

INSTITUTIONAL FRAMEWORK	
Lead agency	No
Funded in national budget	–
National road safety strategy	No
Funding to implement strategy	–
Fatality reduction target	–
SAFER ROADS AND MOBILITY	
Audits or star rating required for new road infrastructure	Yes
Design standards for the safety of pedestrians / cyclists	Yes
Inspections / star rating of existing roads	Yes
Investments to upgrade high risk locations	No
Policies & investment in urban public transport	Yes
SAFER VEHICLES	
Total registered vehicles for 2014	14 433 709
Cars and 4-wheeled light vehicles	9 162 795
Motorized 2- and 3-wheelers	1 725 447
Heavy trucks	2 063 276
Buses	324 151
Other	1 158 040
Vehicle standards applied (UNECE WP.29)	
Frontal impact standard	No
Electronic stability control	No
Pedestrian protection	No
Motorcycle anti-lock braking system	No
POST-CRASH CARE	
National emergency care access number	National, single number
Trauma registry	None
Formal certification for prehospital providers	Yes
National assessment of emergency care systems	No
DATA	
Reported road traffic fatalities (2016)	4 687[a] (76% M, 24% F)
WHO estimated road traffic fatalities (2016)	6 089
WHO estimated rate per 100 000 population (2016)	13.7

[a] State Statistics Service of Ukraine. Unlimited time period following crash

SAFER ROAD USERS	
National speed limit law	Yes
Max urban speed limit	60 km/h
Max rural speed limit	90 km/h
Max motorway speed limit	130 km/h
Local authorities can modify limits	Yes
Enforcement	0 1 2 (3) 4 5 6 7 8 9 10
Predominant type of enforcement	–
National drink-driving law	Yes
BAC limit – general population	≤ 0.02 g/dl
BAC limit – young or novice drivers	≤ 0.02 g/dl
Random breath testing carried out	No
Testing carried out in case of fatal crash	All drivers tested
Enforcement	0 1 2 3 4 (5) 6 7 8 9 10
% road traffic deaths involving alcohol	7%[b]
National motorcycle helmet law	Yes
Applies to drivers and passengers	Yes
Helmet fastening required	Yes
Helmet standard referred to and/or specified	No
Children passengers on motorcycles	Prohibited under 12 yrs/145 cm
Enforcement	0 1 2 (3) 4 5 6 7 8 9 10
Helmet wearing rate	–
National seat-belt law	Yes
Applies to front and rear seat occupants	Yes
Enforcement	0 1 2 (3) 4 5 6 7 8 9 10
Seat-belt wearing rate	–
National child restraint law	Yes[c]
Children seated in front seat	Allowed in a child restraint[d]
Child restraint required	–[c]
Child restraint standard referred to and/or specified	No
Enforcement	0 1 (2) 3 4 5 6 7 8 9 10
% children using child restraints	–
National law on mobile phone use while driving	Yes
Ban on hand-held mobile phone use	Yes
Ban on hands-free mobile phone use	No
National drug-driving law	Yes

[b] 2016, State Statistics Service of Ukraine

[c] The legislation refers to the use of "special means" to be used in conjunction with the seat belt to restrain children under 12 years and 145 cm

[d] No specific reference to child restraint but to "special means" for children under 145 cm and 12 years sitting in the front

Deaths by road user category

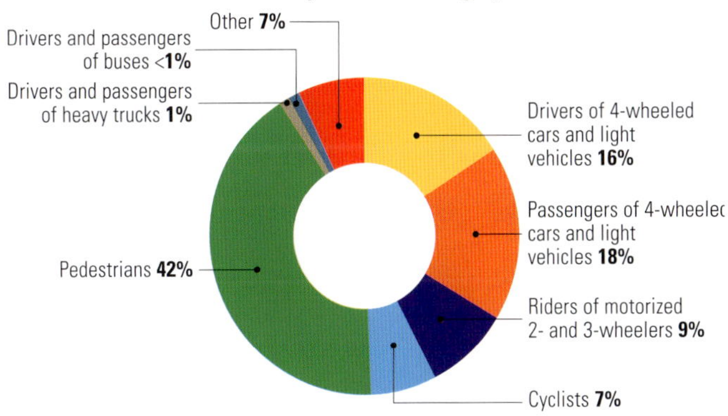

Source: 2016, State Statistics Service of Ukraine

Trends in reported road traffic deaths

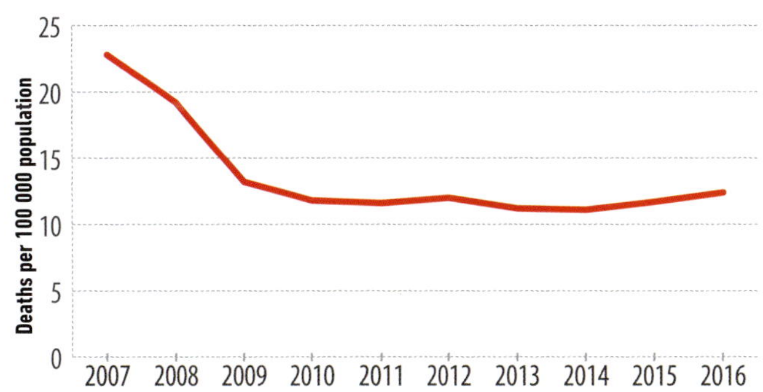

Source: State Statistics Service of Ukraine

Legislative review conducted by WHO. Vehicle safety data from UNECE WP.29. Other data collected by questionnaire.

United Arab Emirates

Population: 9 269 612 | Income group: High | Gross national income per capita: US$ 40 480

INSTITUTIONAL FRAMEWORK	
Lead agency	Traffic Coordination Department, Ministry of Interior
Funded in national budget	Yes
National road safety strategy	Yes
Funding to implement strategy	Partially funded
Fatality reduction target	3 deaths per 100 000 population (2011-2021)
SAFER ROADS AND MOBILITY	
Audits or star rating required for new road infrastructure	Yes
Design standards for the safety of pedestrians / cyclists	Partial
Inspections / star rating of existing roads	Yes
Investments to upgrade high risk locations	Yes
Policies & investment in urban public transport	Yes
SAFER VEHICLES	
Total registered vehicles for 2016	3 391 125
Cars and 4-wheeled light vehicles	2 996 338
Motorized 2- and 3-wheelers	54 581
Heavy trucks	237 427
Buses	102 779
Other	0
Vehicle standards applied (UNECE WP.29)	
Frontal impact standard	No
Electronic stability control	No
Pedestrian protection	No
Motorcycle anti-lock braking system	No
POST-CRASH CARE	
National emergency care access number	National, single number
Trauma registry	Subnational
Formal certification for prehospital providers	Yes
National assessment of emergency care systems	No
DATA	
Reported road traffic fatalities (2016)	725[a] (88% M, 12% F)
WHO estimated road traffic fatalities (2016)	1 678 (95% CI 1 435 - 1 921)
WHO estimated rate per 100 000 population (2016)	18.1

[a] Ministry of Interior (MOI). Died within 30 days of crash

SAFER ROAD USERS	
National speed limit law	Yes
Max urban speed limit	—[b]
Max rural speed limit	—[b]
Max motorway speed limit	—[b]
Local authorities can modify limits	Yes
Enforcement	0 1 2 3 4 5 6 7 8 9 (10)
Predominant type of enforcement	Automated
National drink-driving law	Yes[c]
BAC limit – general population	≤ 0.01 g/dl
BAC limit – young or novice drivers	≤ 0.01 g/dl
Random breath testing carried out	No
Testing carried out in case of fatal crash	All drivers tested
Enforcement	0 1 2 3 4 5 6 7 8 9 (10)
% road traffic deaths involving alcohol	2%[d]
National motorcycle helmet law	Yes
Applies to drivers and passengers	Yes
Helmet fastening required	No
Helmet standard referred to and/or specified	No
Children passengers on motorcycles	Not restricted
Enforcement	0 1 2 3 4 5 6 7 8 9 (10)
Helmet wearing rate	—
National seat-belt law	Yes
Applies to front and rear seat occupants	Yes
Enforcement	0 1 2 3 4 5 6 7 8 9 (10)
Seat-belt wearing rate	—
National child restraint law	Yes
Children seated in front seat	Prohibited under 10 yrs / 145 cm
Child restraint required	Up to 4 yrs[e]
Child restraint standard referred to and/or specified	Yes
Enforcement	0 1 2 3 4 5 6 (7) 8 9 10
% children using child restraints	—
National law on mobile phone use while driving	Yes
Ban on hand-held mobile phone use	Yes
Ban on hands-free mobile phone use	No
National drug-driving law	Yes

[b] Speed limits are established at subnational level per streets' names
[c] Alcohol consumption legally prohibited
[d] 2016, Ministry of Interior (MOI)
[e] Child restraints are required for children aged 4 years and below

Deaths by road user category

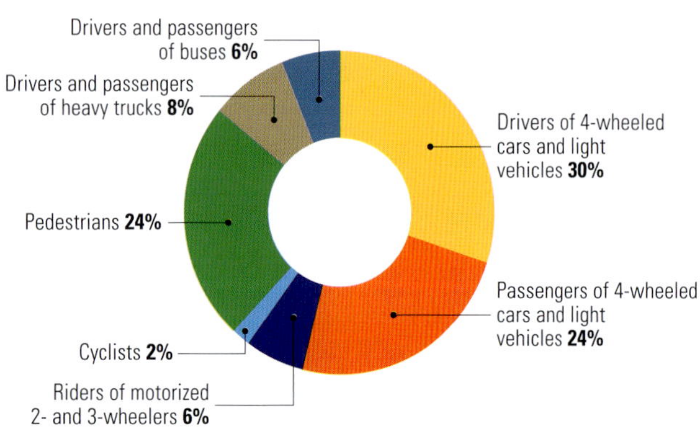

Source: 2016, Ministry of Interior

Trends in reported road traffic deaths

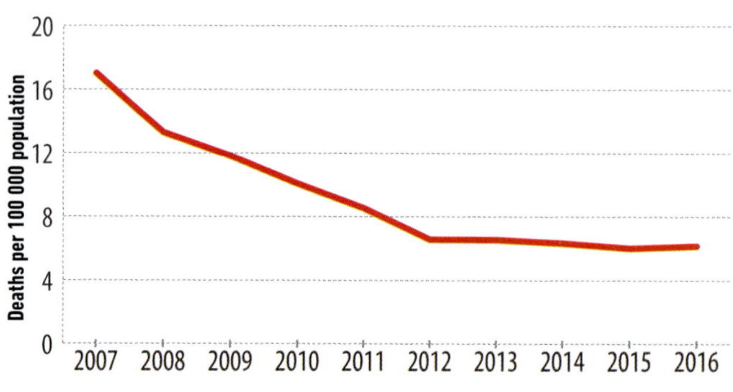

Source: Ministry of Interior

Legislative review conducted by WHO. Vehicle safety data from UNECE WP29. Other data collected by questionnaire and cleared by Ministry of Health and Prevention.

United Kingdom of Great Britain and Northern Ireland

Population: 65 788 572 | Income group: High | Gross national income per capita: US$ 42 390

INSTITUTIONAL FRAMEWORK	
Lead agency	Department for Transport (Great Britain); Transport - Policy, Planning and Partnership Division (Wales); Transport Scotland (Scotland); Department for Infrastructure (Northern Ireland)
Funded in national budget	Yes
National road safety strategy	Yes
Funding to implement strategy	Partially funded
Fatality reduction target	40-60% [a]
SAFER ROADS AND MOBILITY	
Audits or star rating required for new road infrastructure	Yes
Design standards for the safety of pedestrians / cyclists	Yes
Inspections / star rating of existing roads	Yes
Investments to upgrade high risk locations	Yes
Policies & investment in urban public transport	Yes
SAFER VEHICLES	
Total registered vehicles for 2016	38 388 214
Cars and 4-wheeled light vehicles	35 681 940
Motorized 2- and 3-wheelers	1 270 216
Heavy trucks	517 144
Buses	167 056
Other	751 858
Vehicle standards applied (UNECE WP.29)	
Frontal impact standard	Yes
Electronic stability control	Yes
Pedestrian protection	Yes
Motorcycle anti-lock braking system	Yes
POST-CRASH CARE	
National emergency care access number	National, single number
Trauma registry	Subnational
Formal certification for prehospital providers	Yes
National assessment of emergency care systems	No
DATA	
Reported road traffic fatalities (2015)	1 804 [b] (76% M, 24% F)
WHO estimated road traffic fatalities (2016)	2 019
WHO estimated rate per 100 000 population (2016)	3.1

[a] Wales 40%; Scotland 40%; NI at least 60% (2004-2008 average to 2020)
[b] Department for Transport, Road accidents and safety statistics (Great Britain), Police Recorded Injury Road Traffic Collision Statistics (Northern Ireland). Defined as died within 30 days of crash.

SAFER ROAD USERS	
National speed limit law	Yes
Max urban speed limit	~ 48 km/h
Max rural speed limit	~ 96 km/h
Max motorway speed limit	~ 112 km/h
Local authorities can modify limits	Yes
Enforcement	0 1 2 3 4 5 6 7 ⑧ 9 10
Predominant type of enforcement	Automated
National drink-driving law	Yes
BAC limit – general population	≤ 0.08 g/dl [c]
BAC limit – young or novice drivers	≤ 0.08 g/dl [c]
Random breath testing carried out	Yes [d]
Testing carried out in case of fatal crash	All drivers tested
Enforcement	0 1 2 3 4 5 6 7 ⑧ 9 10
% road traffic deaths involving alcohol	13% (GB), 23% (NI) [e]
National motorcycle helmet law	Yes
Applies to drivers and passengers	Yes
Helmet fastening required	Yes
Helmet standard referred to and/or specified	Yes
Children passengers on motorcycles	Not restricted
Enforcement	0 1 2 3 4 5 6 7 8 ⑨ 10
Helmet wearing rate	—
National seat-belt law	Yes
Applies to front and rear seat occupants	Yes
Enforcement	0 1 2 3 4 5 6 7 8 9 ⑩
Seat-belt wearing rate	95% (England and Scotland), 98% (NI) Front seats [f], 90% (England and Scotland), 94% (NI) Rear seats [f]
National child restraint law	Yes
Children seated in front seat	Allowed in a child restraint
Child restraint required	Up to 12 yrs/135 cm
Child restraint standard referred to and/or specified	Yes
Enforcement	0 1 2 3 4 5 6 7 8 9 ⑩
% children using child restraints	95% (NI) [g]
National law on mobile phone use while driving	Yes
Ban on hand-held mobile phone use	Yes
Ban on hands-free mobile phone use	No
National drug-driving law	Yes

[c] In Scotland legal BAC limit is ≤ 0.05g/dl
[d] Legislation requires probable cause to test drivers
[e] 2014, Police Services of Northern Island statistics (NI); Department for Transport Statistical Release 2016 (GB)
[f] 2014, Seatbelt and mobile phone use surveys 2014 (England and Scotland); Survey of Seat Belt Wearing 2014 (NI)
[g] 2014, Northern Ireland Survey of Seat Belt Wearing (figure for all ages and for children seated in the back)

Deaths by road user category

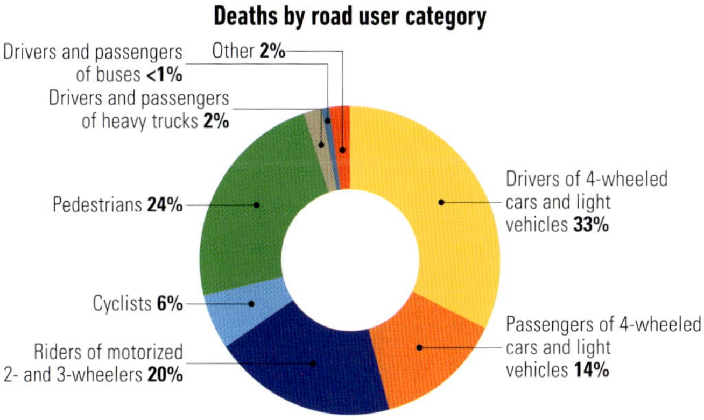

Source: 2015, Department for Transport, Road accidents and safety statistics (Great Britain), Police Recorded Injury Road Traffic Collision Statistics (Northern Ireland)

Trends in reported road traffic deaths

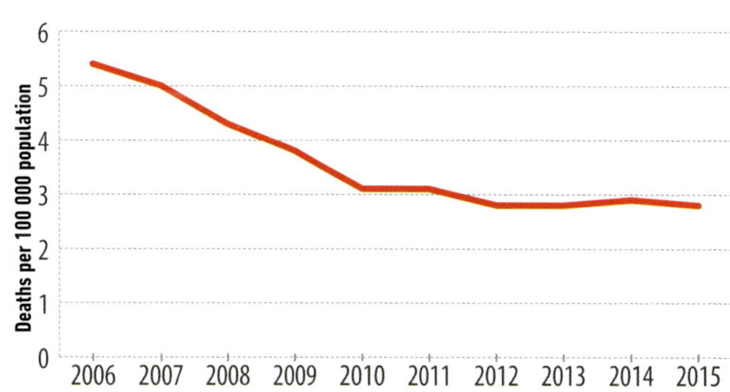

Source: Department for Transport, Road accidents and safety statistics (Great Britain), Police Recorded Injury Road Traffic Collision Statistics (Northern Ireland)

Legislative review conducted by WHO. Vehicle safety data from UNECE WP29. Other data collected by questionnaire and cleared by Department for Transport.

United Republic of Tanzania

Population: 55 572 200 | Income group: Low | Gross national income per capita: US$ 900

INSTITUTIONAL FRAMEWORK

Lead agency	National Road Safety Council (NRSC), Ministry of Home Affairs
Funded in national budget	No
National road safety strategy	Yes
Funding to implement strategy	Partially funded
Fatality reduction target	–

SAFER ROADS AND MOBILITY

Audits or star rating required for new road infrastructure	Yes
Design standards for the safety of pedestrians / cyclists	Partial
Inspections / star rating of existing roads	Yes
Investments to upgrade high risk locations	Yes
Policies & investment in urban public transport	Yes

SAFER VEHICLES

Total registered vehicles for 2016	2 163 623
Cars and 4-wheeled light vehicles	649 127
Motorized 2- and 3-wheelers	1 282 503
Heavy trucks	99 428
Buses	58 247
Other	74 318
Vehicle standards applied (UNECE WP.29)	
Frontal impact standard	No
Electronic stability control	No
Pedestrian protection	No
Motorcycle anti-lock braking system	No

POST-CRASH CARE

National emergency care access number	None
Trauma registry	Subnational
Formal certification for prehospital providers	No
National assessment of emergency care systems	No

DATA

Reported road traffic fatalities (2016)	3 256[a] (79% M, 21% F)
WHO estimated road traffic fatalities (2016)	16 252 (95% CI 13 130 - 19 374)
WHO estimated rate per 100 000 population (2016)	29.2

[a] Traffic Police. Died within 30 days of crash

SAFER ROAD USERS

National speed limit law	Yes
Max urban speed limit	50 km/h
Max rural speed limit	No
Max motorway speed limit	No
Local authorities can modify limits	Yes
Enforcement	0 1 2 3 4 5 6 7 (8) 9 10
Predominant type of enforcement	Manual
National drink-driving law	Yes
BAC limit – general population	≤ 0.08 g/dl
BAC limit – young or novice drivers	≤ 0.08 g/dl
Random breath testing carried out	Yes[b]
Testing carried out in case of fatal crash	No
Enforcement	0 1 2 3 4 5 (6) 7 8 9 10
% road traffic deaths involving alcohol	<1%[c]
National motorcycle helmet law	Yes
Applies to drivers and passengers	No
Helmet fastening required	No
Helmet standard referred to and/or specified	Yes
Children passengers on motorcycles	Not restricted
Enforcement	0 1 2 3 4 5 (6) 7 8 9 10
Helmet wearing rate	–
National seat-belt law	Yes
Applies to front and rear seat occupants	No
Enforcement	0 1 2 3 4 5 6 7 (8) 9 10
Seat-belt wearing rate	–
National child restraint law	No
Children seated in front seat	Not restricted
Child restraint required	–
Child restraint standard referred to and/or specified	–
Enforcement	–
% children using child restraints	–
National law on mobile phone use while driving	No
Ban on hand-held mobile phone use	–
Ban on hands-free mobile phone use	–
National drug-driving law	Yes

[b] Legislation requires probable cause to test drivers or commission of a traffic offence

[c] 2016, Traffic Police

Deaths by road user category

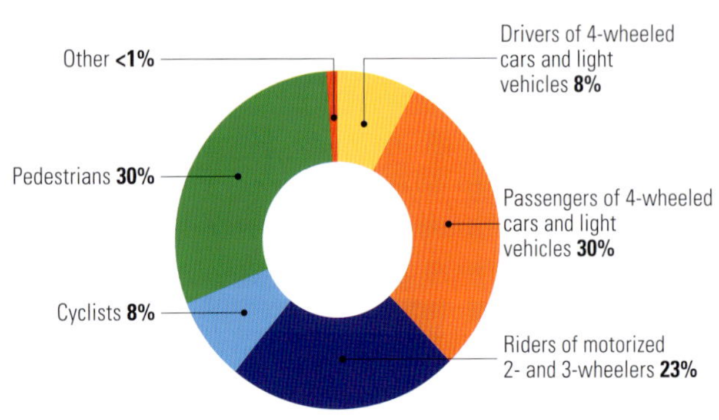

Source: 2016, Traffic Police

Trends in reported road traffic deaths

Source: Traffic Police

Legislative review conducted by WHO. Vehicle safety data from UNECE WP29. Other data collected by questionnaire and cleared by Ministry of Home Affairs

United States of America

Population: 322 179 616 | Income group: High | Gross national income per capita: US$ 56 180

INSTITUTIONAL FRAMEWORK	
Lead agency	National Highway Traffic Safety Administration (NHTSA), Department of Transportation
Funded in national budget	Yes
National road safety strategy	Yes
Funding to implement strategy	Fully funded
Fatality reduction target	1.02 per 100 million miles traveled (VMT) (2018)

SAFER ROADS AND MOBILITY	
Audits or star rating required for new road infrastructure	No
Design standards for the safety of pedestrians / cyclists	No
Inspections / star rating of existing roads	–
Investments to upgrade high risk locations	Yes
Policies & investment in urban public transport	Yes

SAFER VEHICLES	
Total registered vehicles for 2015	281 312 446
Cars and 4-wheeled light vehicles	260 619 419
Motorized 2- and 3-wheelers	8 600 936
Heavy trucks	11 203 184
Buses	888 907
Other	0
Vehicle standards applied (UNECE WP.29)	
Frontal impact standard	Yes
Electronic stability control	Yes
Pedestrian protection	No
Motorcycle anti-lock braking system	No

POST-CRASH CARE	
National emergency care access number	National, single number
Trauma registry	National
Formal certification for prehospital providers	Yes
National assessment of emergency care systems	Yes

DATA	
Reported road traffic fatalities (2015)	35 092[a] (71% M, 29% F)
WHO estimated road traffic fatalities (2016)	39 888
WHO estimated rate per 100 000 population (2016)	12.4

SAFER ROAD USERS*	
National speed limit law	Yes
Max urban speed limit	~ 32 - 128 km/h
Max rural speed limit	~ 40 - 128 km/h
Max motorway speed limit	~ 40 - 128 km/h
Local authorities can modify limits	Yes
Enforcement	–
Predominant type of enforcement	Manual
National drink-driving law	Yes
BAC limit – general population	≤ 0.08 g/dl
BAC limit – young or novice drivers	0.00-0.08 g/dl[b]
Random breath testing carried out	Yes
Testing carried out in case of fatal crash	Some drivers tested
Enforcement	–
% road traffic deaths involving alcohol	29%[c]
National motorcycle helmet law	Yes
Applies to drivers and passengers	No[d]
Helmet fastening required	No
Helmet standard referred to and/or specified	Yes
Children passengers on motorcycles	Not restricted[e]
Enforcement	–
Helmet wearing rate	68% Drivers[f], 53% Passengers[f]
National seat-belt law	Yes
Applies to front and rear seat occupants	No[g]
Enforcement	–
Seat-belt wearing rate	90% Front seats[h], 75% Rear seats[i]
National child restraint law	Yes
Children seated in front seat	Allowed in a child restraint
Child restraint required	–[j]
Child restraint standard referred to and/or specified	Yes
Enforcement	–
% children using child restraints	89%[k]
National law on mobile phone use while driving	Yes
Ban on hand-held mobile phone use	No[l]
Ban on hands-free mobile phone use	No
National drug-driving law	Yes

* These data take into consideration subnational laws. A criteria is answered "Yes" if at least 80% of the subnational entities meet the criteria
[a] Fatality Analysis Reporting System (FARS) Annual Report File. Died within 30 days of crash
[b] Over 90% of the states provide a BAC limit equal or under 0.02 g/dl for young-novice drivers
[c] 2015, National Center for Statistics and Analysis. (2016, December). Alcohol-impaired driving: 2015 data (Traffic Safety Facts. DOT HS 812 350). Washington, DC: National Highway Traffic Safety Administration.
[d] About 40 % of the states require helmets for both drivers and passengers on motorcycles
[e] Less than 10% of the states prohibit that children ride as passengers on motorcycles
[f] 2016, Motorcycle helmet use in 2016 – Overall results. (Traffic Safety Facts Research Note. Report No. DOT HS 812 378), National Highway Traffic Safety Administration.
[g] About 40% of the states do not require seat belt for rear seats passengers
[h] 2016, Seat Belt Use. Overall Results (Traffic Safety Facts Research Note. Report No. DOT HS 812 351), National Highway Traffic Safety Administration.
[i] 2015, Occupant restraint use in 2015: Results from the NOPUS controlled intersection study (Report No. DOT HS 812 330), National Highway Traffic Safety Administration.
[j] Child restraint laws are enacted at subnational level. While all states require the use of child restraints, they provide different age /weight/ height criteria to specify the period for mandatory use of child restraints / booster seats
[k] 2016, the 2015 National Survey of the Use of Booster Seats (NSUBS) (Report No. DOT HS 812 309). Washington, DC: National Highway Traffic Safety Administration.
[l] The majority of states prohibit texting while driving

Deaths by road user category

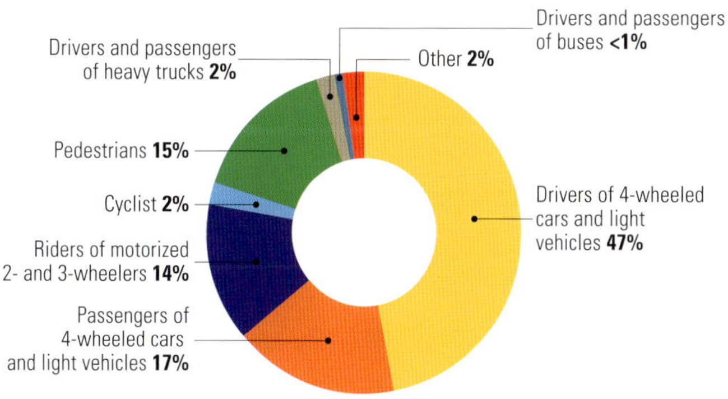

Source: 2015, Fatality Analysis Reporting System (FARS) Annual Report File

Trends in reported road traffic deaths

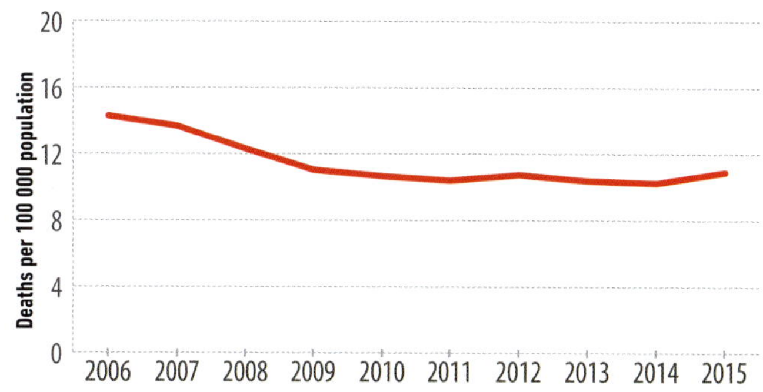

Source: 2006-2010 Fatality Analysis Reporting System (FARS) Annual Final File, and 2015 Fatality Analysis Reporting System (FARS) Annual Report File

Legislative review conducted by WHO. Vehicle safety data from UNECE WP.29. Other data collected by questionnaire and cleared by Department of Health and Human Services.

Uruguay

Population: 3 444 006 | Income group: High | Gross national income per capita: US$ 15 230

INSTITUTIONAL FRAMEWORK	
Lead agency	National Road Safety Unit (UNASEV)
Funded in national budget	Yes
National road safety strategy	No
Funding to implement strategy	–
Fatality reduction target	–
SAFER ROADS AND MOBILITY	
Audits or star rating required for new road infrastructure	No
Design standards for the safety of pedestrians / cyclists	Partial
Inspections / star rating of existing roads	No
Investments to upgrade high risk locations	No
Policies & investment in urban public transport	Yes
SAFER VEHICLES	
Total registered vehicles for 2016	2 342 026
Cars and 4-wheeled light vehicles	1 008 974
Motorized 2- and 3-wheelers	1 252 031
Heavy trucks	71 355
Buses	9 666
Other	0
Vehicle standards applied (UNECE WP.29)	
Frontal impact standard	No
Electronic stability control	No
Pedestrian protection	No
Motorcycle anti-lock braking system	No
POST-CRASH CARE	
National emergency care access number	National, single number
Trauma registry	National
Formal certification for prehospital providers	No
National assessment of emergency care systems	No
DATA	
Reported road traffic fatalities (2016)	446[a] (75% M, 25% F)
WHO estimated road traffic fatalities (2016)	460
WHO estimated rate per 100 000 population (2016)	13.4

[a] National Traffic Information System (SINATRAN). Died within 30 days of crash

SAFER ROAD USERS	
National speed limit law	Yes
Max urban speed limit	45 km/h
Max rural speed limit	90 km/h
Max motorway speed limit	90 km/h
Local authorities can modify limits	Yes
Enforcement	0 1 2 3 4 5 (6) 7 8 9 10
Predominant type of enforcement	Manual and automated
National drink-driving law	Yes
BAC limit – general population	0.00 g/dl
BAC limit – young or novice drivers	0.00 g/dl
Random breath testing carried out	Yes
Testing carried out in case of fatal crash	Some drivers tested
Enforcement	0 1 2 3 4 5 6 7 8 (9) 10
% road traffic deaths involving alcohol	–
National motorcycle helmet law	Yes
Applies to drivers and passengers	Yes
Helmet fastening required	No
Helmet standard referred to and/or specified	Yes
Children passengers on motorcycles	Prohibited[b]
Enforcement	0 1 2 3 4 5 6 (7) 8 9 10
Helmet wearing rate	80% Drivers[c], 71% Passengers[c]
National seat-belt law	Yes
Applies to front and rear seat occupants	Yes
Enforcement	0 1 2 3 4 5 (6) 7 8 9 10
Seat-belt wearing rate	63% Front seats[d], 33% Rear seats[d]
National child restraint law	Yes
Children seated in front seat	Prohibited under 12 yrs/150 cm
Child restraint required	Up to 12 yrs/36 kg/150 cm
Child restraint standard referred to and/or specified	Yes
Enforcement	0 1 2 3 (4) 5 6 7 8 9 10
% children using child restraints	23%[d]
National law on mobile phone use while driving	Yes
Ban on hand-held mobile phone use	Yes
Ban on hands-free mobile phone use	No
National drug-driving law	Yes

[b] Until footrests can be reached
[c] 2016, National Traffic Information System (SINATRAN)
[d] 2016, Observational behavior study in road safety, Uruguay

Deaths by road user category

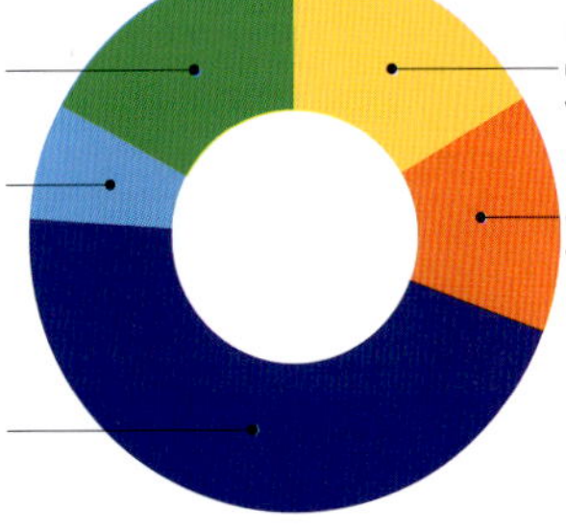

Source: 2016, National Traffic Information System (SINATRAN)

Trends in reported road traffic deaths

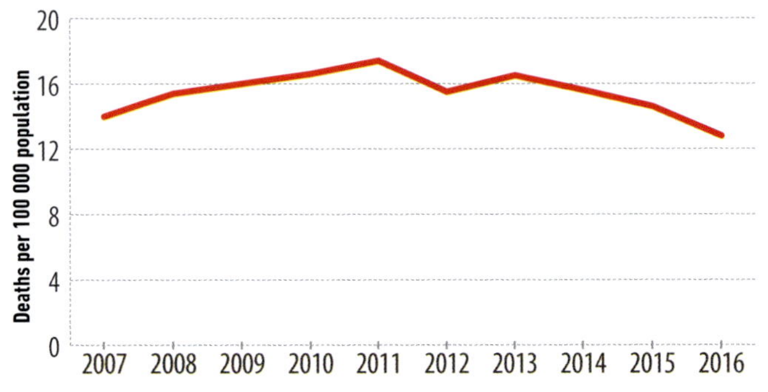

Source: National Traffic Information System (SINATRAN)

Legislative review conducted by WHO. Vehicle safety data from UNECE WP29. Other data collected by questionnaire and cleared by National Road Safety Unit (UNASEV)

Uzbekistan

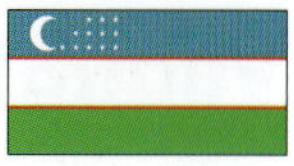

Population: 31 446 796 | Income group: Middle | Gross national income per capita: US$ 2 220

INSTITUTIONAL FRAMEWORK

Lead agency	State Service on Traffic Safety, Ministry of Internal Affairs of Republic of Uzbekistan
Funded in national budget	Yes
National road safety strategy	No
Funding to implement strategy	–
Fatality reduction target	–

SAFER ROADS AND MOBILITY

Audits or star rating required for new road infrastructure	Yes
Design standards for the safety of pedestrians / cyclists	Yes
Inspections / star rating of existing roads	Yes
Investments to upgrade high risk locations	Yes
Policies & investment in urban public transport	Yes

SAFER VEHICLES

Total registered vehicles	–
Cars and 4-wheeled light vehicles	–
Motorized 2- and 3-wheelers	–
Heavy trucks	–
Buses	–
Other	–
Vehicle standards applied (UNECE WP.29)	
Frontal impact standard	No
Electronic stability control	No
Pedestrian protection	No
Motorcycle anti-lock braking system	No

POST-CRASH CARE

National emergency care access number	National, single number
Trauma registry	–
Formal certification for prehospital providers	–
National assessment of emergency care systems	–

DATA

Reported road traffic fatalities (2016)	2 496 [a]
WHO estimated road traffic fatalities (2016)	3 617
WHO estimated rate per 100 000 population (2016)	11.5

[a] State service on Traffic Safety, Ministry of Internal Affairs of Republic of Uzbekistan. Died within 30 days of crash

SAFER ROAD USERS

National speed limit law	Yes
Max urban speed limit	70 km/h
Max rural speed limit	100 km/h
Max motorway speed limit	No
Local authorities can modify limits	No
Enforcement	0 1 2 3 4 5 6 7 (8) 9 10
Predominant type of enforcement	Manual
National drink-driving law	Yes [b]
BAC limit – general population	–
BAC limit – young or novice drivers	–
Random breath testing carried out	Yes
Testing carried out in case of fatal crash	–
Enforcement	0 1 2 3 4 5 6 7 8 9 (10)
% road traffic deaths involving alcohol	4% [c]
National motorcycle helmet law	Yes
Applies to drivers and passengers	Yes
Helmet fastening required	Yes
Helmet standard referred to and/or specified	No
Children passengers on motorcycles	Prohibited under 12 yrs
Enforcement	0 1 2 3 4 5 6 7 8 9 (10)
Helmet wearing rate	–
National seat-belt law	Yes
Applies to front and rear seat occupants	No
Enforcement	0 1 2 3 4 (5) 6 7 8 9 10
Seat-belt wearing rate	–
National child restraint law	No
Children seated in front seat	Allowed in a child restraint
Child restraint required	–
Child restraint standard referred to and/or specified	–
Enforcement	–
% children using child restraints	–
National law on mobile phone use while driving	Yes
Ban on hand-held mobile phone use	Yes
Ban on hands-free mobile phone use	Yes
National drug-driving law	Yes

[b] Not based on BAC
[c] 2016, Statistics of State Road Safety Service

Deaths by road user category

Trends in reported road traffic deaths

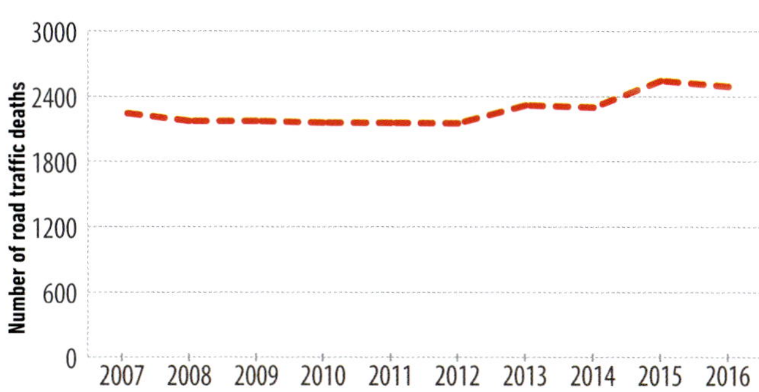

Source: Statistics of State Service on Traffic Safety, Ministry of Internal Affairs of Republic of Uzbekistan

Legislative review conducted by WHO. Vehicle safety data from UNECE WP.29. Other data collected by questionnaire and cleared by Republican specialized scientific-practical medical center of traumatology and orthopedics.

Vanuatu

Population: 270 402 | Income group: Middle | Gross national income per capita: US$ 3 170[a]

INSTITUTIONAL FRAMEWORK

Lead agency	**Vanuatu Police Force, Ministry of Internal Affairs**
Funded in national budget	Yes
National road safety strategy	**Yes**
Funding to implement strategy	Partially funded
Fatality reduction target	–

SAFER ROADS AND MOBILITY

Audits or star rating required for new road infrastructure	Partial
Design standards for the safety of pedestrians / cyclists	Partial
Inspections / star rating of existing roads	No
Investments to upgrade high risk locations	Yes
Policies & investment in urban public transport	Yes

SAFER VEHICLES

Total registered vehicles	**–**
Cars and 4-wheeled light vehicles	–
Motorized 2- and 3-wheelers	–
Heavy trucks	–
Buses	–
Other	–
Vehicle standards applied (UNECE WP.29)	
Frontal impact standard	No
Electronic stability control	No
Pedestrian protection	No
Motorcycle anti-lock braking system	No

POST-CRASH CARE

National emergency care access number	National, single number
Trauma registry	National
Formal certification for prehospital providers	No
National assessment of emergency care systems	No

DATA

Reported road traffic fatalities (2016)	9[b] (67% M, 33% F)
WHO estimated road traffic fatalities (2016)	43 (95% CI 39 - 48)
WHO estimated rate per 100 000 population (2016)	15.9

[a] Data available only for 2014
[b] Vanuatu Police (manual records). Died at scene of crash

SAFER ROAD USERS

National speed limit law	**No**
Max urban speed limit	–
Max rural speed limit	–
Max motorway speed limit	–
Local authorities can modify limits	–
Enforcement	–
Predominant type of enforcement	–
National drink-driving law	**Yes[c]**
BAC limit – general population	–
BAC limit – young or novice drivers	–
Random breath testing carried out	No
Testing carried out in case of fatal crash	No
Enforcement	⓪ 1 2 3 4 5 6 7 8 9 10
% road traffic deaths involving alcohol	67%[d]
National motorcycle helmet law	**Yes**
Applies to drivers and passengers	Yes
Helmet fastening required	Yes
Helmet standard referred to and/or specified	Yes
Children passengers on motorcycles	Not restricted
Enforcement	0 1 2 3 4 5 6 7 ⑧ 9 10
Helmet wearing rate	90% Drivers[e], 90% Passengers[e]
National seat-belt law	**Yes**
Applies to front and rear seat occupants	No
Enforcement	0 1 ② 3 4 5 6 7 8 9 10
Seat-belt wearing rate	20% Front seats[e], 10% Rear seats[e]
National child restraint law	**No[f]**
Children seated in front seat	Allowed in a child restraint[g]
Child restraint required	–
Child restraint standard referred to and/or specified	–
Enforcement	–
% children using child restraints	–
National law on mobile phone use while driving	**No**
Ban on hand-held mobile phone use	–
Ban on hands-free mobile phone use	–
National drug-driving law	**Yes**

[c] Not based on BAC
[d] 2016, Vanuatu Police, Traffic occurrence book
[e] 2016, Vanuatu Police Force
[f] Legislation allows that infants (defined as children under 3 years) be held by a responsible person as an alternative to using special seats
[g] Infant (defined as children under 3 years) shall be placed in a restraining seat while travelling in the front

Deaths by road user category

Trends in reported road traffic deaths

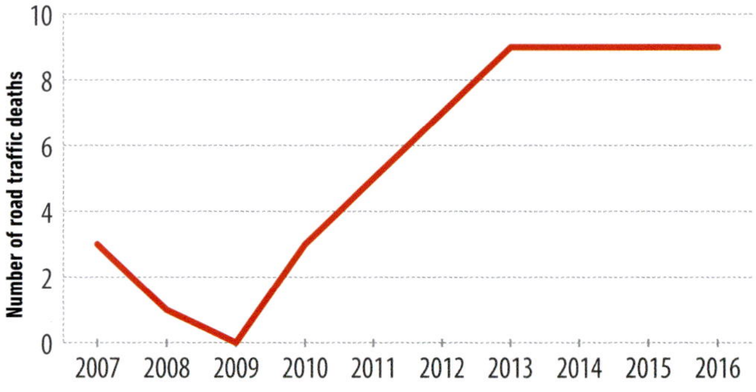

Source: 2013, GSRRS3

Legislative review conducted by WHO. Vehicle safety data from UNECE WP29. Other data collected by questionnaire and cleared by the Ministry of Health.

Venezuela (Bolivarian Republic of)

Population: 31 568 180 | Income group: Middle | Gross national income per capita: US$ 11 760[a]

INSTITUTIONAL FRAMEWORK	
Lead agency	National Institute of Land Transport, Ministry of People's Power for Land Transport
Funded in national budget	Yes
National road safety strategy	Yes
Funding to implement strategy	Fully funded
Fatality reduction target	–
SAFER ROADS AND MOBILITY	
Audits or star rating required for new road infrastructure	Yes
Design standards for the safety of pedestrians / cyclists	Yes
Inspections / star rating of existing roads	–
Investments to upgrade high risk locations	No
Policies & investment in urban public transport	Yes
SAFER VEHICLES	
Total registered vehicles for 2016	7 999 760
Cars and 4-wheeled light vehicles	4 558 246
Motorized 2- and 3-wheelers	1 263 506
Heavy trucks	1 818 649
Buses	336 846
Other	22 513
Vehicle standards applied (UNECE WP.29)	
Frontal impact standard	No
Electronic stability control	No
Pedestrian protection	No
Motorcycle anti-lock braking system	No
POST-CRASH CARE	
National emergency care access number	National, single number
Trauma registry	National
Formal certification for prehospital providers	Yes
National assessment of emergency care systems	No
DATA	
Reported road traffic fatalities (2013)	7 028[b] (83% M, 17% F)
WHO estimated road traffic fatalities (2016)	10 640
WHO estimated rate per 100 000 population (2016)	33.7

[a] Data available only for 2013

[b] 2013 Yearbook Mortality, Ministry of the Popular Power for Health. Died within 30 days of crash

SAFER ROAD USERS	
National speed limit law	No
Max urban speed limit	–
Max rural speed limit	–
Max motorway speed limit	–
Local authorities can modify limits	–
Enforcement	–
Predominant type of enforcement	–
National drink-driving law	Yes[c]
BAC limit – general population	–
BAC limit – young or novice drivers	–
Random breath testing carried out	Yes
Testing carried out in case of fatal crash	All drivers tested
Enforcement	0 1 2 3 (4) 5 6 7 8 9 10
% road traffic deaths involving alcohol	–
National motorcycle helmet law	Yes
Applies to drivers and passengers	Yes
Helmet fastening required	No
Helmet standard referred to and/or specified	No
Children passengers on motorcycles	Prohibited under 10 yrs
Enforcement	0 1 2 (3) 4 5 6 7 8 9 10
Helmet wearing rate	–
National seat-belt law	Yes
Applies to front and rear seat occupants	Yes
Enforcement	0 1 2 3 4 5 (6) 7 8 9 10
Seat-belt wearing rate	–
National child restraint law	Yes[d]
Children seated in front seat	Prohibited under 10 yrs
Child restraint required	–[d]
Child restraint standard referred to and/or specified	No
Enforcement	0 1 2 (3) 4 5 6 7 8 9 10
% children using child restraints	–
National law on mobile phone use while driving	Yes
Ban on hand-held mobile phone use	Yes
Ban on hands-free mobile phone use	No
National drug-driving law	Yes

[c] Not based on BAC

[d] The law requires "infants" to use "special seats for that purpose" but does not specify the age for children falling into the "infants" category

Deaths by road user category

Trends in reported road traffic deaths

Source: 2013 Yearbook Mortality, Ministry of the Popular Power for Health

Legislative review conducted by WHO. Vehicle safety data from UNECE WP29. Other data collected by questionnaire and cleared by Ministry of Ministry of Popular Power for Health.

Viet Nam

Population: 94 569 072 | Income group: Middle | Gross national income per capita: US$ 2 050

INSTITUTIONAL FRAMEWORK	
Lead agency	**National Traffic Safety Committee (NTSC)**
Funded in national budget	Yes
National road safety strategy	**Yes**
Funding to implement strategy	Partially funded
Fatality reduction target	5-10% annually (2012-2020)

SAFER ROADS AND MOBILITY	
Audits or star rating required for new road infrastructure	Yes
Design standards for the safety of pedestrians / cyclists	Partial
Inspections / star rating of existing roads	Yes
Investments to upgrade high risk locations	Yes
Policies & investment in urban public transport	Yes

SAFER VEHICLES	
Total registered vehicles for 2016	**50 666 855**
Cars and 4-wheeled light vehicles	3 033 527
Motorized 2- and 3-wheelers	47 131 928
Heavy trucks	—
Buses	—
Other	501 400
Vehicle standards applied (UNECE WP.29)	
Frontal impact standard	No
Electronic stability control	No
Pedestrian protection	No
Motorcycle anti-lock braking system	No

POST-CRASH CARE	
National emergency care access number	Partial coverage
Trauma registry	National
Formal certification for prehospital providers	No
National assessment of emergency care systems	No

DATA	
Reported road traffic fatalities (2016)	8 417 [a]
WHO estimated road traffic fatalities (2016)	24 970 (95% CI 21 576 - 28 363)
WHO estimated rate per 100 000 population (2016)	26.4

[a] Report of Road Safety Performance Review of Viet Nam, The United Nations Economic and Social Commission for Asia (UNESCAP) and the Pacific and Ministry of Transport of Viet Nam (MOT). Died within 7 days of crash

SAFER ROAD USERS	
National speed limit law	**Yes**
Max urban speed limit	60 km/h
Max rural speed limit	90 km/h
Max motorway speed limit	120 km/h
Local authorities can modify limits	No
Enforcement	0 1 2 3 4 5 6 ⑦ 8 9 10
Predominant type of enforcement	Manual and automated
National drink-driving law	**Yes**
BAC limit – general population	0.00 - 0.05 g/dl [b]
BAC limit – young or novice drivers	0.00 - 0.05 g/dl [b]
Random breath testing carried out	Yes
Testing carried out in case of fatal crash	Some drivers tested
Enforcement	0 1 2 3 4 5 6 7 ⑧ 9 10
% road traffic deaths involving alcohol	—
National motorcycle helmet law	**Yes**
Applies to drivers and passengers	Yes
Helmet fastening required	Yes
Helmet standard referred to and/or specified	Yes
Children passengers on motorcycles	Not restricted
Enforcement	0 1 2 3 4 5 6 7 ⑧ 9 10
Helmet wearing rate	81% Drivers [c], 60% Passengers [c]
National seat-belt law	**Yes**
Applies to front and rear seat occupants	No
Enforcement	0 1 2 3 4 5 ⑥ 7 8 9 10
Seat-belt wearing rate	—
National child restraint law	**No**
Children seated in front seat	Not restricted
Child restraint required	—
Child restraint standard referred to and/or specified	—
Enforcement	—
% children using child restraints	—
National law on mobile phone use while driving	**Yes**
Ban on hand-held mobile phone use	Yes
Ban on hands-free mobile phone use	No
National drug-driving law	**Yes**

[b] Different BAC limits are set depending on the type of vehicle used: for drivers of cars the BAC limit is set at 0.00g/dl while for drivers of motorcycles and mopeds the legal BAC limit is set at 0.05g/dl

[c] 2013, Helmet observation in Ha Noi, BacNinh, Quang Ninh, Da Nang, Vinh Phuc, and Ho Chi Minh city

Deaths by road user category

Trends in reported road traffic deaths

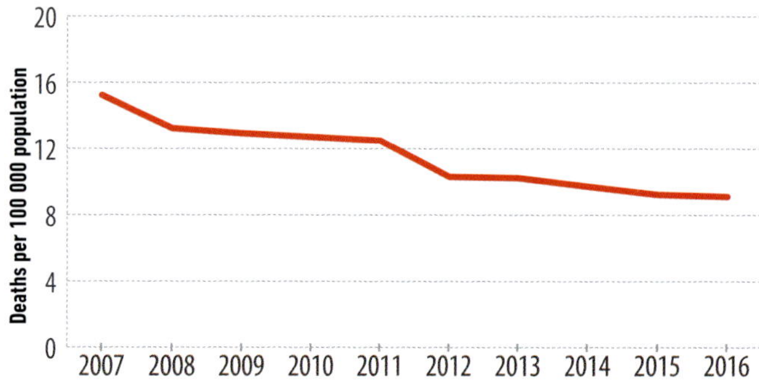

Source: Report of Road Safety Performance Review of Viet Nam, The United Nations Economic and Social Commission for Asia (UNESCAP) and the Pacific and Ministry of Transport of Viet Nam (MOT)

Legislative review conducted by WHO. Vehicle safety data from UNECE WP29. Other data collected by questionnaire and cleared by the Ministry of Transport.

West Bank and Gaza Strip

Population: 4 790 705 | Income group: Middle | Gross national income per capita: US$ 3 230

INSTITUTIONAL FRAMEWORK	
Lead agency	Higher Traffic Council
Funded in budget	Yes
Road safety strategy	Yes
Funding to implement strategy	Partially funded
Fatality reduction target	–
SAFER ROADS AND MOBILITY	
Audits or star rating required for new road infrastructure	Yes
Design standards for the safety of pedestrians / cyclists	No
Inspections / star rating of existing roads	Yes
Investments to upgrade high risk locations	Yes
Policies & investment in urban public transport	Yes
SAFER VEHICLES	
Total registered vehicles for 2015	268 365
Cars and 4-wheeled light vehicles	213 375
Motorized 2- and 3-wheelers	1 670
Heavy trucks	22 277
Buses	2 225
Other	28 818
Vehicle standards applied (UNECE WP.29)	
Frontal impact standard	No
Electronic stability control	No
Pedestrian protection	No
Motorcycle anti-lock braking system	No
POST-CRASH CARE	
Emergency care access number	Single number
Trauma registry	None
Formal certification for prehospital providers	No
National assessment of emergency care systems	No
DATA	
Reported road traffic fatalities (2016)	159[a] (77% M, 23% F)
WHO estimated road traffic fatalities (2016)	252 (95% CI 189 - 333)
WHO estimated rate per 100 000 population (2016)	5.3

[a] Police / Traffic Department, Annual Police Report. Died within 30 days of crash

SAFER ROAD USERS	
Speed limit law	Yes
Max urban speed limit	50 km/h
Max rural speed limit	80 km/h
Max motorway speed limit	110 km/h
Local authorities can modify limits	No
Enforcement	0 1 (2) 3 4 5 6 7 8 9 10
Predominant type of enforcement	Manual
Drink-driving law	Yes[b]
BAC limit – general population	–
BAC limit – young or novice drivers	–
Random breath testing carried out	Yes
Testing carried out in case of fatal crash	No
Enforcement	0 1 2 3 4 (5) 6 7 8 9 10
% road traffic deaths involving alcohol	–
Motorcycle helmet law	Yes
Applies to drivers and passengers	Yes
Helmet fastening required	Yes
Helmet standard referred to and/or specified	Yes
Children passengers on motorcycles	Not restricted
Enforcement	0 1 2 3 4 (5) 6 7 8 9 10
Helmet wearing rate	–
Seat-belt law	Yes
Applies to front and rear seat occupants	Yes
Enforcement	0 1 2 3 4 5 (6) 7 8 9 10
Seat-belt wearing rate	–
Child restraint law	Yes
Children seated in front seat	Allowed in a child restraint
Child restraint required	Up to 14 yrs
Child restraint standard referred to and/or specified	Yes[c]
Enforcement	0 1 2 (3) 4 5 6 7 8 9 10
% children using child restraints	–
Law on mobile phone use while driving	Yes
Ban on hand-held mobile phone use	Yes
Ban on hands-free mobile phone use	No
Drug-driving law	Yes

[b] Not based on BAC
[c] Law refers to a device of the type validated by the licensing authority to restrain children under 14 years

Deaths by road user category

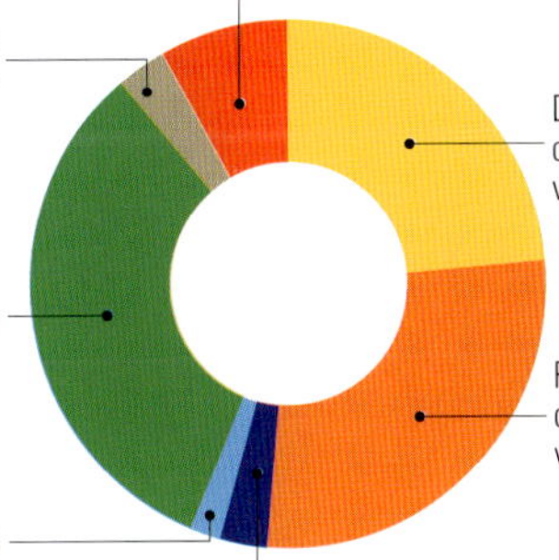

Source: 2016, Police / Traffic Department, Annual Police Report

Trends in reported road traffic deaths

Source: Palestinian Statistics Authority and Police Department

Legislative review conducted by WHO. Vehicle safety data from UNECE WP29. Other data collected by questionnaire and cleared by Ministry of Health.

Zimbabwe

Population: 16 150 362 | Income group: Low | Gross national income per capita: US$ 940

INSTITUTIONAL FRAMEWORK

Lead agency	Traffic Safety Council of Zimbabwe, Ministry of Transport and Infrastructural Development
Funded in national budget	No
National road safety strategy	No
Funding to implement strategy	–
Fatality reduction target	–

SAFER ROADS AND MOBILITY

Audits or star rating required for new road infrastructure	Yes
Design standards for the safety of pedestrians / cyclists	Partial
Inspections / star rating of existing roads	Yes
Investments to upgrade high risk locations	Yes
Policies & investment in urban public transport	Yes

SAFER VEHICLES

Total registered vehicles for June 2017	1 198 584
Cars and 4-wheeled light vehicles	953 852
Motorized 2- and 3-wheelers	46 734
Heavy trucks	123 706
Buses	15 007
Other	59 285
Vehicle standards applied (UNECE WP.29)	
Frontal impact standard	No
Electronic stability control	No
Pedestrian protection	No
Motorcycle anti-lock braking system	No

POST-CRASH CARE

National emergency care access number	National, multiple numbers
Trauma registry	None
Formal certification for prehospital providers	Yes
National assessment of emergency care systems	No

DATA

Reported road traffic fatalities (2016)	1 721[a] (56% M, 44% F)
WHO estimated road traffic fatalities (2016)	5 601 (95% CI 4 602 - 6 599)
WHO estimated rate per 100 000 population (2016)	34.7

[a] Zimbabwe Republic Police. Died within 30 days of crash

SAFER ROAD USERS

National speed limit law	Yes
Max urban speed limit	60 km/h
Max rural speed limit	80 km/h[b]
Max motorway speed limit	120 km/h
Local authorities can modify limits	Yes
Enforcement	0 1 2 3 4 5 (6) 7 8 9 10
Predominant type of enforcement	Manual
National drink-driving law	Yes
BAC limit – general population	< 0.08 g/dl
BAC limit – young or novice drivers	< 0.08 g/dl
Random breath testing carried out	No
Testing carried out in case of fatal crash	Some drivers tested
Enforcement	0 1 2 3 4 (5) 6 7 8 9 10
% road traffic deaths involving alcohol	–
National motorcycle helmet law	Yes
Applies to drivers and passengers	Yes
Helmet fastening required	Yes
Helmet standard referred to and/or specified	Yes
Children passengers on motorcycles	Not restricted
Enforcement	0 1 2 3 4 5 6 7 (8) 9 10
Helmet wearing rate	–
National seat-belt law	Yes
Applies to front and rear seat occupants	No
Enforcement	0 1 2 3 4 5 6 (7) 8 9 10
Seat-belt wearing rate	–
National child restraint law	No
Children seated in front seat	Prohibited under 10 yrs
Child restraint required	–
Child restraint standard referred to and/or specified	–
Enforcement	–
% children using child restraints	–
National law on mobile phone use while driving	Yes
Ban on hand-held mobile phone use	Yes
Ban on hands-free mobile phone use	No
National drug-driving law	Yes

[b] A 120 km/h speed limits applies on roads having a bituminous surface coat of 6 metres or more in width

Deaths by road user category

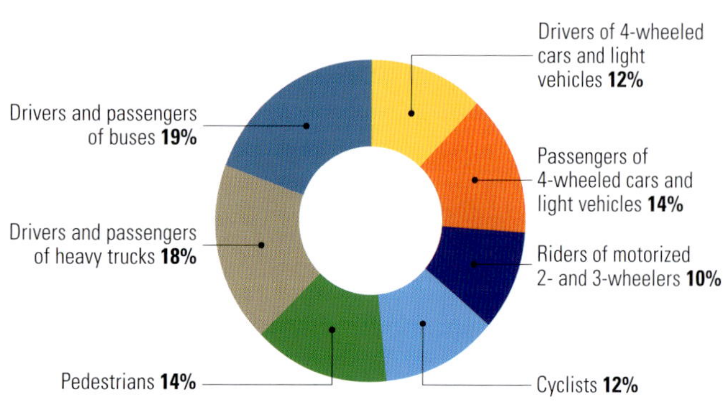

Source: 2016, Zimbabwe Republic Police

Trends in reported road traffic deaths

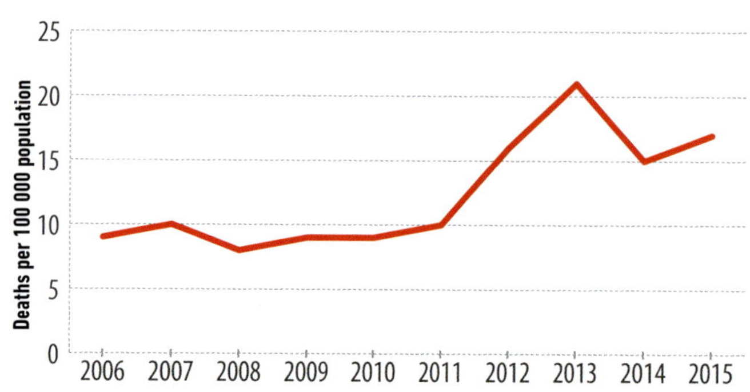

Source: Zimbabwe Republic Police

Legislative review conducted by WHO. Vehicle safety data from UNECE WP29. Other data collected by questionnaire and cleared by Ministry of Health and Child Care.

SECTION 3

EXPLANATORY NOTES AND STATISTICAL ANNEX

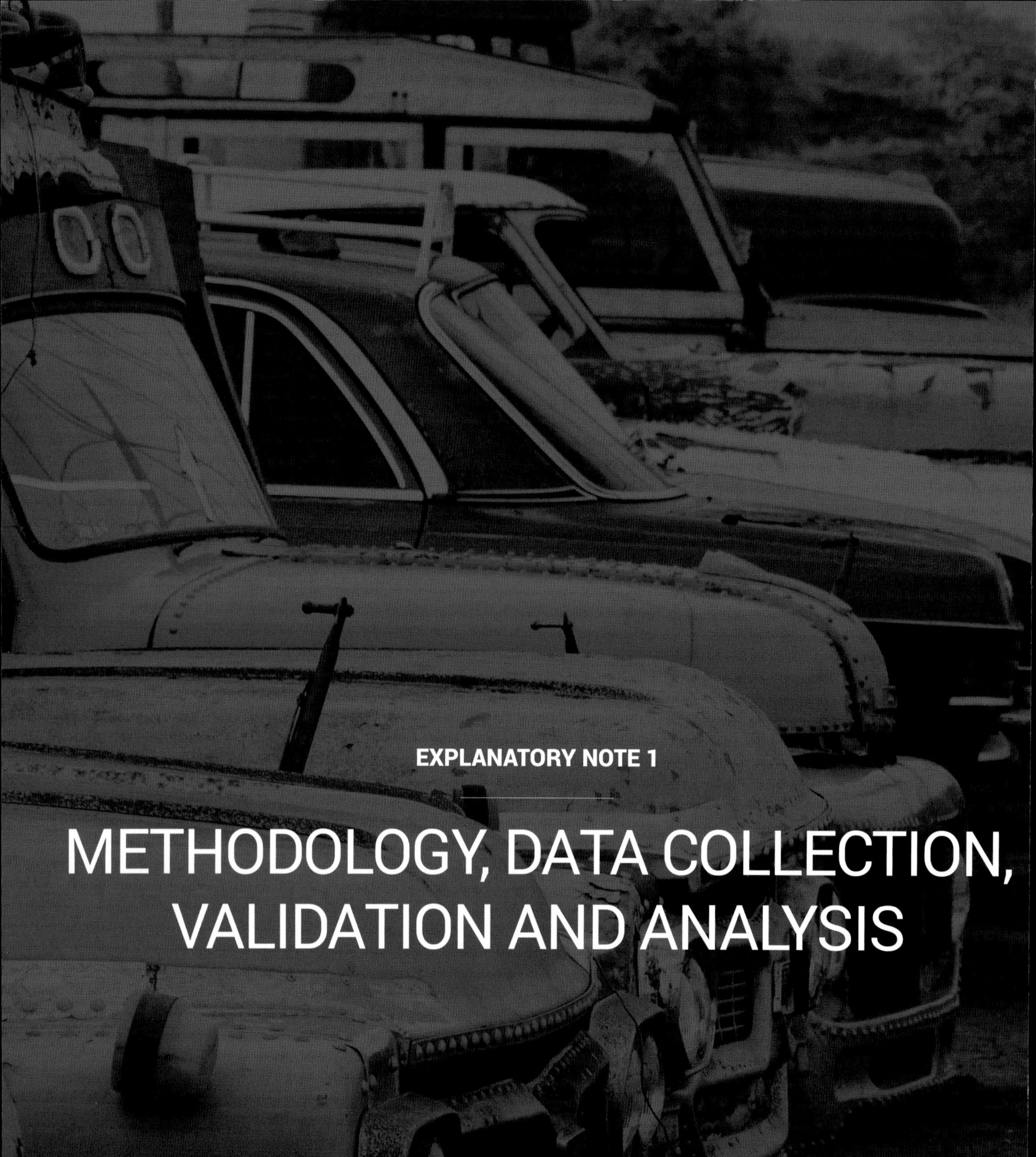

EXPLANATORY NOTE 1

METHODOLOGY, DATA COLLECTION, VALIDATION AND ANALYSIS

Methodology

The methodology involved collecting data from a number of different sectors and stakeholders in each country according to the following process.

National Data Coordinators (NDCs), who were nominated by their governments, were trained in the project methodology. As representatives of their governments, they were required to identify up to eight other road safety experts within their countries from different sectors (e.g. health, police, transport, nongovernmental organizations and/or academia), to facilitate a consensus meeting with the respondents as well as to support the overall management of data collection process. While each expert responded to the questionnaire based on their expertise, the consensus meeting allowed for discussion of all responses, and the group used this discussion to agree on one final set of information that best represented their country's situation at the time (up to 2017, using the most recent data available). This was then submitted to the World Health Organization (WHO) (see Figure E1).

Figure E1: Methodology

National Data Coordinators were asked to submit laws relating to the key behavioural risk factors[1]. All legislative documents were analysed by lawyers at WHO headquarters who extracted the relevant information needed to assess legislation against predetermined criteria. The legal analysis was then shared with National Data Coordinators and a validation process was undertaken to resolve any data conflicts through discussion and/or submission of new legal documents. A new addition to this report is the comparison of legislation status between December 2014 and December 2017 which gives an indication of the pace and nature of legislative changes for the behavioural risk factors reviewed. To ensure the accuracy of the comparison made, the situation at December 2014 was re-evaluated against relevant additional information and documents received in the GSRRS4 data collection process using harmonized interpretation methods. Changes in the legal data published in last report are detailed in the revision guide available at http://www.who.int/violence_injury_prevention/road_safety_status/2018/en.

The methodology used to collect information on vehicle standards was also consistent with the previous report and based on information from the UN World Forum for Harmonization of Vehicle Regulations[2] and interpreted with technical support from Global New Car Assessment Programme (Global NCAP).[3]

The report includes data from 175 countries/areas out of a total of 195, covering 7.3 billion people (98.1% of the world's population). This includes 49 high-income countries, 98 middle-income countries, and 28 low-income countries (see Table E1). Data on legislation and policies represent the country's situation as of 31 December 2017 while data on fatalities and vehicle registration are for 2016, or the most recent year for which these data were available.

Table E1: Participation in the *Global status report on road safety 2018*

Region	Number of participating countries	Number of countries in region	% population participating
African Region	44	47	93.7
Region of the Americas	30	35	98.2
Eastern Mediterranean Region	19	22	95.5
European Region	51	53	99.9
South-East Asian Region	10	11	98.7
Western Pacific Region	21	27	99.9
WORLD	175	195	98.1

1 These behavioural risk factors are speed, drink-driving, drug-driving, the use of mobile phones while driving, failure to use motorcycle helmets, seat-belts and child restraints

2 The UN World Forum for Harmonization of Vehicle Regulations (World Forum the global body responsible for the development of passenger car safety standards), http://www.unece.org/trans/main/wp29/introduction.html

3 Global NCAP is a British organization that conducts testing programmes that will assess the safety of motor vehicles, http://www.globalncap.org/

Data collection and validation

Questionnaire data

The questionnaire used for this report was based on the questionnaire used in the previous report. However, some questions were modified to improve the quality of responses and some were added or deleted. The questionnaire can be downloaded with an accompanying instruction booklet on http://www.who.int/violence_injury_prevention/road_safety_status/2018/methodology/en/.

The questionnaire, protocol and accompanying guidelines and training materials were all available in the six WHO languages (Arabic, Chinese, English, French, Russian and Spanish). Where needed, NDCs coordinated the translation of these documents into local languages and then translated back into English for the data entry stage. All data were entered into an on-line database from where data could be extracted for analysis.

Data collection began in May 2016 and was completed by December 2017. Data validation involved verifying the data against source documents where available and checking for logical inconsistencies. Discrepancies were referred back to the National Data Coordinators where possible for resolution. Following the validation process, the questionnaire data was submitted by the National Data Coordinator to an online database. Final questionnaires were generated from the online data and were sent to respective governments for review and sign-off.

Fatality data

Estimates on number of road traffic deaths relied in part on data from questionnaires as well as from other sources (see Explanatory Note 3). However, countries/areas were also asked to provide a breakdown of deaths by road user type. These proportions (where available) are reflected in the country profiles (see Explanatory Note 2) and were derived from:

→ Country reported data in the current questionnaire;

→ If not available from questionnaires, data that countries reported for the previous reports were used.

These values were then aggregated into regional and global estimates of deaths by road user type.

Legislative data and maps

This report collected information on a number of variables relating to legislation on the five key behavioural risk factors (speed, drink-driving, failure to use helmets, seat-belts and child restraints) as well as on two emerging risk factors, drug-driving and the use of mobile phones while driving.

Criteria analysed for each risk factor are detailed in Table E2 while the interpretation methods for each risk factor are detailed in Explanatory Note 2 on the country profiles.

The information collected was presented in various ways including:

→ Country profiles, representing a summary of information for each country;

→ Statistical annex, representing the full data set for each country;

→ Legislative maps, showing an overview of the situation worldwide for each risk factor.

In order to code the countries for the legislative maps, three categories were used:

→ Countries[4] whose national laws meet all the criteria for best practice: shown in green – criteria considered as representing best practices in light of available evidence[5] are highlighted, for each risk factor, in green in Table E2;

→ Countries[4] whose national laws are encouraging but where additional efforts are needed for best practice to be met: shown in yellow;

→ Countries[4] whose national laws require strong steps to be taken in order to improve their legislation: shown in red.

4 Or, in countries where laws are set at subnational level, where 80% of subnational entities meet selected criteria, except for The Federated States of Micronesia where the threshold was set at 75% as there are 4 subnational entities

5 Peden M et al., editors. World report on road traffic injury prevention. Geneva, World Health Organization, 2004

Vehicle standard data

Data on vehicle standards were collected using information from the UN World Forum for Harmonization of Vehicle Regulations[6], the primary global body responsible for the development of passenger car safety. Technical support on analysing and interpreting this data was provided by Global NCAP[7]. Note that while these data are based on international regulations, in some countries where national regulations are considered to be equivalent to the UN standards (US, Canada, Republic of Korea, China, India, Brazil) these data are used instead. The data collected were based on the following eight variables:

→ Frontal impact: UN regulation 94. Note that US regulation 208 is considered equivalent.

→ Side impact: UN regulation 95. Note that US regulation 214 is considered equivalent.

→ Electronic Stability Control: UN regulation 13H. Note that US regulation FMVSS 126 is considered equivalent.

→ Pedestrian protection: UN Regulation 127

→ Seat-belts: UN regulation 16. Note that US regulation FMVSS 210 is considered equivalent.

→ Seat-belt anchorages: UN regulation 14. Note that US regulation FMVSS 210 is considered equivalent.

→ Child restraints: UN regulations 44 and 129. Note that US regulation FMVSS213 is considered equivalent.

→ Motorcycle anti-lock braking system UN Regulation 78.

More information on each of these regulations is included in Section 3. Data on the three variables considered to be particularly important among these seven (frontal impact, electronic stability control and pedestrian protection) are included in the country profiles. The remaining variables are shown in the Table A12 of the statistical annex.

6 Hosted by the United Nations Economic Commission for Europe (UNECE), the UN World Forum for Harmonization of Vehicle Regulations (World Forum the global body responsible for the development of passenger car safety standards). http://www.unece.org/trans/main/wp29/introduction.html

7 Global New Car Assessment Programme (Global NCAP) is a British organization that conducts testing programmes that will assess the safety of motor vehicles. http://www.globalncap.org/

Table E2: Legislative criteria assessed relating to seven behavioural risk factors

Risk factors	Legislative criteria assessed						
Speed	National speed law in place	Speed limits on urban roads ≤ 50 km/h	Local authorities have the power to modify national speed limits	Speed limit on rural roads	Speed limits on motorways		
Drink-driving	National drink-driving law in place	Drink-driving law is based on BAC or equivalent BrAC	BAC limit for general population ≤ 0.05 g/dl	BAC limit for young/ novice drivers ≤ 0.02 g/dl	BAC limit for commercial/ professional drivers		
Motorcycle helmets	National motorcycle helmet law in place	Law applies to motorcycle drivers and adult passengers	Law applies to all road types	Law applies to all engine types	Law requires helmet to be properly fastened	Law refers to and/or specifies a helmet standard	Law restricts child passengers on motorcycles
Seat-belts	National seat-belt law in place	Law applies to drivers and front seat passengers	Law applies to rear seat passengers				
Child restraints	National child restraint law in place	Law requires child restraint use at least until 10 yrs /135cm	Law refers to and/or specifies a child restraint standard	Law restricts children under a certain age or height from sitting in front seat			
Drug-driving	National Drug-driving law in place						
Mobile phones	National law on mobile phone while driving is in place	Law applies to hand-held phones	Law applies to hands-free phones				

Risk factors

Criteria representing best practices

Additional criteria presented in the country profile and/or the statistical annex

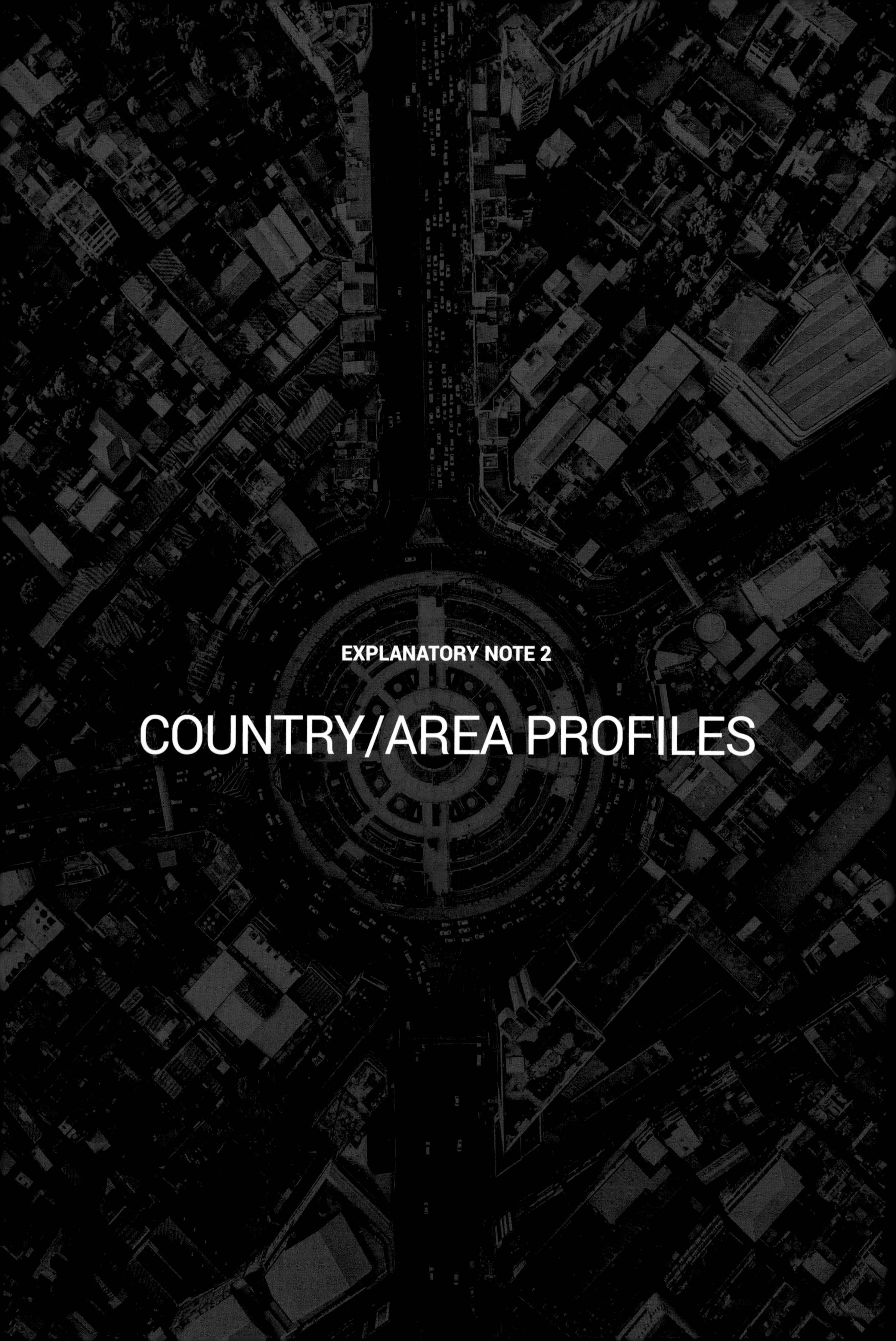

EXPLANATORY NOTE 2

COUNTRY/AREA PROFILES

The country profiles shown on pages 92-267 present a selection of core information about road safety, as reported by each of the 175 participating countries/areas. The country profiles are presented in alphabetical order. Additional national data can also be found in the Tables of the Statistical Annexes (Tables A2–A12).

Data reported for population were extracted from the United Nations Population Division database[8] (1), while gross national income (GNI) per capita for the year 2016 came from World Bank estimates[9] (2). Where no data were available for 2016, published data for the latest year were used. The World Bank Atlas method was used to categorize GNI into bands thus:

→ Low-income = US $ 1 005 or less

→ Middle-income = US $ 1 006 to US $ 12 235

→ High income = US $ 12 236 or more

Flags were obtained from the World Flag Database[10]. Flags and country names were the latest available at the time of finalizing the report (September 2018).

The sections below reflect the way information is structured in each of the Country Profiles. They include details on how data on certain variables are presented and should be interpreted. Variables were coded as "–" if the information was unavailable or non-applicable, or if respondents had ticked a "Don't know" response. Dates provided for data sources refer to the year in which these data were published, rather than the year that the data relate to, unless indicated otherwise.

Data collected by questionnaire were submitted through a consensus meeting (unless otherwise indicated). Each country profile indicates the Ministry that approved this questionnaire data (unless otherwise indicated). Data on legislation were based on WHO's assessment and extensive validation of this information with National Data Coordinators, although it was not officially cleared by the government Ministry.

---

8 Population Division of the Department of Economic and Social Affairs of the United Nations Secretariat (June 2017). World population Prospects: The 2017 Revision, Highlights. New York: United Nations

9 World Development Indicators database, World Bank, November 2017 http://databank.worldbank.org/data/download/site-content/CLASS.xls

10 http://www.flags.net

Institutional framework

A lead agency is considered to be the institution (either stand alone, or within a Ministry) that coordinates road safety at a national level. Information on the existence of a national road safety strategy is indicated as "Yes" or "No". Where countries have multiple national strategies on road safety this is always represented as "Yes".

Where countries indicated they have a fatality reduction target, information on this target is included as well as the relevant time period. Specific fatality targets are indicated either as absolute numbers of deaths, or as a rate per 100 000 population or per vehicle registered, depending on availability.

Safer roads and mobility

→ Information on audits or star rating of new road infrastructure projects is reported as "Yes", "No", or Partial.

→ Information on inspections/star ratings of existing road infrastructure projects is reported as "Yes" or "No". Yes responses where those where respondents answered Yes for existence of formal road safety inspections and/or existence of star rating assessments. Those countries for which respondents answered Yes only for existence of maintenance safety inspections are reported as No.

→ Design standards for the safety of pedestrians and cyclists is reported as "Yes", "No", or "Partial". "Yes" responses included the provision of the following: Managing speed to safe system outcomes (e.g. 20 mph or 30 km/h); Safe crossings for pedestrians and cyclists; and Separation of pedestrians and cyclists from vehicular traffic. If 1-2 of the provisions were met, responses are reflected as "Partial".

Safer vehicles

Total registered vehicles for 2016: Information about the total number of vehicles in the country includes only registered vehicles, and various categories of such vehicles. This is a cumulative number of vehicles in circulation in 2016 (or the most recent year for which data were available) not the number of vehicles brought into circulation in a particular year. In some cases where new data were not available, the figure from the 2015 Global status report has been used and footnoted to indicate this source. In a few countries the number of vehicles in subcategories did not add up to the total number provided. In some countries, respondents noted that a substantial proportion of the vehicle fleet may not be registered.

Vehicle standards applied: Information on vehicle standards presented in this report is derived from UNECE[11] and comprise the following:

- → Frontal impact standard (UN Regulation 94 or equivalent national standard), an important minimum standard for crashworthiness;
- → Electronic stability control and anti-skid system (Regulation 13H or GTR 8), relevant to crash avoidance;
- → Pedestrian protection (Regulation 127 or GTR 9), important for protection of non-car occupants involved in a crash; and
- → Motorcycle anti-lock braking system (Regulation 78) which help the rider maintain control of the motorcycle vehicle during an emergency braking situation

Post-crash care

- → National emergency care access number is reported as "National, single number", "National multiple number", and "Partial coverage". Countries with "National, single number" comprised those that had one single emergency care services access number with total country coverage, and also those having some additional numbers with partial coverage. Countries with "National multiple numbers" comprised those that had multiple emergency care services access numbers that, taken together, provide total country coverage. Countries with "Partial coverage" comprised those that had one or more emergency care services access numbers with partial country coverage overall with areas of the country remaining uncovered.
- → Trauma registry variable indicates whether there was a registry in place and not whether it was regional / national or sentinel in nature.
- → Formal certification pathway for prehospital providers refers to a Government or Government endorsed pathway for medics, technicians, nurses or others to be specifically certified as pre-hospital providers.
- → Assessment of emergency care systems conducted at the national level comprised the comprehensive assessment of the prehospital and facility-based emergency care systems.

11 http://www.unece.org/trans/main/wp29/introduction.html

Data

→ Reported numbers of road traffic deaths are included in the Country Profiles, with a footnote to indicate the source of data and the definition of a road traffic death that was used.

→ The estimated number of road traffic deaths is included based on the methodology described in Explanatory Note 3. Where this number was based on a negative binomial regression model, a 95% Confidence Interval is also shown.

→ The estimated rate per 100 000 population is based on the estimated number of road traffic deaths referred to above.

→ Data on the breakdown by sex may be from a different source to the official road traffic data and are converted to proportions. The proportion of deaths where the sex was unknown has not been reported in the profiles. As a result, proportions may not add up to 100% due to remaining proportions being due to cases of unknown sex. Proportions may also not add up to 100% due to rounding off or when partial information was available (indicated in a footnote).

→ Reported fatality data from different countries are not necessarily comparable, as different definitions and timeframes have been used (these are noted in the footnotes or in brackets behind the data). However, the WHO estimates (both absolute numbers and rate per 100 000) allow for comparisons between countries. For more information on the fatality data see Explanatory Note 3.

→ The standard colour coding of the pie charts used to represent road user deaths in the categories requested in the questionnaire is shown below. Additional categories are represented by non-standard colours as indicated in the specific Country Profiles.

→ Graphs on reported road traffic fatality trends are shown either as road traffic death rates per 100 000 population (solid line) or as an absolute number of road traffic deaths (dotted line), depending on which data were supplied by the country. While many countries track decades' worth of trend data, only a 10-year period is depicted here.

→ For countries providing less than 5 years' road traffic fatality trend data, this information is presented in a tabular format instead of a graph.

→ For countries with small populations where the numbers of deaths are under 50, absolute numbers of deaths rather than rates are shown. Note that in cases where data were only available for regions within a country, this information is indicated in a footnote.

- Drivers 4-wheeled cars and light vehicles
- Occupants 4-wheeled cars and light vehicles
- Passengers 4-wheeled cars and light vehicles
- Riders motorized 2- or 3-wheelers
- Drivers motorized 2- or 3-wheelers
- Pillion riders
- Cyclists
- Pedestrians
- Drivers/passengers heavy trucks
- Drivers/passengers buses
- Other/uspecified
- Drivers (all vehicles)
- Passengers (all vehicles)
- Drivers and passengers (all vehicles)

Safer road users

Data provided in this section is extracted from the questionnaire and the legislative analysis undertaken by WHO Headquarters in collaboration with NDCs.

Enforcement: respondents were asked, as individuals, to rate the effectiveness of enforcement of various elements of national road safety legislation based on their professional opinion or perception. These responses – on a scale of 0 to 10, where 0 is "not effective" and 10 is "highly effective" – are reflected here. A median of these scores is presented. Median enforcement figures are rounded off. It should be noted that these scores are subjective and should be seen only as an indication of how enforcement is perceived in the country. Many respondents expressed difficulty in assessing law enforcement at a national level since it often varies from region to region within a country and the intensity of the enforcement may vary at different times. Some countries did not wish to provide enforcement scores.

Speed: Speed limits reported here (and in the statistical tables) are the default speed limits on urban roads, rural roads and motorways for private passenger cars. The speed limits have been, where needed, converted to kilometres per hour.

'Default speed limit' was interpreted as the maximum speed limit applying in normal circumstances (regardless of weather, roadworks, special events, etc.) on the road type considered.

As road classifications vary greatly from country to country, National Data Coordinators were asked to confirm or correct speed limits reported in the legal analysis for the different types of roads according to the definitions used in the country concerned. In countries, where National Data Coordinators have indicated that motorways do not exist in their country, this is noted with a footnote.

In some countries, the legislation does not articulate speed limits by road type but only by vehicle type. In these countries, the speed limit provided for private passenger cars is reported in the country profile and statistical annex for all road types, with a footnote indicating that this is a speed limit set per vehicle type and not based on the road type.

The criterion «local authorities able to modify speed limit» is answered Yes if the speed limit can be altered at local level in any way (decreased and/or increased). The definition of local authorities is interpreted broadly as any entity that is not from the central system of government (i.e. not from a national ministry) having a jurisdiction over a local area whether the local area is a region, a province, a district, a department or a city. This criterion is automatically answered Yes for countries in which laws are set at subnational level if at least 80% of subnational entities of the country have set their own speed laws.[12]

Drink-driving: Blood alcohol concentration (BAC) limits (or breath alcohol limits converted to BAC limits) refer to the maximum amount of alcohol legally acceptable in the blood of a driver on the road – i.e. the blood alcohol level above which a driver may be punished by law. This figure is provided for the general population, and for young/novice drivers in grams per decilitre (g/dl). This survey gathered information on drink-driving laws regardless of the legal status of alcohol in the country. Where alcohol consumption was legally prohibited in a country, as reported in the final country questionnaire, this is indicated by a footnote. BAC limits are reported with a dash ("–") for countries that have a drink-driving law that is not based on blood (or equivalent breath) alcohol concentration, and with a corresponding footnote.

→ The use of random breath testing is indicated based on countries' reports of whether or not such testing is carried out in practice. Those countries where legislation specifically prohibits primary enforcement of drink-driving laws, and thus random breath testing, are indicated as such in a footnote.

→ Deaths attributable to drink-driving were included only when the estimate was based on a published source. In many cases these are not national estimates (as indicated in the source). These estimates are rounded up.

12 Or in the case of Micronesia (Federated States of), if at least 75% of the subnational entities have enacted speed laws

Motorcycle helmets: A country is interpreted as having a helmet law covering all riders where the law requires helmet use for both the driver and the (adult) passenger, on all road types and for all types of motorcycles (regardless of engine type). A reference to « riders » in the law is understood to include both drivers and passengers. Countries where helmet laws apply only to certain types of roads, at certain times or in certain areas were interpreted as not providing sufficient coverage to be considered as applying to all drivers and passengers.

The criteria «Law refers to and/or specifies a helmet standard» is answered Yes if the law refers to:

→ a specific standard (such as ECE 22 or a national standard), or

→ an authority in charge of setting such a standard, or

→ regulations or rules to specify or develop a standard.

Information on the actual adoption of the regulations prescribing a helmet standard was not always available; in case where the NDCs indicated that the standard had not yet been set, a corresponding footnote was included in the country profile.

The criteria « children passengers on motorcycles » shows whether a country restricts children as passengers on motorcycles and if yes, for what age group.

For information on motorcycle helmet rates (derived from the final country questionnaires), these data were included only when a published source was indicated. The most disaggregated data are presented here, i.e. separate figures are provided for drivers and passengers where this information was provided. Note that the information provided for drivers and passengers does not necessarily represent the same year, nor come from the same source, as indicated in the corresponding footnotes. The data on passenger rates refer to adult passengers unless otherwise indicated. In many cases these are not national estimates (as indicated in the source).

Seat-belts: A country is interpreted as having a seat-belt law covering all occupants where the law requires seat-belt use for the driver, front seat passenger and rear seat passengers at all times and on all roads. Countries where seat-belt laws apply only at certain times or on certain roads were interpreted as having a national seat belt law not applying to all occupants.

For information on seat-belt wearing rates (derived from the final country questionnaires), these data were included only when a published source was indicated. Where available, information on wearing rates disaggregated by front and rear seat occupants was used. Where respondents provided explanatory information on these data, for example, a source or information on geographical coverage, this information is summarized in the footnotes. Note that the information provided for front seat and rear seat occupants does not necessarily represent the same year, nor come from the same source, as indicated in the corresponding footnotes.

Child restraints: A country is interpreted as having a child restraint law where the country requires the mandatory use of child restraint systems for an identified group of children based on either their height and/or their age and/or their weight.

Child restraints include rear-facing child restraints, forward facing child restraints as well as booster seats. Regular (adult) seat-belts, on their own, are not counted as appropriate child restraints. Countries whose legislation required that children within a certain age group/height be restrained either by a seat-belt or in a child restraint use were reported as not having a child restraint law for this age group/height. Countries that referred to child restraint use for children seated in the front only (and not in the rear) were reported as not having a child restraint law. Countries that referred to either child restraint use or "other means" were considered as not meeting the criteria "standard", and this detail was reflected in a footnote in the country profile.

The age and/or height reported for the criteria "child restraint required" corresponds to the period for which only child restraint systems are allowed to restrain children (i.e. no other form of restraint is allowed such as seat-belts only, "other means" etc.).

The criterion «Law refers to and/or specifies a standard» is answered Yes if the law refers to:

→ a specific standard (such as ECE 44 or ECE 129), or

→ an authority in charge of setting such a standard, or

→ regulations or rules to specify or develop a standard.

Information on the actual adoption of the regulations prescribing a standard was not always available; in case where the NDCs indicated that the standard had not yet been set, a corresponding footnote was included in the country profile.

The criterion « children seated in front » shows whether a country restricts children as passengers in the front seat and if so, what is the restriction set (complete ban, or subject to placing the child in a restraint) and for which age group.

Information on rates of child restraint use (derived from the final country questionnaires) are presented when a source was provided for the estimate and are included in the most disaggregated form available. Most countries that provided this data, however, had data on children in restraints that was not broken down by age group. Note that where multiple studies are available this information does not necessarily represent the same year, nor come from the same source, as indicated in the corresponding footnotes.

References

1. Population Division of the Department of Economic and Social Affairs of the United Nations Secretariat (June 2017).
   World population Prospects: The 2017 Revision, Highlights. New York: United Nations.

2. World Development Indicators database, World Bank, November 2017.
   http://databank.worldbank.org/data/reports.aspx?source=World-Development-Indicators

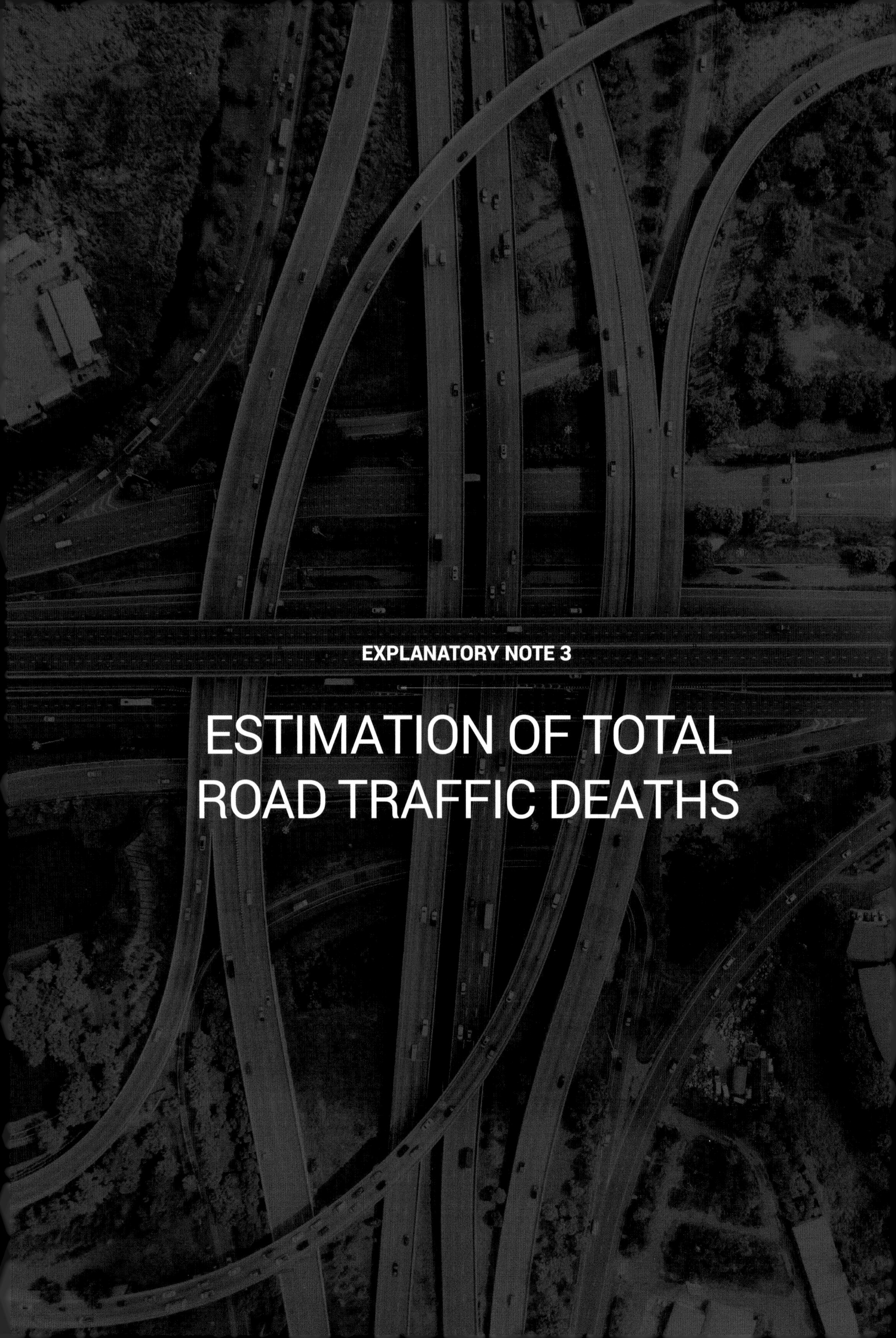

EXPLANATORY NOTE 3

ESTIMATION OF TOTAL ROAD TRAFFIC DEATHS

Background

During the process of preparing the fourth Global status report on road safety, WHO generated estimates of road traffic deaths for 2016 for all Member States. Road traffic deaths were estimated by building on the methods used in the third global report by improving and updating the database of vital registration, the data collection instrument (survey) and the database of the covariates for regressions. These estimates were used to generate regional and global estimates, while estimates for individual countries are included in the report only for the 175 countries that participated in the survey.

Death registration information is submitted to WHO regularly by Ministries of Health from around the world, and most is coded using the International Classification of Diseases 9th or 10th revisions (1, 2, 3). Using this classification all deaths that follow from a road traffic death are counted as such, regardless of the time period in which they occur (unlike many official road traffic surveillance data sources, where road traffic death data are based on a 30-day definition following a road traffic crash). WHO applies certain criteria to ascertain the quality of this death registration data and where the death registration data were considered to be of high quality these data were used for this report[13].

For those countries without such good vital registration data, and for which other sources of information on causes of death were unavailable[14], the estimates were based on covariates (some collected in the survey of Member States, others from available published sources). The regression models were fitted to data for the period 2000–2016, a time series for each covariate was used for this period for each Member States. The improved regression model estimated road traffic deaths (all ages, both sexes) as a function of a set of covariates that include measures of economic development, road transport factors and legislation, road use and safety governance/enforcement and health system access.

Due to the availability of new data, and updated time series for many covariates used in the regression, estimates for the full-time series have been revised. Hence, the WHO 2016 estimates are not directly comparable to previous WHO estimates published in the previous global status reports on road safety (4, 5). The 2018 estimation represents the best estimates of WHO for fatalities that occurred during 2016 and earlier years, based on the evidence available up to September 2018. These estimates are not necessarily the official estimates of Member States for that year and are not necessarily endorsed by Member States. However, during the preparation of the report a consultation letter was sent to each Member State that

13 For details on criteria used to assess quality of vital registration data see reference 3 and Explanatory Note in references 4 and 5.

14 However, in some countries other sources of information on deaths were used: where total deaths reported from the national surveillance system were greater than the deaths estimated from the regression or from the death registration data, these were used.

participated in this fourth Global status report on road safety explaining the methodology used during this estimation process and the latest data used for this purpose. In order to allow global and regional comparisons to previous years, the global and regional estimates for previous years were recalculated based on the new data and methods used for 2016.

Approaches to estimation

As in the second and third reports, there are four groups of countries and the estimation methodology for each group is described in detail below.

1. Countries with death registration data

This group includes 86 countries with death registration data meeting the following completeness criteria: completeness for the year estimated at 80% or more, or average completeness for the decade including the country-year was 80% or more. Total road traffic deaths were calculated from the death registration data and population data reported to WHO as follows. Injury deaths classified as "undetermined intent" were redistributed pro-rata across all unintentional and intentional injury categories within age-sex groups. These data were then used to compute age-sex-specific death rates for road traffic deaths. Where completeness was assessed at less than 100%, death rates were adjusted for incompleteness by multiplying by (100/ completeness %). These death rates were applied to the UN estimates of population by 5-year age group and sex (World Population Prospects 2016) to estimate total road traffic deaths for each country-year.

These countries fall into three categories:

→ Countries with death registration data for year 2016 where the estimated road traffic deaths for 2016 exceeded number reported from the surveillance system. The death-registration based estimate is used. This category contains 9 countries.

→ Countries where the latest death registration data submitted to WHO is earlier than 2015 but not earlier than 2007. Deaths in year 2016 were estimated based on a projection of the most recent death registration data using the trends in reported surveillance data: this category contains 54 countries.

→ Countries where the reported number of road traffic deaths adjusted to unlimited time for 2016 exceeded the estimate based on death registration data. For 23 countries, the reported road traffic deaths were used for year 2016.

2. Countries with other sources of information on causes of death

For India, Thailand and Viet Nam, data on total deaths by cause were available for a single year or very few earlier years. These data sources are documented in Annex B of the Global Burden of Disease: 2004 update report (WHO 2008) and as well as some more recent studies submitted to WHO. For these countries, the regression method described below was used to project forward from the most recent year for which an estimate of total road traffic deaths was available.

3. Countries with populations less than 150 000

For 9 small countries with populations less than 150 000 and which did not have eligible death registration data, regression estimates were not used. The reported deaths were used directly without adjustment.

4. Countries without eligible death registration data

For these countries without death registration data at least 80% complete and with populations greater than 150 000, a regression model was used to estimate total road traffic deaths. As for the first report, we used a negative binomial regression model, appropriate for modeling non-negative integer count data (number of road traffic deaths) (Law 2009, Hilbe 2007). A likelihood ratio test was used to assess that the negative binomial model provided a better fit to the data than a Poisson model (where the variance of the data is constrained to equal the mean).

$$^{(1)}\ \ln N = C + \beta_1 X_1 + \beta_2 X_2 + \ldots + \beta_n X_n + \ln Pop + \varepsilon$$

where N is the total road traffic deaths (for a country-year), C is a constant term, Xi are a set of explanatory covariates, Pop is the population for the country-year, and ε is the negative binomial error term. Population was used as exposure, making it possible to interpret the coefficients (βi) for the independent variables as effects on rates rather than a count. In a previous study, this type of model was used to represent «accident proneness» (Greenwood and Yule, 1920). Karlaftis and Tarko (1998) have also found a negative binomial regression model to be the appropriate for count data such as road traffic fatalities.

The parameters β_1, β_2, β_3 ··· β_n (equation 1) were estimated by fitting the negative binomial regression model to estimated total road traffic deaths for all country-years in the range 2000-2016 meeting the completeness criteria. by using the number of road of traffic deaths from countries from group 1 described above. We chose three models (Models A, B and C) that had good in-sample- and out-of-sample fit, and for which all the covariates were statistically significant and overall estimation is the average of the prediction of these three best models. The table below describes the covariates used for our model:

Table E3: Covariates used in the model

Independent variables	Description	Source of information	Included in models
ln (GDP)	World Development Indicators (2017) and WHO estimates of Gross Domestic Product (GDP) per capita (international dollars or purchasing power parity dollars, 2011 base)	World bank and WHO database	Models A, B, C
ln (vehicles per capita)	Total vehicles per 1000 persons	GSRRS surveys and WHO database	Models A, B, C
Road density	Total roads (km) per 1000 hectares	International Futures database	Models A, B, C
National speed limits on rural roads	The maximum national speed limits on rural roads (km/h) from WHO questionnaire	GSRRS survey	Models A, B, C
National speed limits on urban roads	The maximum national speed limits on urban roads (km/h) from WHO questionnaire	GSRRS survey	Models A, B, C
Health system access	Health system access variable (principal component score based on a set of coverage indicators for each country)	Institute for Health Metrics and Evaluation dataset	Models A, B, C
Alcohol apparent consumption	Liters of alcohol (recorded plus unrecorded) per adult aged 15+	WHO database	Models A, B, C
Population working	Proportion of population aged 15–64 years	World Population Prospects 2017 revision	Models A, B, C
Percentage motorbikes	Per cent of total vehicles that are motorbikes	GSRRS survey	Model B
Corruption index	Control of corruption index (units range from about -2.5 to +2.5 with higher values corresponding to better control of corruption	World Bank (Kaufmann et al 2009), International Futures database	Model B
National policies for walking /cycling	Existence of national policies that encourage walking and / or cycling	GSRRS survey	Model C
Population	Total population (used as offset in negative binomial regression	World Population Prospects 2017 revision (UNDESA)	Models A, B, C

Table E4: Overview of methods used to obtain comparable country estimates

Estimation method	Country
GROUP 1 Countries/areas with good death registration data	Argentina, Australia, Austria, Azerbaijan, Barbados, Belarus, Belgium, Belize, Brazil, Bulgaria, Canada, Chile, China (14, 15), Colombia, Costa Rica, Croatia, Cuba, Cyprus, Czechia, Denmark, Dominican Republic, Ecuador, Egypt, El Salvador, Estonia, Fiji, Finland, France, Georgia, Germany, Greece, Guatemala, Guyana, Hungary, Iceland, Iran (Islamic Republic of), Ireland, Israel, Italy, Jamaica, Japan, Kazakhstan, Kuwait, Kyrgyzstan, Latvia, Lithuania, Luxembourg, Maldives, Malta, Mauritius, Mexico, Montenegro, Netherlands, New Zealand, Norway, Oman, Panama, Paraguay, Philippines, Poland, Portugal, Qatar, Republic of Korea, Republic of Moldova, Romania, Russian Federation, Saint Lucia, Serbia, Singapore, Slovakia, Slovenia, South Africa, Spain, Suriname, Sweden, Switzerland, The former Yugoslav Republic of Macedonia, Trinidad and Tobago, Turkey, Ukraine, United Kingdom, United States of America, Uruguay, Uzbekistan, Venezuela (Bolivarian Republic of), West Bank and Gaza Strip
GROUP 2 Countries with other sources of cause of death information	India (16,17,18), Thailand, Viet Nam
GROUP 3 Countries with populations less than 150 000	Antigua and Barbuda, Cook Islands, Dominica, Grenada, Kiribati, Micronesia (Federated States of), San Marino, Seychelles, Tonga
GROUP 4 Countries without eligible death registration data	Afghanistan, Albania, Angola, Armenia, Bangladesh, Benin, Bhutan, Bolivia (Plurinational State of), Bosnia and Herzegovina, Botswana, Burkina Faso, Burundi, Cabo Verde, Cambodia, Cameroon, Central African Republic, Chad, Comoros, Congo, Côte d'Ivoire, Democratic Republic of the Congo, Equatorial Guinea, Eritrea, Eswatini, Ethiopia, Gabon, Gambia, Ghana, Guinea, Guinea-Bissau, Honduras, Indonesia, Iraq, Jordan, Kenya, Lao People's Democratic Republic, Lebanon, Lesotho, Liberia, Libya, Madagascar, Malawi, Malaysia, Mali, Mauritania, Mongolia, Morocco, Mozambique, Myanmar, Namibia, Nepal, Niger, Nigeria, Pakistan, Papua New Guinea, Peru, Rwanda, Samoa, Sao Tome and Principe, Saudi Arabia, Senegal, Solomon Islands, Somalia, South Sudan, Sri Lanka, Sudan, Syrian Arab Republic, Tajikistan, Timor-Leste, Togo, Tunisia, Turkmenistan, Uganda, United Arab Emirates, United Republic of Tanzania, Vanuatu, Zimbabwe

References

1. World Health Organization. International Classification of Diseases – 9th Revision. Geneva, World Health Organization, 1975.

2. World Health Organization. International Classification of Diseases – 10th Revision. Geneva, World Health Organization, 1990.

3. The global burden of disease: 2004 update. Geneva, World Health Organization, 2008 (http://www.who.int/healthinfo/global_burden_disease/2004_report_update/en/ , accessed 15 September 2015).

4. Global status report on road safety: time for action. Geneva, World Health Organization, 2009.

5. Global status report on road safety 2013 Supporting a Decade of Action. Geneva, World Health Organization, 2013.Global status report on road safety 2015. Geneva, World Health Organization, 2015

6. Population Division of the Department of Economic and Social Affairs of the United Nations Secretariat (June 2013). World population Prospects: The 2012 Revision, Highlights. New York: United Nations.

7. Law TH. The effects of political governance, policy measures and economic growth on the Kuznets relationship in motor vehicle crash deaths. Ph.D thesis, University of London, 2009.

8. Hilbe JM. Negative Binomial Regression. Cambridge University Press, Cambridge, 2007.

9. Greenwood M. Yule GU. An enquiry into the nature of frequency distributions representative of multiple happenings with particular reference to the occurrence of multiple attacks of disease or of repeated accidents. Journal of the Royal Statistical Society (Series A), 1920, 83, 255-279.

10. Karlaftis MG., Tarko AP. Heterogeneity considerations in accident modeling. Accident Analysis and Prevention, 1998, 30:425-433.

11. The International Futures (IFs) modeling system, version 6.5.4. Frederick S. Pardee Center for International Futures, Josef Korbel School of International Studies, University of Denver, www.ifs.du.edu.

12. Myerson R et al. Safe pregnancy and delivery: a systematic analysis of the trends in the coverage of antenatal and intrapartumcare. Presentation at Global Health Metrics and Evaluation Conference 2011: Controversies, Innovation, Accountability, Seattle, Washington, 14–16 March 2011.

13. Kaufmann D, Kraay A, Mastruzzi M. Governance Matters VIII: Governance Indicators for 1996-2008. World Bank Policy Research. 2009

14. Chinese Center for Disease Control and Prevention, **全国疾病监测系统死因监测数据集** [National Disease Surveillance System monitoring causes of death 2012]. Beijing, Military Medical Science Press, 2013.

15. Vital registration data received from Center for Health Statistics and Information Ministry of Healthy, Beijing, China.

16. Causes of death in India in 2001–2003. New Delhi, Registrar General of India, Government of India, 2009.

17. Aleksandrowicz L, Malhotra V, Dikshit R, Gupta P, Kumar R, Sheth J, Rathi S, Suraweera W, Miasnikof P, Jotkar R, Sinha D, Awasthi S, Bhatia P, Jha P. Performance criteria for verbal autopsy-based systems to estimate national causes of death: development and application to the Indian Million Death Study. BMC Medicine 2014, 12:21

18. Registrar General of India and the Centre for Global Health Research. Causes of Death Statistics for India 2010-2013. A Joint Report of the Registrar General of India and the Centre for Global Health Research. Government of India Ministry of Home Affairs – Sample Registration System, 2015. (http://www.censusindia.gov.in/2011- common/Sample_Registration_System.html)

STATISTICAL ANNEX

TABLE A1: NATIONAL DATA COORDINATORS BY COUNTRY / AREA AND WHO REGION

Country / Area	Region	Name of National data coordinator(s)
Angola	Africa	Noélia Loureiro Teixeira
Benin	Africa	Ismaël Mohamed Hoteyi
Botswana	Africa	Amos Kgwefane Motshegwe
Burkina Faso	Africa	Casimir Sanon
Burundi	Africa	Godefroid Kamwenubusa
Cabo Verde	Africa	António Joao Gomes dos Santos
Cameroon	Africa	Christophe Abouna
Central African Republic	Africa	Paul Balekouzou
Chad	Africa	Mahamat Gocke
Comoros	Africa	Nassif Kaissane
Congo	Africa	Yoga Itoua Yoyo Ambianzi
Côte d'Ivoire	Africa	Tidjane Amadou Kamagate
Democratic Republic of the Congo	Africa	Christophe Mwaluka
Equatorial Guinea	Africa	Salvador Emana Edu
Eritrea	Africa	Kahsay Araya Ghebretensae
Eswatini	Africa	Nokuthula Mahlalela
Ethiopia	Africa	Ebriza Mudesir
Gabon	Africa	Vladimir Soami
Gambia	Africa	Essa Drammeh
Ghana	Africa	Gabriel Adu-Sarpong
Guinea	Africa	Luc Kezely Beavogui
Guinea-Bissau	Africa	Cristovao Manjuba
Kenya	Africa	Gladwell Gathecha
Lesotho	Africa	Sejojo Phaaroe
Liberia	Africa	Fulton Shannon II
Madagascar	Africa	Eulalie Razafindranazy
Malawi	Africa	Jones Kaponda Masiye
Mali	Africa	Ousmane Maiga
Mauritania	Africa	Moussa Abdellahi
Mauritius	Africa	Mahmad Saeed Jewon
Mozambique	Africa	Napoleao Salomao Sumbane
Namibia	Africa	Laina Shigwedha
Niger	Africa	Abdou Abdoul-Aziz
Nigeria	Africa	Kayode Olagunju
Rwanda	Africa	Dominique Rurangirwa
Sao Tome and Principe	Africa	Celso Matos
Senegal	Africa	Bineta Sene
Seychelles	Africa	Patrick Andre
South Africa	Africa	Refilwe Mongale
South Sudan	Africa	Komuri Lea Muja Ayub
Togo	Africa	Kossi Dzinyefa Atabuh
Uganda	Africa	Benedict Byamugisha

Country / Area	Region	Name of National data coordinator(s)
United Republic of Tanzania	Africa	Tabitha Makaranga
Zimbabwe	Africa	Lee Nkala
Antigua and Barbuda	Americas	Valarie Williams
Argentina	Americas	Veronica Heler
Barbados	Americas	Denise Carter Taylor
Belize	Americas	Jesse Chun
Bolivia (Plurinational State of)	Americas	Ana María Suxo
Brazil	Americas	Cheila Marina de Lima
Canada	Americas	Paul Boase
Chile	Americas	Carla Medina Aros
Colombia	Americas	Andrea Acero Álvarez
Costa Rica	Americas	Teresa Guzmán
Cuba	Americas	Yania Pla Ramírez
Dominica	Americas	Shalauddin Ahmed
Dominican Republic	Americas	Miguelina Figueroa
Ecuador	Americas	Klever Almerida
El Salvador	Americas	Silvia Argentina Morán de Garcia
Grenada	Americas	Shawn Charles
Guatemala	Americas	Yonni Aguilar
Guyana	Americas	Ramona Doorgen
Honduras	Americas	Dario Roberto Cálix Alvarado
Jamaica	Americas	Andriene Grant
Mexico	Americas	Ricardo Pérez Núñez
Panama	Americas	Rey Fuentes Rodríguez
Paraguay	Americas	Alberto Didier Gonzalez Cabello
Peru	Americas	Joel Gilberto Collazos Carhuay
Saint Lucia	Americas	Phil Leon
Suriname	Americas	Johanna Lakhisaran
Trinidad and Tobago	Americas	Carla Ruiz
United States of America	Americas	Ann Dellinger
Uruguay	Americas	Pablo Posada
Venezuela (Bolivarian Republic of)	Americas	Sarai Patricia Castro Gilly
Afghanistan	Eastern Mediterranean	Adiba Adib
Egypt	Eastern Mediterranean	Ramy Gameel Saied Elnazer
Iran (Islamic Republic of)	Eastern Mediterranean	Mashyaneh Haddadi
Iraq	Eastern Mediterranean	Shakir Kadhim Rubayi Katea
Jordan	Eastern Mediterranean	Mohammad Zaal Mousa Aloudat, Malek Ayed Falah Alhabashneh
Kuwait	Eastern Mediterranean	Jassim Ibrahim Al Kandary
Lebanon	Eastern Mediterranean	Kamel Ibrahim, Ramzi Salamé
Libya	Eastern Mediterranean	Ali Shabban Altounsi
Morocco	Eastern Mediterranean	Ahmad Bardan

Country / Area	Region	Name of National data coordinator(s)
Oman	Eastern Mediterranean	Mohamed Said Alyazidi
Pakistan	Eastern Mediterranean	Samra Mazhar
Qatar	Eastern Mediterranean	Thaera Abdulwahid Muslat
Saudi Arabia	Eastern Mediterranean	Faisal Faisal Murdhi Alanazi
Somalia	Eastern Mediterranean	Farhia Qasim
Sudan	Eastern Mediterranean	Fatima Elhassan Eisa
Syrian Arab Republic	Eastern Mediterranean	Taufik Ismail Hasaba
Tunisia	Eastern Mediterranean	Naoufel Somrani, Henda Chebbi
United Arab Emirates	Eastern Mediterranean	Essam M. N. Howayyer
West Bank and Gaza Strip	Eastern Mediterranean	Imad Aldeen Mahmoud Al Masry
Albania	Europe	Gentiana Qirjako
Armenia	Europe	Kristina Gyurjyan
Austria	Europe	Martin Labuda
Azerbaijan	Europe	Rustam Talishinskiy
Belarus	Europe	Aleksandr Beletski
Belgium	Europe	Wouter Van den Berghe
Bosnia and Herzegovina	Europe	Dalibor Pejovic
Bulgaria	Europe	Galia Tsolova
Croatia	Europe	Ivana Brkic Bilos
Cyprus	Europe	Vasos Scoutellas
Czechia	Europe	Alena Švancarová
Denmark	Europe	Lartey G. Lawson
Estonia	Europe	Reigo Ude
Finland	Europe	Riikka Rajamäki
France	Europe	Joel Valmain
Georgia	Europe	Tamar Chachava
Germany	Europe	Horst Schulzes
Greece	Europe	George Yannis
Hungary	Europe	Péter Csizmadia
Iceland	Europe	Gunnar Geir Gunnarsson
Ireland	Europe	John Carroll
Israel	Europe	Kobi Peleg
Italy	Europe	Maria Giuseppina Lecce
Kazakhstan	Europe	Batpenov Nurlan Dzhumagulovich
Kyrgyzstan	Europe	Samatbek Toimatov
Latvia	Europe	Eva Ramuse
Lithuania	Europe	Aida Laukaitienė
Luxembourg	Europe	Scharel Lehners
Malta	Europe	Beatrice Farrugia
Montenegro	Europe	Svetlana Stojanovic
Netherlands	Europe	Peter M. Mak

Country / Area	Region	Name of National data coordinator(s)
Norway	Europe	Guro Ranes
Poland	Europe	Krystian Warda
Portugal	Europe	Miguel Telo de Arriaga
Republic of Moldova	Europe	Tatiana Zatic Petru
Romania	Europe	Bogdan Pop
Russian Federation	Europe	Sergey Alexanrovich Ryzhov
San Marino	Europe	Andrea Gualtieri
Serbia	Europe	Marija Markovic
Slovakia	Europe	Zora Bucháčová
Slovenia	Europe	Andraž Murkovič
Spain	Europe	Martha Molina Olivas
Sweden	Europe	Matts-Åke Belin
Switzerland	Europe	Maja Ouertani
Tajikistan	Europe	Razzakov Abduvali Abdukhamitovich
The former Yugoslav Republic of Macedonia	Europe	Fimka Tozija
Turkey	Europe	Kayhan Keser
Turkmenistan	Europe	Dry Ata Boppyev
Ukraine	Europe	Yuryi Chornyi
United Kingdom	Europe	Mark Bellis
Uzbekistan	Europe	Mirklhakim Azizov
Bangladesh	South-East Asia	Abdul Alim
Bhutan	South-East Asia	Phuntsho Wangdi
India	South-East Asia	Shri K Guite
Indonesia	South-East Asia	Betsy Ernani
Maldives	South-East Asia	Fathimath Shabana
Myanmar	South-East Asia	Aung Thein Htay
Nepal	South-East Asia	Buland Thapa
Sri Lanka	South-East Asia	Premalal Rathnaweera
Thailand	South-East Asia	Nongnuch Thanthithum
Timor-Leste	South-East Asia	Helder Juvinal Neto da Silva
Australia	Western Pacific	Katrina Cristofani
Cambodia	Western Pacific	Hero Kol
China	Western Pacific	Leilei Duan
Cook Islands	Western Pacific	Edwina Tangaroa
Fiji	Western Pacific	Watilala Fonu
Japan	Western Pacific	Mayuyo Mori
Kiribati	Western Pacific	Mweritonga Rubeiariki
Lao People's Democratic Republic	Western Pacific	Somnuk Mektakul
Malaysia	Western Pacific	Zakira Taib
Micronesia (Federated States of)	Western Pacific	Wincener J. David
Mongolia	Western Pacific	Baatarsuren Purevjav

Country / Area	Region	Name of National data coordinator(s)
New Zealand	Western Pacific	Alec Morrison
Papua New Guinea	Western Pacific	Herman Wakia
Philippines	Western Pacific	Agnes Benegas-Segarra
Republic of Korea	Western Pacific	Soyun Park
Samoa	Western Pacific	Rumanusina Maua
Singapore	Western Pacific	Lay Tin Ong
Solomon Islands	Western Pacific	Brian Surimalefo
Tonga	Western Pacific	Kalo Nofoákifolau
Vanuatu	Western Pacific	Jerry Iaruel
Viet Nam	Western Pacific	Do Minh Trung

TABLE A2: ROAD TRAFFIC DEATHS AND PROPORTION OF ROAD USERS BY COUNTRY / AREA

Country / Area	General information			Road traffic deaths		
	Population numbers for 2016[a]	GNI per capita for 2016 in US dollars[b]	Income level[c]	Reported number of road traffic deaths	Modelled number of road traffic deaths[d]	
					Point estimate	95% Confidence Interval
Afghanistan	34 656 032	580	Low	1 565	5 230	4 502 - 5 958
Albania	2 926 348	4 250	Middle	269	399	369 - 428
Angola	28 813 464	3 440	Middle	2 845	6 797	5 304 - 8 289
Antigua and Barbuda	100 963	13 400	High	8	8	–
Argentina	43 847 432	11 960	Middle	5 530	6 119	–
Armenia	2 924 816	3 760	Middle	267	499	469 - 530
Australia	24 125 848	54 420	High	1 296	1 351	–
Austria	8 712 137	45 230	High	432	452	–
Azerbaijan	9 725 376	4 760	Middle	759	845	–
Bangladesh	162 951 552	1 330	Middle	2 376[e]	24 954	20 730 - 29 177
Barbados	284 996	14 830	High	9	16	–
Belarus	9 480 042	5 600	Middle	588	841	–
Belgium	11 358 379	41 860	High	637	657	–
Belize	366 954	4 410	Middle	101	104	–
Benin	10 872 298	820	Low	637[e]	2 986	2 458 - 3 514
Bhutan	797 765	2 510	Middle	125	139	121 - 157
Bolivia (Plurinational State of)	10 887 882	3 070	Middle	1 259	1 687	1 532 - 1 842
Bosnia and Herzegovina	3 516 816	4 880	Middle	318	552	500 - 603
Botswana	2 250 260	6 610	Middle	450	535	465 - 606
Brazil	207 652 864	8 840	Middle	38 651[e]	41 007	–
Bulgaria	7 131 494	7 470	Middle	708	730	–
Burkina Faso	18 646 432	640	Low	878	5 686	4 499 - 6 872
Burundi	10 524 117	280	Low	112[e]	3 651	2 926 - 4 376
Cabo Verde	539 560	2 970	Middle	41	135	118 - 152
Cambodia	15 762 370	1 140	Middle	1 852	2 803	2 381 - 3 226
Cameroon	23 439 188	1 200	Middle	1 879	7 066	5 670 - 8 463
Canada	36 289 824	43 660	High	1 858[e]	2 118	–
Central African Republic	4 594 621	370	Low	193	1 546	1 209 - 1 884
Chad	14 452 543	720	Low	1 122[f]	3 990	3 110 - 4 870
Chile	17 909 754	13 530	High	1 675	2 245	–
China	1 411 415 375	8 260	Middle	58 022[e]	256 180	–
Colombia	48 653 420	6 320	Middle	7 158	8 987	–

Road traffic deaths	Road user death (%)				
Estimated road traffic death rate per 100 000 population[d]	Drivers/Passengers of 4-wheeled vehicles	Drivers / Passengers of 2- or 3- wheelers	Cyclists	Pedestrians	Other or unspecified users
15.1	–	–	–	–	–
13.6	39.4	11.9	7.8	38.7	2.2
23.6	59.5			40.5	0
7.9	62.5	0	12.5	25	0
14	47.2	22.2	2.4	8.2	20
17.1	59.6	1.5	0.4	34.8	3.7
5.6	60.9	19.3	2.2	14	3.5
5.2	43.8	22	11.1	16.9	6.3
8.7	51.8	0.9	0.9	42	4.3
15.3	–	–	–	–	–
5.6	33.3	33.3	0	22.2	11.1
8.9	48.5		9.2	41.3	1
5.8	57.1	14.4	11.1	12.2	5
28.3	18.8	19.8	11.9	24.8	24.8
27.5	16.8	56.5	0.8	16.8	9.1
17.4	–	–	–	–	–
15.5	60.8	19.7		2.5	17.1
15.7	–	–	–	–	–
23.8	63.1	0	2	24.7	10.2
19.7	23.2	31.4	3.4	18.1	24
10.2	63.8	7.8	4.9	16.7	6.8
30.5	–	–	–	–	–
34.7	–	–	–	–	–
25	–	–	–	–	–
17.8	6.2	73.5	2.3	9.6	8.4
30.1	–	–	–	–	–
5.8	64.3	10.8	2.5	15.2	7.2
33.6	–	–	–	–	–
27.6	–	–	–	–	–
12.5	42	8.7	5.7	36	7.7
18.2	–	–	–	–	–
18.5	8.4	52.5	5.3	26	7.8

Country / Area	General information			Road traffic deaths		
	Population numbers for 2016[a]	GNI per capita for 2016 in US dollars[b]	Income level[c]	Reported number of road traffic deaths	Modelled number of road traffic deaths[d]	
					Point estimate	95% Confidence Interval
Comoros	795 601	760	Low	23	211	177 - 245
Congo	5 125 821	1 710	Middle	308	1 405	1 124 - 1 687
Cook Islands	17 379	–	High	5[e]	3	–
Costa Rica	4 857 274	10 840	Middle	795[e]	812	–
Côte d'Ivoire	23 695 920	1 520	Middle	991	5 582	4 635 - 6 529
Croatia	4 213 265	12 110	Middle	307	340	–
Cuba	11 475 982	6 570[g]	Middle	750	975	–
Cyprus	1 170 125	23 680	High	46	60	–
Czechia	10 610 947	17 570	High	611	630	–
Democratic Republic of the Congo	78 736 152	420	Low	385	26 529	21 142 - 31 915
Denmark	5 711 870	56 730	High	211	227	–
Dominica	73 543	6 750	Middle	10[e]	8	–
Dominican Republic	10 648 791	6 390	Middle	3 118	3 684	–
Ecuador	16 385 068	5 820	Middle	2 894	3 490	–
Egypt	95 688 680	3 460	Middle	8 211	9 287	–
El Salvador	6 344 722	3 920	Middle	1 215	1 411	–
Equatorial Guinea	1 221 490	6 550	Middle	41[e]	300	221 - 379
Eritrea	4 954 645	520[g]	Low	130	1 255	1 025 - 1 485
Estonia	1 312 442	17 750	High	71	80	–
Eswatini	1 343 098	2 830	Middle	203	361	296 - 427
Ethiopia	102 403 200	660	Low	4 352[e]	27 326	21 494 - 33 159
Fiji	898 760	4 840	Middle	60	86	–
Finland	5 503 132	44 730	High	252	260	–
France	64 720 688	38 950	High	3 477	3 585	–
Gabon	1 979 786	7 210	Middle	54[i]	460	382 - 538
Gambia	2 038 501	440	Low	139	605	484 - 726
Georgia	3 925 405	3 810	Middle	581	599	–
Germany	81 914 672	43 660	High	3 206	3 327	–
Ghana	28 206 728	1 380	Middle	1 802[e]	7 018	6 056 - 7 980
Greece	11 183 716	18 960	High	824	1 026	–
Grenada	107 317	8 830	Middle	10	10	–

Road traffic deaths	Road user death (%)				
Estimated road traffic death rate per 100 000 population[d]	Drivers/Passengers of 4-wheeled vehicles	Drivers / Passengers of 2- or 3- wheelers	Cyclists	Pedestrians	Other or unspecified users
26.5	65.2	17.4	0	17.4	0
27.4	–	–	–	–	–
17.3	20	80	0	0	0
16.7	24	40	10.4	24.7	0.9
23.6	11.1	35	0.3	40.2	13.4
8.1	48.2	16	8.8	21.8	5.2
8.5	10.1	15.6	9.9	33.2	31.2
5.1	34.8	21.7	4.3	30.4	8.7
5.9	53.7	10.3	8.7	21.3	6.1
33.7	36.1	11.7	0	51.9	0.3
4	48.3	16.1	14.7	17.1	3.8
10.9	10	0	60	10	20
34.6	11	67	1	17	4
21.3	5.2	19.1	1.8	19.8	54
9.7	45.1	5.5	1.2	26.9	21.2
22.2	32.1	14.2	1.4	49	3.3
24.6	–	–	–	–	–
25.3	36.2	1.5	9.2	25.4	27.7
6.1	52.1	1.4	7	31	8.5
26.9	53.7[h]	0.5	2	43.8	0
26.7	0	–	–	36.7	63.3
9.6	63.3[h]	–	–	36.7	0
4.7	64.7	8.7	9.5	10.7	6.3
5.5	54.4	21.1	4.7	16.1	3.8
23.2	–	–	–	–	–
29.7	–	–	–	–	–
15.3	44.9	0.5	0.7	26.5	27.4
4.1	47.8	18.8	12.3	15.3	5.9
24.9	12	17.9	3.3	46.1	20.7
9.2	40.3	32.4	2.2	18.1	7
9.3	–	–	–	–	–

Country / Area	General information			Road traffic deaths		
	Population numbers for 2016[a]	GNI per capita for 2016 in US dollars[b]	Income level[c]	Reported number of road traffic deaths	Modelled number of road traffic deaths[d]	
					Point estimate	95% Confidence Interval
Guatemala	16 582 469	3 790	Middle	2 058	2 758	–
Guinea	12 395 924	490	Low	458	3 490	2 903 - 4 077
Guinea-Bissau	1 815 698	620	Low	122	565	465 - 664
Guyana	773 303	4 250	Middle	128	190	–
Honduras	9 112 867	2 150	Middle	1 407	1 525	1 388 - 1 661
Hungary	9 753 281	12 570	High	607	756	–
Iceland	332 474	56 990	High	18	22	–
India	1 324 171 392	1 680	Middle	150 785	299 091	–
Indonesia	261 115 456	3 400	Middle	31 282	31 726	27 277 - 36 176
Iran (Islamic Republic of)	80 277 424	6 530[g]	Middle	15 932	16 426	–
Iraq	37 202 572	5 430	Middle	4 134	7 686	6 548 - 8 824
Ireland	4 726 078	52 560	High	188	194	–
Israel	8 191 828	36 190	High	335	345	–
Italy	59 429 936	31 590	High	3 428[e]	3 333	–
Jamaica	2 881 355	4 660	Middle	379	391	–
Japan	127 748 512	38 000	High	4 682	5 224	–
Jordan	9 455 802	3 920	Middle	750	2 306	1 926 - 2 686
Kazakhstan	17 987 736	8 710	Middle	2 625	3 158	–
Kenya	48 461 568	1 380	Middle	2 965	13 463	11 486 - 15 440
Kiribati	114 395	2 380	Middle	5	5	
Kuwait	4 052 584	41 680[g]	High	424	715	–
Kyrgyzstan	5 955 734	1 100	Middle	812	916	–
Lao People's Democratic Republic	6 758 353	2 150	Middle	1 086	1 120	946 - 1 294
Latvia	1 970 530	14 630	High	158	184	–
Lebanon	6 006 668	7 680	Middle	576[e]	1 090	837 - 1 396
Lesotho	2 203 821	1 210	Middle	318	638	544 - 733
Liberia	4 613 823	370	Low	175	1 657	1 299 - 2 015
Libya	6 293 253	4 730[g]	Middle	2 414	1 645	1 234 - 2 171
Lithuania	2 908 249	14 770	High	192	234	–
Luxembourg	575 747	76 660	High	32	36	–
Madagascar	24 894 552	400	Low	340	7 108	5 895 - 8 321

Road traffic deaths	Road user death (%)				
Estimated road traffic death rate per 100 000 population[d]	Drivers/Passengers of 4-wheeled vehicles	Drivers / Passengers of 2- or 3- wheelers	Cyclists	Pedestrians	Other or unspecified users
16.6	19.4	32.7	0.4	39.2	8.3
28.2	–	–	–	–	–
31.1	–	–	–	–	–
24.6	24.2	21.9	12.5	29.7	11.7
16.7	18.6	24.3	4.1	27.9	25.1
7.8	44.3	10.5	12	25	8.1
6.6	72.2	11.1	0	11.1	5.6
22.6	17.9	39.6	1.7	10.4	30.4
12.2	4.9	73.6	3.2	15.5	2.7
20.5	48.7	24.1	0.6	21.6	5
20.7	–	–	–	–	–
4.1	62.2	11.7	5.3	18.6	2.1
4.2	46.3	12.2	2.7	28.7	10.1
5.6	42.8	25.6	7.3	17.6	6.7
13.6	33	28.8	8.4	22.2	7.7
4.1	32.4	17.2	15.1	35	1
24.4	71.3[h]	0	0	28.7	0
17.6	59.8	4.3	1.7	30.9	3.3
27.8	36.4[h]	24.2	2.4	37	0
4.4	40	20	0	40	0
17.6	–	–	–	–	–
15.4	27.6	2.1	0.2	40	30
16.6	–	–	–	–	–
9.3	44.9	12	4.4	34.8	3.8
18.1	42.4[h]	20.7		37	0
28.9	–	–	–	–	–
35.9	–	–	–	–	–
26.1	75	1.9	2.3	20.8	0
8	46.4[h]	5.7	8.9	38	1
6.3	62.5	9.4	3.1	25	0
28.6	52.9[h]	–	–	47.1	0

Country / Area	General information			Road traffic deaths		
	Population numbers for 2016[a]	GNI per capita for 2016 in US dollars[b]	Income level[c]	Reported number of road traffic deaths	Modelled number of road traffic deaths[d]	
					Point estimate	95% Confidence Interval
Malawi	18 091 576	320	Low	1 122	5 601	4 590 - 6 612
Malaysia	31 187 264	9 850	Middle	7 152	7 374	6 482 - 8 266
Maldives	427 756	7 430	Middle	4	4	–
Mali	17 994 836	750	Low	541	4 159	3 404 - 4 914
Malta	429 362	24 140	High	22	26	–
Mauritania	4 301 018	1 120	Middle	184	1 064	891 - 1 236
Mauritius	1 262 132	9 760	Middle	144	173	–
Mexico	127 540 424	9 040	Middle	16 039[e]	16 725	–
Micronesia (Federated States of)	104 937	3 680	Middle	2	2	–
Mongolia	3 027 398	3 550	Middle	484	499	471 - 527
Montenegro	628 615	6 970	Middle	65	67	–
Morocco	35 276 784	2 850	Middle	3 785	6 917	6 109 - 7 726
Mozambique	28 829 476	480	Low	1 379	8 665	7 081 - 10 250
Myanmar	52 885 224	1 190[g]	Middle	4 887	10 540	8 860 - 12 219
Namibia	2 479 713	4 620	Middle	731	754	633 - 875
Nepal	28 982 772	730	Low	2 006[e]	4 622	3 928 - 5 317
Netherlands	16 987 330	46 310	High	621[e]	648	–
New Zealand	4 660 833	39 070	High	327	364	–
Niger	20 672 988	370	Low	978	5 414	4 273 - 6 554
Nigeria	185 989 632	2 450	Middle	5 053	39 802	32 076 - 47 529
Norway	5 254 694	82 330	High	135	143	–
Oman	4 424 762	18 080[g]	High	692	713	–
Pakistan	193 203 472	1 510	Middle	4 448[e]	27 582	23 243 - 31 920
Panama	4 034 119	12 140	Middle	440	575	–
Papua New Guinea	8 084 991	2 160[g]	Middle	158	1 145	991 - 1 298
Paraguay	6 725 308	4 070	Middle	1 202	1 529	–
Peru	31 773 840	5 950	Middle	2 696	4 286	3 898 - 4 674
Philippines	103 320 224	3 580	Middle	10 012[e]	12 690	–
Poland	38 224 408	12 680	High	3 026	3 698	–
Portugal	10 371 627	19 850	High	563	768	–
Qatar	2 569 804	75 660[g]	High	178	239	–

Road traffic deaths	Road user death (%)				
Estimated road traffic death rate per 100 000 population[d]	Drivers/Passengers of 4-wheeled vehicles	Drivers / Passengers of 2- or 3- wheelers	Cyclists	Pedestrians	Other or unspecified users
31	31.1	3.2	16	49.6	0.1
23.6	–	–	–	–	–
0.9	0	75	0	25	0
23.1	27.9	42.3	2.4	11.5	15.9
6.1	18.2	40.9	4.5	27.3	9.1
24.7	–	–	–	–	–
13.7	16.7	45.8	6.9	30.6	0
13.1	18.4[h]	9.6	1.1	28.5	42.4
1.9	50	0	0	50	0
16.5	39.3	18.6	1.2	28.7	12.2
10.7	64.6	15.4	1.5	13.8	4.6
19.6	31.2	28.7	5.9	26.3	7.9
30.1	–	–	–	–	–
19.9	10.8	64.8	3.1	14.2	7.1
30.4	–	–	–	–	–
15.9	–	–	–	–	–
3.8	38	21.4	29.8	9.2	1.6
7.8	68.5	15.9	1.5	7.6	6.4
26.2	–	–	–	–	–
21.4	–	–	–	–	–
2.7	49.6	17	8.9	11.9	12.6
16.1	64.7	3.9	0.7	22.5	8.1
14.3	–	–	–	–	–
14.3	32.3	4.4	5.7	40	17.5
14.2	52.5	–	–	47.5	0
22.7	16.5	52.2	0.2	22.5	8.7
13.5	2.5	0.6	0.2	8.1	88.6
12.3	0.3	4.7	0.1	1	93.9
9.7	46.8	11.2	9	28.7	4.3
7.4	47.6	18.3	5.9	21.8	6.4
9.3	48.3	2.2	2.8	32	14.6

Country / Area	General information			Road traffic deaths		
	Population numbers for 2016[a]	GNI per capita for 2016 in US dollars[b]	Income level[c]	Reported number of road traffic deaths	Modelled number of road traffic deaths[d]	
					Point estimate	95% Confidence Interval
Republic of Korea	50 791 920	27 600	High	4 292	4 990	–
Republic of Moldova	4 059 608	2 120	Middle	346	394	–
Romania	19 778 084	9 470	Middle	1 913	2 044	–
Russian Federation	143 964 512	9 720	Middle	20 308	25 969	–
Rwanda	11 917 508	700	Low	593	3 535	2 690 - 4 380
Saint Lucia	178 015	7 670	Middle	15	63	–
Samoa	195 125	4 100	Middle	17[e]	22	20 - 25
San Marino	33 203	51 810[g]	High	0	0	–
Sao Tome and Principe	199 910	1 730	Middle	23	55	43 - 68
Saudi Arabia	32 275 688	21 750	High	9 031	9 311	8 268 - 10 354
Senegal	15 411 614	950	Low	604	3 609	3 052 - 4 165
Serbia	8 820 083	5 280	Middle	607	649	–
Seychelles	94 228	15 410	High	15	15	–
Singapore	5 622 455	51 880	High	141	155	–
Slovakia	5 444 218	16 810	High	275	330	–
Slovenia	2 077 862	21 660	High	130	134	–
Solomon Islands	599 419	1 880	Middle	11	104	94 - 115
Somalia	14 317 996	–	Low	165	3 884	3 023 - 4 745
South Africa	56 015 472	5 480	Middle	14 071	14 507	–
South Sudan	12 230 730	820[g]	Low	130	3 661	2 976 - 4 346
Spain	46 347 576	27 520	High	1 810	1 922	–
Sri Lanka	20 798 492	3 780	Middle	3 003	3 096	2 777 - 3 415
Sudan	39 578 828	2 140	Middle	2 311	10 178	8 635 - 11 722
Suriname	558 368	7 070	Middle	74	81	–
Sweden	9 837 533	54 630	High	270	278	–
Switzerland	8 401 739	81 240	High	216	223	–
Syrian Arab Republic	18 430 452	1 840[g]	Middle	714	4 890	4 009 - 5 772
Tajikistan	8 734 951	1 110	Middle	427	1 577	1 449 - 1 704
Thailand	68 863 512	5 640	Middle	21 745	22 491	20 265 - 24 717
The former Yugoslav Republic of Macedonia	2 081 206	4 980	Middle	148[e]	134	–
Timor-Leste	1 268 671	2 180[g]	Middle	71	161	138 - 184

Road traffic deaths	Road user death (%)				
Estimated road traffic death rate per 100 000 population[d]	Drivers/Passengers of 4-wheeled vehicles	Drivers / Passengers of 2- or 3- wheelers	Cyclists	Pedestrians	Other or unspecified users
9.8	–	20.5	5.9	39.9	33.7
9.7	17.6	4.3	1.4	18.5	58.1
10.3	46.1	4.4	9	37.2	3.3
18	57.6	5.9	2	29.2	5.3
29.7	–	–	–	–	–
35.4	46.7	20	13.3	13.3	6.7
11.3	41.2	0	5.9	47.1	5.9
0	–	–	–	–	–
27.5	–	–	–	–	–
28.8	–	–	–	–	–
23.4	–	–	–	–	–
7.4	46.3	8.7	9.4	23.1	12.5
15.9	46.7	20	6.7	20	6.7
2.8	7.8	44	14.2	33.3	0.7
6.1	50.2	8.7	7.6	29.1	4.4
6.4	46.9	19.2	10	16.9	6.9
17.4	–	–	–	–	–
27.1	–	–	–	–	–
25.9	44.9	0.3	3.2	38.4	13.1
29.9	–	–	–	–	–
4.1	46.5	21.9	3.7	21.5	6.4
14.9	6.2	50.8	8.1	29.2	5.7
25.7				28.6	71.4
14.5	33.8	45.9	4.1	14.9	1.4
2.8	53.7	16.3	8.1	15.6	6.3
2.7	34.7	22.7	15.3	23.1	4.2
26.5	18.8	6.4	5.9	64.7	4.2
18.1	57.4[h]	–	2.3	40.3	0
32.7	12.3	74.4	3.5	7.6	2.3
6.4	46.6	9.5	6.1	33.1	4.7
12.7	–	–	–	–	–

Country / Area	General information			Road traffic deaths		
	Population numbers for 2016[a]	GNI per capita for 2016 in US dollars[b]	Income level[c]	Reported number of road traffic deaths	Modelled number of road traffic deaths[d]	
					Point estimate	95% Confidence Interval
Togo	7 606 374	540	Low	514	2 224	1 800 - 2 649
Tonga	107 122	4 020	Middle	18	18	–
Trinidad and Tobago	1 364 962	15 680	High	135	165	–
Tunisia	11 403 248	3 690	Middle	1 443	2 595	2 321 - 2 869
Turkey	79 512 424	11 180	Middle	7 300	9 782	–
Turkmenistan	5 662 544	6 670	Middle	543	823	765 - 880
Uganda	41 487 964	660	Low	3 503	12 036	9 454 - 14 618
Ukraine	44 438 624	2 310	Middle	4 687	6 089	–
United Arab Emirates	9 269 612	40 480	High	725	1 678	1 435 - 1 921
United Kingdom	65 788 572	42 390	High	1 804[e]	2 019	–
United Republic of Tanzania	55 572 200	900	Low	3 256	16 252	13 130 - 19 374
United States of America	322 179 616	56 180	High	35 092[e]	39 888	–
Uruguay	3 444 006	15 230	High	446	460	–
Uzbekistan	31 446 796	2 220	Middle	2 496	3 617	–
Vanuatu	270 402	3 170[g]	Middle	9	43	39 - 48
Venezuela (Bolivarian Republic of)	31 568 180	11 760[g]	Middle	7 028[e]	10 640	–
Viet Nam	94 569 072	2 050	Middle	8 417	24 970	21 576 - 28 363
West Bank and Gaza Strip	4 790 705	3 230	Middle	159	252	189 - 333
Zimbabwe	16 150 362	940	Low	1 721	5 601	4 602 - 6 599

Road traffic deaths	Road user death (%)				
Estimated road traffic death rate per 100 000 population[d]	Drivers/Passengers of 4-wheeled vehicles	Drivers / Passengers of 2- or 3- wheelers	Cyclists	Pedestrians	Other or unspecified users
29.2	17.3	71.6	–	–	11.1
16.8	66.7	0	0	27.8	5.6
12.1	57.8	2.2	0.7	31.1	8.1
22.8	49.3[h]	22.9	2.5	24.6	0.7
12.3	21.7	14.9	1.9	23.4	38
14.5					
29	21.3	33.4	5.8	39.5	0
13.7	34	8.7	7.1	41.9	8.4
18.1	54.5	5.5	1.5	24.3	14.2
3.1	46.2	20.5	5.5	23.7	4.1
29.2	38.5	22.7	8	29.9	0.8
12.4	63.9	14.2	2.3	15.3	4.2
13.4	30.7	45.7	7	16.6	0
11.5	–	–	–	–	–
15.9	–	–	–	–	–
33.7	–	–	–	–	–
26.4	–	–	–	–	–
5.3	52.2	2.5	1.9	32.7	10.7
34.7	26.7	10.2	12.2	13.7	37.2

a Population Division of the Department of Economic and Social Affairs of the United Nations Secretariat (June 2017). World population Prospects: The 2017 Revision, Highlights. New York: United Nations.

b Gross National Income (GNI) per capita is the dollar value of a country's final income in a year divided by its population using Atlas methodology. Data from World Development Indicators database, World Bank, November 2017. http://data.worldbank.org/indicator/NY.GNP.PCAP.CD/countries.

c World Development Indicators database: Low income is $1 005 or less, middle income is $1 006 to $12 235, high income is $12 236 or more.

d Modelled using negative binomial regression (see preamble on page 289). Data from countries with good vital registration and countries with a population of less than 150 000 were not included in the model.

e 2016 data not available.

f From Jan-Oct 2016.

g 2016 data not available. Latest available used from World Development Indicators database.

h Drivers and passengers (all vehicles).

i Data for Libreville.

TABLE A3: POST-CRASH RESPONSE BY COUNTRY / AREA

Country / Area	Universal access telephone number	Trauma registry	National assessment of emergency care system
Afghanistan	National, single number	None	No
Albania	National, single number	Subnational	No
Angola	National, multiple numbers	National	Yes
Antigua and Barbuda	National, single number	–	No
Argentina	Partial coverage	Some facilities	No
Armenia	National, single number	National	No
Australia	National, single number	National	No
Austria	National, single number	National	No
Azerbaijan	National, single number	National	No
Bangladesh	Partial coverage	None	No
Barbados	National, multiple numbers	National	No
Belarus	National, single number	None	No
Belgium	National, single number	National	No
Belize	National, single number	None	No
Benin	National, single number	Some facilities	No
Bhutan	National, single number	None	No
Bolivia (Plurinational State of)	Partial coverage	Subnational	No
Bosnia and Herzegovina	National, single number	None	Yes
Botswana	National, multiple numbers	None	No
Brazil	National, single number	None	No
Bulgaria	National, single number	None	No
Burkina Faso	National, single number	Some facilities	Yes
Burundi	None	National	No
Cabo Verde	National, multiple numbers	Some facilities	No
Cambodia	National, multiple numbers	National	No
Cameroon	National, single number	Some facilities	Yes
Canada	Partial coverage	Subnational	No
Central African Republic	–	Some facilities	No
Chad	–	Some facilities	No
Chile	National, single number	National	No
China	National, single number	National	Yes
Colombia	Partial coverage	National	No
Comoros	None	None	No

Provider training and certification				Estimated % road traffic crash victims with permanent disability
Prehospital providers	Nurses	Specialist doctors		
Formal certification pathway	Post graduate courses in emergency and trauma care	Emergency medicine	Trauma surgery	
No	No	Yes	Yes	
Yes	Yes	Yes	No	
Yes	Yes	Yes	Yes	
No	No	No	No	
–	–	–	–	
Yes	Yes	Yes	Yes	
Yes	Yes	Yes	No	15
Yes	No	Yes	Yes	
No	No	Yes	Yes	3
No	No	Yes	Yes	2.4
Yes	No	Yes	Yes	
No	No	Yes	Yes	
Yes	Yes	Yes	Yes	25[a]
No	No	No	No	
Yes	Yes	Yes	Yes	
Yes	No	Yes	Yes	
No	Yes	Yes	No	
Yes	No	Yes	Yes	
–	Yes	Yes	No	
No	Yes	Yes	Yes	23.5
Yes	Yes	Yes	Yes	
No	–	–	No	
No	No	No	Yes	
No	No	–	–	
No	Yes	Yes	Yes	15
No	No	No	No	
–	Yes	Yes	Yes	
–	Yes	–	–	
Yes	No	No	Yes	
No	Yes	Yes	Yes	
Yes	No	No	No	
Yes	Yes	Yes	Yes	5
No	No	No	No	

Country / Area	Universal access telephone number	Trauma registry	National assessment of emergency care system
Congo	Partial coverage	None	No
Cook Islands	National, single number	National	No
Costa Rica	National, single number	Some facilities	No
Côte d'Ivoire	Partial coverage	Some facilities	No
Croatia	National, single number	None	No
Cuba	National, single number	National	No
Cyprus	National, multiple numbers	Subnational	Yes
Czechia	National, single number	National	Yes
Democratic Republic of the Congo	Partial coverage	Some facilities	Yes
Denmark	National, single number	National	Yes
Dominica	National, single number	None	No
Dominican Republic	Partial coverage	National	Yes
Ecuador	National, single number	National	Yes
Egypt	National, single number	National	Yes
El Salvador	National, multiple numbers	National	Yes
Equatorial Guinea	National, multiple numbers	National	Yes
Eritrea	Partial coverage	Some facilities	No
Estonia	National, single number	None	No
Eswatini	National, multiple numbers	None	No
Ethiopia	National, single number	Some facilities	No
Fiji	National, multiple numbers	None	No
Finland	National, single number	National	Yes
France	National, single number	Subnational	No
Gabon	Partial coverage	Some facilities	No
Gambia	None	Subnational	No
Georgia	National, single number	None	No
Germany	National, single number	Some facilities	Yes
Ghana	National, single number	Some facilities	Yes
Greece	National, single number	Some facilities	No
Grenada	National, single number	None	No
Guatemala	National, multiple numbers	Some facilities	No
Guinea	None	Subnational	No

Provider training and certification					
Prehospital providers	Nurses	Specialist doctors		Estimated % road traffic crash victims with permanent disability	
Formal certification pathway	Post graduate courses in emergency and trauma care	Emergency medicine	Trauma surgery		
No	No	No	No		
No	No	No	No		
Yes	Yes	Yes	Yes		
Yes	Yes	Yes	Yes		
Yes	No	Yes	Yes		
Yes	Yes	Yes	Yes		
Yes	Yes	No	No		
Yes	Yes	Yes	Yes		
No	No	No	Yes	40	
–	Yes	No	No		
No	No	No	No		
Yes	No	Yes	No		
Yes	Yes	Yes	Yes		
Yes	Yes	Yes	No		
No	No	No	No		
Yes	Yes	Yes	Yes		
No	No	No	No		
No	Yes	Yes	Yes		
Yes	No	No	No		
Yes	Yes	Yes	Yes		
No	No	Yes	No		
Yes	Yes	Yes	Yes	4	
–	–	–	–	0.8	
Yes	No	Yes	No		
No	No	No	No		
Yes	No	Yes	Yes		
Yes	Yes	Yes	Yes		
Yes	Yes	Yes	Yes		
Yes	Yes	No	No		
No	No	No	No		
Yes	Yes	Yes	Yes		
No	No	No	No		

Country / Area	Universal access telephone number	Trauma registry	National assessment of emergency care system
Guinea-Bissau	National, single number	Some facilities	No
Guyana	Partial coverage	None	No
Honduras	National, single number	Some facilities	No
Hungary	National, single number	None	No
Iceland	National, single number	National	No
India	Partial coverage	Some facilities	No
Indonesia	Partial coverage	None	No
Iran (Islamic Republic of)	National, single number	Subnational	Yes
Iraq	National, single number	Some facilities	Yes
Ireland	National, single number	National	Yes
Israel	National, single number	National	No
Italy	National, single number	Subnational	No
Jamaica	National, single number	Some facilities	No
Japan	National, single number	National	No
Jordan	National, single number	None	No
Kazakhstan	National, single number	National	No
Kenya	National, single number	Some facilities	No
Kiribati	National, multiple numbers	National	No
Kuwait	National, single number	None	No
Kyrgyzstan	National, single number	None	Yes
Lao People's Democratic Republic	Partial coverage	None	No
Latvia	National, single number	National	Yes
Lebanon	National, multiple numbers	None	No
Lesotho	None	None	No
Liberia	National, single number	None	No
Libya	National, single number	National	Yes
Lithuania	National, single number	National	No
Luxembourg	National, single number	Some facilities	No
Madagascar	None	None	No
Malawi	Partial coverage	Some facilities	No
Malaysia	National, single number	None	No
Maldives	Partial coverage	None	No

Provider training and certification				Estimated % road traffic crash victims with permanent disability
Prehospital providers	Nurses	Specialist doctors		
Formal certification pathway	Post graduate courses in emergency and trauma care	Emergency medicine	Trauma surgery	
No	No	No	No	
Yes	Yes	Yes	No	
Yes	–	–	–	
Yes	Yes	Yes	Yes	
Yes	Yes	Yes	No	
Yes	No	Yes	Yes	
Yes	Yes	Yes	Yes	
Yes	Yes	Yes	Yes	5.8
Yes	No	Yes	Yes	
Yes	Yes	Yes	No	
Yes	Yes	Yes	Yes	
Yes	No	Yes	Yes	2.5
No	Yes	Yes	No	1.7
Yes	Yes	Yes	Yes	
Yes	Yes	Yes	Yes	
Yes	Yes	Yes	Yes	5
No	Yes	No	No	
Yes	Yes	Yes	Yes	
Yes	Yes	Yes	No	
Yes	Yes	Yes	Yes	
Yes	Yes	Yes	Yes	
Yes	Yes	Yes	Yes	
No	Yes	Yes	Yes	
Yes	No	No	No	
–	No	No	No	
Yes	Yes	Yes	Yes	
No	Yes	Yes	Yes	
No	Yes	No	No	
No	Yes	Yes	Yes	
No	No	No	No	
Yes	Yes	Yes	Yes	
No	No	No	No	

Country / Area	Universal access telephone number	Trauma registry	National assessment of emergency care system
Mali	Partial coverage	Some facilities	No
Malta	National, single number	National	Yes
Mauritania	–	None	No
Mauritius	National, single number	Subnational	Yes
Mexico	National, single number	National	Yes
Micronesia (Federated States of)	National, multiple numbers	None	No
Mongolia	National, single number	National	No
Montenegro	National, single number	National	Yes
Morocco	National, single number	None	No
Mozambique	National, multiple numbers	Some facilities	No
Myanmar	National, multiple numbers	National	No
Namibia	National, multiple numbers	National	Yes
Nepal	Partial coverage	Some facilities	No
Netherlands	National, single number	National	No
New Zealand	National, single number	National	No
Niger	National, single number	Some facilities	No
Nigeria	National, single number	Some facilities	No
Norway	National, single number	National	Yes
Oman	National, single number	Some facilities	No
Pakistan	National, multiple numbers	Subnational	No
Panama	National, single number	Some facilities	No
Papua New Guinea	Partial coverage	Some facilities	No
Paraguay	National, single number	National	No
Peru	Partial coverage	National	No
Philippines	National, single number	National	No
Poland	National, single number	None	No
Portugal	National, single number	National	No
Qatar	National, single number	National	Yes
Republic of Korea	National, single number	Subnational	Yes
Republic of Moldova	National, multiple numbers	Some facilities	No
Romania	National, single number	None	Yes
Russian Federation	National, single number	Some facilities	No

Provider training and certification				Estimated % road traffic crash victims with permanent disability
Prehospital providers	Nurses	Specialist doctors		
Formal certification pathway	Post graduate courses in emergency and trauma care	Emergency medicine	Trauma surgery	
No	No	No	No	
Yes	No	Yes	Yes	
No	No	No	No	
Yes	Yes	Yes	Yes	
Yes	Yes	Yes	Yes	16.4
No	No	–	–	
No	Yes	Yes	Yes	
Yes	No	Yes	Yes	
No	No	Yes	Yes	
No	No	Yes	No	
No	Yes	Yes	Yes	
Yes	–	No	No	18
No	No	No	No	
No	Yes	Yes	Yes	4 - 7
Yes	Yes	Yes	No	
Yes	Yes	No	No	
Yes	Yes	Yes	Yes	
Yes	Yes	Yes	Yes	
Yes	Yes	Yes	Yes	
No	No	No	No	
Yes	Yes	Yes	No	
Yes	No	Yes	Yes	
No	No	Yes	Yes	
No	Yes	Yes	Yes	3.1
No	Yes	Yes	Yes	
No	Yes	Yes	Yes	
Yes	Yes	Yes	No	
Yes	Yes	Yes	Yes	1
Yes	Yes	Yes	Yes	
Yes	Yes	Yes	Yes	
Yes	Yes	Yes	No	21
Yes	Yes	Yes	Yes	

Country / Area	Universal access telephone number	Trauma registry	National assessment of emergency care system
Rwanda	National, single number	None	No
Saint Lucia	National, single number	–	No
Samoa	National, multiple numbers	None	No
San Marino	National, multiple numbers	None	Yes
Sao Tome and Principe	National, single number	National	No
Saudi Arabia	National, single number	Subnational	No
Senegal	Partial coverage	Some facilities	No
Serbia	National, multiple numbers	Some facilities	Yes
Seychelles	National, single number	None	No
Singapore	National, single number	National	No
Slovakia	National, single number	None	No
Slovenia	National, single number	National	No
Solomon Islands	National, single number	Some facilities	No
Somalia	None	None	No
South Africa	National, multiple numbers	National	No
South Sudan	National, single number	Some facilities	No
Spain	National, single number	Some facilities	No
Sri Lanka	Partial coverage	Some facilities	No
Sudan	National, multiple numbers	Subnational	No
Suriname	Partial coverage	Some facilities	No
Sweden	National, single number	National	No
Switzerland	National, single number	National	No
Syrian Arab Republic	Partial coverage	Subnational	No
Tajikistan	National, single number	National	No
Thailand	National, single number	Some facilities	Yes
The former Yugoslav Republic of Macedonia	National, single number	National	Yes
Timor-Leste	National, single number	National	No
Togo	National, single number	National	No
Tonga	National, multiple numbers	None	No
Trinidad and Tobago	National, multiple numbers	Some facilities	No
Tunisia	National, multiple numbers	None	Yes
Turkey	National, single number	Some facilities	Yes

Provider training and certification				Estimated % road traffic crash victims with permanent disability
Prehospital providers	Nurses	Specialist doctors		
Formal certification pathway	Post graduate courses in emergency and trauma care	Emergency medicine	Trauma surgery	
–	–	–	–	
Yes	No	No	No	
No	No	No	No	
Yes	Yes	No	No	
No	No	No	No	
Yes	Yes	Yes	Yes	
No	No	Yes	Yes	
Yes	Yes	Yes	Yes	
Yes	No	No	No	
Yes	Yes	Yes	Yes	
Yes	Yes	Yes	Yes	
Yes	Yes	Yes	Yes	
No	No	Yes	No	
No	No	No	No	
Yes	Yes	Yes	Yes	
No	No	No	No	
Yes	No	No	Yes	2.1/1 000 inhabitants
No	No	Yes	Yes	
No	No	Yes	No	19
No	No	Yes	No	
No	Yes	Yes	No	17
No	Yes	Yes	Yes	
Yes	Yes	Yes	Yes	
Yes	Yes	Yes	Yes	
Yes	Yes	Yes	Yes	4.6[b]
Yes	Yes	Yes	Yes	11.5
Yes	Yes	No	Yes	
Yes	Yes	Yes	Yes	47
No	No	No	No	
No	Yes	Yes	No	
No	Yes	Yes	Yes	
Yes	Yes	Yes	Yes	

Country / Area	Universal access telephone number	Trauma registry	National assessment of emergency care system
Turkmenistan	National, single number	Some facilities	No
Uganda	National, multiple numbers	Some facilities	Yes
Ukraine	National, single number	None	No
United Arab Emirates	National, single number	Subnational	No
United Kingdom	National, single number	Subnational	No
United Republic of Tanzania	None	Subnational	No
United States of America	National, single number	National	Yes
Uruguay	National, single number	National	No
Uzbekistan	National, single number	–	
Vanuatu	National, single number	National	No
Venezuela (Bolivarian Republic of)	National, single number	National	No
Viet Nam	Partial coverage	National	No
West Bank and Gaza Strip	National, single number	None	No
Zimbabwe	National, multiple numbers	None	No

[a] 25% of all hospitalized MAIS3+ victims incur a long-term disability as a result of the crash

[b] 4.6% of admitted patients estimated

Provider training and certification				Estimated % road traffic crash victims with permanent disability
Prehospital providers	Nurses	Specialist doctors		
Formal certification pathway	Post graduate courses in emergency and trauma care	Emergency medicine	Trauma surgery	
Yes	Yes	Yes	Yes	
No	No	Yes	No	2.8
Yes	Yes	Yes	No	
Yes	No	Yes	No	
Yes	Yes	Yes	Yes	
No	Yes	Yes	Yes	
Yes	Yes	Yes	Yes	
No	No	Yes	Yes	
No	Yes	No	No	
Yes	Yes	Yes	Yes	
No	Yes	Yes	Yes	
No	Yes	Yes	Yes	1
Yes	No	No	No	7.1

TABLE A4: SPEED LAWS AND ENFORCEMENT BY COUNTRY / AREA

Country / Area	National speed limit law	Types of modifications allowed	Maximum default speed limits (km/h)			Enforcement	Predominant type of enforcement
			Urban	Rural	Motorways		
Afghanistan	Yes	No	90 km/h[a]	90 km/h[a]	90 km/h[a]	4	–
Albania	Yes	Yes	40 km/h	80 km/h	110 km/h	4	Manual and automated
Angola	Yes	No	60 km/h	90 km/h	120 km/h	5	Manual
Antigua and Barbuda	Yes	No	~ 32 km/h[b]	~ 64 km/h	No	5	Manual
Argentina	Yes	Yes	60 km/h	110 km/h	130 km/h	5	Manual and automated
Armenia	Yes	No	90 km/h[c]	90 km/h	110 km/h	8	Automated
Australia	Yes	Yes	50 km/h	100 - 130 km/h	100 - 130 km/h	8	Manual and automated
Austria	Yes	Yes	50 km/h	100 km/h	130 km/h		Automated
Azerbaijan	Yes	No	60 km/h	90 km/h	110 km/h	8	Automated
Bangladesh	Yes	No	~ 112 km/h[d]	~ 112 km/h[d]	~ 112 km/h[d]	5	Manual
Barbados	Yes	No	80 km/h[e]	80 km/h[e]	80 km/h[e]	4	Manual
Belarus	Yes	No	60 km/h	90 km/h	110 km/h	7	Manual and automated
Belgium	Yes	Yes	50 km/h	90 km/h[f]	120 km/h	7	Manual and automated
Belize	Yes	No	~ 40 km/h	~ 88 km/h	~ 88 km/h	4	Manual
Benin	No	No	–	–	–	–	–
Bhutan	Yes	No	30 km/h	50 km/h	50 km/h	6	Manual
Bolivia (Plurinational State of)	Yes	Yes	40 km/h[g]	80 km/h[g]	80 km/h	3	Manual
Bosnia and Herzegovina	Yes	No	50 km/h[h]	80 km/h	130 km/h	6	Manual and automated
Botswana	Yes	Yes	60 km/h	80 km/h	120 km/h	8	Manual
Brazil	Yes	Yes	80 km/h[h]	60 km/h[i]	110 km/h	6	Automated
Bulgaria	Yes	No	50 km/h	90 km/h	140 km/h	6	Automated
Burkina Faso	Yes	Yes	50 km/h	90 km/h	No	7	Manual
Burundi	Yes	Yes	50 km/h	100 km/h	100 km/h	0	Manual
Cabo Verde	Yes	Yes	50 km/h	90 km/h	120 km/h	5	Manual
Cambodia	Yes	No	40 km/h	90 km/h	100 km/h	5	Manual
Cameroon	Yes	Yes	60 km/h	110 km/h	No	5	Manual
Canada	Yes	Yes	50 km/h	50 - 100 km/h	80 - 100 km/h	4	Manual
Central African Republic	Yes	Yes	60 km/h	110 km/h	No	–	–

Country / Area	National speed limit law	Types of modifications allowed	Maximum default speed limits (km/h)			Enforcement	Predominant type of enforcement
			Urban	Rural	Motorways		
Chad	Yes	Yes	60 km/h	110 km/h	No	3	–
Chile	Yes	Yes	60 km/h[j]	100 km/h	120 km/h	5	Manual
China	Yes	Yes	50 km/h	70 km/h	120 km/h	8	Automated
Colombia	Yes	Yes	80 km/h	120 km/h	120 km/h	5	Manual and automated
Comoros	Yes[k]	–	–	–	–	3	Manual
Congo	Yes	Yes	60 km/h	110 km/h	No	4	–
Cook Islands	Yes	No	50 km/h[l]	50 km/h[l]	50 km/h[l]	6	Manual
Costa Rica	Yes	No	50 km/h	60 km/h	No	4	Manual
Côte d'Ivoire	Yes	No	60 km/h	110 km/h	120 km/h	5	Manual
Croatia	Yes	Yes	50 km/h[m]	90 km/h	130 km/h	7	Manual and automated
Cuba	Yes	No	50 km/h	90 km/h	100 km/h	7	Manual
Cyprus	Yes	Yes	65 km/h	No	100 km/h	6	Manual
Czechia	Yes	Yes	50 km/h[m]	90 km/h	130 km/h	5	Manual
Democratic Republic of the Congo	Yes	No	60 km/h[n]	90 km/h	120 km/h	3	–
Denmark	Yes	Yes[o]	50 km/h	80 km/h	130 km/h	–	Automated
Dominica	No	No	–	–	–	–	–
Dominican Republic	Yes	No	60 km/h	60 km/h	120 km/h	6	Manual
Ecuador	Yes	Yes	60 km/h	120 km/h	135 km/h	7	Manual and automated
Egypt	Yes	Yes	60 km/h	90 km/h	100 km/h	8	Manual and automated
El Salvador	Yes	No	50 km/h	90 km/h	No	6	Manual
Equatorial Guinea	Yes	Yes	60 km/h	110 km/h	No	0	–
Eritrea	Yes	No	60 km/h	100 km/h	No	6	Manual
Estonia	Yes	Yes	50 km/h[p]	90 km/h	No[q]	7	Automated
Eswatini	Yes	Yes	100 km/h[r]	100 km/h[r]	100 km/h[r]	6	Manual
Ethiopia	Yes	Yes	60 km/h	70 km/h	100 km/h	2	Manual
Fiji	Yes	No	50 km/h	80 km/h	–[q]	7	Manual and automated
Finland	Yes	Yes	50 km/h	80 km/h	120 km/h	8	Manual and automated
France	Yes	Yes	50 km/h	90 km/h	130 km/h	8	Automated
Gabon	Yes	Yes	60 km/h	110 km/h	No	1	–

Country / Area	National speed limit law	Types of modifications allowed	Maximum default speed limits (km/h)			Enforcement	Predominant type of enforcement
			Urban	Rural	Motorways		
Gambia	Yes	Yes	No	No	No	3	Manual
Georgia	Yes	No	60 km/h	90 km/h	110 km/h	6	Automated
Germany	Yes	Yes	50 km/h	100 km/h	No[s]	–	–
Ghana	Yes	No	50 km/h	90 km/h	100 km/h	4	Manual
Greece	Yes	Yes	50 km/h	90 km/h	130 km/h	3	Manual
Grenada	Yes	No	~ 32 km/h	~ 64 km/h	No	6	Manual
Guatemala	Yes	Yes	60 km/h	80 km/h	100 km/h	4	Manual
Guinea	No	–	–	–	–	–	Manual
Guinea-Bissau	Yes	No	50 km/h	80 km/h	100 km/h	1	Manual
Guyana	Yes[t]	No	64 km/h	64 km/h	No	7	Manual
Honduras	Yes[u]	No	–	–	–	6	Manual
Hungary	Yes	Yes	50 km/h	90 km/h	130 km/h	6	Manual and automated
Iceland	Yes	No	50 km/h	90 km/h	100 km/h	7	Automated
India	Yes	Yes	100 km/h[v]	100 km/h[v]	100 km/h[v]	3	Manual
Indonesia	Yes	Yes	50 km/h	80 km/h	100 km/h	8	Manual
Iran (Islamic Republic of)	Yes	No	60 km/h	95 km/h	120 km/h	7	Manual and automated
Iraq	Yes	No	60 km/h	100 km/h	120 km/h	2	Manual
Ireland	Yes	Yes	50 km/h	100 km/h	120 km/h	10	Automated
Israel	Yes	No	50 km/h	80 km/h	110 km/h	5	Automated
Italy	Yes	Yes	50 km/h	110 km/h[w]	150 km/h	8	Automated
Jamaica	Yes	No	~ 48 km/h	~ 80 km/h	No	4	Manual
Japan	Yes	Yes	60 km/h	60 km/h	100 km/h	7	Manual
Jordan	Yes	Yes	90 km/h	120 km/h	120 km/h	7	Manual and automated
Kazakhstan	Yes	No	60 km/h[x]	110 km/h	140 km/h	7	Automated
Kenya	Yes	No	50 km/h	100 km/h	110 km/h	4	Manual
Kiribati	Yes	No	40 km/h	60 km/h	60 km/h	5	Manual
Kuwait	Yes	No	45 km/h	80 km/h	80 km/h	3	Automated
Kyrgyzstan	Yes	No	60 km/h	90 km/h	110 km/h	5	Manual and automated
Lao People's Democratic Republic	Yes	No	40 km/h	90 km/h	–[q]	5	Manual
Latvia	Yes	No	50 km/h	90 km/h	No	7	Manual and automated

Country / Area	National speed limit law	Types of modifications allowed	Maximum default speed limits (km/h)			Enforcement	Predominant type of enforcement
			Urban	Rural	Motorways		
Lebanon	Yes	Yes	50 km/h	70 km/h	100 km/h	5	Manual
Lesotho	Yes	No	50 km/h	80 km/h	No	2	Manual
Liberia	Yes	No	~ 40 km/h	~ 56 km/h	~ 72 km/h	0	Manual
Libya	Yes	No	50 km/h	85 km/h	100 km/h	2	Manual and automated
Lithuania	Yes	No	50 km/h[y]	90 km/h	130 km/h	7	Automated
Luxembourg	Yes	Yes	50 km/h	90 km/h	130 km/h	7	Automated
Madagascar	Yes	Yes	50 km/h[z]	No	No	4	–
Malawi	Yes	No	50 km/h	80 km/h	100 km/h	4	Manual
Malaysia	Yes	Yes	90 km/h[aa]	90 km/h[aa]	110 km/h[aa]	6	Manual
Maldives	Yes	No	30 km/h[ab]	30 km/h[ab]	No	3	Manual
Mali	Yes	Yes	50 km/h	90 km/h	110 km/h	4	Manual
Malta	Yes	No	50 km/h	80 km/h	No	4	Automated
Mauritania	Yes	Yes	80 km/h	100 km/h	100 km/h	4	Manual
Mauritius	Yes	No	90 km/h	90 km/h	110 km/h	6	Manual and automated
Mexico	Yes	Yes	20 - 70 km/h	20 - 90 km/h	45 - 110 km/h	4	Manual and automated
Micronesia (Federated States of)	Yes	Yes[ac]	~ 40 km/h	~ 40 km/h	~ 40 km/h	3	Manual
Mongolia	Yes	No	60 km/h	80 km/h	100 km/h	5	Manual and automated
Montenegro	Yes	No	50 km/h	80 km/h	130 km/h	7	Manual
Morocco	Yes	Yes	60 km/h	100 km/h	120 km/h	7	Manual and automated
Mozambique	Yes	No	60 km/h	120 km/h	No	5	Manual
Myanmar	Yes	No	48 km/h	80 km/h	No	6	Automated
Namibia	Yes	No	60 km/h	120 km/h	120 km/h	4	Manual
Nepal	Yes	No	40 km/h[ad]	80 km/h[ad]	80 km/h[ad]	2	Manual
Netherlands	Yes	Yes	50 km/h	80 km/h	130 km/h	6	Manual and automated
New Zealand	Yes	Yes	50 km/h	100 km/h	100 km/h	7	Manual and automated
Niger	Yes	No	50 km/h	No	No	3	Manual
Nigeria	Yes	Yes	50 km/h	80 km/h	100 km/h	6	Manual
Norway	Yes	Yes	50 km/h	80 km/h	100 km/h	10	Manual and automated

Country / Area	National speed limit law	Types of modifications allowed	Maximum default speed limits (km/h)			Enforcement	Predominant type of enforcement
			Urban	Rural	Motorways		
Oman	Yes	No	–	–	–	10	Manual and automated
Pakistan	Yes	Yes	90 km/h	110 km/h	130 km/h	4	Manual
Panama	Yes	No	80 km/h	100 km/h	120 km/h	4	Manual
Papua New Guinea	Yes	No	60 km/h	75 km/h	–	–	–
Paraguay	Yes	Yes	50 km/h	110 km/h	110 km/h	4	Manual
Peru	Yes	Yes	60 km/h	60 km/h	100 km/h	1	Manual
Philippines	Yes	Yes	40 km/h	80 km/h	No	5	Manual
Poland	Yes	Yes	50 km/h[ae]	90 km/h	140 km/h	8	Manual
Portugal	Yes	No	50 km/h	90 km/h	120 km/h	7	Manual
Qatar	Yes	No	100 km/h	120 km/h	120 km/h	7	Automated
Republic of Korea	Yes	Yes	80 km/h	80 km/h	120 km/h	8	Automated
Republic of Moldova	Yes	No	50 km/h	110 km/h	110 km/h	8	Manual and automated
Romania	Yes	Yes	50 km/h	90 km/h	130 km/h	7	Manual
Russian Federation	Yes	Yes[af]	60 km/h	90 km/h	110 km/h	8	Automated
Rwanda	Yes	Yes	80 km/h[ag]	80 km/h[ag]	80 km/h[ag]	8	Automated
Saint Lucia	Yes	No	~ 24 km/h	~ 24 km/h	~ 56 km/h	0	–
Samoa	Yes	No	~ 56 km/h	~ 56 km/h	–[q]	9	Manual
San Marino	Yes	No	70 km/h	70 km/h	No	6	Manual and automated
Sao Tome and Principe	Yes	No	50 km/h	90 km/h	120 km/h	2	–
Saudi Arabia	Yes	No	80 km/h	120 km/h	No	7	Automated
Senegal	Yes	Yes	No	90 km/h	110 km/h	5	Manual
Serbia	Yes	Yes	50 km/h[ah]	100 km/h	120 km/h	6	Manual
Seychelles	Yes	No	25 - 80 km/h[ai]	80 km/h[ai]	80 km/h[ai]	6	Manual
Singapore	Yes	No	70 km/h[aj]	–[ak]	90 km/h	8	Manual and automated
Slovakia	Yes	No	50 km/h	90 km/h	130 km/h	7	Manual
Slovenia	Yes	No	50 km/h[al]	90 km/h	130 km/h	7	Manual
Solomon Islands	Yes[am]	Yes	–	–	–	5	Manual
Somalia	Yes	Yes	40 km/h	No	No	1	–
South Africa	Yes	Yes	60 km/h	100 km/h	120 km/h	6	Manual and automated

Country / Area	National speed limit law	Types of modifications allowed	Maximum default speed limits (km/h)			Enforcement	Predominant type of enforcement
			Urban	Rural	Motorways		
South Sudan	Yes	No	50 km/h	No	No	3	Manual
Spain	Yes	Yes[an]	50 km/h	90 km/h	120 km/h	8	Manual and automated
Sri Lanka	Yes	No	50 km/h	70 km/h	100 km/h	9	Manual
Sudan	Yes	Yes	50 km/h	90 km/h	No	6	Manual and automated
Suriname	Yes	No	40 km/h	80 km/h	80 km/h	5	Manual
Sweden	Yes	Yes	50 km/h	110 km/h	120 km/h	8	Automated
Switzerland	Yes	No	50 km/h	80 km/h	120 km/h	7	—
Syrian Arab Republic	Yes	Yes	—	—	—	5	Manual and automated
Tajikistan	Yes	No	60 km/h	90 km/h	110 km/h	9	Manual
Thailand	Yes	No	80 km/h	90 km/h	120 km/h	5	Manual
The former Yugoslav Republic of Macedonia	Yes	No	50 km/h[al]	90 km/h	130 km/h	6	Manual
Timor-Leste	Yes	No	50 km/h	90 km/h	120 km/h	5	Manual
Togo	No	No	—	—	—	—	Manual
Tonga	Yes	No	50 km/h	70 km/h	70 km/h	7	Manual
Trinidad and Tobago	Yes	No	50 km/h	80 km/h	No	5	Manual
Tunisia	Yes	Yes	50 km/h	90 km/h	110 km/h	5	Manual
Turkey	Yes	Yes	50 km/h	110 km/h[ao]	120 km/h[ao]	9	Manual and automated
Turkmenistan	Yes	Yes	60 km/h	90 km/h	110 km/h	10	Manual and automated
Uganda	Yes	No	50 km/h	100 km/h	No	7	Manual
Ukraine	Yes	Yes	60 km/h	90 km/h	130 km/h	3	—
United Arab Emirates	Yes	Yes	—[ap]	—[ap]	—[ap]	10	Automated
United Kingdom	Yes	Yes	~ 48 km/h	~ 96 km/h	~ 112 km/h	8	Automated
United Republic of Tanzania	Yes	Yes	50 km/h	No	No	8	Manual
United States of America	Yes	Yes	~ 32 - 128 km/h	~ 40 - 128 km/h	~ 40 - 128 km/h	—	Manual
Uruguay	Yes	Yes	45 km/h	90 km/h	90 km/h	6	Manual and automated
Uzbekistan	Yes	No	70 km/h	100 km/h	No	8	Manual
Vanuatu	No	No	—	—	—	—	—

Country / Area	National speed limit law	Types of modifications allowed	Maximum default speed limits (km/h)			Enforcement	Predominant type of enforcement
			Urban	Rural	Motorways		
Venezuela (Bolivarian Republic of)	No	No	–	–	–	–	–
Viet Nam	Yes	No	60 km/h	90 km/h	120 km/h	7	Manual and automated
West Bank and Gaza Strip	Yes	No	50 km/h	80 km/h	110 km/h	2	Manual
Zimbabwe	Yes	Yes	60 km/h	80 km/h[aq]	120 km/h	6	Manual

a Speed limit set per vehicle type with a maximum speed limit of 90 km/h for fast moving vehicles, decreased by 20 km/h in mountain paths
b Applies in the City of Saint John's and in designated «speed limit areas»
c The limit in residential area is reduced to 60 km/h
d Speed limit set per vehicle type with a maximum speed limit of 70 miles per hour (112 km/h) for light vehicles
e Speed limit set per vehicle type with a maximum speed limit of 80 km/h for specified vehicles including private motor cars
f The 90 km/h speed limit applies on rural areas in Brussels capital region and Wallon region while there is a 70 km/h speed limit in the Flemish region
g Can be increased to an unspecified speed under certain circumstances
h Can be increased up to an unspecified speed
i This limit applies to unpaved roadways while on undivided highway the maximum speed limit is 100 km/h for automobiles, light trucks and motorcycles
j Can be increased up to an unspecified limit under certain circumstances
k Traffic code refers to regulations to set maximum speed limits, regulations not available
l Speed limit applicable on any road, decreased to 30 km/h in reduced speed zones
m Can be increased up to 80 km/h
n Traffic signs may on certain public highways provide for a higher speed limit not exceeding 80 km/h
o Speed limits can be modified at local level by the road authorities and the police
p Can be increased up to 90 km/h on certain conditions
q No motorways in the country
r Speed limit for public roads is 100 km/h for a road with a surface of concrete, bitumen or tar and 80 km/h for other roads
s There is no maximum speed limit on motorways
t Speed limits set per vehicle type and road type - for motor cars, speed limits are: 30 mph (48 km/h) on restricted roads, 60 mph (96 km/h) on Timehri / Linden Highway and 40 mph (64 km/h) elsewhere
u Legislation refers to regulations to set maximum speed limits, regulations not available
v Speed limit set per vehicle type with a maximum speed limit of 100 km/h for passengers cars comprising not more than eight seats in addition to the driver's seat
w 110 km/h for main suburban roads, 90 km/h for secondary suburban roads
x Can be increased up to 90 km/h
y Can be increased or decreased to an unspecified speed under certain circumstances
z Can be modified up to 80 km/h
aa Speed limit set per vehicle and road type with a maximum speed limit for passengers cars of 110 km/h on highways and 90 km/h on other roads
ab Speed limit set per vehicle type with a maximum speed limit of 30 km/h for specified vehicles, except in designated areas with higher speeds
ac Speed limit may be increased by the governor (Kosrae, Yap) or by the director of the department of public safety (Pohnpei)
ad Speed limit set per vehicle type with a maximum speed limit of 80 km/h for specified vehicles including cars, and a maximum limit of 40 km/h in an area with dense settlement

[ae] 60 km/h from 23:00-05:00

[af] Local authorities can modify national speed limits through the posting of speed signs

[ag] Speed limit set per vehicle type with a maximum speed limit of 80 km/h for passengers cars (not exceeding 3500 kg)

[ah] Can be increased to 80 km/h

[ai] Speed limits depend on the geographical area considered: the maximum speed limit is 40 km/h on roads in Greater Victoria and 80 km/h on any other roads; different speed limits are set for the island of praslin and la digue subject respectively to a 65 km/h and 25 km/h speed limit

[aj] Different speed limits are set in urban areas ranging from 30 km/h to 70 km/h

[ak] No rural roads in Singapore

[al] Can be increased up to 70 km/h

[am] Speed limits are established locally per vehicle type and / or per road names or areas

[an] Road authorities can decrease speed limits on both urban and rural roads. Speed limits can only be increased on urban highways

[ao] Ministry of Interior can increase speed limits by 20 km/h for automobiles

[ap] Speed limits are established at subnational level per streets' names

[aq] A 120 km/h speed limits applies on roads having a bituminous surface coat of 6 metres of more in width

TABLE A5: DRINKING AND DRIVING LAWS, ENFORCEMENT AND ROAD TRAFFIC DEATHS ATTRIBUTED TO ALCOHOL BY COUNTRY / AREA

Country / Area	National drink driving law	Based on BAC / BrAC	National maximum legal BAC levels (g/dl)		
			General population	Young / novice drivers	Professional / commercial drivers
Afghanistan	Yes[a]	No	–	–	–
Albania	Yes	Yes	≤0.05	≤0.05	≤0.05
Angola	Yes	Yes	≤ 0.06	≤ 0.06	≤ 0.06
Antigua and Barbuda	Yes[a]	No	–	–	–
Argentina	Yes	Yes	≤0.05[c]	≤0.05[c]	0.00
Armenia	Yes	Yes	≤0.04	≤0.04	≤0.04
Australia	Yes	Yes	< 0.05	0.00	0.00
Austria	Yes	Yes	<0.05	<0.01	<0.01
Azerbaijan	Yes[e]	No	–	–	–
Bangladesh	Yes[a]	No	–	–	–
Barbados	Yes	Yes	≤ 0.08	≤ 0.08	≤ 0.08
Belarus	Yes	Yes	<0.03	<0.03	<0.03
Belgium	Yes	Yes	<0.05	<0.05	<0.02
Belize	Yes	Yes	≤0.08	≤0.08	≤0.08
Benin	Yes[a]	No	–	–	–
Bhutan	Yes	Yes	≤ 0.08	0.00	0.00
Bolivia (Plurinational State of)	Yes	Yes	≤0.05	≤0.05	≤0.05
Bosnia and Herzegovina	Yes	Yes	≤0.03	0.00	0.0
Botswana	Yes	Yes	≤0.05	≤0.05	≤0.025
Brazil	Yes	Yes	0.00	0.00	0.00
Bulgaria	Yes	Yes	≤0.05	≤0.05	≤0.05
Burkina Faso	Yes	Yes	≤0.05	≤0.02	≤0.02
Burundi	Yes	Yes	≤0.08	≤0.08	≤0.08
Cabo Verde	Yes	Yes	<0.08	<0.08	<0.08
Cambodia	Yes	Yes	<0.05	<0.05	<0.05
Cameroon	Yes	Yes	≤0.08	≤0.08	≤0.08
Canada	Yes	Yes	0.04 - 0.08*	0.00 - 0.08	0.04 - 0.08
Central African Republic	Yes	Yes	≤0.08	≤0.08	≤0.08
Chad	Yes	Yes	≤0.08	≤0.08	≤0.08
Chile	Yes	Yes	≤ 0.03	≤ 0.03	≤ 0.03
China	Yes	Yes	<0.02	<0.02	<0.02
Colombia	Yes	Yes	<0.02	<0.02	<0.02
Comoros	Yes[a]	No	–	–	–

Random breath testing carried out	Testing carried out in case of fatal crash	Enforcement	% road traffic deaths involving alcohol	National drug driving law	Alcohol prohibited
Yes	All drivers tested	6	–	Yes	Yes[b]
Yes	Some drivers tested	6	5.2	Yes	No
Yes	Some drivers tested	5	–	Yes	No
No	Some drivers tested	4	0.9	Yes	No
Yes	–	6	17	Yes	No
Yes[d]	All drivers tested	6	1.9	Yes	No
Yes	All drivers tested	8	17	Yes	No
Yes	All drivers tested	–	5.1	Yes	No
Yes	All drivers tested	9	15	Yes	No
Yes	Some drivers tested	2	–	Yes	Yes[b]
Yes[f]	All drivers tested	2	–	Yes	No
Yes[d]	All drivers tested	8	14.3 (Drivers)	Yes	No
Yes	Some drivers tested	6	–	Yes	No
Yes[f]	All drivers tested	4	–	Yes	No
Yes	No	1	–	No	No
Yes	Some drivers tested	6	–	Yes	No
Yes[d]	All drivers tested	4	6.4	Yes	No
Yes	All drivers tested	6	20.8	Yes	No
Yes	Some drivers tested	6	3.8	Yes	No
Yes	Some drivers tested	6	–	Yes	No
Yes	All drivers tested	5	0.9	Yes	No
Yes	No	–	–	Yes	No
Yes[d]	No	1	–	No	No
Yes[g]	No	5	–	No	No
Yes	No	5	13	Yes	No
Yes	No	2	–	No	No
Yes[d]	All drivers tested	8	29.6	Yes	No
No	No	–	–	No	No
No	No	1	–	No	No
Yes	All drivers tested	6	13	Yes	No
Yes[d]	All drivers tested	9	0.4	Yes	No
Yes	All drivers tested	5	–	Yes	No
No	No	2	–	Yes	No

Country / Area	National drink driving law	Based on BAC / BrAC	National maximum legal BAC levels (g/dl)		
			General population	Young / novice drivers	Professional / commercial drivers
Congo	Yes	Yes	≤0.08	≤0.08	≤0.08
Cook Islands	Yes	Yes	≤0.08	≤0.08	≤0.08
Costa Rica	Yes	Yes	≤ 0.05	≤ 0.02	≤ 0.02
Côte d'Ivoire	Yes	Yes	<0.08	<0.08	<0.08
Croatia	Yes	Yes	≤0.05	0.00	0.00
Cuba	Yes	Yes	≤0.01	0.00	0.00
Cyprus	Yes	Yes	≤0.05	≤0.02	≤0.02
Czechia	Yes	Yes	≤0.03	≤0.03	≤0.03
Democratic Republic of the Congo	Yes	Yes	<0.10	<0.10	<0.10
Denmark	Yes	Yes	≤0.05	≤0.05	≤0.05
Dominica	Yes	Yes	≤0.08	≤0.08	≤0.08
Dominican Republic	Yes	Yes	≤0.05	0.00	0.00
Ecuador	Yes	Yes	≤ 0.03	≤ 0.03	≤ 0.01
Egypt	Yes[a]	No	–	–	–
El Salvador	Yes	Yes	<0.05	<0.05	<0.05
Equatorial Guinea	Yes	Yes	≤0.08	≤0.08	≤0.08
Eritrea	Yes	Yes	≤0.05	≤0.05	≤0.03
Estonia	Yes	Yes	<0.02	<0.02	<0.02
Eswatini	Yes	Yes	<0.05	<0.05	<0.02
Ethiopia	Yes	Yes	≤ 0.08	≤ 0.08	≤ 0.08
Fiji	Yes	Yes	≤0.08	0.00	0.00
Finland	Yes	Yes	<0.05	<0.05	<0.05
France	Yes	Yes	<0.05	<0.02	<0.05**
Gabon	Yes	Yes	≤0.08	≤0.08	≤0.08
Gambia	Yes[a]	No	–	–	–
Georgia	Yes	Yes	≤ 0.03	≤ 0.03	≤ 0.03
Germany	Yes	Yes	<0.05	0.00	<0.05
Ghana	Yes	Yes	≤ 0.08	≤ 0.08	≤ 0.08
Greece	Yes	Yes	< 0.05	< 0.05	< 0.05
Grenada	Yes[a]	No	–	–	–
Guatemala	Yes[a]	No	–	–	–
Guinea	Yes	Yes	<0.08	<0.08	<0.08
Guinea-Bissau	Yes	Yes	≤0.05	≤0.05	≤0.05

Random breath testing carried out	Testing carried out in case of fatal crash	Enforcement	% road traffic deaths involving alcohol	National drug driving law	Alcohol prohibited
Yes	No	2	–	No	No
Yes	All drivers tested	6	39	Yes	No
Yes	All drivers tested	4	31.2	Yes	No
Yes	No	3	–	No	No
Yes	Some drivers tested	8	23.8	Yes	No
Yes	All drivers tested	7	33.3	Yes	No
Yes	All drivers tested	7	17.4	Yes	No
Yes	All drivers tested	7	9.5	Yes	No
Yes[d]	No	2	–	No	No
Yes	Some drivers tested	–	–	Yes	No
No	No	1	–	Yes	No
Yes	Some drivers tested	3	–	Yes	No
Yes[d]	All drivers tested	7	6.8	Yes	No
No	Some drivers tested	8	–	Yes	No
Yes	Some drivers tested	7	–	Yes	No
No	–	–	–	No	No
Yes[d]	No	7	–	Yes	No
Yes	All drivers tested	8	10	Yes	No
Yes[d]	No	9	–	Yes	No
Yes[d]	All drivers tested	2	4.3	Yes	No
Yes	Some drivers tested	6	5	Yes	No
Yes	All drivers tested	9	24	Yes	No
Yes	All drivers tested	7	29	Yes	No
Yes	No	1	–	No	No
No	No	1	2.1	Yes	No
Yes[d]	All drivers tested	7	9	Yes	No
Yes	Some drivers tested	–	7	Yes	No
Yes[f]	Some drivers tested	3	–	Yes	No
Yes	All drivers tested	4	25.3	Yes	No
No	No	1	–	Yes	No
Yes	Some drivers tested	4	–	Yes	No
No	No	2	–	No	No
No	Some drivers tested	1	–	Yes	Yes[b]

Country / Area	National drink driving law	Based on BAC / BrAC	National maximum legal BAC levels (g/dl)		
			General population	Young / novice drivers	Professional / commercial drivers
Guyana	Yes	Yes	≤ 0.08	≤ 0.08	≤ 0.08
Honduras	Yes	Yes	<0.07	<0.07	<0.07
Hungary	Yes[h]	Yes	0.00	0.00	0.00
Iceland	Yes	Yes	<0.05	<0.05	<0.05
India	Yes	Yes	≤ 0.03	≤ 0.03	≤ 0.03
Indonesia	Yes[a]	No	—	—	—
Iran (Islamic Republic of)	Yes[a]	No	—	—	—
Iraq	Yes[a]	No	—	—	—
Ireland	Yes	Yes	≤ 0.05	≤ 0.02	≤ 0.02
Israel	Yes	Yes	≤ 0.05	≤ 0.01	≤ 0.01
Italy	Yes	Yes	≤0.05	0.00	0.00
Jamaica	Yes	Yes	≤ 0.08	≤ 0.08	≤ 0.08
Japan	Yes	Yes	<0.03	<0.03	<0.03
Jordan	Yes	Yes	<0.08	<0.08	<0.08
Kazakhstan	Yes	Yes	<0.05	<0.05	<0.05
Kenya	Yes	Yes	≤0.08	≤0.08	≤0.08
Kiribati	Yes	Yes	≤0.05[j]	0.00[j]	0.00[j]
Kuwait	Yes[a]	No	—	—	—
Kyrgyzstan	Yes[a]	No	—	—	—
Lao People's Democratic Republic	Yes	Yes	≤0.05	≤0.05	0.00
Latvia	Yes	Yes	≤ 0.05	≤ 0.02	≤ 0.02
Lebanon	Yes	Yes	≤ 0.05	0.00	0.00
Lesotho	Yes	Yes	≤0.08	≤0.08	≤0.08
Liberia	Yes	Yes	<0.15***	<0.15***	<0.15***
Libya	Yes[a]	No	—	—	—
Lithuania	Yes	Yes	≤0.04	0.00	0.00
Luxembourg	Yes	Yes	< 0.05	< 0.02	< 0.02
Madagascar	Yes	Yes	<0.08	<0.08	<0.08
Malawi	Yes	Yes	<0.08	<0.08	<0.08
Malaysia	Yes	Yes	≤0.08	≤0.08	≤0.08
Maldives	No[b]	No	—	—	—
Mali	Yes	Yes	<0.03	<0.03	<0.03
Malta	Yes	Yes	≤ 0.05	≤ 0.02	≤ 0.02[l]

Random breath testing carried out	Testing carried out in case of fatal crash	Enforcement	% road traffic deaths involving alcohol	National drug driving law	Alcohol prohibited
Yes[d]	No	7	17	Yes	No
Yes[d]	All drivers tested	8	6.8	Yes	No
Yes[d]	All drivers tested	5	7.1	Yes	No
Yes	All drivers tested	7	14	Yes	No
Yes[d]	Some drivers tested	4	4.1	Yes	No
Yes	All drivers tested	9	–	Yes	No
Yes[d]	Some drivers tested	7	1.7	Yes	Yes[b]
Yes	Some drivers tested	2	–	Yes	Yes[b]
Yes	All drivers tested	10	38.5	Yes	No
Yes	All drivers tested	7	3.6	Yes	No
Yes	Some drivers tested	7	20 - 25	Yes	No
Yes[f]	Some drivers tested	2	–	Yes	No
Yes	Some drivers tested	9	5.6	Yes	No
Yes[i]	Some drivers tested	3	–	Yes	No
No	All drivers tested	7	0.3	Yes	Yes[b]
Yes[f]	No	5	–	Yes	No
Yes	No	4	–	Yes	No
No	No	5	–	Yes	Yes[b]
Yes	All drivers tested	5	–	Yes	No
Yes	No	3	–	No[k]	No
Yes[d]	All drivers tested	7	10.8	Yes	No
Yes	Some drivers tested	3	–	Yes	No
Yes	No	2	60	Yes	No
No	All drivers tested	0	–	Yes	No
No	Some drivers tested	7	1.2	Yes	Yes[b]
Yes	All drivers tested	8	9.6	Yes	No
Yes	All drivers tested	6	14	Yes	No
Yes	Some drivers tested	2	–	Yes	No
Yes	No	4	–	Yes	No
Yes	All drivers tested	4	0.1	No	No
No	No	–	–	No	Yes[b]
Yes	No	3	0.4	Yes	No
Yes[d]	All drivers tested	4	–	Yes	No

Country / Area	National drink driving law	Based on BAC / BrAC	National maximum legal BAC levels (g/dl)		
			General population	Young / novice drivers	Professional / commercial drivers
Mauritania	Yes[a]	No	–	–	–
Mauritius	Yes	Yes	≤0.05	≤0.05	≤0.05
Mexico	Yes[m]	No	–	–	–
Micronesia (Federated States of)	Yes[n]	No	–	–	–
Mongolia	Yes	Yes	<0.04[o]	<0.04[o]	<0.04[o]
Montenegro	Yes	Yes	≤0.03	0.00	≤0.03
Morocco	Yes	Yes	<0.02	<0.02	<0.02
Mozambique	Yes	Yes	<0.06	<0.06	<0.06****
Myanmar	Yes[a]	No	–	–	–
Namibia	Yes	Yes	≤0.079	≤0.079	≤0.079
Nepal	Yes[a]	No	–	–	–
Netherlands	Yes	Yes	≤ 0.05	≤ 0.02	≤ 0.05
New Zealand	Yes	Yes	≤0.05	0.00	≤0.05
Niger	Yes[a]	No	–	–	–
Nigeria	Yes	Yes	≤0.05[p]	≤0.002[q]	≤0.000[r]
Norway	Yes	Yes	≤ 0.02	≤ 0.02	≤ 0.02
Oman	Yes[a]	No	–	–	–
Pakistan	Yes[a]	No	–	–	–
Panama	Yes	Yes	≤ 0.05	≤ 0.05	≤ 0.05
Papua New Guinea	Yes[s]	No	–	–	–
Paraguay	Yes	Yes	0.00	0.00	0.00
Peru	Yes	Yes	≤0.05	≤0.05	≤ 0.025
Philippines	Yes	Yes	<0.05	<0.05	0.00
Poland	Yes	Yes	< 0.02	< 0.02	< 0.02
Portugal	Yes	Yes	< 0.05	< 0.02	< 0.02
Qatar	Yes[a]	No	–	–	–
Republic of Korea	Yes	Yes	<0.05	<0.05	<0.05
Republic of Moldova	Yes	Yes	≤ 0.03	≤ 0.03	≤ 0.03
Romania	Yes	Yes	≤ 0.08	≤ 0.08	≤ 0.08
Russian Federation	Yes	Yes	≤0.03[o]	≤0.03[o]	≤0.03[o]
Rwanda	Yes	Yes	≤0.08	≤0.08	≤0.08
Saint Lucia	Yes	Yes	≤0.08	≤0.08	≤0.08
Samoa	Yes	Yes	≤0.08	≤0.08	≤0.08

Random breath testing carried out	Testing carried out in case of fatal crash	Enforcement	% road traffic deaths involving alcohol	National drug driving law	Alcohol prohibited
No	No	8	–	Yes	Yes[b]
Yes[d]	All drivers tested	7	23.6	Yes	No
Yes	Some drivers tested	7	19.5	Yes	No
No	No	5	100	Yes	No
Yes[f]	All drivers tested	8	25	Yes	No
Yes	All drivers tested	7	–	Yes	No
Yes	No	5	3.7	Yes	Yes[b]
Yes	Some drivers tested	6	–	Yes	No
Yes	Some drivers tested	6	21.4	Yes	Yes[b]
Yes	Some drivers tested	4	3.9	Yes	No
Yes	Some drivers tested	8	–	Yes	No
Yes	No	6	11 - 24	Yes	No
Yes	Some drivers tested	7	27	Yes	No
No	No	6	–	Yes	No
Yes	No	4	0.5	Yes	No
Yes	Some drivers tested	10	13	Yes	No
Yes	All drivers tested	10	0.7	Yes	No
No	No	4	–	Yes	Yes[b]
Yes	All drivers tested	5	–	Yes	No
No	No	–	56	Yes	No
Yes	All drivers tested	6	–	Yes	No
Yes	All drivers tested	2	9.3	Yes	No
Yes[d]	Some drivers tested	4	–	Yes	No
Yes	All drivers tested	10	12.7	Yes	No
Yes	All drivers tested	7	29.2	Yes	No
No	All drivers tested	9	2.2	Yes	Yes[b]
Yes[d]	Some drivers tested	7	11.2	Yes	No
Yes	All drivers tested	8	9.4	Yes	No
Yes	All drivers tested	8	5.6	Yes	No
Yes	All drivers tested	6	22.9	Yes	No
Yes[f]	Some drivers tested	9	–	No	No
No	All drivers tested	0	–	Yes	No
Yes	No	8	–	Yes	No

Country / Area	National drink driving law	Based on BAC / BrAC	National maximum legal BAC levels (g/dl)		
			General population	Young / novice drivers	Professional / commercial drivers
San Marino	Yes	Yes	< 0.05	< 0.05	< 0.05
Sao Tome and Principe	Yes	Yes	<0.12	<0.12	<0.12
Saudi Arabia	Yes[a]	No	–	–	–
Senegal	Yes[a]	No	–	–	–
Serbia	Yes	Yes	≤0.03	0.00	0.00
Seychelles	Yes	Yes	≤0.08	≤0.08	≤0.08
Singapore	Yes	Yes	≤0.08	≤0.08	≤0.08
Slovakia	Yes[t]	Yes	0.00	0.00	0.00
Slovenia	Yes	Yes	≤ 0.05	0.00	0.00
Solomon Islands	Yes	Yes	<0.05	<0.05	<0.05
Somalia	Yes[a]	No	–	–	–
South Africa	Yes	Yes	<0.05	<0.05	<0.02
South Sudan	Yes[a]	No	–	–	–
Spain	Yes	Yes	≤ 0.05	≤0.03	≤0.03
Sri Lanka	Yes	Yes	< 0.08	< 0.08	< 0.08
Sudan	Yes[a]	No	–	–	–
Suriname	Yes	Yes	≤ 0.05	≤ 0.05	≤ 0.05
Sweden	Yes	Yes	< 0.02	< 0.02	< 0.02
Switzerland	Yes	Yes	< 0.05	< 0.01	< 0.01
Syrian Arab Republic	Yes[u]	No	–	–	–
Tajikistan	Yes[a]	No	–	–	–
Thailand	Yes	Yes	≤ 0.05	≤ 0.02	0.00
The former Yugoslav Republic of Macedonia	Yes	Yes	≤0.05	< 0.01	≤0.009
Timor-Leste	Yes	Yes	≤ 0.05	≤ 0.05	≤ 0.05
Togo	Yes[a]	No	–	–	–
Tonga	Yes	Yes	<0.03[o]	<0.03[o]	<0.03[o]
Trinidad and Tobago	Yes	Yes	≤0.08	≤0.08	≤0.08
Tunisia	Yes	Yes	<0.03	0.00	0.00
Turkey	Yes	Yes	≤0.05	≤0.05	≤0.02
Turkmenistan	Yes	Yes	< 0.05	< 0.05	< 0.05
Uganda	Yes	Yes	≤0.08	≤0.08	0.00
Ukraine	Yes	Yes	≤ 0.02	≤ 0.02	≤0.02

Random breath testing carried out	Testing carried out in case of fatal crash	Enforcement	% road traffic deaths involving alcohol	National drug driving law	Alcohol prohibited
Yes[d]	All drivers tested	6	–	Yes	No
No	No	2	–	Yes	No
No	Some drivers tested	9	–	Yes	Yes[b]
No	No	3	–	Yes	No
Yes	All drivers tested	5	17	Yes	No
Yes[f]	No	6	–	Yes	No
Yes[f]	All drivers tested	8	6.4	Yes	No
Yes	All drivers tested	8	6.1	Yes	No
Yes	All drivers tested	7	32	Yes	No
Yes	Some drivers tested	7	–	Yes	No
No	No	1	–	Yes	Yes[b]
Yes	Some drivers tested	5	57.5	Yes	No
No	No	0	–	Yes	No
Yes	Some drivers tested	7	17 Males, 6.7 Females	Yes	No
No	Some drivers tested	9	–	Yes	No
Yes	All drivers tested	7	0.3	Yes	Yes[b]
Yes	Some drivers tested	5	–	Yes	No
Yes	All drivers tested	6	24	Yes	No
Yes	Some drivers tested	6	13	Yes	No
Yes	Some drivers tested	7	–	No	No
Yes	All drivers tested	9	4.2	Yes	No
Yes[d]	Some drivers tested	6	14.1	Yes	No
Yes	All drivers tested	5	1.4	Yes	No
No	Some drivers tested	4	–	Yes	No
No	No	0	–	Yes	No
Yes	No	5	77	No	No
Yes[d]	All drivers tested	6	–	Yes	No
No	All drivers tested	3	1.6	Yes	No
Yes	All drivers tested	9	3.3	Yes	No
Yes	All drivers tested	10	–	No	No
Yes[f]	Some drivers tested	6	0.8	Yes	No
No	All drivers tested	5	6.7	Yes	No

Country / Area	National drink driving law	Based on BAC / BrAC	National maximum legal BAC levels (g/dl)		
			General population	Young / novice drivers	Professional / commercial drivers
United Arab Emirates	Yes	Yes	≤ 0.01	≤ 0.01	≤ 0.01
United Kingdom	Yes	Yes	≤ 0.08	≤ 0.08*****	≤0.08*****
United Republic of Tanzania	Yes	Yes	≤0.08	≤0.08	0.00
United States of America	Yes	Yes	≤0.08	0.00 - 0.08******	0.00 - 0.08
Uruguay	Yes	Yes	0.00	0.00	0.00
Uzbekistan	Yes[a]	No	—	—	—
Vanuatu	Yes[a]	No	—	—	—
Venezuela (Bolivarian Republic of)	Yes[a]	No	—	—	—
Viet Nam	Yes[v]	Yes	0.00– 0.05	0.00 – 0.05[v]	0.00 – 0.05
West Bank and Gaza Strip	Yes[a]	No	—	—	—
Zimbabwe	Yes	Yes	<0.08	<0.08	<0.08

[a] Not based on BAC
[b] Alcohol consumption legally prohibited
[c] ≤0.2 g/l for motorcycles drivers
[d] Legislation requires probable cause to test drivers
[e] Law not based on BAC / BrAC
[f] Legislation requires probable cause to test drivers or commission of a traffic offence
[g] Legislation refers to testing in case of crash
[h] Any presence of alcohol in the body is prohibited
[i] Legislation refers to alcohol testing in case of reckless driving or in the case of a crash
[j] BAC limit introduced by the traffic act 2017, at December 2017, the notice of commencment had not yet been signed
[k] Legislation banning drug driving only applies to bus and truck drivers
[l] For commercial drivers limits are as follows: «≤ 9 microgrammes in 100 ml (BrAC), 20 mg in 100 ml (BAC) and 27 mg in 100 ml of urine» while there is a 0 limit For driver of buses, coaches and other vehicles carrying passengers for a fee
[m] Not based on BAC in 19 out of 32 states
[n] In Yap a BAC limit is provided in the law. In Kosrae and Pohnpei, the law is not based on a BAC limit. No data is available for Chuuk
[o] Law based on breath alcohol concentration, values converted to BAC
[p] The legislation, as amended in 2016, refers to an alcohol legal limit of «0.05» for the general population but does not specify the unit to consider
[q] The legislation, as amended in 2016, refers to an alcohol legal limit of «0.002» for young or novice drivers but does not specify the unit to consider
[r] The legislation, as amended in 2016, refers to an alcohol legal limit of «0.000» for commercial drivers» but does not specify the unit to consider
[s] Law not based on BAC
[t] Driving with presence of any alcohol in the body is prohibited
[u] The law refers to regulations to set BAC limit, regulations not available
[v] Different Bac limits are set depending on the type of vehicle used: for drivers of cars the bac limit is set at 0.00g/dl while for drivers of motorcycles and mopeds the legal bac limit is set at 0.05g/dl

Random breath testing carried out	Testing carried out in case of fatal crash	Enforcement	% road traffic deaths involving alcohol	National drug driving law	Alcohol prohibited
No	All drivers tested	10	1.8	Yes	Yes[b]
Yes[d]	All drivers tested	8	13 (GB), 23 (NI)	Yes	No
Yes[f]	No	6	1	Yes	No
Yes	Some drivers tested	–	29	Yes	No
Yes	Some drivers tested	9	–	Yes	No
Yes	–	10	3.6	Yes	No
No	No	0	67	Yes	No
Yes	All drivers tested	4	–	Yes	No
Yes	Some drivers tested	8	–	Yes	No
Yes	No	5	–	Yes	No
No	Some drivers tested	5	–	Yes	No

* National BAC limit is set at 0.08 g/dl. However, in practice all subnational entities have provided their own BAC limits that are reflected in the range above

** Drivers of public transport vehicles are subject to a BAC limit of 0.02 g/dl while other commercial drivers are subject to the BAC limit applicable to the general population (≤0.05g/dl)

*** Over this limit there is a presumption of alcohol impairment (from 0.05 to 0.15 no presumption established but the alcohol concentration can be used to decide on the guilt or innocence of the driver)

**** Except for drivers of public transport and dangerous cargo subject to a blood alcohol concentration limit of 0.00 g/dl

***** In Scotland legal BAC limit is ≤ 0.05 g/dl

****** Over 90% of the states provide a BAC limit equal or under 0.02 g/dl for young-novice drivers

TABLE A6: HELMET LAWS, ENFORCEMENT AND WEARING RATES BY COUNTRY / AREA

Country / Area	Motorcycle helmet law						
	National motorcycle helmet law	Applies to driver	Applies to adult passengers	Applies to all roads	Applies to all engines	Helmet fastening required	Standard referred to and / or specified
Afghanistan	No	–	–	–	–	–	–
Albania	Yes	Yes	Yes	Yes	Yes	No	Yes
Angola	Yes	Yes	Yes	Yes	Yes	Yes	No
Antigua and Barbuda	No	–	–	–	–	–	–
Argentina	Yes	Yes	Yes	Yes	Yes	Yes	Yes
Armenia	Yes	Yes	Yes	Yes	Yes	Yes	No
Australia	Yes	Yes	Yes	Yes	Yes	Yes	Yes
Austria	Yes	Yes	Yes	Yes	Yes	No	Yes
Azerbaijan	Yes	Yes	Yes	Yes	Yes	No	No
Bangladesh	Yes	Yes	Yes	Yes	Yes	No	Yes
Barbados	Yes	Yes	Yes	Yes	Yes	No	Yes
Belarus	Yes	Yes	Yes	Yes	Yes	Yes	Yes
Belgium	Yes	Yes	Yes	Yes	Yes	No	Yes
Belize	Yes	Yes	Yes	No	Yes	Yes	No
Benin	Yes	Yes	Yes	Yes	Yes	Yes	No
Bhutan	Yes	Yes	Yes	Yes	Yes	Yes	Yes
Bolivia (Plurinational State of)	Yes	Yes	Yes	Yes	Yes	No	Yes
Bosnia and Herzegovina	Yes	Yes	Yes	Yes	Yes	No	No
Botswana	Yes	Yes	Yes	Yes	Yes	Yes	Yes
Brazil	Yes	Yes	Yes	Yes	Yes	Yes	Yes
Bulgaria	Yes	Yes	Yes	Yes	Yes	No	No
Burkina Faso	Yes	Yes	Yes	Yes	Yes	No	Yes
Burundi	Yes	Yes	Yes	Yes	Yes	No	No
Cabo Verde	Yes	Yes	Yes	Yes	No	Yes	Yes
Cambodia	Yes	Yes	Yes	Yes	Yes	No	Yes
Cameroon	Yes	Yes	Yes	Yes	Yes	No	No
Canada	Yes	Yes	Yes	Yes	Yes	Yes	Yes
Central African Republic	Yes	Yes	Yes	Yes	No	Yes	No
Chad	Yes	Yes	Yes	Yes	No	No	No
Chile	Yes	Yes	Yes	Yes	Yes	Yes	Yes
China	Yes	Yes	Yes	Yes	Yes	No	Yes
Colombia	Yes	Yes	Yes	Yes	Yes	No	Yes

Children passengers on motorcycles	Enforcement	Helmet wearing rate (%)
Not restricted	–	
Not restricted	6	75% Drivers, 60% Passengers
Prohibited under 7 yrs	7	40% Drivers, 15% Passengers
Not restricted	–	
Not restricted	4	65.4% Drivers, 44.2% Passengers
Prohibited under 12 yrs	9	95% Drivers, 90% Passengers
Prohibited under 8 yrs	8	99% Drivers
Prohibited under 12 yrs		100% All riders
Prohibited under 12 yrs	6	
Not restricted	6	
Not restricted	9	
Prohibited under 12 yrs	8	
Prohibited under 3 /8 yrs[a]	9	99% Drivers, 100% Passengers
Not restricted	5	
Not restricted	3	25% Drivers, 1% Passengers
Not restricted	9	
Not restricted	3	51.9% Drivers, 3% Passengers
Prohibited under 12 yrs	7	
Not restricted	8	
Prohibited under 7 yrs	7	83.4% Drivers, 80.1% Passengers
Prohibited under 12 yrs	5	80% Drivers, 30% Passengers
Prohibited under 5 yrs	4	9% All riders
Not restricted	5	
Prohibited under 7 yrs	8	
Not restricted	6	70% - 43% Drivers, 30 - 13% Passengers[b]
Prohibited under 5 yrs	1	
Not restricted	10	98% Drivers, 98% Passengers
Prohibited under 5 yrs	0	
Prohibited under 5 yrs	5	
Not restricted	9	99% Drivers, 98% Passengers
Prohibited under 12 yrs	6	20% All riders
Not restricted	4	96% Drivers, 79.8% Passengers

Country / Area	Motorcycle helmet law						
	National motorcycle helmet law	Applies to driver	Applies to adult passengers	Applies to all roads	Applies to all engines	Helmet fastening required	Standard referred to and / or specified
Comoros	No	—	—	—	—	—	—
Congo	Yes	Yes	Yes	Yes	No	No	No
Cook Islands	Yes	Yes	Yes	Yes	Yes	No	Yes
Costa Rica	Yes	Yes	Yes	Yes	Yes	No	Yes
Côte d'Ivoire	Yes	Yes	Yes	Yes	Yes	No	Yes
Croatia	Yes	Yes	Yes	Yes	Yes	Yes	Yes
Cuba	Yes	Yes	Yes	Yes	Yes	Yes	No
Cyprus	Yes	Yes	Yes	Yes	Yes	Yes	Yes
Czechia	Yes	Yes	Yes	Yes	Yes	Yes	Yes
Democratic Republic of the Congo	Yes	Yes	Yes	Yes	Yes	No	No
Denmark	Yes	Yes	Yes	Yes	Yes	Yes	Yes
Dominica	No	—	—	—	—	—	—
Dominican Republic	Yes	Yes	Yes	Yes	Yes	No	Yes
Ecuador	Yes	Yes	Yes	Yes	Yes	Yes	Yes
Egypt	Yes	Yes	Yes	Yes	Yes	No	No
El Salvador	Yes	Yes	Yes	Yes	Yes	Yes	No
Equatorial Guinea	Yes	Yes	Yes	Yes	No	No	No
Eritrea	Yes	Yes	Yes	Yes	Yes	No	No
Estonia	Yes	Yes	Yes	Yes	Yes	Yes	Yes
Eswatini	Yes	Yes	Yes	Yes	Yes	Yes	Yes
Ethiopia	Yes	Yes	Yes	Yes	Yes	No	No
Fiji	Yes	Yes	Yes	Yes	Yes	Yes	No
Finland	Yes	Yes	Yes	Yes	Yes	No	No
France	Yes	Yes	Yes	Yes	Yes	Yes	Yes
Gabon	Yes	Yes	Yes	Yes	No	No	No
Gambia	Yes	Yes	Yes	Yes	Yes	No	No
Georgia	Yes	Yes	Yes	Yes	Yes	Yes	No
Germany	Yes	Yes	Yes	Yes	No	No	No
Ghana	Yes	Yes	Yes	Yes	Yes	Yes	Yes
Greece	Yes	Yes	Yes	Yes	Yes	Yes	Yes
Grenada	Yes	Yes	Yes	Yes	Yes	No	Yes
Guatemala	Yes	Yes	Yes	Yes	Yes	No	No

Children passengers on motorcycles	Enforcement	Helmet wearing rate (%)
Not restricted	–	
Prohibited under 5 yrs	3	27% All riders
Not restricted[c]	5	
Prohibited under 5 yrs	5	98.3% Drivers, 91.8% Passengers
Not restricted	4	
Prohibited under 12 yrs	9	95% Drivers, 95% Passengers
Prohibited under 7 yrs	8	95% Drivers, 90% Passengers
Prohibited under 12 yrs	7	75.1% Drivers, 68.3% Passengers
Prohibited under 12 yrs	9	
Not restricted	4	
Prohibited under 5 yrs / 135 cm		98% Drivers
Not restricted	–	
Prohibited under 8 yrs	5	27% Drivers, 2% Passengers
Prohibited under 7 yrs	8	90% Drivers, 12 - 52% Passengers
Not restricted	3	
Not restricted	7	
Prohibited under 5 yrs	0	
Not restricted	8	95% Drivers, 95% Passengers
Prohibited under 12 yrs	9	98% Drivers
Not restricted	5	
Not restricted	2	
Prohibited under 8 yrs[d]	8	80% Drivers, 80% Passengers
Not restricted	9	98.3% All riders
Not restricted	9	98% All riders
Prohibited under 5 yrs	5	
Not restricted	4	
Prohibited under 12 yrs	7	
Not restricted		99% Drivers, 100% Passengers
Not restricted	5	41.8% Drivers, 16.9% Passengers
Prohibited under 5 yrs	4	75% Drivers, 46% Passengers
Not restricted	1	
Not restricted	4	36% Drivers, 11% Passengers

Country / Area	Motorcycle helmet law						
	National motorcycle helmet law	Applies to driver	Applies to adult passengers	Applies to all roads	Applies to all engines	Helmet fastening required	Standard referred to and / or specified
Guinea	Yes	Yes	Yes	Yes	Yes	No	Yes
Guinea-Bissau	Yes	Yes	Yes	Yes	Yes	Yes	Yes
Guyana	No	—	—	—	—	—	—
Honduras	Yes	Yes	Yes	Yes	Yes	No	No
Hungary	Yes	Yes	Yes	Yes	Yes	Yes	Yes
Iceland	Yes	Yes	Yes	Yes	Yes	No	No
India	Yes	Yes	Yes	Yes	Yes	Yes	Yes
Indonesia	Yes	Yes	Yes	Yes	Yes	No	Yes
Iran (Islamic Republic of)	Yes	Yes	Yes	Yes	Yes	No	Yes
Iraq	Yes	Yes	No	Yes	Yes[f]	No	No
Ireland	Yes	Yes	Yes	Yes	Yes	No	Yes
Israel	Yes	Yes	Yes	Yes	Yes	Yes	Yes
Italy	Yes	Yes	Yes	Yes	Yes	Yes	Yes
Jamaica	Yes	Yes	Yes	Yes	Yes	Yes	Yes
Japan	Yes	Yes	Yes	Yes	Yes	No	Yes
Jordan	Yes	Yes	Yes	Yes	Yes	No	Yes
Kazakhstan	Yes	Yes	Yes	Yes	No	Yes	No
Kenya	Yes	Yes	Yes	Yes	Yes	Yes	Yes
Kiribati	Yes[g]	Yes	Yes	Yes	Yes	No	Yes
Kuwait	Yes	Yes	Yes	Yes	Yes	No	No
Kyrgyzstan	Yes	Yes	Yes	Yes	Yes	Yes	No
Lao People's Democratic Republic	Yes	Yes	Yes	Yes	Yes	No	No
Latvia	Yes	Yes	Yes	Yes	Yes	Yes	No
Lebanon	Yes	Yes	Yes	Yes	Yes	Yes	Yes
Lesotho	Yes	Yes	Yes	Yes	No[h]	No	No
Liberia	Yes	Yes	Yes	Yes	Yes	No	No
Libya	Yes	No	No	Yes	Yes	No	No
Lithuania	Yes	Yes	Yes	Yes	Yes	Yes	No
Luxembourg	Yes	Yes	Yes	Yes	Yes	Yes	Yes
Madagascar	Yes	Yes	Yes	Yes	Yes	Yes	Yes
Malawi	Yes	Yes	Yes	Yes	Yes	Yes	No
Malaysia	Yes	Yes	Yes	Yes	Yes	Yes	Yes

Children passengers on motorcycles	Enforcement	Helmet wearing rate (%)
Not restricted	4	7.9% All riders
Prohibited under 6 yrs	4	
Not restricted	–	50% Drivers, 20% Passengers
Not restricted	4	
Not restricted	8	92.3% country roads, 100% Budapest % All riders
Not restricted[e]	9	
Not restricted	4	30% Drivers, <10% Passengers
Not restricted	9	71.4% All riders
Not restricted	5	59% Drivers, 20% Passengers
Not restricted	5	
Not restricted	10	99.9% Drivers
Not restricted	9	98% Drivers, 98% Passengers
Prohibited under 5 yrs	9	98% All riders
Not restricted	2	6% Drivers, 2% Passengers
Not restricted	9	
Not restricted	7	
Prohibited under 12 yrs	7	
Not restricted	3	35.1% Drivers, 2.8% Passengers
Not restricted		
Not restricted	3	
Prohibited under 12 yrs	5	
Not restricted	7	
Prohibited under 150 cm	7	
Prohibited under 10 yrs	5	
Not restricted	8	75% Drivers, 3% Passengers
Prohibited under 13 yrs	1	
Not restricted	1	
Prohibited under 12 yrs	9	
Prohibited under 12 yrs	10	
Not restricted	2	
Not restricted	2	
Not restricted	8	91.2% Drivers, 87% Passengers

Country / Area	Motorcycle helmet law						
	National motorcycle helmet law	Applies to driver	Applies to adult passengers	Applies to all roads	Applies to all engines	Helmet fastening required	Standard referred to and / or specified
Maldives	Yes	No[i]	No[i]	No	Yes	No	No
Mali	Yes	Yes	Yes	Yes	No	Yes	Yes
Malta	Yes	Yes	Yes	Yes	Yes	No	No
Mauritania	Yes	Yes	Yes	Yes	Yes	No	No
Mauritius	Yes	Yes	Yes	Yes	Yes	No	Yes[j]
Mexico	No	No	No	No	No	No	No
Micronesia (Federated States of)	Yes	Yes	Yes	Yes	Yes	No	No
Mongolia	Yes	Yes	Yes	Yes	Yes	No	No
Montenegro	Yes	Yes	Yes	Yes	Yes	Yes	Yes[l]
Morocco	Yes	Yes	Yes	Yes	Yes	Yes	Yes
Mozambique	Yes	Yes	Yes	Yes	Yes	Yes	No
Myanmar	Yes	Yes	Yes	Yes	Yes	Yes	No
Namibia	Yes	Yes	Yes	Yes	Yes	Yes	No
Nepal	Yes	Yes	Yes	Yes	Yes	No	No
Netherlands	Yes	Yes	Yes	Yes	No	Yes	Yes
New Zealand	Yes	Yes	Yes	Yes	Yes	Yes	Yes
Niger	Yes	Yes	Yes	Yes	Yes	No	Yes
Nigeria	Yes	Yes	Yes	Yes	Yes	Yes	Yes
Norway	Yes	Yes	Yes	Yes	Yes	No	Yes
Oman	Yes	Yes	Yes	Yes	Yes	No	No
Pakistan	Yes	Yes	Yes	Yes	Yes	No	No
Panama	Yes	Yes	Yes	Yes	Yes	No	No
Papua New Guinea	Yes	Yes	Yes	Yes	Yes	Yes	Yes
Paraguay	Yes	Yes	Yes	Yes	Yes	Yes	Yes
Peru	Yes	Yes	Yes	Yes	Yes	No	No
Philippines	Yes	Yes	Yes	Yes	Yes	No	Yes
Poland	Yes	Yes	Yes	Yes	Yes	No	Yes
Portugal	Yes	Yes	Yes	Yes	Yes	Yes	Yes
Qatar	Yes	Yes	Yes	Yes	Yes	No	No
Republic of Korea	Yes	Yes	Yes	Yes	Yes	No	Yes
Republic of Moldova	Yes	Yes	Yes	Yes	Yes	Yes	No

Children passengers on motorcycles	Enforcement	Helmet wearing rate (%)
Not restricted	5	
Not restricted	3	6.2% Drivers, 0.4% Passengers
Not restricted	9	
Not restricted	3	
Not restricted	10	
Not restricted	–	83.1% Drivers, 55.4% Passengers
Not restricted	7	
Not restricted[k]	1	
Prohibited under 12 yrs	6	70% Drivers, 30% Passengers
Not restricted	7	64.4% Drivers, 30.5% Passengers
Prohibited under 7 yrs	4	
Prohibited until footrests can be reached	6	32% Drivers, 26.7% Passengers
Not restricted	7	
Not restricted	8	
Not restricted	5	99.9% Drivers, 84% Passengers
Not restricted	9	
Not restricted	5	
Not restricted	4	
Not restricted	10	99% Drivers, 99% Passengers
Not restricted	10	98% Drivers, 92% Passengers
Not restricted	3	10.4% All riders
Not restricted	6	
Not restricted		
Prohibited under 12 yrs	6	
Not restricted	4	69.9% Drivers, 7.7% Passengers
Not restricted[m]	6	51.3% All riders, 86.7% Drivers
Not restricted[n]	7	99% Drivers, 100% Passengers
Prohibited under 7 yrs	9	97.6% Drivers, 97.3% Passengers
Not restricted	9	
Not restricted	6	86% Drivers, 40% Passengers
Prohibited under 12 yrs	8	

Country / Area	Motorcycle helmet law						
	National motorcycle helmet law	Applies to driver	Applies to adult passengers	Applies to all roads	Applies to all engines	Helmet fastening required	Standard referred to and / or specified
Romania	Yes	Yes	Yes	Yes	Yes	No	No
Russian Federation	Yes	Yes	Yes	Yes	Yes	Yes	Yes
Rwanda	Yes	Yes	Yes	Yes	Yes	Yes	No
Saint Lucia	Yes	Yes	Yes	Yes	Yes	No	Yes
Samoa	Yes	Yes	Yes	Yes	Yes	Yes	No
San Marino	Yes	Yes	Yes	Yes	Yes	Yes	Yes
Sao Tome and Principe	Yes	Yes	Yes	Yes	No	Yes	Yes
Saudi Arabia	Yes	Yes	Yes	Yes	Yes	Yes	No
Senegal	Yes	No	Yes	Yes	No	No	No
Serbia	Yes	Yes	Yes	Yes	Yes	Yes	No
Seychelles	Yes	Yes	Yes	Yes	Yes	No	No[p]
Singapore	Yes	Yes	Yes	Yes	Yes	Yes	Yes
Slovakia	Yes	Yes	Yes	Yes	Yes	Yes	No
Slovenia	Yes	Yes	Yes	Yes	Yes	Yes	Yes
Solomon Islands	Yes	Yes	Yes	Yes	Yes	Yes	Yes
Somalia	No	–	–	–	–	–	–
South Africa	Yes	Yes	Yes	Yes	Yes	Yes	No
South Sudan	No	–	–	–	–	–	–
Spain	Yes	Yes	Yes	Yes	Yes	No	Yes
Sri Lanka	Yes	Yes	Yes	Yes	Yes	No	Yes
Sudan	Yes	Yes	Yes	Yes	Yes	No	No
Suriname	Yes	Yes	Yes	Yes	No	Yes	Yes
Sweden	Yes	Yes	Yes	Yes	Yes	Yes	Yes
Switzerland	Yes	Yes	Yes	Yes	Yes	No	Yes
Syrian Arab Republic	Yes	Yes	No	Yes	Yes	No	No
Tajikistan	Yes	Yes	Yes	Yes	Yes	Yes	No
Thailand	Yes	Yes	Yes	Yes	Yes	Yes	Yes
The former Yugoslav Republic of Macedonia	Yes	Yes	Yes	Yes	Yes	No	No
Timor-Leste	Yes	Yes	Yes	Yes	Yes	Yes	Yes
Togo	Yes	Yes	Yes	Yes	Yes	No	No
Tonga	Yes	Yes	Yes	Yes	Yes	Yes	Yes
Trinidad and Tobago	Yes	Yes	Yes	Yes	Yes	No	Yes

Children passengers on motorcycles	Enforcement	Helmet wearing rate (%)
Prohibited under 14 yrs[o]	7	
Prohibited under 12 yrs	4	
Not restricted	10	
Not restricted	2	
Not restricted	10	100% Drivers, 100% Passengers
Not restricted	10	
Prohibited under 7 yrs	7	
Prohibited under 16 yrs	2	
Not restricted	5	
Prohibited under 12 yrs	8	85.7% Drivers,74.3 - 86.5% Passengers
Prohibited under 10 yrs	7	
Prohibited under 10 yrs	9	
Prohibited under 12 yrs	8	
Prohibited under 12 yrs[q]	8	
Not restricted	6	
Not restricted	–	
Not restricted	8	
Not restricted	–	
Prohibited under 7 / 12 yrs	8	99% Drivers, 93.3% Passengers
Not restricted	9	95% All riders
Not restricted	3	
Not restricted	7	95% Drivers, 92% Passengers
Not restricted	8	97 - 99 (97 for moped drivers)% All riders
Not restricted	9	100% Drivers
Not restricted	7	
Prohibited under 12 yrs	6	
Not restricted	6	51% Drivers, 20% Passengers
Not restricted	7	
Not restricted	7	
Not restricted	7	
Not restricted	8	
Not restricted	9	

Country / Area	Motorcycle helmet law						
	National motorcycle helmet law	Applies to driver	Applies to adult passengers	Applies to all roads	Applies to all engines	Helmet fastening required	Standard referred to and / or specified
Tunisia	Yes	Yes	Yes	Yes	Yes	No	Yes
Turkey	Yes	Yes	Yes	Yes	Yes	No	Yes
Turkmenistan	Yes	Yes	Yes	Yes	Yes	No	No
Uganda	Yes	Yes	Yes	Yes	Yes	No	No
Ukraine	Yes	Yes	Yes	Yes	Yes	Yes	No
United Arab Emirates	Yes	Yes	Yes	Yes	Yes	No	No
United Kingdom	Yes	Yes	Yes	Yes	Yes	Yes	Yes
United Republic of Tanzania	Yes	Yes	No	Yes	Yes	No	Yes
United States of America	Yes	No[r]	No[r]	No	No	No	Yes
Uruguay	Yes	Yes	Yes	Yes	Yes	No	Yes
Uzbekistan	Yes	Yes	Yes	Yes	Yes	Yes	No
Vanuatu	Yes	Yes	Yes	No	Yes	Yes	Yes
Venezuela (Bolivarian Republic of)	Yes	Yes	Yes	Yes	Yes	No	No
Viet Nam	Yes	Yes	Yes	Yes	Yes	Yes	Yes
West Bank and Gaza Strip	Yes	Yes	Yes	Yes	Yes	Yes	Yes
Zimbabwe	Yes	Yes	Yes	Yes	Yes	Yes	Yes

[a] Restrictions vary depending on the type of motorcycles: children under 3 years are not allowed on mopeds and motorcycles, children under 8 years are not allowed on motorcycles over 125cc

[b] Percentage are for day - and night -time observations, respectively

[c] Obligation to use a helmet only applies to those riding on a motorcycle travelling above 40 km/h (except for specific provisions in Rarotonga - persons between 16 and 25 and visitors required to wear helmet at all speeds)

[d] Except if motorcycle is fitted with one additional seat designed to transport children

[e] Children who are 7 years or younger shall be placed in an appropriate child seat while children older than 7 years shall be able to have their feet reaching the pedals

[f] Helmet use is required for motorcycles, defined as two or three wheeled vehicles powered by a mechanical engine of 125 cc or more. The use of motorcycles with an engine of less than 125cc is forbidden on public roads

[g] Helmet provisions introduced by the Traffic Act 2017, at december 2017, the notice of commencment had not yet been signed

[h] Does not apply to mopeds

[i] Only required on roads where vehicles may be driven at a speed higher than the normal limit

Children passengers on motorcycles	Enforcement	Helmet wearing rate (%)
Prohibited under 6 yrs	3	
Not restricted	9	75% All riders
Prohibited under 12 yrs	9	
Not restricted	5	49% Drivers, 1% Passengers
Prohibited under 12 yrs / 145 cm	3	
Not restricted	10	
Not restricted	9	
Not restricted	6	
Not restricted[s]		67.8% Drivers, 52.5% Passengers
Prohibited until footrests can be reached	7	80.2% Drivers, 71.2% Passengers
Prohibited under 12 yrs	10	
Not restricted	8	90% Drivers, 90% Passengers
Prohibited under 10 yrs	3	
Not restricted	8	81% Drivers, 60.4% Passengers
Not restricted	5	
Not restricted	8	

j Reference is made to regulations to specify the types, shape and construction of helmets

k Children under 12 can be transported on a motorcycle provided that there is a special support installed in the rear seat

l As prescribed by the responsible state administration

m Restrictions for children to ride as passengers on motorcycles are only set for some types of roads (where there is heavy volume of vehicles, a high density of fast moving vehicles or a speed limit of more that 60 km/h). on these roads conditons for children to be allowed to ride as passengers are follows: child's feet can reach the foot peg of the motorcycle, child's arm can reach and grasp the waist of the driver and child is wearing a standard protective helmet

n Speed limit for motorcycles transporting a child under 7 is limited to 40 km/h

o Children under 14 allowed to be transported in the motorcycle sidecar and must be held in the arms under 7

p Reference is made to regulations to specify helmet types, in 2017 these regulations were in the process of being developed

q Only children older than 12 years old are allowed to ride as passengers on motorcycles

r About 40% of the states require helmets for both drivers and passengers on motorcycles

s Less than 10% of the states prohibit that children ride as passengers on motorcycles

TABLE A7: SEAT-BELT LAWS, ENFORCEMENT AND WEARING RATES BY COUNTRY / AREA

Country / Area	National seat belt law	Seat belt applies to		
		Drivers	Front seat passengers	Rear-seat passengers
Afghanistan	No	–	–	–
Albania	Yes	Yes	Yes	Yes
Angola	Yes	Yes	Yes	Yes
Antigua and Barbuda	No	–	–	–
Argentina	Yes	Yes	Yes	Yes
Armenia	Yes	Yes	Yes	Yes
Australia	Yes	Yes	Yes	Yes
Austria	Yes	Yes	Yes	Yes
Azerbaijan	Yes	No[a]	No[a]	No[a]
Bangladesh	No	–	–	–
Barbados	Yes	Yes	Yes	Yes
Belarus	Yes	Yes	Yes	Yes
Belgium	Yes	Yes	Yes	Yes
Belize	Yes	Yes	Yes	No
Benin	No	–	–	–
Bhutan	Yes	Yes	Yes	Yes
Bolivia (Plurinational State of)	Yes	Yes	No	No
Bosnia and Herzegovina	Yes	Yes	Yes	Yes
Botswana	Yes	Yes	Yes	Yes
Brazil	Yes	Yes	Yes	Yes
Bulgaria	Yes	Yes	Yes	Yes
Burkina Faso	Yes	Yes	Yes	Yes
Burundi	Yes	Yes	Yes	Yes[b]
Cabo Verde	Yes	Yes	Yes	No
Cambodia	Yes	Yes	Yes	No[c]
Cameroon	Yes	Yes	Yes	No
Canada	Yes	Yes	Yes	Yes
Central African Republic	Yes	Yes	Yes	No[d]
Chad	Yes	Yes	Yes	No
Chile	Yes	Yes	Yes	Yes
China	Yes	Yes	Yes	Yes
Colombia	Yes	Yes	Yes	Yes
Comoros	No	–	–	–
Congo	Yes	Yes	Yes	No

Enforcement	Seat-belt wearing rates (%)			
	Drivers only	Front-seat occupants	Rear-seat occupants	All occupants
—				
8	95	85	80	87
6	60	40	10	65
—				
5	50.2	40.8	23.1	43.6
8	70	70		
7		97	96	
—	95	95	93	
7	80	40	20	30
—				
7				
8				
7	91.5	92.2	85.5	91.7
5				
—				
2				
2	20.8	3.5	0.5	9.7
5	48	51	11	
7				
7		79.4	50.2	
5				80
6				
7				
5				
7				
6				
6	95.7	95.2	89.2	95.3
0				
4				
6	76	59	14	49.6
7	36.7			
5	75	64.2	2.2	47.1
—				
2	22	4	4	

Country / Area	National seat belt law	Seat belt applies to		
		Drivers	Front seat passengers	Rear-seat passengers
Cook Islands	No	—	—	—
Costa Rica	Yes	Yes	Yes	Yes
Côte d'Ivoire	Yes	Yes	Yes	No
Croatia	Yes	Yes	Yes	Yes
Cuba	Yes	Yes	Yes	Yes
Cyprus	Yes	Yes	Yes	Yes
Czechia	Yes	Yes	Yes	Yes
Democratic Republic of the Congo	Yes	Yes	Yes	No
Denmark	Yes	Yes	Yes	Yes
Dominica	Yes	Yes	Yes	Yes
Dominican Republic	Yes	Yes	Yes	Yes
Ecuador	Yes	Yes	Yes	Yes
Egypt	Yes	Yes	Yes	No
El Salvador	Yes	Yes	Yes	No
Equatorial Guinea	Yes	Yes	Yes	No
Eritrea	Yes	Yes	Yes	Yes
Estonia	Yes	Yes	Yes	Yes
Eswatini	Yes	Yes	Yes	No
Ethiopia	Yes	Yes	Yes	Yes
Fiji	Yes	Yes	Yes	Yes
Finland	Yes	Yes	Yes	Yes
France	Yes	Yes	Yes	Yes
Gabon	Yes	Yes	Yes	No
Gambia	Yes	Yes	Yes	No
Georgia	Yes	Yes	Yes	No
Germany	Yes	Yes	Yes	Yes
Ghana	Yes	Yes	Yes	Yes
Greece	Yes	Yes	Yes	Yes
Grenada	Yes	Yes	Yes	No
Guatemala	Yes	Yes	Yes	No
Guinea	Yes	Yes	Yes	No
Guinea-Bissau	Yes	Yes	Yes	No
Guyana	Yes	Yes	Yes	No
Honduras	Yes	Yes	Yes	Yes

Enforcement	Seat-belt wearing rates (%)			
	Drivers only	Front-seat occupants	Rear-seat occupants	All occupants
–				
4	77.8	75.1	35.6	76.7
4				
6	61.1	61.9	13.9	58
5	35	30		
6				
8	95	98	72	
5				
–	88/89/96*	96	91	
1				
8	45	18	5	34
8	80	26	2	36
7				
7				
2				
8	80	80		
7	97.8	97.3	81.8	95
9				
5				< 1
7	90	75	5	72
8	96	95	85	94
8		98	88	
7				
6				
8	70	60		
	98	98	99	98
3	55.6	18.4	3.5	35
4	77	74	23	72
8				
4				
3				
1				
8	95	95		42
6				

Country / Area	National seat belt law	Seat belt applies to		
		Drivers	Front seat passengers	Rear-seat passengers
Hungary	Yes	Yes	Yes	Yes
Iceland	Yes	Yes	Yes	Yes
India	Yes	Yes	Yes	Yes
Indonesia	Yes	Yes	Yes	No
Iran (Islamic Republic of)	Yes	Yes	Yes	Yes
Iraq	Yes	Yes	No	No
Ireland	Yes	Yes	Yes	Yes
Israel	Yes	Yes	Yes	Yes
Italy	Yes	Yes	Yes	Yes
Jamaica	Yes	Yes	Yes	Yes
Japan	Yes	Yes	Yes	Yes
Jordan	Yes	Yes	Yes	No
Kazakhstan	Yes	Yes	Yes	Yes
Kenya	Yes	Yes	Yes	Yes
Kiribati	Yes	Yes	Yes	Yes
Kuwait	Yes	Yes	Yes	No
Kyrgyzstan	Yes	No[a]	No[a]	No[a]
Lao People's Democratic Republic	Yes	Yes	Yes	No
Latvia	Yes	Yes	Yes	Yes
Lebanon	Yes	Yes	Yes	Yes
Lesotho	Yes	Yes	Yes	No
Liberia	No	–	–	–
Libya	Yes	Yes	Yes	Yes
Lithuania	Yes	Yes	Yes	Yes
Luxembourg	Yes	Yes	Yes	Yes
Madagascar	Yes	Yes	Yes	No
Malawi	Yes	Yes	Yes	No
Malaysia	Yes	Yes	Yes	No
Maldives	Yes	No[f]	No[f]	No[f]
Mali	Yes[g]	No[g]	No[g]	No[g]
Malta	Yes	Yes	Yes	Yes
Mauritania	Yes	Yes	Yes	No[h]
Mauritius	Yes	Yes	Yes	Yes
Mexico	No	No	No	No

Enforcement	Seat-belt wearing rates (%)			
	Drivers only	Front-seat occupants	Rear-seat occupants	All occupants
7	81.7	82.8	38.5	81
9	90	93	86	90
3	14 - 40	3.5 - 11		
8				69
8	95	93	15	68.5
5				
10	92	94	74	91
7	91.2	88.7	69.7	87.9
7		61.9	15.4	
3	51	54	4	
7	99.5/98.5[e]	98/94.9[e]	71.8/36[e]	94.9/89.5[e]
6				
7				
4				
0				
5				
7				
2				
7	81	84.7	53.0	
4				
7				
–				
7				
7		97	30	94
7	93	90	76	92
5				
3	25.8	21		
4	82.9	73.8	9.6	48.4
5				
4	20			
6				
3				
5	93.8	97.4	0.2	
6	81.4	49	5.6	58.9

Country / Area	National seat belt law	Seat belt applies to		
		Drivers	Front seat passengers	Rear-seat passengers
Micronesia (Federated States of)	No	—	—	—
Mongolia	Yes	Yes	Yes	Yes
Montenegro	Yes	Yes	Yes	Yes
Morocco	Yes	Yes	Yes	No[i]
Mozambique	Yes	Yes	Yes	Yes
Myanmar	Yes	Yes	Yes	Yes
Namibia	Yes	Yes	Yes	Yes
Nepal	Yes	Yes	Yes	No
Netherlands	Yes	Yes	Yes	Yes
New Zealand	Yes	Yes	Yes	Yes
Niger	No	—	—	—
Nigeria	Yes	Yes	Yes	Yes
Norway	Yes	Yes	Yes	Yes
Oman	Yes	Yes	Yes	Yes
Pakistan	Yes	Yes	No	No
Panama	Yes	Yes	Yes	Yes
Papua New Guinea	Yes	Yes	Yes	Yes
Paraguay	Yes	Yes	Yes	Yes
Peru	Yes	Yes	Yes	Yes
Philippines	Yes	Yes	Yes	Yes
Poland	Yes	Yes	Yes	Yes
Portugal	Yes	Yes	Yes	Yes
Qatar	Yes	Yes	Yes	No
Republic of Korea	Yes	Yes	Yes	Yes
Republic of Moldova	Yes	Yes	Yes	Yes
Romania	Yes	Yes	Yes	Yes
Russian Federation	Yes	Yes	Yes	Yes
Rwanda	Yes	Yes	Yes	No
Saint Lucia	Yes	Yes	Yes	No
Samoa	Yes	Yes	Yes	No
San Marino	Yes	Yes	Yes	Yes
Sao Tome and Principe	Yes	Yes	Yes	No
Saudi Arabia	Yes	Yes	Yes	Yes
Senegal	Yes	Yes	Yes	No

Enforcement	Seat-belt wearing rates (%)			
	Drivers only	Front-seat occupants	Rear-seat occupants	All occupants
—				
5				
6	60	40	5	35
8	66.7	63.2	22.3	64
6				
7	7.4			
7				
5				
6	96.9	96.6	82	95.8
7	97	97	92	
—				
9				
10	95.9 - 97.7[j]	95.2 - 95.7[j]		94.7 - 96[j]
10	98			
6				
7				
—				
6				
5	58.2	15.8	0.4	32.3
6	79.7			
8	95	96	76	94
8	96.4	95.7	77.2	94.9
7				
8	94	83	30	84
8	65.5	61.8	17.5	
7				
5	76 - 86	66 - 83	20 - 50	
8				
7				
10	100	100	100	100
8				
2				
3				
6				

Country / Area	National seat belt law	Seat belt applies to		
		Drivers	Front seat passengers	Rear-seat passengers
Serbia	Yes	Yes	Yes	Yes
Seychelles	Yes	Yes	Yes	Yes
Singapore	Yes	Yes	Yes	Yes
Slovakia	Yes	Yes	Yes	Yes
Slovenia	Yes	Yes	Yes	Yes
Solomon Islands	No	–	–	–
Somalia	No	–	–	–
South Africa	Yes	Yes	Yes	Yes
South Sudan	No	–	–	–
Spain	Yes	Yes	Yes	Yes
Sri Lanka	Yes	Yes	Yes	No
Sudan	Yes	Yes	Yes	No
Suriname	Yes	Yes	Yes	Yes
Sweden	Yes	Yes	Yes	Yes
Switzerland	Yes	Yes	Yes	Yes
Syrian Arab Republic	Yes	Yes	Yes	No
Tajikistan	Yes	Yes	Yes	No
Thailand	Yes	Yes	Yes	Yes
The former Yugoslav Republic of Macedonia	Yes	Yes	Yes	Yes
Timor-Leste	Yes	Yes	Yes	Yes
Togo	Yes	Yes	Yes	Yes
Tonga	No	–	–	–
Trinidad and Tobago	Yes	Yes	Yes	No
Tunisia	Yes	Yes	Yes	Yes
Turkey	Yes	Yes	Yes	Yes
Turkmenistan	Yes	Yes	Yes	Yes
Uganda	Yes	Yes	Yes	Yes
Ukraine	Yes	Yes	Yes	Yes
United Arab Emirates	Yes	Yes	Yes	Yes
United Kingdom	Yes	Yes	Yes	Yes
United Republic of Tanzania	Yes	Yes	Yes	No
United States of America	Yes	Yes	Yes	No[l]
Uruguay	Yes	Yes	Yes	Yes

Enforcement	Seat-belt wearing rates (%)			
	Drivers only	Front-seat occupants	Rear-seat occupants	All occupants
6	77.0	75.1	10.1	66.2
7				
8				
8				
9	90.4	91.8	68.6	82.2
—				
—				
5	33	31		
—				
8	90.3	90.5	80.6	88.3
8	75	75	75	
5				
7	75	75	8	
6	98	96	90	97
8	94	94	86	
7	90	90		
3				
6	58	40		
5	21	19.8	3.1	14.6
2				
6				
—				
8				
3				
9	50.1	40.6		
10				
4				
3				
10				
10	95.3 - 98[k]	94.6 - 98[k]	90.3 - 94[k]	97.5 - 98[k]
8				
—	90.5	90.1	74.8	90.1
6	69.1	62.8	33	62.8

Country / Area	National seat belt law	Seat belt applies to		
		Drivers	Front seat passengers	Rear-seat passengers
Uzbekistan	Yes	Yes	No	No
Vanuatu	Yes	Yes	Yes	No
Venezuela (Bolivarian Republic of)	Yes	Yes	Yes	Yes
Viet Nam	Yes	Yes	Yes	No
West Bank and Gaza Strip	Yes	Yes	Yes	Yes
Zimbabwe	Yes	Yes	Yes	No

[a] The obligation to use seat belt does not apply in residential areas nor for children under 12
[b] Legislation requires drivers and passengers «and particularly those sitting in the front» to use a seat belt
[c] Obligation to use seat belts for all passengers only applies outside cities and densely populated areas. Inside cities and densely populated areas, only the driver and front seat passenger sare required to wear a seat belt
[d] Rear seat passengers as children under 12 are not subject to the obligation to use a seat belt
[e] Percentage are for expressways and other roads, respectively
[f] Only required on roads where vehicles may be driven at a speed higher than the normal limit
[g] Seat belts are only required outside cities
[h] The use of seat belt for rear seat passengers is only required outside urban areas
[i] For rear seat passengers, seat-belt required only outside cities
[j] Percentages reflect «urban» and «outside urban» areas, respectively
[k] Percentage are for «England and Scotland» and «NI», respectively
[l] About 40% of the states do not require seat belt for rear seats passengers
[*] 96% for cars; 89% for vans; 88% for taxi

Enforcement	Seat-belt wearing rates (%)			
	Drivers only	Front-seat occupants	Rear-seat occupants	All occupants
5				
2	41	20	10	20
6				
6				
6				
7				

TABLE A8: CHILD RESTRAINTS LAWS, ENFORCEMENT AND PERCENTAGE/ RATES OF CHILD RESTRAINT USE BY COUNTRY / AREA

Country / Area	Child restraint systems law			Children seated in front seat	Enforcement	Percentage of children using child restraints
	National child restraint law	Child restraints required	Standard referred to and / or specified			
Afghanistan	No	–	–	Not restricted	–	–
Albania	Yes	Up to 4 yrs	Yes	Allowed in a child restraint[a]	6	–
Angola	Yes	Up to 12 yrs / 36 kg / 150 cm	Yes	Prohibited under 12 yrs /150 cm	5	–
Antigua and Barbuda	No	–	–	Not restricted	–	–
Argentina	Yes	Up to 4 yrs[b]	No	Prohibited under 10 yrs	–	26.4
Armenia	No	–	–	Allowed in a child restraint[c]	–	–
Australia	Yes	Up to 7 yrs	Yes	Prohibited under 7 yrs[d]	7	–
Austria	Yes	Up to 14 yrs / 150 cm	Yes	Allowed in a child restraint	–	97 (Rear seats)
Azerbaijan	No[e]	–	–	Allowed in a child restraint[e]	–	–
Bangladesh	No	–	–	Not restricted	–	–
Barbados	Yes	Up to 4 yrs	Yes	Prohibited under 4 yrs	4	–
Belarus	Yes	Up to 5 yrs[f]	Yes	Allowed in a child restraint[g]	8	–
Belgium	Yes	Up to 18 yrs / 135 cm	Yes[h]	Allowed in a child restraint[i]	5	89
Belize	No	–	–	Not restricted	–	–
Benin	No	–	–	Not restricted	–	–
Bhutan	No	–	–	Not restricted	–	–
Bolivia (Plurinational State of)	No	–	–	Not restricted	–	–
Bosnia and Herzegovina	Yes	Up to 12 yrs[j]	No	Prohibited under 12 yrs[k]	8[l]	40
Botswana	Yes	Up to 5 yrs	No	Prohibited under 5 yrs	5	–
Brazil	Yes	Up to 7.5 yrs	Yes	Prohibited under 10 yrs	7	57
Bulgaria	Yes	Up to 150 cm	Yes	Allowed in a child restraint[i]	6	–
Burkina Faso	Yes	Up to 8 yrs	No	Prohibited under 7 yrs	0	–
Burundi	No	–	–	Prohibited under 13 yrs	–	–
Cabo Verde	No[m]	–	–	Allowed in a child restraint[n]	–	–
Cambodia	Yes[o]	Up to 4 yrs	No	Prohibited under 10 yrs[p]	0	–
Cameroon	No	–	–	Not restricted	–	–
Canada	Yes	–[q]	Yes	Allowed in a child restraint	8	91
Central African Republic	No	–	–	Not restricted[r]	–	–
Chad	No	–	–	Not restricted	–	–

Country / Area	Child restraint systems law			Children seated in front seat	Enforcement	Percentage of children using child restraints
	National child restraint law	Child restraints required	Standard referred to and / or specified			
Chile	Yes	Up to 8 yrs / 33 kg / 135 cm	Yes	Prohibited under 12 yrs	4	73
China	No	–	–	Not restricted	–	–
Colombia	No[s]	–	–	Prohibited under 10 yrs	–	7.1
Comoros	No	–	–	Not restricted	–	–
Congo	No	–	–	Not restricted	–	–
Cook Islands	No	–	–	Not restricted	–	–
Costa Rica	Yes	Up to 12 yrs / 145 cm	No	Prohibited under 12 yrs / 145 cm	5	–
Côte d'Ivoire	No	–	–	Not restricted	–	–
Croatia	Yes	Up to 135 - 150 cm[t]	No	Prohibited under 150 cm	5	–
Cuba	No[u]	–	–	Prohibited under 12 yrs	–	–
Cyprus	Yes	Up to 135 - 150 cm[t]	Yes	Allowed in a child restraint[i]	6	–
Czechia	Yes	Up to 36 kg / 150 cm	Yes	Allowed in a child restraint[i]	8	–
Democratic Republic of the Congo	No	–	–	Prohibited under 12 yrs	–	–
Denmark	Yes	Up to 135 cm	Yes	Allowed in a child restraint[v]	–	97
Dominica	No	–	–	Not restricted	–	–
Dominican Republic	Yes	Up to 6 yrs[w]	Yes	Prohibited under 12 yrs	4	–
Ecuador	Yes[x]	–[x]	No	Prohibited under 12 yrs	5	15
Egypt	No	–	–	Prohibited under 7 yrs	–	–
El Salvador	Yes	Up to 2 yrs / 15 kg	No	Not restricted[y]	–	–
Equatorial Guinea	No	–	–	Not restricted	–	–
Eritrea	No[z]	–	–	Prohibited under 9 yrs[aa]	–	–
Estonia	Yes[ab]	–	No	Not restricted	8	98
Eswatini	No	–	–	Not restricted	–	–
Ethiopia	No[ac]	–	–	Prohibited under 13 yrs	–	–
Fiji	Yes[ad]	Up to 8 yrs	No	Allowed in a child restraint	3	–
Finland	Yes	Up to 135 cm	Yes	Allowed in a child restraint[i]	8	97
France	Yes	Up to 10 yrs	Yes	Prohibited under 10 yrs[ae]	9	–

Country / Area	Child restraint systems law			Children seated in front seat	Enforcement	Percentage of children using child restraints
	National child restraint law	Child restraints required	Standard referred to and / or specified			
Gabon	No	–	–	Not restricted	–	–
Gambia	Yes	Up to 5 yrs	No	Allowed in a child restraint	–	–
Georgia	No	–	–	Prohibited under 12 yrs	–	–
Germany	Yes	Up to 12 yrs / 150 cm	Yes	Allowed in a child restraint	–	97 - 99
Ghana	No	–	–	Prohibited under 5 yrs[af]	–	–
Greece	Yes	Up to 135 - 150 cm[ag]	Yes	Allowed in a child restraint	2	67
Grenada	No	–	–	Not restricted	–	–
Guatemala	No	–	–	Not restricted	–	–
Guinea	Yes	Up to 18 mths[ah]	No	Prohibited under 10 yrs	–	–
Guinea-Bissau	Yes	Up to 12 yrs /135 cm	No	Prohibited under 12 yrs / 135 cm	0	–
Guyana	Yes[ai]	–	No	Not restricted	0	–
Honduras	No[aj]	–	–	Prohibited under 12 yrs	–	–
Hungary	Yes	Up to 135 - 150 cm[ak]	Yes	Allowed in a child restraint	7	67
Iceland	Yes	Up to 135 cm	Yes	Allowed in a child restraint[al]	9	93
India	No	–	–	Not restricted	–	–
Indonesia	No	–	–	Not restricted	–	–
Iran (Islamic Republic of)	No	–	–	Prohibited under 12 yrs	–	–
Iraq	No	–	–	Prohibited[am]	–	–
Ireland	Yes	Up to 36 kg / 150 cm	Yes	Allowed in a child restraint[i]	10	–
Israel	Yes	Up to 8 yrs[an]	Yes	Allowed in a child restraint	6	52
Italy	Yes	Up to 150 cm	Yes	Allowed in a child restraint[i]	6	38
Jamaica	Yes[ai]	–	Yes	Not restricted	2	–
Japan	Yes	Up to 6 yrs	Yes	Allowed in a child restraint	7	64
Jordan	No	–	–	Prohibited under 10 yrs	–	–
Kazakhstan	Yes	–[ao]	Yes[ao]	Allowed in a child restraint	7	–
Kenya	No	–	–	Not restricted	–	–
Kiribati	No[ap]	–	–	Not restricted	–	–
Kuwait	No	–	–	Prohibited under 10 yrs	–	–

Country / Area	Child restraint systems law			Children seated in front seat	Enforcement	Percentage of children using child restraints
	National child restraint law	Child restraints required	Standard referred to and / or specified			
Kyrgyzstan	No[aq]	–	–	Allowed in a child restraint[ar]	–	–
Lao People's Democratic Republic	Yes[as]	–	No	Not restricted	1	–
Latvia	Yes	Up to 150 cm	No	Allowed in a child restraint[at]	7	–
Lebanon	Yes	Up to 5 yrs[au]	No	Prohibited under 10 yrs	3	–
Lesotho	No	–	–	Not restricted	–	–
Liberia	No	–	–	Not restricted	–	–
Libya	No	–	–	Not restricted	–	–
Lithuania	Yes	Up to 135 cm	Yes	Allowed in a child restraint[av]	8	–
Luxembourg	Yes	Up to 17 yrs / 150 cm	Yes	Allowed in a child restraint[i]	8	–
Madagascar	No	–	–	Prohibited under 5 yrs	–	–
Malawi	No	–	–	Not restricted	–	–
Malaysia	No	–	–	Not restricted	–	–
Maldives	No	–	–	Not restricted	–	–
Mali	No[aw]	–	–	Prohibited under 10 yrs	–	–
Malta	Yes	Up to 3 yrs[ax]	Yes	Allowed in a child restraint	3	–
Mauritania	No	–	–	Prohibited under 10 yrs	–	–
Mauritius	No	–	–	Prohibited under 10 yrs	–	–
Mexico	No	–	–	Not restricted	–	13.7
Micronesia (Federated States of)	No	–	–	Not restricted	–	–
Mongolia	No	–	–	Not restricted	–	–
Montenegro	Yes	Up to 5 yrs	No	Prohibited under 12 yrs[ay]	4	–
Morocco	No	–	–	Prohibited under 10 yrs	–	–
Mozambique	Yes	Up to 12 yrs	No	Prohibited under 12 yrs[az]	4	–
Myanmar	No	–	–	Not restricted	–	–
Namibia	No[ba]	–	–	Not restricted	–	–
Nepal	No	–	–	Not restricted	–	–
Netherlands	Yes	Up to 18 yrs / 135 cm	Yes	Allowed in a child restraint[i]	6	–
New Zealand	Yes	Up to 7 yrs	No	Allowed in a child restraint	8	93 and 95[bb]
Niger	No	–	–	Not restricted	–	–

Country / Area	Child restraint systems law			Children seated in front seat	Enforcement	Percentage of children using child restraints
	National child restraint law	Child restraints required	Standard referred to and / or specified			
Nigeria	Yes	Up to 7 yrs	No	Prohibited under 7 yrs	3	–
Norway	Yes	Up to 135 - 150 cm[bc]	Yes	Allowed in a child restraint[i]	10	–
Oman	Yes	Up to 4 yrs	No	Prohibited under 10 yrs	7	–
Pakistan	No	–	–	Not restricted	–	–
Panama	No[bd]	–	–	Prohibited under 5 yrs	–	–
Papua New Guinea	No	–	–	Not restricted[be]	–	–
Paraguay	Yes	Up to 5 yrs	No	Prohibited under 10 yrs	2	–
Peru	Yes	Up to 3 yrs[bf]	Yes	Prohibited under 12 yrs	1	<1
Philippines	No	–	–	Prohibited under 6 yrs[bg]	–	–
Poland	Yes	Up to 135 - 150 cm[bc]	Yes	Allowed in a child restraint[i]	7	93
Portugal	Yes	Up to 12 yrs / 135 cm	Yes	Prohibited under 12 yrs /135 cm[bh]	8	91 - 100
Qatar	No	–	–	Prohibited under 10 yrs	–	72
Republic of Korea	No[bi]	–	–	Allowed in a child restraint[bj]	–	40 - 42
Republic of Moldova	Yes[bk]	–	No	Prohibited under 12 yrs	8	50
Romania	Yes	Up to 135 cm	Yes	Allowed in a child restraint[bl]	7	–
Russian Federation	Yes[bm]	Up to 7 yrs[bn]	Yes	Allowed in a child restraint[bo]	7	49 - 52
Rwanda	No	–	–	Not restricted	–	–
Saint Lucia	No	–	–	Not restricted	–	–
Samoa	No[bp]	–	–	Not restricted[bq]	–	–
San Marino	Yes	Up to 150 cm	Yes	Allowed in a child restraint	8	–
Sao Tome and Principe	No[br]	–	–	Prohibited under 12 yrs / 150 cm[bs]	–	–
Saudi Arabia	Yes	–[bt]	No	Prohibited under 10 yrs	1	–
Senegal	No	–	–	Not restricted	–	–
Serbia	Yes	Up to 3 yrs	Yes	Prohibited under 12 yrs[bu]	3	28
Seychelles	Yes[bv]	–[bw]	No	Not restricted	5	–
Singapore	Yes	Up to 135 cm	Yes	Allowed in a child restraint	8	–
Slovakia	Yes	Up to 150 cm	Yes	Allowed in a child restraint[i]	8	–
Slovenia	Yes	Up to 150 cm	No	Allowed in a child restraint[i]	9	–

Country / Area	Child restraint systems law			Children seated in front seat	Enforcement	Percentage of children using child restraints
	National child restraint law	Child restraints required	Standard referred to and / or specified			
Solomon Islands	No	–	–	Not restricted	–	–
Somalia	No	–	–	Not restricted	–	–
South Africa	Yes	Up to 3 yrs	Yes	Not restricted[bx]	5	–
South Sudan	No	–	–	Not restricted	–	–
Spain	Yes	Up to 135 cm	Yes	Prohibited under 135 cm[by]	8	88
Sri Lanka	No	–	–	Not restricted	–	–
Sudan	No	–	–	Prohibited under 10 yrs	–	–
Suriname	Yes[bz]	–[bz]	No	Allowed in a child restraint	4	–
Sweden	Yes	Up to 135 cm	Yes	Allowed in a child restraint[i]	6	96
Switzerland	Yes	Up to 12 yrs / 150 cm[ca]	Yes	Allowed in a child restraint	7	93
Syrian Arab Republic	No	–	–	Prohibited under 12 yrs	–	–
Tajikistan	No[cb]	–	–	Allowed in a child restraint[cc]	–	–
Thailand	No	–	–	Not restricted	–	–
The former Yugoslav Republic of Macedonia	Yes	Up to 5 yrs	No	Prohibited under 12 yrs[cd]	7	–
Timor-Leste	No	–	–	Prohibited under 12 yrs[ce]	–	–
Togo	No	–	–	Not restricted	–	–
Tonga	No	–	–	Not restricted	–	–
Trinidad and Tobago	Yes	Up to 5 yrs	Yes	Prohibited under 5 yrs	3	–
Tunisia	No	–	–	Prohibited under 10 yrs	–	–
Turkey	Yes	Up to 36 kg / 135 - 150 cm[cf]	Yes	Allowed in a child restraint[i]	9	–
Turkmenistan	No[cg]	–	–	Allowed in a child restraint[ch]	–	–
Uganda	No	–	–	Not restricted	–	–
Ukraine	Yes[ci]	–	No	Allowed in a child restraint[cj]	2	–
United Arab Emirates	Yes	Up to 4 yrs [ck]	Yes	Prohibited under 10 yrs / 145 cm	7	–
United Kingdom	Yes	Up to 12 yrs / 135 cm	Yes	Allowed in a child restraint	10	95 (NI)
United Republic of Tanzania	No	–	–	Not restricted	–	–
United States of America	Yes	–[cl]	Yes	Allowed in a child restraint	–	89

Country / Area	Child restraint systems law			Children seated in front seat	Enforcement	Percentage of children using child restraints
	National child restraint law	Child restraints required	Standard referred to and / or specified			
Uruguay	Yes	Up to 12 yrs / 36 kg / 150 cm	Yes	Prohibited under 12 yrs / 150 cm	4	23
Uzbekistan	No	–	–	Allowed in a child restraint	–	–
Vanuatu	No[cm]	–	–	Allowed in a child restraint[cn]	–	–
Venezuela (Bolivarian Republic of)	Yes[co]	–	No	Prohibited under 10 yrs	3	–
Viet Nam	No	–	–	Not restricted	–	–
West Bank and Gaza Strip	Yes	Up to 14 yrs	Yes[cp]	Allowed in a child restraint	3	–
Zimbabwe	No	–	–	Prohibited under 10 yrs	–	–

a Children under 12 years can travel in the front if placed in an appropriate restraining device (with airbag deactivated for rear-facing restraint)
b A 2018 amendment (not covered in the review period ending at December 2017) raised the age for mandatory child restraint use to 10 years old
c Transport of children under 12 years in the front seat shall be made in a «child protecting device»
d In no circumstances are children under 4 years allowed to sit in the front. Children from 4 to 7 years can sit in the front only if there is no room for them in the back due to the back seats being occupied by other children under 7 years
e Child restraint systems are only required for children under 12 years seated in the front
f For children aged 5-12 years, either CRS or «other means» (than CRS) can be used to secure the child using the seat belt
g If rear-facing child restraints, airbag shall be deactivated
h All child restraints sold in Belgium must comply with UNECE regulation
i Provided that airbag is deactivated if child is in a rear-facing child restraint system
j Children aged 5-12 years can be either restrained in a booster seat or in a child restraint
k By exception, a child under 2 years can be seated in the front if there is no airbag installed or if the airbag is deactivated when the child is seated in a rear-facing seat
l Data only for Republic of Srpska
m The legislation refers to the use of either child restraint systems or seat-belts for children
n Children under 12 yrs / 150 cm shall normally sit in the rear except if placed in a suitable restraint
o Enters into force in January 2020
p Ban on children under 10 years travelling in front seats enters into force in January 2020
q Child restraint laws are enacted at subnational level. While all provinces require the use of child restraints, they provide different age / height criteria to specify the period for mandatory use of child restraint / booster seats
r Legislation only recommends («as far as possible») to place children under 12 years in the rear
s A child under 2 years travelling with a driver only shall be placed in a child restraint. If there is an adult passenger, the child can be held by the adult instead of being placed in a child restraint.
t A child of height 135-150 cm can be restrained with an adult seat belt only provided that this child sits in the rear of the car
u Children under 2 years shall be either accompanied by adults or restrained with special accessories

v Provided that airbag is deactivated if a rear-facing restraint is used
w Children aged 6-12 years shall be placed in a booster seat
x The legislation refers to seat belt or child restraints for children under 12 years but does not yet specify a minimum age / height / weight under which only child restraint systems can be used
y Except for children under 2 yrs old or 15 kg who are required to be transported in a child restraint
z Legislation refers to the use of child restraint or seat belts for «children over 9» while children under 3 years are required to be placed in a restraint only while seated in the front
aa Except for an infant under 3 years fitted in a proper restraint
ab The legislation generally states that children not tall enough to wear a seat belt must be secured by a safety device corresponding to the height and weight of the child but does not specify age / height / weight group covered
ac Legislation requires that children under 7 years be either accompanied by an adult or «hugged by an instrument made for safety purpose»
ad The obligation to use a child restraint for children under 8 years sitting in the rear is subject to the availability of a restraint system in the car
ae By exception, children under 10 years can sit in the front if placed in a rear-facing child restraint (if front airbag is deactivated) or if there are no available rear seats
af Under the road traffic act, children aged 5 years and below shall not sit in the front, while under the road traffic regulations they can sit in the front if placed in a child restraint
ag The use of seat belt is allowed for children of height 135-150 cm sitting in the rear
ah The legislation refers to homologated seats for children under 18 months and to cribs and hammocks for children under 10 years
ai The legislation refers to child restraint system for children but does not specify the age / height group covered by this obligation
aj Legislation refers to the protection of children under 5 years but does not specify which form this protection takes
ak Children of height 135 - 150 cm can be restrained with seat belts only if they sit in the back
al Seating of children under 150 cm allowed in the front only if front airbag deactivated
am The law prohibits children to sit in the front but does not specify the age, size or weight of children concerned
an For children under 3 years, a child restraint is required (an a rear facing child restraint for children under one year) while for children aged 3-8 years the legislation refers either to child restraint or booster seat use
ao The legislation requires that children under 12 years be placed in a child restraint or «other means» used in conjunction with a seat belt
ap The traffic act 2017 requires children aged 1-16 years to be either seated in the back with a seat belt or restrained by passenger over 16 yrs
aq Legislation only refers to the use of child restraints for children under 12 years travelling in the front
ar Children under 12 years travelling in the front of a car must be placed in a child restraint
as The law states that children unable to wear normal seat belts must be placed in a child restraint seat but no specific age / weight / height is specified
at Except if no seat belt is fitted in the vehicle, in which case children under 150 cm shall be travelling in the rear
au Legislation refers to regulations to further specify the child restraint rules
av If transported in rear facing restraints, airbag must be deactivated
aw Children under 13 years can be restrained either by a child restraint systems or a seat belt
ax Legislation refers to child restraint use for children up to 12 yrs /150 cm but allows children aged 3 year and over, in the absence of an available restraint, to travel in the rear without a restraint. For children under 3 years, a child restraint shall be mandatorily used
ay By exception, a child under 3 years can be transported in the front of the vehicle if placed in a rear-facing restraint provided that airbag is deactivated
az Except for infants under 3 years in a rear-facing child restraint air airbag deactivated
ba The law requires the use of child restraints for children (defined as people between the age of 3 and 14) if available or the use of a seat belt if a child restraint is not available if an unoccupied seat fitted with a seat belt is available
bb 93% 0-4 years, 95% 5-9 years
bc Child restraints are required for children under 150 cm. By exception, children of height 135-150 cm can be restrained with a seat belt only if sitting in the rear
bd Children under 2 years shall be placed in a child restraint only where there is no other passenger seated in the rear
be Children can sit in the front as long as they are using a seat belt
bf Legislation requires the use of the seat belt for children from 3-12 years old
bg Ban on front seating set for children aged 6 years and below
bh Except for children under 3 years in a rear-facing child restraint with airbag deactivated
bi Only required for small children (defined as children under 6) sitting in the front
bj Safety seats required for small children (defined as children under 6) sitting in the front
bk The legislation refers to the use of child restraint systems or other means to transport children under 12 years
bl If in accordance with the manufacturer's instruction and for rear-facing restraint if airbag is deactivated
bm Since 2017, child restraint systems are the only form of restraint allowed for children under 7 years old (before the 2017 revision, children under 12 were to be restrained either in a child restraint or by «other means»)
bn For children aged 7-11 years old (included) sitting in the rear, child restraint or seat belt can be used
bo Children up to 11 years old (included) while sitting in the front shall be placed in a child restraint, children aged 12 years and more can sit in the front without a child restraint
bp Legislation refers to either child restraint or seat belt to restrain children under 12 years
bq Except if child restraint or seat belt are available in the front seat
br Legislation refers to either child restraint or seat belt use to transport children
bs Except if the vehicle does not have rear seats provided and such transportation is made in a child restraint (with airbag deactivated if a rear-facing restraint is being used)
bt Reference is made to special seats to be used for children with no details as to the specific age / height under which children should be mandatorily placed in them
bu Except for children under 3 years if airbag is deactivated
bv The legislation refers to the use of child restraint systems for infant or child passenger but does not refer to a specific age/ height up to which the use of child restraint is mandatory

[bw] Obligation not based on age / height or weight

[bx] Obligation to place children in the rear only applies in vehicles not fitted with seat belts and having rear seats

[by] Front seating for children under 135 cm is only allowed as an exception if there are no seats in the back or all other seats are occupied by children

[bz] For children under 10 years, the legislation refers to the use of child restraint system (CRS) where available and appropriate, and specifies that in the absence of child restraint, seat belts are to be used

[ca] Children under 12 years and less than 150 cm shall be placed in a child restraint

[cb] Legislation refers to the use of child restraints or «other means» to secure children up to 12 years old but allows the transport of children under 12 years on the knees of an adult passenger seated in the back with the seat belt fastened

[cc] Front seating of children under 12 years allowed if a child restraint is being used

[cd] Except for children under 2 years in a rear-facing child restraint if airbag is deactivated

[ce] Unless the vehicle does not have a back seat and such transportation is carried out by using an approved child restraint, appropriate to the child's size and weight

[cf] Child restraints are required for children under 150 cm, by exception, children of height 135-150 cm can be restrained with a seat belt only if they sit in the back

[cg] Special seating equipment for children under 12 years is only mentioned only in relation with front seating

[ch] Law does not specifically refer to child restraint system but to «special seating equipment» for children under 12 years

[ci] The legislation refers to the use of «special means» to be used in conjunction with the seat belt to restraint children under 12 years and 145 cm

[cj] No specific reference to child restraint but to «special means» for children under 145 cm and 12 years sitting in the front

[ck] Child restraints are required for children aged 4 and below

[cl] Child restraint laws are enacted at subnational level. While all states require the use of child restraints, they provide different age / weight / height criteria to specify the period for mandatory use of child restraints/ booster seats

[cm] Legislation allows that infants (defined as children under 3 years) be held by a responsible person as an alternative to using special seats

[cn] Infant (defined as children under 3 years) shall be placed in a restraining seat while travelling in the front

[co] The law requires «infants» to use «special seats for that purpose» but does not specify the age for children falling into the «infants» category

[cp] Law refers to a device of the type validated by the licensing authority to restraint children under 14 years

TABLE A9: MOBILE PHONE LAWS BY COUNTRY / AREA

Country / Area	National mobile phone law	Mobile phone law		Any data on use of mobile phone while driving
		Applies to hand-held phone use	Applies to hands-free phone use	
Afghanistan	No	–	–	No
Albania	Yes	Yes	No	Yes
Angola	Yes	Yes	No	Yes
Antigua and Barbuda	No	–	–	No
Argentina	Yes	Yes	Yes	Yes
Armenia	Yes	Yes	No	Yes
Australia	Yes	Yes	No	Yes
Austria	Yes	Yes	No	Yes[a]
Azerbaijan	Yes	Yes	No	No
Bangladesh	No	–	–	No
Barbados	Yes	Yes	No	No
Belarus	Yes	Yes	No	Yes
Belgium	Yes	Yes	No	Yes[a]
Belize	No	–	–	No
Benin	Yes	Yes	Yes	No
Bhutan	Yes	Yes	No	No
Bolivia (Plurinational State of)	No	–	–	No
Bosnia and Herzegovina	Yes	Yes	No	Yes[a]
Botswana	Yes	Yes	No	Yes
Brazil	Yes	Yes	Yes	Yes[a]
Bulgaria	Yes	Yes	No	No
Burkina Faso	Yes	Yes	No	No
Burundi	Yes	Yes	Yes	No
Cabo Verde	Yes	Yes	No	Yes
Cambodia	Yes	Yes	No	No
Cameroon	Yes	Yes	Yes	No
Canada	Yes	Yes	No	Yes[a]
Central African Republic	Yes	Yes	Yes	No
Chad	Yes	Yes	Yes	No
Chile	Yes	Yes	No	Yes
China	Yes	Yes	No	Yes
Colombia	Yes	Yes	No	No
Comoros	No	–	–	No
Congo	Yes	Yes	Yes	No

Country / Area	National mobile phone law	Mobile phone law		Any data on use of mobile phone while driving
		Applies to hand-held phone use	Applies to hands-free phone use	
Cook Islands	No	–	–	No
Costa Rica	Yes	Yes	No	Yes
Côte d'Ivoire	Yes	Yes	Yes	No
Croatia	Yes	Yes	No	Yes[a]
Cuba	Yes	Yes	Yes	Yes
Cyprus	Yes	Yes	No	Yes
Czechia	Yes	Yes	No	Yes[a]
Democratic Republic of the Congo	No	–	–	No
Denmark	Yes	Yes	No	No
Dominica	No	–	–	–
Dominican Republic	Yes	Yes	No	Yes[a]
Ecuador	Yes	Yes	No	Yes
Egypt	Yes	Yes	No	No
El Salvador	Yes	Yes	Yes	Yes
Equatorial Guinea	Yes	Yes	Yes	No
Eritrea	Yes	Yes	No	Yes
Estonia	Yes	Yes	No	Yes
Eswatini	Yes	Yes	No	No
Ethiopia	Yes	Yes	Yes	Yes
Fiji	Yes	Yes	Yes	Yes
Finland	Yes	Yes	No	Yes[a]
France	Yes	Yes	No	Yes
Gabon	Yes	Yes	Yes	No
Gambia	Yes	Yes	No	No
Georgia	Yes	Yes	No	Yes
Germany	Yes	Yes	No	Yes[a]
Ghana	Yes	Yes	No	No
Greece	Yes	Yes	No	Yes[a]
Grenada	No	–	–	No
Guatemala	Yes	Yes	No	Yes
Guinea	Yes	Yes	No	No
Guinea-Bissau	Yes	Yes	No	Yes
Guyana	Yes	Yes	No	Yes

Country / Area	National mobile phone law	Mobile phone law		Any data on use of mobile phone while driving
		Applies to hand-held phone use	Applies to hands-free phone use	
Honduras	Yes	Yes	Yes	Yes
Hungary	Yes	Yes	No	Yes
Iceland	Yes	Yes	No	Yes
India	Yes	Yes	Yes	Yes
Indonesia	Yes	No	No	Yes
Iran (Islamic Republic of)	Yes	Yes	Yes	No
Iraq	Yes	Yes	Yes	No
Ireland	Yes	Yes	No	Yes
Israel	Yes	Yes	No	–
Italy	Yes	Yes	No	Yes[a]
Jamaica	No	–	–	Yes
Japan	Yes	Yes	No	Yes
Jordan	Yes	Yes	No	No
Kazakhstan	Yes	Yes	No	Yes
Kenya	Yes	Yes	No	No
Kiribati	Yes	Yes	No	No
Kuwait	Yes	Yes	No	No
Kyrgyzstan	Yes	Yes	No	Yes
Lao People's Democratic Republic	Yes	Yes	Yes	No
Latvia	Yes	Yes	No	No
Lebanon	Yes	Yes	Yes	No
Lesotho	No	–	–	No
Liberia	No	–	–	No
Libya	Yes	No	No	Yes
Lithuania	Yes	Yes	No	Yes
Luxembourg	Yes	Yes	No	No
Madagascar	Yes	Yes	No	No
Malawi	Yes	Yes	No	Yes[a]
Malaysia	Yes	Yes	No	Yes[a]
Maldives	Yes	Yes	No	No
Mali	Yes	Yes	No	Yes[a]
Malta	Yes	Yes	No	No
Mauritania	Yes	Yes	Yes	Yes

Country / Area	National mobile phone law	Mobile phone law		Any data on use of mobile phone while driving
		Applies to hand-held phone use	Applies to hands-free phone use	
Mauritius	Yes	Yes	Yes	Yes
Mexico	No	No	No	Yes[a]
Micronesia (Federated States of)	No	—	—	No
Mongolia	Yes	Yes	No	No
Montenegro	Yes	Yes	Yes	Yes
Morocco	Yes	Yes	No	Yes[a]
Mozambique	Yes	Yes	No	No
Myanmar	No	—	—	No
Namibia	Yes	Yes	No	No
Nepal	No	—	—	No
Netherlands	Yes	Yes	No	Yes
New Zealand	Yes	Yes	No	Yes
Niger	Yes	Yes	Yes	No
Nigeria	Yes	Yes	Yes	Yes
Norway	Yes	Yes	No	No
Oman	Yes	Yes	No	Yes
Pakistan	Yes	Yes	No	No
Panama	Yes	Yes	Yes	No
Papua New Guinea	No	—	—	No
Paraguay	Yes	Yes	Yes	No
Peru	Yes	Yes	No	Yes[a]
Philippines	Yes	Yes	No	Yes
Poland	Yes	Yes	No	Yes[a]
Portugal	Yes	Yes	No	No
Qatar	Yes	Yes	No	Yes
Republic of Korea	Yes	Yes	No	Yes[a]
Republic of Moldova	Yes	Yes	No	No
Romania	Yes	Yes	No	No
Russian Federation	Yes	Yes	No	Yes[a]
Rwanda	No	—	—	No
Saint Lucia	Yes	No	No	No
Samoa	Yes	Yes	No	Yes
San Marino	Yes	Yes	No	No

Country / Area	National mobile phone law	Mobile phone law		Any data on use of mobile phone while driving
		Applies to hand-held phone use	Applies to hands-free phone use	
Sao Tome and Principe	Yes	Yes	No	No
Saudi Arabia	Yes	Yes	No	Yes
Senegal	Yes	Yes	Yes	No
Serbia	Yes	Yes	No	Yes
Seychelles	Yes	Yes	No	Yes
Singapore	Yes	Yes	No	No
Slovakia	Yes	Yes	No	Yes
Slovenia	Yes	Yes	No	No
Solomon Islands	No	–	–	No
Somalia	No	–	–	No
South Africa	Yes	Yes	No	Yes
South Sudan	No	–	–	No
Spain	Yes	Yes	No	Yes
Sri Lanka	Yes	Yes	No	No
Sudan	Yes	Yes	Yes	No
Suriname	Yes	Yes	No	Yes
Sweden	Yes	No	No	No
Switzerland	Yes	Yes	No	Yes
Syrian Arab Republic	Yes	Yes	Yes	Yes
Tajikistan	Yes	Yes	No	No
Thailand	Yes	Yes	No	No
The former Yugoslav Republic of Macedonia	Yes	Yes	No	Yes
Timor-Leste	Yes	Yes	No	No
Togo	Yes	Yes	Yes	No
Tonga	No	–	–	No
Trinidad and Tobago	Yes	Yes	No	Yes
Tunisia	Yes	Yes	No	No
Turkey	Yes	Yes	Yes	Yes
Turkmenistan	Yes	Yes	Yes	Yes
Uganda	Yes	Yes	No	No
Ukraine	Yes	Yes	No	No
United Arab Emirates	Yes	Yes	No	Yes
United Kingdom	Yes	Yes	No	Yes

Country / Area	National mobile phone law	Mobile phone law		Any data on use of mobile phone while driving
		Applies to hand-held phone use	Applies to hands-free phone use	
United Republic of Tanzania	No	–	–	No
United States of America	Yes	No[b]	No	Yes
Uruguay	Yes	Yes	No	Yes
Uzbekistan	Yes	Yes	Yes	Yes
Vanuatu	No	–	–	No
Venezuela (Bolivarian Republic of)	Yes	Yes	No	No
Viet Nam	Yes	Yes	No	No
West Bank and Gaza Strip	Yes	Yes	No	No
Zimbabwe	Yes	Yes	No	No

[a] Only some specific studies

[b] The majority of states prohibit texting while driving

TABLE A10: ROAD SAFETY MANAGEMENT, STRATEGIES AND TARGETS BY COUNTRY / AREA

Country / Area	Lead agency		Functions of the lead agency			Road safety strategies		Road safety targets	
	A lead agency is present	The lead agency is funded	Coordination	Legislation	Monitoring & evaluation	There is a national road safety strategy	The strategy is funded	Fatal	Non-fatal
Afghanistan	No	–	–	–	–	No	–	–	–
Albania	Yes	Yes	Yes	Yes	Yes	Yes	Partially funded	Yes	Yes
Angola	Yes	No	Yes	Yes	Yes	Yes	Partially funded	–	–
Antigua and Barbuda	Yes	No	Yes	Yes	Yes	No	–	–	–
Argentina	Yes	Yes	Yes	Yes	Yes	Yes	Fully funded	Yes	No
Armenia	Yes	Yes	Yes	Yes	Yes	No	–	–	–
Australia	Yes	Yes	Yes	No	Yes	Yes	Not funded	Yes	Yes
Austria	Yes	Yes	Yes	Yes	Yes	Yes	Partially funded	Yes	Yes
Azerbaijan	Yes	Yes	Yes	Yes	Yes	No	–	–	–
Bangladesh	Yes	No	Yes	Yes	Yes	Yes	Partially funded	Yes	No
Barbados	Yes	No	Yes	Yes	Yes	No	–	–	–
Belarus	Yes	Yes	Yes	Yes	No	Yes	Partially funded	Yes	No
Belgium	No	–	–	–	–	Yes	Partially funded	Yes	Yes
Belize	Yes	Yes	Yes	Yes	Yes	Yes	Partially funded	Yes	Yes
Benin	Yes	No	Yes	No	Yes	No	–	–	–
Bhutan	Yes	Yes	Yes	Yes	Yes	Yes	Partially funded	Yes	Yes
Bolivia (Plurinational State of)	Yes	Yes	Yes	Yes	Yes	Yes	Partially funded	Yes	Yes
Bosnia and Herzegovina	Yes	Yes	Yes	Yes	Yes	Yes	Partially funded	Yes	Yes
Botswana	Yes	Yes	Yes	Yes	Yes	Yes	Fully funded	Yes	No
Brazil	Yes	Yes	Yes	Yes	Yes	Yes	Partially funded	No	No
Bulgaria	Yes	Yes	Yes	Yes	Yes	Yes	Partially funded	Yes	Yes
Burkina Faso	Yes	Yes	Yes	Yes	Yes	Yes	Partially funded	Yes	Yes
Burundi	Yes	Yes	Yes	Yes	No	No	–	–	–
Cabo Verde	Yes	Yes	Yes	Yes	Yes	Yes	Partially funded	Yes	Yes
Cambodia	Yes	Yes	Yes	Yes	Yes	Yes	Partially funded	Yes	No
Cameroon	No	–	–	–	–	Yes	Partially funded	No	No
Canada	Yes	No[a]	Yes	Yes	Yes	Yes	Partially funded	Yes	Yes
Central African Republic	Yes	Yes	Yes	Yes	Yes	–	–	–	–
Chad	Yes	Yes	Yes	Yes	No	Yes	Partially funded	Yes	Yes

Country / Area	Lead agency		Functions of the lead agency			Road safety strategies		Road safety targets	
	A lead agency is present	The lead agency is funded	Coordination	Legislation	Monitoring & evaluation	There is a national road safety strategy	The strategy is funded	Fatal	Non-fatal
Chile	Yes	No	Yes	Yes	Yes	Yes	Partially funded	No	No
China	Yes	Yes	Yes	Yes	Yes	Yes	Partially funded	Yes	No
Colombia	Yes	No	Yes	Yes	Yes	Yes	Partially funded	Yes	Yes
Comoros	Yes	No	Yes	Yes	Yes	No	–	–	–
Congo	Yes	No	Yes	Yes	Yes	Yes	Partially funded	Yes	Yes
Cook Islands	Yes	Yes	Yes	Yes	Yes	Yes	Partially funded	Yes	Yes
Costa Rica	Yes	No	Yes	Yes	Yes	Yes	Fully funded	Yes	No
Côte d'Ivoire	Yes	Yes	Yes	Yes	Yes	Yes	Fully funded	Yes	Yes
Croatia	No	–	–	–	–	Yes	Fully funded	Yes	No
Cuba	Yes	Yes	Yes	Yes	Yes	Yes	Fully funded	Yes	No
Cyprus	Yes	Yes	Yes	Yes	Yes	Yes	Partially funded	Yes	Yes
Czechia	Yes	Yes	Yes	Yes	Yes	Yes	Partially funded	Yes	Yes
Democratic Republic of the Congo	Yes	Yes	Yes	Yes	Yes	Yes	Partially funded	No	–
Denmark	No	–	–	–	–	Yes	Partially funded	Yes	Yes
Dominica	Yes	No	Yes	Yes	Yes	No	–	–	–
Dominican Republic	Yes	Yes	Yes	Yes	Yes	Yes	Partially funded	Yes	No
Ecuador	Yes	Yes	Yes	Yes	Yes	Yes	Partially funded	Yes	Yes
Egypt	Yes	No	Yes	Yes	No	Yes	Partially funded	Yes	No
El Salvador	Yes	Yes	Yes	Yes	Yes	Yes	Partially funded	Yes	Yes
Equatorial Guinea	Yes	Yes	Yes	Yes	No	No	–	–	–
Eritrea	Yes	Yes	Yes	Yes	Yes	Yes	Partially funded	Yes	Yes
Estonia	Yes	Yes	Yes	Yes	No	Yes	Partially funded	Yes	Yes
Eswatini	Yes	Yes	Yes	Yes	Yes	No	–	–	–
Ethiopia	Yes	Yes	Yes	Yes	Yes	Yes	Partially funded	Yes	No
Fiji	Yes	Yes	Yes	Yes	Yes	Yes	Partially funded	Yes	Yes
Finland	Yes	Yes	Yes	Yes	No	Yes	Partially funded	Yes	No
France	Yes	Yes	Yes	Yes	Yes	Yes	Fully funded	Yes	No
Gabon	Yes	Yes	Yes	Yes	Yes	Yes	Not funded	–	–
Gambia	Yes	Yes	Yes	No	No	No	–	–	–

Country / Area	Lead agency		Functions of the lead agency			Road safety strategies		Road safety targets	
	A lead agency is present	The lead agency is funded	Coordination	Legislation	Monitoring & evaluation	There is a national road safety strategy	The strategy is funded	Fatal	Non-fatal
Georgia	Yes	Yes	Yes	Yes	Yes	Yes	Partially funded	No	No
Germany	Yes	Yes	Yes	Yes	No	Yes	Partially funded	Yes	No
Ghana	Yes	Yes	Yes	Yes	Yes	Yes	Partially funded	Yes	Yes
Greece	Yes	No	Yes	Yes	Yes	Yes	Partially funded	Yes	No
Grenada	Yes	Yes	Yes	Yes	Yes	No	–	–	–
Guatemala	Yes	Yes	Yes	Yes	Yes	Yes	Partially funded	Yes	No
Guinea	Yes	–	Yes	–	–	No	–	–	–
Guinea-Bissau	No	–	–	–	–	No	–	–	–
Guyana	Yes	Yes	Yes	Yes	Yes	Yes	Partially funded	Yes	No
Honduras	Yes	Yes	Yes	Yes	Yes	Yes	Partially funded	No	No
Hungary	No	–	–	–	–	Yes	Partially funded	Yes	No
Iceland	Yes	Yes	Yes	Yes	Yes	Yes	Partially funded	–	–
India	Yes	Yes	Yes	Yes	Yes	Yes	Partially funded	Yes	No
Indonesia	Yes	Yes	Yes	No	No	Yes	Partially funded	Yes	No
Iran (Islamic Republic of)	Yes	No	Yes	Yes	Yes	Yes	Partially funded	Yes	No
Iraq	Yes	No	Yes	Yes	Yes	Yes	Not funded	No	No
Ireland	Yes	No	Yes	No	Yes	Yes	Fully funded	Yes	Yes
Israel	Yes	Yes	Yes	Yes	Yes	Yes	Fully funded	No	No
Italy	Yes	Yes	Yes	Yes	Yes	Yes	Partially funded	Yes	No
Jamaica	Yes	Yes	Yes	No	No	Yes	Partially funded	Yes	No
Japan	Yes	Yes	No	No	No	Yes	Fully funded	Yes	Yes
Jordan	No	–	–	–	–	No	–	–	–
Kazakhstan	Yes	Yes	Yes	Yes	Yes	Yes	Partially funded	Yes	Yes
Kenya	Yes	Yes	Yes	Yes	Yes	No	–	–	–
Kiribati	No	–	–	–	–	Yes	Partially funded	Yes	Yes
Kuwait	Yes	Yes	Yes	No	No	No	–	–	–
Kyrgyzstan	Yes	Yes	Yes	Yes	Yes	Yes	Partially funded	Yes	–
Lao People's Democratic Republic	Yes	Yes	Yes	Yes	Yes	Yes	Partially funded	Yes	No
Latvia	No	–	–	–	–	Yes	Not funded	Yes	Yes

Country / Area	Lead agency		Functions of the lead agency			Road safety strategies		Road safety targets	
	A lead agency is present	The lead agency is funded	Coordination	Legislation	Monitoring & evaluation	There is a national road safety strategy	The strategy is funded	Fatal	Non-fatal
Lebanon	Yes	Yes	Yes	Yes	Yes	No	–	–	–
Lesotho	Yes	Yes	Yes	Yes	Yes	No	–	–	–
Liberia	No	–	–	–	–	No	–	–	–
Libya	Yes	No	Yes	Yes	Yes	Yes	Not funded	Yes	Yes
Lithuania	Yes	Yes	Yes	Yes	Yes	Yes	Partially funded	Yes	Yes
Luxembourg	Yes	Yes	Yes	Yes	Yes	Yes	Partially funded	Yes	Yes
Madagascar	Yes	Yes	Yes	Yes	Yes	Yes	Partially funded	Yes	Yes
Malawi	Yes	Yes	Yes	Yes	Yes	Yes	Partially funded	Yes	Yes
Malaysia	Yes	Yes	Yes	Yes	Yes	Yes	Partially funded	Yes	No
Maldives	Yes	Yes	Yes	Yes	Yes	Yes	Not funded	No	No
Mali	Yes	Yes	Yes	Yes	Yes	Yes	Partially funded	Yes	Yes
Malta	Yes	Yes	Yes	Yes	Yes	Yes	Fully funded	Yes	Yes
Mauritania	Yes	Yes	Yes	Yes	Yes	Yes	Partially funded	Yes	Yes
Mauritius	Yes	Yes	Yes	Yes	Yes	Yes	Fully funded	Yes	Yes
Mexico	Yes	Yes	Yes	Yes	Yes	Yes	Partially funded	Yes	No
Micronesia (Federated States of)	No	–	–	–	–	No	–	–	–
Mongolia	Yes	Yes	Yes	Yes	Yes	Yes	Partially funded	Yes	Yes
Montenegro	Yes	Yes	Yes	Yes	Yes	Yes	Partially funded	Yes	Yes
Morocco	Yes	Yes	Yes	Yes	Yes	Yes	Fully funded	Yes	No
Mozambique	Yes	Yes	Yes	Yes	Yes	Yes	Partially funded	No	No
Myanmar	Yes	No	Yes	Yes	Yes	Yes	Not funded	Yes	No
Namibia	Yes	Yes	Yes	No	Yes	Yes	Partially funded	Yes	Yes
Nepal	Yes	Yes	Yes	Yes	Yes	Yes	Partially funded	–	–
Netherlands	Yes	Yes	Yes	Yes	Yes	Yes	Partially funded	Yes	Yes
New Zealand	Yes	Yes	Yes	Yes	Yes	Yes	Fully funded	Yes	No
Niger	Yes	Yes	Yes	Yes	Yes	Yes	Partially funded	No	Yes
Nigeria	Yes	Yes	Yes	Yes	Yes	Yes	Fully funded	Yes	Yes
Norway	Yes	Yes	Yes	Yes	Yes	Yes	Fully funded	Yes	Yes
Oman	Yes	Yes	Yes	Yes	Yes	Yes	Fully funded	Yes	Yes
Pakistan	Yes	Yes	Yes	Yes	Yes	Yes	Fully funded	No	No

Country / Area	Lead agency		Functions of the lead agency			Road safety strategies		Road safety targets	
	A lead agency is present	The lead agency is funded	Coordination	Legislation	Monitoring & evaluation	There is a national road safety strategy	The strategy is funded	Fatal	Non-fatal
Panama	Yes	Yes	Yes	Yes	Yes	Yes	Partially funded	Yes	Yes
Papua New Guinea	Yes	Yes	Yes	Yes	Yes	Yes	Partially funded	No	No
Paraguay	Yes	Yes	Yes	Yes	Yes	Yes	Partially funded	Yes	Yes
Peru	Yes	Yes	Yes	Yes	Yes	Yes	Partially funded	Yes	Yes
Philippines	Yes	Yes	Yes	Yes	Yes	Yes	Fully funded	Yes	Yes
Poland	Yes	Yes	Yes	Yes	Yes	Yes	Partially funded	Yes	Yes
Portugal	Yes	Yes	Yes	Yes	Yes	Yes	Partially funded	Yes	Yes
Qatar	Yes	Yes	Yes	Yes	Yes	Yes	Fully funded	Yes	Yes
Republic of Korea	Yes	Yes	Yes	Yes	Yes	Yes	Partially funded	Yes	Yes
Republic of Moldova	Yes	No	Yes	Yes	Yes	Yes	Partially funded	Yes	Yes
Romania	Yes	No	Yes	Yes	Yes	Yes	Partially funded	Yes	No
Russian Federation	Yes	Yes	Yes	Yes	Yes	Yes	Partially funded	Yes	No
Rwanda	Yes	Yes	Yes	Yes	Yes	Yes	Partially funded	No	Yes
Saint Lucia	Yes	Yes	Yes	Yes	Yes	No	–	–	–
Samoa	Yes	Yes	Yes	Yes	Yes	Yes	Partially funded	Yes	No
San Marino	Yes	No	Yes	Yes	Yes	Yes	Partially funded	No	No
Sao Tome and Principe	Yes	No	Yes	Yes	Yes	No	–	–	–
Saudi Arabia	Yes	Yes	Yes	Yes	Yes	Yes	Partially funded	–	–
Senegal	Yes	Yes	Yes	Yes	Yes	Yes	Partially funded	Yes	Yes
Serbia	Yes	Yes	Yes	Yes	No	Yes	Partially funded	Yes	Yes
Seychelles	Yes	Yes	Yes	Yes	Yes	Yes	Partially funded	No	No
Singapore	Yes	Yes	Yes	Yes	Yes	Yes	Partially funded	No	No
Slovakia	Yes	Yes	Yes	Yes	Yes	Yes	Partially funded	Yes	No
Slovenia	Yes	Yes	Yes	Yes	Yes	Yes	Partially funded	Yes	Yes
Solomon Islands	Yes	Yes	Yes	Yes	Yes	No	–	–	–
Somalia	Yes	Yes	Yes	Yes	Yes	Yes	Not funded	No	No
South Africa	Yes	Yes	Yes	Yes	Yes	Yes	Partially funded	Yes	No
South Sudan	Yes	Yes	Yes	Yes	Yes	No	–	–	–

Country / Area	Lead agency		Functions of the lead agency			Road safety strategies		Road safety targets	
	A lead agency is present	The lead agency is funded	Coordination	Legislation	Monitoring & evaluation	There is a national road safety strategy	The strategy is funded	Fatal	Non-fatal
Spain	Yes	Yes	Yes	Yes	Yes	Yes	Fully funded	Yes	Yes
Sri Lanka	Yes	No	Yes	Yes	Yes	Yes	Partially funded	Yes	Yes
Sudan	Yes	No	Yes	Yes	Yes	Yes	Partially funded	Yes	Yes
Suriname	No	–	–	–	–	No	–	–	–
Sweden	Yes	Yes	Yes	Yes	Yes	Yes	Partially funded	Yes	Yes
Switzerland	Yes	Yes	Yes	Yes	Yes	No	–	–	–
Syrian Arab Republic	Yes	No	Yes	Yes	Yes	Yes	Partially funded	No	No
Tajikistan	Yes	Yes	Yes	Yes	Yes	Yes	Partially funded	No	No
Thailand	Yes	Yes	Yes	Yes	Yes	Yes	Partially funded	Yes	No
The former Yugoslav Republic of Macedonia	Yes	Yes	Yes	Yes	Yes	Yes	Partially funded	Yes	Yes
Timor-Leste	Yes	Yes	Yes	Yes	Yes	Yes	Partially funded	No	No
Togo	Yes	No	Yes	Yes	Yes	No	–	–	–
Tonga	Yes	Yes	Yes	Yes	Yes	Yes	Partially funded	Yes	Yes
Trinidad and Tobago	Yes	No	No	No	No	Yes	Partially funded	No	No
Tunisia	Yes	Yes	Yes	No	Yes	No	–	–	–
Turkey	Yes	No	Yes	Yes	Yes	Yes	Fully funded	Yes	Yes
Turkmenistan	Yes	Yes	Yes	Yes	Yes	Yes	Fully funded	No	–
Uganda	Yes	Yes	Yes	Yes	Yes	Yes	Partially funded	Yes	No
Ukraine	No	–	–	–	–	No	–	–	–
United Arab Emirates	Yes	Yes	Yes	Yes	Yes	Yes	Partially funded	Yes	Yes
United Kingdom	Yes	Yes	Yes	Yes	Yes	Yes	Partially funded	Yes	Yes
United Republic of Tanzania	Yes	No	Yes	Yes	Yes	Yes	Partially funded	Yes	No
United States of America	Yes	Yes	Yes	Yes	Yes	Yes	Fully funded	Yes	Yes
Uruguay	Yes	Yes	Yes	Yes	Yes	No	–	–	–
Uzbekistan	Yes	Yes	Yes	Yes	Yes	No	–	–	–
Vanuatu	Yes	Yes	Yes	Yes	No	Yes	Partially funded	–	–

Country / Area	Lead agency		Functions of the lead agency			Road safety strategies		Road safety targets	
	A lead agency is present	The lead agency is funded	Coordination	Legislation	Monitoring & evaluation	There is a national road safety strategy	The strategy is funded	Fatal	Non-fatal
Venezuela (Bolivarian Republic of)	Yes	Yes	Yes	Yes	Yes	Yes	Fully funded	No	No
Viet Nam	Yes	Yes	Yes	Yes	Yes	Yes	Partially funded	Yes	No
West Bank and Gaza Strip	Yes	Yes	Yes	Yes	Yes	Yes	Partially funded	No	No
Zimbabwe	Yes	No	Yes	Yes	Yes	No	–	–	–

[a] A self-sustaining prganisation through membership fees and data services.

TABLE A11: SAFER MOBILITY BY COUNTRY / AREA

Country / Area	Number of registered vehicles	Audits or star rating required for new road infrastructure	Inspections / star rating of existing roads	Design standards for the safety of pedestrians / cyclists	Investments to upgrade high risk locations	Policies & investment in urban public transport	Policies promoting walking and cycling
Afghanistan	655 357	Partial	–	Partial	Yes	Yes	No
Albania	563 106	Yes	No	Partial	Yes	Yes	Subnational
Angola		No	No	Partial	Yes	Yes	Yes
Antigua and Barbuda	36 030	Partial	No	Partial	No	No	No
Argentina	21 633 587	Partial	Yes	Yes	Yes	Yes	Yes
Armenia		Yes	Yes	Partial	Yes	Yes	No
Australia	18 326 236	Yes	Yes	Yes	Yes	No	Yes
Austria	7 421 647	Yes	Yes	Yes	Yes	Yes	Yes
Azerbaijan	1 330 551	Partial	Yes	Partial	No	Yes	No
Bangladesh	2 879 708	Partial	Yes	Yes	Yes	Yes	No
Barbados	117 104	No	Yes	Partial	No	Yes	No
Belarus	4 192 291	No	Yes	Yes	Yes	Yes	Yes
Belgium	7 330 718	Yes	Yes	Yes	Yes	Yes	Subnational
Belize	56 094	Yes	Yes	Yes	No	No	No
Benin	469 761	Partial	No	Partial	Yes	No	No
Bhutan	86 981	Yes	Yes	Yes	Yes	Yes	Yes
Bolivia (Plurinational State of)	1 711 005	Yes	Yes	Yes	No	Yes	Subnational
Bosnia and Herzegovina	978 229	Partial	Yes	Yes	Yes	No	Subnational
Botswana	653 274	Yes	Yes	Yes	Yes	No	No
Brazil	93 867 016	Yes	No	Partial	Yes	Yes	Yes
Bulgaria	4 031 748	Partial	No	Yes	No	Yes	Yes
Burkina Faso	2 106 292	Partial	Yes	Yes	Yes	No	No
Burundi	111 236	Partial	No	No	No	No	No
Cabo Verde	64 955	Yes	Yes	Partial	Yes	Yes	No
Cambodia	3 751 715	Yes	Yes	No	Yes	No	No
Cameroon	758 145	Partial	Yes	Partial	Yes	Yes	No
Canada	23 923 806	Partial	Yes	Yes	Yes	Yes	Subnational
Central African Republic	37 475	Partial	Yes	Partial	Yes	No	No
Chad	1 124 000	Yes	No	Yes	Yes	No	No
Chile	4 960 945	No	No	Partial	No	Yes	Subnational

Country / Area	Number of registered vehicles	Audits or star rating required for new road infrastructure	Inspections / star rating of existing roads	Design standards for the safety of pedestrians / cyclists	Investments to upgrade high risk locations	Policies & investment in urban public transport	Policies promoting walking and cycling
China	294 694 457	Yes	Yes	Yes	Yes	Yes	Yes
Colombia	13 477 996	Partial	No	No	No	Yes	No
Comoros	34 898	No	No	No	Yes	No	No
Congo		Yes	No	Partial	No	No	No
Cook Islands	12 453	Partial	Yes	Partial	Yes	No	Yes
Costa Rica	1 991 398	No	–	No	No	Yes	Subnational
Côte d'Ivoire	905 537	Partial	No	Partial	Yes	Yes	No
Croatia	1 996 056	Partial	Yes	Yes	Yes	Yes	Yes
Cuba	633 369	No	Yes	Partial	Yes	Yes	No
Cyprus	650 805	Partial	Yes	Yes	Yes	Yes	Yes
Czechia	7 325 789	Partial	Yes	Yes	No	Yes	Yes
Democratic Republic of the Congo		–	No	Partial	No	No	Subnational
Denmark	3 131 673	Partial	Yes	Yes	Yes	Yes	Yes
Dominica	35 796	–	No	Partial	No	No	No
Dominican Republic	3 854 038	Yes	No	Partial	Yes	Yes	Yes
Ecuador	1 925 368	Yes	Yes	Partial	No	Yes	Yes
Egypt	8 412 673	Yes	Yes	Partial	Yes	Yes	Subnational
El Salvador	1 008 080	Partial	No	Partial	No	Yes	Yes
Equatorial Guinea	143 000	No	–	No		No	No
Eritrea	72 405	Partial	Yes	Yes	Yes	Yes	Yes
Estonia	865 040	Partial	Yes	Yes	Yes	No	Yes
Eswatini	99 830	Yes	Yes	Partial	No	Yes	No
Ethiopia	708 416	No	No	Partial	No	Yes	No
Fiji	110 763	Yes	Yes	Partial	Yes	Yes	Yes
Finland	5 217 850	Yes	Yes	Yes	Yes	Yes	Yes
France	42 363 000	Partial	Yes	Yes	Yes	Yes	Yes
Gabon		–	–	No	Yes	Yes	No
Gambia	84 963	Partial	No	Partial	Yes	No	No
Georgia	1 126 470	Yes	No	Partial	Yes	Yes	Yes
Germany	56 622 000	Yes	Yes	Yes	Yes	No	No
Ghana	2 066 943	Yes	Yes	Yes	Yes	Yes	Yes

Country / Area	Number of registered vehicles	Audits or star rating required for new road infrastructure	Inspections / star rating of existing roads	Design standards for the safety of pedestrians / cyclists	Investments to upgrade high risk locations	Policies & investment in urban public transport	Policies promoting walking and cycling
Greece	9 489 299	Partial	Yes	Partial	Yes	Yes	Subnational
Grenada	27 266	Partial	Yes	Partial	Yes	No	No
Guatemala	3 250 194	Partial	No	Partial	Yes	Yes	Subnational
Guinea	259 731	Yes	No	No	No	Yes	No
Guinea-Bissau	62 239	No	No	No	No	No	No
Guyana	15 694	Yes	No	Partial	No	No	No
Honduras	1 694 504	Yes	No	Yes	Yes	No	No
Hungary	4 022 798	Yes	Yes	Yes	No	No	Subnational
Iceland	289 501	Yes	Yes	Partial	Yes	Yes	Yes
India	210 023 289	Partial	Yes	Yes	Yes	Yes	No
Indonesia	128 398 594	Yes	Yes	Yes	Yes	Yes	Subnational
Iran (Islamic Republic of)	30 377 065	Yes	Yes	Partial	Yes	Yes	Subnational
Iraq	5 775 777	Partial	No	Partial	No	Yes	No
Ireland	2 573 961	Partial	Yes	Yes	Yes	Yes	Yes
Israel	3 239 305	Yes	Yes	Partial	Yes	Yes	Yes
Italy	52 581 575	Yes	Yes	Yes	No	Yes	Yes
Jamaica	541 316	Yes	Yes	Partial	No	Yes	Yes
Japan	81 602 046	Yes	Yes	Yes	Yes	Yes	Yes
Jordan	1 502 420	Yes	Yes	Partial	Yes	Yes	No
Kazakhstan	4 383 120	Yes	Yes	Yes	Yes	Yes	No
Kenya	2 979 910	Partial	No	Partial	Yes	Yes	Subnational
Kiribati	3 706	Yes	No	Partial	Yes	Yes	Yes
Kuwait	2 001 940	Yes	–	No	No	No	No
Kyrgyzstan	993 000	Yes	No	Partial	Yes	Yes	
Lao People's Democratic Republic	1 850 020	Partial	No	Partial	Yes	No	Yes
Latvia	803 628	Yes	Yes	Yes	Yes	No	No
Lebanon	1 866 407	Partial	–	Partial	No	No	No
Lesotho		Yes	Yes	No	No	No	No
Liberia	1 085 075	Yes	Yes	Partial	No	Yes	Yes
Libya	3 553 497	Yes	No	Partial	Yes	Yes	No
Lithuania	1 391 568	Partial	Yes	Yes	Yes	Yes	Yes

Country / Area	Number of registered vehicles	Audits or star rating required for new road infrastructure	Inspections / star rating of existing roads	Design standards for the safety of pedestrians / cyclists	Investments to upgrade high risk locations	Policies & investment in urban public transport	Policies promoting walking and cycling
Luxembourg	466 472	Partial	Yes	Yes	Yes	Yes	Yes
Madagascar	236 979	Yes	Yes	Partial	No	No	No
Malawi		Partial	No	Yes	No	No	No
Malaysia	27 613 120	Yes	Yes	Yes	Yes	Yes	Yes
Maldives	92 983	No	Yes	Partial	No	Yes	No
Mali	344 345	Yes	Yes	Partial	Yes	No	No
Malta	358 947	Partial	Yes	Partial	No	Yes	Yes
Mauritania		No	No	No	Yes	No	No
Mauritius	507 676	Yes	Yes	Partial	Yes	Yes	No
Mexico	40 205 671	No	Yes	Yes	Yes	Yes	Yes
Micronesia (Federated States of)	5 673	Partial	Yes	Partial	No	No	No
Mongolia	841 537	Yes	No	Partial	No	Yes	Yes
Montenegro	211 219	Yes	Yes	Yes	Yes	No	Yes
Morocco	3 791 469	Partial	Yes	No	Yes	Yes	Yes
Mozambique	698 864	No	No	Partial	No	No	No
Myanmar	6 381 136	Yes	Yes	Yes	Yes	Yes	Yes
Namibia	371 281	No	No	Partial	Yes	Yes	Yes
Nepal	2 339 169	Partial	Yes	Partial	No	Yes	No
Netherlands	10 757 655	Yes	Yes	Yes	Yes	Yes	Yes
New Zealand	3 656 300	Yes	Yes	Yes	Yes	Yes	Yes
Niger	436 420	Partial	No	Yes	No	No	No
Nigeria	11 733 425	Yes	Yes	Partial	Yes	Yes	Yes
Norway	3 969 612	Yes	Yes	Partial	Yes	Yes	Yes
Oman	1 370 913	Yes	Yes	Yes	Yes	Yes	Subnational
Pakistan	18 352 500	Yes	Yes	Partial	Yes	Yes	No
Panama	1 288 573	No	No	Partial	No	Yes	Subnational
Papua New Guinea	100 993	Partial	Yes	Partial	No	No	Subnational
Paraguay	1 871 947	Yes	Yes	Partial	No	Yes	Subnational
Peru	5 604 789	No	–	No	Yes	No	Yes
Philippines	9 251 565	Yes	Yes	Partial	Yes	Yes	Yes
Poland	27 409 106	Partial	Yes	Yes	Yes	Yes	Yes

Country / Area	Number of registered vehicles	Audits or star rating required for new road infrastructure	Inspections / star rating of existing roads	Design standards for the safety of pedestrians / cyclists	Investments to upgrade high risk locations	Policies & investment in urban public transport	Policies promoting walking and cycling
Portugal	6 590 094	Partial	Yes	Yes	No	Yes	Yes
Qatar	1 330 487	Yes	Yes	Yes	Yes	Yes	Yes
Republic of Korea	25 680 967	Yes	Yes	Yes	Yes	Yes	Yes
Republic of Moldova	894 253	Yes	Yes	Yes	Yes	Yes	Yes
Romania	7 014 661	Yes	Yes	Yes	No	Yes	No
Russian Federation	54 014 259	Yes	No	Yes	Yes	Yes	Subnational
Rwanda	180 137	Yes	Yes	Yes	Yes	Yes	Yes
Saint Lucia	35 681	No	No	Partial	No	No	No
Samoa	25 235	Yes	Yes	Partial	Yes	Yes	Subnational
San Marino	54 956	Partial	No	Partial	Yes	Yes	No
Sao Tome and Principe	34 050	No	No	Partial	No	No	No
Saudi Arabia	6 895 799	Partial	Yes	Partial	Yes	Yes	Subnational
Senegal	468 051	Yes	Yes	No	No	Yes	No
Serbia	2 282 401	No	No	Yes	Yes	Yes	No
Seychelles	23 076	Partial	Yes	Yes	Yes	Yes	Yes
Singapore	933 534	Yes	Yes	Yes	No	Yes	Yes
Slovakia	2 606 412	Partial	Yes	Yes	Yes	Yes	Yes
Slovenia	1 468 439	Partial	Yes	Yes	Yes	Yes	Yes
Solomon Islands		Yes	Yes	Yes	No	Yes	No
Somalia	59 457	No	–	No	No	No	No
South Africa		Partial	Yes	Partial	Yes	Yes	Yes
South Sudan	69 647	No	Yes	Partial	No	No	No
Spain	32 986 384	Yes	Yes	Yes	Yes	Yes	Yes
Sri Lanka	6 795 469	Partial	No	Partial	Yes	No	Subnational
Sudan	1 252 740	Yes	Yes	Partial	No	Yes	No
Suriname	228 388	No	No	Partial	No	Yes	No
Sweden	6 102 914	Partial	Yes	Yes	Yes	Yes	Yes
Switzerland	5 980 512	Partial	Yes	No	Yes	Yes	Yes
Syrian Arab Republic	2 396 544	Partial	Yes	Partial	Yes	Yes	Yes
Tajikistan	439 972	Yes	Yes	Partial	Yes	Yes	No
Thailand	37 338 139	Partial	Yes	Partial	Yes	Yes	Yes

Country / Area	Number of registered vehicles	Audits or star rating required for new road infrastructure	Inspections / star rating of existing roads	Design standards for the safety of pedestrians / cyclists	Investments to upgrade high risk locations	Policies & investment in urban public transport	Policies promoting walking and cycling
The former Yugoslav Republic of Macedonia	442 962	Partial	Yes	Yes	No	Yes	Yes
Timor-Leste	146 596	Partial	No	Yes	No	Yes	Yes
Togo	64 118	Partial	No	Partial	Yes	Yes	No
Tonga	8 154	Yes	Yes	Partial	Yes	No	Subnational
Trinidad and Tobago	831 803	Partial	No	Yes	No	Yes	No
Tunisia	2 015 601	Partial	–	Partial	Yes	Yes	No
Turkey	21 090 424	Partial	Yes	Yes	Yes	Yes	Yes
Turkmenistan		Yes	No	Partial	Yes	Yes	Yes
Uganda	1 594 962	Yes	Yes	Partial	Yes	No	Yes
Ukraine	14 433 709	Yes	Yes	Yes	No	Yes	Subnational
United Arab Emirates	3 391 125	Yes	Yes	Partial	Yes	Yes	Subnational
United Kingdom	38 388 214	Yes	Yes	Yes	Yes	Yes	Yes
United Republic of Tanzania	2 163 623	Yes	Yes	Partial	Yes	Yes	No
United States of America	281 312 446	No	–	No	Yes	Yes	Yes
Uruguay	2 342 026	No	No	Partial	No	Yes	Yes
Uzbekistan		Yes	Yes	Yes	Yes	Yes	No
Vanuatu		Partial	No	Partial	Yes	Yes	No
Venezuela (Bolivarian Republic of)	7 999 760	Yes	–	Yes	No	Yes	No
Viet Nam	50 666 855	Yes	Yes	Partial	Yes	Yes	Subnational
West Bank and Gaza Strip	268 365	Yes	Yes	No	Yes	Yes	No
Zimbabwe	1 198 584	Yes	Yes	Partial	Yes	Yes	No

TABLE A12: VEHICLE STANDARDS BY COUNTRY / AREA

Country / Area	Vehicle standards							
	Seat-belts	Seat-belt anchorages	Frontal impact	Side impact	Electronic stability control	Pedestrian protection	Child seats	Motorcycle anti-lock bracking system
Afghanistan	No	No	No	No	No	No	No	No
Albania	No	No	No	No	No	No	No	No
Angola	No	No	No	No	No	No	No	No
Antigua and Barbuda	No	No	No	No	No	No	No	No
Argentina	Yes	Yes	Yes[a]	Yes[b]	No[c]	No	No	No
Armenia	No	No	No	No	No	No	No	No
Australia	Yes	Yes	Yes	Yes	Yes	Yes[d]	No	Yes
Austria	Yes	Yes	Yes	Yes	Yes	Yes	Yes	Yes
Azerbaijan	No	No	No	No	No	No	No	No
Bangladesh	No	No	No	No	No	No	No	No
Barbados	No	No	No	No	No	No	No	No
Belarus	No	No	No	No	No	No	No	No
Belgium	Yes	Yes	Yes	Yes	Yes	Yes	Yes	Yes
Belize	No	No	No	No	No	No	No	No
Benin	No	No	No	No	No	No	No	No
Bhutan	No	No	No	No	No	No	No	No
Bolivia (Plurinational State of)	No	No	No	No	No	No	No	No
Bosnia and Herzegovina	No	No	No	No	No	No	No	No
Botswana	No	No	No	No	No	No	No	No
Brazil	Yes	Yes	Yes	No[e]	No	No	Yes	Yes
Bulgaria	Yes	Yes	Yes	Yes	Yes	Yes	Yes	Yes
Burkina Faso	No	No	No	No	No	No	No	No
Burundi	No	No	No	No	No	No	No	No
Cabo Verde	No	No	No	No	No	No	No	No
Cambodia	No	No	No	No	No	No	No	No
Cameroon	No	No	No	No	No	No	No	No
Canada	Yes	Yes	Yes	Yes	Yes	No	Yes	No
Central African Republic	No	No	No	No	No	No	No	No
Chad	No	No	No	No	No	No	No	No
Chile	No	No	No	No	No	No	No	No
China	Yes	Yes	Yes	Yes	No[f]	No	No	No

Country / Area	Vehicle standards							
	Seat-belts	Seat-belt anchorages	Frontal impact	Side impact	Electronic stability control	Pedestrian protection	Child seats	Motorcycle anti-lock bracking system
Colombia	No	No	No	No	No	No	No	No
Comoros	No	No	No	No	No	No	No	No
Congo	No	No	No	No	No	No	No	No
Cook Islands	No	No	No	No	No	No	No	No
Costa Rica	No	No	No	No	No	No	No	No
Côte d'Ivoire	No	No	No	No	No	No	No	No
Croatia	Yes	Yes	Yes	Yes	Yes	Yes	Yes	Yes
Cuba	No	No	No	No	No	No	No	No
Cyprus	Yes	Yes	Yes	Yes	Yes	Yes	Yes	Yes
Czechia	Yes	Yes	Yes	Yes	Yes	Yes	Yes	Yes
Democratic Republic of the Congo	No	No	No	No	No	No	No	No
Denmark	Yes	Yes	Yes	Yes	Yes	Yes	Yes	Yes
Dominica	No	No	No	No	No	No	No	No
Dominican Republic	No	No	No	No	No	No	No	No
Ecuador	Yes	Yes	Yes	Yes	Yes	No	No	No
Egypt	Yes	Yes	Yes	Yes	Yes	Yes	Yes	No
El Salvador	No	No	No	No	No	No	No	No
Equatorial Guinea	No	No	No	No	No	No	No	No
Eritrea	No	No	No	No	No	No	No	No
Estonia	Yes	Yes	Yes	Yes	Yes	Yes	Yes	Yes
Eswatini	No	No	No	No	No	No	No	No
Ethiopia	No	No	No	No	No	No	No	No
Fiji	No	No	No	No	No	No	No	No
Finland	Yes	Yes	Yes	Yes	Yes	Yes	Yes	Yes
France	Yes	Yes	Yes	Yes	Yes	Yes	Yes	Yes
Gabon	No	No	No	No	No	No	No	No
Gambia	No	No	No	No	No	No	No	No
Georgia	No	No	No	No	No	No	No	No
Germany	Yes	Yes	Yes	Yes	Yes	Yes	Yes	Yes
Ghana	No	No	No	No	No	No	No	No
Greece	Yes	Yes	Yes	Yes	Yes	Yes	Yes	Yes
Grenada	No	No	No	No	No	No	No	No

Country / Area	Vehicle standards							
	Seat-belts	Seat-belt anchorages	Frontal impact	Side impact	Electronic stability control	Pedestrian protection	Child seats	Motorcycle anti-lock bracking system
Guatemala	No	No	No	No	No	No	No	No
Guinea	No	No	No	No	No	No	No	No
Guinea-Bissau	No	No	No	No	No	No	No	No
Guyana	No	No	No	No	No	No	No	No
Honduras	No	No	No	No	No	No	No	No
Hungary	Yes	Yes	Yes	Yes	Yes	Yes	Yes	Yes
Iceland	Yes	Yes	Yes	Yes	Yes	Yes	Yes	Yes
India	Yes	Yes	Yes	Yes	No	Yes[g]	No	Yes
Indonesia	No	No	No	No	No	No	No	No
Iran (Islamic Republic of)	No	No	No	No	No	No	No	No
Iraq	No	No	No	No	No	No	No	No
Ireland	Yes	Yes	Yes	Yes	Yes	Yes	Yes	Yes
Israel	Yes[h]	Yes[h]	Yes[h]	Yes[h]	Yes[h]	No	Yes	No
Italy	Yes	Yes	Yes	Yes	Yes	Yes	Yes	Yes
Jamaica	No	No	No	No	No	No	No	No
Japan	Yes	Yes	Yes	Yes	Yes	Yes	Yes	Yes
Jordan	No	No	No	No	No	No	No	No
Kazakhstan	No	No	No	No	No	No	No	No
Kenya	No	No	No	No	No	No	No	No
Kiribati	No	No	No	No	No	No	No	No
Kuwait	No	No	No	No	No	No	No	No
Kyrgyzstan	No	No	No	No	No	No	No	No
Lao People's Democratic Republic	No	No	No	No	No	No	No	No
Latvia	Yes	Yes	Yes	Yes	Yes	Yes	Yes	Yes
Lebanon	No	No	No	No	No	No	No	No
Lesotho	No	No	No	No	No	No	No	No
Liberia	No	No	No	No	No	No	No	No
Libya	No	No	No	No	No	No	No	No
Lithuania	Yes	Yes	Yes	Yes	Yes	Yes	Yes	Yes
Luxembourg	Yes	Yes	Yes	Yes	Yes	Yes	Yes	Yes
Madagascar	No	No	No	No	No	No	No	No

Country / Area	Vehicle standards							
	Seat-belts	Seat-belt anchorages	Frontal impact	Side impact	Electronic stability control	Pedestrian protection	Child seats	Motorcycle anti-lock bracking system
Malawi	No	No	No	No	No	No	No	No
Malaysia	Yes	Yes	Yes	Yes	Yes	Yes	Yes	No
Maldives	No	No	No	No	No	No	No	No
Mali	No	No	No	No	No	No	No	No
Malta	Yes	Yes	Yes	Yes	Yes	Yes	Yes	Yes
Mauritania	No	No	No	No	No	No	No	No
Mauritius	No	No	No	No	No	No	No	No
Mexico	Yes	No	No	No	No	No	No	No
Micronesia (Federated States of)	No	No	No	No	No	No	No	No
Mongolia	No	No	No	No	No	No	No	No
Montenegro	No	No	No	No	No	No	No	No
Morocco	No	No	No	No	No	No	No	No
Mozambique	No	No	No	No	No	No	No	No
Myanmar	No	No	No	No	No	No	No	No
Namibia	No	No	No	No	No	No	No	No
Nepal	No	No	No	No	No	No	No	No
Netherlands	Yes	Yes	Yes	Yes	Yes	Yes	Yes	Yes
New Zealand	Yes	Yes	Yes	Yes	Yes[i]	Yes	Yes	No
Niger	No	No	No	No	No	No	No	No
Nigeria	No	No	No	No	No	No	No	No
Norway	Yes	Yes	Yes	Yes	Yes	Yes	Yes	Yes
Oman	No	No	No	No	No	No	No	No
Pakistan	No	No	No	No	No	No	No	No
Panama	No	No	No	No	No	No	No	No
Papua New Guinea	No	No	No	No	No	No	No	No
Paraguay	No	No	No	No	No	No	No	No
Peru	No	No	No	No	No	No	No	No
Philippines	No	No	No	No	No	No	No	No
Poland	Yes	Yes	Yes	Yes	Yes	Yes	Yes	Yes
Portugal	Yes	Yes	Yes	Yes	Yes	Yes	Yes	Yes
Qatar	No	No	No	No	No	No	No	No
Republic of Korea	Yes	Yes	Yes	Yes	Yes	Yes	Yes	No

Country / Area	Vehicle standards							
	Seat-belts	Seat-belt anchorages	Frontal impact	Side impact	Electronic stability control	Pedestrian protection	Child seats	Motorcycle anti-lock bracking system
Republic of Moldova	No	No	No	No	No	No	No	No
Romania	Yes	Yes	Yes	Yes	Yes	Yes	Yes	Yes
Russian Federation	Yes	Yes	Yes	Yes	Yes	Yes	Yes	No
Rwanda	No	No	No	No	No	No	No	No
Saint Lucia	No	No	No	No	No	No	No	No
Samoa	No	No	No	No	No	No	No	No
San Marino	Yes	Yes	Yes	Yes	Yes	Yes	Yes	No
Sao Tome and Principe	No	No	No	No	No	No	No	No
Saudi Arabia	No	No	No	No	No	No	No	No
Senegal	No	No	No	No	No	No	No	No
Serbia	No	No	No	No	No	No	No	No
Seychelles	No	No	No	No	No	No	No	No
Singapore	No	No	No	No	No	No	No	No
Slovakia	Yes	Yes	Yes	Yes	Yes	Yes	Yes	Yes
Slovenia	Yes	Yes	Yes	Yes	Yes	Yes	Yes	Yes
Solomon Islands	No	No	No	No	No	No	No	No
Somalia	No	No	No	No	No	No	No	No
South Africa	No	Yes	No	No	Yes	Yes	Yes	No
South Sudan	No	No	No	No	No	No	No	No
Spain	Yes	Yes	Yes	Yes	Yes	Yes	Yes	Yes
Sri Lanka	No	No	No	No	No	No	No	No
Sudan	No	No	No	No	No	No	No	No
Suriname	No	No	No	No	No	No	No	No
Sweden	Yes	Yes	Yes	Yes	Yes	Yes	Yes	Yes
Switzerland	Yes	Yes	Yes	Yes	Yes	Yes	Yes	Yes
Syrian Arab Republic	No	No	No	No	No	No	No	No
Tajikistan	No	No	No	No	No	No	No	No
Thailand	Yes	Yes	No[j,k]	No[j,k]	No[k]	Yes	No	No
The former Yugoslav Republic of Macedonia	No	No	No	No	No	No	No	No
Timor-Leste	No	No	No	No	No	No	No	No
Togo	No	No	No	No	No	No	No	No

Country / Area	Vehicle standards							
	Seat-belts	Seat-belt anchorages	Frontal impact	Side impact	Electronic stability control	Pedestrian protection	Child seats	Motorcycle anti-lock bracking system
Tonga	No	No	No	No	No	No	No	No
Trinidad and Tobago	No	No	No	No	No	No	No	No
Tunisia	No	No	No	No	No	No	No	No
Turkey	Yes	Yes	Yes	Yes	Yes	Yes	Yes	No
Turkmenistan	No	No	No	No	No	No	No	No
Uganda	No	No	No	No	No	No	No	No
Ukraine	No	No	No	No	No	No	No	No
United Arab Emirates	No	No	No	No	No	No	No	No
United Kingdom	Yes	Yes	Yes	Yes	Yes	Yes	Yes	Yes
United Republic of Tanzania	No	No	No	No	No	No	No	No
United States of America	Yes	Yes	Yes	Yes	Yes	No	Yes	No
Uruguay	Yes	Yes	No	No	No	No	Yes	No
Uzbekistan	No	No	No	No	No	No	No	No
Vanuatu	No	No	No	No	No	No	No	No
Venezuela (Bolivarian Republic of)	No	No	No	No	No	No	No	No
Viet Nam	No	No	No	No	No	No	No	No
West Bank and Gaza Strip	No	No	No	No	No	No	No	No
Zimbabwe	No	No	No	No	No	No	No	No

[a] Only for new models
[b] For new models as from 2018
[c] Mandatory as from 2018 under voluntary agreement with car makers but postponed to 2022 by the new government following Brazil ESC mandatory date
[d] Australia has signed the UN127 for Pedestrian Protection as a Contracting Party but is not enforcing it
[e] Brazil included the requirement for side impact for new vehicles from 2020
[f] However top 12 car makers (more than 70% of sales volume) commited to ESC standard as from 2018
[g] Mandatory from October 2018
[h] Required for cars made under US regulations - for European cars, no requirements further than ESC
[i] For new models as from 2018
[j] According to representatives information the regulation will be mandatory as from 2020
[k] Thailand launched an ECO-CAR program with tax incentives for cars with ESC but this is not mandatory for all cars

PHOTO CREDITS

Page iii	AdobeStock
Page vii	WHO
Page ix	Bloomberg
Page xii	AdobeStock
Page xv	AdobeStock
Page xvi	AdobeStock
Page 9	WHO
Page 12	AdobeStock
Page 13	AdobeStock
Page 14	AdobeStock
Page 17	WHO
Page 21	AdobeStock
Page 22	AdobeStock
Page 30	AdobeStock
Page 34	WHO
Page 37	AdobeStock
Page 44	AdobeStock
Page 47	AdobeStock
Page 48	AdobeStock
Page 49	AdobeStock
Page 51	WHO
Page 55	Edward Echwalu
Page 56	AdobeStock
Page 60	AdobeStock
Page 63	AdobeStock
Page 65	AdobeStock
Page 66	AdobeStock
Page 71	AdobeStock
Page 73	AdobeStock
Page 74	AdobeStock
Page 76	AdobeStock
Page 80	AdobeStock
Page 270	AdobeStock
Page 278	AdobeStock
Page 288	AdobeStock
Page 288	AdobeStock